Archaeology and the Emergence of Greece

Anthony Snodgrass

CORNELL UNIVERSITY PRESS
Ithaca, New York

First published in the U.K. by Edinburgh University Press

Printed and bound in Great Britain by The Cromwell Press, Trowbridge, Wilts

First published in the United States of America in 2006
by Cornell University Press

Librarians: Library of Congress Cataloging-in-Publication Data are available.

ISBN   978-0-8014-4528-6 (cloth)
ISBN   978-0-8014-7354-8 (paperback)

Cloth printing   10 9 8 7 6 5 4 3 2 1
Paperback printing   10 9 8 7 6 5 4 3 2 1

Contents

Part III   The Early *Polis* at Home and Abroad

Part IV   The Early *Polis* at War

Part V   Early Greek Art

Part VI   Archaeological Survey

Acknowledgements

The Editors of the following periodicals were kind enough to grant permission for the reproduction in this book of previously published articles: *American Journal of Archaeology, Annali di Archeologia e Storia Antica (Istituto Universitario Orientale, Napoli), Cambridge Archaeological Journal, Classical Antiquity, Dialogues d'Histoire Ancienne, Journal of Hellenic Studies, Proceedings of the Cambridge Philological Society, Scienze dell'Antichità (Università di Roma 'La Sapienza')*.

Equally generously, the holders of Copyright for chapters and essays in collective volumes, and of separate publications, allowed me to reproduce certain pieces here: the Cambridge University Press (Chs. 1, 11 and 13), Dr Michael Krumme (Ch. 5), Professor R. A. Crossland and Dr A. Birchall (Ch. 6), Verlag Bibliopolis, Möhnesee (Ch. 9), Professor P. D. A. Garnsey and Mr C. R. Whittaker (Ch. 12), Éditions du CNRS, Paris (Ch. 18), the Oxford University Press, USA (Ch. 23), La Maison de l'Orient Méditerranéen, Lyon (Ch. 25). The full references to all these works will be found at the foot of the first page of each Chapter.

The following acknowledgements are due for the re-use of illustrations: for *Figure 13.10* and *21.9*, Copyright Hirmer Verlag, München; for *Figure 21.2*, Photograph Copyright 1981 Museum of Fine Arts, Boston; for *Figure 21.5*, Cliché Bibliothèque nationale de France, Paris; for *Figure 21.13*, Copyright the Trustees of the British Museum; for *Figure 21.14*, American School of Classical Studies at Athens: Agora Excavations. I am grateful to the Cartoon Bank, New York, for allowing me to reproduce the cartoon *Figure 4.1*, and to Faber and Faber Ltd in respect of the lines from the poem quoted on pp. 217–18.

Finally, I think the staff of the Edinburgh University Press and especially John Davey, whose idea this book was.

Preface

The papers here presented cover forty years of research – a time which has seen vast changes within a small discipline. I would sum up these changes by saying that, about halfway through this period, Classical archaeology suddenly began to turn into a branch of archaeology. If an obvious question then is: 'Was it ever anything else ?', the answer is that, to the contrary, when I myself graduated forty-five years ago it was implicitly assumed that there were two quite distinct subjects, 'archaeology' and 'Classical archaeology', and that the similarity of their names did not bind them much more closely together than did that between 'history' and 'natural history'. This dichotomy was equally accepted, whether with resignation or with relief, on both sides of the divide. The aims, methods and, above all, the preferred subject matter of the two subjects differed greatly: the things that they found interesting and worth studying hardly coincided at all. Today this is no longer universally, perhaps not even broadly, true.

General readers, weaned on a traditional diet of great monuments and beautiful objects, may be disappointed by what they find here. Instead, the papers presume to try to bring about change in the discipline by straying across the traditional boundaries, hitherto tacitly observed, with the domains of prehistorians, ancient historians or literary critics. In this very conservative subject, it had been regarded as somehow out of order for Classical archaeologists to meddle with social, political and economic history; or with topics that involved the entire Old World, like the transition from bronze- to iron-using; or with the study of the Aegean Bronze Age; or with testing the historical veracity of ancient authors like Homer or Pausanias; or with the intellectual presuppositions of ancient artists; or, for a Hellenist, with provincial Roman history; or with surface survey and its scope for broadening our view of Classical history. At heart, my experience has been not so much of swimming against the tide, as of working across the grain of the subject.

A lesser but recurrent feature here is a growing concern with quantification and measurement. I make no bones about the source of the influence: from the time of the first edition of David Clarke's *Analytical Archaeology* in 1968, quantitative change through time has been proclaimed by prehistorians as an unusually appropriate object of archaeological investigation, and it has been as prominent in my own work as in that of the prehistorians who have most influenced me. Admitting to such influences was in itself a cause for estrangement from some Classical archaeologists. Yet at the same time, a failure to embrace other goals that then had wide appeal among prehistorians – the search for universal findings that could be extended from one period or culture to the whole human past; or the disparaging view of the nature of history and historical research; or the enthusiasm for 'interconnecting jargon' which Clarke once voiced – set up another barrier on their side and were, I think, seen as, respectively, pusillanimous, deferential and old-fashioned. If there is any message for the prehistorian in these pages, it is that the prodigious wealth of the database of which Classical archaeology disposes, and the relative security and testability of its inferences, are things that deserve attention.

It would be idle to expect Classical archaeology to recover the place at the apex of world archaeology which it held, against an utterly different intellectual background, 200 years ago. In those days, an unquestioning deference still operated towards the Classical past. The early nineteenth century was a time when ancient Greece and Rome were, together or as rivals, the only serious contenders from the human past for unqualified admiration or serious emulation. A major element of this was the high regard for the physical remains of the Classical past. Egypt might be equally the object of wonder and admiration, but it was Greece and Rome that were usually paid the supreme compliment of imitation. Thus a knowledge of the architecture and visual arts of Greece and Rome had become not just knowledge for its own sake, but knowledge that could be applied. To describe beautiful buildings and objects accurately and illustrate them faithfully were not just necessary virtues, but sufficient ones. Such assumptions, we can safely assume, have vanished for ever from the wider intellectual scene. Any claim to attention which Classical archaeology makes today must be based strictly on its own merits as a discipline.

Some of these generalisations do not apply to the papers in the first section which, perhaps tellingly, have been the ones more favourably received and more often cited. In the first of them, I drew attention (p. 10) to a 'positivist fallacy' which disfigured much earlier work in the discipline: the belief that the observable phenomena are identical with the significant phenomena; that the data we have are by definition the data which matter. At the time of writing, I was unaware that I had myself fallen victim to a glaring example of this fallacy a few years earlier: I had argued that the steep increase in the frequency of burials in and around Athens during the eighth century BC could only be explained by an equally steep rise in population (Ch. 11, pp. 204–6). What I had overlooked was the fact that these were only the *observable* burials: that archaeologically invisible burial was not merely a theoretical possibility, but one which closer study could show to have prevailed widely at the time. Appropriately (and not for the last time) it was my then graduate pupil Ian Morris who presently undertook that closer study and showed that the population rise, probably real but much more gradual, was a less significant factor than the changing Athenian practice in determining admissibility to formal burial (Morris 1987: 72–109).

It may be chastening, but it is also heartening to find that a failing which you have identified is exemplified in your own work: it seems, to the writer at least, to increase the chances of the failing being a real one. It is not, I think, perverse to find more satisfaction in such a step-by-step advancement of understanding than in that rather commoner scholarly practice, the determined defence of an earlier thesis against radical revision. I have included one example of this in Chs. 17 and 19 (on which see below, pp. 344–5) – the fact that these two papers are reproduced again here shows that in this case I retain my faith in a thesis that is in essence much older than my own contributions to it – but the makings of another such controversy could perhaps be detected in the introduction to Ch. 7 (pp. 126–8 below).

If there is a final theme that runs through all these writings, it is one that is somewhat paradoxical in the light of what was said earlier, and one that I was barely conscious of following myself: a recurrent assertion of the *independence* of the archaeological study of the Classical cultures. This is something that is by no means necessarily healthy or desirable; already it is to some extent being dissolved in the fruitful alliances which more broad-minded successors have made with other disciplines. Certainly, no enlightened Classical archaeologist would wish independence to be equated with a hermetically-sealed isolation, the very weakness that has dogged the discipline in the past. But here it is seen most obviously in an assumption of independence from Classical literary scholarship, to which the subject was so long subordinated both intellectually and, as a direct result, institutionally. In an allied sense, there is a certain claim to independence of thought and method, which acts to distinguish Classical archaeology from the archaeology of certain other historical societies, such as those of Egypt, the Near East or China where, for historical periods, the texts are still the usual starting-point. There is separation of a different kind (one which I much regret) from world prehistory, inherited as we saw from previous generations and still persisting to some extent today; and a consequent distancing from those disciplines, such as anthropology, with which prehistory has sought to make common cause. There is the distinctiveness of the subject's contribution to the study of ancient art which, by contextualising art within material culture as a whole, serves to contrast it with most other fields of art history. There is even an independence of method which is maintained in by far its most fruitful partnership so far, that with ancient history.

What this all amounts to is, I hope, something like the newly-won independence of a people or nation, earned after a series of more or less bruising conflicts which have inevitably biased their outlook, but conferring on them, for the first time and for better or worse, a freedom to design their own constitution and set their own policies and priorities.

Variegated as this collection may appear, there are recognisable omissions from it, made in the cause of either coherence or general readability: little on the Aegean Bronze Age, little or nothing on Cyprus, no contributions to reports of excavation and fieldwork, and little on the interpretation of the findings made, in Sicily, Crete, Laconia and Boeotia. A paper devoted to early hero-cult, which might otherwise have been included, has already been anthologised elsewhere (in *Oxford Readings in Greek Religion*, ed. Richard Buxton, Oxford: Oxford University Press, 2000, pp. 180–90). What remains is presented under six successive themes, of gradually decreasing generality.

I should finally add that the opportunity has been taken to correct the very few misprints which appeared in the published versions of these papers.

BIBLIOGRAPHY

Morris, I. (1987) *Burial and Ancient Society*, Cambridge: Cambridge University Press.

A Credo

INTRODUCTION TO PART I

I should begin with a note of apology for the practice, employed in certain passages of the first few papers, of referring to 'the archaeologist', 'the excavator' or indeed 'the historian', as 'he'. This was a presumption that, even twenty years ago, had begun to attract objections and most readers will be glad to see it later disappear. It may seem no more than a trivial indiscretion, but it exemplifies the very attitude that was being implicitly criticised: the unquestioning continuation of past practice. For these papers all, in one way or another, spring from a kind of dissatisfaction with traditional views, traditional proprieties and traditional aims in Classical archaeology. As one might expect, they have been more warmly welcomed by exponents of other disciplines, and by younger colleagues, than by contemporaries in the subject.

CHAPTER 1

Archaeology

This piece, intended as an overall survey and forming a chapter in a book essentially addressed to historians, is perhaps the least controversial of these papers. I should apologise for the repetition, the first of several in this book, in the treatment of two particular problems, Herodotus' account of Saite Egyptian history and the foundation-dates of Greek settlements in Sicily, between pages 11–13 and 18 respectively and Ch. 2 below (pp. 52–6), even if there is a difference of emphasis and context in the two passages. In retrospect, I am struck by the naivety of the expectation that some of the current debates of 1983, on chronology and other issues, would be fairly quickly resolved to general satisfaction: more than twenty years later, this has still to happen. The chronology of the Greek Archaic and Classical periods in general (pp. 15–19); the detailed application of dendrochronology, even to the specific case of Gordion (pp. 19–22); the attribution of the 'Tomb of Philip' at Vergina (p. 40) – each of these has been strenuously challenged since 1983.

As is inevitable with such a survey, these and other aspects require an updated treatment after this length of time; I should, without using up too much space, indicate the most important of them. On *chronology*, the period down to the late fourth century BC is now covered in greater detail by Whitley (2001: 60–74), who also cites in his bibliography an extended series of articles criticising the orthodox chronology by E. D. Francis and M. Vickers, and by Vickers alone (early instalments in this series are briefly referred to in Ch. 2, p. 52).

The then 806-year-long dendrochronological sequence of juniper specimens at Gordion has been matched with a sequence from other Anatolian sites of about twice that length, reaching from the Bronze Age into historical times (Kuniholm *et al.* (1996)), still not precisely anchored to absolute historical dates but susceptible to a complex process of matching with fluctuations in the curve of the calibrated radiocarbon dates for samples taken from the same timbers, which in some opinions fixes the sequence within fairly close limits. For Gordion itself Kuniholm and his colleagues, persuaded by the arguments for the choice adopted at the end of my treatment (pp. 21–2), at first set the closing of the Great Tumulus and the cutting of the trees used for its outer chamber at 718 BC (Kuniholm *et al.* 1996), a date later (Manning *et al.* 2001) raised to within a very few years of 740 BC. This solution has implications for the dating of a whole series of earlier and later episodes which we need not address here: one of them is the eruption of Thera, briefly referred to in a later paper (below, Ch. 3, p. 74).

Regional divisions in the early history both Greece and Italy (pp. 27–8) have been illuminated in a whole series of recent studies concentrating on those regions which lay outside the system of the *polis*, among which Morgan (2003) stands out for the breadth of its scope. Intensive archaeological survey (pp. 32–3) has continued and grown apace, although a recent judgment holds that its impact, even within archaeology, has been minimal (Osborne 2004: 89): more will be said on this topic under Part VI below.

On the 'Tomb of Philip', finally (p. 40), the past twenty years have seen a series of challenges to the dating of the tomb and consequently the identity of its occupant, and even to the identification of Vergina with Aigeae: these are again summarised in Whitley (2001), 407–10.

BIBLIOGRAPHY

Kuniholm, P. I., B. Kromer, S. W. Manning, M. Newton, C. E. Latini and M. J. Bruce (1996), 'Anatolian tree rings and the absolute chronology of the eastern Mediterranean', *Nature* 381 (27 June 1996): 780–3.

Manning, S. W., B. Kromer, P. I. Kuniholm and M. Newton (2001), 'Anatolian tree rings and a new chronology for the East Mediterranean Bronze-Iron Ages', *Science* 294: 2532–5.

Morgan, C. (2003), *Early Greek States Beyond the Polis*, London: Routledge.

Osborne, R. (2004), 'Greek Archaeology: a survey of recent work', *American Journal of Archaeology* 108: 87–102.

Whitley, J. (2001), *The Archaeology of Ancient Greece*, Cambridge: Cambridge University Press.

Nowhere are the distinctive assets and liabilities of archaeology as a source shown up so conspicuously as in Greek and Roman history. While the decisive theoretical battles of archaeology have long been fought out on other fields and between bigger battalions, it is in the closer encounters of Classical archaeology that the more continuous attrition of empirical testing takes place. The experience has not had much influence on wider archaeological thought, but it has revealed certain assets on the part of archaeological evidence in an historical context: four of these, which I would single out as the most important, are its independence, its directness, its experimental character, and its unlimited potential for future extension. None of these qualities should be understood as implying objectivity. In so far as the ideal of total objectivity can be pursued at all, it is no more at the command of the archaeologist than of the historian. Less widely acknowledged, but in the long run just as important, are the peculiar liabilities of archaeological evidence. It is impossible simply to give a list of these; a great part of the discussion in this chapter arises from their existence. But one can say at the outset that archaeological evidence particularly lends itself to misunderstanding of one form or another: occasionally, to misunderstanding by the archaeologist of the identity of what he himself has discovered; much more often, to his misunderstanding of the *meaning* of his own and others' discoveries; equally frequently, to misunderstanding by historians of what is the scope of permissible inference from archaeological data in general or from a particular discovery. To these and other failures of understanding and communication, we must turn presently.

First, however, the assets. The 'independence' of archaeological evidence consists in the fact that the hypotheses and arguments of the archaeologist are part of a great nexus of general archaeological theory and practice, which is something entirely independent of historical theory, if only because it has evolved partly from the findings of archaeologists working on fields that are not historically documented. To give a simple example: in 1904 G. E. Fox argued that a suite of rooms in the Roman villa at Chedworth in Gloucestershire had served as a *fullonica*, an establishment for the fulling of cloth.[1] The references to the British textile industry in documentary sources such as Diocletian's Price Edict and the *Notitia Dignitatum* provided a natural

'Archaeology', from M. H. Crawford (ed.), *Sources for Ancient History*, Cambridge: Cambridge University Press, 1983, pp. 137–84.

incentive for this interpretation; but it was also based on the analogy of actual fulling-installations such as that found at Pompeii, and especially on representations in wall-paintings of fulling operations. Because the establishment was manifestly too large for the needs of one villa and therefore argued a commercial purpose, Fox's observations were widely taken up in general accounts of the rural economy of Roman Britain. It was not until two generations later that I. A. Richmond re-examined this part of the site at Chedworth.[2] By close study of the stratigraphy he was able to show that the supposedly complementary parts of the *fullonica* had not after all been contemporary with each other in construction and use, while his great knowledge of bath-installations in other Romano-British buildings helped him to perceive the true explanation, that these rooms belonged to successive rearrangements of the villa's bath-suite. This kind of experience, though often in a less clear-cut form, is by no means uncommon in archaeology: even when the rightness of the new explanation is less than demonstrable, the doubts cast on the old one can be salutary. Part of the significance of this particular illustration is that Fox's reasoning was probably in part *a priori*, and based on the natural desire to match the material remains with the historical and iconographical sources; it stood to be corrected by the purely archaeological arguments (characteristically empirical in their basis) of Richmond. It is often, and in my opinion rightly, argued that archaeology has the same ultimate aims as history. But the two disciplines use different techniques and different data. It is also true that, just as there are aspects of history for which archaeology cannot be used, so there are fields of archaeology which lie beyond the reach of historical evidence.

In speaking of the 'directness' of archaeological evidence, I am partly drawing a contrast with the quality of some of the other evidence used in ancient history, which is not always acknowledged by its practitioners. Ancient historians use the word 'source' with a latitude which most students of later periods would repudiate: Herodotus is a 'source' for the history of Saïte Egypt (*c.* 664–525 BC), Thucydides for the conspiracy of the Tyrannicides, Tacitus for the reign of Tiberius, and Plutarch for the life of Themistocles. One weakness of this usage is that it leaves one without a distinctive term for the documents or other contemporary records from which these much later writers derived their accounts and which may in some cases still survive. It is this very circumstance which gives archaeological evidence some of its value in ancient studies: the excavated physical remains, at least at the moment of their discovery, do bring us closer to some kind of historical reality than we are ever likely to get through any other medium. They represent what somebody once did, not what some contemporary or later writer says that they did. But this moment soon passes: the material cannot be given a truly historical meaning until it has been subjected to a series of processes, all in one sense or another very hazardous. In many cases, these include removal from its immediate physical environment (which is itself presently destroyed), cleaning, identification, verbal description, dating, establishment of geographical origin, drawing, photography, conservation, preliminary and final publication. The possibility of human error hangs over every stage. By the end, the true facts may become as distorted, obliterated, even forgotten, as in any written account of past events. Indeed, at a trivial level an excavation report *is* a piece of written history, a point underlined in the last twenty years by the case of Sir Arthur Evans' account of his own excavations at Knossos which has at times been handled in a way reminiscent of the treatment given to, say, Rameses II's account of the Battle of Kadesh. But the fact remains that the starting-point of an excavation report is often eye-witness observation, and always contemporary documentation of some kind. That is an asset not to be despised.

The experimental quality of archaeology is closely linked with the fourth and final factor that we shall consider in a moment – the supply of fresh archaeological evidence. It is this which enables archaeology to proceed, at times, by the kind of experimentation which is more often associated with the natural sciences. The archaeologist can form hypotheses, ranging from straightforward historical propositions ('The Vikings reached North America') to complex models of human behaviour, and then test them by searching for evidence that is entirely new, either because it lies undiscovered beneath the ground or because it has never before been applied to this particular end. Or he can pose open-ended questions or problems ('Did the peasants of the ancient Mediterranean world live predominantly on their land or in towns?') and similarly search for the evidence that will provide an answer. The historian working only with non-archaeological sources cannot normally use this procedure, least of all in ancient history, because discoveries of new documentary material, though not as rare as is widely believed, are almost entirely unpredictable. Archaeology can also on occasion operate in a more literally experimental way, by producing replicas of ancient structures, artefacts and processes and then testing them in action.

That the soil of Greece and Italy should still, after more than a century of intensive exploitation, be producing archaeological material in apparently endless quantity is always a source of surprise to laymen. There is a natural tendency to suspect that little of this material is of real significance. The suspicion is justified in one sense only: there is little chance that any future discovery will have quite the breadth of impact that was produced, for example, by the bringing of the Elgin Marbles to London or the discovery of the great Bronze Age civilisations of the Aegean. But this is largely because we are better informed today. There have been discoveries in the past decade, and there will be many more in the future, which would have dumbfounded educated people everywhere if they had occurred a century or two earlier (as they could well have done); on the modern world, their impact is more muted. It is, on the other hand, a complete mistake to imagine that we are by now well supplied with evidence on all important aspects of ancient history, as a few almost random examples will show: how many Republican villas in Italy have been excavated? how many Messenian sanctuaries, Spartan cemeteries or Boeotian town-sites? how many Classical village-settlements from the countryside of Attica? how many Bronze Age settlement-sites in Arcadia? how many Greek colonies on the Mediterranean coasts west of Sicily? The answer to each question is to be reckoned, if at all, on the fingers of one hand. Yet today the rate of work is increasing, to an almost alarming degree. Many excavations are occasioned by modern building-operations, but many others are not. In the unoccupied zone of the island of Cyprus alone, there were fourteen foreign and six Cypriot expeditions excavating in 1978; 120 excavations of Roman sites in Britain are to be expected in a normal year. Clearly there is going to be, for the foreseeable future, a colossal influx of new archaeological evidence for ancient history. To the obvious question, through what medium this evidence is to be communicated to historians and to the world at large, the only answer is by excavation reports, monographs and syntheses, of which the first two must be written by professional archaeologists and even the third requires someone expert enough to pick out the significant details mentioned in passing by a summary or provisional account. Ideally this work should be given priority over that of actual excavation; in practice it will lag far behind. Yet the means of communication are more highly developed today than in the days when one had to travel to hear the excavator's oral account of his newest discoveries. If only a portion of the seed falls on good ground, there will still be a crop for historians to harvest.

Next, a word about definitions. There are those who would include inscriptions and coins as a part of the archaeological evidence, but this seems to me to be valid only in the unimportant sense that they too are often found by excavation: once discovered, their interpretation proceeds by techniques quite separate from those of the archaeologist, and that is why they are treated elsewhere in this volume. On the other hand, there is a field of essentially archaeological activity, of swift and comparatively recent growth, which is often overlooked: field survey and other field-work not involving excavation. There are several areas where this has already proved itself potentially or actually a more fruitful source of evidence than the excavation of sites. There is also the growth, more recent still, of the use of the techniques of the physical sciences, which has made some important contributions to Classical archaeology. Yet among the public and even among some professional scholars working in other fields, the impression remains that archaeology *is* excavation. This is about as accurate as saying that medicine is surgery. The earlier remarks (see p. 8) about the stages in the communication of archaeological results were intended to show how illusory, in one aspect, this belief is; but beyond that there is a kind of collective misapprehension that, at least sub-consciously, pervades the belief of many people, archaeologists included. It could perhaps be called the positivist fallacy of archaeology. It holds that archaeological prominence and historical importance are much the same thing; that the observable phenomena are by definition the significant phenomena.

One cure for the illusion is first-hand experience. Twenty-five years ago, T. J. Dunbabin in his lectures 'The Greeks and their Eastern Neighbours' argued that the serious historian of early Greece 'must be prepared to forget that he is an historian and to study archaeology for its own sake'; the best prescription was to work on an excavation or study intensively an object or class of objects.[3] He was right, though some of his readers at the time must have found this hope more pious than realistic. It seems less so today, and there are now many ancient historians who by following this prescription have acquired as clear a grasp of the archaeological realities as many archaeologists have. But for most people it will always remain true that 'historical' statements about the remains are more interesting than archaeological ones; this is why propositions that are not merely false but, on closer analysis, devoid of actual meaning ('Stonehenge was built by the Druids'; 'This is the tub in which Telemachus took the bath described in the *Odyssey*'), still retain some of their hold. One can only trust that this tendency will weaken with the passage of time; and that there will not always be disappointment at the discovery that the Curia in Rome, besides being restored, preserves the form of a period 300 years after Cicero, or that the walls of Phyle are of a building-style which makes it impossible to associate them with the famous events of 403 BC.

The illusion can also be cured by reflection. On an urban site, for example, the most fully preserved architectural phase will belong, other things being equal, not to the period of greatest historical importance, but to the latest period when the site had any economic importance at all. Among the portable archaeological finds, many potentially significant classes of material will be absent because of their perishability or intrinsic value; by contrast, broken pottery, lacking these qualities, will have a quantitative predominance which is out of all proportion to its historical significance. In rejecting a fallacy of this kind, one is tempted as often to go to the opposite extreme and say that the truth about archaeology is the reverse: that the function of archaeology has been not to buttress the historical account nor even to supplement it, but to undermine it. Certainly there is no shortage of examples in which the result of excavation appears at first sight to have been exactly that. Take, for instance, the statements of Herodotus about the Greeks in Egypt during the reign of the Pharaoh Amasis (569–525 BC).[4] He says (II 178) that Amasis 'gave' the Greeks the city of Naucratis to settle in; that Greek trade was concentrated at Naucratis to the exclusion of other sites (II 179); and that Amasis withdrew a settlement of Greek mercenaries, established nearly a century earlier at a place called Stratopeda on the eastern frontier of Egypt (II 154), and brought them to Memphis to act as his own bodyguard. What does archaeology suggest? The excavation of Naucratis from 1884 onwards provided conclusive evidence that Greeks were permanently settled there well before the reign of Amasis. There are inscriptions in Greek and an unmistakeably Greek temple in the Ionic order as well as much pottery ranging from the late seventh century BC down to Amasis' period. Greek pottery belonging to the time of Amasis has, however, also been discovered at a number of Egyptian sites outside Naucratis, making it hard to accept the picture of the concentration of trade from Greece, or at least to associate it with this Pharaoh. At Tel Defenneh a major settlement of Greek mercenaries, in the general area of 'Stratopeda' if not identical with it, was also partially excavated and provided no evidence, either for establishment a century earlier than Amasis or for abandonment in his reign; on the contrary, its Greek pottery-finds began if anything later than those from Naucratis and were positively concentrated in his reign. A very similar pattern was found at Memphis, to which the mercenaries were supposed to have been withdrawn; occupation by mercenaries seems to have covered much the same period at the two sites. Thus matters remained for many years, until in 1978 Dr E. D. Oren reported the discovery of a dozen further sites with evidence (including burials) for the settlements of Greeks in the north-eastern Delta, the vicinity of 'Stratopeda'.[5] Again, the pottery-finds cover much of the sixth century BC (including Amasis' reign); furthermore one of these sites is heavily fortified and makes as plausible a candidate for identification with 'Stratopeda' as does Tel Defenneh. The archaeological evidence thus tells a coherent story: a community of Greeks was settled at Naucratis from before 600 BC; presently, with all the air of a planned movement, groups of Greeks, probably mercenaries, were very widely stationed at strategic points on the eastern frontier of Egypt, and at Memphis; meanwhile, items of Greek trade were occasionally finding their way to yet other places in Egypt. The subsequent accession of Amasis has no detectable impact on conditions at Naucratis, nor does it lead to the withdrawal of the mercenaries from any of the frontier posts so far found; still less does it bring a curtailment of the distribution of Greek finds on other Egyptian sites.

Has the evidence of excavation therefore destroyed the credit of Herodotus' account? Not really, I would argue. On the questions of detail, it is perfectly possible that even now the particular site called 'Stratopeda' has not been located, that the Greek pottery at places outside Naucratis was traded by non-Greek middlemen, and (though this is the hardest obstacle to overcome) that Herodotus' phrase about 'giving the Greeks Naucratis' was intended to cover some purely institutional change of the kind that leaves no material trace. But it also seems to me that, at a more theoretical level, the claim that Herodotus' account has been falsified by archaeology is a relapse into another variant of the 'positivist fallacy'. It assumes that archaeology and history are operating in essentially the same order of historical reality; that archaeological observations are made, so to speak, in the same language as historical statements. In fact the overlap between the two is small and occurs, in the main, only in those cases where the activities of a significant part of the community are directly influenced by contemporary historical events. Historical events of this kind seldom occur, as can be confirmed by consulting, say, criminal records or proceedings of private societies during periods of political and military crisis; much of life goes on unchanged. Thus it is with the evidence from Egypt that we have been considering. The archaeological evidence has displayed exactly the qualities – directness, potential for expansion and above all independence – which we attributed to it earlier. In so doing, it has revealed Herodotus' account as being a very inadequate summary of the history of the Greek presence in Egypt in these years; on the use of Greek mercenaries, for example, any future account of the episode will probably give at least as much prominence to the archaeological findings as to Herodotus' statements. But it has not destroyed the entire credibility of Herodotus' account, because it is not in the nature of archaeological evidence to do so. What it has rather done is to cast doubt on the chosen *emphasis* of the historian's version. It is this subtler kind of contradiction which W. H. Auden had in mind when he wrote:

> From Archaeology
> one moral, at least, may be drawn,
> to wit, that all
>
> our school text-books lie.
> What they call History
> is nothing to vaunt of,
>
> being made, as it is,
> by the criminal in us:
> goodness is timeless.
>
> ('Archaeology', in *Thank you, fog*; London:
> Faber and Faber, 1974)

To attempt to make any corresponding statement about the limits of the historian's inferences would be presumptuous, and perhaps impossible. It is enough to say that the more broadly the ancient historian interprets the scope of his subject, the more likely he is to find archaeological evidence helpful to him. This is best illustrated by taking examples of different historical approaches, as I shall now try to do, and showing how archaeological evidence can be used or misused in the service of history. The ancient historian has, perhaps paradoxically, an advantage here in that the quality of his documentary evidence has never been good enough for him to subscribe to the old, naïve notion of history as the mere recording of past events, or to aim at the goal of pure objective description. Such notions, though long since abandoned by professional historians, continue to survive in some outsiders' views of history. The absurdity of total description as a goal for the historian can be illustrated by a recent use of it, taken (as it had to be) not from history but from historical fiction, where as a narrative device it serves a different purpose:

> The rearmost shell of this salvo exploded seventy-one feet from Löwenherz's port engine. The theoretical lethal radius of an exploding 10.5 cm. shell was fifty feet. This one fragmented into 4,573 pieces of which twelve weighed over one ounce, 1,525 weighed between one ounce and a fiftieth of an ounce, and 3,036 were fragments of less than a fiftieth of an ounce. Twenty-eight fragments hit Löwenherz's Junkers. Four pieces penetrated the port motor...
>
> (Len Deighton, *Bomber* (1978), 434)

It is as well that the recording, in this way, of every particle of relevant information is not within the powers of the historian, and of the ancient historian least of all. Interpretation, vital in any study of the past, is the life-blood of ancient history. Perhaps less readily, ancient historians have learned from those working in later periods that cultural, social and economic history, local history, demography, historical geography, the history of science, the history of ideas, and other sub-disciplines can be fruitfully pursued for antiquity as well. Whether or not this is pure gain for ancient history as a whole, it is certainly beneficial for the collaboration of historian and archaeologist, as already hinted.

A corresponding breadth of approach is also, however, required of the Classical archaeologist. The traditional art-historical bias of the subject, from this point of view, needs to be shifted. For a long time, the subject has remained imbued with that spirit in which Lord Charlemont wrote two centuries ago: 'We have reason to believe that the World is still in Possession of a Portion at least of those Masterpieces which have been the Admiration of all Antiquity; and we cannot but flatter ourselves that we have had the Glory of being the Discoverers of this inestimable Treasure...'.

However, this must not be taken to imply an elimination of art history, which makes a central contribution to our understanding of cultural history as a whole. 'When time gives historians the perspective to judge our age,' writes a despairing commentator on twentieth-century Britain, 'they may epitomise its barbarism not in our violence, intolerance and irrationality, but in the suicide of western art.' (Paul Johnson, *The offshore islanders* (1972), 584). If that is indeed their conclusion, it will be reached only after much art-historical and archaeological research of the kind which has long been devoted to antiquity. (A quite different but interesting point is that the same research may lead them to a very different view from that of the contemporary commentator.) But alongside the art of a civilisation, there are many other aspects of its material culture whose significance we can instantly recognise in a present-day case and about which, in the case of the past, we can therefore reasonably ask archaeology to inform us. With some of these, long the object of research in non-Classical fields, Classical archaeologists have only recently begun to concern themselves seriously: animal husbandry, agriculture, diet and pathology, and industrial techniques of various kinds, especially metallurgy – to name only a few. The process is analogous to the one taking place in ancient history. But the important thing is that it is happening at all. It is a real pleasure to be able to write, in concluding this section, that the prospects for future collaboration between ancient historians and archaeologists are becoming more favourable every year, and that this is already giving new vitality to both disciplines.

We may now consider one by one the different aspects of ancient historical research to which archaeological evidence may be applicable.

CHRONOLOGY

Traditionally, this aspect has played the dominant role in the handling of archaeological evidence for historical purposes, and for this reason it may be taken first. For the dating of events in periods too early to be covered by written records, or in regions on the fringe of the literate Classical world, archaeology has a long-recognised utility. It is also in the chronological field that the more recently available scientific techniques have been most prominently employed. Many of these last have too wide a margin of potential error to be useful in a period as well documented as that of Classical antiquity but, as we shall see, there is an exception in the case of dendrochronology.

For much of the period between 750 BC and AD 600, a chronological framework covering certain of the finer wares of Greek and Roman pottery is now generally agreed among archaeologists.[6] As the years pass, the framework is subjected to repeated tests (though with decreasing frequency) as new finds occur in historically dated contexts. Over the last generation or more, it has usually passed these tests with no more than minor inaccuracies being revealed, which suggests that within this period it cannot be very far wrong. It is a matter of opinion what degree of precision the framework possesses as a result of this, but in the best-studied periods an error of more than fifteen or twenty years would now be surprising. The deficiencies of the framework are that the finer wares in question cover only a tiny fraction of the pottery in production at any one time, are geographically uneven in their distribution and are not uninterruptedly consecutive in time. This means that many excavations in ancient Mediterranean sites are largely or entirely deprived of the help that these diagnostic wares can give; the chronology has instead to be established at the first or second remove, by using other wares or objects altogether, which have been found elsewhere in association with the more closely dated series and acquire a looser and more indirect dating from them. But there is a deeper underlying weakness about the framework which affects it at many points: we can see this as soon as we ask the question, how was the framework established in the first place?

The answer is that with a few negligible exceptions (such as the Panathenaic prize amphorae in fourth- and third-century Athens which are inscribed with the name of the annual magistrate, or the funerary urns from Ptolemaic Egypt marked with regnal years), each fixed point has been derived either from the discovery of pottery in a context believed to be associated with a dated event in history or, less often, from its association with more closely dated objects such as coins. But a message of this chapter has been that archaeological material and historical events are hard to bring together, because they represent different facets of human existence. Thus, for example, there is an easily intelligible process, well known to archaeologists, whereby a deposit of material becomes 'sealed', that is cut off from later intrusions either by having a continuous layer of soil superimposed on it, or through concealment in a grave. It is usually possible to detect whether anyone has subsequently dug through the stratum, or robbed or re-used the grave. The process of sealing will thus provide a lower chronological limit, a *terminus ante quem*, for all the material in the deposit. But how often is such a sealing process even plausibly, let alone demonstrably, associated with a dated historical event? The commonest circumstance is the destruction of a settlement, especially helpful when it is followed by total abandonment. But first, the possibility of other unrecorded destructions, accidental or otherwise, has to be excluded; then there remains the problem of the extent of most settlement-sites. If the sealed deposit in effect covers several acres, it is of course the latest material in any part of this deposit which provides the fixed dating-point. The difficulty in pinning down this latest material, even in relative terms, is exemplified by several instances in prehistory. What stage in the pottery-sequence had been reached when the palatial site at Knossos was destroyed? 'The end of Late Minoan II', said Sir Arthur Evans; 'Late Minoan III A 1', said others who had accepted his stratigraphy but refined his pottery-classification; 'the beginning of Late Minoan III A 2', say yet others, a generation later, to make no mention of those who reject Evans' scheme of stratification altogether. A similar process of scrutiny and downward revision seems to have begun with the Mycenaean pottery from Tell el Amarna in Egypt, a settlement not destroyed but abandoned after a brief occupation. Much the same has also been attempted for the pottery from the settlement on Thera, destroyed by volcanic disturbances a century or more earlier.[7] In these cases there was no close link with any dated historical event; the aim was the more modest one of establishing which material could be used to date the sealing of the deposit. Closer examination leads to new refinements of typology and some of these may reveal the presence of supposedly later features. Then either the scheme of relative chronology has to be adjusted, or the whole typological sequence is revised so that the chronology can be kept. All this tends to undermine confidence.

The same method can be used, often with better results, with graves or communal burials which have a known date. Here the process of 'sealing' is less equivocal and the problems caused by the quantity of material scarcely arise. Once again, it is in Aegean prehistory that there is the greatest dependence on this method, when Minoan and Mycenaean pottery has been found in Egyptian tombs which can be dated to the reign of a specific Pharaoh. The main danger lies in the fact that the pottery has by definition been imported over quite long distances, comprises only a small fraction of the grave-goods in any one burial, and may have been highly prized; it may therefore have been made appreciably earlier than the date of the tomb in which it is found. Archaeologists sometimes resort too readily to this 'heirloom' explanation, but enough unquestionable instances have occurred to show that it must apply at times in antiquity. But in historical times, such dated burials are in any case not common; they have mainly occurred in the form of communal graves associated with important battles, such as Marathon (490 BC), Delion (424) or Chaeronea (338), or the grave of the Lacedaemonians killed in 403 BC, which was discovered in 1930 in the Athenian Kerameikos.[8] Apart from lingering doubts over the identity of these tombs (as with the 'tumulus of the

Plataeans' at Marathon, below, pages 28–9), these finds on the whole offer the best dating evidence for ancient pottery of any period; the circumstances make the use of heirlooms relatively unlikely.

Less satisfactory is the dating evidence gained from the foundation of a dated settlement. Here the element of 'sealing' is absent; it is merely a question of pursuing excavation over a wide area of the site until one is satisfied that some of the earliest deposits have been found, or the graves of the earliest settlers identified. The risk is the same as that of extensive destruction-levels, only in reverse; further examination may at any time reveal deposits earlier than the earliest that were previously known, and on which chronological equations have already been based. The conclusions must therefore remain provisional. Some examples of this process, by now notorious among specialists, have occurred on Greek colonial sites in Sicily, notably Megara Hyblaea and Selinus; Thucydides (VI 4, 2) offers credible foundation-dates (728 and 628 BC respectively in these particular cases), and excavations had progressed far enough for the earliest pottery at each site to be provisionally identified; an absolute chronology for early Greek pottery was established which leaned heavily on these and a few other such fixed points; then re-examination of the material at both sites revealed stylistic phases hitherto undetected and apparently earlier.

Yet the very fact that the chronology of Greek painted pottery is based on this range of different kinds of evidence gives it a cumulative strength which is lacking in any single category. When inferences based on destruction-dates in one area agree with those based on foundation-dates in another, it is reasonable to conclude that both are approximately correct. So far this question has been discussed in terms of Greek painted wares which, with their rapid and logical development and their wealth of iconographical detail, establish a more or less adequate framework for the years between c. 750 and 300 BC. For about a century and a half after that we have a series of dated Hellenistic deposits, but they are more thinly distributed and affect a narrower range of wares. There then ensues a hiatus before the process is resumed, first by the Italian and then by the provincial *terra sigillata*. In most important respects this fills the same role as the Greek pottery but with rather more precision. Attribution to individual craftsmen, instead of resting on stylistic observation supplemented by occasional signatures, is assured by the frequent occurrence of potters' stamps; dating contexts are often potentially more accurate thanks to the fuller documentation of Roman military history and the narrower dating-range of Roman Imperial coins. From the accession of Augustus to the end of Trajan's principate we have a series of military sites in Gaul, Germany and Britain whose occupation is historically attested and was often brief, which have been scientifically excavated and which have produced *terra sigillata* in adequate quantities. When this evidence falls away in the later Empire there remains the evidence of provincial cemeteries where pottery is associated with Imperial coins, extending to after AD 400. Occasional correlations for other Roman wares are possible later still: there are deposits containing 'Late Roman C' ware which are dated by a great earthquake at Antioch on the Orontes in AD 526; the Slav invasions in the late sixth century of our era, and those of the Persians and Arabs in the earlier seventh, offer at least the possibility of further fixed points in the ceramic series.[9]

For the traditional methods of determining chronology, pottery is the only class of archaeological material which stands comparison with coins and inscriptions; at times it is more accurately datable than either. In default of any of these, other materials must be used – sculpture, architecture, terracottas, metalwork – but on closer examination these usually prove to depend ultimately on the original three sources of dating evidence; they thus offer chronological information of the same type, but less direct and accurate. For the historical period, the very different method of dating by techniques based on the physical properties of objects – radiocarbon, thermo-luminescence, thermo-remanent magnetism – provide even less precision and are therefore seldom of use except in the detection of modern fakes. But in recent years, such great advances have been made with dendrochronological dating that one day it can be expected to bring about, in ancient history, a minor but significant sequel to the undoubted revolution that it is creating in prehistoric chronologies. In prehistory, this has been achieved mainly through its use in conjunction with the radiocarbon technique, to correct and refine the less reliable but more widely available evidence which the latter offers. In ancient history, its contribution will be more direct, by confronting the archaeological dates which have been derived, by the traditional means that we have been reviewing, from historical events. The prospect is rather stimulating.

Dendrochronology involves the slow and painstaking build-up of a tree-ring sequence over a long period, as is suggested by the fact that it was already being pioneered in the early years of this century by the American astronomer A. E. Douglass. It was no accident that it first evolved in the New World, where exceptionally long-lived species like the sequoia and the bristlecone-pine are available. In Europe, where few trees live to a great age, this technique was developed through B. Huber's studies in the years from 1938 onwards, and had to proceed by laborious compilation through the establishment of 'overlaps' between relatively short sequences, each within a restricted geographical area. The preservation of substantial pieces of timber in archaeological contexts, on which the application of dendrochronology depends, is best favoured by the more temperate climate-zones of Europe. A 'master' tree-ring chronology, extending back thousands of years, could thus be built up for northern and western Europe. From the viewpoint of history, some of the most valuable early results were achieved in regions only briefly in touch with the Mediterranean civilisations, where archaeological contexts existed which were already approximately datable. One thinks especially of the work of E. Hollstein and H. Cüppers on Roman bridge-timbers from the Rhineland, which was helped by the fact that approximate historical dates existed for some of the structures; of these, that of AD 310 for a bridge at Cologne was the most precise. This gave a fixed point which, by reversing the normal application of dendrochronological dates, itself 'anchored' a useful early sequence covering as much as 1,060 years. In the Mediterranean world, no epoch of Classical history can yet be covered by such absolutely-dated sequences, but even when there is a 'floating' sequence available the results can be both illuminating and startling, as has been shown recently by P. I. Kuniholm's work at Gordion.[10] He has used the 806-year floating sequence earlier derived from the timbers in the burial-chamber of the Great Tumulus at Gordion, known to have been constructed in the earlier Iron Age and approximately dated to the late eighth century BC by cross-links with Assyrian types of vessel portrayed on reliefs at Khorsabad. Other timbers, both from Gordion and from other sites on the Anatolian plateau, could thus be dated relatively to the construction of the Great Tumulus; but it was within the tumulus itself that the main surprise was encountered.

The tomb-chamber is in the form of a cabin composed of squared timber beams, from which a few tree-rings might therefore have been trimmed; but the cabin was enclosed in a loose outer casing of unsquared logs (some of these found with traces of their bark attached) held in place by rubble backing. The whole was then covered by a gigantic mound of earth. What Kuniholm has found is that the latest preserved tree-ring on the timbers of the inner chamber conforms to reasonable expectations: it is very close in date to those of two other monuments whose finds are of similar date, 'Tumulus P' and

'Tumulus Koerte III'. All three should date to the late eighth century BC, and their latest tree-rings range from the 612th to the 623rd years of the 'floating' Gordion sequence, the Great Tumulus timber being the latest within this very narrow spread. The epoch when the trees were felled and the three tombs constructed can therefore be reasonably equated with these years of the tree-ring sequence. But when the logs of the *outer* casing of Great Tumulus (unsquared) were examined, no less than three of them proved to have the very same year for their final ring and it was the 806th year of the 'floating' sequence – 183 years later than the last year found in the inner tomb. So far there is no insuperable difficulty: the 183 outermost rings of the carefully squared timbers of the inner chamber could simply have been removed by the carpenters. But then Kuniholm finds that, in the whole area of the settlement and cemeteries of Gordion, only one monument produced a tree-ring later than the 806th year of the outer structure of the Great Tumulus. Most were very substantially earlier, even when the tree-rings were associated with Persian buildings in the city, dated archaeologically to the *sixth* century BC. The range for these and other 'late' buildings was from the 303rd to the 727th years of the sequence, with just one outlier from the 853rd year.

Most archaeologists would conclude that there is but one sensible interpretation of these facts: that the 806th year of the sequence represents the approximate date of the Great Tumulus and that the earlier tree-ring dates are explained by the trimming off of the outermost rings. But this will mean that, with one exception, every single structure so far tested at Gordion was composed of timbers which had either been drastically trimmed, or were being re-used after centuries had elapsed, and were thus very aged. There will also be the coincidence that three of these structures, at roughly the same date in the late eighth century, had almost the same number of rings removed so as to leave on the surface a ring of rather before 900 BC. There is also a third difficulty not yet mentioned: some of these same timbers had also been used for radio-carbon tests and the results, allowing for any conceivable adjustment, still came out as substantially later than the venerable dates which we have been inferring for the surviving beams. For these reasons, Kuniholm himself is more drawn to the only other possible alternative: that it is the *623rd* year which marks the approximate date of the construction of the tomb. The radiocarbon dates will then fit nicely, and the other Gordion timbers will be about 183 years less 'aged' than we had thought, several of them coming fairly close to the archaeological date of their associated structures. But there is now a serious new objection: the outer chamber of the tomb, and consequently the whole superimposed tumulus, will have to belong to the mid sixth century BC; the inner chamber with its precious contents will have stood unprotected yet unplundered through an era of well-attested violence and unrest in the city's history; and, one might add, Professor R. S. Young who excavated the tumulus with great skill in 1957 will have missed a major discrepancy, of about 183 years, in the two stages of its construction.

Both alternatives thus bristle with difficulties, and there seems to be no third possibility. When one of the first applications of a new and precise dating technique to a documented historical context produces such results as these, the way seems open to all sorts of sceptical and disparaging conclusions, either about the validity of the traditional dating methods or about the accuracy of the new one. Personally I would conclude, not without some agonising, that it is after all the *former* of the two alternative interpretations which involves the less intractable problems. A somewhat later date than the late eighth century for the Tumulus (and thus for the 806th year of the sequence) is archaeologically possible and would marginally ease the problems. The other interpretation, by contrast, seems to me acceptable only if combined with some further and totally hypothetical assumption – for instance, that a temporary (and no doubt smaller) earth tumulus had protected the inner tomb during the unstable epoch between its two stages of construction.

POLITICAL AND INSTITUTIONAL HISTORY

This might seem the very last aspect of history on which archaeology could be expected to throw light. It is, of course, true that a political system is itself an elusive thing in material terms; only in rare cases like that of Classical Athens, where we have a wealth of historical and topographical documentation, and the help of epigraphy into the bargain, has it proved possible to match the architectural remains to an already-known political structure. In different circumstances, where the details of the political system are not a given element, attempts have sometimes been made to reconstruct such a system from almost exclusively material evidence, as for example in the Minoan city at Mallia; or from evidence partly of this kind, as on certain Archaic sites; but inevitably they have attracted controversy. In general, our understanding of the political development of prehistoric and even of proto-historic societies (that of the Etruscans for instance) remains flimsy in the extreme. What hope then is there of turning archaeological evidence to profitable use in such a field?

It is obvious that, here as elsewhere, the more broadly archaeological research and political history are defined, the greater the possibilities for using the one as a source for the other. What is more debatable is the claim that this collaboration has already produced results which could not have been achieved otherwise, and which are important, even central, to the understanding of ancient political history. But it is, after all, essentially a political act to found a settlement in the first place; thereafter, the introduction of urban development and planning, the establishment of official cults, the allocation of land, the devolution of power to local centres, the organisation of the army, the formation of alliances and the extension of territory are all elements of political history. And for each of these activities archaeological evidence is available for use, if not necessarily in the ways in which it has traditionally been applied. Sometimes experience has taught us that certain of the more obvious archaeological criteria do not have the significance that they have been thought to possess; equally, our understanding of some statements in historical sources has had to be modified from the literal or anachronistic interpretation of them which had prevailed previously. In the foundation of settlements, for example, it has become clear that fortification is a criterion of very variable significance. From reading ancient sources which mostly date from a mature period in the growth of the ancient states, one is left with the impression that fortification-walls surrounding the settlement-area were a normal feature of any well-equipped city; such indeed they had become, but things had not always been so. Many fortifications on colonial or provincial sites have been proved to date from a century or more after the original foundation; that is, when a cross-section has been taken through the wall, the pottery underlying the very earliest structure has proved to date from at least a century after the earliest pottery found elsewhere on the site. This is as widely true of Greek and Phoenician colonies in Sicily (where some excavators have shown a reluctance to accept it) as it is of Roman towns in central and northern Gaul and Britain. In the homelands of Greece and Italy, town-walls were if anything even slower to appear: it is doubtful whether either Athens or Rome was walled by 500 BC. This throws an interesting light on the simultaneous advance of civilisation and insecurity.

Archaeology has also provided one of the explanations, at least in the Archaic period, for the delay in the fortification of cities: that previously there had been nothing which merited fortifying. Here again, there had been a tendency to take in a literal sense the statements of Classical writers which incorporated terms like *polis* and *synoikismos*; ambiguous though both these words were known to be, scholars still envisaged an urban settlement ('polis') as the invariable product of the union of settlements under one capital ('synoecism') when they read these passages. There had of course to have been an earlier stage in urban growth, and there was a *locus classicus* to illustrate it: the repeated phrase of Thucydides in his account of early Greece (15, 1; 10, 2), to describe the form of the primitive city composed of villages (*kata kōmas oikoumenē*). The revelation has been that this kind of 'city' persisted so late, at least in the non-colonial areas. For urbanisation in its true sense, the great age appears to have been the first half of the sixth century BC; Thucydides, whether he realised it or not, was describing an era scarcely more remote from his times than Regency London is from ours.

On other political questions, a wider range of archaeological techniques can be brought to bear. At several periods of ancient history, notably in Archaic Greece and late Republican and early Imperial Rome, there were few more burning issues than that of the allocation of land. To find any extant physical traces of this process was a forbidding task: that substantial areas of the ancient agricultural landscape have been recovered is one of the great triumphs of aerial photography, whose techniques were pioneered in the 1920s but developed with a new rigour and insight through military experience in World War II. The best-known achievement has been the recognition of large tracts of land in the Po valley, in Apulia and in Tunisia, with smaller nuclei in other areas such as southern Gaul and Greece, which had been centuriated – that is, divided up into carefully-surveyed rectangular plots in the manner employed by the Romans when allocating land to retired veterans. Already this has changed and enlarged our understanding of the circumstances in which centuriation was applied. At the same time, physical evidence has been recovered for other types of land-division used by the Romans and, on occasion, by the Greeks before them. Outstanding work was done by Père A. Poidebard on the Syrian *limes*, by Colonel J. Baradez in Algeria, by R. G. Goodchild in Tripolitania and in Roman Britain by a whole series of pioneers, most recently Professor J. K. S. St Joseph. For an earlier age, D. Adamesteanu has made remarkable discoveries, using air-photographs, as to the Archaic land-apportionment in the territory of the Greek colony of Metapontum; nor should

John Bradford's study of Classical fields and terracing in Attica be forgotten.[11]

A growing recognition of the political importance of religious cults has been a feature of recent historical work, and this is another field to which archaeology can contribute. Indeed, archaeological evidence is so obviously germane to the study of cult that in this case the appropriate note to sound is one of warning. It is unfortunate that the excavation of sanctuaries, that time-honoured area of Mediterranean archaeological activity, proceeded too far too soon; for in fact it presents peculiarly complex problems of stratification and association. Isolated classes of artefacts have been published superbly – Adolf Furtwängler's volume of 1895 on the Olympia bronzes is still a shining example today;[12] individual sacred buildings, even when very fragmentary, have been measured, analysed and reconstructed on paper with great skill; but the historical interpretation of the sites as a whole has lagged far behind. We still have only a hazy notion of how a major sanctuary actually worked, the aspect about which written sources tell us least. Again, to understand the political significance of a cult, it is necessary to be able to identify the deity to which a sanctuary is dedicated and, in Greece at least, there is a long list of instances where this has proved impossible, even where temples are preserved. As a result, there are potentially valuable bodies of documentary and epigraphic evidence which cannot be related to the physical remains. Particular difficulties surround the question of chronology: the better-preserved buildings can be dated with reasonable accuracy, but many sanctuaries show a long antecedent period of dedications with no accompanying structures. How were the early dedications housed? When and why were they jettisoned like so much rubbish, as excavation has proved them often to have been? Above all why, in the case of many major Greek sanctuaries, do dedications of the Archaic period predominate so heavily over those of later periods? These are some of the questions which archaeology has failed not only to answer but usually even to ask.

One other area of political activity calls for special treatment because, unlike those discussed so far, it has long been seen as a promising area for applying archaeological evidence – perhaps unjustifiably so. This is the whole field of inter-state relations, from diplomatic and commercial links to wars, conquests and, in cases where there is no documentary evidence, relationships of a colonial nature. Once again, it is mainly the Greek world that is involved, if only because the superior documentation of Roman history removes many areas of doubt. The favourite basis for such interpretations is of course the Greek pottery-styles, which offer a standing temptation because of the uniquely precise determination of their geographical and chronological positions. There are two levels of objection to this practice, of which the first and much the less important is that this determination may not be so precise, particularly in geographical terms, as it has been claimed to be. In recent years there has been a small but disquieting series of findings, based on scientific tests of one kind or another (usually trace element analysis) as to the provenance of Greek regional wares. While in most cases this has confirmed the views previously held of the associations of particular *decorative styles* with particular regions, it is otherwise with the questions of *fabric*. It has revealed that decorative styles could be, and were, imitated closely enough to pass the test of ordinary visual inspection and be accepted as the 'real thing'; only fabric-analysis has shown that a different centre of production, possibly hundreds of miles away from the originating region, is involved.[13] In simple terms, the result is that numerous 'imported' pots are now revealed as locally-made, and that suspicion therefore falls on many other cases where no such tests have yet been applied. Of course, the imitation of the artefacts of another community may be just as important, in historical terms, as the importation of them, and neither is necessarily susceptible to explanation in terms of political influence.

Far more substantial, however, are the objections to applying the evidence of pottery to such ends in the first place. The question of the commercial significance of pottery is not directly relevant here except in the comparative sense, that any doubt which hangs over this aspect applies, *a fortiori*, to the question of its political significance. If, as most archaeologists now accept, the production and circulation of pottery reflected the policy of the state hardly at all, then clearly we must be very cautious indeed in using it to interpret inter-state relations. If Region A exports a large quantity of pottery to Region B, or exercises obvious influence over the styles employed there, the inference that there is some political influence over Region B may still be quite unjustified. It may reflect nothing more than the fact that Region B was short of suitable potter's clay deposits, or that Region A had an acknowledged pre-eminence in that particular industry. We are back once more in the shadow of the 'positivist fallacy': pottery is nearly always the most plentiful and sometimes the only material evidence available – if we cannot use it, where else can we turn? One answer is that in fact there usually are other categories of evidence available, only they have not yet been studied with the same thoroughness as pottery, so that their implications are less clear. With sculpture, terracottas, architectural detail, roof-tiles, grave-types, weapons or bronze dress-accessories, understanding of regional style is progressing steadily: one day it may be possible to use these as indications of external contact and, if so, several of them could have greater historical significance than pottery. Yet the example of present-day experience, as often in archaeology, is a standing warning against using artefacts as indicators of political relationships.

Political relations, however, are merely a function of political *entities*. Archaeologists outside the Classical field have become increasingly uneasy about the validity and application of the whole concept of 'cultures', that is geographical assemblages based on similarity of artefact-types. Here they would do well to consider the evidence, both for and against, offered by the results obtained in Classical lands; and we in turn should consider how far this concept is tacitly applied in the ancient Mediterranean world, and what material evidence is used. I believe that here the potential for archaeological evidence may offer grounds for optimism. For example, one of the most fundamental and most neglected facts of Greek and of Italian history is the persistence, right down to our own times, of certain regional divisions of culture, material and otherwise. These divisions cannot have their origins in the period when the Greek states of the historical era were in the process of formation, first because the regions are in many cases larger than the individual historical states, secondly because they are perceptibly earlier than the latter. For Greece, the Late Bronze Age is the very latest period by which the regional divisions must have taken shape, since they can already then be recognised in terms of material culture. It is true that prehistoric archaeologists have consciously looked for these divisions on the analogy of those existing in historical times; but the fact remains that they have found them. 'Boeotian', 'Attic', 'Messenian' are identifiable archaeological categories, at least by the later phases of the Bronze Age. It is possible that the boundaries of such regions coincided with those of the Mycenaean kingdoms, but that is a hotly disputed question and not essential to the argument. What is not debated is that by the early historical period, five hundred years later, these divisions have acquired a political (and incidentally a linguistic) significance. In Greece, some of the regions embrace the territories of a number of smaller states, largely independent of each other but owing a wider allegiance to their region, sometimes by means of a formal league (Achaea, Arcadia,

Boeotia); some house unitary states of an 'ethnic' nature even in historical times (Locris, Acarnania, Aetolia). In one case (Attica) a whole region has coalesced into a single city-state, while in another (Laconia and Messenia) two such regions are forcibly amalgamated. By about 700 BC, they are all in some sense political entities, and they may have been so earlier; the fact remains that they are first detectable as archaeological groupings, linked by similarities of burial-customs and of pottery-style and fabric. In other words, they are archaeological 'cultures'. It is encouraging that M. Pallottino has recently used similar evidence from Italy to reach much the same conclusion there: that the ethnic and linguistic structure of ancient Italy, as we know it from later historical sources, must have been established at this same early date.[14] There may be lessons here for both archaeologist and historian.

MILITARY HISTORY

The contribution of archaeology here is more predictable, in form and in importance; yet its value is not exactly what it is often imagined as being. The most obvious and substantial physical relics, namely fortification-works, can certainly at times be related to historical accounts of wars, or else extend them. But when it comes to the topography of individual campaigns and battles, the historian often turns to archaeology in vain. It is worth pausing a moment to consider why this should be so. The fundamental discrepancy between archaeology and 'event-orientated' history is and will always be their very different time-scales. In ancient warfare, a campaign of huge scale and significance, like the Persian invasion of Greece in 480/79 BC, could be prepared and carried out virtually without leaving any permanent and positive (as distinct from destructive) physical trace. This is partly because of its short duration, partly because of incidental factors like the relatively backward development of ancient siege-craft. As a result, excavation has not much light to throw on the great wars of the ancient world; a destruction-level here, a monument there, a communal grave elsewhere, are the most that can be produced. An apparent exception arose with the discovery in 1970 of the 'tumulus of the Plataeans' at Marathon; its precise location was so unexpected and hard to reconcile with any natural interpretation of the ancient sources for the battle that it seemed that archaeology was re-writing a famous chapter in history. Yet by 1977 the identification of the tumulus was already being seriously questioned, mainly on archaeological grounds.[15] The episode in my view reflects not just problems of a particular kind, but the general nature of archaeological evidence: it seldom speaks the language of historical events.

That a lasting contribution has been made by archaeology to ancient military history is in part the result of incidental historical factors whose effects are detectable by excavation; and in part, yet again, through the extension of archaeological techniques far beyond excavation. Because the ancients, at certain periods, practised burial with arms; because they regularly dedicated military spoils at sanctuaries; above all, because they introduced the human figure as the dominant element in their art and were especially addicted to military subjects – these are the prime reasons why so much light can be thrown on their military development. Such evidence is obviously appropriate not to events but to processes: it enables us to build up a background of technical, tactical and even organisational development, against which the known campaigns can then be set. Its value lies in the fact that this background was largely impossible to reconstruct from documentary evidence.

But a contribution of a much more specific kind has been possible (as with land-systems) through the development of archaeological air survey and, to a lesser extent, of field-work on the ground as well. A classic instance is that of the history of Roman military operations in northern Britain. As long ago as 1747, in the aftermath of the Battle of Culloden, a young lieutenant of engineers (the future Major-General William Roy) was appointed to army mapping duties in Scotland and indefatigably planned and recorded the Roman military installations which he found. Thus began the process of filling out by archaeological observation the exiguous documentary sources for these operations. The activities of Agricola between AD 79 and 84 seemed to provide the best opportunities. In 1918, excavation at Camelon produced the first positive material indications of Agricola's presence in Scotland; the picture was soon extended. Then in the years from 1945 on, J. K. S. St Joseph developed to a new degree of refinement the recognition of military sites from the air. A number of permanent forts, hitherto unknown, were discovered; in several cases excavation later proved them to be of Agricolan date. Much more numerous, however, were the temporary marching-camps found; here the main contribution of excavation was to relate series of overlapping camps on the same site, thus building up a relative sequence; a typology was constructed in which camps of different size and plan could be assigned to different periods. When the camps occur further north than

Strathtay, historical evidence confines their possible date to the two
alternatives of Agricola's and Septimius Severus' campaigns. In this
way, not only have Agricola's steps been traced at least as far north
as Banffshire, but in the process the course of Severus' expeditions of
AD 208 and 209 have been even more fully reconstructed.[16] This is a
remarkable achievement, and one which it may prove possible to repli-
cate in some of the less built-up regions around the Mediterranean.
It also provides a good instance of a problem (an unusually specific
one in this case) which was posed by historians, or at least by the
study of history, and was left for archaeologists to try to answer. This
is often the best procedure for advancing the co-operation of the two
disciplines; problems posed by the archaeologists themselves have a
habit of not being historically very significant and, to be still more
candid, much archaeology has never been directed at the solution of
problems at all. These observations are particularly relevant to the
next section.

ECONOMIC AND SOCIAL HISTORY

There is a sense in which every archaeological find ever made contributes to economic and social history; but it is not a very helpful
sense. To expect historians to monitor the entire output of excavation in Classical lands would, as we have said, be preposterous. A
better procedure is for archaeologists to provide, in their excavation
reports and monographs, a primary treatment of the more relevant
finds that is oriented towards economic and social history, and for
the help of like-minded historians (as suggested above, page 10) to
be enlisted in this study. Archaeologists, even if not disposed to explore the economic implications themselves, can make it far easier for
others to do so by improving their communications: that is, by not
even claiming to pursue the will-o'-the-wisp of total objectivity in presenting the 'facts', but acknowledging the interpretative nature of all
archaeological reporting; by describing, in excavation reports, their
stratification in terms intelligible to those unfamiliar with excavation;
by cataloguing their finds by function rather than by the material of
which they are made; by grouping together deposits which belong
together, rather than abstracting, from *all* the deposits, each class of
finds in turn. Several of these suggestions are taken from an article
by Mrs S. C. Humphreys which has become something of a classic
since it was first published in 1967.[17] For the archaeologist writing a
monograph on a particular category of archaeological evidence, one

can only urge that his treatment (and as a reflection of this, his title) be in some degree aimed at those students in other fields who, if they only know it, will be able to extract valuable information from his book.

But these are only the first steps; there is still a long way to go. Younger archaeologists, with whom the primary initiative lies, are showing (at least in the English-speaking countries) a strong tendency to work in those prehistoric and proto-historic fields where the problem of mastering the ancient sources hardly arises. To some extent this gap is being filled by the increasing familiarity with archaeological method on the part of the younger ancient historians. This should take care of some immediate needs, and there is, after all, a certain unreality about making specific programmatic demands for the future development of a discipline. It is more fruitful to ask for a change in attitudes, and here the signs are already more favourable. In the past, whereas it was universally recognised that the essence of historical enquiry was the search for explanations and causes, the same was not seen to be so clearly true of archaeology; in fact, many archaeologists acted as if it were not. Today Classical archaeologists (and not only those of the younger generation) are more often asking themselves the questions 'why?' and 'how?'. Pottery studies provide a good example. After generations of study of the stylistic development of Greek pottery by art-historical methods, the moment was felt to be ripe, in the period between the two World Wars, to harness this material to far-reaching economic arguments. This episode continued strongly into the 1950s and is not yet entirely over. But in the last generation a third approach has grown up which is in every sense critical of the other two. The pottery industry has been studied as an industrial phenomenon, not just as a sort of artists' collective. In the process, some absolute estimate of its scale has been reached. As a result of this in turn, the economic significance of pottery exchanges has been scrutinised; many earlier conclusions about trade, economic policy and even political influence (cf. pages 25–7) have been undermined.[18]

These recent developments have probably been influenced by the changes of emphasis in ancient history, whereby social and economic problems have come more to the forefront and increased attention has been paid to the methods of anthropology. Certainly there were audible criticisms of the earlier approaches from historians and anthropologists. For example, the shape of a pot, instead of being seen as the result of factors in the personality of an individual craftsman, is now more often looked at in terms of its function, both literal and social; its decoration, similarly, being designed for a market of some kind, is scrutinised for other influences besides the purely artistic ones; its geographical origins and the distribution of its type are less often taken as evidence for the operation of an undifferentiated 'trade', but are looked at in a more sophisticated way which takes account of the exact context (whether the type is found, for example, only in graves, or as dedications at sanctuaries, in Greek or in non-Greek settlements, in regular association with other wares, in strictly contemporary or also in later contexts, in a restricted social milieu; and so on).

All this is part of a wider and essentially beneficial phenomenon: the realisation, on the part of the archaeologist, of the distinctive contribution that he can make to social and economic history. It is no exaggeration to say that in the past Classical archaeologists were often unaware of the potential value of their own findings in this respect. Purely 'archaeological' data such as the relative chronology of mosaic pavements in Romano-British villas, or the discontinuation of burial with arms in Archaic Greece, once they were put into the hands of historians, have proved rich sources of historical inference. It has been a similar story with much wider principles like that of the quantification of data. For a hundred years and more, Classical archaeologists have been handling bodies of material which are of sufficient size to be susceptible of quantification, and even to form statistically significant samples: the numbers of temples belonging to successive phases of architectural development, the numbers of pots from a given site or from the output of a given workshop, the numbers of grave-goods from the successive phases of a cemetery, the incidence of different types of statue (at any rate in the Archaic era) or of carved grave-stelai (in Classical Athens) – the potential of many such groups of data, long since available, is now at last being exploited.

Quantification is also an essential feature of the technique of archaeological survey which, more clearly here than in any other aspect of history, has an almost unlimited contribution to make. By recording systematically the traces of all settlements of all periods in a given region (or, more realistically, in a sample of a given region), survey work can provide, ready-made, the data for demographic studies and, less directly, material for the study of environmental change, agricultural practices, land-holdings, market organisation, communications and a dozen other aspects of local history. Solutions range from one-man surveys of small political and geographical units (such as islands) to large centralised projects like the *Forma Italiae* series, produced by the Unione Accademica Nazionale, which already comprises over twenty volumes covering thousands of square kilometres of the Italian landscape. Another distinctive asset of survey is that, in its nature, it is more likely to throw light on rural as opposed to urban settlement, whereas the bias of the documentary sources is in the opposite direction, emanating as it does from the ancient city and reflecting in the main its workings and tastes. By survey, the archaeologist can amass more relevant information for the economic development of a region than he can by excavating a single site, however rich; particularly when one reflects that nearly all excavations, too, are confined to a sample of the site. Excavation, being slower and more labour-intensive, is also more costly in proportion to its results. As so often, the initiative in this field has in the first instance lain outside Classical lands and, when introduced to Greece, Italy and the Mediterranean, has tended to concentrate on areas and periods where documentation is thin or non-existent. But as well as being a substitute for historical documents, survey results can supplement them in a very substantial way, as has been made clear when expeditions have included in their coverage, or even been centred on, historical communities.

Consider, for example, a question already posed hypothetically (above, page 8): where did the peasants of the ancient world actually live? For Roman Italy, a well-reasoned answer has now been put forward by P. D. A. Garnsey, drawing on the detailed results of field-survey expeditions in southern Etruria, Molise and northern Apulia: an answer not the less interesting because it runs counter to some of the best-known statements of the ancient literary sources for this question.[19] In brief, he finds that the traditional picture of a landscape largely depopulated of a free peasantry by later Republican times, of agriculturalists concentrated in towns, and of the progressive extension of slave labour on rural estates, cannot be entirely reconciled with the results of field survey. One final effect of archaeological survey whose value will be most widely appreciated is that it, and it alone, can produce an accurate large-scale historical map, at any rate of a small region. All Classical archaeologists and most other Classicists have at some time felt the acute shortage of such maps; now, at last, some are taking the initiative to remedy that lack.

CULTURAL HISTORY

Under this perhaps amorphous heading I group those aspects of history on which Classical archaeology, as traditionally practised, could reasonably be expected to throw most light. The time-honoured study of works of art, their content, their place in the historical development, their relationship with other contemporary art (including literature) would appear to be nothing if not a contribution to cultural history. Yet once again one must acknowledge that the results have been disappointing from this point of view, and once again the cause is a familiar one. Just as Classical archaeologists have been unaffected by some of the recent changes in archaeological theory and practice, so they have stood apart, for a much longer period and with less obvious reason, from developments in the approach of the art historian in non-Classical fields. The whole notion of the *function* of art, the appreciation that the visual arts are directly shaped by the society for which they are practised, and that they therefore directly reflect the nature of that society – these are not deeply engrained in archaeological thinking. Here too, the question 'why?' is not very often asked. Instead, a good part of the energies of Classical art historians (and thus of the whole activity of Classical archaeology) is taken up with the largely descriptive discipline of classification: that is, the locating of works of art, with increasing accuracy and detail, in a framework of chronological and geographical categories, if possible extending to attribution to individual artists and workshops. This is an essential preliminary to art history, but would not elsewhere be regarded as art history itself. Not only does it not bring much illumination to the broader field of cultural history if it stops there; but as far as Greek art is concerned, it does not do so for traditional political history either, for the particular reason that Greek art happens to have extraordinarily little directly historical content. The result is, yet again, a tendency towards the isolation of the discipline of ancient art history; it may be no coincidence that the formative years of the subject coincided with the birth of the doctrine of 'art for art's sake'.

Yet the art of the ancient world provides real scope for the writing of cultural history: it survives in relatively large quantities; there is a by no means negligible body of ancient literature devoted to it; and the fact that the status of the artist in antiquity had a lower place in the social hierarchy than it has today, so far from forming a serious obstacle, can actually be turned to advantage when we are using art as a medium for examining society as a whole. It means that the artist was continually the object of external pressures – social, religious and professional – to a degree which is hard for us to picture with our accepted notions of the independent artist and his free inspiration. It means that he can occasionally show the ordinary man's reaction to those pressures, in a way that few ancient writers could afford to do, even when they were equipped to: one thinks particularly of the vase-painter, whose product was not of great intrinsic value and not often directly commissioned by the patron; and who could introduce with impunity caricature scenes, vernacular versions of myths or a generally 'debunking' style to his work. It means, therefore, that he can fill an important gap in our understanding of ancient societies.

But there are more difficulties here than meet the eye. The language of Greek and Roman art is usually thought of as direct, widely intelligible and not in need of the detailed interpretation and careful translation without which the works of ancient literature cannot be communicated to the world. In fact, both stand in the same danger of being misunderstood, but for different reasons: with literature, the risk is that of our being misled by error in interpretation; with works of art, it is that we do not see the need for an interpretation at all. There are books in plenty to describe, classify and date them; to explain their subjects; but not, usually, to explain the works themselves. In some cases, this is because our knowledge is too limited to provide such an explanation; the result is that the spectator becomes habituated to not being given one. This is true of sculpture above all. Yet there can hardly have been a single piece of large-scale Greek or Roman sculpture which did not have a meaning, religious or secular; which did not carry an intelligible message to contemporaries. Sometimes we must confess outright that the message is lost to us, at least for the time being: until it can be established, for example, whether the famous bronze statue from Artemision represents Zeus, or Poseidon, or not a deity at all, our understanding of this work is essentially defective. Similarly, to know whether the head no. 437 in the National Museum at Athens does or does not represent Julius Caesar is critical to our understanding both of the work and of the subject. Sometimes we are offered a whole choice of interpretations, most or all of which must be false, as for example with the mid fifth-century BC relief known as the 'Mourning Athena', which is thereby placed almost on a par with an undeciphered text. Sometimes a long-accepted interpretation of a familiar monument is suddenly called into question, as has happened recently with no less a work than the Parthenon frieze; if it does *not* represent the Panathenaic procession, then there is no end to the false suppositions which, consciously or unconsciously, have been based on the belief that it does.[20] Faced with hazards of this kind, it is not surprising that many Classical archaeologists prefer to stick to the relatively secure ground of artistic evaluation and classification.

Yet when more enterprising approaches have been tried, they have usually proved fruitful, often by advancing our knowledge and understanding and almost always in intellectual stimulation. In certain areas of ancient art history, the achievement stands beyond dispute, but is often forgotten: for instance, in the interpretation of mythical scenes, especially on vases. As long ago as 1880, Carl Robert began a series of painstaking iconographic studies, culminating in the great work of his old age, *Archäologische Hermeneutik*, a classic account of the means adopted by Greek artists to convey a mythological narrative. This has been, in its main outlines, so universally accepted ever since that it is seldom acknowledged any longer; indeed, only in recent years has there been a revival of discussion of the whole question with which Robert was dealing.[21] Yet what could be more fundamental, both to the art history of this and many subsequent periods, and to the broader interpretation of Greek myth? The successive solutions which artists found to these problems of narrative are vital steps in the intellectual development of their times. In particular, the discovery in Archaic Greece of a means of representing a whole myth by one single 'closed' composition makes extremely interesting comparisons, first with the narrative methods employed by early Greek poets; then with the contrasting means used by Greek artists of the Classical period to portray myth; and finally with the essentially Roman device of 'continuous narrative', which Robert's contemporary Franz Wickhoff had expounded in 1895, and which prevailed in Western art for some fifteen centuries.[22] This is the very stuff of cultural history.

Portraiture is a medium which in its nature brings art very close to history. Most studies of it have nevertheless treated ancient portraits as isolated art-objects and (since the majority of surviving examples are in the form of sculpture) as illustrations of a particular stage in the development of the sculptor's art. To do this is to side-step the really important (and, I would argue, the really interesting) questions about portraiture in the ancient world: such as, why was it scarcely existent in Archaic society? Why, when athletic portrait-statues of living subjects had long since been tolerated, were other kinds of private portrait apparently only acceptable when they were posthumous? (I am of course assuming that the degree of individual characterisation that made a portrait recognisable as such, even when of an unknown subject, was approximately the same for contemporaries as it is for us two millennia later). How, when the demand for personal portraiture eventually became irresistible, did the portrait manage to take over such a central place in the social transactions of the Hellenistic age? It might be possible to give answers to all these questions in purely artistic terms, but the answers would certainly be inadequate and probably wrong as well. Here as in some other respects, historians of Roman art, less preoccupied than the Hellenists with the sheer quality of the works and confronted with a more overtly political message, have progressed rather further in their understanding.

To give a simple illustration of one of the problems: consider our own reactions, on the one hand when we encounter a portrait in an exhibition devoted to a single artist or theme; and on the other hand, when we enter a portrait gallery – perhaps a sculptural one like the 'Walhalla' erected by King Ludwig I of Bavaria on the banks of the Danube near Regensburg. In the first case, we are interested in the style of the artist, the way in which he adapted it to the portrait, the common features of his portraits generally; in the second, we are more concerned with the subjects, their place in history, the principles on which they have been chosen and the purpose of the gallery generally. At Walhalla, where the vast majority of the busts were carved in a homogeneous style between 1807 and 1842, it is only when we are brought up short by the starkness of the features of Bruckner, Stifter and Strauss (carved respectively in 1937, 1954 and 1973) that artistic considerations suddenly become uppermost. In our study of Greek portraits (though again this is less true of Roman), we adopt exclusively the former, 'exhibition' type of approach; yet the evidence shows that Greek contemporaries invariably encountered the portrait in the latter, 'gallery' type of context; a reading of Pausanias shows that this was still true in the second century AD. The appearance of Dieter Metzler's *Porträt und Gesellschaft* in 1971 was therefore a welcome innovation, and a similar approach to a broader range of sculpture has now been adopted in the closing chapter of Andrew Stewart's *Attika* (1979).[23]

One advantage of this type of research is that it is not necessary to be an archaeologist to carry it out with distinction. Other Classical scholars who have familiarised themselves thoroughly with the evidence, and who possess the courage of their convictions in matters artistic, have produced masterly treatments of cultural questions in which much of the primary evidence is archaeological. Again one tends to think first of religion, where in the last two generations the work of men like M. P. Nilsson and A. B. Cook has set a standard for future approaches by showing the indispensability of the archaeological material.[24] As a result, there are deities, such as Artemis in the Greek pantheon, for whose early evolution and for many of the details of whose cults archaeology has provided as much evidence as all the surviving written sources. Excavated sites, such as the Sanctuary of the Great Gods on Samothrace, have brought to light a range of religious practices previously quite unsuspected, several of them pre-Greek in origin but absorbed into the ritual of the sanctuary. But there are numerous other fields for this kind of activity as well. An excellent example was given recently by Sir Kenneth Dover's study *Greek homosexuality* (1978). For centuries scholars have been more or less uneasily aware of the prevalence in Greek imagination of homosexual love; but until the widely different categories of evidence could be brought together, as they are in Dover's book, it was impossible to evaluate the phenomenon properly. Now we have an indication of the date from which overt homosexual practices became acceptable to Greek society; of the differential standards that were adopted in judging different acts within homosexual behaviour generally; of the geographical unevenness in our evidence and the undoubted local variations in attitudes; and of much else. Most of this would have been impossible without the detailed study of the 500-odd vase-paintings listed in Dover's text.

But this is only one notable recent example. There are several other areas of cultural life where the artistic and archaeological evidence has proved itself indispensable long since, and is nowadays handled with due respect. Among the most obvious are ancient music and musical instruments, poetic recitation, theatre-production, athletics, domestic entertainment, education and reading, marriages and funerals, racial attitudes and the role of women. It would be true to say that our knowledge and judgement of many of these aspects of ancient life has been radically modified from that of earlier generations, since this broadening of approach took place.

By treating its subject in terms of the various branches of *historical* studies, this account has left many specific aspects of archaeological evidence out of consideration. One of these aspects, the archaeology of graves, deserves a few words in its own right, since it does not fall squarely within any of the categories used here. The prominence of grave-excavation in Mediterranean archaeology can be expected to continue, even if in the future excavation is increasingly confined to rescue operations arising from urban building and the construction of roads and pipe-lines. One great asset of cemeteries is that they consist of easily quantifiable units: throughout much of Classical history, single burial was practised, so that each grave represents a single act of interment and its grave-goods form a single closed deposit. A cemetery whose graves cover several generations may give a cross-section of a society more representative of the range of prosperity, as well as being chronologically wider, than will an excavated settlement of the same date, where most of the finds and architecture will belong to the final stages, and where the discovery of the full range of housing of all levels of society will be, at best, a costly and long-drawn-out process; or indeed than a sanctuary-deposit, in which most links of personal ownership are lost. Yet there are several obscure variables in funerary studies; above all, that of the relation between social hierarchy and funerary hierarchy, between a society's wealth and the wealth and elaboration of its graves. This makes it an urgent task to develop a more systematic approach to grave-archaeology; we need some kind of theory of funerary sociology and indeed funerary ideology. Fortunately there are signs that this need is now appreciated: an international colloquium on the latter topic was held in Naples in December 1977.[25]

Several of the larger published cemeteries of the Greek and Roman world have also been made the subject of valuable syntheses and statistical analyses. Predictably, these have concentrated on the earlier periods when there is less competition from other, more historically-oriented classes of evidence. The cist-tombs of the Early Bronze Age in the Cyclades, for example, were analysed in some detail by A. C. Renfrew in 1972; the size of the sample was large enough to justify the use of a computer. The graves of the important Early Iron Age cemetery in the Kerameikos at Athens were studied through the medium of their metalwork by H. Müller-Karpe in 1962, and through that of their stratigraphy and pottery by R. Hachmann in 1963. A broader study of the burials of the same period in the Argolid was published by R. Hägg in 1974, while J. B. Ward-Perkins and others have contributed comparable studies of the graves of the large Quattro Fontanili cemetery at Veii in Etruria. Surveys of the whole field of burial customs have been undertaken, for Greece by D. Kurtz and J. Boardman in 1971, for Rome by J. M. C. Toynbee (1971) and in a very useful collection of papers edited by R. Reece in 1977.[26] Excavators of cemeteries are themselves beginning to incorporate statistical studies of their material in the primary publication. But there are many fresh fields of synthesis to be conquered: among the most obvious (and the most formidable) are the hundreds of graves now recorded from Classical Athens and Rome.

Alongside these broader studies, the discoveries of exceptional individual burials continue to make contributions to archaeological knowledge. Even here, the conclusions have often been more

problematic than one would expect from the relatively simple process of interment on a single occasion: as witness the instances from
Marathon, from Gordion and from the Egyptian tombs containing
Minoan and Mycenaean pottery which have been mentioned earlier.
It is fitting to end with the most celebrated recent find, the royal tomb
at Vergina in Macedonia which was opened in November 1977 and
which its discoverer, Professor M. Andronikos, tentatively identifies
as that of Philip II.[27] If his identification proves right, this alone will
contribute a certain amount of evidence that will be useful to historians of the period. But a greater value attaches to the inferences
which will stand irrespective of the correctness of the identification.
To begin with, we now have, thanks to this impressive discovery, a
new and almost certain localisation for the site of Aigeae, mentioned
in several ancient sources as the place of burial of the Macedonian
kings, but hitherto placed by most modern scholars some distance to
the north, at Edessa; this will affect many questions of ancient topography. We have for the first time a standard of Macedonian royal
burial by which to judge other rich tombs. We have much new information on the military equipment of the era. We have a whole new
chapter in the history of Greek tomb-paintings, a fragmentary field
but one which throws unique and contemporary light on the whole
lost achievement of Greek free painting. It will be years before the
wealth of potential knowledge yielded by this one discovery can be
exploited to the full, and this process will outlast the dazzlement of
the intrinsic wealth of the finds.

The recurrent message of this chapter has been that, for the full
value of archaeology's contribution to ancient history to be realised,
the same qualities need to be shown by scholars in both disciplines:
understanding of the different problems that confront each side in the
pursuit of a common aim, and of the even more clearly different status
of the evidence that each side has to offer; and above all, breadth of
approach in interpreting the whole nature of historical enquiry.

APPENDIX

It may be helpful to give here, in addition to the works cited in the
footnotes, some examples of books which successfully apply archaeological evidence to some period or theme of ancient history.

On the questions of the *theory and method* of the application
of archaeological evidence to ancient history, there is a fundamental difficulty, alluded to in the opening sentences of the chapter: that

most works on archaeological theory studiously avoid making more than passing refences to Classical archaeology. This is even true of Bruce Trigger's *Time and Traditions: essays in archaeological interpretation* (Edinburgh, 1978), even though most classicists will derive substantial benefit from his chapter 2 in particular. One corner of the Classical world which does sometimes come into consideration is Roman Britain, and for this field (and by implication for other historical cultures) there is real enlightenment to be gained from I. R. Hodder and C. Orton's *Spatial Analysis in Archaeology* (Cambridge, 1976).

On *chronology*, although there are several thorough treatments of the non-archaeological evidence (see most recently A. E. Samuel, *Greek and Roman Chronology: Calendars and years in Classical antiquity (Handbuch der Altertumswissenschaft* I, 7) (Munich 1969), there is no work which systematically integrates the material evidence with this. R. W. Ehrich (ed.), *Chronologies in Old World Archaeology* (Chicago, 1965) is characteristic in leaving its readers to discover that the chronologies end in *c.* 2000 BC. One can only refer the reader to the works cited in notes 6–10. above, dealing with particular aspects.

Political and institutional history

One may single out a few basically historical works for their perceptive use of archaeological material, notably W. G. Forrest's *The Emergence of Greek Democracy* (London, 1966) and, on a regional level, P. A. Cartledge's *Sparta and Laconia: a regional history* (London, 1979).

Economic and social history

Here the field is much richer. One way of achieving the necessary range of expertise is by collaborative works, and an outstanding example of these is M. I. Finley (ed.), *Problèmes de la terre en Grèce ancienne* (Paris/The Hague, 1973). Notable recent studies and monographs include: C. G. Starr, *The Economic and Social Growth of Early Greece* (New York, 1977); A. Burford, *The Greek Temple-builders at Epidauros* (Liverpool, 1969) and *Craftsmen in Greek and Roman Society* (London, 1972); L. A. Moritz, *Grain-mills and Flour in Classical Antiquity* (Oxford, 1958); G. E. Rickman, *Roman Granaries and Store Buildings* (Cambridge, 1971).

Military history

Here again, collaboration has produced some of the most fruit-
ful results in J.-P. Vernant (ed.), *Problèmes de la guerre en Grèce
ancienne*, and J.-P. Brisson (ed.), *Problèmes de la guerre è Rome*
(Paris/The Hague, 1968 and 1969 respectively). But see also P. A. L.
Greenhalgh, *Early Greek Warfare: horsemen and chariots in Archaic
Greece* (Cambridge, 1973); J. S. Morrison and R. T. Williams, *Greek
Oared Ships, 900–322 BC* (Cambridge, 1968); W. K. Pritchett, *Ancient
Greek Military Practices* I, and *The Greek State at War* II (Berkeley/
Los Angeles, 1971 and 1974); J. K. Anderson, *Military Theory and
Practice in the Age of Xenophon* (Berkeley Los Angeles/ London,
1970).

Cultural history

A welcome move here is the 'Fontana History of the Ancient World'
series, in which there have appeared so far: R. M. Ogilvie, *Early
Rome and the Etruscans* (1976); J. K. Davies, *Democracy and Clas-
sical Greece* (1978); M. H. Crawford, *Republican Rome* (1978);
O.Murray, *Early Greece* (1980); and F. W. Walbank *The Hellenistic
World* (1981). One work of art history certainly deserves mention
here because of its unusual breadth of approach: Martin Robertson's
A History of Greek Art (Cambridge, 1975).

  In a separate class are the books written by archaeologists on periods accounted fully historical: R. M. Cook's *The Greeks till Alexander*
(London, 1962); John Boardman's *The Greek Overseas* (revised ed.,
London, 1980); F. Chamoux' *The Civilisation of Greece* (London,
1965); A. W. Johnston's *The Emergence of Greece* (Oxford, 1976);
and my *Archaic Greece* (London, 1980) all come under this heading on the Greek side, while the obvious Roman counterpart is the
'History of the Provinces of the Roman Empire' series, in which have
appeared S. S. Frere, *Britannia*; J. J. Wilkes, *Dalmatia* (London, 1967
and 1969).

NOTES

1. 'Notes on some probable traces of Roman fulling in Britain', *Archaeologia* 59.2 (1904), 207–32.
2. 'The Roman villa at Chedworth', *Transactions of the Bristol and
   Gloucester Archaeological Society* 78 (1959), 5–23.

3. *The Greeks and their Eastern Neighbours* (Society for the Promotion of Hellenic Studies, Supplementary Paper VIII, 1957), 15.
4. Discussed by M. M. Austin in *Greece and Egypt in the Archaic Age* (Cambridge Philological Society, Supplementary Volume II, 1970).
5. In *Greece and Italy in the Classical World* (Acta of the XIth International Congress of Classical Archaeology, London, 1978) (1979), 199.
6. For convenient discussions, see R. M. Cook, *Greek Painted Pottery*[2] (1972), Ch. 11; J. W. Hayes, *Late Roman Pottery* (1972), *passim*; F. Oswald and T. Davies Pryce, *An Introduction to the Study of Terra Sigillata* (1920), Ch. 3.
7. See for example M. R. Popham, *The Destruction of the Palace at Knossos* (Göteborg, 1970); V. Hankey and P. M. Warren, 'The absolute chronology of the Aegean Late Bronze Age', *BICS* 21 (1974), 142–52; several papers in C. Doumas and H. C. Puchelt (eds.), *Thera and the Aegean World* 1 (1978).
8. See F. Willemsen 'Zu den Lakedämoniergräbern im Kerameikos', *Athenische Mitteilungen* 92 (1977), 117–57.
9. See Roman references in n.6 above.
10. P. I. Kuniholm, *Dendrochronology at Gordion* (dissertation University of Pennsylvania, 1977, available in microfilm), *passim*; especially pages 45–53.
11. For earlier references, see J. Bradford, *Ancient Landscapes* (1957); also D. Adamesteanu, 'Le suddivisioni di terra nel Metapontino' in *Problèmes de la terre en Grèce ancienne*, ed. M. I. Finley (The Hague, 1973), 49–61.
12. *Olympia IV: die Bronzen* (Berlin, 1895).
13. For four recent instances, see G. Vallet and F. Villard, *Mégara Hyblaea II: la céramique archaïque* (1964); J. P. Morel, 'L'expansion phocéenne en Occident' (*BCH* 81(1957), 853–96), on 'Aeolic grey bucchero' at Massalia and elsewhere; M. Farnsworth, I. Perlman and F. Asaro, 'Corinth and Corfu: a neutron activation study of their pottery', *AJA* 81 (1977), 455–68; M. Coja and P. Dupont, *Histria v: les ateliers céramiques* (Bucharest and Paris, 1979).
14. 'Problemi attuali della protostoria Italiana nel quadro dello sviluppo del mondo classico', in *Greece and Italy in the Classical World* (above, n. 5), 57–71, especially 60–4.
15. See P. G. Themelis, 'Marathon', *Arkhaiologikon Deltion* 29 (1974), A (1977), 226–44, 297–8.
16. Well summarised by J. K. S. St Joseph, 'Types and dates of temporary camps in Scotland', *JRS* 63 (1973), 228–33; see also 'The camp at Durno and Mons Graupius', *Britannia* 9 (1978), 271–87.
17. 'Archaeology and the social and economic history of Classical Greece', *Parola del Passato* 116 (1967), 374–400 (also printed in *Anthropology and the Greeks* (1978), Ch. 4).

18. See particularly R. M. Cook's article 'Die Bedeutung der bemalten Keramik', *JdI* 74 (1959), 114–23, on general principles; for a specific example, F. Villard, *La céramique grecque de Marseille* (Paris, 1960), 72–161.

19. 'Where did Italian peasants live?', *Proceedings of the Cambridge Philological Society* 205 (1979), 1–25.

20. See F. Chamoux, 'L'Athéna mélancolique', *BCH* 81 (1957), 141–59; J. Boardman, 'The Parthenon frieze: another view', in *Festschrift für Frank Brommer* (Mainz, 1977), 39–49.

21. See especially N. Himmelmann-Wildschütz, 'Erzählung und Figur in der archaischen Kunst', *Abhandlungen der Akademie der Wissenschaften und der Literatur (Geistes- und Sozialwissenschaftliche Klasse)* (Mainz, 1967), 73–100; P. G. P. Meyboom, 'Some observations on narration in Greek art', *Mededelingen van het Nederlands Instituut te Rome* 40 (1978), 55–82; and, more elementary, J. E. Henle, *Greek Myths: a Vase-Painter's Notebook* (Bloomington and London, 1973).

22. Wilhelm Ritter von Härtel and F. Wickhoff. *Die Wiener Genesis* (Vienna, 1895); Wickhoff's contribution was translated and edited by Mrs E. S. Strong as *Roman Art* (1900).

23. D.Metzler, *Porträt and Gesellschaft: über die Entstehung der griechischen Porträts in der Klassik* (Münster, 1971); A.Stewart, *Attika: studies in Athenian sculpture of the Hellenistic age* (Society for the Promotion of Hellenic Studies, Supplementary Paper xiv, 1979).

24. See especially M. P. Nilsson, *Geschichte der griechischen Religion I–II* (Munich, 1941–50); A. B. Cook, *Zeus I–III* (1914–40).

25. *L'idéologie funéraire dans le monde antique*, to be published by the Cambridge University Press (see now below, p. 76, n. 8).

26. D. Kurtz and J. Boardman, *Greek Burial Customs* (1971); J. M. C. Toynbee, *Death and Burial in the Roman World* (1971); R. Reece (ed.), *Burial in the Roman World* (Council for British Archaeology Research Report xxii, 1977).

27. 'The tombs at the Great Tumulus of Vergina', in *Greece and Italy in the Classical World* (above, n. 5), 39–56.

CHAPTER 2

Greek Archaeology and Greek History

Here some more specific targets for criticism are selected – un-
due deference to the ancient sources, event-oriented archaeological narratives, and the apparently irresistible urge to match
the two with each other. On the proposed revision of earlier
Greek chronology by Francis and Vickers (p. 52), see above under Ch. 1. Little else need be added, save that the excavations
at Lefkandi (pp. 59–60), after the publication of an admirable
series of volumes dealing mainly with the cemeteries, have now
(2003) made a welcome return to further investigation of the
main settlement at Xeropolis (Whitley 2004: 39–40).

BIBLIOGRAPHY

Whitley, J. (2004), 'Archaeology in Greece, 2003–2004', *Archaeological Reports* 50: 1–92.

At certain points, the disciplines of history and archaeology converge;
and some of the closest rapprochements have traditionally taken place
in the field of Classics. I am concerned here with one quite specific
form of close relationship that can exist only between certain kinds
of historical and archaeological approach. These must be defined at
the outset.

The historian who bases his account fairly and squarely on the
ancient sources will tend to construct a narrative account that deals
in concepts similar to theirs: an account, that is, couched mainly in
terms of political, constitutional, and military events. To this view
of history, archaeological work for the most part can make little or
no contribution. But there is one large area of exception. The careful

'Greek archaeology and Greek history', *Classical Antiquity* 4, 1985, 193–207.

excavation of a site – particularly of a settlement-site – is likely to reveal episodes in the site's history: e.g., the construction, the extension,
the rebuilding, or the destruction of some part or parts of a settlement;
the deposition of a hoard; the reinforcement of a fortification or perhaps the failure to build one at all. Other kinds of site, though less
obviously, can yield evidence for their own types of 'episode': the appearance of a burial or burials in a cemetery in circumstances that
invite speculation as to the occasion on which they took place or even
as to the identity of the deceased, or a change in the nature or quantity
of dedications at a sanctuary.

To bring together this type of historical approach and this category of archaeological finding is to adopt an assumption that is very
widespread, but usually unspoken, in both disciplines. This assumption is that the kinds of event likely to feature in a conventional historical narrative and the kinds of episode likely to be detectable by
the excavation of a site (primarily, a *settlement*-site) substantially coincide. Put in such terms, the assumption appears both specific and
banal. This must explain why it is not discussed in the investigations of the higher-order relation between archaeology and history
that continue to appear.[1] It has also escaped the scrutiny which has
been directed, especially over the last twenty years, at the principles
and nature of archaeology. That fact is less surprising, since the assumption is not directly relevant to studies of prehistory, to which
this scrutiny has been mainly confined. Even here, however, when the
'events' are modern constructs – the Maya collapse, the coming of
the Greeks – the assumption can still operate in a secondary form.
The reconstructed accounts, by assimilating themselves with historical narrative, contain the kinds of event that an ancient source (had
there been one) would certainly have recorded.

In setting out to criticize this assumption, as I now do, I am by
no means advancing a general indictment of the practices either of
ancient history or of Classical archaeology today. The history to which
archaeology has so often been assimilated in this way is, after all, only
one kind of history, the kind that most of the surviving ancient sources
purvey. But once we extend the realm of history, as modern historians
now do, to include a range of *processes* as well as of events, then this
criticism is no longer relevant. Such processes – economic, social,
cultural, demographic – are essentially too slow-moving to be either
narrated in most of our documentary sources or recognized in the
kind of archaeological episode that I have described. This does not
mean that they are not susceptible to archaeological investigation: on

the contrary, it could be argued that archaeology excels in throwing light on just such long-term, recurrent, often unnoticed developments, which can only be extrapolated from a careful analysis of a large body of documentary material. It is here that, in my view, the alliance of history and archaeology becomes most fruitful. Thus what may appear, in these pages, to be a pessimistic and negative critique is really a plea for the redirection of effort.

We return, then, to the assumption that is under scrutiny; namely, that the kinds of historical event that the ancient sources found worthy of recording, and the kinds of episode detectable by archaeological investigations, are frequently (I do not think that anyone would argue that they are *always*) one and the same. This is to state the assumption in its original and most specific form. We shall see later that it has modifications, enabling it, for example, to be used to equate entities rather than events, between documentary and archaeological sources of knowledge, or extending its scope to the whole field of Classical art history, where its function is to make possible identifications between those works of art mentioned in ancient sources and those recovered by archaeology. These modifications can be subsumed under one general set of attitudes: the belief that archaeological results can speak to us in a language that is essentially the same as the language used by documentary sources. But we should begin with the original version of the assumption, which is made in terms of historical narrative and archaeological stratigraphy.

One should not pretend that there can be no overlap between the two categories. The eruption of Vesuvius in AD 79, for example, was an event indelible in both the historical record and the stratigraphy of the adjacent settlements. But this instance may serve to bring out an important limitation: that of spatial extent. The Vesuvius eruption was found historically noteworthy only within a limited geographical area and is detectable by excavation only within another, much smaller area. The issue of space, usually on a much smaller scale, lies close to the heart of the argument, inasmuch as a connection has sometimes been assumed between a fairly momentous historical event and an archaeological episode which is later found not to be represented over even the whole of one site; and this temptation will remain so long as archaeological fieldwork continues to be directed primarily at the individual site (or, rather, at that sample of a site which is accessible at the time, or whose excavation the funds permit).

What has led me to question this assumption is not the spirit of the true revolutionary; it could hardly be, when in the past I have championed the assumption as enthusiastically as anyone. Rather, it is a suspicion directed at those preconceptions whose function is, at least in part, to give comfort and to reinforce existing attitudes, and whose presence may therefore be as easily explained in psychological terms as it can be founded on objective evidence. That description fits the present assumption: by appearing to give independent confirmation of the statements of ancient sources, it reinforces the historian's trust in his authorities; by giving his discoveries the sanction of ancient documentation, it boosts the self-confidence of the excavator. Both parties have something to gain, and little to lose, from sharing in such a preconception; and the same is true of the layman, for whose benefit the exercise (at least on the archaeological side, in these days of cultural tourism) is partly designed. Laymen naturally prefer a clear-cut narrative account to a series of fragmented archaeological observations, especially if the account comprises episodes already familiar to them.

There are several different standpoints from which one could begin to criticize such an assumption, and I aim to take as many of them as possible. But first, since the exercise is bound to be unpopular, I look around anxiously for allies. Within Classical archaeology, they are hard to find. Within ancient history, they certainly exist, and perhaps especially (if paradoxically) among that conservative fraternity that has never had any use for archaeological evidence anyway; but it would be against their nature to say so openly, and the question is of little moment to them. As often, it is from non-Classical Archaeology that the earliest statements of similar views have come. Here, the late David Clarke was among the most authoritative figures of recent years, and I quote from the opening chapter of his most influential work:

> The danger of historical narrative as a vehicle for archaeological results is that it pleases by virtue of its smooth coverage and apparent finality, whilst the data on which it is based are never comprehensive, never capable of supporting but one interpretation and rest upon complex probabilities. Archaeological data are not historical data and consequently archaeology is not history.[2]

This incompleteness, ambiguity, and complexity on the part of archaeological findings will provide the *obbligato* to my own account also. A particularly telling phrase in Clarke's statement is the 'apparent finality' he attributes to historical narrative. The historian, ancient or modern, will always build his narrative around a backbone of propositions about past events which he must assume will never be seriously challenged, however interpretative the nature of that narrative may otherwise be. The question at issue is how often (if ever) the excavator of an archaeological site can advance, or assume, propositions about the results of his excavation that have a similar truth-value. Clarke has indicated, at least in an *a priori* manner, some of the reasons for giving a pessimistic answer to that question.

From *a priori* generalization, I turn to an *a posteriori* argument of a particular kind. Consider the built environment that surrounds us today. The buildings in which we live and work, whether they are five, fifty, or five hundred years old, owe their construction to certain past decisions and may have been altered as a result of further decisions; moreover, they have stood as mute witnesses to various major or minor historical events, some of which may have had an effect on their immediate vicinity. But what chance would a future excavator (whom we must imagine to possess basic historical texts for the period in question) have of detecting stratigraphical features that were in any way linked with the events related in these texts or, conversely, of identifying in the texts events that influenced, even indirectly, the decisions that produced the buildings? A little reflection will show that, in most cases, the links will simply never have been there for him to find: the two levels of activity are, both in scale and in kind, too widely separated.

Let me give a real and more or less contemporary example, for which I am indebted to Prof. Pierre Ducrey of the University of Lausanne.[3] On 1 May 1951 the Grand-Théâtre de Genève was destroyed by fire. On 4 August 1964 the Bâtiment Electoral, only 250 meters away, suffered a similar fire. Consider the plight of the future excavator of Geneva. He extends his soundings far enough to discover traces, first of one fire and then of the other. He possesses sufficiently detailed historical records to know that World War II lasted, in Europe, from 1939 to 1945, and that the frontier of a country involved in the war, France, ran within less than five miles of Geneva. His knowledge, in short, is about on a par with ours in respect to Classical Antiquity. He is, therefore, unlikely to be able to distinguish, in terms of purely material culture, a chronological interval as fine as that between 1945 and 1951, nor perhaps that between 1951 and 1964. If we further assume that his lines of reasoning also follow those of the present-day Classical archaeologist (admittedly a pessimistic hypothesis), then we can confidently predict the conclusion at which he will arrive. It is perverse (he reasons) not to link the two fires, so close to each other in space and time, with the same episode; and since the most cursory examination of the historical record will point to an obvious historical occasion for that episode, his reconstruction is easily completed. Geneva suffered, in the course of the war, a bombardment severe enough to burn two of its main public buildings; and (since his readers will expect this of him) he must also speculate as to whether this happened by accident or, more interestingly, because Switzerland, which he probably knows to have been neutral through at least a part of the war, eventually decided to take sides. Archaeology will thus have fruitfully enlarged on the bare documentary record.

There is nothing in this hypothetical prediction that would be in the least fanciful when applied to the contemporary archaeology of Greece and Rome. Let us test this claim by considering a recent instance that has arisen in one of the better-documented periods of antiquity, the Roman Empire in the second century after Christ. This is an epoch where we know the regnal dates of the emperors to the month, and often to the day; and where the circulation of an imperial coinage bearing the likenesses of these emperors enables us to date the coins, again with extreme precision in many cases. This in turn, with the aid of Imperial inscriptions, makes possible a strictly archaeological chronology that is also relatively accurate, being based for the Western Empire primarily on the pottery-series of the workshops of Eastern and Central Gaul.

Within, or rather at the edge of, this Western Empire lies the Antonine Wall, which for a period formed its extreme northwestern frontier. The ancient sources attribute the construction of this wall to the emperor Antoninus Pius, and date it to approximately AD 142. It ran across the narrowest point on the British mainland, the isthmus between the estuaries of the Forth and the Clyde, and the material traces of the fortification were first recognized, and then scientifically examined, many years ago. Let us then put the fairly straightforward question: when was the wall abandoned by the Romans? Archaeological excavation has contributed one further important point, not directly attested by an ancient source, which is also a first step toward answering our question: the Romans occupied the wall, briefly abandoned it (with some evidence of local destruction), and then rebuilt and reoccupied it. The sequence thus far can, it seems, be compressed into a short space of time, since a consensus has now been reached that the reoccupation still lies within the principate of Antoninus, who died in AD 161. What, though, of the date of the final abandonment?

A very recent authority, Dr. D. J. Breeze, gives us an answer as precise as it is candid:

> Over the last 100 years the suggested dates have ranged from the 160's through the 180's to 197 and 207 and finally back to the 160's. There is no guarantee that the date of about 163, which is the one now accepted by most scholars, is correct; it is merely the most probable in the light of the evidence available at the present time.[4]

We note, first, the apparent precision of some of the rival dates offered: a sure sign that the abandonment has been connected with major political upheavals in the affairs of the Empire. We further note that the absolute range covered by the variant dates is more than twice as great as that involved in our example of modern Geneva; and, finally, that the discrepancy in relative terms for the length of the reoccupation stands, between the earliest and the latest suggested dates (and taking the accession of Marcus Aurelius in 161 as a starting point), in a ratio of 23 to 1 – a telling observation when we come to consider the force of archaeological stratification as a means of estimating the approximate lapse of time. In the ensuing pages of his account, Breeze points to some of the difficulties, whether peculiar to the study of Roman military antiquities (like the habit of the Roman army of destroying its own forts before withdrawal, in order to deny them to an enemy), or present in all field archaeology (the incapacity of excavation to demonstrate the reason for, as opposed to the fact of, rebuilding, abandonment, or destruction), which have dogged this controversy.

The lesson of the Antonine Wall is a sobering one, particularly when we reflect on the high standard of most recent excavation of Roman military sites in Britain, and of research on the prime archaeological dating material, the pottery.[5] The excavators of the Antonine Wall have also had the advantage that their sites are, by the standards of the Classical world, exceptionally small and therefore in many cases susceptible to fairly exhaustive excavation. For all these reasons, it seems justifiable to base on this instance arguments of an *a fortiori* nature when turning to the Greek world, where all the parameters are less exact: dated official inscriptions are rare, and the chronology of both coins and of pottery is somewhat less accurate.

I shall resist the temptation to cite here any of the numerous examples offered by the archaeology of the Aegean Late Bronze Age, some of which I have referred to elsewhere.[6] It will be enough to say that the recent exercise of calibrating the radiocarbon dates, which many scholars believe to be dictated by the results of dendrochronological study, would widen the margin of uncertainty as to the dates of certain major archaeological episodes from a generation or two to a century or two, but that scholars continue, undismayed, the attempts to reconstruct some sort of historical narrative out of these same episodes. Inasmuch as these attempts also often pay heed to Greek heroic legend, the resultant narratives are not exclusively 'prehistoric' in nature. But it would be fairer to direct our investigation to better-documented periods of Greek history, which warrant fuller comparison with both the Roman and the modern examples.

A first symptom of the residual uncertainty which exists, or can be argued to exist, in the earlier part of the historical period can be found in the current program of E. D. Francis and M. Vickers, advanced in a series of articles published[7] and forthcoming, for revising the chronology of Archaic Greek art. If their overall aim is thus an art-historical one, their arguments nevertheless in part involve archaeological questions – that is, the interpretation of the results of excavation. The value of their work lies partly in showing that a different interpretation may be possible for each of the findings which make up the skeleton of the archaeological chronology of the period, and partly in exposing the very small number of such findings. Thus there would be lessons to be learned from hearing their case, even if it were to meet with universal rejection. If I do not rush to enlist their arguments in support of my own case here, this is mainly because I feel that their radically new chronology (which results in the removal of much art from the Archaic period altogether) is just as dependent on the assumption that I am criticizing as the conventional chronology that they reject. Both reveal an expectation that the material record will directly reflect certain historical events that are reported in the ancient sources. The instances dealt with in their publications so far are the career of the Athenian general Leagros, the historical circumstances concerning the Island of Siphnos which led the inhabitants to build a treasury at Delphi, and the destruction of the Temple of Apollo at Eretria by the Persians. All of these involve questions of the positive identification of archaeological remains, yet of the historical episodes in question, only the erection of the Siphnian Treasury belongs to the class which could be confidently expected to leave unmistakeable traces in the material record, and that thanks only to the exhaustive exploration of the Delphic sanctuary and an unusually specific statement by Herodotus (3.57.4).

Let us return to those cases that involve our original issue, the interpretation of excavated settlement-sites. I have used elsewhere the example of Herodotus' account of the Greek infiltration of Egypt in the time of the Saïte Dynasty.[8] The historian says that the Pharaoh Psammetichos (ca. 664–609 BC) established Greek and Carian mercenaries at a place called Stratopeda on the eastern frontier of Egypt (2.154), and that the later Pharoah Amasis (569–525 BC) moved these troops to Memphis and also gave the Greeks Naukratis to settle in, confining Greek trade to Naukratis thereafter (2.178–79). Evidence from the excavation of Naukratis, Memphis, what may be Stratopeda, and other sites has been used to verify, or more often to cast doubt on, Herodotus' account, in both cases on the clear assumption that the episodes related by him will have left archaeological traces. We may, instead, pose a series of questions in the following vein: is it possible that 'Stratopeda' is not among the sites so far discovered in the eastern frontier area? Is it possible that Naukratis had already been enjoying, for a generation or two before Amasis' decision, a Greek presence such as would lead to the building of an Ionic temple and the writing of inscriptions in Greek? Is it possible that Greek pottery continued, for a while thereafter, to reach other Egyptian sites, perhaps by indirect means, notwithstanding his decision? Only if we could with reasonable certainty answer no to these questions could archaeology be said to have destroyed Herodotus' credibility in this matter; and if, in order to vindicate the account that he gives, we have to propose a complete revision of the chronology of early Greek art, along the lines advanced by Francis and Vickers (supra n. 7), then that proposal must surely first be justified by a series of strong external arguments. The plain fact is that Herodotus need not be understood as talking in categories identical, nor even perhaps comparable, with those the material record can be expected to reflect. When an Egyptian pharaoh designates Naucratis as a Greek entrepôt or moves his bodyguard from 'Stratopeda' to Memphis, is it at all realistic to expect that these changes will be reflected in the small sample of the material culture of these sites that is recoverable? Yet the traditional archaeologist, together with the majority of his readers, seems happy to work on this expectation.

The same lesson may be inculcated by other examples. Let us turn to the topic of early Greek colonization: a suitable subject in that, today, it is recognized as involving archaeological evidence to at least the same degree as historical, but is yet of prime historical importance. For the nature, causation, and dating of the earlier Greek colonies, the evidence from the excavation of the relevant sites has long been accepted as fundamental. From an orthodox viewpoint,

the experience of combining this evidence with that of the documentary sources has been a reassuring one: the ancient sources have at
times been satisfactorily vindicated, at times usefully supplemented.
A dissident minority has, in a few cases, taken the opposing view: the
results of excavation are not always compatible with the documentary
accounts and, where the two clash, can be pressed home to the point
of destroying the credit of those accounts. The two sides, once again,
share the assumption that their categories of evidence are mutually
independent, yet can be made to impinge significantly on each other.

A few instances will serve as a testing ground. It is natural to begin
with the first Greek colonies in Sicily, because Thucydides, in a few
vital sentences near the beginning of his sixth book, offers us not only
a narrative account but also specific dates for their foundations.[9] The
next step in the story precisely recalls the case of the Greeks in Saïte
Egypt: excavation of some of the relevant sites, in the late nineteenth
and early twentieth centuries, brought to light pottery in sufficient
quantities to encourage the belief that some of the earliest deposits
on each site were included. Then, in the next generation, scholars
worked to establish, by means of these two classes of evidence, an
accurate chronology for the early Greek pottery-styles, which had not
previously been attainable. It may be helpful to express their reasoning
in the syllogistic form which it implicitly took, using the example of
Gela on the southern coast of Sicily.

Major premiss: Gela was founded in 689/8 BC, because that is the
date that emerges from Thucydides.

Minor premiss: The earliest Corinthian pottery found at Gela is of
the beginning of the Middle Protocorinthian phase.

Ergo: The Middle Protocorinthian phase should begin close to 690
BC.[10]

Thus far, the argumentation was sound enough. Further discoveries
of pottery of the same phase (and no earlier phase) at Gela would
presumably serve to substantiate this archaeological fixed point, while
the discovery of appropriately earlier or later pottery elsewhere, in the
first deposits at colonies dated earlier or later by Thucydides, would
reinforce trust in Thucydides' account as a whole. But what if later
excavation, at any one of the relevant sites, were instead to produce
discordant results?

Let us pause for a moment to reflect, in what I hope is a spirit
of common sense. Humfry Payne published in 1931 a chronological
scheme for Corinthian pottery[11] using the evidence described above,
and building on the work of several predecessors – which won wide

acceptance. Therefore only evidence that has come to light since 1931, or which Payne can be shown not to have used, can be used to test his scheme. All other arguments run a grave risk of circularity, especially through forgetting the fact that Payne's scheme *assumed* the trustworthiness of Thucydides' dates.

The site whose evidence played the biggest part in Payne's formulation of the later chronology of Corinthian pottery was Selinus, in western Sicily. Here, Thucydides' date for the foundation, though not the only one on offer in the ancient sources, was understandably judged to be the most reliable. Accordingly, the implicit syllogism ran on the following lines.

Major Premiss: Selinus was founded in 629/8 BC, because that is the date that emerges from Thucydides and he is our best source.

Minor premiss: The earliest Corinthian pottery found at Selinus is of the beginning of the (Early) Ripe Corinthian phase, or just before.

Ergo: The Ripe Corinthian phase should begin close to 625 BC.

But with Selinus there arose, in its most conspicuous form, the issue of fresh and apparently discordant evidence – an issue which, on any realistic view, was almost bound to present itself sooner or later. After all, was it really likely that the body of evidence available to Payne and his predecessors was representative in every detail? Only if it were could their answers be expected to be uniformly correct. If new evidence had been offered to them before they went into print, would they not have gladly revised their conclusions while there was yet time? The actual sequel, which came some years after Payne's death, is instructively different.

There came to light, in the storerooms of the museum at Palermo, a quantity of hitherto unpublished pottery which appeared to have come from the excavation of one of the cemeteries of Selinus. What was disturbing was that it included a number of pieces of Protocorinthian ware, from a phase very much earlier than the earliest Ripe Corinthian.[12] This suggested that the minor premiss in the syllogism given above was inaccurate: the first burials containing a substantial element of Greek pottery were appreciably earlier than the material on which Payne and his predecessors had based their dating scheme. Now when a logician discovers that his minor premiss is mistaken, one expects him instantly to suspend belief in his conclusion, pending the reexamination of his whole argument. This is not what most of the archaeologists did. By the 1950s (when the new evidence was published) they had become too attached to their conclusion – that Ripe Corinthian begins ca. 625 BC – to give it up. Instead, they either sought arguments that would keep the syllogism precariously intact (such as the hypothesis of a pre-colonial Greek presence on the site) or, more radically, they jettisoned their own *major* premiss in the effort to salvage the conclusion. Thucydides was not after all our best source; a different date for the founding of Selinus, ca. 650 BC, preserved in later and otherwise less reliable sources, was to be preferred.[13] Thus the chronology for Corinthian pottery, which by now could claim additional support from quite independent evidence, could be preserved unchanged. Few appeared to be dismayed either by the painful lack of logical rigor in this procedure or by the magnitude of what had been sacrificed thereby. For if Thucydides' dates could be rejected when they gave inconvenient results, then there would be serious repercussions for those earlier cases, in the eighth century BC, for which his evidence had been generally accepted.

Arguments of this kind do not necessarily lead to wrong conclusions: it may be that Thucydides was inaccurate in one or even all the dates he gave for these episodes of early Greek history. But it is beyond question that such arguments depend, tacitly, on the assumption that formed our starting point: that the evidence of excavation can be expected to speak in the same clear language as that of the historical event. Once again, a series of questions will serve to remind us of the incompleteness, ambiguity, and complexity of the former class of evidence. Can we be sure that the site of a colony has produced some of its very earliest material before that site has been completely excavated (a condition often impossible to fulfill)? Can we be sure that the word *colony* (*apoikia*) in our sources has a constant meaning in terms of material culture? Can we take the presence of Greek pottery in graves, when the full circumstances of their finding have not been published, to indicate the presence of Greek settlers? Can we even, at a more trivial level, be sure of the provenience of pots found, without full documentation, in museum basements? It was, in fact, a negative answer to the third of these questions which was to provide at least a temporary solution to the Selinus problem: extensive later excavation of the settlement and sanctuaries of Selinus yielded nothing, anywhere, that was of the same early date as the pieces said to have come from the cemeteries.[14] Payne's chronological scheme and the Thucydidean evidence on which it rested have thus been reassuringly vindicated; but the sighs of relief must not be allowed to drown all misgivings about the assumptions on which the whole argument, from its very beginning, can be seen to rest.

There are more fundamental questions about a colony than that of its date of foundation: for example, that of its historical existence. For the Phocaean expansion in the western Mediterranean area, we have to reckon without the specific testimony of a Thucydides: all the same, the existence of some of the Phocaean colonies seems to be posited by the compiler of the early *Periplous* – in many opinions, of a date no later than ca. 600 BC – which is partially preserved in the much later text of the *Ora Maritima* of Avienus. General historical considerations make it unlikely that their foundation, if it was really by Phocaeans, took place later than the sixth century BC. They include two especially problematic cases, Mainake and Hemeroskopeion, on the Mediterranean coast of Spain. Here a difficulty, not present in the Sicilian cases just considered, interposes itself: we are not certain of the geographical location of either place, though general placings – for Hemeroskopeion, in the vicinity of Cabo de la Náo south of Valencia; for Mainake, on the coast east of Malaga – may be agreed on. The disquieting thing has been the failure of archaeology to identify anything like the material traces of an Archaic Ionian colony in either area. These and other factors lead J.-P. Morel, in 1966, to ask whether Mainake, in particular, had ever been in reality a Phocaean colony;[15] in 1971, M. Tarradell went so far as to describe both colonies as 'phantoms';[16] and in 1980 H.-G. Niemeyer proposed a different interpretation: Mainake was in fact the Phoenician site that he had been excavating for twenty years past. It had never been a Phocaean colony in the strict sense, but Phocaean settlers had perhaps been tolerated in a much older Phoenician community.[17] Niemeyer's view overcomes one of the difficulties, since there is Archaic Greek pottery on his site. But it tacitly concedes one of the points made just now, the difficulty of achieving a universally valid definition of a Greek colony in material terms. The criteria of the ancient geographer and the modern archaeologist may not always coincide.

We should therefore hesitate before accepting the claim that archaeology has discredited, any more than the claim that it has vindicated, the documentary evidence. A similar case could be made in respect to another Thucydidean problem, this time involving the Phoenician rather than the Greek settlements in Sicily.[18] At 6.2.6, Thucydides states or implies, within the compass of a single sentence, a whole series of propositions about the Phoenicians in Sicily:

> There were Phoenicians living all around Sicily, who had settled on promontories and off-shore islands, the better to trade with the Sikels; but when the Greeks began to arrive by sea in large numbers,

they withdrew from most of these places and concentrated in Motya, Soloeis and Panormos, near to the Elymians, both because they trusted in the alliance with the Elymians and because from there the sea-passage to Carthage is shortest.

Given that the context of this sentence is the time of the arrival of the Greeks (from 735/4 BC, as Thucydides is about to state in the immediately following passage), a careful reading of it will show that Thucydides believed that: (1) the Phoenicians were in this area before 735 BC; (2) one of their main objectives was trade with the Sikels; (3) their Sicilian settlements already included one or more of the trio of sites Motya, Soloeis, and Panormos; and (4) they had also by then settled Carthage. I have chosen the four propositions which appear most properly testable by archaeology, and tested they have been, in many archaeologists' opinions at least. With propositions (3) and (4), a prime purpose (as with the historian's comparable statements about the Greek colonies in Sicily) was the chronological one; with propositions (1) and (2), the question boiled down to one of sheer historical reality, recalling the case of the Phocaean settlements in Spain. On each count, the findings have been negative: no evidence for a Phoenician presence demonstrably earlier than 735 BC in Carthage, still less in the Phoenician sites of Sicily; no evidence for a Phoenician presence *at all* from the examination of likely promontory and island sites elsewhere in Sicily or from the excavation of Sikel cemeteries. Yet there are ways around this apparent contradiction which would not have the effect of discrediting a highly esteemed historical authority: the chronology of Phoenician pottery, certainly problematic, may need revision;[19] the archaeological record, being as always incomplete, may come up with surprises in future;[20] the recognition of Phoenician activity, if sought in other media than that of pottery, might be established over a very much wider time span and geographical area.[21] I need only add that while the material traces of a Greek colony may be hard to identify with certainty, those of a Phoenician trading-post may present even greater difficulties. That Thucydides' 'Phoenicians living all round Sicily' are archaeologically elusive does not necessarily means that they were historically negligible, still less that they were nonexistent.

One could easily add to the list of illustrations of the optimistic assumption, on the part of archaeologists and historians alike, that their data can be interrelated in such an uncomplicated way. It is one of the few shibboleths which survive the years in Classical Archaeology, to appear in as straightforward a form in, say, the 1985 number of a journal as in the 1885 one. I shall take an example from the less recent past, because it is exceptional in offering a precisely quantifiable maximum probability. Pliny the Elder (*Nat. Hist.* 36.95) tells us that in the fourth-century Artemision at Ephesus, thirty-six of the columns bore relief sculpture and (unless his text is corrupt, as has been maintained) that one of these was the work of Skopas. British excavations of the nineteenth century produced one column-drum of fine quality and relatively good preservation which seemed to come from this set, three others of which fairly substantial parts survived, and fragments of about eight others. Thus, if no doubts about identification are assumed and if stylistic considerations based on our evidence for Skopas' style are set on one side, the odds against the first-mentioned drum being by Skopas were at least 35:1; those against our having any substantial trace of his workmanship here are at least 8:1; those against the survival of any Skopasian fragment, however small, at least 2:1. To give the stylistic arguments precedence over the statistical is surely to embark on treacherous ground. Yet the pieces had not been long excavated before the attribution of the finest drum to Skopas began to be advanced and, as late as 1952, P. E. Arias in surveying the question could report that this opinion 'trova vari consensi.'[22] Several excellent judges have dismissed the stylistic arguments for any attribution to Skopas, and one may suspect that their real foundation lay in a special version of that devotion to the ancient sources that we have detected elsewhere. The 'source' in this case belonged more than four centuries later than the time in question and, as we have seen, there are suspicions about the quality of his text, yet the mere existence of that text gave rise to this whole episode of scholarly discussion.

This instance, however, belongs to that special application of our original assumption to art-historical questions that was described near the outset (supra p. 47). Let us therefore end where we began, with the correlation of the results of archaeological excavation with the events narrated by the ancient sources. A justly famous episode of Greek archaeology in the last twenty years has been the excavation of the settlement and cemeteries at Lefkandi, near Eretria in Euboea.[23] The discovery that at least one building-complex here had been abandoned, after being destroyed by fire, has led to much speculation about the involvement of the site in a documented conflict, the Lelantine War, which seems to have taken place at about the time of this abandonment, that is, close to 700 BC. Obviously, our interpretation of the destruction and abandonment will depend on whether the history of this building is representative of the fate of the settlement as a whole. Yet what proportion of the probable settlement-area has been excavated? From a perusal of the overall plan,[24] it is difficult to arrive at a fraction much higher than 2 percent. Likewise, references to the desertion of the site should be qualified by the observation that a little pottery of the mid-sixth century BC – some 150 years later than the fire – was also found on the site.[25] I am not implying criticism here of the excavators, who have published the evidence with exemplary clarity, but of the apparently irresistible urge to make archaeological discovery speak in historical language. The issue of spatial extent, which was identified (supra p. 47) as being critical, is at the heart of this instance.

The aim of this paper has not been simply to issue negative warnings and to inculcate blind caution. There are many positive lessons to be drawn and many grounds for optimism in the immediate future. Just as ancient historians, in increasing numbers, are turning their attention to those approaches that best lend themselves to elucidation by archaeological means (whether or not they have chosen them for that reason), so archaeologists are moving, if more slowly, away from the assumption that the individual *site* is the only legitimate focus for their field operations and are adopting a regional perspective. These tendencies can be expected not only to modify the attitude that I have been criticizing but to replace it by more fruitful ones. A whole field of the illuminating of historical processes by archaeological means awaits exploration. Those of us who are archaeologists must bear in mind the important difference between man the maker, almost by definition the ideal quarry for the archaeologist, and man the doer, whose record forms the annals of documented history but who is archaeologically most elusive.

NOTES

The text of this paper substantially coincides with that of the second of the Sather Classical Lectures, under the general title 'An Archaeology of Greece,' which I gave at Berkeley in the fall of 1984, and which are to be published in book form by the University of California Press.

1. For example, in Ph. Bruneau, 'Sources textuelles et vestiges matériels: réflexions sur l'interprétation archéologique,' in *Mélanges helléniques offert à Georges Daux* (Paris 1974) 33–42; M. I. Finley, 'Archaeology and History,' chapter 5 in *The Use and Abuse of History* (London

and New York 1975); B. G. Trigger, *Time and Traditions: Essays in Archaeological Interpretation* (Edinburgh 1978); T. B. Jones, 'Archaeology and History,' pp. 23–35 in *Contributions to Aegean Archaeology: Studies in Honor of William A. McDonald* (Minneapolis 1985).

2. D. L. Clarke, *Analytical Archaeology* (London 1968) 12.

3. P. Ducrey, 'Menaces sur le passé,' *Etudes de Lettres* 3, 10 (1977) 2, 1–18, at 13.

4. D. J. Breeze, *The Northern Frontiers of Roman Britain* (London 1982) 118.

5. See, e.g., B. R. Hartley, 'The Roman Occupations of Scotland: The Evidence of the Samian Ware,' *Britannia* 3 (1972) 1–55.

6. 'The New Archaeology and the Classical Archaeologist,' *AJA* 89 (1985) 31–37.

7. 'Leagros Kalos,' *PCPS* 207 (1981) 97–136; 'Kaloi, Ostraka and the Wells of Athens,' *AJA* 86 (1982) 264; '*Signa priscae artis:* Eretria and Siphnos,' *JHS* 103 (1983) 49–67.

8. M. H. Crawford, ed., *Sources for Ancient History* (London 1983) 144–46.

9. Thucydides 6.3.1–4.3.

10. This presents the original form of the argument; later finds have modified the minor premiss in much the same way as for Selinus (infra). See J. N. Coldstream, *Greek Geometric Pottery* (London 1968) 326–27.

11. H. G. G. Payne, *Necrocorinthia* (London 1931) 21–27, an account which built on earlier work by K. Friis Johansen and others.

12. See G. Vallet and F. Villard, 'La date de fondation de Sélinonte: les données archéologiques,' *BCH* 82 (1958) 16–26.

13. Vallet and Villard (supra n.12). It is worth noting that they had anticipated the identical conclusion, on independent grounds, in their earlier paper 'Les dates de fondation de Megara Hyblaea et de Syracuse,' *BCH* 76 (1952), 318–21.

14. R. Martin, 'Histoire de Sélinonte d'aprés les fouilles récentes,' *CRAI* 1977, 46–63, esp. 50–51.

15. The citation is from *La parola del passato* 21 (1966) 391; but see more fully idem, 'L'expansion phocéenne en occident,' *BCH* 99 (1975), 853–96, esp. 886–92.

16. Cited by J.-P. Morel, 'Colonisations d'occident,' *MEFRA* 84 (1972) 721–33, at 731.

17. H.-G. Niemeyer, 'Auf der Suche nach Mainake: Der Konflikt zwischen literarischer und archäologischer Überlieferung,' *Historia* 29 (1980) 165–89.

18. Perhaps the best discussion of this problem remains that of E. Frézouls, 'Une nouvelle hypothèse sur la fondation de Carthage,' *BCH* 79 (1955) 153–76.

19. As was proposed by P. Cintas, *La céramique punique* (Tunis 1950).

20. Implied by J. Heurgon, 'The Inscriptions of Pyrgi,' *JRS* 56 (1966) 1–13, esp. 1–3.
21. G. F. Bass, Jr., *Cape Gelidonya: A Bronze Age Shipwreck, Transactions of the American Philosophical Society* 57, part 8 (1967) 165–67.
22. P. Arias, *Skopas* (Rome 1952) 111–12. Especially instructive is W. R. Lethaby, 'Further Notes on the Sculpture of the Later Temple of Artemis at Ephesus,' *JHS* 34 (1914) 76–88; at p. 85, he strives directly to reduce the odds against the conclusion that he will advance at p. 86. On the whole question, see A. F. Stewart, *Skopas of Paros* (Park Ridge 1977) 103, 124, 132 no. 33, 152 n. 1(3).
23. M. R. Popham, L. H. Sackett, and P. G. Themelis, *Lefkandi 1: The Iron Age* ([Text] London 1980).
24. Popham et al. (supra n.23) ([Plates] London 1979), pl. 4.
25. Popham et al. (supra n.23) 78.

CHAPTER 3

The New Archaeology and the Classical Archaeologist

Originally delivered as a lecture to a New York audience, this paper wears a more dated look today, if only because the 'New Archaeology' has since lost its vogue for many prehistorians. The general expectation of a brighter future for Aegean Bronze Age studies, voiced near the end of the paper, has found a measure of fulfilment in the diminishing concern with 'events'. This has not, however, resulted from any definitive solutions to the old controversies, where hopes were once again revealed as naive. Twenty years on, radical differences of opinion persist on the chronology, the significance and, in some cases, the reality of the list of 'events' given on p. 73: nowhere more so than with the date of the Thera eruption, where more than a century separates the two rival factions, with their mutually incompatible methodologies: those who rely on the calibrated radiocarbon dates, now reinforced and given added precision by dendrochronology, and those who maintain the synchronisms derived from dated episodes in Egypt and the Near East. Each side can claim fresh external support for its view: for the former, there are the very widespread environmental phenomena which cluster around the date of 1628 BC and point to a single cataclysmic eruption in the northern hemisphere at that time; for the latter, there are new concordances which once more support the traditional dating, over a century later.

The neglected victim of this and other debates remains the series of radiocarbon dates from within the Bronze Age Aegean itself, which is seldom subjected to systematic analysis in its own right – most Aegean prehistorians find it too deficient in precision to be useful to them – much less brought into confrontation with those from other parts of Europe (pp. 73–4).

The topic of this paper is no longer a novel one. It is now over four years since my colleague at Cambridge, Professor Colin Renfrew, delivered a clarion call in the shape of his lecture at the Centennial celebrations of the Archaeological Institute of America, 'The Great Tradition versus the Great Divide.'[1] Since then, we have had Stephen Dyson's conciliatory paper 'A Classical Archaeologist's Response to the New Archaeology,' in the *Bulletin of the American Schools of Oriental Research* for 1981, not to mention a few other attempts by American and British archaeologists to address themselves, briefly and usually in passing, to similar questions;[2] while from France has come the one really extended treatment of the problem, emanating from within what Renfrew called the 'Great Tradition' and taking a searchingly critical look across his 'Great Divide': Paul Courbin's consistently witty and often scathing book of 1982, *Qu'est-ce que l'Archéologie?*[3]

What is the issue that has so agitated all of us? Roughly speaking (and there is no analysis of the problem that would command universal acceptance), it is this. There exists a more-than-century-old tradition of archaeology in the Mediterranean lands and the Near East. Because of the historical importance of the civilizations with which it deals, it occupies some place in the intellectual background of every educated man, woman or child. Because of the material brilliance of these same cultures, it has filled half the museums of the world with impressive objects. Because of the select recruiting ground from which many of its practitioners have come, it has produced a literature which contains its fair share of works, whether excavation reports or syntheses, which have become 'classics.' Without being by any means universally accepted as a university discipline – a point on which we might reflect – it is in every other way an established subject, occupying the time of a small army of academics and government employees in every developed country, and enjoying at least the status of an up-market hobby among tens of thousands of others. For many laymen, and for the whole of the entertainment industry, it represents what the word 'archaeology' actually means: indeed there is one language, German, in which it actually *is* a large part of what

'The new archaeology and the Classical archaeologist', *American Journal of Archaeology* 89, 1985, 31–7.
This article was presented as the first in a series of lectures on archaeology sponsored jointly by the Archaeological Institute of America and the 92nd Street YMHA in New York City in April 1984. I am most grateful to Paul Halstead for guidance amid unfamiliar literature.

the word 'Archäologie' means, in contradistinction to another term, 'Prähistorie' or 'Vorgeschichte,' which is used for the archaeology of all pre-literate and most non-literate cultures. Archaeology in the Mediterranean world and the Near East is closely linked with, and was indeed for a long time merely an integral part of, the linguistic, literary and historical study of the corresponding parts of the globe in antiquity.

The New Archaeology, by contrast, is even today less than twenty years old, and is generally describable in terms of a polarity with the kind of archaeology that I have just described. It and its practitioners have little or nothing to do with linguistic, literary or historical studies. It deals primarily with past cultures which are not recognized as having had an important role in history, and it is emphatically not orientated toward the recovery of objects, beautiful or otherwise. Geographically, its origins lie in two areas of research, North America and northern Europe; but from this base it has expanded its scope to cover work in Africa (which is still 'Vorgeschichte'), in Latin America (thus entering the domain of 'Archäologie'), and even in certain periods of the past of lands like Mesopotamia, Greece and Italy, thus at least marginally overlapping with the field of the traditional archaeology that I spoke of first. It has a tremendous following among archaeologists under the age of about 35; it has established a definite niche, as an intellectual approach, among a somewhat wider range of disciplines, mostly lying within the social sciences; but it has, as yet, made little impact on the imagination of the educated general public. Its commonest stance in regard to the traditional school of archaeology ranges from reasoned criticism and remonstrance to contemptuous indifference. The main charges brought against the traditional archaeology are those at which my earlier description perhaps hinted. It is an undisciplined discipline. It is pragmatic, and employs no explicit body of theory. Lulled into complacency by the benevolent interest of the educated public, it is content with the goal of description. It describes everything, analyzes and synthesizes a restricted range of aspects, and explains nothing. It is concerned with the unique and the particular, not with generalities: the classic works in its literature, which I mentioned earlier, betray this position by their titles: books like *Ur of the Chaldees, The Palace of Minos, The Tomb of Tutankhamen* are unashamedly books about a single site. They rely on the importance of Ur, Knossos or the Valley of the Kings to determine the importance of what they describe. They use archaeology as a means of adding to what was already known about these sites; they do not use their sites as exemplifications of the principles and methods of archaeology, and anyone who used one of them as a handbook to help in the excavation of, say, a pueblo in Arizona would be bitterly disappointed in the outcome. Where such books go beyond pure description and become interpretative, the interpretations that they offer are not testable by any objective criterion: rather, they reflect the unspoken prejudices of their authors – by any European writing in the 1920s, for instance, imperialism and its concomitant features had been unconsciously assimilated as a way of life, and this acceptance affected his view of the past too.

Thus there has grown up what Colin Renfrew called the 'Great Divide.' His own appeal was directed to the bridging of this divide by means of some splendid, no doubt cantilevered structure, which was to be built from both ends until it met in the middle, thus letting loose an intense two-way traffic which would enormously enrich both sides of the gap. Stephen Dyson's proposal, on the other hand, seems to be for a more modest rope-bridge over the gulf, which would allow some part of the intellectual baggage of the New Archaeology to be humped across into the 'Great Tradition'; while the result of Courbin's meticulous feasibility study is that, on balance, the huge costs of building a bridge would not be justified by the meager benefits that it would bring.

Most of these writers, and several others whom I have not mentioned, have approached the problem from one side of the divide: they ask themselves the question, 'What (if anything) is Classical Archaeology going to do about the New Archaeology?' I wish to begin by raising the converse question: 'What is the New Archaeology going to do about Classical Archaeology?' (and the other components of the 'Great Tradition'). Now Classical Archaeology, from within which I speak, surely lies at the very heart of the traditional archaeology that has lately been put under scrutiny. It is the oldest component of the 'Great Tradition' in archaeology, and it is the biggest, in terms of the number of its practitioners and its students, and of its published output. In its own estimation at least, it is also probably the most distinguished component of that tradition. To adopt a more critical vein, if the assemblage of data and the tidy ordering of material are activities that epitomize the sterility of the traditional archaeology, then what branch of it can offer a mass so large and so thoroughly ordered as Classical Archaeology? If the aim of mere description, however full, is stigmatized as an unworthy one for a discipline such as archaeology, then what branch of it has accepted that aim with more complacency than Classical Archaeology? If a concentration on the particular at the expense of the universal was one of the flaws at the heart of traditional archaeological thinking, then what could be more particularized than Classical Archaeology, in which half a dozen books may be devoted to a single building, and even two or three to a single statue, and in which everything is conceived in terms of its impact on a single culture?

All of this suggests that a re-orientation of the discipline of archaeology might be expected to begin with Classical Archaeology and its methods, as a paradigm of the approach that had been practiced hitherto, and that must now be either abandoned as sterile, or deflected into a more productive channel. But nothing of the kind has happened. The pioneers of the New Archaeology have in the main ignored Classical Archaeology, whether for praise or for blame, almost as if it did not exist. The 'traditional archaeology' which they have held up for scrutiny and ultimate dismissal, where it has been clearly specified, has appeared to be a version of European archaeology in the generation after Gordon Childe, or of Mesoamerican archaeology (one thinks of that riotously funny and not entirely fictitious 'straw man' created by Kent V. Flannery, the 'Real Mesoamerican Archaeologist'[4]) of the same period. Thus most Classical Archaeologists have been left with the feeling that they are outside the target area of the new criticisms, and that the conflict provoked by these hardly concerned them. Let me give a statistic. One other major event in the four years since Colin Renfrew's address has been the appearance of a volume of collected pieces by Lewis H. Binford, under the title *In Pursuit of the Past*.[5] This extremely stimulating work contains a bibliography of, on my count, 293 items. Of this total, there is (again on my count) not a single one which is primarily concerned with any part of the Mediterranean world at any period: the nearest approach, geographically, is perhaps Gordon Childe's *The Danube in Prehistory*. As a statistic, this may seem amazing, but it is not untypical or freakish in respect of the output of the New Archaeology. What attitudes or motives does it imply? One explanation that may suggest itself is a discreditable one that I shall not adopt: it is that the New Archaeologists are afraid of venturing into a specialist domain where a vast body of pre-existing knowledge has to be assimilated. I do not advance this view, first because there are examples of distinguished work which has been undertaken in areas like the archaeology of Roman Britain,[6] where the difficulty mentioned exists in almost as intense a form as in Mediterranean lands; and secondly because the problems of such an undertaking could anyway be readily overcome by collaboration between a theory-oriented New Archaeologist and a sympathetic Classicist (as we have seen, this latter breed does exist). A more likely explanation is surely that New Archaeologists do not consider that such an attempt would be worthwhile or justifiable.

Nor would such an attitude – if I have correctly diagnosed it – be altogether an injustice to the sentiments of Classical Archaeologists themselves. The view that, for example, the general principles of archaeology consist of nothing more than common sense, or that archaeology is not an independent branch of knowledge, is sufficiently widespread among Classical Archaeologists to need no individual attribution. It constitutes a major deterrent to New Archaeologists, against holding up their principles to potential discredit by testing them in a context which the practitioners themselves often do not consider a fair and comparable one; where the formulation of free hypotheses is constrained on every side by the body of pre-existing knowledge – and I am not referring only, nor even mainly, to the knowledge provided by documentary and historical sources: the body of purely *archaeological* knowledge is, in its own right, colossal, as may be seen by comparing the size of holdings of a really well stocked library of Classical Archaeology and a comparable one of general archaeology: the sheer volume will bear no resemblance whatever to the proportions of the two geographical areas covered, and will indeed be by no means disparate in absolute terms.

But, whatever the reasons for it, the gulf undeniably persists: the criticisms of the New Archaeologists are primarily directed at, and the rejoinders primarily come from, the non-Classical fields of traditional archaeology. The New Archaeology has not pressed home any criticism of Classical Archaeology, and Classical Archaeology has therefore felt free to ignore both the criticisms and the constructive proposals.

But there are Classical Archaeologists who do not share this feeling, and it is because I am one of them that I am speaking on this subject. Like Stephen Dyson, like James Wiseman,[7] I feel that Classical Archaeology could learn salutary lessons from the writings and the example of the New Archaeology. Indeed, I shall go further than they might wish to go, and certainly I do not want to saddle them with any complicity in what I am going to say next. I feel that traditional archaeology has, in the past generation, entered some kind of minor intellectual crisis, at least in Britain and in some other European countries that I could name. The traditionally minded archaeologists

seem to me rather cut off from the mainstream of that kind of intellectual advance which can manifest itself in several disciplines at
the same time. Their work does not elicit productive response from
people in other subjects, beyond the immediately adjacent ones (such
as the historians of the same culture whose archaeology they themselves practice.) It is not easy for them to point to exciting theoretical
or methodological advances in the recent history of their subject, as
distinct from the new application of technical advances made in other
disciplines: obvious examples here are the 'radiocarbon revolution' of
more than a generation ago, and the 'dendrochronological revolution'
of twenty years later, where the advances in ideas seem confined to the
more or less common-sense deductions that follow from the discovery
that a group of finds is much earlier (or less often, much later) than
had previously been thought. Real conceptual advances are seldom
sought, and even less often achieved. Consider, for example, the chilly
reception that has been given, outside and at times even inside France,
to the work of the 'Paris School' in recent years. Here is a group of
people studying the Classical world through what may (very roughly)
be called a structuralist approach: an approach in which the methods
of Classical Archaeology, or some of them, are closely integrated with
the anthropological tradition of Louis Gernet and others, and applied
to many different aspects of ancient society, especially religious cult
and ritual, but also ancient literary works of many kinds. If there is
anywhere in the world where the material of Classical Archaeology
is being put to novel uses, and the subject as a whole embroiled in
wide intellectual explorations, it is here.[8] Yet the reward has been, in
general, the unjust one of being read, or at least taken seriously, by
very few of their colleagues in Classical Archaeology, and none at all
of their counterparts on the other side of the Atlantic, the New Archaeologists who are also (although in a very different way) linking
the approaches of archaeology and anthropology.

One reason for Classical Archaeologists to welcome the challenge
of the New Archaeology is thus, in my view at least, the fact that they
badly need the stimulus which it can offer. A second reason is that
there are already at least one or two encouraging precedents, such as
the case of Aegean Bronze Age archaeology to which I shall turn in a
moment. First, however, I should state clearly what it is that I think the
New Archaeology has to offer. Even in its short life so far, the new discipline has undergone some rather drastic re-orientations. A leading
figure like Lewis Binford has to expend some of his energies in rebuk-
ing over-enthusiastic followers, who have pressed new doctrines too

far.[9] The early insistence on pursuing universal laws of human behavior, exemplified in the archaeological record, has (probably justifiably) met with recent discouragement from within the New Archaeology. This process of distillation has been salutary: it dispenses the rest of the archaeological world from the arrogant and laborious operation of 'choosing the best' out of what the New Archaeology has to offer, since this operation has already been carried out, at least in part. And the contribution that remains is still an important one. It is to the New Archaeology that we owe our growing self-awareness, our realization of the highly debatable nature of what we are doing when we make archaeological inferences. Another of its services has been to inculcate respect for the quantitative method: so many of the arguments and generalizations in traditional archaeology have a covertly quantitative basis, yet only recently has it become common to express this basis in numerical terms – the *size* of a sample, the *degree* of a preponderance, the *changes* in a proportion through time – so that a preliminary evaluation of the argument becomes possible, before one moves on to the more critical task of evaluating the basis itself – is the sample valid? is the proportion biased? and so on. It is in this latter area, I believe, that the New Archaeology has made its most significant contribution of all. Here we enter the territory of what Binford calls 'Middle Range Theory,'[10] of what David Clarke called 'Predepositional and Depositional Theory,'[11] of what still others call 'Behavioral Archaeology.' The differences in terminology should not disguise the fact that, most of the time, these different authorities are talking about the same kind of thing: that is, the true *meaning* of the archaeological record. For some of these insights, we should not have had to wait for the enlightenment given by the New Archaeology: the lessons could have been learned from quite a different source, namely the view of archaeology taken by the outside world. A good starting point would have been the cartoons of the *New Yorker* or *Punch*: the image of the archaeologist here is often that of an enterprising person, perhaps a lucky person, but not usually a very clever person. A recurrent theme is the misinterpretation, by archaeologists of the future, of some bizarre creation of our contemporary culture. The main point of such humor may be to ridicule the eccentricities of modern society, but a second implication is that these very eccentricities are what make society so difficult to understand, and so easy to misinterpret, for those who belong to another age.

Now it would be possible to argue that Classical Archaeology has long been practicing, under different names, the very procedures that the New Archaeology is advocating when it urges the development of middle range theory, for instance. It would be a satisfying indulgence for me to develop this line of argument, but I am not sure that it would serve any greater purpose than to boost the self-confidence of Classical Archaeologists. What I will assert, however, is that Classical Archaeology still offers an incomparable field for putting into further practice the principles of the New Archaeologists. Let it not be forgotten that David Clarke himself once offered encouragement: 'Text-aided archaeology,' he wrote, would 'provide vital experiments' by offering the control of documentary sources over purely material-based inferences, as long as the inherent biases of each were borne in mind.[12] Was this a declaration of intent, or an invitation to others? Whichever it was, he made the statement in 1973; three years later, he was dead; and his colleagues have not shown much inclination to follow his lead. Yet I am convinced that he was right, and that a phase of intensive experiment within a 'controlled' field like that of Classical Archaeology would work wonders for the mutual respect, and the general credibility, of both sides.

There are, of course, major discouragements still in the way. There is a deep difference of mentality on the two sides, shown by what each regards as 'interesting.'[13] For Binford, particularizing approaches are in their nature 'trivial' and 'uninteresting.' Now it is possible, in mathematics or philosophy for instance, to use the word 'interesting' in a way that at least purports to be objective; that is, to use it of findings and arguments which have repercussions or implications beyond the immediate context in which they arose. It may be that Binford uses these words, at times, in some such sense; but I am sure that he also means them in their familiar everyday sense (as indeed is suggested by his also using the word 'boring' of particularizing approaches), and I am equally sure that he is sincere. Yet many Classical Archaeologists pursue the particularized precisely because they personally do find it *interesting*; a conclusion about fifth century Athens, even if valid for no other society in history, nevertheless interests them very much. All that this shows is that the mentality of late twentieth century western man is still a very heterogeneous one. There is also the issue of language[14] – the language in which the two sides express themselves: an especially sensitive area for Classicists, who are trained, often from their early youth, in the habit, whenever they use a word, of automatically asking themselves its exact meaning. But I promised myself that I would say nothing about this, and I shall try to keep my promise.

It is time, instead, to turn to what I consider the strongest argument in favor of collaboration between the New Archaeology and traditional Classical Archaeology in its strict sense: namely, the precedent offered by recent experience in the closely allied field of Aegean Bronze Age archaeology. What I am going to say now will not, I fear, make me many friends – especially not in Britain, that longstanding stronghold of Aegean Bronze Age studies. But for some twenty years past I have been experiencing a feeling of growing unease about the progress of this subject, quite distinct from that aroused by contemplation of Classical Archaeology proper. In the Bronze Age field, the feeling relates not so much to the methods, or the narrowness of the aspects usually studied, but to something harder to describe. I felt it again very strongly when, two years ago, I read a statement by one of the most thoughtful American practitioners of the subject: 'After more than a century of scholarship', writes Philip Betancourt, 'Mycenaean studies are still in their vigorous youth.'[15] What is worrying about this statement is that it is so absolutely true. The vigor of Aegean Bronze Age studies is of course a matter for satisfaction, but should they not by now have outgrown their youth? One is glad that the subject is a volatile and exciting one, but one would expect it to have acquired maturity as well. One of the connotations of youth is conveyed by a remark of William Pitt the elder (from a speech made in his late middle age): 'Youth is the season of credulity.' In Aegean Bronze Age archaeology, indeed, too much has been believed too readily, and repeated in a series of secondary treatments to the point where it acquired the status of an axiom. The great names in Aegean Bronze Age archaeology are the names not of its thinkers nor of its masters of the visual approach (as is largely true in Classical Archaeology), but of its excavators. The place which in Classical Archaeology is occupied by the ancient sources, and in Near Eastern archaeology by the cuneiform and hieroglyphic texts and the Bible, is taken in the Aegean Bronze Age by the early excavators' interpretations of their own discoveries (and, much more sporadically, by Homer). By this I mean, not that these men's every word is believed until it is proved false, which today especially would be manifestly untrue, but that their vision of Aegean prehistory has been perpetuated as a framework within which everyone has worked – until, that is, the advent of a new approach in the last fifteen years or so, a point to which I shall return.

What was that vision like? Essentially, the early excavators felt called upon to present their reconstructions in a historical form, of the most traditional kind. In these reconstructions, events dominated.

A handful of these supposed events has survived, until recently, as the main landmarks for most research, and almost all teaching, of the Aegean Bronze Age: the Coming of the Greeks, the Rise of Mycenae, the Eruption of Thera, the Mycenaean Ascendancy in Crete, the Fall of Knossos, the Trojan War, the Fall of Mycenaean Civilization and the Dorian Invasion. Most text books offer approximate dates for these events, and much research is devoted to refining the dates and investigating their causes, nature and effects. Why did the early excavators feel called upon to offer a reconstruction so much more 'event'-ful than what has been proposed for other areas and epochs with a similar kind of archaeological record? The answer is in part that the strictly archaeological record is *not* the only one available in the Bronze Age Aegean. There is also Greek heroic legend, the avenue which first gave access to this field of study; legends deal, at the superficial level, with deeds and events; most people still believe that the Greek legends in *some* degree reflect the realities of the later Bronze Age, and in the past scholars went much further, accepting them in detail and trying to match them with the archaeological record. A further answer lies in the decipherment of Linear B. For a time in the 1950s there were some – and I was one of them – who really thought that the later Aegean Bronze Age was going to emerge as a semi-historical epoch. A better understanding of the nature of the texts, together with the fact that no major archives have been found since, has brought this view – probably permanently – into eclipse. Finally, and more objectively, it is true that the archaeological record of the period is rich in destruction layers. To collate these destruction deposits into broad 'horizons' of destruction is a more questionable step, but it is an extremely tempting one. Its attractions are still powerfully at work today, and I would argue that they exercise a patent influence on the discussion of the dates of such controversial episodes as the Thera eruption and the destruction of the palace at Thebes.

But why should it be thought misleading to see the Bronze Age of the Aegean in such terms? I would argue that the prime objection arises from the nature of the archaeological chronology. The basis for the dating of the Aegean Bronze Age consists of a small group of associations, some of them at second or third remove, between Aegean artifacts and datable Egyptian or Near Eastern contexts, or vice versa. The flimsy nature of this structure of dates is not always remembered. One episode which cast some doubt on it was the emergence of radiocarbon dating and, more particularly, the calibration of radiocarbon dates by cross-reference to dendrochronology, which for this period results in a distinctly 'higher' chronology. The impact on the debate about the Thera eruption was especially interesting. Here, the archaeologists were in dispute over a margin of about fifty years: was the eruption to be equated with the end of Late Minoan IA (conventionally 'ca. 1500 BC') or the end of IB ('ca. 1450')? By 1976, a scientist was claiming on the basis of calibrated radiocarbon dates that it must have happened 150 to 200 years before the earlier of these two dates.[16] The view was received with some derision in many circles, and taken as an illustration of the crudity and unreliability of 'scientific' dating methods as compared with the relative accuracy of the traditional, 'protohistorical' chronology. But then in 1980 a book[17] appeared which, by a close re-examination of the *traditional* basis of dating and altogether independently of the radiocarbon evidence, reached a rather similar conclusion: in the earlier part of the Aegean Late Bronze Age, the accepted dates might indeed be more than a century too late.

But does the absolute chronology really matter? Is it not the *relative* dating of the episodes within the Aegean area which really counts, and does this not stand independently of actual dates in years? The answer is that absolute chronology matters very much, as soon as connections are drawn (as they often are) between Aegean developments and the more securely attested episodes of early Near Eastern history and, I might add, between the Aegean and other cultures dated by radiocarbon only. There is a rather important point involved in this last connection. Some years ago I argued – twice over, although that did not appear to increase the impact of the claim[18] – that the series of radiocarbon dates available from the Aegean Bronze Age itself must be taken seriously, as an independent alternative to the conventional chronology described just now. If an irreconcilable discrepancy emerged between the two – and the then recent calibration of the radiocarbon dates made it more clear than ever that it did emerge – then one (or both) of two conclusions must surely follow. Either radiocarbon dates, which elsewhere were often exclusively relied on for the dating of archaeological sequences, should not be relied on after all; or the conventional chronology was significantly wrong. This is just the sort of challenge that I have in mind for the New Archaeology to test its theories on in the Classical context. But the first alternative was widely found repugnant; the second seemed very unlikely; and the point was not generally taken up.[19] What the sequel has shown is perhaps that the second alternative is *not* after all to be excluded; the conventional chronology may indeed be less trustworthy than had been thought, although this in itself does not necessarily reassure us on the other count – the radiocarbon dates could be wrong too. The real lesson, reinforced by the appearance of further radiocarbon dates from the Aegean, is surely that we *must* use these radiocarbon dates as the basis for all chronological comparisons between the Aegean and other radiocarbon dated sequences; for such *relative* dating, they are not only in the appropriate form, but they may also be the best evidence that we have. By comparison with this fact, arguments about the choice between different 'calibration curves,' to establish the *absolute* dating, are a side-issue.

My central point, however, concerns the Aegean itself. Even where only the internal chronology is involved, the arguments are sometimes based on the absolute duration of periods: is a century long enough for this development? is fifty years too long for this interval? and so on. It is surely clear that any kind of 'historical' narrative, for a culture in which any of the dates may be even fifty years out, let alone two hundred, in either direction, is an impossibility. The very language of political developments and military episodes, in which narratives of the Aegean Bronze Age have for long been couched, seems inappropriate.

But we come at last to the dénouement of the story. In the last fifteen years or so of research in the Aegean Bronze Age, the approach that I have been criticizing has no longer been unchallenged. Alongside it have emerged the exponents, in ever-increasing numbers, of a very different kind of archaeology. The newcomers deal, not in events, but in processes; they reconstruct not immutable political and military events, but variegated systems; they study some previously neglected classes of evidence, but they also apply the traditional materials – including, conspicuously, the Linear B tablets – to the investigation of new problems. In short, they share many or all of the aims of the New Archaeology. I am speaking subjectively, I know, but I find that these recent developments offer Aegean Bronze Age studies a brighter future than their past, in terms of intellectual vitality, notwithstanding the glamour of the early discoveries in the field.

Can this initiative be extended to Classical Archaeology proper? For the New Archaeologists, as we have seen, Classical Archaeology seems at best to be a small regional application of their subject; and at worst, not to be counted as archaeology at all. The most natural response to this position is also the one which will do most to reinforce the existing attitudes of the New Archaeologists: it is to stress the *content* of Classical Archaeology, that is, the unique cultural achievements of the Greeks and Romans. This is not a good line to pursue; and in any case, most features of Greek and Roman material culture are far from unique. A much better reply is one based on the state of the subject: the huge body of purely archaeological knowledge, and the close association with other, non-archaeological disciplines which have reached a high level of sophistication. Even if the charge is true that all this knowledge was amassed in order to answer 'yesterday's questions, if any,' which is highly debatable,[20] does not the whole history of science teach us that such knowledge, acquired for different reasons or out of sheer disinterested curiosity, can be put to dramatically innovatory use?

NOTES

1. C. Renfrew, 'The Great Tradition versus the Great Divide: Archaeology as Anthropology?' *AJA* 84 (1980) 287–98.
2. S. Dyson, 'A Classical Archaeologist's Response to the "New Archaeology",' *BASOR* 242 (1981) 7–13. Compare also J. Wiseman, 'Conflicts in Archaeology: Education and Practice,' *JFA* 10 (1983) 1–9, with references to earlier papers; J. Boardman in briefer references, e.g., *CR* 25 (1975) 118–20; 'The Athenian Pottery Trade,' *Expedition* (1979) 33–39; 'Remnants of History,' *Encounter* 40.4 (April 1973) 67–69.
3. P. Courbin, *Qu'est-ce que l'Archéologie?* (Paris 1982).
4. K. V. Flannery ed., *The Early Mesoamerican Village* (New York 1976).
5. L. H. Binford, *In Pursuit of the Past: Decoding the Archaeological Record* (London 1983, J. F. Cherry and R. Torrence eds.)
6. See, e.g., I. A. Hodder and C. Orton, *Spatial Analysis in Archaeology* (Cambridge 1976); Renfrew (supra n. 1) 297, ns. 28–33.
7. See supra n. 2.
8. See, e.g., G. Gnoli and J.-P. Vernant eds., *La mort, les morts dans les sociétés anciennes* (Cambridge 1982); Institut d'archéologie et d'histoire ancienne (Lausanne) and Centre de recherches comparées sur les sociétés anciennes (Paris), *La cité des images* (Paris 1984).
9. Binford (supra n. 5) 15, 106–108.
10. Binford (supra n. 5) 76, 194–95, citing Binford ed., *For Theory Building in Archaeology* (New York 1977) 1–10.
11. Cf. D. Clarke, 'Archaeology: The Loss of Innocence,' *Antiquity* 47 (1973) 6–18 (16).
12. Clarke (supra n. 11) 18.
13. Cf. Courbin (supra n. 3) 211–12.
14. Courbin (supra n. 3) 130–35, 147–48.

15. P. P. Betancourt, 'Introduction,' *Sixth Temple University Aegean Symposium* (Philadelphia 1981) 1.
16. H. N. Michael, 'Radiocarbon Dates from Akrotiri on Thera,' *(First) Temple University Aegean Symposium* (Philadelphia 1976) 7–9.
17. B. J. Kemp and R. Merrillees, *Minoan Pottery in Second-Millennium Egypt* (Mainz 1980).
18. A. M. Snodgrass, 'Mycenae, Northern Europe and Radiocarbon Dates,' *Archaeologica Atlantica* 1 (1975) 33–48; 'An Outsider's View of Radiocarbon Calibration,' in T. F. Watkins ed., *Radiocarbon: Calibration and Prehistory* (Edinburgh 1975) 39–46.
19. See, however, C. Renfrew, *Problems in European Prehistory* (Edinburgh 1979) 281–82, 326.
20. Renfrew (supra n. 1) 295.

CHAPTER 4

A Paradigm Shift in Classical Archaeology?

This, the most recent of all these papers, makes claims which some would find premature or downright presumptuous. Another, yet more recent survey (Osborne 2004) gives a more nuanced picture: many of the same fresh directions of research are noted as here – 'rural life, domestic life, neglected periods, dedications, burial, the more backward regions of Greece', to quote p. 87 below – but some of the aims set out twenty years ago have undergone reorientation. The emphasis on the origins of the Greek state has given way to study of its spatial articulation, the 'brave new world of cemetery studies' has yet to arrive (at least for mainland Greece), the quantification of dedications has matured into a contribution to the wider study of regional variation, in which H.-J. Gehrke's 'Third Greece' has at last begun to play a prominent part (Osborne: 90–2). All this is not only true, but in general to be welcomed. Those who might contest the reality of a paradigm shift will still presumably be gratified to read that the subject is today 'more self-aware ... more systematic and more sophisticated' (Osborne: 95).

BIBLIOGRAPHY

Osborne, R. (2004), 'Greek archaeology: a survey of recent work', *American Journal of Archaeology* 108: 87–102.

This article, a revised version of the 13th McDonald Lecture given on 21 November 2001, sets the recent and partial transformation in the content and practice of Classical archaeological against the background of Kuhn's well-known work, first published in 1962, on

'A paradigm shift in Classical archaeology?', *Cambridge Archaeological Journal* 12, 2002, 179–93.

paradigm and revolution in the scientific disciplines. Perhaps the most important question in this context – how would we know when a change in paradigm had taken place? – is harder to answer for a humanities discipline than for a science. But the attempt is made, first to set out a traditional paradigm for the subject; then to give examples of new approaches which seem to satisfy many of Kuhn's criteria for the introduction of a new paradigm; and, more briefly, to show that other approaches, innovatory though they may be, by their nature cannot bring about such a change. Whether a true paradigm shift has been set in motion, the future alone will show.

The first half of my title comes, of course, from that non-scientist's bible of the operations of the physical sciences, Thomas S. Kuhn's *The Structure of Scientific Revolutions*, first published in 1962 and since hailed, by the *Times Literary Supplement*, as one of 'The Hundred Most Influential Books since the Second World War'. I said 'of course', but that may have been a mistake. Note that I called the book 'the *non*-scientist's bible', and that it was *The Times Literary Supplement* that rated it so highly. These are hints that, quite apart from the fact that Kuhn's central propositions have become increasingly contested over the years (see for example Fuller 2000), his achievement anyway never acquired quite the same standing among practising scientists. In fact, a private poll that I have conducted has so far failed to yield a single one who has read the book: the explanation being invariably along those lines, so familiar from quite other contexts, that 'They're too busy doing it to want to read about it'.

So a word or two is in place about Kuhn's analysis of how revolutions happen in the sciences, noting his view that, on an initially small scale, they happen very frequently. As he later admitted in response to his critics (the best source for such elucidations and modifications of his original position is the 'Postscript – 1969' in Kuhn 1996, 174–210), he had used the word 'paradigm' in two senses. First, the sociological one, on which we shall mainly concentrate: 'the entire constellation of beliefs, values, techniques . . . shared by the members of a given (scientific) community'. Secondly, 'the exemplary past achievements' to which those members share in paying homage (Kuhn 1996, 175). You will notice how important the concepts of 'sharing' and 'community' are to both definitions. A 'paradigm shift' is what occurs when, perhaps at first in only one small part of one discipline, new beliefs, values and techniques are embraced. Such episodes are often preceded by a kind of crisis, which Kuhn defines very simply: 'the common awareness that something has gone wrong' (Kuhn 1996, 181). They are followed by a phase of competition, but this 'is usually quickly ended', one way or the other (Kuhn 1996, 177). Either the case of this innovatory sub-group is rapidly proved to rest on error or misunderstanding; or it quietly prevails, first in its own small corner, then more widely. In the latter case, a further consequence of such assimilation is that it often has the effect of creating a different kind of crisis elsewhere, in other parts of the discipline or in other disciplines altogether: nobody there had thought that 'something had gone wrong', the majority probably still don't, but eventually the new paradigm is shown to yield more robust results, with fewer anomalies, than the old one.

Really important paradigm shifts are ones which seriously interrupt the progress of the other main element of Kuhn's antithesis, 'normal science.' Normal science is predicated on the assumption that, broadly speaking, the scientific community knows what the world is like. Most scientists will spend most of their careers in extending the frontiers of that assumption, discovering new applications and solving residual problems. After a successful paradigm shift some of them, and eventually all of them in the areas affected, will switch to a completely different set of problems, and to completely different standards by which to judge their solution. The rules have changed, and the relevant part of the community gradually acknowledges that it had not after all known 'what the world was like'.

That is probably enough of my facile reprise of Kuhn's analysis. More pressing questions urge themselves upon us. First and most obvious, what has the practice of the 'hard sciences' to do with a humanities discipline? Can paradigm shifts occur in communities which, nowadays at any rate, would seldom lay claim to knowing what their subject-matter 'was like'? To historians, any such assertion about life in their chosen periods would be an invitation to debate, just as literary scholars would hesitate to accept it about the mind of their chosen authors. Is there a place for the paradigm in subjects which abound in competing schools, whose challenge to each other, far from being 'quickly ended', may continue for generations on end? To this last question, Kuhn had the ultimate answer: that his theses were actually 'borrowed from other disciplines', namely the humanities, which commonly see their subjects in terms of 'revolutionary breaks in style, taste and institutional structure' (1996, 208); his own originality, if any, consisted in applying the same concepts to the sciences which had been thought to behave quite differently. There remain, of course, important differences between the two cases: in the hard sciences, the old and the new paradigms are often absolutely incompatible with each other, as is seldom if ever true in the humanities; likewise, the necessity for common standards of validation is much more prevalent in the sciences. But that should still help to answer this first misgiving.

There are others, however. They include one whose point will become apparent presently: how wide does the field have to be in which the original paradigm shift is held to have taken place? Here Kuhn gives an equally explicit answer: it doesn't have to be wide at all. The change 'need not seem revolutionary to those outside a single community, consisting perhaps of fewer than twenty-five people' (1996, 181). What it does is to reconstruct 'the group commitments' of these people (notice again the stress on the factor of community) and in due course, if it is successful, those of others too. That sets to rest another source of doubt which I entertained when using the title for this article.

Then there is the all-embracing question: how would we know when a paradigm shift, in whatever subject, had taken place? I do not think that this is an insurmountable difficulty either. One obvious test is to take a long view of other people's disciplines and see how much they have changed since we last studied them ourselves. On this evidence, I think that Geography is the first example that comes to mind. Rather than falling back on vague definitions of the process, such as 'change in the way subject-matter is perceived and organized', or in 'the framework for thought and practice within the discipline', we can retrieve a more operational criterion, in one last phrase before we say good-bye to Thomas S. Kuhn: paradigm debates involve confronting the question 'Which problems is it more significant to have solved?' (1996, 110).

This is a quotation worth bearing in mind throughout: the debate that follows on an attempted paradigm shift, as Kuhn notes, will tend to involve progressively wider audiences. Thus, 'What would be most useful and applicable in your field, as a fellow-scientist?' 'What would you as a fellow-academic find more intellectually challenging?' 'What would most interest you as a member of the educated public?' 'What would *you* in the world at large find of the greatest benefit to humanity?' Francis Crick's alleged claim, at the bar of the 'Eagle' in 1953, that he and James Watson had just discovered 'the secret of life' (Watson 1968, 126), would have easily satisfied all those criteria of significance, as a genuine paradigm shift always would.

So we turn to one small humanities discipline, Classical archaeology, to see what has happened there. We have been looking only at the first of Kuhn's two senses of 'paradigm', but now I am going to start with the second, that of the 'exemplary past achievements'. No achievement in the history of the subject has more often served as an exemplary paradigm than the work of Sir John Beazley. And deservedly so: in his long life (1885–1970) Beazley achieved, on a gigantic scale and with near-complete success, what dozens of his predecessors and hundreds of his successors have undertaken, in smaller fields and with results that have never commanded quite the same authority. A sizeable sector of the 'normal science' of Classical archaeology has followed the paradigm first set up by Beazley's early papers of the 1910s and 1920s. There are many reassuring aspects of working by this kind of paradigm. Its progress is readily measurable and, in consequence, there is a striking degree of consensus about the value of individual contributions to that progress. Beazley exemplifies, to perfection, this consensus (see in general Kurtz 1985; for a critical re-assessment, Whitley 1997).

Even at the time when his studies began, the numbers of Athenian black-figure and red-figure vases in the world's collections, major and minor, were to be numbered in the tens of thousands (today there are more still). Beazley found a system whereby a substantial proportion of these could, for the first time, be definitively organized: that of associating each of them with the individual hand which had been responsible, not for their shaping, but for their surface decoration. Others before him had attempted this approach: mostly, they had started out from the fact that some of these painted scenes were actually signed with an artist's name. The trouble was that there were too few of these: they were to be counted only in hundreds, not nearly enough to establish control over the field. Beazley therefore set this criterion on one side, and concentrated instead on the purely visual technique of observing tiny stylistic details in each painter's method: the rendering of an eye-lid, an ear-lobe or a toe. These, he believed – not the conscious effects that the painter was aiming for, but the unconsciously-repeated features of his work – were the most tell-tale indicators of individual style. Several analogies have been drawn for this procedure, in the somewhat earlier intellectual activities of the late nineteenth century: most obviously, with the success achieved by Giovanni Morelli with unattributed Renaissance works, which it has never quite been proved that Beazley used as a model (this is contested by Williams 1996, 241–2); or, more laterally, with the rise of the science of detection, through which a criminal betrays his identity in the unthinking repetition of certain small details which give a pattern to his crimes, much as Beazley's vase-painters gave up their secrets to him (Beard 1986; Elsner 1990).

Thus Beazley assembled, by tens, fifties, in some cases a few hundreds, the works by each single hand. Where – as most often – no signed piece was among them, he had to invent names for the painters that he had discovered. Intellectually, an amazing aspect of this achievement was the visual memory it required: Beazley travelled assiduously to each major collection in Europe and North America, drawing and photographing; but it was obviously necessary for him to retain, for years on end, some means of visual recollection for each individual piece, until the time came to fit it into his framework. From this, it was for Beazley a secondary step, for everyone else a vitally important one, to arrange these artists in chronological groups. Sometimes Beazley could do this in the most direct way possible, by showing that a painter in generation 'Y' had actually learned his craft from an older predecessor in generation 'X'. But more broadly, each one of his artists could be grouped with their apparent contemporaries, by observing such features as common advances in anatomical rendering. Thus a whole, vast field was for the first time organized into a system applicable by many other scholars to their own work.

I should like now to establish a simple point, again exemplified (though on a huge scale) by Beazley. Before, during and since Beazley's time, traditional Classical archaeology has been defined in terms of subject-matter, of specific *classes of material*. These classes of material were, in a sense, already laid down for the discipline by external factors. There were geographical categories – Greek, Italian, Ionian, Sicilian, Athenian. There were (on an even more important and defining level) chronological ones – Archaic, Classical, Hellenistic, Imperial Roman. Then there were those largely peculiar to this branch of archaeology, the categories determined by *individual* past activity. In art-historical studies (always the most prestigious branch of the subject) these involved the handiwork of individual artists and schools. But there was also that category, only found in this branch of archaeology, which was determined by the writers of ancient texts, of which the outstanding example is (or was) 'Homeric archaeology', a branch of the subject whose whole *raison d'être* lay in the survival of two literary works, the *Iliad* and *Odyssey*, and whose primary aim was to throw light on their interpretation.

The traditional practice of the subject was to take one such class of material and (to employ the verb in commonest use), 'do' it. As often, an anecdote will save pages of description. At some date in the 1950s H.R.W. Smith, the revered Professor of Classical Archaeology at Berkeley and a former Beazley pupil, was interviewing a potential graduate research pupil, a young woman. Enthusiastic about her potential, he is said to have offered her this encouragement: 'With five years and a bit of luck, Miss X., I can make you the Miss Haspels of the Etruscan undecorated *oinochoai*'. The story has an excellent source and I find no difficulty in believing it to be true. What Smith was offering to his potential pupil was the status of a counterpart to Émilie Haspels, author of *Attic Black-figure Lekythoi* (1936). This was a considerable and much-admired piece of work. Haspels, a contemporary admirer of Beazley's method rather than a pupil, had applied that method to a large sub-category of Athenian pottery, the so-called *lekythos* shape. She had produced a typology of variant sub-forms, a chronological scheme, and a series of attributions to individual painters, with such success that, when Beazley came to publish his own *magnum opus* on black-figured pottery twenty years later, he was content to refer his readers to 'her fine work' (1956, viii), to omit the hundreds of specimens of the *lekythos* which she had listed and to adopt her attributions, except when he had something to add – from him, a unique accolade.

But 'the Etruscan undecorated *oinochoai*'? They can be beautifully-made artefacts but, as their name suggests, they lack surface decoration. This eliminated, at a stroke, some of the approaches used by Haspels or Beazley: the whole, multi-faceted approach of connoisseurship including, in all probability, attributions to individual hands. This would reduce drastically the potential impact of the proposed piece of work, and perhaps the young woman realized this. At all events, the sequel to the story is not without relevance to my theme: she changed her mind, withdrew her application and (it is said) married a Sergeant of Marines soon afterwards; but that is not the aspect of the story that I find so depressing.

One could describe the thinking behind Smith's offer, according to taste, as positivistic, empirical, conservative or purely cumulative. The classes of material, themselves the most traditional of concepts, were mentally arranged in a three-dimensional matrix of pigeon-holes, with the geographical as one dimension, chronological as the second, and descriptive category as the third. The Etruscan undecorated *oinochoai* were one of the (by now rapidly diminishing) number of empty holes. As the sub-divisions of the subject were pigeon-holed, so did its practitioners come to be. I myself, as a graduate student, worked on Greek military equipment; today, 35 years after I ceased to do so I am still greeted at conferences as 'the armour man'. When my colleague Nigel Spivey was about to produce his prize-winning book *Understanding Greek Sculpture* – the title in itself shows some kind of rejection of the disciplinary tradition I have described – a foreign colleague is said to have protested 'But he's a pot man!'. But that is enough of anecdotal evidence.

That disciplinary tradition required you to do certain things, sophisticated yet of a largely descriptive nature, with your class of material. Prolonged reflection on the *function* of the artefacts was not necessarily one of these requirements; nor on what valuation had been put upon them in antiquity; nor on what lessons could be learned from their geographical description outside the centre of production; nor even on the vital question of the precise archaeological contexts in which they had been deposited, beyond the mere names of the find-spots. In short, the tradition gave short shrift to the whole *social* context (not to speak of the cognitive aspects) of the class of objects in question. Each contribution was destined to be an inward one, to other studies of other, parallel classes of object in a bracket of ancient time and space: nor was one often encouraged to cross even the minor, parochial boundaries between these classes.

Eventually, even Beazley's work in vase-painting studies began to be questioned, not for one moment for its accuracy and validity, but precisely for its value as a paradigm. To attribute 245 vases to 'The Berlin Painter', it was asked: what exactly does this contribute to the further development of the subject? One very obvious contribution, not intended by Beazley and not even lying within the field of academic research, lies in the benefit to the art market, where the individual attributions by himself and his successors have greatly enhanced the price of vases (see Fig. 4.1). But the widest and most useful application of Beazley's attributions was as a guide to the chronology of any kind of discovery, made in any part of the world that had contact, direct or indirect, with the ancient Greeks between the sixth and the fourth centuries BC: this world extended from the Yemen to southern England. If there was no decorated Athenian pottery in an excavation-find, there would almost invariably be other objects, which elsewhere had been associated with yet other objects, which could in turn be

*"A red-figure volute krater attributed to a painter of the Syleus
sequence! Maynard, you shouldn't have!"*

Figure 4.1 (© The New Yorker Collection 1999 George Booth from
cartoonbank.com. All Rights Reserved.)

dated in terms of Beazley's classification. But for this purpose, a piece
by a mediocre contemporary of the Berlin Painter would serve as well
as one from the hand of this artist.

Even art-historically, what kind of figure is this Berlin Painter? We
know nothing of his place in contemporary society, not even his name;
we do not know that he was not a woman rather than a man; it has
even been argued that his and his lesser colleagues' talents lay, not
in the original creation of their figures but, rather in their skill in
copying them from drawings of works in precious metals (Vickers &
Gill 1994, ch. 6; and, for the ancient monetary valuation of this very

painter's work, p. 86). In the last analysis, the Berlin Painter has not just his origin, but his only real existence as an individual, in the uniquely sensitive perception of Beazley.

Such questioning of ruling paradigms began to spread more widely, in a series of new orientations which will form the subject of the rest of this article. I will leave it to others to decide whether they constitute a paradigm shift, but I think I can show that they satisfy one of the more testable of Kuhn's criteria: they have certainly given rise to the posing of that question, 'Which problems would it be more significant to have solved?'. First, though, another general point. Earlier on, I alluded to the influence exercised by the ancient texts, and Classical archaeology is often stigmatized, by its many critics, as being 'text-driven'. In a superficial sense, this is palpably false: most Classical archaeologists do their work, and always have done, without directly consulting an ancient text for days or weeks on end. The entire corpus of work on Greek pottery, for instance, from before Beazley's time to the present day, was undertaken in defiance of the fact that there is scarcely a line in ancient literature referring to this field of activity. What the criticism implies is something deeper: that the subject takes its orientation from, and adapts its whole narrative to, the lead given by the literary sources. Thus the archaeology of Roman Britain has been built around Tacitus' narrative of conquest; the study of Greek art around the text of the Elder Pliny; the archaeology of fifth-century Athens around the narratives supplied by Herodotus, Thucydides and Xenophon; that of Republican Rome similarly around those of Livy and Diodorus; that of Sicily again around Thucydides; and most notoriously, that of Aegean prehistory and protohistory around Homer. There is something in this, even if it still conspicuously fails to cover the case of Greek vase-painting.

But there is a deeper level still. Traditional Classical archaeology is stated, this time I think with complete truth, to have directed its energies at those *aspects* of the ancient world on which the written sources, taken as a whole, throw light. Thus, on urban but not on rural life; on public and civic, but not on domestic activity; on periods seen as historically important, but not on the obscurer ones; on the permanent physical manifestations of religion, but not on the temporary ones – sacrifice, patterns of dedication, ritual meals, pilgrimage; on the artefacts interred in burials, but not on burial itself; on the historically prominent states – in Greece, Athens and Sparta – but not on what has recently been called 'the Third Greece' (Gehrke 1986); and so on. The decisive stage in the recent history of the subject came, in my view, when Classical Archaeologists began to ask themselves: why not study this aspect, not because the ancient sources throw light on it, but precisely because they do *not* throw light on it? The examples I shall give illustrate how, usually in combination, some of these Cinderellas have recently been brought to the ball: rural life, domestic life, neglected periods, dedications, burial, the more backward regions of Greece. There have also been changes in *method*: not only were new problems investigated, but they were approached in unprecedented ways.

Let us take, as an example of the 'new way', the project presented in Joseph Coleman Carter's *The Chora of Metaponto* ii: *the Necropoleis* (Carter 1998). The first thing to notice about this publication is that it was produced as part of the results of surface survey of the rural territory, or *chora*, of a Greek city in southern Italy. I shall have more to say in a moment about this technique of field survey which, thirty years ago, first began to offer a serious alternative to excavation, at least on the part of English-speaking archaeologists working either at home or overseas; and which, at least in quantitative terms, has now almost reached a point of parity in activity. In fact the outlying cemeteries at Metaponto were discovered as a part of the study of the city's land-allotment grid, first detected from the air; the main rural cemetery, at Pantanello, lines the sides of two of the main arterial roads on which the grid was based. Pantanello is 3.5 kilometres from the city (Fig. 4.2): there are plenty of other cemeteries in what is the more normal location, on the edges of the built-up area, so some other group was buried here: who were they? The answer is pretty obvious: it was those forgotten people of Greek history, the country-dwellers – and, sure enough, their farmsteads were also found, spaced at approximately one per land-holding, all around the area (Fig. 4.3).

This was an inhumation-cemetery of about 330 graves, in reasonably good preservation, and perhaps the most interesting point is what was done with the skeletons. They were submitted for testing of their blood-groups and epigenetic traits, as well as for aging and sexing. An important detail is that this was done partly 'blindfold': that is, the biologists were not told of the archaeological indications of age, gender and date provided by the grave-goods, though they did know how the graves lay on the ground. In the event, it did indeed prove possible to distribute over 250 of the skeletons into some 45 small groups, each with biological linkages. This is an example of what I call the 'quantitative bonus' of Mediterranean archaeology:

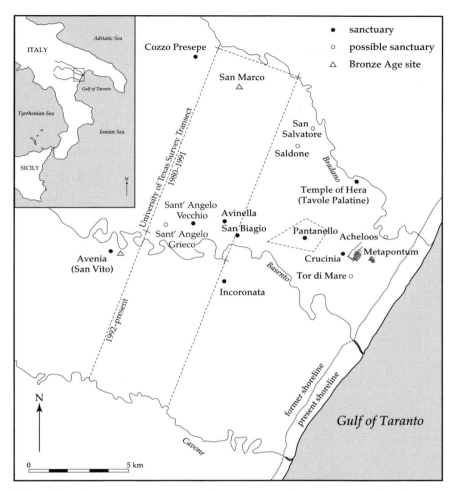

Figure 4.2 Map of the territory of ancient Metapontum, showing the relative positions of the city itself (right centre) and of Pantanello.

the greater size of sample forms a correspondingly better basis for inference.

Further, the relatively precise chronology (Beazley can take a posthumous bow) meant that these groups could be set out as family trees (Fig. 4.4), with a series of generations indicated with their approximate life-spans. The shaded rectangles here indicate the possible range of date for the *birth*, not the death, of each individual; gender is indicated by the white symbol, approximate age at death

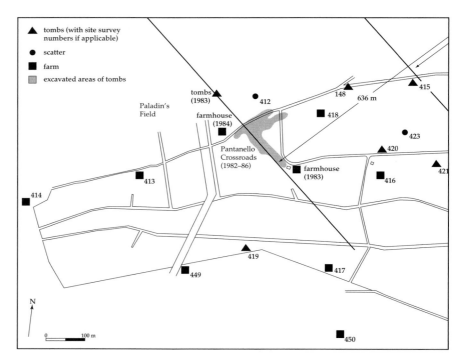

Figure 4.3 The Pantanello cemetery (shaded) straddling one of the parallel roads of the ancient land-allotment grid (arrowed), with the adjacent farmhouses (square symbols).

by the numeral within it. Thus in this illustration, we see what is taken to be a married couple, both born rather before the mid-fourth century BC and both living to a ripe old age. But their children fared less well: both the married son (buried as was usual with his family of origin, in Tomb 85) and the presumed daughter-in-law (Tomb 99) died young, while the grandson (Tomb 94) lived an even shorter time. More problematic is the case of the female, taken to be the daughter of the original couple, in Tomb 100: she is associated with a male (Tomb 103) who, for reasons of blood-group, cannot be her younger brother, and should not, in the light of the already-mentioned rule of patrilocal burial for married sons, be her husband. If he is then her son, why is she not buried elsewhere with her husband? Have we a case here of a child born out of wedlock, or of a husband killed far away in battle? In any case, both these individuals also died young, leaving the old couple to outlive not only their children, but even perhaps their grandchildren.

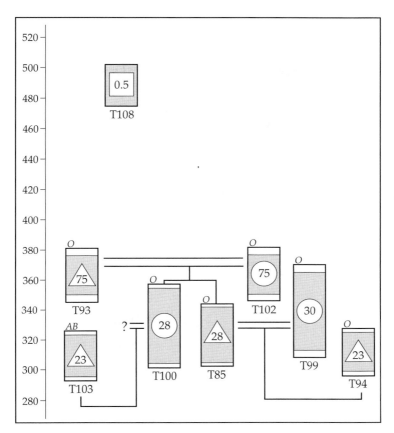

Figure 4.4 One of the proposed family trees, N6.7, of the Pantanello burial group (see pp. 89–91).

The most satisfying feature was that, when the family groups were plotted on to the cemetery, they proved to fall into fairly neat rectangles (Fig. 4.5), of standard dimensions, with little 'trespassing'. As well as being a remarkable objective vindication of the method, this last finding validated, at a stroke, one of the oldest hypotheses in the book of funerary archaeology: that closer groupings within a formal cemetery are indeed *family* groupings. Before this, parallel claims had been founded on much smaller samples; common sense had long since suggested that the hypothesis was a likely one; study of modern cemeteries, where over long periods families were often grouped in plots, had reinforced it; but for the more distant past, a hypothesis is what it had remained.

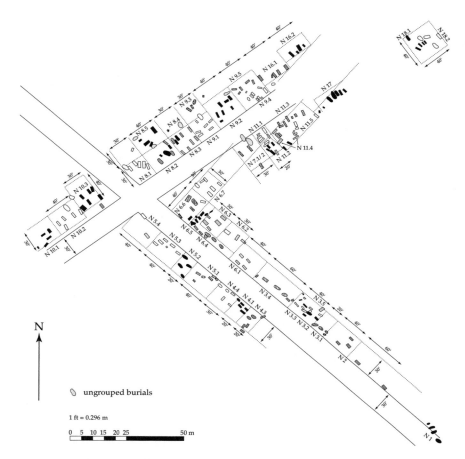

Figure 4.5 The Pantanello cemetery divided into family plots. The groups of burials shown as differentially-shaded rectangles are each biologically linked (N6.7 can be seen right of the crossroads, with one member 'trespassing' on to the plot of N6.6).

Of the many merits of this project – the skill of the excavation, the scientific objectivity of the skeletal testing, the exhaustive detail of the interpretation, individual by individual, the precision of the dating which made it all possible, and the relatively large sample size which makes it all credible – some you would expect in any good project, but I should be surprised to find the last two in any field of archaeology but the Classical. Yet the contrast with the traditional Classical cemetery report is also intense. No doubt there are still those who would have preferred to have the finds published on their own, set out according to the traditional classes and sub-classes, ready to use, as they would once have been. But for anyone interested in the broader aspects of Classical Greek culture, I would guess that the Metaponto volume offers about a hundred times as much new and serviceable knowledge as a traditional publication. For good measure, the preservation of the Metaponto bones made possible one last touch: the re-construction of the faces of the fifth-and fourth-century dead (Carter 1998, 521–5).

But Metaponto lies fairly near the outer fringe of the Greek world, and the evidence presented in the report relates primarily, though by no means exclusively, to burial practices. So what about something much nearer home, and throwing light on the living rather than the dead? Here again, the new fashion for rural surface survey during the 1980s and 1990s can come up with exciting finds. In the far south of Attica, near the tip of the peninsula at Sunion and only a little over 20 miles from Athens, the German archaeologist Hans Lohmann carried out a one-man survey (Lohmann 1993) of an unusually dry, hilly stretch of terrain. It would be interesting to know what, if anything, his more conservative seniors had expected him to find: some fortifications, perhaps, a few graves, and the odd rural sanctuary? In fact his most important discovery was of a whole network of isolated farmsteads, less regularly laid out than their Metaponto counterparts, as one might expect in such terrain, but concentrated into a similar period: mainly the fifth and earlier fourth centuries BC. This indeed seems to have been one of the the few periods in its whole history when it was thought worth cultivating this impoverished land at all intensively, a testimony to the burgeoning population of Attica in these years. Mainly as a direct result of this later neglect of the land, Lohmann found clear traces of the farm-buildings still visible above ground, together with a number of their appurtenances (Fig. 4.6): terracing, threshing-floors, boundary-walls, even boundary-inscriptions, and once again burial-plots, but this time separate ones for each farm, not grouped into cemeteries. The original appearance of the bestpreserved establishments could be readily reconstructed (Fig. 4.7).

Notice that both the prize examples of innovatory Classical archaeology that I have produced stem from field-survey projects. If there is one huge aspect that contrasts the new approaches from the old, it is this switch from the urban to the rural, undertaken in disregard of the near-silence of the literary sources and pushed through, I might add, in the face of indifference (to use no stronger term) from those of a more traditional cast of mind today. Neglect of organic materials

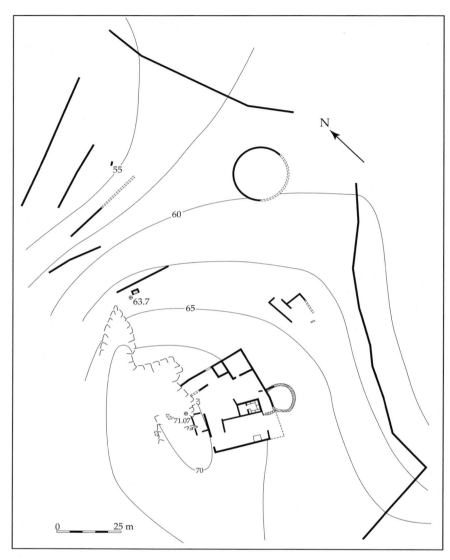

Figure 4.6 Plan of the farm LE 16 of H. Lohmann's survey in southern Attica, showing the farmstead and out-buildings, with a boundary wall (above and right), terrace wall (upper left) and a threshing floor (above, centre).

has been another characteristic of the subject, so let me give an extreme and perhaps distasteful counter-example. We have just seen, from Italy and from Attica, that it was only by surface survey that the rural landscape was found to have been dotted with small, isolated sites which offer convincing evidence of having been inhabited:

Figure 4.7 Model of the farm LE 17 of Lohmann's survey, showing the farmstead and out-buildings (here including a tower), enclosures and, again, a threshing floor.

roof-tiles, tableware, cooking vessels, storage-vessels, lamps and so on. Perhaps the next big finding, however, was one that is not present in all parts of the Mediterranean landscape: that even between these small sites, much of the landscape is frequently carpeted with broken pottery and tiles, mainly of the Greek and Roman periods, much less commonly of the ages that came before and after. The closer you are to one of the Classical sites, the denser the scatter (Fig. 4.8). What is this material and how did it get there?

Here we are still in the realms of theory, because the answer is very hard to demonstrate. But the most convincing proposal, I think, is a more-or-less common-sense one: that Classical farmers are known to have fertilized their land, using domestic refuse and animal manure to do so. This rubbish would be collected over the year in some sort of compost-heap, then spread on the fields, roughly concentrically out from each farm. While it was being collected, broken pot and tile would be thrown into the same heap, become embedded in the refuse, and be taken out with it. The refuse would turn into soil, the potsherds and tile would not. Provided that the land remained

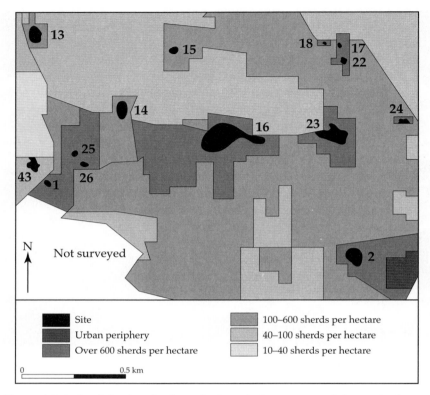

Figure 4.8 A sherd-density plot from the Boeotia Survey, central Greece, in the
territory of ancient Thespiai: the 'urban periphery' (lower right) shows the
proximity of the city itself. The ground slopes at first from north to south, then is
virtually level in the southern half of the map.

in cultivation over the following centuries, ploughing would always
bring a proportion of it to the surface. The earlier stages of this process, as ethnoarchaeological study has shown, are something which
can still be witnessed in the more traditional agricultural régimes of
Greece, with plastics taking the place of ceramics, and other, more
perishable materials such as textiles also embedded in the refuse. This
explanation – indeed, mere discussion of the issue – is so unattractive
to some of our colleagues, perhaps so out of keeping with 'the glory
that was Greece', that it has provoked protest on what seem primarily
aesthetic grounds: 'Making a mountain out of a manure-hill will leave
many readers with a ludicrous view of survey archaeology' (Morris
1995, 185).

But at any rate I have given my explanation, of something which needs explaining: for none of the easy answers, whereby environmental, climatic or *recent* agricultural factors might have gradually spread the material out from the site centre, will really do – for a start, the scatters run uphill as well as downhill from the sites. Mediterranean conditions, I should add, prove to be especially favourable to generating these scatters, as can be seen by comparing the density of Roman pottery emanating from Roman sites in Essex (Williamson 1984, esp. fig. 2), where 'more than 4 sherds per hectare' counts as 'dense scatter', with that of Greek pottery from Classical sites in the project I have jointly directed with Professor J. L. Bintliff in Boeotia, Central Greece (from which comes Fig. 4.8), where the higher densities, outside the actual sites, exceed 600 pieces per hectare, 150 times as high. The 'quantitative bonus' of Mediterranean archaeology has struck again.

In this case, the difference is so striking that, in turn, it opens up a set of new problems. Are climatic factors alone responsible for this change in orders of magnitude as between Britain and Greece? That they played some rôle is suggested by the fact that even single-period Roman sites in Greece generate far more pottery than Roman sites in Britain. But Martin Millett has developed an alternative and powerful line of explanation: that the production, per unit of time, and the supply and consumption, per head, of ceramics showed major fluctuations in different epochs and regions (Millett 1991). As a simple statement of fact, this must be true; and it probably also carries considerable weight as one of the explanations.

I have not yet mentioned one work in the Classical field, so weighty and so uniquely influential that there must be many people, in the United States at least, who would automatically suppose that a title like mine must be intended to refer to it: *Black Athena* (Bernal 1987; 1991). The book has been taken seriously enough to be incorporated into American school curricula and would, in some quarters, unquestionably be judged to have generated a paradigm shift, in a much wider field than that of Classical archaeology, but there as well. For me, it offers a classic example of a work of genuine originality and radical implications which is nevertheless, in its nature, unable to give rise to such a shift within the professional community. This is partly, I would argue, because its aims are anyway not directed only at changing professional practice, partly because little of its methods and evidence is new. Interestingly enough, Martin Bernal himself conceded at the outset (Bernal 1987, 1) that 'the changes of view that I am proposing are not paradigmatic in the strict sense of the word'.

To take my first argument, it is entirely desirable to seek to undermine European racism in general, and in particular to show that
it was an attitude that extended to much nineteenth- and twentieth-
century scholarship. But in professional practice, the presence of this
last factor had been widely accepted, and adjustments made for it,
even before it was so brilliantly documented in volume 1 of the book.
There was no 'common awareness that something had gone wrong';
there was no perception of unsolved problems. Instead, the question
that has since been asked by many archaeologists is: if every word
of *Black Athena* were accepted and absorbed by us, what difference
would this make to our actual practices? Or, loosely re-phrasing the
question in terms of the distant past: by re-writing the origins of a
culture how, if at all, do you change its nature?

As for the methods employed in the work, they are familiar enough:
in Jonathan Hall's words (1990, 252), 'the stage and a great deal
of the scenery and props remain fundamentally the same'. Volume
I offers, first and foremost, re-study of ancient literary texts, then
of modern receptions of them; volume II addresses other documents
including archaeological finds; while linguistic evidence, etymology
and place-names are promised for III, and religion and mythology for
IV. Those who set out to refute its propositions are easily drawn into
using equally traditional evidence to do so. Any such fundamental re-
orientations as, say, the rejection of the 'Indo-European hypothesis',
are absent.

All this makes it particularly fascinating to read of a direct encounter in 1989, shortly before an academic meeting where volume
I of *Black Athena* was to be discussed, between Bernal and Kuhn
himself (Bernal 1991, xix). Whatever Bernal was expecting (he had
prefaced his first volume with a quotation from Kuhn), the comments
of the sage reported by him are rather non-committal. Two of them are
still worth recording here: that the meeting was being held much too
soon (about two years) after the publication, but that the important
thing was the legitimating effect of holding it at all. Encouragement,
but not yet validation.

It is not an entirely frivolous point (though perhaps an unkind
one) to observe that more or less the same means are employed by
infinitely less-serious writers to argue for far more extravagant conclusions. An example might be the author of *Where Troy Once Stood*
(Wilkens 1990), who has set the Trojan War close to Cambridge,
with Troy itself located at Wandlebury on the Gog Magog hills; and
has extended the travels of the *Odyssey* far afield, not just to his
native Netherlands but to the Azores, the Cape Verde Islands and

even Cuba. The method here is, again, close analysis of Homer's text, supplemented by the evidence of etymology and place-names, with briefer glances at religion and mythology; and again, if serious researchers spared the time to refute Wilkens' thesis, they would do so partly by use of equally traditional evidence, partly in this case by common-sense observations (Homer's references to continuous rain and occasional snow are not, in themselves, a proof that the *Iliad* is set in Britain). Both examples, in my view, serve a useful purpose by exemplifying certain of the means by which a paradigm shift is *not* to be achieved.

Even before this last digression, we had strayed into questions whose interest would be, has indeed been seen to be, incomprehensible to some practitioners of the subject. We have tried our hands at explanation, not in the past regarded as necessarily one of its objectives. We have indulged in a little mild quantification, again an activity long regarded as the province of less well-endowed branches of archaeology. We have looked at the claims on our attention of organic materials. There is, finally, the issue of the neglected periods of antiquity. I should perhaps have begun with this, the only area for which I can point to a published claim (not made by myself) that a paradigm shift has taken place. In traditional archaeology, these periods were neglected mainly because they were seen as 'uninteresting'. Crudely decoded, this means what one would by now expect: they were periods of which our ancient sources had little to say, or which showed a dearth of beautiful artefacts. Prime examples are: the Middle Bronze Age of Greece (but not the Late Bronze Age of the Mycenaean palaces); most of the Early Iron Age everywhere; much of the Hellenistic and Roman Imperial ages in Greece; later Roman Imperial Italy and, above all, the period after the capital was transferred to Constantinople.

One of these periods is the Greek Early Iron Age. In so far as it entered the traditional consciousness at all, it was there as a component of 'Homeric archaeology', already noted as a prize specimen of a sub-discipline that took not only its lead, but its very name, from the fact of survival of literary texts. But by the 1970s, writes Ian Morris (1996, 123), there had grown up 'a methodological distinction between a text-based model of the 500 years after the destruction of the (Mycenaean) palaces as a Heroic Age, and an artefact-based model of it as a Dark Age'. One might have expected archaeologists, of any persuasion, to lean towards the second of these models, but this had not always been the case. I still cherish the rhetorical question put by a reviewer of my own first book: 'Is it being old-fashioned to suggest that the special value, and special delight, of Classical Archaeology is that it helps us to interpret the Classics, and not the other way about?' (Anderson 1966, 269). Although this is a sentiment which I have never shared, I have always respected it for its candour, and for the consequent clarity with which the issue is posed.

But turn now to what, according to Ian Morris, happened next. 'At this point, we might expect to find an academic debate to rival the fury of that of the 1880s' (referring to the conflict then aroused by the palpable incompatibilities between the discoveries of Heinrich Schliemann at Late Bronze Age Troy and Mycenae, and the Homeric picture). 'Instead', Morris continues, 'there was a classic example of the paradigm shift . . . with hardly any sustained debate in print, the archaeological model quietly swept the field'. He goes on to illustrate this by the institutional evidence (something which Kuhn stressed but which I have so far omitted from this article), by pointing to the successive elections to chairs at University College London, Cambridge and Oxford; and adds that 'Outside Britain, the published versions of the three major international conferences on Greece between 1200 and 700 BC also suggest that by the 1980's the British scholars' archaeological model . . . was simply taken for granted by most linguists and philologists, as well as by archaeologists' (1996, 123). It all sounds just like what Morris calls it, a paradigm shift. But there is one jarring note: 'with hardly any sustained debate'. Why did this not happen? Was it because so few people were at all interested? Was it because the shift was so palpably overdue? I myself put it down to the maturity and fair-mindedness of Classical scholarship as a whole, but then I am a partial witness. Morris, another partial witness, thinks that, in 'This extraordinary success . . . the crucial factor was that the archaeologists simply produced fuller and more dynamic pictures than the philologists' (1996, 124).

Be that as it may, circumstances are crowding me into breaking my promise to avoid parochialism, and offering an answer to a final, unspoken question: does this have anything especially to do with Cambridge? It would be possible to answer in positive terms by pointing out that Ian Morris is himself one of the group of graduate products of Cambridge Classical archaeology in the 1980s and 1990s. It is significant that most of this group maintain links with prehistoric world archaeology: some (James Whitley, Catherine Morgan, Michael Shanks) actually had part of their original formation in the famous Cambridge school of that discipline. This is the moment to acknowledge that there is a causal link here: much of the innovation

achieved in recent Classical archaeology does indeed stem from familiarity with the current advances in the wider discipline. And talking of
institutional evidence, this and other fields within Classical archaeology are now energetically professed by those named, and by their
former Cambridge fellow-students, in the universities of Chicago,
Florida, Lehigh, Michigan, Princeton, Stanford, Birmingham, Cardiff,
Glasgow, King's College London, University College London, the
Open University, the Open University of Greece, Oxford, Reading,
Sheffield and, in the person of the newly-elected Professor of Ancient
History, right here in Cambridge. But it would be tasteless to continue in this vein: even now, we are within Kuhn's ceiling of 'fewer
than twenty-five people'. Instead, I will appeal to a fairer source: our
opponents and critics.

That there has been some form of backlash is, in view of what was
said above, reassuring. It was rather slow in coming and it took a
rather unexpected form, but here are a few quotations, all from the
last decade, to illustrate it:

> What is a mirage is the Dark Age and the deliberate distance main-
> tained between the second millennium and the culture of Classical
> Greece (Papadopoulos 1993, 195);

> Greek civilization . . . would certainly be better served if the spectre
> of the Dark Age, a phantom that has haunted the 'musty confines
> of Cambridge' . . . for too long, is finally laid to rest (Papadopoulos
> 1993, 196–7).

From this, it transpires that what is now criticized is no longer the
preference for an archaeological interpretation of the centuries after
the fall of Mycenae, but the specific and negative nature of that interpretation: the 'Dark Age'. This is a slightly different charge from that
of turning one's back on the Homeric picture for that period, but there
are features in common: a similar hankering can be detected, for a
return to the picture of a glorious continuity, or a continuity of glory,
extending from the Greece of Agamemnon to that of Perikles, which
has been rudely interrupted by the insertion of a spurious Dark Age in
between. A third, and perhaps less transparent, quotation addresses
one of the accompaniments to this interruption:

> Early Greek archaeology [has been turned] into exclusive grist for
> the mill of the polis, the only currently acceptable goal for politically
> correct scholarship (S. Morris 1997, 64).

The charge here is that, to reinforce and underwrite this interruption
in Greek culture, there has been a parallel concern to over-emphasize

what is supposed to have happened at its end: the rise of a new, fresh Greek civilization of the polis, from the long-cold ashes of Mycenaean Greece. If we set aside questions of opinion and evaluation, these criticisms can claim to present the factual state of affairs in tolerably accurate terms, and I shall not engage in debate with them. The charge of 'political correctness', as often, is an acknowledgement that the party under attack has made some progress in the exercise of persuasion. But these comments are also relevant because they point the finger, explicitly or implicitly, at Cambridge as the villain of the piece. This is something that had not previously emerged.

So did the changes which began in the 1970s, in Cambridge and elsewhere, constitute a paradigm shift? The feeling that 'something had gone wrong' was certainly present in the minds of some, though they were only a minority. The narrowness of the field from which the changes began is, as we have seen, not an insuperable barrier. The institutional evidence at least says something about the change in the shared beliefs of the disciplinary community. Opinions have visibly changed on 'which problems it would be more significant to have solved'. Previous views of what the prehistoric, proto-historic and Classical Greek worlds (to say nothing of the Roman) 'were like' have certainly been adjusted. 'Normal science' in Classical archaeology, in dozens of universities, no longer means what it used to. Irrespective of any possible paradigm shift, by far the most important result of the changes has been, in my own opinion, to make of Classical archaeology a much more intellectually challenging discipline. But as I said before, others must judge.

ACKNOWLEDGEMENTS

I should like to thank my colleagues Dr Patricia Fara and Dr Timothy Lewens for their generous help in the interpretation of the work of Thomas S. Kuhn; Todd Whitelaw for invaluable ethnoarchaeological information; and Professor Joseph C. Carter and Dr Hans Lohmann for their kind permission to use Figures 4.2–5 and 4.6–7 respectively.

REFERENCES

Anderson, J. K., 1966. Review of A. Snodgrass, *Early Greek Armour and Weapons. Classical Philology* 61, 278–80.
Beard, M., 1986. Signed against unsigned. (Review of Kurtz (ed.), 1985). *Times Literary Supplement*, 12th September, 1013.

Beazley, J. D., 1956. *Attic Black-figure Vase Painters.* Oxford: Oxford University Press.

Bernal, M., 1987. *Black Athena: the Afroasiatic Roots of Classical Civilization,* vol. I: *The Fabrication of Ancient Greece, 1785–1985.* London: Free Association Books.

Bernal, M., 1991. *Black Athena: the Afroasiatic Roots of Classical Civilization,* vol. II: *The Archaeological and Documentary Evidence.* London: Free Association Books.

Carter, J. C., 1998. *The Chora of Metaponto,* vol. 1: *the Nekropoleis.* Austin (TX): University of Texas Press.

Elsner, J., 1990. Significant details: systems, certainties and the art-historian as detective. *Antiquity* 64, 950–52.

Fuller, S., 2000. *Thomas Kuhn: a Philosophical History for our Times.* Chicago (IL): University of Chicago Press.

Gehrke, H-J., 1986. *Jenseits von Athen und Sparta: das dritte Griechenland und seine Staatenwelt.* Munich: C. H. Beck.

Hall, J., 1990. Black Athena: a sheep in wolf's clothing? (Review of Bernal, 1987). *Journal of Mediterranean Archaeology* 3(2), 247–54.

Kuhn, T. S., 1996. *The Structure of Scientific Revolutions.* 3rd edition. Chicago (IL): University of Chicago Press.

Kurtz, D. C. (ed.), 1985. *Beazley and Oxford.* (Oxford University Committee for Classical Archaeology, Monograph 10.) Oxford: Oxford University Press.

Lohmann, H., 1993. *Atene: Forschungen zu Siedlungs- und Wirtschaftsstruktur des klassischen Attika.* Cologne, Weimar & Vienna: Böhlau Verlag.

Millett, M., 1991. Pottery: population or supply patterns? The Ager Tarraconensis approach, in *Roman Landscapes: Archaeological Survey in the Mediterranean Region,* eds. G. Barker & J. Lloyd. (Archaeological Monographs of the British School at Rome 2.) London: British School at Rome, 18–26.

Morris, I., 1996. Periodization and the heroes, in *Inventing Ancient Culture: Historicism, Periodization and the Ancient World,* eds. M. Golden & P. Toohey. London: Routledge, 96–131.

Morris, S. P., 1995. From modernism to manure. (Review of I. Morris (ed.), *Classical Greece: Ancient Histories and Modern Archaeologies). Antiquity* 69, 182–5.

Morris, S. P., 1997. Greek and Near Eastern art in the Age of Homer, in *New Light on a Dark Age: Exploring the Culture of Geometric Greece,* ed. S. Langdon. Columbia (SC): University of Missouri Press, 56–71.

Papadopoulos, J. K., 1993. To kill a cemetery: the Athenian Kerameikos and the Early Iron Age in the Aegean. *Journal of Mediterranean Archaeology* 6(2), 175–206.

Vickers, M. & D. Gill, 1994. *Artful Crafts: Ancient Greek Silverware and Pottery.* Oxford: Clarendon Press.

Watson, J. D., 1968. *The Double Helix: a Personal Account of the Discovery of the Structure of DNA.* New York (NY): Atheneum Publishers.

Whitley, J., 1997. Beazley as theorist. *Antiquity* 71, 40–47.

Wilkens, I., 1990. *Where Troy Once Stood.* London, Sydney, Auckland & Johannesburg: Rider Books.

Williams, D., 1996. Refiguring Attic red-figure: a review article. *Revue Archéologique* 6, 227–52.

Williamson, T. M., 1984. The Roman countryside: settlement and agriculture in N. W. Essex. *Britannia* 15, 225–30.

Separate Tables? A Story of Two Traditions within One Discipline

This was delivered at a conference, essentially for historians, in Berlin. It may seem to sit oddly here but, in a more allusive way, it is concerned with the same fundamental issue as the first four papers: Is there a problem with traditional Classical archaeology, and if so what is it? The effective loss of 'ownership', by British Classical archaeology, of one of its former components, the archaeology of Roman Britain, gives some food for thought, regardless of any comparison with that of Roman Germany.

BIBLIOGRAPHY

Bradley, R. (1990), *The Passage of Arms: An Archaeological Analysis of Prehistoric Hoards and Votive Objects*, Cambridge: Cambridge University Press.

Junker, K. (1998), 'Research under dictatorship: the German Archaeological Institute, 1929–1945', *Antiquity* 72: 282–92.

Künzl, E. (1996), 'Gladiusdekorationen der frühen römischen Kaiserzeit', *Jahrbuch des Römisch-Germanischen Zentralmuseums* 43: 385–475.

Marchand, S. L. (1996), *Down from Olympus: Archaeology and Philhellenism in Germany 1750–1970*, Princeton: Princeton University Press.

Wheeler, R. E. M. (1961), Review of *The Journal of Roman Studies* 50 (1960), *Antiquity* 35: 157–9.

Wheeler, R. E. M. (1968), Review of I. A. Richmond *et al.*, *Hod Hill* ii (1968), *Antiquity* 42: 149–50.

Two non-Mediterranean countries – yours and mine – only remotely linked with ancient Greek culture, were each brought partially into the Classical world through Roman conquest. In both cases, the territory of the modern nation-state was only partly under Roman rule (though the proportions are very different). The territory of each is therefore traversed by a *limes* which, on its own account, has absorbed a substantial proportion of the research into the Roman province – in Britain, I would put it at something like 20%; in Germany, the greater length of the *limes* and the much shallower depth of the Roman-occupied territory have probably combined to make the figure higher. The two provinces enclosed by these *limites* have become, I suppose, archaeologically the two best-documented provinces of the entire Roman empire. Each of them, finally, provided the setting of a monograph by Tacitus.

Such are the obvious common features in the earlier historical past of Germany and Britain. Thanks to Suzanne Marchand's fine book of 1996,[1] we now have a profound insight into the way in which Classical scholarship in general, Classical archaeology in particular, and the specific example on which I am going to focus today, the archaeology of Roman Germany, have developed in German intellectual life. In the superficially parallel case of Britain, no remotely comparable study yet exists. But even without one, it requires no great insight to see that the two cases are in fact profoundly different in almost every respect. I shall follow one of Suzanne Marchand's leads in looking first at the institutions of the two countries, as a guide to the underlying assumptions that they embody.

The first fundamental difference between the two cases is to be found, however, in political rather than academic institutions. Whereas the modern capital of Britain did not merely lie within, but was the largest town of Roman *Britannia*, here in Berlin, the pre-1945 capital which will soon resume its status, we are deep into *Germania libera*. This fact, in what has anyway always been a less centralised country, soon raised questions about the proper location for the central bodies controlling Romano-German archaeology, of a kind which did not, and could hardly, arise in Britain. Nor could their outcome, whereby the Römisch-Germanische Kommission (RGK) and the older Römisch-Germanisches Zentralmuseum (RGZM) were located in Frankfurt and in Mainz respectively. Yet in both countries a common issue has been: whose institutional property is the archaeology of the Romanised part of the country?

'Separate tables? A story of two traditions within one discipline', from S. Altekamp, M. R. Hofter and M. Krumme (ed.), *Posthumanistische Klassische Archäologie*, Munich: Hirmer Verlag, 2001, pp. 105–12.

The unification of Germany set in motion a whole series of schemes, backed by much-increased funding, in which archaeology played a much more central rôle than would be imaginable in Britain. The rapid emergence of the renamed Deutsches Archäologisches Institut (DAI), and the inauguration of one of its most famous undertakings, the excavation of Olympia in 1875, were some of the earliest fruits of this. With the combination of the century-old German Philhellenism and of the newly-arisen Italian nationalism, which meant that the scope for large-scale undertakings on Italian soil would be very limited, it was not surprising that German eyes should have looked first to Greece rather than Rome: much the same was true of Britain. But by the 1890's, the interests of German Romanists, more obviously than in Britain, were turning to the other area where they could naturally be given play, *Germania* – a field which, in the German sense of the term *Archäologie*, could be strongly argued to fall within the Institute's purview.

Thus the interests of the Institute came into at least potential conflict with those of a whole array of other organisations. With one group, the local *Vereine*, there is a similarity with Britain where, in the early study of Roman provincial archaeology, local associations such as the Field Clubs had also played a central rôle. But other strong interests were represented, from the highest levels downward, which have no British parallel. The Ministry of the Interior which had, from the 1870's, funded *limes* research under the old Reichslimeskommission, found itself embroiled with the Foreign Ministry which controlled the Institute. The Berliner Gesellschaft für Archäologie, Ethnographie und Urgeschichte, led by the natural scientist Rudolf Virchow, distrusted the Classicists of the Institute and resented their new claim to an area which they had previously scorned for decades. The local *Vereine* were against centralisation anyway, but especially if it were to take place under what they regarded as Berlin-based aesthetes. There was even the army which, at least in the heady days of the elder Moltke, wanted a share in the direction of Romano-German archaeological excavations and publications.

It is not so much the political and institutional battles of the late 19th century that are baffling to a British archaeologist – more than once, for example, our own Foreign Office has been approached with the proposal that it take charge at least of the British archaeological institutes abroad – but first, their outcome, and second, their purely archaeological implications. The best illustration one could wish for of the different values of the Germans and the British is the fact that, in Germany, the Institute should have won against the combination of all the other forces: the new RGK, when it at last came into being in 1899, did so as a component of the DAI. Not even Alfred Rosenberg succeeded in overturning this arrangement when, under National Socialism, the DAI again defended itself with some success against the encroachments of the dictatorship (as shown in Klaus Junker's very recent article[2]).

This positioning of the RGK implies, explicitly rather than implicitly, the subordination of archaeology at home to archaeology overseas. That the RGK in turn presides over the study of prehistoric Germany, and that the RGZM likewise contains a large prehistoric department, are also a cause for surprise in Britain. There, the term 'Römisch-Germanisch' is in fact widely misunderstood as being analogous to 'Romano-British', and *Germania* is primarily thought of as merely a Roman province. This comes from forgetting that it is *Germania libera* that was always seen as the more vital part of the ancestry of the German nation-state, whereas Roman Britain is by contrast seen as a formative stage in the history of almost the whole island of Great Britain.

But these differences mask what is for me the more fundamental distinction to be made between the thought of the two countries in relation to their past: that, in Britain, prehistory has for centuries been accepted as the dominant component of archaeology. This domination, which we British now take for granted, is a constant source of surprise in most other European countries. Only perhaps in the Scandinavian countries, in Switzerland and more obviously in the Netherlands, could such a relative evaluation be matched – not at all in the Mediterranean countries, nor in France, least of all in Germany.

This high British evaluation of prehistory goes right back to the time of William Camden and William Stukeley. Today, its supremacy has come to extend to the particular case of Romano-British studies as well. Yet this last supremacy was won only fairly recently and only after a long battle. One could give numerous illustrations of this struggle. Their range covers everything from the iconography of modern public sculpture – where an initially Classicizing figure of Boadicea was transformed into the British warrior-heroine Boudicca – to museum lay-out. The Prehistoric room in the Museum of London, the only 'compulsory' gallery in the sense that all visitors must pass through it, is a sign too obvious to need pointing out. A much earlier symptom of the same kind was the decision of the British Museum to name one of its Departments as, first 'British and Medieval', later 'Prehistoric and Romano-British', both incorporating Romano-British, both in clear distinction from 'Greek and Roman'. But that was a sign of the beginning, not the end of the battle.

For things did not change all at once. The roll-call of early excavators of Romano-British sites includes, remarkably, two Directors of the British School at Athens (Robert Carr Bosanquet at Housesteads and Dolaucothi, Arthur Maurice Woodward at Rudston villa and Slack and Ilkley forts), plus John Percival Droop of the Artemis Orthia team at Sparta (who later worked at Bainbridge and Lancaster) and Hugh G. Evelyn-White, better-known for Loeb translations from the Greek (who dug at Castell Collen and Cawthorn). For a long time, too, it was the Roman Society that cherished Romano-British studies: indeed, there were phases when it looked almost as if things were the other way round – that it was the Romano-British specialists who were running Roman archaeology as a whole.

Look for example at the contents of the Jubilee Volume of the *Journal of Roman Studies* (vol. 50 [1960]). There is quite a lot of archaeology there, but unlike the other disciplines, it is heavily, almost exclusively concentrated in two regions, Central Italy and Britain. Contrast the localism of the archaeological surveys of the past 50 years by Kenneth A. Steer and Ian Archibald Richmond with the universalism of those for other disciplines by Alexander Hermann McDonald, Chester G. Starr, Herbert Jennings Rose and Joyce Reynolds. The Jubilee had fallen at an opportune time, for who was President but Ian Richmond, and who was Editor (and latest ex-President) but Margery Taylor? To look back, who had been the founder-President of the Roman Society but Francis Haverfield, remembered almost exclusively as the founding father of Romano-British studies as a scientific discipline? And how had Margery Taylor's career begun? As Haverfield's secretary. Among the other ex-Presidents of the Roman Society were Sir George MacDonald, Dr. Harold Idris Bell and M. P. Charlesworth, all noted exponents of Roman Britain. Nor was Richmond to be the last primarily Romano-British scholar to hold the office: in the early 1980's, there were two in succession, Leo Rivet and Sheppard Frere. But will there ever be another? A telling change was made when the *Journal of Roman Studies* shed its Adam's Rib, in the shape of the journal *Britannia*, in 1970. *Éloignement* from Classics was taking place at the same time as the embrace of a new foster-mother, prehistory.

Many British archaeologists know of the *cause célèbre* in the pages of *Antiquity* 42 (1968), when Mortimer Wheeler's posthumous but candid review of Ian Richmond's *Hod Hill* volume 2 in June[3] ('the last book of one's oldest friend') led to deeply wounded rejoinders from Aileen Fox, Jocelyn Toynbee, Sheppard Frere, Kenneth St. Joseph and George Boon in December, printed together with a scathing riposte from Wheeler. Wheeler of course had written as an all-round archaeologist, a significant part of whose reputation rested on his work at Romano-British sites: he was thus not out to disparage the achievements of Romano-British archaeology itself. The burden of his case was rather that, in the person of its most famous exponent, it had somehow let 'us' prehistorians down, through Richmond's dilatoriness in publishing Chedworth, Bath and Inchtuthil, the shortcomings of his volume on Hod Hill, his inability to manage excavation-teams and his preference for playing a lone hand. The unspoken assumption, not really questioned by his challengers, was that the methods and priorities of prehistory could be applied *in toto* to Romano-British fieldwork.

In his later riposte Wheeler spared, alone of his assailants, Aileen Fox, perhaps because she was primarily a prehistorian. He dismissed the remaining four with the words 'The testimony of a distinguished art-historian, a superb air photographer and two defaulting excavators adds little to [Richmond's] case'. Everyone noticed the insult contained in the last phrase about the excavators, directed at Frere and Boon. It has been less appreciated that the first phrase, 'a distinguished art-historian' (referring to Jocelyn Toynbee) was intended to be at least as wounding, implying as it did that a scholar of that kind had no standing in Romano-British field archaeology. In Wheeler's mental framework, it is arguable that such a label was worse than the accusation of doing the right thing, but too slowly.

Much less well-known is a piece which Wheeler had published in the same periodical seven years earlier,[4] which may have softened the shock of his later piece for Richmond's injured friends. This was a review of none other than the Jubilee Volume of the *Journal of Roman Studies*, which Wheeler ended a familiar mode, with the words 'And if that doesn't shake the local circulation of *Antiquity*, I don't know what will'. He used the occasion to give a magisterial summing-up of the contributions to Romano-British archaeology of Francis Haverfield, Margery Taylor and, more briefly, Robin George Collingwood and Ian Richmond. He concluded: 'Haverfield's work was not merely a monument, it was a tombstone'. He maintained that although 'the path of minor progress will continue to be strewn with Ph. D.'s and DPhil's', yet 'for the major attainments of mankind, the young scholar ... must now look to other periods, other lands'. This premature obituary for Romano-British archaeology, now itself 38 years old, seems to me far more arrogant than what Wheeler wrote in the Hod Hill controversy.

For conditions have greatly improved in the generation since then: British prehistory has changed not only its own orientation in general, but its attitude to Roman Britain in particular. The intellectual level has risen appreciably, in both fields. British prehistory has shed some of its long-standing insularity. High standards in excavation are often, and rightly, exemplified by Romano-British sites as well as prehistoric ones. The only discordant (if welcome) trend of recent years is that Romano-British archaeology is now increasingly practised by scholars who have extensive field experience in other parts of the Empire, including the metropolis itself. This in its way shows the growth, or the revival, of an affinity with at any rate one branch of 'mainstream' Classical scholarship, which is as much as one could hope for in the circumstances. For, whether or not Romano-British archaeology would have done better to throw in its lot at the outset with Classical Archaeology, as in the German case, the truth is that this simply could not have happened in Britain. It may be difficult to try to imagine a German Wheeler, but it is far more so to think of the direction of Romano-British excavation being in the hands of an Institute presided over by Sir John Beazley.

This process of the steady *éloignement* of Roman provincial archaeology (in Britain and the Netherlands at least) from mainstream Classical scholarship, though seldom now accompanied by any animosity, has continued down to the present day. I give one final illustration of it, taken from as recently as 1996. This time, the example is a theoretical and methodological one: it concerns the interpretation of *Flußfunde*, the finds of objects (in this case of Roman date) in the beds of rivers, a context of longstanding familiarity in northern Europe. British prehistorians have long been preoccupied with this phenomenon: the orthodox assumption, which emerged many years ago, was that the majority of such finds, at least in prehistoric periods, could be interpreted as votive offerings. In 1990 Richard Bradley put this assumption on a much more systematic footing in an influential book, *The passage of Arms: an archaeological analysis of prehistoric hoards and votive objects*.[5] As its title suggests, Bradley's treatment gave prime emphasis to the dedication of weapons; and finds from rivers provided a substantial part of the evidence. Bradley's conclusions were then taken up by specialists in the Roman period, above all in two northern European countries, Britain and the Netherlands. The numerous river-finds of Roman weapons and other metal objects were now interpreted in the same way, as offerings made to water deities. This research was conducted by essentially the same methods as if the material were prehistoric: the use of documentary sources did not enter the picture.

Eventually in 1996 Ernst Künzl of the RGZM, who had published the huge deposit of late Roman metalwork from the old bed of the Rhine at Neupotz, was moved to protest at the blanket application of this prehistorians' view to Roman times.[6] He was able to show that, especially in the case of the Rhine at Mainz (an unusually rich source), finds of Roman weapons were, first, suspiciously concentrated in the vicinity of a known bridge-crossing but, secondly, antedated the probable date of the building of the first bridge there. The most natural conclusion is that they were not dedications but accidental losses from the time when crossings were still made by ferry. He was able to draw clear distinctions in the archaeological record between river-finds and water-offerings of other kinds (at springs, wells and lakes); and between weapons and other metalwork (vessels – often inscribed – and above all coins); and to cite a few references in Latin sources (the Elder Pliny, Seneca) which again described conditions for water-offerings without ever specifying a combination of major rivers and weapons. The 'votive' theory of the prehistorians had, predictably, made no use of this kind of detailed argument from distribution, backed up by texts.

To me the really interesting aspect is not the question of which interpretation is correct, but the head-on conflict between two completely different modes of thinking, more or less along national lines: Künzl cites, as supporters of the votive theory in the Roman context, three British archaeologists, four Dutch, and the cover-illustrations of a Dutch conference-publication and of a British journal, together with one German article in the same British journal number, and one reference from a German scholar who also works on prehistory.[7] The preference for a generalising, almost timeless explanation, which comes naturally to a prehistorian of the processualist persuasion, and is then adopted by Romanists with a prehistorian's cast of mind, runs up against the more culture-specific method of Classical archaeology. This example will serve as well as any, not only to draw the contrast between the German and the British, the Romanist and the prehistoric theoretical approaches; but also to explain how difficult the two will find it ever to merge together.

My title, 'Separate Tables', is taken from a once very successful short play of 1954 by Terence Rattigan. The setting is the dining-room of a seaside boarding-house, and the curtain rises to show the room crowded with diners: at one extremity of the stage a woman sits alone, at the other, a lone man. Presently the room empties apart from these last two: they address each other, and we in the audience suddenly realise that they are an estranged husband and wife who have come by chance to the same hotel. The eponymous play ends with them moving together again to the wife's table, now laid for two. Can we expect that, one day, the same thing will happen with the German and British traditions in Roman provincial archaeology? And if so, which party will make the move?

NOTES

1. Marchand (1996).
2. Junker (1998).
3. Wheeler (1968).
4. Wheeler (1961).
5. Bradley (1990).
6. Künzl (1996).
7. Künzl (1996) 441: M. Millett (n. 226), M. C. Bishop and J. C. Coulston (n. 224), H. van Enckevort, J. H. Willems, N. Roymans (n. 224) and A. M. J. Derks (n. 226); Leiden Conference and cover of *Roman Military Equipment Studies* (both in 1994) (n. 225); article by A. Thiel and W. Zanier in the latter, with L. Pauli (n. 224).

The Early Iron Age in Greece

INTRODUCTION TO PART II

With these papers, we begin to address the more specific issues with which traditional archaeology concerns itself. In a year when the Edinburgh University Press alone has announced the imminent publication of two edited volumes of papers on this period, I have felt the need to be unusually selective here.

From the time when I began to work on issues within the Early Iron Age forty-five years ago, I sensed that European prehistory might have a relevance to such studies, comparable with that of the traditionally much more favoured archaeology of the ancient Near Eastern cultures, and the first two papers reflect this interest.

CHAPTER 6

Metalwork as Evidence for Immigration in the Late Bronze Age

This was a journeyman piece, delivered at a colloquium organised by the Departments of Greek and Ancient History of the
University of Sheffield in March 1970. Among other contributions, I have a vivid memory of the paper delivered by Colin
Renfrew at the end of the conference, which contained the germ
of his much later book *Archaeology and Language* (Renfrew
1987). In the context of the Aegean Bronze Age, both our talks
were seen as contributions to the anti-migrationist school of interpretation, which was then beginning to sweep the archaeological landscape and to a large extent still does so.

BIBLIOGRAPHY

Renfrew, C. (1987), *Archaeology and Language*, London: Jonathan
Cape.

The great wave of destruction and abandonment of Mycenaean sites
at or near the end of the Late Helladic IIIB period is one of the inescapable landmarks of the Aegean Late Bronze Age. For the past
twenty years and more, however, many scholars have also seen it as
something else: as the occasion of a mass-immigration and permanent
settlement in Greece of non-Mycenaean peoples.

The prime basis for this conclusion is the occurrence of new metal
types in Greece at this time; it is true that much other evidence has
been adduced as well, but this supporting evidence is not, on its
own, decisive. There is first of all the mere fact of the destructions;

'Metal-work as evidence for immigration in the Late Bronze Age', from R. A.
Crossland and A. Birchall (ed.), *Bronze Age Migrations in the Aegean*, London:
Duckworth, 1974, pp. 209–14.

but these (like other destructions in prehistory) in themselves betray nothing about the agency behind them; still less do they imply anything about the subsequent settlement of the destroyers in Greece. Thus Miss N. K. Sandars, in her review-article on V. R. Desborough's work (Desborough 1964), proposed attributing these destructions to raiders who afterwards withdrew (Sandars 1964: 259). Next, there is the fortification-wall built at this period at the Isthmus of Corinth: we must now accept this as a northward-facing wall which ran right across the isthmus, in the light of O. Broneer's latest investigations (Broneer 1966 and 1968). But the wall in itself does not imply a threat from beyond the Mycenaean world, rather than from, say, central Greece. Again, we have the undoubtedly significant coincidence of this epoch with the activities of the land and sea raiders recorded in Egyptian and Hittite documents; but these texts scarcely suggest that this agency lay behind the Aegean destructions, and they give no hint of permanent settlement by the raiders in Greece.

When we examine the other archaeological evidence from the Aegean, we find that the testimony of architecture, of funerary practices, of grave goods, and above all of pottery, so far from giving any suggestion of the arrival of a non-Mycenaean population, presents an almost uniform picture of the post-destruction period, the earlier part of Late Helladic IIIC, as a survival of its predecessor. It is the new metal types, and they alone, which form the corner-stone of the case for mass-migration. Most of the scholars who incline to accept that this occurred regard it as immigration, or perhaps merely infiltration, from the north. It is unnecessary here to review the voluminous literature on this question, beyond acknowledging the influence of V. Milojčić's initial paper (Milojčić 1949), and beyond citing one or two important recent authorities, such as Professor M. Gimbutas (Gimbutas 1965: especially 339), and the late Professor E. Grumach who harnessed this evidence to the radical theory that the first coming of the Greek-speakers of any kind took place at this time, and that their point of departure was the western Danube basin (Grumach 1969: 50).

Let us therefore scrutinize these metal types (they are all bronzes) more closely, and see how far they justify the inference of immigration and permanent settlement from their regions of origin. None is more important than the *violin-bow fibula* (Fig. 6.1A; for good recent discussions, see Desborough 1964: 54–8; Gimbutas 1965: 113–16), and to its case we may apply certain particular arguments. Those who cite this type as evidence for migration of Central European peoples

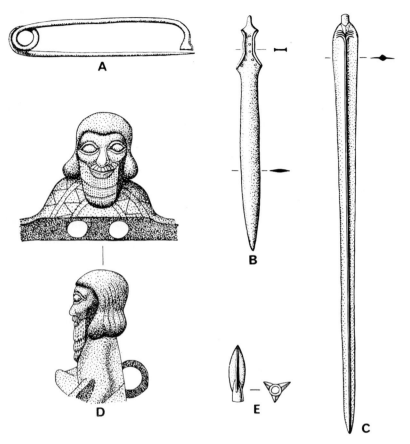

Figure 6.1 'Intrusive' bronze types in the Aegean area.
A, violin-bow fibula (Mycenae). Scale 1:2.
B, flange-hilted cut-and-thrust sword (*Griffzungenschwert*) (Siteia region, Crete). Scale 1:8.
C, Minoan rapier (Karo's type A) (Arkalokhori, Crete). Scale 1:8.
D, 'Siren'-attachment from cauldron (Olympia). Scale 1:2.
E, 'Scythian' arrowhead (Athens). Scale 1:2.

southwards into Greece seem to me to be positing an odd historical coincidence. For all authorities agree that the violin-bow fibula makes its first appearances, whether in the proto-Urnfield phase of central Europe, in the Terremare of northern Italy, or in the Aegean of LH IIIB–C, at roughly the same time. It is not any clear indication of temporal priority in the north that leads most people to ascribe a northern origin to the type, so much as the association of the fibula with thicker clothing and therefore with a cooler climate. Thus, on the 'migration' hypothesis, it follows that the invention of the violin-bow fibula in one of these three areas must have been followed by a strangely swift *diaspora* of its wearers to the other two regions. This would have to be coincidental, since the fibula could hardly be causally linked to a migration. But if, on the other hand, we ascribe the diffusion of the fibula to its own merits, however humble, as a form of dress-fastening, then the element of coincidence disappears: it spread swiftly because it was a good idea.

The factor of climatic change in Europe in the thirteenth and twelfth centuries BC has also been introduced into this problem; but I do not think that it alters the arguments. The fibula and its associated costume may well have been first adopted in the middle Danube region because the climate had become cooler and wetter there; and it seems to have got relatively cooler and wetter in the Aegean area too, although in neither case are the climatological data precise in terms of date (Frenzel 1966: 113, 118). This change was no doubt a contributory cause for the adoption and retention of the fibula in Greece. But this argument is not easily combined with the hypothesis of a southward migration, unless one supposes that the climate in Greece, for some centuries after 1200 BC, was colder and wetter than that of Czechoslovakia and Hungary hitherto; for fibulae of this type and its successors were commonly worn in Greece right down to the seventh century BC.

If we turn from fibulae to weapons, and especially to that weapon whose chronology, diffusion and significance seem to have much in common with those of the violin-bow fibula, namely the *Griffzungenschwert* (flange-hilted cut-and-thrust sword; Fig. 6.1B), then the case changes. First, the degree of coincidence involved in a hypothesis of southward migration is slighter: for the development of a new weapon might serve as a spur to an armed migration, or at least ensure its successful outcome, and so a causal connection could exist. Once again, it is true that the *Griffzungenschwert* was an important new development whose very wide diffusion began soon after its perfection (Cowen 1966). In this situation, I can only say that I again find it a more attractive hypothesis to believe that the qualities of the sword itself, appreciable as they are, were responsible for its wide distribution, rather than the mass-migration of its bearers.

There is a further argument, relevant to both these bronze types, which there is not time to develop here, but which I regard as of great significance for this problem: namely, that these intrusive bronzes are now attested in Mycenaean graves of pure LH IIIB date, and were thus demonstrably used by Mycenaeans before the horizon of the great destructions.

I now wish to cite briefly one or two cases of new metal types and practices from other periods in the Aegean, which seem to me further to weaken the hypothesis of migration if based on intrusive metal-work.

First, there were few steps in Greek metallurgy more important than the introduction of the full-length sword to the Greek mainland. It appears in the two circles of shaft-graves at Mycenae; here, from my own calculations based on the available publications (Karo 1930; Mylonas 1957: 128–75; Sandars 1961), out of 56 traceable swords from these graves, at least 41 are of a long type of rapier (Fig. 6.1C; Karo's type A) which most scholars agree to be of Minoan derivation. Yet few today would claim that the shaft-grave rulers, or the inhabitants of other parts of the Greek mainland who soon adopted this sword, were Cretan immigrants.

Secondly, and conversely, an era for which almost all scholars agree in accepting a wave of immigration and permanent settlement in Greece is Early Helladic III and the early part of Middle Helladic. Yet how far is this belief founded on innovations in metallurgy? I suspect that not only is the answer 'Not at all', but that on the contrary the new era was marked by something of a metallurgical recession (Vermeule 1964: 75).

Next, by overstepping the chronological limits of this colloquium it is possible to attain greater certainty. A major innovation in Greek metal-work of a later period, around 700 BC, was the adoption of the Oriental type of bronze tripod-stand with separate cauldron. This ousted, almost totally, the old Geometric Greek type of one-piece tripod cauldron, and became a characteristic article of domestic and sacral metal-work in seventh-century Greece. A common variety had siren-attachments round its rim (Fig. 6.1D), and a recent authority has shown that out of 49 such attachments known from Greece, 37 are of actual Oriental workmanship and only 12 are Greek adaptations (Herrmann 1966: 30–2, 57–8 as against 91–2, 102). Yet mass-immigration of Orientals into Greece at this date is out of the question, and even the theory of immigrant craftsmen is hotly debated.

Later still, in the seventh, sixth and fifth centuries BC, Greece whole-heartedly adopted a new type of arrow-head, the tiny socketed bronze form, usually of roughly triangular outline, and this is overall by far the commonest type on Greek sites of these periods (Fig. 6.1E;

Snodgrass 1964: 148–54). It had been devised by the Cimmerians or Scyths and partly diffused, it is true, by their warlike migrations in western Asia. But we have no evidence that a Cimmerian or Scyth ever discharged a bow in anger on the soil of mainland Greece or the islands, at least until the later sixth century BC.

Although I wish to confine my arguments to the Aegean area, and indeed largely to the Greek mainland proper, I suspect that supporting evidence could be adduced from Etruria, either from the sudden increase in the range and quantity of fibulae in the graves at Quattro Fontanili, Veii, about 800 BC (Close-Brooks 1968: 323–9), or from the more general and massive influx of foreign metal-work in Etruscan graves about a century later; for a major immigration into Etruria at either time is coming to appear increasingly unlikely.

In these later instances, there is historical evidence which helps to provide an ultimate barrier to any hypothesis of mass-immigration. For the Aegean Late Bronze Age such evidence is largely absent, though not entirely so. The later cases provide archaeological evidence of other kinds, from pottery and other materials, and from continuity of settlements and cemeteries, which I think would have been on its own a strong deterrent to such a hypothesis. Archaeological evidence of this kind is present in the Aegean Late Bronze Age, for all the violence of the destructions around 1200 BC, and it is at least arguable that its collective weight is greater than that of the new 'northern' bronzes. I have concentrated on those types which make their appearance in the era of the great destructions, but it should be observed that hypotheses of foreign immigration have been founded, at least in part, not only on the later series of bronzes which appear in Mycenaean graves from the late twelfth century onwards (the so-called 'second wave'; e.g. Desborough 1964: 70–2), but also on the introduction of practical iron-working to Greece in the eleventh and tenth centuries (e.g. Kimmig 1964: 241–4).

My own belief is that the civilization of the Aegean in the Late Bronze Age (and probably in the other periods referred to in the list of examples above) was a culture too sophisticated in its organization, with trade-contacts that were too long-standing and widespread, and perhaps with a degree of specialization in labour that was too high, for us to be able to base hypotheses of foreign immigration on the appearance of new metal types in its area, in a way that is the common and undoubtedly justified practice with some other prehistoric cultures. I would finally stress that I am arguing not against the incidence of violence and turmoil in the Aegean of *c.* 1200 BC, since that is self-evident; nor against the presence of individual foreigners, whether as traders, pirates or mercenary soldiers, from central Europe and elsewhere, since this too seems extremely likely; but against assumption of the mass-immigration and permanent settlement of non-Mycenaeans in Greece, when this theory depends to any considerable degree on the appearance of new metal types and practices there.

DISCUSSION

Jan Bouzek: The fibula is a development of the European pin, not of Mycenaean buttons, and therefore could hardly have originated in Mycenaean Greece, where buttons were used only exceptionally. The distribution of many metal objects over a vast area of Europe and the eastern Mediterranean between the thirteenth and twelfth centuries BC is a unique event which has no parallel throughout the whole of the rest of the Bronze Age and the early Iron Age. Unlike the later diffusion of metal types, which was never so wide or so homogeneous, that of the late thirteenth century and the early twelfth is contemporaneous with the large-scale downfall of a complete culture; cities were destroyed and only partially rebuilt in much impoverished style, arts and crafts declined, writing and fine *objets d'art* disappeared, population decreased; at the same time many new elements were introduced in pottery and probably also in architecture (oval houses; and cf. hut models from Crete). Most historically attested migrations have left considerably less archaeological evidence of such kinds.

REFERENCES

Broneer, O. 1966. 'The Cyclopean wall at the Isthmus of Corinth and its bearing on Late Bronze Age chronology.' *Hesperia*, 35: 346–62.
——. 1968. 'The Cyclopean wall at the Isthmus of Corinth and its bearing on Late Bronze Age chronology: Addendum.' *Hesperia*, 37: 25–35.
Close-Brooks, J. 1968. 'Considerazioni sulla cronologia delle facies arcaiche dell' Etruria.' *StEtr*, 35: 323–9.
Cowen, J. D. 1966. 'The origins of the flange-hilted sword of bronze in Continental Europe.' *ProcPS*, 32: 262–312.
Desborough, V. R. d' A 1964. *The last Mycenaeans and their Successors.* Oxford.
Frenzel, B. 1966. 'The Atlantic/Sub-Boreal transition.' *World Climate from 8000 to 0 BC.* (Royal Meteorological Society): 99–123.
Gimbutas, M. 1965. *Bronze Age Cultures in Central and Eastern Europe.* The Hague.

Grumach, E. 1969. *The Coming of the Greeks* (reprinted from *Bulletin of the John Rylands Library*, 51, 1 and 2). Manchester.

Herrmann, H. V. 1966. 'Die Kessel der orientalisierenden Zeit, I.' *Olympische Forschungen*, 6. Berlin.

Karo, G. 1930. *Die Schachtgräber von Mykenai*. Munich.

Kimmig, W. 1964. 'Seevölkerbewegung und Urnenfelderkultur'; in R. von Uslar and K. J. Narr, *Studien aus Alteuropa* I (*Beihefte der BonnJbb*, 10/1; Cologne): 220–83.

Milojčić, V. 1949. 'Die dorische Wanderung im lichte der vorgeschichtlichen Funde.' *JdI/AA*, 63/64 (1948/49) *Beiblatt*: 11–30.

Mylonas, G. 1957. *Ancient Mycenae*. London.

Sandars, N. K. 1961. 'The First Aegean swords and their ancestry.' *AJA*, 65: 17–29.

——. 1964. 'The Last Mycenaeans and the European Late Bronze Age.' *Antiquity*, 38: 258–62.

Snodgrass, A. M. 1964. *Early Greek Armour and Weapons*. Edinburgh.

Vermeule, E. T. 1964. *Greece in the Bronze Age*. Chicago.

CHAPTER 7

The Coming of the Iron Age in Greece: Europe's Earliest Bronze / Iron Transition

This paper was (not for the last time in this collection) commissioned for inclusion in a set of papers otherwise largely contributed by prehistorians. It contains a series of propositions about the nature of the bronze / iron transition in Greece which I would still uphold today; but in two places, one marginal and the other much more central, different views have since been expressed and need to be indicated. First, the brief passage on depopulation (p. 133), as acknowledged earlier (above, p. viii), rests in part on the fallacy that the recovered burials from this time are representative of the entire population at each settlement. The evidence has now convinced me that they are not: absolute figures are thus inappropriate, even though relative depopulation remains an almost universally acknowledged reality. But this issue is not important to the general thrust of the argument.

Much more fundamental is the case advanced, at the very time when I was writing this paper, by Ian Morris in another article (Morris 1989), for a different explanation of the apparently abrupt switch to the economic use of iron in the Aegean area. Morris proposes what he calls the 'deposition model' for the prevalence of iron, in preference to my 'circulation model' (below, pp. 135–38). That is, the prime factor which lies behind the temporary but apparently intense recourse to iron during the eleventh and tenth centuries BC was not that bronze and its vital component, tin, were in short supply (the 'circulation model'), but that iron had suddenly acquired a new prestige which made it the metal of choice for deposition in graves (the 'deposition model'). Morris contends (p. 508) that, though the burial finds are compatible with the explanation of a bronze shortage, those from settlements, together with the evidence of technical analyses, are not. Rather, the settlement evidence suggests that iron was if anything scarcer than bronze. The technical tests had already been dealt with in part by me (below, p. 137), but Morris adds the argument that the (very low) tin content of the large 'bronze' tripods – in fact, often of almost pure copper – continued to prevail down to the eighth century, when there is independent evidence that any shortage of tin had long since passed. Therefore, their composition was dictated, not by availability of raw materials but by conscious choice.

This counter-argument exemplifies the many correctives which, in prehistoric circles, 'Post-Processual' archaeology was just then offering to the work of the Processualists. In general, I am sympathetic to these correctives; yet in this instance, I resist. Is this simply the old story of over-attachment to one's own theories? Perhaps; but I would point in turn to three points of weakness which surely affect the 'deposition model'.

First, the settlement evidence, which lies at its heart, consists of a very few samples, each characterised by Morris himself as 'tiny' or 'small'. Metals in general and iron especially are indeed thinly represented; but other possible explanations exist for what is so often the case in settlement excavations of many different periods and regions. Second, there is more technical evidence, this time from iron objects rather than bronze, to bring into consideration: I had briefly alluded to some of it (p. 136 below). The apparent intensity of the drive to improve the hardness of early iron, in both Cyprus and Greece, sits less easily with the notion of iron as a material conferring prestige in itself, than it does with hard economic necessity as a driving force. It places practical considerations above prestige, function above display. A third point of weakness is broader: iron must be, of all metals, the most difficult to control or ration, as the 'deposition model' requires (Morris, pp. 506–7). Iron ore occurs too widely and its working in the smithy has always tended to be a public activity – as it had certainly become by Hesiod's time (*Works and Days*, 492–4).

These are not conclusive arguments, and the best model for Greece will not necessarily hold good elsewhere – especially not in regions with ready access to copper and tin. The starting point of my hypothesis was indeed precisely that Greece was not such a region.

BIBLIOGRAPHY

Morris, I. (1989), 'Circulation, deposition and the formation of the
Greek Iron Age', *Man* n.s. 24: 505–19.

The concept of an 'Iron Age' is one of the least analysed in European prehistory, though as an expression it is constantly on the lips
of every prehistorian of Europe. There are many reasons for this. In
the first place, the replacement of bronze by iron for a specific range
of practical purposes, important change though it was, was clearly a
less fundamental step than the original introduction of metallurgy; so
it is hardly surprising that only a small proportion of the amount of
research devoted to that earlier process has gone into the study of the
bronze / iron transition. A second factor, as influential as it is banal,
is the simple fact that iron survives so much less well than bronze,
and so presents a much less attractive field for investigation to the
archaeologist, whether he or she is interested in typology, function,
surface-wear, compositional analysis, or some other aspect. A third
influence has, I think, been operative to a special degree during the
past fifteen years of the great theoretical revolution in archaeology.
Many of the doctrines of the New Archaeology have evolved in the
New World, and have been tested by application to the material record
there. Now the New World, like Africa, does not belong to that portion of the globe where the sequence of stone to bronze to iron, which
Europeans have come to think of as the 'natural' one, ran its course
in the 'natural' way. True, there was a sophisticated metallurgy, based
on bronze and other copper alloys, in the region of the Central Andes, which lasted until the Spanish conquest (Lechtman 1980). But in
many other areas, the use of stone tools gave way directly, and at a
relatively recent date, to the use of iron. The transition from bronze to
iron was thus not a topic likely to make an early claim on the attention
of the new school of thought, and even the Andean transition took
place in circumstances – an invasion in an historically documented

'The coming of the Iron Age in Greece: Europe's earliest Bronze / Iron Transition',
from M. L. Stig Sørensen and R. Thomas (ed.), *The Bronze Age–Iron Age Transition in Europe: Aspects of Continuity and Change in European Societies c. 1200 to
500 BC*, Oxford: British Archaeological Reports, International Series 483, 1989, i,
pp. 22–35.

period – which would make it an unpromising field for many of the new approaches.

For European prehistorians, however, there is a test case available which involves part of their continent. It sets the transition to iron in a fairly closely studied and accurately dated context; it has temporal priority over most other local occurrences of this transition in the world, and it is thus more likely to exemplify the process in its 'natural' form; and finally, it had direct or indirect repercussions on the parallel but later transitions in many other parts of Europe. The test case I mean, of course, is the bronze/iron transition in Greece and the Aegean area. The history of its study reproduces, in microcosm, many of the features of the history of this discussion in general. Here, too, the transition to iron has received very much less attention than the earlier episode of the first Aegean metallurgy. In this case, there is, however, also a specific local influence at work: the preceding Late Bronze Age of the Aegean enjoys a privileged status in everyone's minds, as having formed the historical basis (such as it is) for the body of Greek heroic legends, as well as for the brilliance of its material record. As for the ensuing Classical period of Greek civilisation, its place is an even more obviously privileged one, and anyone who referred to it by such a generalised name as the 'Middle Iron Age' would be assumed to be making a rather obscure joke.

As a result, the Early Iron Age of Greece is seldom referred to by that name, being more commonly designated by some label that indicates an unfavourable comparison with its more famous antecedent and sequel: it is 'post-Mycenaean', a 'Dark Age', 'proto-historic', 'pre-Classical', or it is the 'Greek Middle Ages' from which only a 'Renaissance' could bring relief. Yet, the conversion of the Greeks to the practical use of iron was one of the most significant material advances in several thousand years of history in the Aegean – on account of its exceptionally early date, we may even say in Europe. Nor should we lose sight of the advantages, referred to above, which this area offers as a field of study, by comparison with other European instances of the bronze / iron transition.

Let me be more specific about these advantages of the Aegean as a study area. First, the relatively precise chronology enables us to say that, between about 1050 and 1000 BC, several parts of the Aegean entered what is in the fullest sense of the words an Iron Age. That is to say, they adopted iron as the *predominant* metal for tools and weapons of practical use. Of wider application, however, are the inferences that we can draw for the periods before and after this. First, we can now see, in the Aegean and in certain areas of the Near East, the essential irrelevance of the earlier, somewhat desultory experiments with iron in the preceding thousand years or more. These clearly demonstrate that a culture may be familiar with the rudiments of iron-working, and even produce functional artefacts in iron, for centuries before entering a true Iron Age. This generalisation may be illustrated from finds in the Aegean area, but a much clearer example is provided by Egypt. Here iron objects occur from about 4000 BC onwards; here too the tomb of Tutankhamun (c. 1340 BC) produced 19 iron objects. One of these was a ceremonial dagger with an iron blade (significantly, its companion piece was a dagger with a blade of hardened gold). Yet it was almost six centuries after the date of this latter find that Egypt entered a true Iron Age, in the sense that its economy became substantially based upon iron-working: and that, surely, is the sense in which we *should* use the term 'Iron Age'. In practice, most European archaeologists apply the name much more loosely to cultures which merely display some familiarity with iron; just as the Egyptologist Petrie was led, by finds like those of Tutankhamun's tomb, to speak of a 'Sporadic Iron Age' in the Second Millennium BC in Egypt (van der Merwe 1980: 466). Such careless terminology may on occasion throw some light on the origins of an isolated innovation; but it only serves to obscure the far more important questions of the *economic* consequences of adopting iron, which do not arise until a society has committed itself to practical iron-working in preference to bronze.

A case like that of the Aegean, where the term 'Iron Age' is used only of the period when it actually means what it says, is a salutary exception in this respect. It is much too late today to bring about a change in the looser usage whereby, for example, the Villanovan period in northern Italy and the Hallstatt A of Central Europe are designated as Iron Age phases; but one must always bear in mind that the pattern of iron use that they display is at most comparable with that of the later phases of the Aegean Bronze Age, or of the Late Cypriot III period (12th and earlier 11th centuries BC) in Cyprus (Snodgrass 1980a: 340ff.)

Likewise, the relatively rich documentation of the later Iron Age of the Aegean enables us to see clearly the paradoxical fact that a developed Iron Age culture may be characterised by the richness of its bronze industry. Anyone who has visited a representative collection of Classical Greek artefacts will appreciate that, after clay and marble, the most copious and significant material present is bronze

especially decorative bronze-work. But if we are tempted by this fact
into treating a culture like that of Classical Greece as in some way
'transitional' between Bronze and Iron Age, then once again we are
misleading ourselves as to the meaning of the term 'Iron Age'. The
range of artefacts which an iron based culture actually makes out
of iron is quantitatively quite a narrow one, for all its vital significance. It consists in the main of the 'working' parts of implements
and weapons; the parts, that is, that come into direct contact with
the material that is to be cut, pierced, broken up, split or joined. The
fact that containers, defensive armour or art-work continue to be executed in bronze is as irrelevant as the fact that wood is used for the
shafts of iron spears and axes. As for the decoration of bronze- work,
one of the most significant steps was the creation of the iron tools
which facilitated it. This explains why, for example, Classical Greece
was richer in respect of bronze-work than Mycenaean Greece.

The relative precision of the Aegean chronology also enables one
to test theories devised for other parts of Europe. Take, for example,
the very interesting suggestion recently made that the phenomenon
of bronze hoards in the European Late Bronze Age might be seen as
an attempt to manipulate the metals market, by boosting the price of
bronze against the threat of the ever-extending use of iron (Rowlands
1980: 46). Whatever the attractions of this explanation elsewhere,
chronology alone forbids its adoption as an explanation of the phenomenon in the Aegean area. Bronze hoards are indeed a well known
feature of Aegean Late Bronze Age archaeology; but their chronological range is a narrow one, being essentially confined to the transition
between the Late Helladic IIIB and IIIC periods – that is close to
the date 1200 BC (Spyropoulos 1972). This date lies between 50 and
150 years before the time when any serious preoccupation with practical iron-working manifests itself in the archaeological record of the
Aegean. It is difficult, therefore, to see any causal connection between
the two episodes; and the traditional interpretation of the Aegean
bronze hoards, as one further sign of the acute insecurity which prevailed in the area at this time, must be preferred in this case.

Yet, for all my insistence on the unique value of the Aegean evidence as a test case for the bronze/iron transition in Europe, I must
at the same time concede that several of its features are unlikely to
be representative of the European pattern as a whole, and many may
even turn out to be peculiar to Greece. The instance of the bronze
hoards, just cited, illustrates this. It may prove hard to find other
cases in European prehistory where the incidence of bronze hoards

coincides so exactly with an independently attested horizon of insecurity and destruction. Furthermore, the widespread breakdown
of the Aegean palatial systems, with their re-distributive functions
and their use of writing, is a process that is directly linked with the
question of the bronze supply, though not with the advent of iron. The
Mycenaean palace at Pylos, to cite the best known case, was involved
in the procurement and distribution of bronze on a colossal scale.
The 'Jn' series of tablets from Pylos, on its own, records and mon-
itors the distribution of over 800 kg of bronze among 193 'active'
and 81 'inactive' bronze-smiths. This total of 274 smiths (*ka-ke-we*)
served by the palace, even if spread over a fairly wide geographical
area, is extraordinarily high (Ventris and Chadwick 1959: 352ff.). It
implies the extreme centralisation of the bronze industry, and it also
hints at the complex organisation needed for supplies of the raw materials. Whether the copper was imported from Aegean sources, from
Cyprus, or from yet other copper-mining areas, it seems today an inescapable fact that the necessary sources of tin cannot have lain within
a circle of a thousand mile radius of Pylos (or any other mainland
Mycenaean centre). The palace-centred importation and redistribu-
tion of the metals was certainly not a necessary mechanism for the
maintenance of a bronze-based economy; but since it had become a
fact of Aegean life, its removal was bound to lead to urgent adjustment
and improvisation.

From the sequel, we can at least infer that some of these adjustments must have been fairly effective. Mycenaean culture did not
vanish, and it remained for much of its final phase (Late Helladic
III C) a bronze-based economy. Foreign contacts were maintained in
certain directions, especially eastwards to the Levant and westwards
to southern Italy – perhaps partly with a view to sustaining the copper and tin supplies. Emigration was rife, and population evidently
began to decline – a factor which takes on some importance when we
consider the other natural means of obtaining copper and tin, namely
by the melting down and reuse of existing bronze artefacts. A reduced
remnant could survive far longer on the accumulated wealth of a former, much larger population. The progressive abandonment of sites,
particularly the smaller, outlying ones, is a feature which supports the
notion of increasing difficulties in obtaining metals. Regional differences within the Greek world become steadily more apparent in the

material record suggesting increased decentralisation; whereas one of the features of the palace system had been the maintenance of a sort of Aegean cultural *koine*, doubtless founded on the close communications, at a high level, between the ruling classes of each region.

Presently, in the later part of the Late Helladic III C period, these processes accelerated. It will be simplest if I give a bare list of the major changes apparent from the archaeological record which lie on either side of the phenomenon that we are seeking to explain, the advent of an Iron Age. First, in the later twelfth century BC and thus decidedly earlier than the conversion to iron, we have the sudden upsurge in single burial which is opposed to the previous widespread Mycenaean custom of burial in family vaults (Dickinson 1983). In the same general period, we have also more marked signs of depopulation, leading to a situation where, in the Early Iron Age, we have no single cemetery that attests to a community population of much more than 50 people at any one time; and no settlement whose area, unless improbably densely settled, suggest a figure of more than about ten times that number (Snodgrass 1983a). By this time Cyprus, though not yet part of the Aegean world, is showing an intense interest in applying iron to practical uses, especially in the production of knives (Snodgrass 1980a; 1983b). We know that the Greeks were in at least intermittent contact with Cyprus throughout this period, and there can be little doubt that we have here the immediate source of the later conversion of the Aegean world to the use of iron: not that that constitutes an *explanation* of its spread to Greece, and thus to Continental Europe. Next, and still more or less synchronous with the adoption of single burials, there is a change of custom which leads to the deposition of hand-made coarse pottery in graves, alongside the wheel-made painted ware which had predominated for centuries in funerary contexts (though settlement material tells a slightly different story).

We have now reached the horizon of the first true Iron Age in Greece; and there are two other phenomena which coincide almost exactly in time with the adoption of iron as the preferred metal for practical uses. One is the advent of cremation; and the other is the adoption of a new style of wheel-made pottery, the Protogeometric. This pottery is distinguished by the use of two trivial but diagnostic mechanical aids, the compass and the multiple brush, in its decoration. But the interesting thing is that, like iron itself, both these innovations are found only in selected areas of Greece; and that the areas in question do *not* coincide for each of the three innovations. Thus, the north-eastern Peloponnese, which is forward in the adoption of both iron and the Protogeometric style, almost entirely rejects cremation; while central Crete embraces iron and cremation long before it adopts the Protogeometric system of decoration (on these questions see most conveniently Snodgrass 1971: 55ff. (pottery); 147ff. and 164ff. (cremation); 217ff. and 249ff. (iron)). Finally, and on present evidence not detectable until some way into the Iron Age, we have an architectural change that is likewise restricted in its geographical extent, but which likewise fails to coincide in its scope with any of the earlier innovations. This change consists of an adoption of curvilinear building plans, whether sub-elliptical or (much more commonly) apsidal. This feature is characteristic only of the Greek mainland and of the Greek-speaking settlements on the western coast of Asia Minor and its off-shore islands. In Crete and the Cyclades, by contrast, rectilinear plans still prevail.

Thus, within a space of about 150 years since the breakdown of the palace system, a far-reaching transformation had taken place in the material culture of mainland Greece: the settlement-pattern had been drastically thinned; regional differences had been accentuated; building-types had altered; burial-forms and rites, together with other funerary depositional practices, had undergone a series of changes; and a new style of painted pottery had arrived.

What social changes are suggested by this accumulation of changes in the material record? And how can they be brought to bear on the question of the adoption of iron?

All manner of speculative answers have been given to the first of these questions. To mention only two recent and intriguing ones: the hypothesis of a reversion to pastoral nomadism or transhumance in the Early Iron Age has been advanced on the evidence of one or other of the phenomena just listed. Sakellariou (1980: 118ff.), for example, argued that the apsidal house-plan, a reversion to a building-form much favoured in pre-Mycenaean Greece, was characteristic of nomadic populations; while Kirsten (1983: 437, n. 64) has thrown off the suggestion that the increased incidence of hand-made pottery in Early Iron Age Greece betokens an upsurge in transhumance. These hypotheses were intrinsically attractive to me, since I had been arguing for many years (Snodgrass 1971: 379f; 1980b: 35f) that pastoralism was widespread in Greece during the earlier part of the Iron Age. It could even be argued that a metal like iron, widely available from native sources in Greece, would present distinctly greater attractions to a mobile, pastoralist population than would bronze, an alloy of metals obtainable only by long-distance exchange. However, I shall forswear any attempt to press the case further, since I have been assured by all my prehistorian colleagues that the evidence produced in support of this view (which now includes the only available sample of animal-bones from an Iron Age settlement site (Sloan and Duncan 1978) not only has failed to establish the argument, but is in principle incapable of ever doing so, and I shall instead fall back on a less controversial interpretation of the same body of evidence.

One thing that clearly emerges from the changes in the archaeological record at the end of the Bronze Age in Greece is that a decentralisation of political control took place, leading to an increased local independence. The disappearance of the palace economies, the thinning of the settlement pattern, the more obvious diversity of the material culture – all these are manifestations of that process. One natural consequence of small communities being thrown back on their own resources is the simplification of certain social practices and technological processes. Thus, among the cultural changes we have considered, the abandonment of burial in family tombs will have come naturally to people who either have just changed their place of habitation (as there is reason to believe many Mycenaean communities did, on a purely local scale, in the Late Helladic IIIC period) or expect to do so in the fairly near future. The adoption of apsidal building plans, in regions like mainland Greece and Ionia where mud brick had been the standard building material, can also be seen as a consequence of the abandonment of a standard, centrally determined size of brick, and the reversion to 'do-it-yourself' practices (Gullini 1983). Thus, again, the progressive substitution of hand-made for wheel-made coarse pottery may reflect nothing more than a restricted access to the products of professional potter's workshops. Phenomena such as these have been characterised by Dickinson (1983: 67) as exemplifying the principle of economy of effort; and my view merely provides a context for the emergence of that principle.

How will this reflect on the adoption of iron? The answer is fairly obvious. Bronze-working, quite apart from the special circumstances which, in the Aegean, had come to link it with a palace-centred redistributive economy, acquires from its very nature an aura of mystique as well as of artisanship. The bronze-smith operates with raw material that comes from different sources, in many cases exotic to his native region; he mixes them in carefully-observed proportions; thus providing a material which with the necessary skills can be given an attractive appearance even before any surface decoration is attempted;

if and when it is, the aesthetic considerations assume an even more important place alongside the purely technical ones. Above all, the raw materials and more especially the finished product are, at most periods, likely to be *expensive*. All of this encourages an attitude of deference: to the material, to those who procure it and to those who can work it. Iron, once it is turned to practical uses, presents a contrast in almost all respects. It is of widespread occurrence; its aesthetic potential is almost non-existent; its working requires different skills, and much more hard work of an unremarkable kind, than that of bronze. This contrast was appreciated in the Classical period, as is shown by a remark of Plutarch's which, although it refers to an unspecified period in the past and although it was inspired by bronze statuary, is very much to the point:

> '*Was there then some compounding process, some sorcery on the part of the ancient workers in bronze, like the so-called quenching of swords, whose abandonment led to a truce on bronze in warfare?*' (*Moralia 395 B*).

Quenching is, of course, a process appropriate to iron-working, not bronze, as Plutarch well knew (*Moralia* 156 B); so that the phrase in the middle of this quotation represents an analogy, not an exemplification. Plutarch is comparing the most spectacular process of the blacksmith's trade, which he and his readers understand, with the 'secret' skills of the bronze-smith which are much less easily intelligible. Elsewhere in the same passage he expresses similar awe about the means by which a patina was produced on bronze statues. But he links these observations to one of the most important episodes in metallurgical history, the abandonment of bronze for weapons.

The independent chieftains in their tiny Iron Age communities will have shared none of Plutarch's sentiments (apart, perhaps, from the aesthetic deference). To them, iron-working represented self-sufficiency, in the same way that single burial or hand-made pottery did. Furthermore, it now seems that in Greece, as was already known to be the case in Cyprus, they and their technicians rapidly achieved an added advantage: they learned how to produce iron that was clearly superior to even the best bronze, in respect of its hardness and cutting power (Varoufakis 1983; cf. Maddin 1983). As more examples of early Cypriot and Aegean iron weapons and tools are tested by analysis, the result has been to push back almost to the beginning of the Iron Age the date at which the processes of carburising, tempering and quenching were mastered, and at which wrought iron was thus effectively converted into mild steel. This is an important discovery.

It explains, not why iron was originally adopted, but why its initial adoption, beginning perhaps as a experiment made under the pressure of constraint, then led to an irreversible process of change that swept across half the world. Those regions of Europe which made the transition to iron-use under the direct influence of the Greeks, as some later did, could thus benefit not merely from a change in raw materials, but from a rapidly achieved expertise in handling the new material which made it actually superior to the old. This must in part explain why regions which were well supplied with copper and tin, and which therefore suffered from none of the constraints which had pushed the Greeks into exploring the potential of iron, nevertheless followed them along the same path. I do not mean to assert that every part of Europe made this transition under Greek or Eastern Mediterranean influence, although I do think that a careful reconsideration of the local chronological sequences, observing the criteria which I suggested earlier, and isolating the point at which *economic* dependence on iron became paramount, will reveal that this is at least a historical possibility.

In referring to the 'constraints' that operated in the Greek case, I am maintaining the view which I first put forward some years ago (Snodgrass 1971: 237ff.) that the very first steps in Greek ironworking may have been motivated by the shortage of bronze supplies and in particular tin. I do this despite the emergence of two awkward pieces of evidence from the analysis of Early Iron Age artefacts at Nichoria (Rapp, Jones, Cooke and Henrickson 1978) and at Lefkandi (Jones 1980). These analyses revealed that *bronze* objects of Early Iron Age date had a tin content which, far from indicating shortage of tin supplies, was excessively high: at Nichoria it surpassed 22%, at Lefkandi 20%, as against an optimal proportion of about 10% in bronze. But Catling, in a later volume of the Nichoria report (Catling 1983: 283f.), has pointed to what is surely the correct explanation of these aberrations. The objects tested at both sites have all been tiny and all decorative. Their high tin content is thus of little significance in terms of absolute quantity: what it reflects is rather the desire to make decorative bronzes, such as dress-pins, more attractive by boosting the tin content to the point where the resultant alloy might even be confused with gold. In Greece, at least, the other evidence still conforms to the idea that bronze, and especially tin, may have been difficult to obtain in any quantity. Particularly notable in Greece is the temporary recourse, especially in the tenth century BC, to making iron versions of such objects as fibulae, for which bronze was a very much more appropriate material. Inasmuch as the same practice, followed by a parallel reversion to bronze in later times, occurs also in Cyprus, Cilicia, southern Italy, Sicily and France (Snodgrass 1980a: 368), there are grounds for thinking that some such constraints may have operated well beyond Greece: all these regions, it may be noted, lie at some distance from tin sources.

We may learn something, finally, from the sequel to this early period of iron-use in Greece: a sequel whose character has already emerged, by implication, earlier in this paper. Decentralisation and independence fostered individual enterprise; and it was individual enterprise which enabled the Aegean communities to escape from the initial austerity of the age of iron, and to achieve that fusion of iron technology and affluence in bronze which is characteristic of most developed Iron Age cultures. Here at last we may draw on the one great literary asset which the Greek Early Iron Age has to set against the glamour of the Late Bronze Age: the Homeric poems, by which I mean not the content of the legends that they retail, but the incidental light which the poet at times throws on later periods, especially his own lifetime, through his similes and other non- traditional passages. It is Homer, after all, who in a gruesome simile provides our earliest literary proof of the Greek knowledge of quenching (*Odyssey* 10: 459), in words that are unlikely to have been composed much later than 700 BC. It is Homer, too, who gives us our earliest, indeed almost our only picture of the means – so different from that of the Mycenaean palace at Pylos – whereby an individual in the reviving world of the developed Iron Age in Greece might supply his community with bronze:

> "... *sailing across the wine-dark sea to foreign parts, to Temese, after copper, and carrying with me shining iron*" (*i.e., for exchange*) (*Odyssey* 1: 183f.*)

The speaker is the goddess Athena, but in her disguise as Mentes, a prominent gentleman from a neighbouring island who has called in at Ithaka. Whether Temese is to be identified with Tamassos in Cyprus (preferable on grounds of the commodity sought) or Tempsa in the toe of Italy (preferable in that its people are described as 'foreign', that is non-Greek speakers), the significant feature is that it is thought to be a convincing 'cover' in the world of the *Odyssey* for a Greek to be exchanging native iron for foreign copper.

Here, for once, we have explicit acknowledgement of the feature which, by inference, I have been attributing to developed Iron Age societies in Europe: their hunger for bronze. The evidence is familiar everywhere, but the inference still seems a paradoxical one. It puzzles archaeologists, and I think that it misled even Gordon Childe. His famous pronouncement (Childe 1942: 183), 'Cheap iron democratised agriculture and industry and warfare too', was, I would argue, entirely sound in its instincts. Nothing could be more egalitarian than a strictly and exclusively iron-based economy. The example of Greece (which Childe probably had in mind) would seem to bear out his claim, but only for the brief duration of that period at the beginning of the Iron Age when Greece had such an economy. What Childe did not allow for was the fact that an Iron Age society, once it could get its hands on adequate supplies of bronze, would find itself able to put them to even better use than a Bronze Age society, thanks in part to the availability of iron tools to work them. Conversely, one aspect of the value of discovering native iron nearby was that it formed a commodity for exchange with copper and tin from remoter sources. The fact that many Iron Age societies in Europe in due course come to show an even greater concentration of political and economic power than in the preceding Bronze Age is surely in part a reflection of this process: an elite which disposed of all the advantages of *both* metals was indeed strongly placed. Neither Childe nor some of his successors have appreciated this factor: he himself expressed a puzzled partial retraction of his generalisation a few years later (1950: 222), when confronting with typical honesty the inescapably hierarchical structure of Iron Age societies in barbarian Europe.

The Greek case is, I would admit once again, untypical in many respects. Few European societies can have combined the same features, of being on the one hand so badly placed to maintain supplies of copper and tin, and on the other hand so readily innovative in exploiting the potential of iron. That is no doubt the reason why the bronze/iron transition appears in such a clear-cut form in the Aegean area. Perhaps I may end by illustrating the sequence. In the eleventh, tenth and ninth centuries BC almost the exclusive source of metal finds from Greece is that of grave-goods. But in the eighth century, this source begins to decline, as funerary practices change. At the same period, and rather abruptly, a different context for metalwork, the dedications at sanctuaries, becomes prominent; and in the seventh and sixth centuries, it is the sanctuary-finds which predominate as exclusively as the grave-goods had earlier.

A selection of the metal finds from five of the richest cemeteries of Early Iron Age Greece is presented in Fig. 7.1. The types have been arranged, from left to right, in the order according to which iron was introduced in place of bronze for each particular type. I have singled

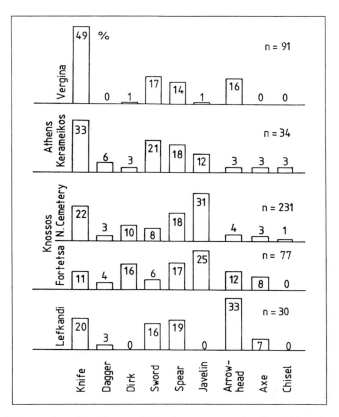

Figure 7.1 Proportional incidence of nine iron types at five Early Iron Age Greek cemeteries.

out the classes of weapon and tool for which the adoption of iron was critical. The predominance of iron over bronze, in these classes of object and at the period in question (between the outher limits of c. 1100 and c. 700 BC in every case), is in fact almost total. It ranges between 92 and 99% at the sites in question and the exceptional bronze pieces are all early and mostly spearheads. The distribution of types clearly illustrates the prevalence of regionalism in Greece: note how the two Cretan cemeteries (both at Knossos) are distinguished by their preference for the javelin over the thrusting-spear, for instance, and how closely their profiles in general resemble each other. The two mainland cemeteries, the Kerameikos in Athens and Vergina in Macedonia, are notable for their weighting towards the left-hand side of the histogram. The predominance of the 'early' iron types – knife, dagger, dirk, sword – in Athens and at Vergina may possibly reflect the fact that these cemeteries lie in areas which were pioneering the use of iron in Greece, without much guidance from outside. There are some independent grounds for believing this, just as there is evidence that the other sites (Lefkandi in Euboea, Knossos in Crete) in some respects were following behind the leaders, at a detectable interval. But this is speculation, and the differences may indicate nothing more than the different needs of local communities within Greece.

What is not debatable is the sequel, as portrayed by the finds from Greek sanctuaries. The change in context – the replacement of short-lived private ostentation by permanent, often communal display – is indeed of great significance in itself, but it does not directly relate to our subject here. What I wish to emphasise is instead the abrupt change in the balance of metals. There are indeed iron objects dedicated in Greek sanctuaries (Kilian 1983), but they make an unimpressive show in the publications, and this is not primarily a function of the excavators' preference for publishing bronzes. The truth is that from the eighth century BC onwards, bronze objects were being dedicated at sanctuaries in almost unimaginable quantities. It is idle to speculate as to what proportion of the original total is represented by the surviving finds, whose context in most cases shows that they were jettisoned (and thus safely buried) because of overcrowding. But even they offer some quite impressive figures (see Snodgrass 1980b: 52ff., 104ff., 131 for some examples), and many of them are of substantial size. Bronze tripod-cauldrons at the sanctuaries of male deities, and bronze dress-accessories of those of female, are the commonest classes in the eighth century; in the seventh and sixth, the latter continue, while the place of the former is taken by pieces of bronze armour. The prevalence of bronze extends not only to the types where we would expect it – decorative pieces and objects of sheet metal – but also to offensive weapons: in the case of arrowheads, this can be explained by the ease of multiple casting, but this rationale can hardly be applied to the spearheads, among which bronze shows a notable resurgence, half a millennium after the end of the Bronze Age proper. It is, without doubt, the rediscovery of the time-honoured attributes of bronze, the metal of affluence and artistry, which is reflected here (cf. Burgess 1979: 278).

When the evidence is so rich in paradox and complexity, it is hardly surprising that the implications of the transition from Bronze Age to Iron Age have been imperfectly understood. To unravel the many strands of this process will be arduous, and we have already found reason to think that the solution adopted for one part of Europe will not necessarily, nor even probably, be appropriate elsewhere. I would only claim that the case of the Aegean area, because of its early context and the relative precision of its evidence, is one that merits the attention of anyone working in later European prehistory.

BIBLIOGRAPHY

Burgess, C., 1979. 'A find from Boyton, Suffolk, and the end of the Bronze Age in Britain and Ireland'. In Burgess, C., and Coombs, D.,(eds.) *Bronze Age Hoards – some finds old and new*, British Archaeological Report 67, 269–283 (Oxford: BAR).

Catling, H. W., 1983. 'The small finds'. In McDonald, W. A., Coulson, W. D. E., and Rosser, J. (eds.) *Excavations at Nichoria in South West Greece iii: Dark Age and Byzantine occupation*, 273–287 (Minneapolis: University of Minnesota Press).

Childe, V. G., 1942. *What happened in History.* (Harmondsworth: Pelican Books).

Childe, V. G., 1950. *Prehistoric Migrations in Europe.* (Oslo: Institut for Sammenlignende Kulturforskning).

Dickinson, O. T. P. K., 1983. 'Cist graves and chamber tombs'. *Annual of the Brit. Sch., Athens* 78, 55–67.

Gullini, G., 1983. 'Discussion intervention'. *Atti del Convegno Internazionale: Grecia, Italia e Sicilia nell' VIII e VII secole a./c. (Annuario della Scuola Archeologica di Atene* 59, n.s. 43, 1981), 344.

Jones, R. E., 1980. 'Analyses of bronze and other base metal objects from the cemeteries'. In Popham, M. R., Sackett, L. H., and Themelis, P. G., (eds.) *Lefkandi i: the Iron Age*, 447–459 (London: Thames and Hudson).

Kilian, K., 1983. 'Weihungen aus Eisen und Eisenvorbereitung im Heiligtum zu Philia (Thessalien)'. In Hägg, R., (ed.) *The Greek Renaissance of the Eighth Century* BC: *Tradition and Innovation*, Skrifter utgivna av Svenska Institutet i Athen, 4°, 30, 131–146 (Athen: Svenska Institutet i Athen).

Kirsten, E., 1983. 'Gebirgshirtentum und Sesshaftigkeit'. In Deger-Jalkotzy, S., (ed.) *Griechenland, die Ägäis und die Levante während der Dark Ages*, (Wien: Verlag der Österreichischen Akademie der Wissenschaften).

Lechtman, H., 1980. 'The Central Andes: Metallurgy without iron'. In Wertime, T. A., and Muhly, J. D., (eds.) *The Coming of the Age of Iron*, 267–334 (New Haven: Yale University Press).

Maddin, R., 1983. 'Early iron technology in Cyprus'. In Maddin, R., and Muhly, J. D., (eds.) *Acta of the International Archaeological Symposium: Early metallurgy in Cyprus*, 303–314 (Larnaka: the Pierides Foundation).

Rapp, G. R., Jones, R. E., Cooke, S. R. B., and Henrickson, E. L., 1978. 'Analysis of the metal objects'. In Rapp, G. R., and Aschenbrenner, S. E., (eds.) *Excavations at Nichoria in South West Greece i: Site, Environs and Techniques*, 166–181 (Minneapolis: University of Minnesota Press).

Rowlands, M. J., 1980. 'Kinship, alliance and exchange in the European Bronze Age'. In Barrett, J., and Bradley, R., (eds.) *Settlement and Society in the British later Bronze Age*, British Archaeological Report 83, 15–55 (Oxford: BAR).

Sakellariou, M., 1980. *Les Proto-Grecs*. (Athens: Ekdotike Athenon).

Sloan, R. E. and Duncan, M. A., 1978. 'Zooarchaeology of Nichoria'. In Rapp, G. R., and Aschenbrenner, S. E., (eds.) *Excavations at Nichoria in South West Greece i: Site, Environs and Techniques*, 60–77 (Minneapolis: University of Minnesota Press).

Snodgrass, A. M., 1971. *The Dark Age of Greece*. (Edinburgh: Edinburgh University Press).

Snodgrass, A. M., 1980a. 'Iron and early metallurgy in the Mediterranean'. In Wertime, T. A., and Muhly, J. D., (eds.) *The Coming of the Age of Iron*, 335–374 (New Haven: Yale University Press).

Snodgrass, A. M., 1980b. *Archaic Greece: the Age of Experiment*. (London: J. M. Dent).

Snodgrass, A. M., 1983a. 'Two demographic notes'. In Hägg, R., (ed.)*The Greek Renaissance of the Eighth Century* BC: *Tradition and Innovation*, Skrifter utgivna av Svenska Institutet i Athen, 4°, 30, 167–171 (Athen: Svenska Institutet i Athen).

Snodgrass, A. M., 1983b. 'Cyprus and the beginning of iron metallurgy in the Eastern Mediterranean'. In Maddin, R., and Muhly, J. D., (eds.) *Acta of the International Archaeological Symposium: Early metallurgy in Cyprus*, 285–296 (Larnaka: the Pierides Foundation).

Spyropoulos, T. G., 1972. *Hysteromykenaikoi Helladikoi Thesauroi*. (Athens: Bibliotheke tes en Athenais Arkhaiologikes Etaireias 72).

van der Merwe, N. J., 1980. 'The advent of iron in Africa'. In Wertime, T. A., and Muhly, J. D., (eds.) *The Coming of the Age of Iron*, 463–506 (New Haven: Yale University Press).

Varoufakis, G., 1983. 'The origin of the Mycenaean and Geometric iron on the Greek mainland and in the Aegean islands'. In Maddin, R., and Muhly, J. D., (eds.) *Acta of the International Archaeological Symposium: Early metallurgy in Cyprus*, 315–324 (Larnaka: the Pierides Foundation).

Ventris, M. and Chadwick, J., 1959. *Documents in Mycenaean Greek*. (Cambridge: Cambridge University Press).

CHAPTER 8

The Euboeans in Macedonia: A New Precedent for Westward Expansion?

This appeared in a volume celebrating the eightieth birthday of the late Giorgio Buchner. It shifts the scene away from central and southern Greece, to a question on which history and archaeology alike had long failed to throw much light: the early movements from those regions to Macedonia and especially to the Chalkidike, where a spate of new discoveries in the 1980s had changed the whole picture.

The underlying issue here is what constitutes evidence for overseas settlement. Mere resemblances in pottery style, even when reinforced by actual imports of the class being imitated, should not be judged sufficient proof of a population movement (as I myself have insisted, above, Ch. 1, pp. 25–7). It is on the supporting evidence of other kinds that one must base any suspicion that people from Euboea had actually settled here: perhaps the strongest hint comes in the fact that a curious practice attested in the cemeteries of Euboean Lefkandi, whereby sizeable cist tombs were built and then apparently used to accommodate, not the corpse but token fragments of the ashes and bones deriving from its cremation elsewhere, is matched at Koukos in the Chalkidike (p. 151 below; but see Lemos (2002: 162–3) for a possible alternative explanation of such burials).

The case for such (unexpectedly early) settlement has nevertheless been contested by one of the excavation team at the important nearby site of Torone (Papadopoulos 1996); one of the excavators of Lefkandi is also more guarded on the issue (Lemos 2002: 183–4, 207). Both are better placed than I am to judge. It may be that the case here advanced is premature: certainly I confess to discomfort at taking up a thesis opposed to the one I had adopted in other, roughly comparable instances. But in this case one can be fairly confident that further discoveries will settle the question one way or the other.

BIBLIOGRAPHY

Lemos, I. (2002), *The Protogeometric Aegean: The Archaeology of the Late Eleventh and Tenth Centuries* BC, Oxford: Oxford University Press.
Papadopoulos, J. K. (1996), 'Euboeans in Macedonia? A closer look', *Oxford Journal of Archaeology* 15: 151–81.

The Euboeans are the great discovery of early Greek archaeology since World War II – a discovery that might conceivably never have happened but for Giorgio Buchner's decision to begin excavation at Pithekoussai in 1952. Long before that time, the insistent appearance of the Euboeans in the literary record of early colonisation had pointed to either a gap or a failure of recognition on the archaeological side. But the 1950s were the watershed for archaeology: in the syntheses of this time, the Euboeans as yet scarcely exist,[1] but the primary research was already under way, and not only through the medium of excavation. In 1957, John Boardman had published the second of his papers on Euboean pottery, in which he began to discern the historical and geographical significance of the regional style of Euboea: not only could it be distinguished within the broader category of 'Thessalo-Cycladic' in which it had been placed, but it could be recognised in some far-flung appearances, especially at Al Mina in Syria.[2] Then in 1964 began both the excavation of Lefkandi and the work of the Greco-Swiss expedition at Eretria, and for the first time these exports could be securely traced to some of their points of origin,[3] and when to these was added the important exploration of the cemeteries and wells of Chalkis, from 1976, by Dr Angeliki Andreiomenou, both of the historically-documented colonising cities of Euboea had begun to re-enter the light of day.[4] In quite a short space of time, the early overseas enterprises of the Euboeans had become common knowledge; by the 1970s conferences were being devoted to them in their own right, and in 1980 they were given a chapter of their own in a cultural history of early Greece.[5]

In the consensual narrative of this episode that now emerged, there was an awkward transition that was made with some difficulty. The

'The Euboeans in Macedonia: a new precedent for westward expansion', *Annali di Archeologia e Storia Antica (Istituto Universitario Orientale)*, n.s. 1, 1994, 87–93.

Euboeans could be shown to have been the first Greeks to open the sea-lanes of the eastern and central Mediterranean as mariners and, in most opinions, as traders; but at a certain point these roles were exchanged for that of leading the way in permanent, colonising settlement, in Italy, Sicily and on the northern coast of the Aegean. Tradition suggested only a minor Euboean contribution to the known migrations of the pre-colonial era, and the nearest thing to a precedent for the sudden outburst of western colonisation was to be found in the surmise, made plausible by the archaeological material, that emigrant Euboeans had participated in establishing new settlements on certain neighbouring Aegean islands, such as Andros, Tenos and Skyros, in the tenth or ninth centuries BC.[6] The abruptness of the transition was further mitigated by two instances that were claimed to represent intermediate stages: at Al Mina and possibly at Tell Sukas, it was argued that Euboean settlers had joined foreign communities on the Asiatic coast, at a date earlier than that of the colonising movement; while at Pithekoussai, the earliest western settlement, a quite widely held view was that the Euboean enterprise was not yet truly colonial in nature – it lacked the characteristic founding traditions and the territorial element of a normal colony, and its population (as in the East) had been a cosmopolitan one. As it happens, each of these views has recently been challenged;[7] but even while accepting their validity, scholars must have felt some intermittent unease at the weight of argument that was being rested on the purely archaeological evidence from Al Mina, and on the rather unsatisfactory literary traditions about Pithekoussai.

Throughout these developments, there was little discussion of one potentially important episode: the Euboean settlement of the northern coast of the Aegean, in the Chalkidike peninsula in Macedonia and, somewhat later, in their colonies further to the East, in Thrace. Here again, the literary evidence was far from satisfactory, being confined almost entirely to much later authors; the arguments based on it were at best inferential. More surprisingly, archaeological exploration had given no such clear answers as in the case of the western colonies.[8] Such chronological evidence as was available suggested that the Euboean colonising activity here had been broadly contemporary with that in the West; but to this there was the obvious commonsense objection that the same cities, Chalkis and Eretria, had been involved in both instances, and that their resources can hardly have measured up to mounting two such operations simultaneously. These considerations led some scholars to postulate that the original northern venture, in the Chalkidike, had been undertaken somewhat earlier than the western, others that it had been rather later;[9] my impression is that the latter view had the more adherents, but the range of speculation mainly illustrates the poverty of the evidence and, as I have said, the issue was anyway not often discussed.

In the past fourteen years, new excavation at several sites in the Chalkidike has put the matter decisively beyond further speculation. My aim in the remainder of this paper is to communicate briefly some of the results of this work but, more important, to stress their profound implications for early Greek history in general, and in particular for the foundation of Pithekoussai and its successor-sites in the West. This new archaeological contribution may have been overdue, but it is none the less welcome for that.

The story begins in the 1981 season of the joint Greco-Australian excavations at Torone, on the middle (Sithonian) prong of the triple promontory of Chalkidike. One can only guess at what exactly the excavators had expected to find in their earliest levels when they began work here in 1975: here was a site traditionally colonised by the Euboean Chalkidians at some date no later than the first half of the seventh century BC, and the evidence gathered from the first three seasons had been generally in accord with that tradition, although prehistoric pottery extending back to the Early Bronze Age was present in one part of the site, the 'Lekythos' named in Thucydides IV, 113 ('Promontory 1'). More significantly in the light of later events, a handful of Early Iron Age sherds had also been gathered at points inland, assignable to the Protogeometric and Sub-Protogeometric phases. Then in 1981 came the discovery of a large cemetery, consisting mainly of cremations, on 'Terrace V', underlying the architecture of the Classical city: its chronological range was impressively long and early, extending from the later part of the Submycenaean phase until the end of the Sub-Protogeometric: that is, according to the prevailing chronology, at least from ca. 1075 to ca. 825 BC, a period of two and a half centuries lying entirely in the 'pre-colonial' phase. By the end of the 1984 season, a total of 134 graves had been opened, 118 of them cremations; and these had yielded over 500 complete and fragmentary pots. Some of the pottery could be identified as imports from central and southern Greece, while other vessels were local imitations of these; others again were hand-made. Presently, a further very important conclusion emerged: the Attic element was prevalent in the earlier imports, but for the last century or so of the cemetery's life Euboean wares and influence dominated.[10]

What was the identity and context of the group using this cemetery? The sheer numbers of the imported vessels, and the practice of
imitating them on the spot, gave a suggestion that the actual burying
group had included immigrants from central Greece; but the next evidence chronologically that supported such a conclusion was as yet
to be found only in a nearby potter's kiln which had been used for
the production of painted pottery of Late Geometric date, as well as
of storage pithoi.[11] The likeliest inference still seemed to be that a
Chalkidian colony of the later eighth century had been preceded by a
prolonged venture of more than three centuries earlier, with an interruption between the two. But the discoveries of 1988–1990 made it
slightly harder to maintain that view. Excavation had now resumed its
focus on the 'Lekythos' promontory investigated in the 1970s: here, in
one of a set of trenches laid out near the landward end of the promontory, substantial settlement evidence of the Late Geometric period for
the first time came to light. It included four storage pithoi found *in
situ*; a fifth such pithos was recovered in 1990, some distance away towards the northern, seaward tip of the peninsula, suggesting that storage facilities extended over a considerable area. The adjacent pottery,
mostly incorporated in a deposit of fill laid around and over the pithoi
in the Archaic period, included 'especially plentiful . . . fragments of
Late Protogeometric and notably Sub-Protogeometric vessels'.[12] Continuity between the period of the cemetery and that of the kiln began to seem more likely, now that material comparable with both
had been found in the same location, even if there remained an
apparent chronological gap between the notional end of the Sub-
Protogeometric and the beginning of the Late Geometric.

But continuity was beginning to be hinted at in the other direction
as well: here and elsewhere on the site, repeated finds of Middle and
Late Bronze Age pottery, some of it imported from further south, were
prolonging the sequence begun with the Early Bronze Age finds of the
1970s: the main emphasis was given to the finds of Early Mycenaean
(LH I–II) date, because their occurrence on a Macedonian site was
without precedent. Stratigraphic proof of continuous occupation until
the beginning of the cemetery in the Submycenaean period is not yet
forthcoming, but it is at least clear that the carriers of the imported
pottery from the cemetery were following in the tracks of much older
predecessors; and that any chronological interval at Torone was very
much shorter than in the case of the western colonies where parallel
explanations, in terms of memory of Bronze Age forerunners, have at
times been offered. It is perhaps just worth recording here the tradition

recorded by Stephanus of Byzantium s.v. 'Τορώνη', with the words:
'Torone: a city of Thrace, from Torone, the daughter of either Proteus
or Poseidon and of Phoinike; and there is another Torone too, founded
after the Trojan War'. No other city of the name existed; instead,
Stephanus must have stumbled on two conflicting traditions, one of
which ascribed to Torone a foundation during the Heroic Age, the
other later, and concluded that they applied to two different places.

The next site of great significance for this period is Mende, traditionally an Eretrian colonial foundation of the same general period as
Chalkidian Torone, but lying this time on the westernmost of the three
promontories, Pallene. Here Dr Julia Vokotopoulou began in 1986
a most fruitful examination of the site. In the first two seasons of
excavations, there took place discoveries that would have occasioned
great surprise but for what had already emerged at Torone.[13] On the
plateau of Vigla, the highest point of the Classical city, were discovered
a series of bins and pits of varying shapes and sizes, evidently designed
for storage, since some of them were lined with clay. At some point no
later than the early seventh century BC, they were used for the disposal
of pottery, building materials, bones and other unwanted materials,
and in some cases sealed off with stones. The pottery ranged in date
from late Mycenaean of the twelfth century, through Submycenaean,
Protogeometric and Geometric to Sub-Geometric. In this case, the
material of the earlier phases, down to and including the Protogeometric, was notably similar to that from Lefkandi in Euboea, and the
Geometric material included Eretrian and East Greek imports. The
link with Euboea appeared to cover some four centuries.

Meanwhile, work was also undertaken in a quite different part of
the site, close to the sea-shore and about 150 m. away to the east.
Here, in contrast to the Vigla site, stratified occupation-deposits were
preserved, extending from the fourth century BC right back to at least
the ninth: in 1988, a floor of Late Protogeometric date was found at
the great depth of 4.50 m. The pottery, here mostly of local fabric,
is remarked on for its resemblances in part to the material from the
Early Iron Age cemetery at Torone, in part to that found at Lefkandi:
there was even a leg from a zoomorphic plastic vase reminiscent of
the famous 'Lefkandi centaur'.[14] Finds in the same area in the following season, 1989, prompted caution about the absolute chronology of the local material, when sherds of the local Geometric were
found in close association with an imported Middle Protocorinthian
kotyle of the earlier seventh century BC. In the same year, an extensive child cemetery further along the beach began to be systematically

explored, and was found to extend back to at least 700 BC.[15] Finally in 1990, the last season of excavation in this quarter, a major stratigraphic sounding was carried even deeper than previously, almost to the present sea-level; much further pottery of Protogeometric and Sub-Protogeometric style was found, including later versions of the pendent-semicircle skyphos, and imported pieces of possible Thessalian origin, as well as Euboean. On the revised chronology, occupation in the coastal part of the site may not go back beyond c. 850 BC, in contrast to the much earlier material from Vigla. Two small circular paved areas and part of a third, lying inside one of the houses and dating to the third quarter of the eighth century BC, at once recalled the structures of similar date found against the outer walls of houses at Lefkandi some years earlier.[16]

Mende thus provides a fuller picture than, as yet, Torone does, of what seems to be much the same phenomenon: a long-standing 'pre-colonial' interest in the area of the Chalkidike on the part of Euboeans and others. In both cases, the material belongs to several different types of context, and comes from more than one area of the site. At Mende, the Euboean presence appears to extend, at least intermittently and possibly continuously, over some four centuries before the inferred date of the Eretrian colony.

A third site in the Chalkidike strongly reinforces the evidence from Mende: this is Koukos near Sykia, which lies towards the end of the Sithonia promonory, but some way eastwards from Torone, on a hilltop towards the opposite coast. As the use of the modern toponym shows, this is not a site for which an ancient identification can yet be proposed, and the suggestion has been made that its history may have resembled that of Lefkandi and of Zagora on Andros, with decline and abandonment taking place at the threshhold of the historical era. Work began here in 1987, initially in the area of an Early Iron Age cemetery but later incorporating a fortified settlement of similar date as well: like Torone this was a joint Greco-Australian project. Five seasons (1987–1990, 1992) have been reported on to date. In the first four years a total of 98 graves, all cremations of varying types, were opened in the cemetery: as at Torone, there was a mixture of wheel-made and hand-made pottery, but although there was a chronological overlap with the cemetery there, the Koukos cremations extend distinctly later, from the late tenth century to the end of the eighth, thus neatly bridging the chronological gap between the Torone graves and the child-cemetery on the beach at Mende. Here the predominance of locally-made pottery seems to be great, but by 1988 it was being noted that the imported pieces, once again, recalled Euboean wares; and furthermore, there was a correspondence in burial-practices with Lefkandi in the use of cists for secondary cremations, with only microscopic traces of burnt bone in the fill of the graves.[17]

From 1988 on, the settlement and its fortification-wall were tested as well. The contemporaneity of the fortification could not be conclusively established, but the settlement produced apsidal houses, a possible ash altar and, in 1992, a soap-stone mould and other apparent traces of metalworking.

It has often happened in archaeology that an initially unexpected discovery rapidly stimulates comparable finds on other sites not far away; and that has certainly happened with these three excavations in the Chalkidike. The revelation of this early activity on the part of people from further south in the Aegean is of course the major surprise, but what makes it important for the early western colonies is the indisputable prominence in this activity of the Euboeans. We are not dealing, as in the case of the early Euboean appearances in the Levant, with a mere dispersion of pottery. These are durable settlements, planted on a continental coast, with many intrusive features alongside an undoubted indigenous element. The natural comparison is with the Ionian Migration, with which there must have been, at least in the case of Mende, a substantial chronological overlap. While Athenians and others, as tradition recalled, led the way there, in the Chalkidike it was the Euboeans who evidently came to prevail. The evidence for this view is to be found in the imported pottery from all three sites; in the architectural evidence of the circular platforms at Mende and perhaps in the leg of the figurine from the same site; in many features of the Early Iron Age cemetery at Torone; in the architecture and especially in the burial-practices at Koukos. It seems very likely that emigrant Euboeans were settling on this coast for generations before they began their documented western ventures. The historical destiny of Torone and Mende as city-states recalls that of their respective traditional foundresses, Chalkis and Eretria, just as the apparent demise of Koukos, and the probable loss of its ancient name, echoes the fate of Lefkandi.

The discoveries are also acutely relevant to a notorious problem in the early history of Macedonia, which may have some relevance for Pithekoussai as well. This is the issue of the mysterious 'Chalkidian *genos*' twice mentioned by Herodotus (VII, 185, 2; VIII, 127) in the context of this region; the ethnic denotation of the 'Thraceward Chalkidians' in Thucydides (I, 57, 5) and the 'Thraceward Ionians' by Demosthenes (*apud* Stephanus of Byzantium, s.v. 'Ἀπολλωνία') has often been taken to refer to the same group, and the most explicit statement comes from Polybius, who writes (IX, 28, 2) of a 'confederation (σύστημα) of Thraceward Greeks founded by Athens and Chalkis'. This problem is confronted, in the light of the new archaeological evidence, in a forthcoming paper by Professor N. G. L. Hammond, whose greater mastery of the complex evidence will enable me to be brief here.[18]

The most important point is that these 'Chalkidians' are clearly distinguished from the inhabitants of the coastal colonies founded by Chalkis. The first Herodotean passage positively enforces this conclusion: at VII, 185, 2 we hear that the 'Chalkidian *genos*' provided infantry for Xerxes in 480 BC., whereas earlier the colonies (Torone specifically included) had been mentioned as furnishing ships and crews (VII, 122). This and other arguments had indeed led several scholars, following a powerfully-argued article by E. Harrison as long ago as 1912, to suggest that the '*genos* of the Chalkidians' had only a coincidence of name in common with the city in Euboea, and were in reality a little-known indigenous Macedonian tribe; and that the tradition of colonial foundations in the area by Euboean Chalkis had at least in part arisen through the confusion in names.[19] But as Hammond convincingly argues, a much better solution to the problem is now at hand: the pre-colonial activity of Euboean settlers, at Torone and elsewhere, could have led to the establishment of a group in the Chalkidike who retained the name of one of the Euboean cities from which they had originally set out; and who in later history were distinguished from, and at times at odds with, the inhabitants of the formal colonies established from the late eighth century on, even though many of the latter hailed from the same place; for there is no need to reject the strong tradition that Chalkidian colonies of the normal type, conforming to the model of the *polis*, followed on in this region in later centuries. To revert for a moment to the archaeology, it may be opportune to observe here that on the evidence of the Torone excavations, the builders of the Classical period were clearly unaware of, or indifferent to, the presence of the Early Iron Age cemetery underneath their city.

What makes this finding exceptionally interesting from the point of view of early colonisation is the fact that the first group of 'Chalkidians' were called just that; that they retained the ethnic denomination and organisation appropriate to the era before the rise of the *polis*, and to the regions where the *polis* system did not prevail. Do we perhaps have here a glimpse of the nature of many 'pre-colonial' ventures, when the new settlers adopted what was in all probability the only form of organisation known to them, that of an ethnic, 'tribal' or federal grouping, in which the population of a number of separate settlements, including small hill-top hamlets like Koukos, would combine? And, much more speculatively, could this have any bearing on the case of Pithekoussai where, as we have seen (p. 146) there has been a widespread tendency to regard this earliest Greek settlement in the West as having been in some way 'pre-colonial', or 'pre-*polis*', in its nature and organisation?

On this point I find the recent arguments of Coldstream (above, n. 7) convincing. A maturer consideration of the topography of Pithekoussai and Ischia suggests that this tendency should be reversed; in particular, Giorgio Buchner's recent discoveries of rural settlements elsewhere on the island, contemporary with the early years of Pithekoussai, give a strong hint that the *chora* of the settlement – that is, the rest of the island – was being exploited from early on, as we should expect in a 'normal' colonial foundation. In any case, the topographical conditions on Ischia were so far removed from those of the continental territory in which the 'Chalkidian *genos*' had formed during the preceding centuries that even an identical form of organisation on the part of the colonisers would have produced different results.

The precedent of the dark age settlements of Euboeans in Macedonia is thus not an unqualified parallel. The eighth – even the early eighth – century was a very different era from the thirteenth, twelfth or eleventh. To be more specific, the Greek homeland was witnessing the growth of nucleated settlemets which saw their neighbours as potential rivals rather than associates, a growth which was probably already bringing into being the familiar world of the independent *polis*; and there is no clearer example of the process than the triad of settlements around the Lelantine Plain of Euboea, Chalkis, Lefkandi and Eretria. Eretria was growing rapidly and Chalkis must have been as well; Lefkandi's time was nearly over. An obscurer drama with a similar plot was apparently running its course in that other area of Euboean settlement, the Chalkidike, where Torone and Mende were to survive as *poleis* on their respective promontories, but the smaller fortified settlement at Koukos was apparently to share the fate of Lefkandi. Whether Chalkis or Eretria or both participated in founding Pithekoussai, the founders are more likely to have designed their new settlement in their own image, that of nucleated communities sharing a preoccupation with arable land.

In a recent paper on the general theme of western colonisation (above, n. 7), I have drawn attention to two other fundamental differences between the earlier Euboean ventures in the Chalkidike and the later ones at Pithekoussai and its successor settlements. The contrast in the length and hazard of the necessary sea-voyage is so obvious as to need no further emphasis; but a second distinction deserves rehearsing once again. This is the marked difference in the *density* of the Greek settlement, Euboean and other, in the two regions. In the Chalkidike, more than perhaps in any other area of Greek colonisation, one is struck by how closely the settlements are crowded on to this exceptionally indented coastline. In Italy, Sicily and the West, a much wider pattern of spacing prevails, as a glance at the map will show. This need for distancing seems to have been accepted by the various colonising cities from the very start of the movement to settle in the West; even when infilling occurred in the course of time, the density never came to approach that in the northern Aegean. Whatever kind of explanatory model we adopt for the contrast in density, it is likely to include some element of intentional policy: the new venture in the West was seen to require a change of scale, as well as of distance. Among the few exceptions to this rule are the first Megarian colony at Megara Hyblaea, which was located uncomfortably and, in the very long term, fatally close to Syracuse; and, interestingly, the very first Euboean settlements in the West at Pithekoussai and Kyme, which faced each other across a strip of water only 15 kilometres wide. In the latter case, this only held true of the comparatively short period when the two colonies co-existed, and we cannot assume that their simultaneous occupation was part of the original design of the founders of Pithekoussai; yet it may have some significance as an example of a transitional phase of policy, when the practices of Euboean settlers much nearer home were still felt to be appropriate to the western Mediterranean.

The value of the recent discoveries on the Macedonian coast, not least for the field of western settlement, remains considerable in spite of these palpable differences. They show that the people of the Euboean communities had been not only far-travelled mariners, but also founders of durable overseas settlements, for centuries before they turned their eyes to the Bay of Naples – something which fell far short of proof in the case of their Levantine ventures, even where Al Mina was concerned (above, p. 146). They show them transplanting their own established cultural features – architectural and funerary as well as ceramic and, at least at Torone, involving the manufacture as well as the importation of pottery – to a continental shore, and maintaining them in the face of local inhabitants who, as later Macedonian history shows, could turn hostile. They give us our best glimpse to date of the operation, and indeed the feasibility, of such settlements in an era which undoubtedly preceded the rise of the *polis* in the Greek homeland: we can no longer assume *a priori* that the existence of the *polis* system at home was a precondition for the onset of the colonising movement abroad. This is an impressive series of gains to emerge from little more than a decade of excavation in one small area of the ancient world. The Euboean pioneers of the Chalkidike have claims on the attention of anyone with a serious interest in the rise of Greek colonisation in Italy and Sicily – and no one alive has demonstrated this interest more profoundly, or to better effect, than Giorgio Buchner.

Notes

1. Euboea makes a fleeting appearance in V. R. Desborough's *Protogeometric pottery*, Oxford 1952, pp. 194–196, 199, but none at all in T. J. Dunbabin's, *The Greeks and their eastern neighbours* (Society for the Promotion of Hellenic Studies, Supplementary Paper 8), London 1957.
2. 'Early Euboean pottery and history', in *BSA* 52, 1957, pp. 1–29; and more fully in his *The Greeks overseas* (first edition), Harmondsworth 1964, pp. 38–45, 52–53.
3. M. R. Popham-L. H. Sackett (a cura di), *Excavations at Lefkandi, 1964–66*, Preliminary Report, London 1968; K. Schefold, 'Die Grabungen in Eretria im Herbst 1964 und 1965', in *AntK* 9, 1966, pp. 106–124.
4. A. Andreiomenou, 'Skyphoi de l'atelier de Chalcis', in *BCH* 108, 1984, pp. 37–69, with continuation *ibidem* 109, 1985, pp. 49–75; *eadem*, 'Vases protogéometriques et subprotogéometriques I-II de l'atelier de Chalcis', in *BCH* 110, 1986, pp. 89–120.
5. *Contribution à l'étude de la société et de la colonisation eubéennes* (Cahiers du Centre Jean Bérard 2), Naples 1975 and *Gli Eubei in Occidente*, Atti del 18° Convegno di Studi sulla Magna Grecia, Taranto 1979; O. Murray, *Early Greece*, Glasgow 1980, chapter 5, 'Euboean society and trade'.
6. Tentatively suggested already in J. N. Coldstream, *Greek Geometric pottery*, London 1968, p. 342; and in V. R. d'A. Desborough, *The Greek Dark Ages*, London 1972, pp. 185–186, 201–202, 348–349.
7. For the case of Al Mina, A. M. Snodgrass, 'The nature and standing of the western colonies', in G. R. Tsetskhladze–F de Angelis (a cura di), *The archaeology of Greek colonisation*, Oxford 1994, pp. 1–10, citing

some other very recent opinions to the same effect; for Pithekoussai, J. N. Coldstream, 'Prospectors and pioneers: Pithekoussai, Kyme and Central Italy', *ibidem*, pp. 47–59.

8. The whole position is well summed up by A. J. Graham in J. Boardman *et al.* (a cura di), in *CAH* (2nd ed.) 3.3, Cambridge 1982, pp. 113–118 and 160–162.

9. Earlier, e.g. D. W. Bradeen, 'The Chalcidians in Thrace', in *AJP* 73, 1952, pp. 356–380, especially pp. 378–380; later, e.g. R. M. Cook, 'Ionia and Greece in the eighth and seventh centuries BC', in *JHS* 66, 1946, pp. 67–98, at p. 71.

10. See A. Cambitoglou–J. K. Papadopoulos, 'Excavations at Torone, 1986: a preliminary report', in *Mediterranean Archaeology* 1, 1988, pp. 180–217, with a useful summary of the earlier seasons' work at pp. 180–188.

11. J. K. Papadopoulos, 'An Early Iron Age potter's kiln at Torone', in *Mediterranean Archaeology* 2, 1989, pp. 9–44.

12. The fullest reports of these' seasons are to be found in A. Cambitoglou–J. K. Papadopoulos, 'Excavations at Torone, 1988', in *Mediterranean Archaeology* 3, 1990, pp. 93–142 and 4, 1991, pp. 147–171; quotation from p. 152. For 1990, A. Cambitoglou, 'Torone', in *Ergon* 1990, pp. 89–93.

13. For Mende (and for Koukos, the next site) the fullest reports are to be found in the recently-founded periodical Το Ἀρχαιολογικό ῎Εργο στη Μακεδονία και Θράκη (hereafter *AEMTH*), with intermittent briefer accounts in *Deltion* and *AR*. For the Vigla pits, I. Vokotopoulou, in *AEMTH* 1, 1987, pp. 281 and 528, pl. 7; *Deltion* 41, 1986, Chronika pp. 147–149 and 42, 1987, Chronika pp. 368–369; H.W. Catling, in *AR* 35, 1988–89, p. 72 and E. B. French, in *AR* 39, 1992–93, p. 54.

14. I. Vokotopoulou, 'Ἀνασκαφή Μένδης 1988', in *AEMTH* 2, 1988, pp. 331–345, at pp. 332, 337 and *Deltion* 43, 1988, Chronika p. 361.

15. I. Vokotopoulou, 'Ἀνασκαφή Μένδης 1989', in *AEMTH* 3, 1988, pp. 409–423, at pp. 413–415, 418.

16. I. Vokotopoulou, 'Μένδη-Ποσείδι 1990', in *AEMTH* 4, 1990, pp. 399–410, at pp. 399–401 and 404, pls. 1–6; E.B. French, in *AR* 39, 1992–93, p. 54.

17. See I. Vokotopoulou, 'Ἀνασκαφικές ἔρευνες στη Χαλκιδική', *AEMTH*, 1, 1987, pp. 284–285 and 528, with H. W. Catling, in *AR* 34, 1987–88, p. 49; J. Carington-Smith-I. Vokotopoulou, 'Ἀνασκαφή στον Κούκο Συκίας', in *AEMTH* 2, 1988, pp. 357–370, with specific observations cited at pp. 364 (history), 362 (imported pottery) and 360 (burial customs); 3, 1989, pp. 425–438; 4, 1990, pp. 439–454; with respective summaries by H. W. Catling, in *AR* 35, 1988–89, pp. 72–73; E. B. French, in *AR* 36, 1989–90, p. 52; 37, 1990–91, p. 49. For the 1992 season, *eadem*, in *AR* 39, 1992–93, p. 54.

18. 'The Chalcidians' and 'Apollonia of the Thraceward Ionians' *BSA* 90, 1995, 307–15. I thank Professor Hammond most warmly for showing me the text of this paper in advance of publication.
19. E. Harrison, 'Chalkidike', in *CQ* 6, 1912, pp. 93–103 and 165–178; followed by, e.g. M. Zahrnt, *Olyntb und die Chalkidier* (Vestigia 14), München 1971, pp. 12–27; S. C. Bakhuizen, *Chalkis in Euboea, iron and the Chalcidians abroad* (Chalcidian Studies 3), Leiden 1976, pp. 14–15, 18–19.

CHAPTER 9

The Rejection of Mycenaean Culture and the Oriental Connection

This paper fitted a little awkwardly into the agenda of a 1998 Mainz conference devoted to Greco-Oriental contacts at the turn of the second and first millennia BC. For the second time, I must apologise for the overlap between its opening paragraphs and the closing passage of ch. 4 above. This time, the central concern is with continuities and discontinuities: essentially with the question of the ancestry of the Greek world of the Early Iron Age and thus, less directly, of Archaic and Classical Greece. It will become clear that there is a profound incompatibility in the rival views as to what is evidence for continuity, and at which levels it operated. Here, a case is based on resemblances, extending down to a relatively humble social level, between the archaeological record of two quite widely separated eras – resemblances which I think would survive the test of the 'Post-Processual' view that this record, rather than simply reflecting contemporary realities, is partly shaped by ideology. But another issue central to this paper is, once again, that of regionalism and regional variety within mainland Greece.

I begin with a miscellany of recent quotations, which are representative of what is today a coherent and quite widely-held view, embodying certain fundamental tenets. First:

> The polis arose not in the eighth century, but from the recently dissolved Mycenaean world, enriched by new arrivals from the East... The world of early Greece... is neither Bronze Age nor Archaic but both, nor is it more Greek than it is oriental.[1]

'The rejection of Mycenaean culture and the Oriental connection', from E. A. Braun-Holzinger and H. Matthäus (ed.), *Die nahöstlichen Kulturen und Griechenland an der Wende vom 2. zum 1. Jahrtausend v. Chr.*, Möhnesee-Wamel: Bibliopolis, 2002, pp. 1–9.

The 'new arrivals from the East' of course form the central theme of this conference. But I wish first to turn away from them, in the direction of an even more central feature of the statement, the claim of unbroken continuity from the 'recently dissolved' Mycenaean world to that of Archaic Greece. The implicit assumption here is that there was no clean break, no interruption of institutions, of contacts, of material culture, between these two episodes in pre-Classical Greece. Elsewhere, this assumption becomes explicit:

'What is a mirage is the Dark Age and the deliberate distance maintained between the second millennium and the culture of Classical Greece'.[2]

Here, belief in some form of 'Dark Age' is seen, and rightly, as the main positive obstacle to the narrative as so far constructed. To believe in a prolonged episode in the history of Greek culture which is palpably different in pattern, both from the Late Bronze Age and from the Archaic period, is close to being a rejection of any continuous cultural tradition between the former and the latter; it maintains 'a deliberate distance'. True, it does not exclude the possibility of revivals; but these would be a conscious phenomenon, one that acknowledges the existence of an interruption by the very attempt to overcome it. This is something different from the case put forward, in which the polis 'arose . . . from the . . . Mycenaean world'.

The mention of the polis brings in a second obstruction, one which – as the words 'not in the eighth century' imply – again derives from conventional belief and practice. By making 'the rise of the polis' into a central theme for archaeological (as well as historical) research, and especially by centering our investigation on the eighth century BC, we prolong the opposing narrative into a further stage:

'Early Greek archaeology [has been turned] into exclusive grist for the mill of the polis, the only currently acceptable goal for politically correct scholarship'.[3]

Finally, both the Late Bronze Age Aegean and Archaic Greece are strongly Orientalising periods. In the field of the visual arts, many of the most impressive Greco-Oriental parallels are between Near Eastern monuments of Bronze Age date, and Greek ones of the seventh and sixth centuries BC; while in literature and mythology, predictably, a similar state of affairs exists, with the earliest Greek testimony coming from Hesiod and Homer. This common debt to the Orient, shared by both Bronze Age and early historical Greece, binds the two of them to each other, as well as bringing them closer to the cultures of the Near East. Indeed,

'The period called 'Orientalising' extends from the Bronze Age to late antiquity, and remains better understood as a dimension of Greek culture rather than a phase'.[4]

At least three separate strands are thus woven together in this series of arguments: first, that the Bronze Age culture of the Aegean has been unwarrantably separated off from its successors of the historical period; secondly, that the instrument used for this amputation has been the narrow focus, in the early historical period, on the rise of the polis; thirdly, that a continuous theme of the debt to the Orient is obscured or even denied by the traditional narrative. These three strands are closely intertwined. The hypothesis of a Dark Age, in which the Orient exercises no significant effect on Greece, interrupts continuity both in general and in this vital respect: hence the call for its elimination. Equally, concentration on the Greek polis, whose exclusivity tended to be ethnic rather than social, discourages paying great attention to the supposed debts to the Near East: hence the call for a wider perspective.

This is not the place to attempt to answer all these arguments. Instead, I shall be concentrating on one particular phase, the end of the Bronze Age. If any separation of Bronze Age from later Greek culture is to be justified, then this is the place to begin. In Greece, it is a time when not only Oriental connections, but also state forms of organisation are, to all appearances, about to cease to exist. If these appearances are not to be dismissed as either illusory, or short-lived and insignificant, phenomena, then some more positive picture of the severance of links with the preceding Mycenaean age can be constructed. That is what I aim to provide in this paper.

My subject is not the 'Bronze Age revival' which so often crops up in the archaeology of Greece in later periods, almost all of it relating to spiritual, artistic and intellectual imagination, and almost all of it concerning practices which first show themselves quite a long time after the end of the Bronze Age. I am concerned instead with much more mundane things: with staying alive (or failing to stay alive and thus needing burial) at a much earlier time, the close of the Bronze Age itself and the immediately ensuing period.

Even when I wrote about it in 1971, it was hardly a new observation that there were strong resemblances between the material culture of mainland Greece in two widely-separated periods, the MBA (Middle Helladic) and the Bronze Age / Iron Age transition, two periods separated by fully five centuries of the Mycenaean age.[5] Axel Persson's observation of 1938, about the 'astounding similarity' in the hand-made pottery found at Asine in the MH settlement and in the PG tombs of the tenth century BC, was an early acknowledgement of one small aspect of this resemblance.[6] I take his statement as a confession that the Asine team could not really tell the two wares apart, from his hint[7] that only the association of the later ware in tombs with painted, wheel-made PG pottery put its dating beyond dispute.

But the real founding father of the broader idea was the late Jean Deshayes, basing his arguments on the burials in the Deiras cemetery at Argos. He argued[8] for the localised survival of unpretentious single burial, most often in cists, right through the Mycenaean age, a period when multiple burial in tholos- and chamber-tombs was prevalent and, in some opinions, pretty well universal. This view clashed with the prevalent opinion, then recently propounded by Vincent Desborough, that single burial was an intrusive re-introduction, from northern Greece, in the closing phase of the Bronze Age. Perhaps unsurprisingly, Deshayes' theory of the survival of a Middle Bronze Age substrate met with a chilly reception from the Mycenologists, who did not like the thought of pockets of recusant provincials marring the grandeur of their vision of imperial Mycenae and, worse still, outliving that grandeur to inherit its legacy themselves.

Undeterred, I tried to work Deshayes' observations into a wider pattern of survival (rather than mere revival) of Middle Helladic material culture down to this much later age: tomb-types, and especially cist-burial, might form the heart of this case, but it could be extended into at least three other areas, domestic architecture, pottery manufacture and decoration, and metal-use (or rather non-use); and to yet broader aspects, such as the complete absence of fortified settlements at both periods. I think it is a fair summary to say that, in the narrower respect of the origins of tomb-types, the 'Helladic survival' view has come to prevail over the 'northern intruder' explanation; but that the broader idea has been largely neglected.

Briefly to sketch the similarities between the two main periods under discussion: in the burial sphere, variations of the cist, using rougher stones rather than well-shaped slabs, simple pit-burials in the earth, and vessel-burials, for adults as well as for children, are also very widespread in both the Middle Helladic and the final Bronze to early Iron Ages. Many specimens of cists in, for example, the Middle Helladic cemetery at Asine[9] show resemblances to later practices of the Early Iron Age. The resemblances are not limited to the basic use of single burial in slab-cists, but also show the phenomenon of contracted burial in very similar pose, bridging some 1000 years from beginning to end. This is important, because it is one of the things that tells against the 'intrusive northerners' theory of the later wave of cist-burial: many cists exist in contemporary northern Greece, but the burials in them are invariably extended. One other, very local parallel at Asine in the Argolid should be noted here: the Middle Helladic cemetery contained a number of stone structures which were at first taken for tombs and then, when they proved to be either solid or empty, reinterpreted as grave-altars: the same feature recurs among the Protogeometric graves there.[10]

With domestic architecture, the salient fact is a very obvious one: apsidal plans are the commonest house-form, apparently at all levels of society, in both Middle Bronze and Early Iron Ages, but not in between. Classic examples such as those from Middle Helladic Lerna V[11] can be closely compared with the biggest unit in Iron Age Nichoria, IV.1.[12] All manner of explanations have been given for the adoption of, or reversion to, apsidal plans, ranging from the desire to avoid projecting corners for mud-brick walls, to a break-down of standard brick-sizes, or a deep-seated appeal of the apsidal plan to nomadic mentalities. Fascinating though this topic is, nothing approaching a consensus has been achieved and I pass over it for now: it is enough to stress that choosing the form for a domestic structure is a very basic cultural decision, taken only after deliberation about much profounder issues than mere fashion. If, as I believe, the internal organisation of room-use was also closely similar in both periods, then that is even more important.

We have already touched on ceramic issues, with Axel Persson's early observation about the resemblances in hand-made pottery. One could broaden this by emphasizing that the mere prevalence of hand-made pottery, both in Middle Helladic times and in the final Bronze and earliest Iron Ages, is something far stronger than in the intervening Mycenaean period. A Middle Helladic woman at Asine[13] symbolically clutches such a jar, and five centuries later similar things were again appearing. On decorated wheel-made pottery, one cannot make so forceful a claim, and I am not going to pretend that excavators have difficulty in distinguishing Middle Helladic matt-painted from Submycenaean or Protogeometric wares. I am going to say, however, that the actual makers of these wares sometimes show a strikingly similar decorative repertoire. For example, a painted early MH jug from Asine[14] is a kind of portable anthology of motifs which were to enjoy a long after-life, particularly if we concentrate on the 'peripheral' zones of the Early Iron Age, where what we think of as characteristic Protogeometric motifs like the concentric semicircle did not prevail. What we have here, instead, is cross-hatched triangles, swastikas and zig-zag lines. In a group of sherds from Iron Age Nichoria[15] we can see, not just triangles, but cross-hatched triangles, with the notion of parallel outer frames for the triangles. Plenty of other examples could be given from Western Greek 'Dark Age ware'.

On metal usage, I can be brief. We call the Middle Helladic the middle period of the Bronze Age, but all specialists who study settlement material know what a misnomer this is. In what is much the clearest study of a single Middle Helladic settlement in its own right, Gullög Nordquist[16] catalogues from MH Asine some 26 bronze objects, plus 17 lead and 4 in other metals. Set this against her 102 finds in bone, antler and tusk, 124 in ground stone, and 67 in obsidian, flint and chert and you get a representative picture of settlement debris: under 8% of the implements in the so-called Middle Bronze Age were actually of bronze. Of course, as she points out, the inhabitants may well have taken greater care to retain the metal objects when abandoning the site. But the comparison remains fair with the use of iron in the Early Iron Age settlements studied in Ian Morris' article on the early use of iron,[17] where again we are not dealing with destruction-levels, but with peaceful abandonment of sites. Once again (with iron replacing bronze in most contexts) we find that we are in an age where ordinary domestic life seems to have depended little on metal, and much more on tools of stone and bone (Karphi is a prize example from the final Bronze Age, Thorikos, Zagora and Koukounaries of the developed Iron Age). The one exception that Morris acknowledges is in buildings that had a prominent social or religious function: Unit IV. 1 at Nichoria (and for that matter Room 17 at Vrokastro in Crete) are instances where metals were found in quantity in and round an abandoned building. This is important in showing that, in certain circumstances, metal *could* survive the desertion of the site, and it strengthens the significance of its absence from the more standard domestic assemblages. Dark Age Nichoria evidently enjoyed freer use of metals than MH Asine, over a period of perhaps similar length, but its metal inventory is boosted by the particular status of Unit IV.1, which on its own produced nearly half the metal objects of the earliest phase. On the other hand, ninth-century Thorikos in Attica (apparently no metals at all), eighth-century Lefkandi (one or two iron finds against a large number of stone tools), and the eighth-century settlement at Zagora on Andros, where obsidian and other stone finds outnumber metal ones, even in the choice selection of finds exhibited in the museum, do strongly recall the Middle Helladic picture.[18]

My first attempt to sketch these parallels was tentative because, like everyone else, I was overawed by the sheer length of the chronological gap which it seemed to involve: 500 years at the least. But there are in fact not one but two alternative lines of explanation, competing or complementary, for what I shall describe: first, in terms of local revival after a chronological gap; secondly, in terms of geographical spread. What I shall be suggesting today is that recent discoveries have enabled us to explore the second, to switch our attention away from the narrowly chronological problem, to take account of a more complex *geographical* pattern. As well as searching for stray surviving strands to bridge the gap of time in the Mycenaean heartlands, we should look away to the peripheral lands to the immediate west and north, where the penetration of Mycenaean material culture had always been shallower. The Middle Helladic culture, by contrast, was *everyone's* heritage in mainland Greece. Today, after a century of concentration on the heart of Mycenaean culture in the Late Bronze Age and the excavation of its central sites, archaeological activity has suddenly burgeoned in these peripheral areas.

The map of the four larger Aegean 'super-regions' in Ian Morris' recent chapter in *New Light on a Dark Age*[19] demarcates exactly the area that I shall mostly talk about, the horizontally-shaded zone which he calls 'Western Greece' – an approximate name, since it extends eastwards almost to the longitude of Athens, but it will do. Morris was out to distinguish its material culture in a much later period, but it is distinctive already at the close of the Bronze Age, as we shall see. We shall carry out a rapid tour of this zone, concentrating on the two periods that concern us today. The kind of sites we shall be looking at are, ideally, those where both the Middle Helladic and the very end of the Bronze Age are strongly represented, but where the site's importance in the Mycenaean age appears to have been slighter: Nichoria in Messenia is an example that comes to mind; Lefkandi in Euboea is another (though its Middle Helladic levels have yet to be fully published). But there are whole regions elsewhere where something similar seems to hold good.

I begin with a preliminary demographic point, illustrated by Maps 4 and 5 in the Hope Simpson / Dickinson *Gazetteer of Aegean Civilisation in the Bronze Age*.[20] The map covering the 14th and 13th centuries, the Mycenaean heyday, and the corresponding one for the final phase of the Bronze Age, show, predictably, not only very different overall densities of sites, with a large reduction in the later period; but also a swing in the balance in distribution. In the Late Helladic IIIA2/IIIB map, there is a reasonable balance between the 'Central Greece' and 'Western Greece' zones as defined in Ian Morris' map, with the major cluster in Messenia being more or less matched by the cluster extending from the Argolid up into Attica and Boeotia. In the IIIC/Submycenaean map, there is clearly a better tendency for survival in the 'Western Greek' sector: about 50 of the 80-odd sites lie here. The shift is in itself entirely predictable and has often been noted: whatever the forces that overthrew the Mycenaean palatial centres, their impact would be expected to be less pronounced, the further you move away from the palaces.

But it introduces us to the importance of this 'peripheral zone'. Within it, Messenia is exemplified by Nichoria, at which we have already looked: a site well away from the palatial centre at Pylos, a site whose importance in the Middle Helladic and Early Iron Age periods seems to have been greater, relative to that of its peers, than in the intervening Mycenaean age. But neither this nor any other Messenian site seems to offer the classic evidence of Middle Helladic survival that I am looking for: cists and other single burials, for example, are not characteristic of this region. Nor are these features represented very fully in the other Peloponnesian regions of this 'western zone': all that we can say is that they include some rare cases, north of the Alpheios valley, where the *absolute* count of sites remains the same on the second map as the first.

For a more positive picture, it is north of the Corinthian Gulf that we have to look. We begin with the case of Aitolia, represented by that really interesting sanctuary-site, Thermon. Here the enigmatic sequence of buildings has taken the best part of a century to unravel, through the cumulative efforts of Sotiriadis, Rhomaios, Drerup, Wesenburg, Mazarakis-Ainian and now Papapostolou.[21] It is the oldest structure, Megaron A, which is of greatest interest here. The latest investigations by Ioannis Papapostolou have, I think, established three major points about its history. First, although its apsidal plan had led many architectural specialists to assume a Middle Helladic date for it, this is not certainly the case. There was Middle Helladic activity at Thermon, but all that we know for sure is that the other, probably contemporary, curvilinear buildings round Megaron A underwent destruction in Late Helladic IIA, to which all the dateable pottery belongs; and there is no reason to think that they had existed for anything approaching a period of centuries before that.

(In passing, it is fascinating to know that in 1907 Sotiriadis, the first excavator, took Megaron A to be Geometric (8th century) in , date – perhaps the first archaeologist to fall victim to the deceptive resemblances which this paper is about). Secondly, it is now known that Megaron A was both visible and respected, continuously down to that moment when Megaron B, which so exactly copies the orientation of Megaron A, was constructed, and probably for a while longer. Thirdly, that moment has been shown to have been decidedly earlier than many of us had held, belonging close to the beginning of the Iron Age and certainly not later than the 10th century BC. These findings have the effect of bringing Megara A and B together in time. They have also provided us with an example of a major apsidal building, probably built and certainly standing in the earlier Mycenaean period. But, more important still, they offer a clear instance of the direct influence of essentially Middle Bronze Age material culture on that of the Iron Age: hitherto, this had been no more than a surmise in the case of Thermon. Perhaps the Iron Age 'Head Man' saw a genuine Bronze Age chieftain's house as a fit model.

Moving eastwards into Phokis, we come to another rural sanctuary site that has acquired recent fame, Kalapodi, near ancient Hyampolis. Here it is less the structures than the dedications which have provided us with the best-documented case, on the whole of the Greek mainland, for continuity of worship from the very late (LHIIIC) Bronze Age right down into the historical period, by which time it had acquired the identity of a joint sanctuary of Artemis and Apollo.[22] The first built temple here was also probably very early. A whole picture is beginning to form, in this area of central Greece, in which instead of a terminal disaster near the close of the Bronze Age, a strong element of survival and continuity through into the Iron Age is the dominant theme.

That on its own, however, is not enough for my case. I have to show that the Bronze Age culture that survived itself preserved traces of the much earlier Middle Bronze Age. We have already seen one significant hint of this in the apsidal form of Megaron A at Thermon, a probable 'Mycenaean' structure in terms of conventional chronology, but of a form that belongs firmly in the Middle Helladic. But for the best exemplification of this, we move to my concluding region, Eastern Lokris, and the excavations of Phanouria Dakoronia, the Ephor at Lamia. When we 'home in' on the scene of her main activities in the 1980's and 1990's (well shown in one of her published maps),[23] a series of major sites enter the picture.

The map in question covers only a very restricted area of coastal Lokris, running inland from the Gulf of Atalanti and today dominated by the sizeable town of Atalanti itself. We encounter a kind of funerary time-warp with several different dimensions: from Pyrgos Livanaton in the north, with its intra-mural burials in both Middle Helladic and the Early Iron Age, to a site near Megaplatanos where a cemetery of pithos-burials proved to belong to the fifth and fourth centuries BC – connoisseurs of prehistoric burial-forms will recognize this as an extraordinarily late survival of its kind – to Atalanti (where there are graves of the 8th century which, from their external appearance, might well have been assigned to the 18th). For Eastern Lokris at last delivers the missing central piece of the jigsaw, the retention of single burial, especially but not only in cists, right the way through the Middle and Late Bronze Ages and beyond – though not to the exclusion of chamber-tombs, which occur at the two sites called Palaiokastra, in one case showing re-use down to Roman times!

But the perfect demonstration comes from an earlier and much remoter site in central Greece, some way to the west. I have several times in this paper referred to the difficulties encountered by excavators in deciding the date of pottery, of structures, and especially of graves, as between the Middle Helladic period and much later times. Now we come to an instance where the debate has involved others besides the excavator, and has already lasted more than a decade. This is the cemetery site of Marmara, of which Ph. Dakoronia gave a full and informative publication in 1987. It lies almost literally 'off the map', on the western slopes of Mt. Oeta.[24]

The first thing to stress about Marmara is its altitude. Oeta itself rises to over 7000 feet (some 2200m.), and the Marmara tumuli are around the 1300m. contour: to compare it with two other notoriously high-lying archaeological sites in Greece, the peak of Megali Koprana above Karphi is itself only just over 1200m., with Karphi lying in the saddle below it; while the settlement at Vitsa Zagoriou in Epiros has the 1040m. contour running through it, with the cemeteries lying just above. So the Marmara burials outdo both of these in altitude; the accompanying settlement has yet to be found, but one assumes it cannot have been inconveniently far below.

Here among the pine trees, a series of nine low tumuli were excavated, and each of them proved to cover a cluster of cist-tombs (on average, just over six). The burials were contracted, and the excavator induced one of her workmen to demonstrate their capacity to accommodate an adult, in the familiar pose which we have seen in so many periods that we almost come to think of it as timeless.[25] The grave-goods were very sparse, but fortunately enough to be – in my opinion if not those of all Bronze Age experts – chronologically decisive. Most of the pottery-shapes, in the excavator's words, 'remind [us] intensely of Middle Helladic'. Indeed they do: there are hand-made vessels reminiscent of the very first Middle Helladic specimens that we looked at from Asine.[26] The arrangement of the cists under tumuli did nothing to undermine this apparent dating, because tumulus-burial prevails over a wide area of the western Greek mainland from at least the Middle Helladic period on. But one or two of the burials contained metal objects which threw out this whole pattern of dating. There were two bronze dress-pins, one indeed of a Middle Helladic type, the other[27] a disc-and-globe-headed pin of a type which makes a sudden and unprecedented appearance in Greece in the cemeteries of the very end of the Bronze Age. They place the burial unquestionably no earlier than the eleventh century BC. The vessel in this same interment, A2, is an amphora with the form and decoration of similar date. Again, there are three bronze knives in two different interments, of which two are loosely Mycenaean, the third[28] with the flange-hilted form of Sandars Type F, which is not known anywhere till just before 1200 BC. There are also two pots from yet other graves which imitate 13th-century shapes, one of them a hand-made alabastron or pyxis,[29] providing at least a *terminus post quem* for two more cists. (Note that each one of the finds that I have listed comes from a different burial). So what is going on here? Have we a burial-site which was used intermittently for 500 years? Against this perhaps natural inference, there is the excavator's word that 'the resemblance in the technique of all the pots (clay and baking) shows that there is no great length of time among them'; and, following her own logic, she dates the entire cemetery to the eleventh century BC. The interpretation of this site is complex. All the same, I was surprised when I consulted Bronze Age specialists to ask 'what the word was' about Marmara, and was told 'It's essentially a Middle Helladic site'.[30] This opinion violates a central principle of archaeology, that we date a deposit by its latest element. Of course, the possibility of continuous use over a half-millennium can be argued for; but that line of reasoning seems to me to involve just the kind of rigidly traditionalist thought, based above all on pottery-styles, which I have been trying to escape from in this paper. It seems to me much more likely that Dakoronia is simply right: that she has found a remote burial-site of the eleventh century in which the funerary practices and much of the pottery testify to an unbroken tradition reaching far back into the past.

Marmara thus exemplifies to perfection what was missing from my argument of 1971: a peripheral survival of an essentially Middle Helladic culture to the very end of the Bronze Age, a phenomenon which we now learn is especially well documented in the region of Dolopia and Eastern Lokris, but some aspects of which appear all round the western and northern fringes of the Mycenaean heart-land, and which surfaces even in more or less central, but at the time relatively minor, sites like Asine and Argos. What we have seen is, to put it plainly, that a material culture that once prevailed all over central and southern Greece (in the Middle Helladic) was largely, but not entirely, pushed out to the margins of the succeeding culture (the Mycenaean), before once again prevailing over a large part of the original area, in the final Bronze and initial Iron Ages. Even in the Mycenaean heart-land, single burial may have been relatively rare, but this misses the main point. The question is not whether cists and other single tombs were *common* in the Late Bronze Age – although they certainly were in the peripheral regions, including Thessaly[31] which I have left out of my account – but whether they were known at all.

If this summary account be accepted, then it remains to suggest how it affects our broader interpretation of the culture processes at work in such cases. How are we to understand the significance of such a pattern of resemblances? I have concentrated on the funerary side because so many of the sites offer only this kind of evidence. But clearly the similarity in house-plans is of at least equal significance: standing apsidal houses in, say, 1100 BC could probably be seen much nearer to the Mycenaean heartland than at Thermon. The parallel reversion to stone and bone tools, at the expense of metal ones, tells us that circumstances were similar in one absolutely vital field, technology and the working of materials. The re-emergence of pottery-techniques and fabrics, in a form hard to distinguish from Middle Helladic, illustrates the position in one particular branch of technology. Only the reappearance of MH motifs in decorated pottery can be dismissed as a matter of fashion. In other words, as I said at the outset, this is not so much a question of conscious cultural imitation, as of the serious adaptation or readaptation of life's fundamental activities to a time-honoured pattern. I would cite here the late James Hooker's summing-up of the funerary case in 1977: he ascribed the resurgence of single burial 'not to the advent of newcomers who had not known the Mycenaeans, but to a deliberate rejection of

former practice by those who knew them all too well'.[32] This is perhaps an over-enthusiastic claim; apart from anything else, it raises the
unwanted spectre of an ethnic difference between the Mycenaeans
and the 'single buriers', whereas my case is one of essential ethnic
continuity.

The recently-propounded view that the Dark Age itself is an out-
dated fantasy depends crucially on a belief that the societies of the
Early Iron Age retained most of what had been significant in Mycenaean culture – including its political structures and especially the
links of Mycenaean culture with the Eastern Mediterranean. Personally, I hold that they retained rather little, and that that little then
dwindled away to almost nothing, until some elements were artifi-
cially revived in the late eighth century BC and later. But quite apart
from that, my account of the processes at the very end of the Bronze
Age, if accepted, would make for the worst possible circumstances
for retaining those overseas links. The revival of the practices of the
Middle Helladic culture, perhaps the least 'Orientalizing' one in
Greece after Neolithic times, implied among other things the dis-
carding of all the mechanisms by which the Mycenaean palaces had
maintained contact with Western Asia. By accepting Middle Helladic
ways as appropriate for resumption in their own world, the population of mainland Greece were implicitly turning their backs on all
such connections.

It is a nice irony that Lefkandi, the site without which none of
the arguments cited at the beginning would have been advanced in
so strong a form (whether about the continuity of the polis, or more
especially about the survival of the oriental links of the Mycenaean
world) was a Middle Helladic site with a thin Mycenaean occupation, to which a return in force was evidently made only in the final
stages of the Bronze Age. By their very choice of such a site, one
group of Greeks in the twelfth century BC made a kind of statement about the rejection of Mycenaean culture, leaving it to their
descendants to rebuild the Near Eastern links on an entirely fresh
basis.

NOTES

1. Sarah P. Morris, *Daidalos and the Origins of Greek Art* (Princeton,
   1992), p. 124.
2. John K. Papadopoulos, 'To Kill a Cemetery: The Athenian Kerameikos
   and the Early Iron Age in the Aegean' *JMA* 6 (1993), p. 195.

3. Sarah P. Morris, 'Greek and Near Eastern art in the Age of Homer', in S. Langdon (ed.), *New Light on a Dark Age: Exploring the Culture of Geometric Greece* (Columbia, Mo., 1997), pp. 56–71, at p. 64.

4. Morris, *Daidalos* (n. 1 above), p. 130.

5. In *The Dark Age of Greece* (Edinburgh, 1971), pp. 383–86.

6. In O. Frödin–A. W. Persson, *Asine* (Stockholm, 1938), p. 279.

7. *Ibid.*, p. 436.

8. In *Argos: Les fouilles de la Deiras* (Paris, 1966), pp. 240–42, 249–50.

9. As shown in G. Nordquist, *A Middle Helladic Village: Asine in the Argolid* (Uppsala, 1987), p. 192, fig. 95.

10. Persson, *op.cit.* (above, n. 6), pp. 347, 426; but for a different interpretation of the 'tomb-altars', see Nordquist, *op.cit.* (above, n. 9), 105.

11. As in J. L. Caskey, 'Excavations at Lerna, 1952–53', *Hesperia* 23 (1954), pp. 3–30, fig. 2 at p. 13.

12. W. A. McDonald and others, *Excavations at Nichoria* iii: *the Dark Age and Byzantine Occupations* (Minneapolis, 1983), pp. 19–42.

13. Nordquist(above, n. 9), p. 9, fig. 1.

14. Nordquist (above, n. 9), p. 167, fig. 34.

15. McDonald and others (above, n. 12), p. 149, fig. 3–33.

16. Nordquist (above, n. 9), pp. 112–127.

17. 'Circulation, Deposition and the Formation of the Greek Iron Age', *Man* 24 (1989), pp. 502–519.

18. Nichoria is discussed by Morris, *ibid.*, pp. 511–12; for Thorikos, no metal finds seem to be mentioned in the preliminary publications of the Geometric settlement (in H. F. Mussche and others, *Thorikos* ii: *1964* and iii *1965* (both Bruxelles, 1967); for Lefkandi, see M. R. Popham – L. H. Sackett–P. G. Themelis, *Lefkandi* i: *the Iron Age* (Londong, 1980), and compare the number of tools in stone and bone at pp. 85, nos. 1–8, 11–15 (with comment at pp. 81–2) and p. 88, nos. 88–90, with the metal tools or weapons at p. 88, nos. 76–82 (bronze) and 86–87 (iron); for Zagora, see A. Cambitoglou and others, *Zagora* ii (Athens, 1988) for the ten obsidian tools (pp. 230, 245–47), one or two bronze (p. 232, [d],[e]) and six iron tools (pp. 233–34, [a]–[d]) found in the 1969 excavation; and for the museum exhibits, A. Cambitoglou, *The Archaeological Museum of Andros* (Athens, 1981), pp. 76, 79–80 (some 27 stone and obsidian utilitarian objects) with pp. 34–5 (6 iron objects from Areas I–II) and 81 (2 bronze and 2 iron from Area V), from the settlement areas only.

19. 'The art of citizenship', in S. Langdon (ed.), *New Light on a Dark Age* (above, n. 3), pp. 9–43; map, fig. 2 at p. 19.

20. R. Hope Simpson–O. T. P. K. Dickinson, *Gazetteer of Aegean Civilisation in the Bronze Age i: The Mainland and Islands* (Göteborg, 1979), Maps 4 and 5.

21. I. A. Papapostolou, 'Thermos', *ADelt* 1990, pp. 191–200.

22. See most recently R. Felsch, 'Kalapodi Bericht 1978–82', *AA* 1987, 1–99 and *Kalapodi* i (Mainz, 1996).

23. See Ph. Dakoronia, 'Homeric Towns in Eastern Lokris: Problems of Identification', *Hesperia* 62 (1993), pp. 115–27; map, fig. 1 at p. 116.

24. Ph. Dakoronia, *Marmara: ta ypomykenaika nekrotafeia ton tymbon* (Athens, 1987). Had the site been found before 1979, it would appear towards the bottom right-hand corner of Map J in Hope Simpson and Dickinson's *Gazetteer* (above, n. 20).

25. Dakoronia, *op.cit.* (above, n. 24), fig. 117.

26. For example, Dakoronia, *ap.cit.* (above, n. 24), figs. 64 and 92, from tombs D2 and E5.

27. Dakoronia, *op.cit.* (above, n. 24), fig. 6, from Tomb A2.

28. Dakoronia, *op.cit.* (above, n. 24), fig. 89, from Tomb E4.

29. Dakoronia, *op.cit.* (above, n. 24), fig. 68, from Tomb D4.

30. Doubtless influenced by the arguments of Joseph Maran, 'Zur Zeitstellung der Grabhügel von Marmara (Mittelgriechenland)', *Archäologisches Korrespondenzblatt* 18 (1988), pp. 341–55.

31. See the important Late Bronze Age cist cemetery at Iolkos, D. R. and M. Theocharis, 'Iolkos', *AAA* 3 (1970), pp. 198–203, with a later report in *Archaeological Reports* 38 (1991–92), p. 40.

32. J. T. Hooker, *Mycenaean Greece* (London, 1977), p. 179.

CHAPTER 10

An Historical Homeric Society?

This is a paper, now over thirty years old, which I was persuaded, against my first inclination, to include in this collection. It poses a rhetorical question to which my own answer was a resounding 'no'. It exemplifies a rare excursion into social anthropology, but that was not the reason for my original intention to exclude it. Rather, it was the long and detailed critique of some its arguments in yet another paper by Ian Morris (Morris 1986: 105–14), and his pertinent implication that I had done less than justice to the earlier article by W. K. Lacey cited in notes 14 and 21.

The issues this time are not ones that can be empirically tested by archaeological discovery. Nor should they be settled by counting heads: here, it is enough to say that, since the publication of Morris's article in 1986, both sides have, remarkably, continued to enlist more or less equally weighty support: Raaflaub 1998, 174 with nn. 24, 25 and Burgess 2001, 50 with n. 10 offer helpful roll-calls of the holders of the rival views.

There are two important factors which differentially affect the 'playing field' on which this controversy is enacted. First, the supporters of a unified and historical Homeric society have to face (as their opponents do not) the immediately ensuing question: so when did such a society exist in Greece? It is interesting, to say the least, that they have given such conflicting answers to this second question: the tenth and ninth centuries BC (Finley 1956, 55, in the fundamental study that provoked my paper), the late ninth and early eighth centuries (Raaflaub 1993, 45 and 1996, 628), the eighth century (Morris 1986: 127–9) or the seventh (Taplin 1992: 33–5). The intended effect of the last two answers was to make this 'Homeric society' the one in which the poet himself lived. The difficulties have since been compounded by another recent tendency, in which some of these writers have themselves joined (see again Burgess's note, above), to move the date of Homer's lifetime down into the seventh century.

Second, believers in a unified Homeric society have to reckon with the fact that, even if the conclusions that I reached about the inconsistencies in the specific field of marriages in Homer are entirely flawed, the unitary nature of that society is not thereby proven: there are plenty of other categories of evidence which would need to be examined first.

The controversy is one that will long continue: a notable recent instalment is to be found in Raaflaub 1998. This contribution to it is offered in full acceptance of that fact.

BIBLIOGRAPHY

Burgess, J. S. (2001), *The Tradition of the Trojan War in Homer and the Epic Cycle*, Baltimore and London: Johns Hopkins University Press.

Finley, M. I. (1956), *The World of Odysseus* (rev. edn.), London: Chatto and Windus.

Morris, I. (1986), 'The use and abuse of Homer', *Classical Antiquity* 5: 81–138.

Raaflaub, K. (1993), 'Homer to Solon: the rise of the polis: the written sources', in *The Ancient Greek City-State*, ed. M. H. Hansen, Copenhagen: Munksgaard, pp. 41–105.

Raaflaub, K. (1996), 'Homeric society', in *A New Companion to Homer*, ed. I. Morris and B. Powell, Leiden: E. J. Brill, pp. 624–48.

Raaflaub, K. (1998), 'A historian's headache: how to read "Homeric society"?', in *Archaic Greece: New Approaches and New Evidence*, ed. N. Fisher and H. Van Wees, London: Duckworth, pp. 169–93.

Taplin, O. (1992), *Homeric Soundings*, Oxford: Clarendon Press.

I begin with two modern texts, both as it happens printed on the first page of earlier issues of this journal, and each, I think, expressive of a strong body of opinion in Homeric scholarship, at least in the English-speaking countries, at the time of their writing. First, Miss Dorothea Gray in 1954: 'Belief in an historical Homeric society dies hard'.[1] Secondly, Professor Adkins in 1971: 'I find it impossible to believe . . . that the bards of the oral tradition invented out of their own imaginations a society with institutions, values, beliefs and attitudes

'An historical Homeric society?', *Journal of Hellenic Studies* 94, 1974, 114–25.

all so coherent and mutually appropriate as I believe myself to discern in the Homeric poems. This aspect of the poems is based upon some society's experience'.[2] Miss Gray's prophecy, whether or not one shares the misgivings that it embodied, was thus soundly-based: the seventeen years between these two quotations have indeed witnessed a powerful revival of the belief that the social system portrayed in the Homeric poems, and with it such attendant features as the ethical code and the political structure, are in large measure both unitary and historical. One good reason for the vitality of this belief is the simple fact that it has been alive since Classical times. Another is that it has received support from several influential recent works: if pride of place should be given to M. I. Finley's *The World of Odysseus*, on whose conclusions Professor Adkins expressly says that he takes his stand,[3] a number of others should be acknowledged also. Whereas Finley located the social system of the *Odyssey* most probably in the tenth and ninth centuries BC, A. Andrewes in his book *The Greeks* extends this type of inference when he argues for an historical origin in the 'migration period' of the twelfth and eleventh centuries for the Homeric political system.[4] As influences on the other side, one may mention T. B. L. Webster's work in isolating Mycenaean practices and features, whose divisive effect on the social pattern is apparent;[5] while G. S. Kirk has a significantly entitled chapter in his *The Songs of Homer*, 'The cultural and linguistic *amalgam*' (my italics).[6] Most recently, the early chapters in the German *Archaeologia Homerica*[7] have shown a certain tendency to discern a consistent and historical pattern in the allied area of the material and technological practices of the poems. It is true that in one chapter the author is led to conclude that the metallurgical picture of the *Iliad* is substantially earlier than that of the *Odyssey*, and that the date of composition of the former poem must accordingly be very much earlier.[8] But this is only because he is pressing the arguments for the 'historical' case one step further: the historical consistency of the metallurgical pictures in each of the two poems is, for him, so apparent and so precise that each can and must be given an historical setting, even if the two are separated by a long period.

Unity of authorship and background between the *Iliad* and *Odyssey* is indeed a quite separate issue, though an important one; the division of opinion here may cut right across the line of division as to whether Homeric society is historical or not. But it is an important element of Professor Adkins' argument that he maintains the identity of the social system as between the *Iliad* and *Odyssey*; and that he links the equally unitary Homeric ethical code with this social system. Not all scholars would agree with this; indeed the 'fundamental differences ... in their social and ethical relations' were among the factors which led Professor Page[9] to conclude that the same man did not compose the *Iliad* and *Odyssey*. I do not wish to enter this debate, since to do so would be to beg the question on which I wish to argue, namely whether the social system is consistent and identical *within* each poem. But, for what it is worth, my inclination is to fall back on the familiar observation that the one poem shows the heroic world on a war footing, while the other shows it at peace; and to attribute the differences rather to this than to any deeper dichotomy.

If, therefore, it seems reasonable to follow Adkins in speaking of a 'Homeric society' common to both poems, we can now proceed to the central question. Do the features of this society show the degree of coherence and mutual appropriateness that Professor Adkins sees, and which is perhaps a necessary precondition of that society's being historical?[10] First, there is a subsidiary question which may arise, since a precondition need not be a guarantee: even if the society is shown to be so cohesive, will that necessarily make it historical? Could there not be other explanations of such a picture, if it were shown to exist? Perhaps an oral poèt of genius could construct a truly consistent society, by sifting and selecting the traditional material at his disposal, and shaping it to fit the elements of his own creation – one more consistent, indeed, than the untidy compromises which history often produces. At least one scholar[11] has pursued this line of argument, to arrive at the opposite conclusion to that of Adkins: Homer's society is idealised, and cannot represent any single historical society, because it is *too* cohesive and unmixed. Another approach is that of A. A. Long, who has both expressed doubt about Adkins' conclusion and challenged the basis for it; 'The plain fact is', he writes, 'that a consistent pattern of society does not emerge from Homer'.[12] This and other arguments lead him to doubt Adkins' assumptions that Homeric society has 'some autonomous existence, outside the poems', or that Homer is concerned to represent 'the life and values of any actual society'.[13] Faced with this bewildering conflict of views, one might be tempted to abandon all hope of reaching a conclusion. Let us, however, postpone such despair until it is forced upon us, and return to our primary question.

It is perhaps most fruitful to concentrate on institutions, where the arguments have a better chance of being of a factual nature. The field of marriage settlements has long proved an attractive one here.

Homeric marriages present a number of apparently inconsistent features; but scholars have argued that these 'inconsistencies' are in part the result of misunderstanding,[14] or alternatively that, though real, they are nevertheless compatible with a single and historical social system.[15] Let us first look at the Homeric evidence. It is commonplace, in both poems, for a marriage to be accompanied or preceded by lavish gifts from the suitor to the bride's kin.[16] But alongside this picture of what E. R. Dodds has called 'women at a premium', we also have 'women at a discount'; again, instances of the situation in which a dowry is paid by the bride's kin to the bride and bridegroom occur in both poems.[17] Rather than simply asking whether both practices could co-exist in a single social system, we should do better to call in anthropological evidence on this whole matter. For a start, this will tell us that any simple division into 'bride-price' and 'dowry' practices is misleading. Human societies also show a third common practice known as 'indirect dowry', in which the groom pays over property to the bride, which is then used to endow the newly-established household. It is called indirect dowry because it shares with the plain dowry system this aim of conferring property upon the newly-married couple. But if marriage-settlements are described in careless or poetic language, there is a likelihood that *indirect dowry* and *bride-price* will become confused, since these are the two situations in which the bridegroom has to pay.

To return to Homer. It could be argued that the confusion just mentioned has happened in the interpretation of the Homeric poems; that some or all of the so-called 'bride-price' practices noted in Homer (above, n. 16) are in reality cases of indirect dowry; indeed a somewhat similar line of argument, although with very different terminology, was followed as long ago as 1912 by G. Finsler.[18] If this were true, it would much increase the likelihood that Homer's picture of marriage-settlements is unified and consistent, for dowry and indirect dowry were and are to this day often found together in the same society. But this explanation, although attractive in a number of cases, fails when it encounters a hard core of episodes which cannot be cases of indirect dowry, since we are explicitly told that it is the bride's kin (usually her father) who secure the suitor's gifts, and not the bride.[19] To cite three *Odyssey* passages: Eumaeus relates that King Laertes and his wife married their daughter off to someone in Same, ʽΣάμηνδ᾽ ἔδοσαν καὶ μυρί᾽ ἕλοντο (ο 367); then there is the story of Neleus offering his daughter's hand in return for the cattle of Phylakos (ο 231); again and most explicit of all, Hephaistos on detecting Aphrodite in adultery threatens to make her father Zeus hand back '$\pi\acute{\alpha}\nu\tau\alpha$ .... $\overset{,}{\dot{\epsilon}}\epsilon\delta\nu\alpha$ | $\overset{,}{o}\sigma\sigma\alpha$ $o\overset{,}{\iota}$ $\dot{\epsilon}\gamma\gamma\upsilon\acute{\alpha}\lambda\iota\xi\alpha$ $\kappa\upsilon\nu\acute{\omega}\pi\iota\delta o\varsigma$ $\epsilon\overset{,}{\iota}\nu\epsilon\kappa\alpha$ $\kappa o\acute{\upsilon}\rho\eta\varsigma$' ($\theta$ 318). It seems more than likely that each of the three forms of marriage prestation mentioned above is present in Homer.

What is the likelihood of the co-existence of all these practices in a single society? It will probably be sufficient to concentrate on the two extreme practices of dowry and 'bride-price' (I retain the inverted commas for a reason that will shortly be explained), for a society combining these two might be expected to take indirect dowry in its stride. Theoretically at least, one and the same society could combine these two practices in one and the same marriage; or it could use them on different marriage-occasions in the same social milieu; or it could practise them in marriages at two different social levels. The third of these possibilities is the easiest to envisage, and is indeed well-attested in the anthropological record;[20] but it will not do for Homer, since the Homeric passages on marriage are almost exclusively concerned with the practices of one class, the $\overset{,}{\alpha}\rho\iota\sigma\tau o\iota$. There remain the other two alternatives. Of these the first possibility, whereby both practices take place together on the same occasion, has been advocated in another closely-argued study by M. I. Finley (above, n. 14). He believes that the so-called 'bride-price' in Homer is not a price at all, but a gift of goods passing from the bridegroom (and sometimes also from unsuccessful suitors) to the bride's father, which had its recompense in a counter-gift or dowry, from which he and his wife would benefit, and in the wife herself; together these would be equated in value, as far as possible, with the gifts passing in the other direction, to make a fair exchange. To this view there is at least one objection: that in all the Homeric reference to marriages, there is only one doubtful case, so far as I know, in which the two contrasting practices seem to be associated with one and the same marriage. The possible instance is the marriage of Hektor and Andromache.[21] In X 472 we are told that Hektor won his wife '$\dot{\epsilon}\pi\epsilon\grave{\iota}$ $\pi\acute{o}\rho\epsilon$ $\mu\upsilon\rho\acute{\iota}\alpha$ $\overset{,}{\epsilon}\delta\nu\alpha$'; while in Z 394 and X 88 Andromache is described as $\pi o\lambda\acute{\upsilon}\delta\omega\rho o\varsigma$. Both phrases are in some degree ambiguous: the former, a much-repeated formula, does not identify the recipient of the $\mu\upsilon\rho\acute{\iota}\alpha$ $\overset{,}{\epsilon}\delta\nu\alpha$, and so could easily be seen as a description of indirect dowry rather than of bride-price; while the adjective $\pi o\lambda\acute{\upsilon}\delta\omega\rho o\varsigma$ (with parallel words like $\overset{,}{\eta}\pi\iota\acute{o}\delta\omega\rho o\varsigma$) has a wide variety of possible meanings besides the favoured interpretation of 'richly dowered'. This latter, I admit, is the translation supported by the scholiasts; on the assumption that it is correct, I am more inclined to believe that we have here an instance of the commonly-attested (above, p. 177) combination of dowry and indirect dowry, than that this passage alone should be proof of the exchange of gifts on the same marriage-occasion. It is relevant, if hardly conclusive, to cite here the famous offer of Agamemnon to Achilles in *I* 146 (=*I* 288), where Agamemnon expressly renounces the one practice (apparent bride-price) in favour of the other (lavish dowry). I appreciate that Finley's type of exchange transaction would conform exactly to the pattern of gift-exchange whose operation, in a wide variety of other Homeric situations, he himself has so clearly demonstrated. But these other situations are in general 'open-ended' ones in whose field etiquette operates unfettered – hospitality, departure, diplomacy, payments for services rendered, desired or anticipated – whereas a marriage is a formal and contractual thing. A much more substantial point, to my mind, is that anthropological evidence shows the exchange of gifts at marriages, in the way envisaged by Finley, to be exceedingly rare in Eurasia and Africa at any time. Where it does occur (mainly in America and the Pacific), it is largely confined to the simpler societies which do not practise agriculture. For Homer's society, it would be unexpected and indeed inappropriate.[22] There is, besides, the argument to be considered below (pp. 181–2): that bride-price and dowry are but respective parts of two contrasting modes of property-transmission. Both modes, together with other more or less closely associated practices, are clearly detectable in Homer, which should make it easier to accept that true bride-price is present too.

It remains to consider briefly the remaining possibility mentioned earlier: that marriages among the Homeric ἄριστοι were sometimes attended by bride-price practice, sometimes by dowry (with or without indirect dowry). If this were so, there would have to be factors influencing the choice of practice. The likeliest would perhaps be that, according to fine social gradations within the general class of the nobility, the relative status of the bride's family and the bridegroom's would decide in which direction the gifts passed. Marriage-settlements have often contributed to the nuances of social precedence dear to the hearts of aristocrats; the rationale is usually that the preponderance of gifts should pass from the less socially elevated side of the marriage to the more elevated.[23] But again we have to ask, is this true of Homer? And again the answer must be negative. By what rationale should Hektor, the eldest and most prominent son of the king of Troy, be required to offer a lavish bride-price (or indirect dowry) for the daughter of the relatively obscure king of Thebe? (*X* 472). Or

the great Neleus of Pylos to do likewise for the daughter of a king
of Orchomenos? (λ 281). Conversely, why should King Ikarios offer his much-admired daughter Penelope to an unspecified nobleman
from Dulichion, Same, wooded Zakynthos or rocky Ithaka with a
large dowry, as it is repeatedly predicted that he will? (α 277 etc.).
The explanation in terms of 'marriage up or down', it seems, will
hardly fit the Homeric patten. Nor, to be briefer still, will another
possible way of rationalising different practices, namely the incidence
of marriage abroad. There is no consistent differentiation between
marriages contracted locally and those involving more distant families: each kind of marriage shows both kinds of practice.[24] For other
potential bases of differentiation, the Homeric descriptions are not
sufficiently circumstantial to provide the evidence.

It seems to me that another, altogether simpler explanation of the
diversity of Homeric marriage-settlements is beginning to force itself
upon us: namely, that Homer is describing a mixture of practices,
derived from a diversity of historical sources. For such a conclusion
there is, I think, some further support which emerges from broadening
the scope of the anthropological argument; for marriage-settlement
is, after all, but a part of the whole spectrum of inheritance, property and kinship patterns. Before calling on this evidence, however,
let me freely confess to the dangers attendant on such a procedure;
dangers which go beyond the invariable disadvantages of appealing
to a different discipline in which one is not well versed. My justification for using this evidence is that I shall not claim that it is in any
way decisive or final, for it manifestly is not; merely it seems to me to
suggest *tendencies* which, taken together, appear to shift the balance
of probability in favour of the tentative conclusion, reached above in
the particular context of marriage-settlements, and capable of a wider
application in the social system as a whole: that Homer's picture is
composite.

From the enormous body of data tabulated in G. P. Murdock's
World Ethnographic Atlas, which cover no less than 863 human societies from all over the world, and of many different stages of development, Dr J. R. Goody has in a recent paper extracted some interesting conclusions in the field of inheritance, property and marriage.[25]
I am aware that a compilation such as the *Ethnographic Atlas* must
present a simplified picture of human institutions, in which the various components have to be isolated and coded in a way that must
gloss over many individual variants: to take an example, one of the

features whose presence or absence is recorded is endogamy, which is extended to cover any tendency to marry within a certain range of kin, caste or local group – whereas one might argue that in reality these are not all merely variants of the same phenomenon. Nevertheless, when consistent and repeated patterns emerge from such data, it is surely legitimate to identify the patterns and to offer one's explanation for them. This is what Goody has done.

In categorising the societies, Goody shows that *transmission of property* is an important variable, often determining other practices in associated fields. He demonstrates this by dividing the societies into two categories based on property-transmission, and then testing the correlation of these categories with other variables. The results seem to me to be sufficiently positive to be significant. His first category consists of those societies which exhibit 'diverging devolution', whereby property is distributed among kin of both sexes; his second, of the 'homogeneous devolution' societies, where property passes through kin of the same sex only. In the first, diverging devolution category, there is a very strong association with the nuclear family; this, rather than any broader descent-group, is the emphasised social unit. Another very common form of diverging devolution is the system of dowry and/or indirect dowry,[26] a point particularly relevant to the previous section of this discussion. Again within the field of marriage, there is a further, if looser, correlation with the tendency to celebrate weddings with elaborate ceremonial.[27] But from this point on, Goody tests the correlation of diverging devolution with a number of quite diverse variables; they number a dozen or so, of which perhaps six allow for some sort of check with the Homeric evidence. I give these in order of the strength of the correlation with diverging devolution:

A Monogamy.
B The use of the plough.
C A complex stratification by caste or by class.
D A kinship terminology sufficiently complex to distinguish siblings from from cousins.
E Alternative residence for married couples with either group of 'in-laws' ('ambilocal') or independently ('neolocal'), rather than automatic residence with either the wife's family ('uxorilocal') or the husband's ('virilocal').
F Endogamy, as defined above.

Goody's second category, that of the homogeneous devolution societies, naturally tends to be associated with the opposite features to the above. For example, such societies tend to allow wide freedom in the choice of spouse, and to practise polygamy (invariably in the form of polygyny on the part of the men); they are also often associated with 'classificatory' kinship-terminology, and with no elaborate social stratification. More important is their correlation with the reverse of the more or less definitional characteristics of diverging devolution which were mentioned earlier: homogeneous devolution societies are based on the patrilineal or matrilineal descent group, even though they may well retain the nuclear family within this; and (again important for our purposes) they practise bride-price rather than dowry or indirect dowry.

Where does Homeric society stand in relation to these two contrasting patterns? Hellenists will at once recognise several features of the first, diverging devolution type of social system as being familiar from Homer. A dowry system (with, less certainly, indirect dowry as well) is as we have seen present in Homer. Actual marriage ceremonial, to judge from the double wedding celebrated at Menelaos' palace in δ 3 ff., and from the scenes on the Shield of Achilles (Σ 491 ff.), is quite elaborate. Turning to the other variables listed above, it will probably be agreed that in its strict sense monogamy (A) is common practice for the Homeric hero (though not invariable, as will be shown below); perhaps the clearest case is that of Menelaos who, when it becomes clear that Helen can bear him no further children after Hermione, begets a son and heir by a slave-woman rather than take a second wife (δ 11). Use of the plough (B), it goes without saying, is familiar in Homer. As to kinship-terminology (D), it is certainly true that Homer once uses the word ἀνέψιος (I 464), thus making the distinction between cousin and brother (ἀδελφεός) in much the same way that later Greeks did; but here there is again some contrary evidence to take into account (see below). On the residence of married couples (E), there is perhaps enough evidence to show that Homer's picture corresponds once again to the diverging devolution pattern: for example, it seems that the presence of an heiress such as Nausikaa (ζ 244–5) or the daughters of Priam or Nestor (below, p. 183), could lead to an 'uxorilocal' marriage even though the general pattern may have been 'virilocal'. The remaining two variables, (C) and (F), I find it difficult to evaluate with respect to Homer. In many respects his society is very highly stratified (C), and there seems to be a corresponding inhibition against marrying outside one's class (F); yet the forms of endogamy whereby marriage within a kinship or a local group is favoured seem largely foreign to Homer. But as hinted above (p. 181), there is perhaps a methodological flaw here in the compilation of the data. Overall, the evidence so far considered encourages the view that Homer's society is broadly of the diverging devolution type.

Once we turn to the contrasting pattern of homogeneous devolution, however, we find equally positive correspondences with Homer. These begin at the most basic level. The *oikos* is the hub of Homer's whole social system, as champions of the historical Homeric society like Finley[28] and Adkins[29] have rightly insisted. But what are the characteristics of the Homeric *oikos*? In most of the cases where we have explicit description, it is no more nor less than the patrilineal extended family of the homogeneous devolution pattern in ancient dress. The nuclear family, although known to Homer, is to say the least not his general norm. It might seem possible to explain away the extravagantly diffuse *oikos* of Priam, which includes fifty sons and their wives, and twelve daughters and their husband (Z 242 ff.), as a piece of foreign exoticism contrasted with Achaean practice. But then we find that Nestor's *oikos* similarly includes both sons and sons-in-law (γ 387 etc.); that Menelaos' son (though not his daughter) is apparently destined to live at home after marriage (δ 10 f.); and that the less conventional ménage of Aeolus (κ 5–12) also represents a larger descent group under one roof. As Finley writes,[30] 'Normally, the poems seem to say, although the evidence is not altogether clear and consistent, the sons remained with their father in his lifetime' – and the same is frequently true of the daughters. Here then we seem to find a basic characteristic of homogeneous devolution represented in Homeric society. Nor is it the only one. As we have seen, bride-price is apparently embedded in the Homeric tradition. Polygamy rears its head in Troy, where Priam is resolutely polygynous (X 48 etc.); the temptation may again be felt to treat this as conscious exoticism, but the example of Priam's *oikos* (see above) does not encourage such an explanation. Next, under the heading of kinship-terminology ((D) on p. 181), let us note the curious occurrence of κασίγνητος, a word frequently used elsewhere to denote a sibling, in the sense of 'first cousin' in O 545;[31] this imprecision contrasts sharply with the usage of ἀνέψιος noted previously (p. 182). Finally, if it can legitimately be counted as a feature of homogeneous devolution, let us recall Homer's apparent avoidance of certain important forms of endogamy (above).

On the criterion of property-transmission, therefore – and I stress that this is the basis of the dichotomy employed here – it appears that the Homeric social system has characteristics of two different patterns of society. How much does this imply? The two patterns are opposed; not, however, totally inter-exclusive. I am not for one moment claiming that all the features so far noted could not be *observed* in one and the same society; anthropological laws are not so inflexible as that. Nor, incidentally, in the matter of marriage-settlements, are linguistic laws sufficiently restrictive to prevent the same society from using the same word, such as ἕδνα, along with its cognates, to cover every possible form of marriage-prestation – bride-price, dowry, indirect dowry – as seems to be the case in Homer. In all such cases, a degree of overlap between different systems would not be unexpected, and such overlap would most naturally occur in the circumstances either of a geographically marginal, or of a chronologically transitional culture, between opposed norms. There is little to prevent anyone from explaining the Homeric picture in such a way, and thus seeking to preserve its unitary and historical quality. The evidence, as I said at the outset, is not finally decisive; I have rehearsed it simply because, cumulatively, it seems to me difficult to reconcile with the belief that Homer's society is unitary and historical. The evidence is naturally strongest where Homer seems to portray, as *normal* features of his society, practices which are not often combined in reality. To give one example, homogeneous devolution features such as bride-price and the patrilineal descent-group are seldom found together with diverging devolution features such as monogamy;[32] in this particular instance, of 344 homogeneous devolution societies in the *Ethnographic Atlas*, monogamy was present in only 29. Yet Homer, it seems to me, presents all the three features mentioned as being normal in his society. Even here, I concede that there is subjectivity involved in assessing what is 'normal' for Homer; and in these circumstances it would be unwarranted to try to press this evidence any further. I will leave it to exert such persuasive force as it may possess on its own.

To return briefly to the matter of marriage-settlement with which we were originally concerned, it may be thought significant that the marriage practices of each of the main types are described by Homer in strongly formulaic language. One may cite the repeated formula for bride-price or indirect dowry, 'ἐπεὶ πόρε μυρία ἕδνα' (the subject of πόρε being the bridegroom), and the pair of lines twice used of the bride's kinsmen in the dowry situation, 'οἱ δὲ γάμον τεύξουσι καὶ ἀρτυνέουσιν ἔεδνα |πολλὰ μάλ᾽, ὅσσα ἔοικε φίλης ἐπὶ παιδὸς ἕπεσθαι'. This fact, however, will hardly be used by Homeric scholars these days as an argument for the great antiquity, still less the historical contemporaneity, of the practices so described. On the latter point at least, it must now be accepted that formulae relating to the same area of activity could and did originate in different periods of the growth of the Epic. In another article, Miss Gray showed[33] that, for example, the traditional shield-phrases 'ἀσπίδος εὐκύκλου' and 'ἀσπίδος ἀμφιβρότης' should derive from two different historical stages in the development of the shield.

Those who maintain that Homeric society is unitary and historical are bound to ask themselves the question, to what time and place that society belongs.[34] The two answers which might seem, *prima facie*, to be the likeliest, can be shown to be improbable on other grounds: namely the historical period in which the story of the poems is ostensibly set, the later Mycenaean age, and the period in which the poems reached their final form and in which the historical Homer most probably lived, the eighth century BC. A fully Mycenaean setting is rendered almost impossible by the evidence of the Linear B tablets, whose picture has been shown, by Finley more than anyone else, to be quite inconsistent with Homer, especially in the field of social and political structure. A purely contemporary origin, though it may not be excluded by the ubiquitous and pervasive presence of formulae, affecting social life as much as other aspects, would surely be in utter conflict with the other evidence that we have for eighth-century society, from Hesiod and from archaeological sources. It is a surprise to encounter such primitive features as bride-price and polygamy in Homer at all; that they should have been taken, as normal features, from the Greek society of his own day is almost unthinkable. This means that, if one is set on an historical explanation, the likely models are narrowed down to two periods, the 'Age of Migrations' between the fall of the Mycenaean citadels around 1200, and a lower date in the region of 1000; and the ensuing two centuries, a more settled period which in my view forms the central part of the Dark Age.

In inclining as he does towards tenth- and ninth-century Greece as the historical basis for the world of Odysseus (see n. 34), Finley makes a telling point. 'If it is to be placed in time', he writes, '*as everything we know about heroic poetry says it must ...* ' (my italics), and so on. I concede the general truth of this. Finley's favoured comparisons are with the *Chanson de Roland* and the *Nibelungenlied*, of which this is evidently true; and to these one could add a parallel not used by him, the 'Ulster Cycle' of prose epic about which my Edinburgh colleague Professor K. H. Jackson has written with such authority. 'This whole picture of the ancient Irish heroic way of life', he concludes,[35] 'as it is seen in the oldest tales is self-consistent, of a very marked individuality, and highly circumstantial. One can hardly doubt that it represents a genuine tradition of a society that once existed'. This is independent and striking confirmation for Finley's view. But there is a well-tried counter to such analogy between Homer and other Epic: this is to say that the qualitative distinction between Homeric and most other, perhaps all other Epic is such as to invalidate these analogies.[36] The argument may perhaps be too well-worn today to carry the conviction that it once did, without detailed substantiation of a kind that I am not competent to provide. Nevertheless I firmly believe that it is soundly based. In support of this whole position, I wish now to draw some analogies, not outside but within the Homeric Epic, that is with topics other than the social system.

Inevitably, it is with the material aspects of culture that we have the most secure external evidence. I wish to discuss briefly certain aspects[37] – specifically, metal-usage, burial-practices, military equipment and temples – which figure in the cultural background of the poems, and which may provide valid analogies with the social features.

For metal-working, it should be generally appreciated as a result of Miss Gray's article with which I began (see n. 1), that Homer's picture is a very curious one. His exclusive use of bronze, for every sword and every spearhead mentioned in both poems, is the point of greatest significance; for these are the two supreme weapons of the Epic. There is no period of Greek history or prehistory, later than the first half of the eleventh century BC, of which such a picture would be representative. Professor Kirk rightly observes[38] that afterwards bronze continued to be used 'often enough, for spear- and arrowheads and even for axes'. But for Homer, arrowheads and axes are of secondary importance; and for Homer bronze is used, for the two prime offensive weapons, not 'often enough' but always. Such a culture never existed after the end of the Bronze Age; the formulae on which the picture is based – although the language is not exclusively formulaic – can only have originated in either the full Mycenaean period or its immediate aftermath. But this simple assertion at once faces us with the other aspects of Homer's metallurgy which conflict utterly with this: first and foremost, that iron is not only known to Homer as a working metal and a trading commodity, but is actually the normal metal for his agricultural and industrial tools. Historically, iron for tools was adopted, if anything, rather later than iron for weapons; it follows therefore that no historical society, at least in the relevant part of the ancient world, ever showed even fleetingly the combination of metal-usages found in Homer. The central era of the Dark Age, the tenth and ninth centuries, is in some ways the least appropriate of all periods to look to for an historical setting for Homer's metallurgy, for at this time the dependence on iron reached its peak, to recede a little in the eighth and seventh centuries and give way to that partial recourse to bronze which prompted Professor Kirk's statement quoted above.

On burial-practices, there is no unanimity today, any more than in the past. To quote two very recent books, Professor Finley in his *Early Greece* still holds that 'The *Iliad* and *Odyssey* remain firmly anchored in the earlier Dark Age on this point (*sc.* burial rite)'; while Dr Kurtz and Mr Boardman are equally sure that Homer's picture 'is almost wholly in keeping with Geometric and later Greek practice', which is not at all the same thing.[39] My own view, predictably, is that Homer's burial practices are not firmly anchored in, nor wholly in keeping with, anything. His heroes cremate each other, maybe, because that was the rite with which Homer was most familiar. But from this point on, historical verisimilitude disappears. For it is not true that at any one period all Greece, nor even all Ionia, cremated. In Homer, the heroes are cremated singly or *en masse* according to the dictates of the story. When, as regularly happens, a tumulus is erected over a single cremation (whereas historically the tumulus almost always contains a multiple burial), we may again suspect that the requirements of the plot are the overriding factor. A few elements of the funerary practice may be culled from the Bronze Age: the fairly lavish provision of possessions for the deceased, the occasional use of horse-sacrifice, the idea of cenotaphs, possibly the funerary games. Although it is agreed that the great Homeric funerals are among the most magnificent set-pieces in the poems, it seems certain that no Greek ever witnessed in real life the precise sequence of events narrated in Patroklos' funeral. Life may imitate art, but it cannot match it.

What need be said about Homeric fighting-equipment beyond the fact, today I hope accepted, that it is composite and shows internal inconsistency? To illustrate this, it may be enough to recall that the same hero repeatedly sets out to fight with a pair of throwing-spears and is then found in action with a single heavy thrusting-spear (*cf.* e.g. *Γ* 18 and 338; *Λ* 43 and 260; *Π* 139 and 801). But there is another conclusion to be drawn from Homeric weaponry and armour: this is, that whatever conspicuous item of equipment we choose to focus our attention on – the fairly common bronze corslets, bronze greaves, and bronze helmets, the pair of throwing-spears which is clearly the hero's regular armament, the occasionally metal-faced shield, the silver-studded sword-hilt – argument may rage as to whether their historical origin lies in the Mycenaean period or in the improved equipment of the poet's own day, the eighth century; but the one period at which virtually no evidence for their existence is to be found is the tenth and ninth centuries, and it could be added that there is but slight indication of their presence in the preceding Age of Migrations.[40]

Something of a pattern may thus be emerging from the categories of material culture that we have been considering. The historical models for each feature can be looked for either early (that is in the full Bronze Age) or late (that is in the poet's own times). They show a remark-able reluctance to reveal themselves in the intervening four centuries, between about 1200 and 800. The same lesson is provided by the study of the Homeric temple. There are now free-standing religious buildings, worthy of the name νηός and conforming to the Homeric references, known from Bronze Age Greece. I would cite the structure found by Professor Caskey at Ayia Irini on Keos, and the temples of Mycenaean date at Kition in Cyprus which Dr Karageorghis has re-cently excavated. There is also the smaller shrine which Lord William Taylour has uncovered at Mycenae. At the other end of the time-scale, the revival of the temple in historical times, in the light of the latest chronological evidence, can barely if at all be traced back before 800 BC on any Greek site. Of the earlier so-called temples that have been claimed, either the identification as a temple, or the ascription to the ninth century (occasionally the tenth) is doubtful – sometimes both.[41]

This archaeological evidence has, I fear, been rather summarily presented here. But my aim is the fairly limited one of showing that, in certain aspects of the material world he portrays, Homer, besides in some cases combining features from different historical eras, also displays certain tendencies in the choice of those eras. The reasons for these tendencies may be of the simplest kind – perhaps that the poet's desire is to portray a materially impressive culture, and that this inevitably leads to the choice of cither the Mycenaean world which had been impressive in this way, or to the contemporary world which was becoming so, but to avoid the less well-endowed intervening periods. But a question remains: would similar factors operate in the more intangible world of social relations?

Professor Finley again has a ready answer to such suggestions:[42] 'The comparative study of heroic poetry shows, I think decisively, that the society portrayed tends to be relatively (though not entirely) 'modern', for all the pretence of great antiquity and for all the archaism of the armour and the political geography'. I would disagree with him over one point: what we have in Homer is surely not just archaism in material culture, but artificial conflations of historical practices, a few features such as the provision of twin spears being probably of decidedly recent origin. But this must not be allowed to distract us from the fundamental question: is it possible to have social institutions operating quite independently of material culture in a literary world? I wish to argue, not that it is quite impossible, but that it is unlikely to have happened with Homer.

For consider certain of the characteristics of Homeric society that Finley and Adkins have described so well. It is strongly success-orientated and strongly materialistic; among its most pervasive features are the ceremonial exchange of gifts in a wide variety of situations, in which it insists on the actual exchange value and not merely the aesthetic or sentimental value of the gifts, and also the equally ceremonial feasting. These are activities whose successful operation demands quite a high material standard of living: for kings to exchange mean gifts is not merely unheroic from a literary point of view, it is socially ineffective in real life; for a host to entertain an uninvited group of long-term guests on skimpy fare is, equally, not merely unheroic but historically improbable. A society that cannot afford to perform such ceremonial lavishly will not practise it at all. Now all the evidence yielded by the archaeology of the settlements and graves of the earlier Dark Age suggests that here, at any rate, was a society that could afford nothing of the kind. Precious metals are for long totally unknown; bronze utensils and other large metal objects are exceedingly rare; while in one particular field, that of the funerary feasts, we are luckily able to make a precise comparison between Homer and archaeology. We find differences not only in degree, but in kind. The quantities of animal bones found beside Dark Age graves are relatively modest, and represent cut joints of meat rather than Homer's whole carcasses; furthermore, the beef and pork so prominent in Homer are far eclipsed by the cheaper mutton and goat's meat.[43] If challenged on the validity of archaeological evidence in such contexts, I would point not only to the obvious contrast with Mycenaean Greece, but to the example of a contemporary society in another part of Europe, the Urnfield Culture of East Central Europe, whose cemetery-sites produce evidence of just such a lavish society as we would expect from Homer's description: graves with quantities of elaborate bronzework, and with the accoutrements of feasting and of war particularly conspicuous. Another instance could be found in the rich tombs of the eighth century at Salamis in Cyprus.[44] Clearly, therefore, it is possible for archaeological evidence to match up to a literary picture thus far.

If, on the other hand, the objection were made that Homer's picture, though glorified by poetic licence, is yet fundamentally rooted in the historical society of the Dark Age, then one could indicate other qualities in the archaeological record of the period, which would have required Homer not merely to exaggerate but positively to contradict. There are, for instance, signs of drastic depopulation, and of the interrupted communications which naturally accompanied this. Homeric society does not admit of either circumstance. Another point about the centuries of the Dark Age is that their memory was not retained, let alone treasured, by any Greek writer of whom we know. Hesiod regarded the era as one of unrelieved disaster; later Greeks found themselves embarrassed by their total ignorance of these years. It is fair to ask how this happened, if Greek society of that period possessed anything resembling the striking qualities of Homeric society, its self-reliance, its extreme competitiveness, its prodigious acquisitiveness and generosity, the functional simplicity of its ethics. If such a society had flourished at so relatively recent a time, would not its ideals and values have inevitably seeded themselves more widely in early Greek thought?

In the later part of this paper I have concentrated on one particular period, roughly the tenth and ninth centuries BC, in order to assess its claim to have provided the model for Homeric society. It may be felt that the preceding Age of Migrations, for example, has escaped scrutiny in this connection. But I hope to have made clear that some at least of these arguments apply to any identification, of whatever period, of an historical society which might be faithfully reflected in Homer. For it seems to me that such identifications involve, in one respect, a certain derogation from Homer's artistic standing. If Homer really preserved, like a faded sepia photograph, a faithful image of a real society that belonged, not to his own times nor to the period which had provided such historical background as there was for the actual events he described but to the period which happened to be most influential in the formation of this aspect of the Epic tradition; then indeed he was on a footing with the forgotten and anonymous authors of the *Chanson de Roland* or the *Cattle Raid of Cooley* or any one of the numerous epics and sagas of normal type. For an oral poet who adopts, entire, from his predecessors of a certain period, something as pervasive as a social framework, becomes in my view not merely traditional but derivative. To an important extent, he can make his characters behave in the way that people actually behaved at that time, and in no other way. The scope for creative contributions is sharply inhibited. If he does extend this social pattern himself, he must do it with such scrupulous care as to obliterate his own tracks completely. This is no doubt one reason why no author's name has survived for the *Nibelungenlied,* the Ulster Cycle, some Icelandic sagas and those others of even the finest non-Homeric epics in which such social and historical verisimilitude is to be found. By contrast, a poet who is also traditional, and ultimately just as indebted to predecessors, but who depends on predecessors of *many* periods, and admits elements from his own experience and imagination into the bargain, is far freer. He can select, he can conflate, he can idealise. Unless he is pedantically careful, minor inconsistencies will creep in, of the kind we have been discussing; but his scope for creativity, even though the picture he paints is not truly fictional, will be greater. This is a subjective argument to end with, but the fact that the Homeric poems are attached to a name, and that, even if we doubt the existence of an eighth-century poet called Homer, we are nevertheless aware, in reading the *Iliad* and *Odyssey,* of being at least intermittently in the presence of poetic genius, is a strong hint that Homeric Epic conforms to the second of the two pictures sketched above, and not the first. At all events. I offer this as a further argument against the existence of an historical Homeric society.[45]

Notes

1. *JHS* 74 (1954), 1.
2. *JHS* 91 (1971), 1.
3. *Ibid.,* 2.
4. *The Greeks* (1967), 45.
5. See e.g. *From Mycenae to Homer* (1958), chapter 4; and in *A Companion to Homer* (ed. A. J. B. Wace and F. H. Stubbings, 1963), 452–62.
6. *The Songs of Homer* (1962), chapter 9.
7. *Archaeologia Homerica* (ed. F. Matz and H.-G. Buchholz), Göttingen, 1967–.
8. *Ibid.,* Kapitel C, E. Bielefeld, *Schmuck* (1968), 65; *cf.* more fully *Gnomon* 42 (1970), 157–9.
9. *The Homeric Odyssey* (1955), 157.

10. By 'historical', throughout this paper, I mean 'derived from one single period of history'; a conflation of features from a diversity of historical periods I prefer to call 'composite'.

11. Alasdair MacIntyre, *A short history of Ethics* (1968), 8.

12. *JHS* 90 (1970), 137, n. 58.

13. *Ibid.*, 122.

14. M. I. Finley in *Revue Internationale des Droits de l'Antiquité* (3ᵉ ser.), 2 (1955), 167–94, followed in this important respect by W. K. Lacey, *JHS* 86 (1966), 55–69.

15. G. M. Calhoun in *A Companion to Homer* (above, n. 5), 452.

16. I give a bald list of those passages which seem to me to illustrate this: Λ 243, N 365 (where the 'price' is a feat rather than a payment), Π 178, 190, X 472, θ 318, λ 281, o 16, 231, 367, π 391, τ 529, φ 161.

17. Again, while several instances are ambiguous, this practice seems exemplified by Z 191, 251, 394, I 147 = 269, X 51, α 277 = β 196, β 54, 132, δ 736, η 311, υ 341, ψ 227, ω 294.

18. *Hermes* 47 (1912), 414–21. The interpretation of ἕδνα as meaning 'indirect dowry' in certain passages receives notable support from the scholiasts, *ibid.*, 419.

19. *Cf.* Finley, *op. cit.* (above, n. 14).

20. See e.g. Nur Yalman, *Under the Bo Tree* (Berkeley and Los Angeles, 1967), esp. chapter 8 and pp. 303-4.

21. There is a further case where both practices appear to be associated with a hypothetical future occasion, the re-marriage of Penelope: contrast o 16 etc. (apparent bride-price) with α 277 etc. (dowry). But the case is weaker because the identity of the bridegroom is undecided, and in any case I would apply here the same explanation (*mutatis mutandis*) as in the case of Hektor and Andromache. The marital fortunes of Penelope are indeed a constant embarrassment to those who believe in a consistent social pattern in Homer, since the ultimate responsibility is distributed between herself, her father and her son, and the political control of Ithaka is also implicated. Even Finley describes the case as an 'often self-contradictory amalgam of strands' [*op. cit.* (above, n. 14), 172, n. 19]. W. K. Lacey (above, n. 14, 61-6) has bravely striven to discern consistent principles behind the various situations envisaged for Penelope; but his explanation seems to me to posit an improbable and indeed almost legalistic fidelity on the poet's part.

22. See J. R. Goody, 'Bridewealth and Dowry in Africa and Eurasia', especially Appendix II, in *Bridewealth and Dowry* (Cambridge Papers in Social Anthropology), ed. J. R. Goody and S. J. Tambiah, forthcoming.

23. I think especially of the hilarious negotiations between Baron Ochs and the Marschallin's notary in the first act of *Der Rosenkavalier*.

24. Contrast Neleus and Chloris (λ 281, see above) with Odysseus and Nausikaa (hypothetical, η 314) for marriages abroad; Polymela and

Echekles (*Π* 190) with Laothoe and Priam (*X* 51) for more local marriages.

25. 'Inheritance, Property and Marriage in Africa and Eurasia', *Sociology* 3 (1969), 55–76.
26. *Ibid.*, 56.
27. *Ibid.*, 57.
28. E.g. *The World of Odysseus* (1956), 66 f.
29. E.g. *Merit and Responsibility* (1960), 35 f.
30. *Op. cit.* (above, n. 28), 72.
31. I am indebted to Mrs S. C. Le M. Humphreys for this and several other valuable observations.
32. Goody, *op. cit.* (above, n. 25), 62–3 with Table V.
33. *CQ* 41 (1947), 109–21, esp. 120–1.
34. E.g. Adkins, *JHS* 91 (1971) 1; Finley, *The World of Odysseus*, 55.
35. *The Oldest Irish Tradition* (1964), 28.
36. *Cf.*, on methods of composition, Kirk, *The Songs of Homer*, 95.
37. Some of these points are discussed in my book *The Dark Age of Greece* (1971), 388–94.
38. *The Songs of Homer*, 182.
39. M. I. Finley, *Early Greece: the Bronze and Archaic Ages* (1970), 84; D. Kurtz and J. Boardman, *Greek Burial Customs* (1971), 186.
40. I refrain from introducing chariots into this question, since the widespread assumption that Homer's chariotry is a half-understood memory of the true Bronze Age practice has been questioned by J. K. Anderson (AJA 69 (1965), 349–52). But it remains true that, for chariots as well, the tenth and ninth (and indeed the eleventh) centuries in Greece have little or no evidence to offer.
41. Cf. *The Dark Age of Greece*, 408–12, 422–3.
42. *Historia* 6 (1957), 147, n. 1.
43. Cf. *The Dark Age of Greece*, 379–80 and n. 20.
44. As was kindly pointed out to me by Mr V. R. d'A. Desborough.
45. An earlier version of the paper was delivered to the Oxford Philological Society on May 12, 1972. It would be invidious to single out any of the numerous members from whose contributions to the subsequent discussion I benefited. But on the anthropological side I gratefully acknowledge my debt to Dr Jack Goody and my colleague, Professor James Littlejohn, much as I fear I have over-simplified their views on complex subjects; while among Classical colleagues I owe a special debt to Mr D. B. Robinson.

The Early Polis at Home and Abroad

INTRODUCTION TO PART III

This group of papers largely dates from the heyday of a movement which, as previously hinted (see above, under Ch. 4) has now passed into diverging channels. The initial stimulus arose from the feeling that the rise of the Greek *polis* – best translated, with Runciman (1982) as 'citizen state' – was a topic to which archaeological evidence might have much to contribute. A hundred years earlier in the history of scholarship, a somewhat parallel development had taken place with Homeric studies: there, as here, the effect was to bring external evidence to bear on questions which had previously been answered largely from the internal indications given in the relevant texts. The outcome of that older intervention has been clear: there is an array of Homeric questions which not even the severest philologist can now address without recourse to the archaeological evidence. In this case, there are signs of a similar outcome for historical research, though it would still be presumptuous to press the case further than that.

If there is one large area of enquiry which is largely neglected in these pages, it is that of the relation of the *polis* to its region. The persistence of often identical regional divisions in the culture of Greece (and indeed Italy), from prehistory right down to our own times, is a subject briefly touched upon in the opening paper (Ch. 1, pp. 27–8) and even more fleetingly in two of those to come (Ch. 12, p. 225, Ch. 14, pp. 282–3). These regional divisions, as archaeology can demonstrate, were much older than the rise of the *polis*, just as they were to survive its decline, sometimes in the formal political shape of regional federations. Their durability is founded on the natural geographical constants, to a degree which is not true of the *polis*. Yet the relationship between these two spatial entities, something eminently susceptible to both historical and archaeological investigation, has not been fully exploited by either. Not surprisingly, greater progress has been made with those regions which remained outside the *polis* system (Morgan 2003), where there is usually an equifinality between the political and the geographical entities.

BIBLIOGRAPHY

Morgan, C. (2003), *Early Greek States Beyond the Polis*, London: Routledge.
Runciman, W. G. (1982), 'Origins of states: the case of Archaic Greece', *Comparative Studies in Society and History* 24: 351–77.

CHAPTER 11

Archaeology and the Rise of the Greek State

An Inaugural Lecture of 1977, this can be seen as an early attempt to set agenda for a new deployment of archaeology. I have
already referred (above, p. x) to the flawed basis of the demographic calculations in pp. 204–6. Other arguments too have
been overtaken by later insights: they include the passages in
which appeal is made to the early prevalence of a 'tribal order'
(p. 203 and again in the passage on regionalism, p. 209) – a system in which most historians no longer believe. Even as I spoke
in 1977, two French studies (Roussel 1976; Bourriot 1976) had
just appeared, in which the twin political concepts of the *phyle*
('tribe') and *genos* ('clan') were exhaustively analysed and were
found, far from being inherited from a pre-political era of the
past, to be artificial constructs of the developed *polis*. Reconstructions of Greek society in the era between the Mycenaean
age and the rise of the *polis* may therefore need to be expressed
in different terms, and suggestions (e.g. Whitley 1991) have not
been lacking.

But I shall not proceed in this way through the other occurrences of obsolete or 'dated' points of view: the reader may be
sure that the writer is equally aware of them. By far the most
lasting thesis has proved to be that advanced on pp. 211–14,
about the building of a monumental temple as an index of the
advent of the *polis*; and the most fruitful development of it
has been that initiated by François de Polignac. From his early
book (de Polignac 1984) which first established the link between
the themes of sanctuary and territory, making especial use of
the Greek settlements in the West, he has developed the study
of the rural sanctuary to an entirely new level, subtly refining
his original thesis in a series of publications over the next two
decades, of which de Polignac 1994 is a prime example.

BIBLIOGRAPHY

Bourriot, F. (1976), *Recherches sur la nature du genos*, Lille and Paris:
Librairie Honoré Champion.

de Polignac, F. (1984), *La naissance de la cité grecque: cultes, espace et société, VIIIᵉ–VIIᵉ siècles avant J.-C.*, Paris: Editions la Découverte.

de Polignac, F. (1994), 'Mediation, competition, and sovereignty: the evolution of rural sanctuaries in Geometric Greece', in *Placing the Gods: Sanctuaries and Sacred Space in Ancient Greece*, ed. S. E. Alcock and R. G. Osborne, Oxford: Clarendon Press, pp. 3–18.

Roussel, D. (1976), *Tribu et Cité (Annales Littéraires de l'Université de Besançon*, 193), Paris: Les Belles Lettres.

Whitley, J. (1991), 'Social diversity in dark age Greece', *BSA (Annual of the British School of Athens)* 86: 341–65.

Humility, which people in my situation always profess, is in this case sincere and unforced. I stand before you as a newcomer to Cambridge, the first to invade this particular sanctum since the Laurence Chair was founded in 1931; as a specialist in none of the traditionally central fields of Classical Archaeology; as a late-comer, even, to the subject as a whole. It is impossible to take on unabashed a mantle once worn by A. B. Cook and Alan Wace, men who were so much more than Classical Archaeologists, but their breadth of interests is stimulating as well as daunting. I can but plead, in mitigation of the first shortcoming mentioned above, that I began research as a pupil of a Cambridge man, John Boardman; and that my first learned publication was a favourable review of a book by Professor Robert Cook in a journal edited by Professor Glyn Daniel. This at least provides an entrée to my ultimate theme of cooperation between different branches of archaeology, and to my immediate one, the work of my predecessor. I have no wish to requite Robert Cook's many kindnesses to me by embarrassing him, but I want to say that, in thirty-one years as Reader and Professor, he has represented his discipline and his University to the outside world with real honour. To say that he was a worthy colleague and natural successor to Arnold Lawrence and Jocelyn Toynbee might in itself seem praise enough; it is good to know, by the way, that all three are still active, and I hope they will tell me if I let them down. But Robert Cook has also a notably individual approach, with an unmistakable Laconian brevity of style and accuracy of expression. No lazy assumption is safe in his literary presence; you have to count your platitudes when he leaves. Nor can there be many scholars so fertile in suggestions for new work; I regard some of the themes that I shall follow today as mere extensions of his thoughts.

Archaeology and the Rise of the Greek State. Inaugural Lecture, 1st March, 1977, Cambridge: Cambridge University Press [37 pp.].

Some adjectives have the power to transform the meaning of any noun to which they are attached, and it seems that 'Classical' is one of them. At any rate, Classical Archaeology has come to be understood as something generically different from Archaeology: different in the training that it presupposes, in the kind of people who practise it, in the matter with which it deals, in its manner of execution and in its language of expression. It is almost as if the resemblances of names, like that between History and Natural History, resulted from the survival of an obsolete usage. I think that it is time that this was changed. This feeling is reinforced by fifteen years' experience of the Scottish University system: at Edinburgh I was able to teach not only students taking Honours degrees in Classics and in Archaeology, but also those taking Honours in History of Art, as well as some practising Art students and some who were taking general degrees. From this diversity there was much to be learned: for example, that for the understanding of how Greek and Roman works of art came into being, much else is useful besides a Classical background; or that for the interpretation of Greek and Roman civilisation, many techniques lie to hand which not only could be, but should long since have been applied by Classicists.

One factor is that of the intellectual make-up of different kinds of people, whether students or teachers. A Cambridge man who went to Edinburgh, Professor Liam Hudson, threw interesting light on this question in his study of English schoolboys, *Contrary imaginations*.[1] He categorised their intellects over a range extending between two poles, the convergers and the divergers. Convergers, to simplify, are people who do much better at intelligence tests of the standard type – 'Brick is to house as plank is to . . . nail/walk/saw/ladder/boat?' – than they do at questions of an open-ended form – 'How many uses can you think of for a brick?' Divergers are those who do much better at the second than at the first. All-rounders fare equally at both. When it comes to the choice of academic subjects, it proves possible to predict, on the basis of performance in such tests, in which subject the school-leaver will specialise. It then hardly needs Professor Hudson to tell us that Classicists, along with Mathematicians and Physical Scientists, tend to be recruited from the extreme converger end of the scale, the people who excel in getting the right answer when there *is* a right answer. Contrariwise, those studying History and allied subjects, no doubt including Art History and Archaeology, tend to be divergers. In a system where the only area of recruitment for Classical Archae-ologists is from among Classicists, it is likely that those working in an allied field such as European Prehistory or Renaissance Art History, who have arrived there by a quite different route of specialisation, will have less intellectual *rapport* with Classical Archaeologists than is to be desired. Indeed, one has seen the operation of this factor all too often, and I hazard the guess that it is not unknown in the parallel case of Ancient and Modern History. However, just as it is now becoming accepted that not every Ancient Historian should have a Classical training, so I would argue that the same holds for Classical Archaeology. But this is not the only available remedy: one could go altogether further – as a converger myself, I feel emboldened to say this – and suggest that the field of Classical studies as a whole might benefit from a larger injection of divergent intellects. I am not thinking here of any narrow partisan advantage for my own subject, although the status of Classical Archaeology within Classics might in time be affected by such changes.

I hope no one will be too offended if I say that that status has not hitherto been particularly high. It seems to me that the subject at present falls between two ideals; that many of its objectives are such as neither to satisfy the intelligence of the outstanding convergers that it might hope to draw from among Classicists, nor to attract the more imaginative divergers who are making revolutionary contributions in non-Classical Archaeology. Yet is not Classical Archaeology in a position to deploy the whole range of methods, and to pursue many of the aims, with which Archaeology elsewhere is now, to its own great advantage, experimenting, as well as drawing on certain peculiar assets of its own? I have in mind here not just those general aids that come from studying historically documented cultures, but more specific advantages. To name but two of them, there is first the exceptionally thorough coverage through field-work of certain parts of the ancient Mediterranean: how many areas are there, up to sixty miles by thirty, which have more than 650 established ancient sites, as Messenia has? Secondly, there is the possibility of recognising the handiwork of a single artist in a series of works: by this means, some precision can be given to the chronology of Greek pottery in the eighth century BC, with results that we shall consider presently; and it is this, more surprisingly, which enables two crucial episodes eight hundred years earlier still, the burials in the shaft-graves at Mycenae and the volcanic eruption of Thera, to be shown to be contemporary. Do not such features as these make Classical Archaeology an exemplary testing-ground for theories otherwise hard to validate? Such was certainly the view of a man whose colleague I had much looked forward to becoming, the late Dr David Clarke.[2] There are of course already fields, such as the archaeology of the Roman provinces or of the prehistoric Aegean, whose practitioners exemplify this sort of bridge-building across to the wider field of general archaeology, and it is gratifying that both of these have noted exponents in Cambridge.

To say that we know too much, from written sources, to need to deploy an armoury of techniques derived from very different circumstances, is an obvious but in my view an invalid objection. There are topics of which this is largely true but, if they have hitherto comprised a major part of the study of Classical Archaeology, should they continue to do so for ever? Are there not still long-standing questions in Classical antiquity for which our written sources largely fail us, but on which a broadened archaeological approach could throw much light? I believe that there are topics of central importance to Greek and Roman History in every sense but the chronological one: that is, they are fundamental to our understanding of Classical civilisation, yet they are set in periods which lie at or beyond the limits of the field illuminated by our historical sources. Greek colonisation is certainly such a topic; at the other end of Classical history, the breakdown of Roman government in the provinces may be another. It is on a third such subject, the rise of the Greek polis, that I should like now to speak.

In this case, there exists a considerable historical literature, and a not very considerable archaeological one. Certain points have been established which, although they command less than universal agreement, I shall in fact be using as prior assumptions. First, the Classical polis can be minimally defined as an autonomous political unit, incorporating a town and its territory as the inseparable parts of that unit. As such, it had certain differences from its only plausible ancestor as a state-organisation on Greek soil, the Mycenaean kingdom. A number of towns usually fell under the rule of one Mycenaean monarch, and his palace often exercised a detailed, almost obsessive control over production and exchange within his kingdom; this palace was normally located within a strongly fortified citadel, with much of the settlement lying beyond the walls, and it normally incorporated any identifiable centres of cult as an integral part of itself. Under the polis system, by contrast, the majority of towns either had, or aspired to, political independence from each other; they exercised little economic control over their citizens; their fortifications, when present, usually enclosed the bulk of the settlement; and an independent temple-building was a feature, often the outstanding architectural feature, of a polis. One could elaborate this dichotomy further, but I hope that this is enough to show that it exists. Next, the immediate predecessor of the Classical polis was in any case not the Mycenaean citadel but a quite different form of organisation, the tribal order, in which the community was defined less in terms of location than of kinship, real or pretended, with each unit being ruled by a chieftain. Tribal organisation was mobile and diffuse, linking men with their distant relatives who might be in another part of the country; it was compatible with nomadism, but once the tribe was settled, the family and the household formed the effective unit for many activities. At an intermediate level, however, there was normally the clan, gradually associated with a single locality and often dominated by one family. In the tribal order, stock-rearing often preponderated, both occupationally and as a medium of wealth, which also helped mobility. To many of these features, the polis presented a complete contrast; agriculturally, for example, its emphasis moved strongly in the direction of arable farming. Next, the polis although characteristically Greek was not the only state-form prevalent in Classical Greece; alongside it, as a less sophisticated contemporary (and, one might add, as a more durable survivor), there existed the ethnos, a unit much closer to the tribal order in that it lacked a single urban centre (though it could, like Arcadia, have several), and covered a geographical area which was often based on that occupied by an earlier tribe or group of tribes. Next, an effect of Greek colonisation once it began was that the polis became virtually the only 'export model' of Greek state, though that may not have any automatic implications for the political development of the homeland at the time of colonisation. Finally, the polis itself, together with practically every one of its subdivisions however small, was intimately linked with a religious cult-organisation of corresponding size. At the highest level, to quote Victor Ehrenberg, 'the god...became the monarch of a state which had ceased to be monarchical'.[3]

If we set aside a few questions on which archaeology is unlikely to throw much light – such as one raised by that last quotation, the survival or disappearance of hereditary kingship – then it seems to me that these are legitimate areas for the application of archaeological methods. I am not going to argue, that material objects necessarily imply institutions; as Alcaeus said, it is not houses or walls but men who make up a city;[4] but there are some institutions which presuppose some physical features, and institutions on their own are, after all, hard to pin down. Just how difficult, is shown by considering three modern opinions on a thorny question which each authority had thoroughly pondered: the question as to how far the Homeric poems reflect or do not reflect the rise of the polis. Between them, they bracket almost the whole range of defensible views. First, 'In Homer we find cities of the classical Greek type ... and they imply a new conception of city life in which every citizen has his share'; secondly, 'The *Iliad* shows no trace of the existence of the polis, whereas the *Odyssey* does'; thirdly, 'Neither poem has any trace of a polis in its classical political sense.'[5] I do not think that these three writers are using terms in different senses, but even if they were, it would at least suggest a dire ambiguity in the terminology.

Let us first consider the question of population trends. I avoid the more hazardous field of *absolute* estimates of ancient populations; even the array of sources available for fifth-century Athens has not sufficed to harmonize the dissident views, and it may be that the future lies with quite different computational methods. But even for *relative* change in population, I must inevitably resort to a few figures. The following statistics refer to Athens and Attica in the years between about 1000 and 700 BC; they summarise the finds of the more precisely datable graves, published up to 1976. Because a degree of accuracy is needed, I have excluded those burials which are only very loosely datable; the overall figures would be considerably higher. The pottery-phases which form our best guide to the chronology of this period are of different lengths, so I have converted each total into a figure of burials per notional generation of thirty years, to give a fair basis for comparison. These latter figures are the significant ones.[6] (Fig. 11.1)

Protogeometric	129		26	
Early Geometric	43	graves	26	
Middle Geometric I	46	or	28	per
Middle Geometric II	47	about	35	generation
Late Geometric	408		204	

The increase in the last figure is startling, and justifies closer investigation. To anticipate some natural queries, no, there is no sign of a plague or of mass infant mortality in the Late Geometric period, nor is there any change in the basic practice of single burial throughout the period; no, the level in the Late Geometric period is not likely to be a temporary peak; no, the figures are not distorted by the chance discovery of a large one-period cemetery; yes, the burials are made with a fairly constant level of ceremony, and have a spread of some twenty separate cemeteries outside Athens, and perhaps as

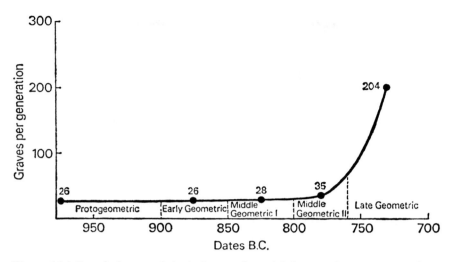

Figure 11.1 Population trends in Attica, tenth to eighth centuries BC, expressed in terms of burials per generation.

many inside. Unless the laws of probability have been unaccountably flouted, we must conclude that the population of Attica rose very gradually for a long period, and then almost meteorically from a date early in the eighth century, in time to be reflected in the deaths from about 760 BC onwards. Is this credible? Let me first quote some words which Malthus wrote about the remoter inland settlements of North America in the years before AD 1800: 'In the back settlements, where agriculture was the sole employment, and where vicious customs and unwholesome occupations were little known, the population has been found to double itself within fifteen years.'[7] Such a growth- rate, involving an annual increase of over 4%, is about as steep as the one that I shall posit for eighth-century Attica; nor shall I be going against what Dr E. A. Wrigley has said in his *Population and history*:[8] 'Four per cent has very rarely been attained, and then only briefly. Three is a rapid rate of growth.' There appears to be a steeper rise for the region outside Athens than for Athens itself, suggesting a net emigration from city to country, but there are no grounds for believing in immigration from outside Attica at this date.

There is however a further aspect of these population figures which took on a new significance for me when I read Professor Colin Renfrew's recent paper 'Megaliths, territories and populations.[9] This is, that a growth-rate like that of eighth-century Attica is exponential, and as such has only been known to take place in unrestricted circumstances, such as in newly-colonised territory, or at least after the discovery of some revolutionary advance in production which enables the same territory to support a much larger population. The moment that a population begins to approach a level that would exhaust the available resources, the rate of increase drops and instead of the exponential curve we get what is called a 'logistic curve', in a roughly symmetrical S-shape. Now, the statistics for Late Geometric Attica are capable of further refinement, since the pottery-style is subdivided into Late Geometric I and II; the difficulty is that not all the graves are published in such detail as will enable us to apportion them between the two sub-phases. We have about 234 burials that are so divisible however; and if we assume that the remaining 174 Late Geometric graves divide in the same proportion, then we obtain the results shown in Fig. 11.2. The most plausible line of curve does seem to me to be of 'logistic' type, with an even steeper rise between Middle Geometric II and Late Geometric I than we previously suspected, and a drop in the growth-rate thereafter. At its steepest, it just exceeds Malthus' rate, which suggests that its shape may be slightly exaggerated, or perhaps that the duration of the pottery-styles, which cannot be *far* wrong at this late stage in the Geometric style, needs a small adjustment.

   This evidence seems to me to come near to proving what has not been universally accepted, that the depopulation of the centuries before 800 BC had been so drastic as to create the near-vacuum in which

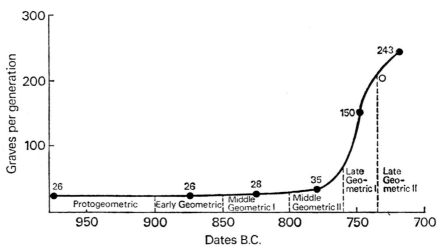

Figure 11.2 The same, with extrapolated figures for the subdivisions of Late Geometric.

such a growth-rate can occur. It does not quite prove it, because of the possible operation of another factor which I have mentioned, an agricultural revolution, for which there is some independent evidence from Attica at this time. Certain Attic graves, beginning around 850 and with increasing frequency in the eighth century, contain painted terracotta model granaries of a new kind.[10] These are surely the burials of agricultural land-owners and their families, specialising in arable farming. Beyond Attica, there is the evidence of the Epic poets: Hesiod wrote a whole poem, the *Works and Days*, to inculcate the first principles of arable farming, and even the Homeric poems, for all their lavish descriptions of heroes eating meat, betray casually the recognition that 'bread is the marrow of man'.[11] Whatever its causes, the population explosion of the eighth century is to be taken into account in any picture of urbanisation in Greece. Outside Attica, the evidence collected in Robin Hägg's *Die Gräber der Argolis*[12] shows another region where this period witnessed a substantial though less spectacular rise. With the Attic rate of increase, five neighbouring villages of 200 inhabitants each would find themselves, one generation later, coalesced into a town of over 4,000. No social or administrative structure could survive that sort of thing without radical change.

It may be interjected here that the case of Attica was unusual, in that it was an exceptionally early and large-scale act of synoecism which brought into existence a single state, with a thousand square miles of territory, adopting Athens as their political centre. Many scholars have rejected the traditional ascription of this act to Theseus, and thus to the Mycenaean period; whether or not we follow them, it seems to me that any act of unification in the Bronze Age would have had to be implemented afresh after the period of desertion of the Attic countryside – that is, after about 900 BC It is true that the ninth and eighth centuries have produced some rich graves in centres outside Athens: one thinks of Eleusis to the west, Spata in the interior and Anavyssos in the far south, but there are also gold bands and other jewellery from Koropi, Menidi and Thorikos.[13] But this does not actually contradict our earliest account of the synoecism, that of Thucydides;[14] indeed, he goes out of his way to say that the people were induced to adopt only the one political centre, even though they might still enjoy their properties as before. These burials can perfectly well represent rich land-owners living or at least dying on their estates, after synoecism had come into effect. Fig. 11.3 shows the evidence for the settlement of the Attic countryside down to about 700 BC; each

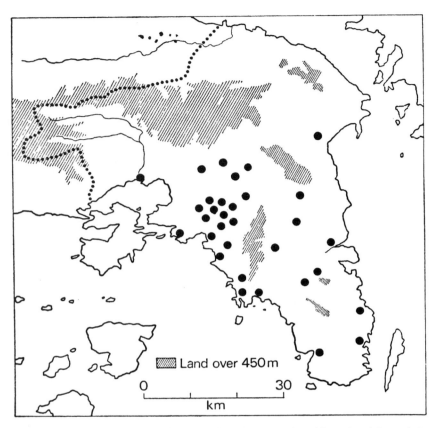

Figure 11.3 Historical demes of Attica which have produced burials of the eighth
century BC The locations of the demes are based on the work of J. S. Traill, *The
political organisation of Attica* (*Hesperia* Supplement XIV, 1975). The demes likely
to be represented are:

City demes	*Coastal demes*	*Inland demes*
Alopeke	Aixone	Acharnae
Diomeia	Anagyrous	Erchia
Euonymon	Anaphlystos	Ionidai
Halimous	Eleusis	Kephisia
Koile	Halai Aixonides	Kolonos
Kollytos	Kephale	Kropidai
Kydathenaion	Marathon	Phlya
Lakiadai	Myrrhinous	Prospalta
Melite	Philaidai	Sphettos
Oion Kerameikon	Thorikos	Sypalettos
Phaleron		
Piraeus		
Skambonidai		

symbol represents one of the demes of Classical Attica, in which graves of the eighth century have been found; there were probably originally 139 of them, and eighth-century settlement is already proved in nearly a quarter of these.

The relatively large pool of resources and land thus available may have conferred advantages on the Athenians; it could have facilitated the agricultural revolution, and it could have contributed to the artistic leadership which, at this phase though not in the following one, the Athenians exercised in Greece. But an even greater ingredient in their success, for which a large territory was not an obvious advantage, was surely that rare achievement, an urbanisation which did not set up a conflict of interest between town and country. In a successful polis, town and country were equal and complementary partners in the state. It is the failure to match this achievement which has bedevilled almost all advanced cultures before and since, including our own. Occasional political leaders have had the vision to realise this; in the words of one of them: 'The labour of the country-dweller fertilised the life of the town, but he was shut out from its excitements . . . When the countryside is neglected, it always takes its revenge. Unless country and town march together in reciprocal activity, civilisation will limp on one foot.' These observations from Aneurin Bevan's *In place of fear*[15] are justified by countless historical instances, but if history can also provide an exception, it is surely the Greek polis at its height.

Pottery-classification, one of the oldest concerns of archaeology, may be brought to bear afresh on this question, thanks to the development of new techniques. First, however, we may note that even its application in the traditional manner can throw light on conditions in the preceding era, the period of the tribal order. For the regional uniformity of pottery-decoration, over quite large but thinly-populated areas,[16] conforms to a pattern which can be explained in terms of the tribal system. What was it that led, say, the people of Mycenae to decorate their pottery in much the same way as the people of Troezen, forty miles away, and quite differently from the people of Cleonae, ten miles away, if not some sense of community based on tribe and kinship, which set off the Argolid from Corinthia? These divisions of style also largely survived the rise of the polis. There is today, however, a possibility of extracting more precise information, from the technique of trace element analysis in pottery fabrics. By comparing the composition of fabrics in this way, actual locations of production can be suggested, and they may come as a surprise. The Fitch Laboratory in the British School at Athens, itself a welcome recent example of the kind of initiative from which Classical Archaeology can derive great benefit, has recently, at the initiative of Dr Barbara Bohen, investigated samples from the very milieu that we were considering earlier, eighth-century Attica. Pottery from a rich rural cemetery at Anavyssos near Cape Sunion, of quite fine quality, was compared with fine pottery from graves in the Kerameikos at Athens. Both would probably have been classed, according to the traditional methods, as sophisticated, metropolitan ware, presumably made therefore in Athens and purchased by the well-heeled relatives of the deceased in rural Anaphlystos (the ancient deme located at Anavyssos). What the tests have shown is that, on the contrary, even some of the finest ware from Anavyssos has a different composition from that standard in Athens, though the manner of decoration is closely similar. It was therefore presumably made locally, or at any rate not in Athens. Nor is this all: some pieces with the characteristic Anavyssos composition were actually found in the Kerameikos material from Athens.[17] The possible inferences are many; one that is at least compatible with the evidence is that now in the eighth century, with synoecism becoming a reality and the status of Athens as political and judicial centre for all Attica accepted, the cultural influence of the city was fostered by the repeated journeys of the countrymen to and from it, so that they learned to produce pottery indistinguishable in style and quality from that of the city; and that they were able to sell some of it in the city.

From pottery we turn to what should be the most direct evidence for the rise of the Greek state: that which comes from the excavation of early Greek settlement-sites. Here the discoveries have revealed at least two quite distinct patterns of development. A series of towns in Ionia and the Cyclades have been dug since World War II, and in almost all of them, fortification is the feature which first attracts attention. At Old Smyrna,[18] in whose excavation Mr R. V. Nicholls played such a noted part, the first wall, which at that date enclosed the whole town, was found to date from about 850 BC. The settlement itself is however older still, and begins by about 1000. Was there then no wall to protect the settlement in its first years? If there was, it was in some place other than the natural line of defence; for here the excavators found only a much earlier prehistoric wall, which was already totally ruinous and can have offered no defence at all, and then the series of fortifications beginning about 850. The likeliest conclusion seems to me that the infant Smyrna, being perhaps neither very concentrated nor very substantial, did without a wall. As we shall see, even 850 is an exceptionally early date for a Greek fortification. The other important feature at Smyrna is the early temple – or rather the lack of a very early temple.[19] Only at a date just after 700 BC did the city acquire a traceable temple, though it has a possible predecessor, which could have stood on a platform of uncertain use, constructed about 750 BC. Once again, as with the wall, there is the theoretical possibility that the people of Smyrna, for no known reason and against normal Greek practice, may have built a really early temple in some other undiscovered spot, and then moved its site; but once again the likelier alternative is that there was none, and that the city waited until about 750, perhaps until after 700 for the first temple of its patron goddess.

The site of Zagora on Andros is perhaps the next example to take.[20] Here the fortification-wall, in the light of the most recent excavation, has turned out to be, if anything, somewhat earlier than the bulk of the material from the settlement which it protects. Its construction seems to belong around 800 BC; the material from the houses, after several seasons of excavation, has been found to be very largely of late-eighth-century date; yet, as at Smyrna, there are signs of an original settlement well before either date, to judge from isolated burials. In each case the sequence is one of a small, unfortified settlement; then a decision to fortify; then a gradual growth of urbanisation in the protection of the wall. As for the temple at Zagora, the remarkable fact is that it dates to a period when the settlement had been deserted for something like 150 years, though there had probably been a sanctuary of some kind during the lifetime of the town.

Next, Emporio on Chios;[21] founded perhaps around 800 BC, it is closer geographically to Smyrna and chronologically to Zagora; but it differs from either in being on the site of a former Mycenaean settlement, and this may explain certain rather backward-looking features that it exhibits. Its fortifications, miserable as they were, enclosed only the acropolis at the highest point of the town; a single large building, probably a chieftain's house, was prominent on the acropolis, but most of the houses lay outside. Here again, the extant temple of Athena dates from well after the lifetime of the settlement, when it was in effect a rural shrine, although once more there are signs of dedications being offered during the occupation of the town. Emporio has been claimed – not by its excavators – as an exemplar of the kind of state that Homer describes;[22] but there are several discordant features, to say nothing of the vexed question of the discrepancy in architectural standards, to which I believe that Dr Plommer will be drawing attention in a forthcoming paper, as forcefully as only he can.

There are other sites of this period which could be brought into the discussion. One of them, Iasos in Caria,[23] offers a fortification-wall which may not be much later than Smyrna's, but which again is not as old as the first settlement on the site. Two more recent discoveries are Agios Andreas, on the Cycladic island of Siphnos, where in the eighth century a deserted Bronze Age fortress was repaired and rebuilt with new housing;[24] and the settlement of the ninth and eighth centuries on the tiny island of Donoussa, less than ten square miles in area, where walls and houses are apparently contemporary.[25] Neither place has produced a recognisable temple.

I wish to argue that the implication of fortification-walls, for questions of institutional development, may be less decisive than we have hitherto tended to think; and more specifically that their presence is not a guarantee of the attainment of independent polis status. By contrast, the building of a monumental temple, to a recognised patron deity, especially when it is the first of a long line on the same site, may be our clearest physical indication that the emergent polis has arrived, or is at hand. It shows, to echo Ehrenberg's words, that the god has taken over the monarchy. By this reckoning, Smyrna may have become a polis only after about 750 BC; Zagora and Emporio were abandoned before they could reach this status, and their posthumous temples have a quite different rôle; Agios Andreas and the Donoussa site also failed to achieve polis status. Such conclusions win support from certain other evidence. For a start, we at least know that Smyrna became a polis sooner or later. By contrast, in the Emporio report Mr Boardman disclaims polis status for his site,[26] while the excavators of Zagora have gone further and suggested that the occasion for the desertion of their site was the move to the historical polis of Andros, a few miles to the north;[27] this then would be an act of synoecism in its fullest physical sense. On Siphnos, we at least know that there was another settlement in existence, during and after the lifetime of the Agios Andreas site, and that this other place has remained a principal town of the island to our own times.[28] Even on tiny Donoussa, occasion was found to move away to some other spot, perhaps off the island altogether, around 700 BC. There is indeed a clear case of the opposite end of this process, in a Greek town whose site was shifted, probably in the early eighth century, from an uncertain site to a known one, and this is Eretria in Euboea.[29]

There is nothing new in the suggestion, which follows from what I have been saying, that the formative period for the polis, at least in Ionia and the islands, was the eighth century BC and perhaps the early seventh. I would like to reinforce it, however, by appealing more broadly to the criterion of a monumental temple to a patron deity. All over the Greek world, we now have stratigraphic evidence for the first construction of temples on historic sites, usually in cities: at Eretria, Perachora, Mycenae, probably Tiryns, the Argive Heraeum, Asine, Mantinea, Sparta, Thermon in Aetolia, Antissa on Lesbos, the Samian Heraeum, Dreros. At Athens and Eleusis we have buildings of peculiar form which are nevertheless associated with cult.[30] None of these is much later than 700 BC, and most are a little earlier; yet not one of them has been convincingly shown to be earlier than 800. By contrast, I wonder whether the early fortifications on such sites as Smyrna, Iasos and Zagora are not a precocious development prompted by regional factors of security; for on the Ionian coast, we can point to the example of Miletus, where even the Mycenaeans had so far forgotten their standard practice as to put a defensive wall round the whole settlement. Need there be any profound political implications in all this?

There is in any case a second and quite different pattern of development discernible on the Greek mainland. Athens, uniquely fortunate in the sheer quantity of isolated finds brought to light in the development of the modern city, is uniquely *un*fortunate in the way that these same operations have obliterated the broader picture of the early city. But for the eleventh and tenth centuries BC, in the lifetime of the Protogeometric style, we can confidently say that Athens consisted of a number of separate, discontinuous, unfortified villages. The Acropolis may have been the focus of settlement, but a unified community living there could hardly have used all the far-flung cemeteries that are known from this period (Fig. 11.4), extending to a thousand yards from the Acropolis rock. Even in the ensuing Geometric period, when the population-boom presently brought a thicker spread of settlement, it is hard to think of the area enclosed by the cemeteries (Fig. 11.5) as being built up. There is one other documented case which recalls that of Athens: a recent study by Carl Roebuck has shown that Corinth, even at the time of her great colonial enterprises beginning in the 730s, was still no more than a group of villages.[31] The evidence from the temples at both sites may also prove to harmonise. The American excavators now incline to push back the date of the first Apollo temple to the very beginning of the seventh century.[32] At Athens, the case is more obscure although the location of the early Athena temple, on the site of the former Mycenaean palace, between the later Parthenon and Erechtheum, is generally agreed. The only substantial

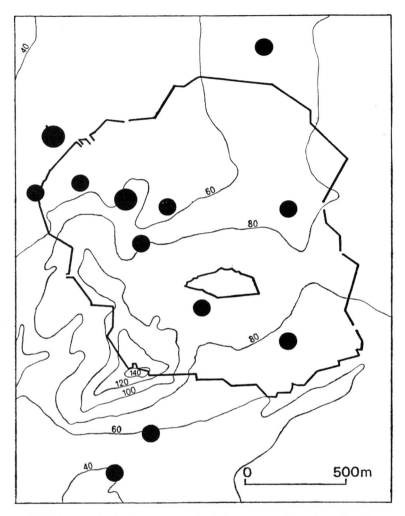

Figure 11.4 Cemeteries in Protogeometric Athens (later eleventh and tenth centuries BC). The larger symbols indicate close groupings of 25 or more graves.

evidence comes from two column-bases, which were for long thought to belong to the Mycenaean palace itself. In 1962, however, two different scholars working quite independently, Professor Iakovidis and Dr Carl Nylander, came to the conclusion that the bases were more readily comparable with bases from temples of the eighth and seventh centuries.[33] Perhaps, therefore, these two great cities can be added to the list of those who first erected a monumental temple in the years around 700 BC.

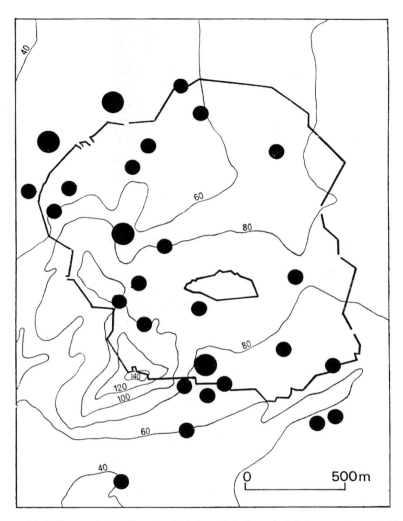

Figure 11.5 Cemeteries in Geometric Athens (ninth and eighth centuries BC). The larger symbols indicate close groupings of 25 or more graves.

It is fitting to place the final emphasis on religion, perhaps the most important single medium for articulating Greek society. If we turn for a moment from city to countryside, we find a different type of worship, which has received considerable attention recently: this is the strange phenomenon of hero-cults at prehistoric graves, and occasionally at other kinds of prehistoric site. I have said enough about this elsewhere, and am anyway saved from the need of lengthy explanation by the timely appearance last month of an article by Professor

Nicolas Coldstream.[34] To put things in one sentence: between 750 and 700 BC, Greeks in several parts of the country show a sudden interest in making offerings at graves belonging to an age between 500 and 1,000 years earlier. Why? The evidence of discontinuity of population proves, if proof were needed, that any claim to hereditary connection with the dead would have been bogus. The worshippers can have had not the faintest notion of the real identity of the people buried in the graves, as they occasionally prove to us when they reveal whom they *pretended* to identify. What is interesting is that the pretence was thought worth while. At a time when the Greeks were establishing a form of society in which land-ownership was the secure path to citizenship, it was doubtless helpful to establish a link with a territory through the medium of its earlier inhabitants. For the distribution of these cults, Professor Coldstream's ingenious explanation is that it coincided with the areas where the form of monumental tomb used in the Heroic Age had vanished – *omne ignotum pro magnifico* – and that where these types of tomb were still familiar, the cults were absent. One alternative explanation however occurs to me: that the absence of these cults from, most conspicuously, Thessaly, Laconia and Crete is significant of the fact that these were the regions where a truly free and independent peasantry did not come into being in Classical times. Such rustic propaganda-practices were beyond the aspirations of landless serfs, and beneath the consideration of an entrenched landowning class. I see them as private, family cults, not as early examples of the state-regulated hero-cults of which we read in historical sources and inscriptions; these latter were often moved into the city (as happened with the worship of Eurysakes, son of Ajax, established in the Athenian deme of Melite some time before the late sixth century[35]), whereas our cults at tombs can continue at the original site until the Classical period.

The great official sanctuaries which stood apart from the individual cities, and in a sense above them, are a different thing again. The date of their rise is a controversial question on which, once again, I have had my say elsewhere. Let me therefore support it by resorting again to some figures, provided by other scholars who can hardly have been influenced by anything I have written. In the last few years, the bronze figurines from Delphi have been published by Claude Rolley,[36] as have the early bronzes from Delos;[37] Jean Ducat has published the early pottery and bronzes from the Ptoan sanctuary in Boeotia,[38] Klaus Kilian the fibulae from the sanctuary of Artemis Enodia at Pherae in Thessaly[39] and Wolf-Dieter Heilmeyer the early terracottas from Olympia, the site which is universally agreed to have the earliest range of dedications in mainland Greece.[40] Between them, these publications include nearly 3,000 objects of a date of the seventh century BC or earlier; of these, the authors date 2.9% to before 800 BC, 97.1% to after. Were it not for the Olympia finds, the figures would be 0.4% before and 99.6% after. Approximate though their judgements of date must be, I hope that this message is clear: the eighth century witnessed, among other things, a huge increase in activity at the inter-state sanctuaries. It is not easy to explain why it had suddenly become so pressing a need to secure the favour of Zeus or Hera, Apollo or Artemis, unless it was that the inter-state sanctuaries were attracting dedications from the ethnē and other elements who had no easy access to the new city-temples of these same deities.

There are other questions to do with the rise of the polis on which archaeological evidence could yet throw light. There is no time to do more than ask one or two of them. Does the evidence of the first colonial polis-sites, and particularly of the earliest of all, Pithekoussai on Ischia, imply the same degree of physical and institutional development in the mother-cities which sent them out? Or is it possible that the example of the colonies may have accelerated developments at home? We may recall that some colonists came from regions like Lokris and Achaea where the polis *never* became the norm. Again, why is it that Homer's picture of the city appears to fit only a late stage of the process that I have been sketching, if the social system he portrays is one untouched by any of its accompaniments?

Our clearest finding, however, is that nowhere after the Bronze Age is there anything resembling an urban concentration to be seen before about 850 BC. In the whole 150-year-long Protogeometric period, for example, the largest cemeteries in southern Greece and the Aegean have produced fewer than a hundred graves; one example with some claim to thorough exploration is the Athenian Kerameikos, which has about 62.[41] On the generous assumption of a normal life-expectation of thirty years, this represents the graves of a community averaging twelve to fifteen people. A simple definition that we can give of this dark age is as the period when there were no towns. I am reminded of a description of the Shield of Achilles, given not by Homer but by W. H. Auden.[42]

> She looked over his shoulder
> For vines and olive-trees,
> Marble well-governed cities
> And ships upon untamed seas,
> But there on the shining metal
> His hands had put instead

An artificial wilderness
And a sky like lead.

.   .   .   .   .

She looked over his shoulder
For athletes at their games,
Men and women in a dance
Moving their sweet limbs
Quick, quick to the music,
But there on the shining shield
His hands had set no dancing-floor
But a weed-choked field.

Nowhere in the description of the Shield in the *Iliad,* and still less in our *a posteriori* visions of 'marble well-governed cities', do I find such correspondences with the picture that is emerging of the dark age of Greece, as in this poetic image. If there is any truth in such a view, it makes all the more astounding the creation, against such a setting, of the historical Greek state.

This Inaugural Lecture was delivered in the University of Cambridge on 1 March 1977.

NOTES

1. London, 1966.
2. See especially *Antiquity* 47 (1973), 18.
3. *The Greek state* (2nd ed., London, 1969), 15.
4. Fr. Z 103 (Lobel and Page).
5. J. M. Cook, *The Greeks in Ionia and the East* (London, 1962), 37–8; V. Ehrenberg, *Journal of Hellenic Studies* 57 (1937), 155 and compare *The Greek state²*, 242; M. I. Finley, *The world of Odysseus* (Pelican, Harmondsworth, 1962), 39.
6. The references for Attic sites can be found in my *The Dark Age of Greece* (Edinburgh, 1971), 202–3 or, for Geometric only but with a greater precision in the specification of periods, in J. N. Coldstream, *Greek Geometric pottery* (London, 1968; see especially site index, pp. 399–403). To these must be added the more recently published finds: for Athens, in *Arkhaiologikon Deltion* 23 (1968), *Chronika*, 48–50; 55–7; 67; 73–5; 79–84; 88–9; 89–92; vol. 24 (1969), *Chr.*, 37–41; vol. 25 (1970), *Chr.*, 55–8; vol. 27 (1972), *Chr.*, 62; 93–7; vol. 28 (1973), *Meletimata*, 1–63; *Athens Annals of Archaeology* 1 (1968), 20–7; 5 (1972), 165–76; *Athenische Mitteilungen* 81 (1966), 4–12 and 112–16; 89 (1974), 1–25; *Hesperia* 43 (1974), 325–90; for the Athenian Agora, the map in Eva T. H. Brann, *Agora* VIII (Princeton, 1962), plate 45 is helpful; for Eleusis, G. E. Mylonas, To *Dutikon Nekrotapheion tis Eleusinos* (Athens,

1975); for Thorikos, H. F. Mussche *et al., Thorikos* vols. II (1967), 33, n. 1; III (1967), 31–56; IV (1969), 71–109; further Attic references in *Arkhaiologikon Deltion* are (Argyroupolis) 23 (1968), *Chr.*, 112–13; (Merenda, ancient Myrrhinous) 25 (1970), *Chr.*, 127–9; (Markopoulo) 26 (1971), *Chr.*, 38–40. For Trachones, finally, see *Athenische Mitteilungen* 88 (1973), 1–54.

7. *An essay on the principle of population* (Everyman ed., London, 1958), vol. 1, 7.

8. (London, 1969), 54.

9. In *Acculturation and continuity in Atlantic Europe* (*Dissertationes Archaeologicae Gandenses*, vol. 16): Papers presented at the IVth Atlantic Colloquium, Ghent, 1975, 198–220.

10. See Evelyn L. Smithson in *Hesperia* 37 (1968), 83, 92–7, plates 23–7.

11. *Odyssey* 2.290; 20.108.

12. *Die Gräber der Argolis in Submykenischer, Protogeometrischer und Geometrischer Zeit* (*Boreas* VII: 1), Uppsala, 1974.

13. Especially the Isis Grave at Eleusis (Coldstream, *op. cit.* (above, n. 6), 21 with references); Spata, *Arkhaiologikon Deltion* 6 (1920), *Parartima*, 131ff. and Anavyssos, *ibid.* 21 (1966), *Chr.*, 97–8; Koropi, *Annual of the British School at Athens* 46 (1951), 45–9; Menidi, *Archäologischer Anzeiger* 1904, 40; Thorikos, the silver fibula mentioned by R. Hampe, *Frühe griechische Sagenbilder in Böotien* (1936), 90, no. 10.

14. 11.15.2.

15. 2nd edition (London, 1961), 60

16. See especially the works of V. R. d'A. Desborough, *Protogeometric pottery* (Oxford, 1952) and J. N. Coldstream (*op. cit.* above, n. 6).

17. I am extremely grateful to Dr Bohen, and to Dr R. E. Jones of the Marc and Ismene Fitch Research Laboratory of the British School, Athens, for permission to refer more fully to their findings, briefly referred to in the *Annual Report of the Managing Committee, British School at Athens* for 1975–76, page 19.

18. See J. M. Cook and R. V. Nicholls, *Annual of the British School at Athens* 53–4 (1958–9), 1–137, especially 121–3.

19. *Ibid.* 75–81 and n. 189.

20. A. Cambitoglou, J. J. Coulton, J. Birmingham and J. R. Green, *Zagora* 1 (Sydney, 1971); for the fortification-wall, add *Praktika tis Arkhaiologikis Etaireias* 1972, 269–73 and 1974, 163–80.

21. J. Boardman, *Excavations in Chios, 1952–5: Greek Emporio* (London, 1967).

22. Cf. T. B. L. Webster in A. J. B. Wace and F. H. Stubbings (edd.), *A companion to Homer* (London, 1962), 454.

23. See *Annuario della Scuola Archeologica in Atene* 39–40 (n.s. 23–4) (1961–2), 527–34 (D. Levi).

24. *Arkhaiologikon Deltion* 25 (1970), *Chr.*, 431–4 (B. Philippaki).

25. *Ibid.* 22 (1967), *Chr.*, 467; 24 (1969), *Chr.*, 390–3; 25 (1970), *Chr.*, 426–8; 26 (1971), *Chr.*, 465–7; *Athens Annals of Archaeology* 4 (1971), 210–16 and 6 (1973), 256–9 (Ph. Zaphiropoulou).
26. *Op. cit.* (above, n. 21), 249.
27. *Op. cit* (above, n. 20), II.
28. See *Annual of the British School at Athens* 44 (1949), 1–92 (J. K. Brock and G. Mackworth Young).
29. See most recently C Bérard, *Eretria* III: *L' Hérôon à la porte de l'ouest* (Berne, 1970), 68, nn. 25–6.
30. Site-references are conveniently given in H. Drerup, *Griechische Baukunst in geometrischer Zeit* (Kapitel 'O' of *Archaeologia Homerica*, edd. F. Matz and H.-G. Buchholz, Göttingen, 1969), with the exception of Mantinea, *Arkhaiologikon Deltion* 18 (1963), *Chr.*, 88–9 (Th. Karagiorga).
31. *Hesperia* 41 (1972), 96–127.
32. *Ibid.* 99, n. 6.
33. Sp. Iakovidis, *I Mukinaiki Akropolis tôn Athinôn* (Athens, 1962), especially 62–5; C. Nylander, *Opuscula Atheniensia* 4 (1962), 31–57.
34. *Journal of Hellenic Studies* 96 (1976), 8–17.
35. See W. S. Ferguson in *Hesperia* 7 (1938), 1–74, especially 15ff.; M. P. Nilsson, *Cults, myths, oracles and politics in Ancient Greece* (*Skrifter utgivna av Svenska Institutet i Athen*, 8°, I, Lund, 1951), 29–34.
36. *Fouilles de Delphes* V, 2 (Paris, 1969); *Les Statuettes de Bronze.*
37. *Études Déliennes* (*Bulletin de Correspondance Hellénique*, Supplément I, Paris, 1973), 491–524.
38. *Les Kouroi du Ptoion* (*Bibliothèque des Écoles françaises d' Athènes et de Rome*, fasc. 219, Paris, 1971), 49–55, 58–65.
39. *Fibeln in Thessalien* (*Prähistorische Bronzefunde* xiv, 2, Munich, 1975).
40. *Frühe Olympische Tonfiguren* (*Olympische Forschungen* VII, Berlin, 1972).
41. See W. Kraiker and K. Kübler, *Kerameikos* I (Berlin, 1939), 89–130; K. Kübler, *Kerameikos* IV (1943); *Athenische Mitteilungen* 81 (1966), 4–10.
42. *The Shield of Achilles* (London, 1955), 35–7 (quoted by permission of Faber & Faber Ltd, London, and Random House Inc, New York).

I should finally like to acknowledge with gratitude the help give me by Mr P. L. J. Halstead over demographic questions, by Dr W. G. A. Cavanagh over the dating of some Attic graves, and by Mr J. G. Howie in the understanding of significance of hero-cults.

CHAPTER 12

Heavy Freight in Archaic Greece

This was a paper that attracted some predictable criticisms – for over-insistence on the use of oared galleys for overseas enterprise by Greeks of the Archaic period (pp. 223–4), for example: see Reed 1984: 39–40; Macdonald 1986. On the numerical side, one important change must be made: the measurements of the *Schiffsfundament* on Samos (p. 223), taken from a small-scale drawing, were underestimated by me: Wallinga (1993: 49–53) makes them roughly 23.33 by 3.22 m – a significant increase in the width especially – though he supports the identification of a pentekontor here. But he also stresses (42 and n. 31) the likelihood of variation in the beam of galleys, which would open wider possibilities for the transport of heavy goods and answer some of the earlier criticisms.

Behind this paper, there also lurks a spectre of its time (the 1980s): the ubiquity of the 'commercial imperative' and the rise (or return) of an extreme modernist view of past economies. While politicians extolled the limitless merits of wealth creation through commercial enterprise, and economists inculcated the doctrine that the only social duty of a public company to society was to make a profit for its shareholders, students of past cultures – often, I think, quite unconscious of the effects exerted on them by the thought of their own times – began to impute similar values to the historical, and indeed the distant prehistoric past. Yet it is overwhelmingly likely that there were long periods in the past when quite other priorities and values were given precedence: indeed Sahlins (1972) had earlier used anthropological and other evidence, to classic effect, to demonstrate this. This paper was partly conceived as a reaction to this tendency, in the firm belief that ancient Greece was also a culture in which quite different motives often prevailed.

BIBLIOGRAPHY

Macdonald, B. R. (1986), 'The Diolkos', *Journal of Hellenic Studies* 96, 191–5.
Reed, C. M. (1984), 'Maritime traders in the Archaic Greek world: a typology of those engaged in the long-distance transfer of goods by sea', *The Ancient World* 10: 31–43.
Sahlins, M. (1972), *Stone Age Economics*, Hawthorne, NY: Aldine de Gruyter.
Wallinga, H. T. (1993), *Ships and Sea-Power before the Great Persian War: The Ancestry of the Ancient Trireme*, Leiden: E. J. Brill.

The larger aim of this paper is to convince historians that archaeological evidence can truly be brought to bear on problems that are of central concern to them, and that it can be perilous to ignore it. In public, of course, most historians would indignantly deny that they needed any such convincing; but in the heat of discussion a deeper stratum of scepticism and downright mistrust sometimes comes to the surface. I choose the topic of sea-borne freight as just such a central problem, omitting land-transport, partly because it has been effectively dealt with by Burford (1960), partly because the inherent advantages of sea-over land-transport in the ancient world must have been further enhanced when it was a question of carrying heavy loads, sometimes (as in the case of marble) in the form of large indivisible units. In archaic times, especially, one suspects that the provision of good roads was such as to widen rather than narrow the gap.

This brings us, however, to the question of the facilities for maritime transport in archaic Greece, and above all to the ships. The author of the most interesting recent paper on archaic sea-trade, Bravo (1977), disclaims such knowledge of archaeology as would enable him to make use of its evidence; nor does the later work of Mele (1979) set out to fill this particular gap. But I shall be taking as a working hypothesis Bravo's intriguing theory of rich, land-holding ship-owners and of 'agents', who either did not belong to the land-owning class or else were merely not rich, undertaking the actual voyages; coupling this with Humphreys' gloss that the ships used for these enterprises in the archaic period were, in the main, not purpose-built merchantmen but

'Heavy freight in Archaic Greece', from P. Garnsey, K. Hopkins and C. R. Whittaker (ed.), *Trade in the Ancient Economy*, London: Chatto & Windus, 1983, pp. 16–26.

dual-purpose galleys, often pentekontors (Humphreys (1978) 166–8 and n. 13). There is in fact supporting evidence for this hypothesis which has not been used.

Herodotus tells us (1 163.2) that the Phocaeans used pentekontors, not merchantmen, for long-distance trade. Plutarch (*Pericles* XXVI 3–4) ascribes an origin in sixth-century Samos to the type of ship called *Samaina*, a kind of super-pentekontor enlarged to take bigger cargoes. If two of the most prominent Archaic trading states at least sometimes preferred oared galleys, then the burden of proof is on those who believe that purpose-built, sail-driven merchantmen were the norm elsewhere at this period. The archaeological evidence will not support them. The vase-paintings for a long time depict only oared vessels (cf. Morrison and Williams (1968)); this could be explained in terms of the greater social prestige of such ships, but the explanation wears thin when it is applied to the Corinthian votive plaques dedicated to Poseidon in his sanctuary on Pentescuphia (Acrocorinth), presumably on successful completion of a voyage – especially since one plaque shows a cargo of pots loaded on a vessel of a type indistinguishable from the war-galleys on other plaques.[1] A Samian coin of *c*.490 BC (Morrison and Williams (1968), 111, pl. 20(e)) shows the bows of what must be a *Samaina*, to judge from its close correspondence with Plutarch's description and inferences therefrom. It looks very like the Corinthian ships on the plaques; we are reminded of Thucydides 1 13.2 on the naval links between these two states.

The pentekontor was a fair-sized vessel with a length to beam ratio of about 10:1. Casson (1971) 54–5 estimates its length at 38 m, its beam at 3.95 m; Landels (1978) 142 at 30.4 m and 3.04 m respectively. But nobody seems to have taken account of the 'Schiffsfundament' at the Samian Heraion, a row of nine parallel oblong stone blocks with the shortest ones at the ends and the longest one in the middle;[2] these acted as supports for a complete dedicated ship and were set up around 600 BC. No part of the ship was found, but the approximate dimensions given appear rather smaller than the above estimates, about 21.9 m long and 2.1 m in the beam. The German excavators[3] did however also find a series of wooden miniature dedications and once again they are all of war-galley type, though one might expect at least some of these Samian sanctuary-dedications to commemorate merchant enterprises rather than sea-battles. When in the last quarter of the sixth century pictures of sail-driven 'round ships' at last begin to appear on Athenian vases, there continue to be pictures of what are clearly oared merchantmen too (see Casson

(1971) 66, Fig. 91). The significance of all this is that a galley required a crew of 50 (or more: Humphreys (1978) 300, n. 10) trained
oarsmen who had either to be paid or to take a share in the profits
of a venture. Humphreys (1978) 168 notes the telling point that in
Herodotus IV 152.4 the *whole* crew of the ship of Colaeus of Samos
makes the dedication of the tithe.

Now I turn to the question of the cargoes carried. Trade nowadays
is usually quantified in terms of the value of goods exchanged (e.g. in
balance of payments calculations), but even for the best-documented
periods of antiquity this type of calculation is hardly an imaginable
possibility: the more so for Archaic times when it would have to
be estimated in man-hours of labour as a proportion of the total
labour input. But the next most significant index of trade is perhaps
that of tonnage (as in wartime shipping losses), and for antiquity
this is not quite such a hopeless proposition. We can make some
progress by isolating the heaviest and bulkiest commodities which
we know to have been exported and imported, and thus try to reach
conclusions about a fairly substantial sample of the total volume of
overseas exchanges. Here I believe that *marble* and *metal ores* between
them must have composed an important part of the tonnage of sea-
transport in the Archaic world. This would seem to be particularly
true of the earlier Archaic period, when the import of grain had barely
entered the picture and when the necessary supplies of timber, though
certainly large, may still have been mainly met from local resources.
As for the slave-trade, even if we do not follow Starr in his restricted
view ((1977) 91) of the scope of industrial and especially of agrarian
slavery in archaic Greece, the fact remains that slaves could walk,
and might therefore, unlike inanimate cargoes, be more economically
moved overland in many cases. Anyway, I would observe that a block
for a single life-sized Archaic marble statue weighed as much as about
12 slaves.

With marble, we have to reckon with two main uses, in sculpture
from about 650 BC and in marble building-stone from about 550; both
become increasingly common down to the very late Archaic period,
when for sculpture marble begins to give way to bronze. The problem
now arises of distinguishing the provenances of Aegean marbles with
a sufficient degree of precision: as we were reminded a few years ago
by the rather sharp exchange which took place in the pages of the
Annual of the British School at Athens (Renfrew and Peacey (1968),
Ashmole (1970), Wycherley (1973)). Most younger archaeologists felt
a fervent sympathy with Renfrew's scientific approach in that debate,

but time has reinforced Ashmole's argument that no scientific test is yet capable of yielding results that are definite. Even the prospects of isotope identification as a method seem to have dimmed in the last year or two (see Germann *et al.* (1980), Lazzarini *et al.* (1980)). Further, it was a serious defect of the original case that no account was taken of ancient documentary and epigraphical evidence for the origin of marbles in buildings which still survive (as Wycherley observed for the Periclean buildings in Athens). Even for the Archaic period, we have a few precious pieces of evidence of this kind: Herodotus states flatly (V 62.3) that in the years after 513 BC exiled Athenian aristocrats built a temple at Delphi with extensive use of Parian marble. Two earlier buildings at Delphi are also built of marble, the Treasuries of Cnidos (*c.* 560–50) and of Siphnos (*c.* 525); classicists call this 'Parian' marble too, partly because it is very like that of the temple, partly (in the latter case) because Herodotus again clearly tells us (III 57.4) that the people of Siphnos, at the time when they were building their treasury, also fitted out the meeting-place and town-hall of their native island with Parian marble. More generally, the plain fact is that there are many regions of Greece which lack marble deposits, especially those of the fine white marbles which were increasingly demanded; and that many important sites for sculpture and architecture (and this means above all sanctuaries) lie within such regions. So that although a degree of scepticism is proper, I do not think that this can prevent us from concluding that marble often had to be shipped.

With sculptural marble, the epigraphic evidence throws some important light, not indeed on the provenance of the marbles used for the statues, but on an allied question: the origins of the artists who carved them. They show that beyond any doubt it was a frequent occurrence in the Archaic period for a statue in city A to be carved by a sculptor from city B. On its own, this may not appear to prove very much; theoretically this could happen without the sculptor travelling, as he could simply have the finished statue shipped from B to A. Luckily, however, we can call on much written testimony to show that Archaic sculptors often did travel: we read of Cretans in Arcadia, the Argolid, Sicyon and Aetolia; Corinthian exiles in Etruria; an Ionian in Sparta; Spartans at Olympia; an Athenian in Ionia; a Sicyonian in Miletus.[4] In all these cases, either we are told in so many words that the artist travelled to carry out the commission, or the size and elaboration of the work were such as to make execution on the spot essential. There are anyway the common-sense arguments that a fully-finished marble statue of any size would be a fragile thing to transport, and that ascertaining the client's desires and securing his approval would be much easier if the artist travelled. In the case of Archaic temple-building, where the presence of the architect was essential, there is also a high incidence of non-native architects in the surviving accounts. To return to sculpture, it would be valuable to establish that not only was a statue at A made by a sculptor from B, but also that it was carved out of *marble* from B. This we can seldom do with complete certainty but we can get close: there is for example in Taranto an unfinished female statue in imported (presumably Greek) marble, and the work-manship does not look local.[5] But when we put together the copious archaeological evidence of imported marbles with the frequent liter-ary attestation of travelling sculptors it is I think a fair conclusion that many Archaic statues were finished *in situ* by the sculptor or his apprentices. So we have the artists fairly firmly pinned down at one end – that of the destination – of the Archaic marble-shipping process.

Interestingly enough, we also have some evidence to pin them down at the other end as well. At three sites on Naxos and on Mt Pentelikon in Attica, there are unfinished Archaic statues in or near ancient quarry sites, in some cases still attached to the living rock. The extraordinary thing about them is the degree to which they have been worked: in one case on Naxos, it is possible to detect the stage of anatomical knowledge which the statue reflects, and therefore its probable date.[6] This must mean, either that the sculptor himself roughed out the statue in the quarry, or that he briefed the quarryman in some detail to do so. In either case, he would have to spend time at the quarry; and anyway we know from Renaissance and later evidence that sculptors like to pick out their block in the quarry. From all this, the likeliest reconstruction of the process of creation of an Archaic statue emerges as follows:

   (i) client commissions artist
  (ii) artist goes to marble source
 (iii) artist pays quarry-owner and contractor for extracting marble
 (iv) artist pays for land and sea transport of part-worked statue
  (v) client pays artist's and assistants' maintenance for period of
        work (which would be up to a year for a life-sized statue)

The artist will of course try to ensure that the payment under (v) exceeds the sum of those under (ii), (iii) and (iv).

We can perhaps use the analogy of the fourth-century architec-tural and sculptural work at Epidaurus (Burford (1969)) to throw some light on the last three stages of the sequence. To take (iii), the transaction at the quarry, first: Burford reasonably asks (172) – Did quarry-stone cost anything? Her answer for Epidaurus is that the intrinsic value of the stone cannot have been a major factor compared with the cost of labour and transport. This means that it is not very important whether quarries belonged more often to the state or to private individuals; what really counted were the other costs, and the evidence from Naxos and Mt Pentelikon (see above, p. 226) again suggests that the sculptor will have paid any charges at this stage, no doubt with an advance from the client. For building-stone, the picture at Epidaurus is different, but even more clear: a third party, the private contractor who had tendered for supplying each lot of stone, had to cover all stages from the quarry to the building-site (in this instance anything up to 80 km, partly by sea). There were swingeing fines for late delivery (e.g. Burford (1969) 149). At Epidaurus it is clear that, of our stages (iii) and (iv), the former was the more costly: for Corinthian limestone, which had to be brought about 48 km by land, sea and then land again, the ratio of quarrying costs to transport costs was nevertheless between 2:1 and 3:1 (cf. Burford (1969) 189–91, 193–4 and n. 3 for example). To return to sculpture and to our stage (v): we should look for an all-inclusive and therefore high payment here: Epidaurus shows that the sculptors, like the building-stone contractors, accepted an 'all-in' contract which in most cases required a guarantor.

With sculptural marble we can make some attempt, however crude, at overall quantification. In her catalogue of the commonest type of Archaic statue, the *kouros*, Richter lists about 177 works in stone. Nineteen of these come from one particular sanctuary, that of Apollo on Mt Ptoön in Boeotia. But another and much more detailed study[7] has been made of the sculpture from this same sanctuary; and once all the fragmentary evidence, too insubstantial to be included in Richter's book, has been taken into account, the number of *kouroi* which can be shown to have been dedicated here is at least 120, a number greater by a factor of $6\frac{1}{2}$ than the figure in Richter. If this increase is typical, we can infer that traces of about 1,120 *kouroi* from the Archaic period have actually been found. What proportion of the original total are these likely to represent? Here we really enter the realm of surmise, but allowing for incomplete excavation, and for the ravages of the lime-kiln over 2,500 years, I would doubt whether they represent as much as 5 per cent: a study of a particular form of clay vessel of this period, the Panathenaic amphora, has suggested that the surviving proportion is only about $\frac{1}{4}$ of 1 per cent (Cook (1959) 120). We can therefore safely multiply by twenty to give an original total of well over 20,000 archaic *kouroi*. What proportion of Archaic stone sculpture is represented by *kouroi*? Very roughly, one-third, since the corresponding female statues appear to be only slightly less numerous, while other types are individually rarer but collectively would amount to a similar quantity. So there would be at least 60,000 '*kouros*-units' to reckon with. How heavy was the average *kouros*? Our very earliest life-sized marble statue, around 650 BC, is actually female, and its simplified form helps to keep its weight down to about $\frac{1}{4}$ of a ton: but by about 600, we begin to have over-life-sized statues, such as the Sounion *kouros* which weighs about 2 tons even after carving. One gigantic example on Delos, most of which has now vanished, will have weighed some 23 tons, while its surviving base (of which more below) is 34 tons.[8] It will not be excessive to work on a mean figure of three-quarters of a ton per life-sized statue, at least before final carving. Archaic marble sculpture covers a span of about 170 years. A fair guess might be that in any single year of the Archaic period, an absolute minimum of 270 tons (350 '*kouros*-units') of sculptural marble would be travelling round the Aegean: the great bulk of this tonnage would have to do most of its travelling by sea, if only because the island marbles were the most favoured at this time. Inscriptions show that the Cyclades were also a major source of sculptural talent, though the sculptors did most of their work away from home. On to this sculptural total, we have to add the marble used for building-operations in the later part of the period; this would be required on fewer occasions, but of course in much larger quantities: the fragmentary inscriptions which happen to survive for the Temple of Asclepius at Epidaurus show that this modest-sized building required, for part of its cella alone, enough Pentelic marble (about 160 cubic metres) for over 500 life-sized *kouroi*.

So marble was a commodity that made big demands on Archaic shipping resources. The biggest Archaic marble block which we know to have been shipped (*pace* Renfrew and Peacey) is the base of the Colossus of the Naxians on Delos, mentioned above; it appears to be of Naxian marble (as its own boastful inscription perhaps hints), and it dates to about 600 BC.[9] It is 5.14 m by 3.47 m by 0.71 m and, given the measurements for oared galleys on page 223, I can see no way that it could have been safely carried on one of these; so here is perhaps an instance where either a specially-built raft or a merchant 'round ship' must be inferred in earlier Archaic times. But our average statue-block, 1.83 m by 0.61 m by 0.3 m or so, weighing three-quarters of a ton, could most certainly be loaded on a pentekontor. We even have a documented case of this happening with finished statues: Hdt. I 164.3 (the flight of the Phocaeans).[10] When local stone (even local marble) was involved, Coulton's table shows that archaic architects were prepared to move around blocks of up to 73 tons.

It is time to turn to the transport of metals. Beyond saying that the quantities of iron transported must have been very large, while those of copper would have been somewhat smaller but would have to travel much longer distances on average, I shrink from attempting any quantification. There is, however, some useful evidence for the *stage* at which metal-shipments took place. Theoretically, three stages of transportation could be involved:

(i) from the point of extraction to the smelting-location
(ii) from smelting-location to craftsman's shop
(iii) from workshop, perhaps *via* a middleman, to the ultimate owner.

What the Archaic Greek evidence however shows is that stage (ii) was regularly eliminated; in other words, that smelting and forging, casting or working took place at the same site (and in passing one may note that there is evidence from Late Bronze Age Kea to suggest that the same may have been true in prehistoric Greece). Our two best examples involve island-sites with no metal sources of their own. At Pithecusae in Ischia (Buchner (1970) 97–8) quantities of iron slag, together with half-finished iron artefacts, tuyères and other iron-foundry debris, tell their own story; what is more, the slag when analysed proved to be traceable to one particular vein of ore from Elba, which lies about 400 km away to the north-west. This is interesting not least because it flatly contradicts the literary evidence, at least for a later period, of Diodorus (V 13.1–2), who describes how the ore was smelted more or less *in situ* on Elba and then exported in the form of 'sponge' iron (blooms) to Puteoli and elsewhere, where it was marketed: a clear instance of the discrepancy between Archaic and Classical practice. The smaller island of Motya produced traces of iron-smelting on the spot, as well as numerous iron artefacts.[11] Equally striking in a different way is the evidence from the sanctuary of Apollo at Bassae, which lies over 1,000 m up in the mountains of Arcadia but nevertheless showed proof of iron-smelting on the site – presumably for the production of objects for the pilgrims to dedicate.[12]

What does all this suggest? Clearly, that for preference, in Archaic times, iron was often transported in the form of ore, either over sea-voyages up to 400 km in length, or by arduous uphill portages on land. A few years ago, I found this a surprising conclusion, and was rash enough to say so, only to fall prey to a reviewer who described himself as 'a former sailor in the Swedish ore trade'.[13] Where I had thought that iron ore was an 'extravagant and bulky' medium for transport, he assured his readers that it was 'the embodiment of non-bulkiness', and we must take his word for it. Clearly, in the Archaic period it was a frequent practice for base metals to be shipped, for the bulk of the distance over which they had to travel, in ore form; and in fact I know of no really strong evidence to the contrary at this period.

But what about stage (iii) of our theoretical model of transmission of metalwork? There is a certain amount of evidence that it was often a short and relatively trivial undertaking, and that the spectacular distances over which archaic Greek artefacts sometimes travelled were covered *after* the objects entered their final owners' possession. This is certainly true of one of the most famous cases, the gigantic bronze cauldron found in a princess' tomb at Vix in Burgundy, which was made to order and probably assembled at its destination by a craftsman who travelled there with it. Other similar cases – the Greek helmet from a river in south-western Spain, the harness-plate in the shape of a fish from northern Germany – are probably susceptible of a similar explanation (see Boardman (1981) 221 figs. 261–2; 214 fig. 254; 262 fig. 306). Within Greece, the great bulk of 'internal imports' of metalwork are found at sanctuaries, where it is far easier to believe that they have been dedicated by pilgrims from elsewhere in Greece than that they have been imported in bulk and sold to local customers: thus, there are many dedications of bronzes from the Italian colonies at Olympia and of Cretan ones at Delphi, and in both cases we know that visitors from the areas in question were frequent. Only in rare cases does a commercial interpretation appear to force itself on us: for instance, at Samos where the excavators found 132 Egyptian bronzes in the sanctuary of Hera (Jantzen (1972). Since there is no evidence at all for Egyptian visitors to Samos, and since we know that Samians were prominent among the Greeks who were using the *emporium* of Naucratis in the Nile delta at the period in question, it is only sensible to conclude that these are the offerings of Samians returning from mercantile ventures in Egypt. But even here, the evidence is indirect: the actual *objects* will not have got there by commerce – they merely reflect commercial activity on the part of their owners (and without written evidence we could not even know that much).

Returning to the sites that were mentioned earlier (see above p. 229), we can be pretty sure that at Bassae, the journey from craftsman to ultimate owner – stage (iii) in our model – was just a few yards long, from the forge to the nearby temple. No one would carry iron ore up to a 1,000 m mountaintop just for the sake of the favourable breeze for the smelting-furnace, and then bring it down again! There are numerous iron dedications in the Archaic temple-deposits to confirm the natural interpretation. On the small islands of Ischia and Motya, in default of evidence to the contrary, we can likewise assume that the smelting and forging activities were, to a considerable extent, for the benefit of local customers: on Ischia, at least, the installations are of a size more appropriate for this than for servicing an overseas trade in finished artefacts.

The common feature of these two case-studies is their bearing on Archaic Greek trade as a whole. I have suggested that, in terms of tonnage, metal ores and marble between them represented a very substantial slice of Archaic sea-borne exchanges in Greece. In the case of iron ores, three particular factors will have tended to increase the tonnage shipped: the first is simply the very heavy dependence on iron as a practical metal at this period; the second is the fact that (unlike bronze) iron cannot be effectively re-worked, so that a constant supply of new ore is needed; the third, again pointing a contrast with copper and tin, is that iron ore is much less wasteful in that it yields a much higher proportional weight of usable metal (see above, p. 230), so that there was less of a deterrent to shipping it before smelting. Yet in the whole process of transmission from the mining of the ore to the sale of the finished artefact, only this ore-shipping operation could even potentially be classed as long-distance trade. In many cases, too, there would be a factor to counteract the three maximizing factors just listed: if a major centre of metal-production lay close to the metal sources (and Chalcis and Eretria in Euboea are well-known examples), then the services of the ore-shipper, the most 'commercial' of the participants in the process, would not after all be needed. Whether they were or not, however, the location of a network of foundries to serve the needs of their immediate localities was a feature of Archaic Greece which, among other things, had the effect of cutting down to a minimum the operation of commerce in the field of metals. Iron ore must have been vastly cheaper, per unit of weight, than finished metalwork. If this was to any degree a deliberate policy, then we may see a possible motivation for it in the very limited resources of contemporary merchant shipping, for which I argued in the first part of this paper. As in so many aspects of the Archaic economy, the practice – whether or not it corresponded to a conscious aim – was to support oneself as far as was feasible from internal resources, of labour if not of materials.

With sculptural marble, the case is even more clear-cut. There is no single stage in the process summarized on page 226 which can be classed as a 'marble trade'. The marble block is paid for at the quarry in the same way, whether it is for subsequent export or not. If it is to travel overseas at all, it does so (we have inferred) as the property of the sculptor who is travelling with it. If he has paid for it with an advance from the client, then this and his other subsequent payments, a large part of which will in any case consist of maintenance, are unlikely to be 'repatriated' if his practice is to travel further to find another commission.

If 'trade' is defined in the narrow sense of the purchase and movement of goods without the knowledge or identification of a further purchaser, then it seems that a substantial component of Archaic Greek maritime shipments could not be classified as trade. How far such a conclusion could be extended to other cultures of the period, I leave it to others to judge; but let us not forget that even the most obvious counter-example, the Phoenicians, could turn into agriculturalists at the drop of a habitat, as at Carthage. I have the feeling, too, that other categories of the traditional archaeological evidence for 'trade' in Archaic Greece will, when scrutinized more closely, begin to evaporate; the 'commercial export' of painted pottery is one such element which already shows signs of doing so (cf. Snodgrass (1980) 128–9, 224)[14]

NOTES

1. *Deutsches arch. Inst., Antike Denkmäler herausgegeben vom Kaiserlich Deutschen arch. Inst.* I 1 (1887) pl. 8, 3a; cf. II 3 (1898) pl. 29, 12.
2. See H. Walter, K. Vierneisel, 'Heraion von Samos: die Funde der Kampagnen 1958 und 1959', *A. M.* 74 (1959) 10–34, at 11, fig. 1 and Tafel, squares M–N 11–13.
3. H. Kyrieleis, 'Archaische Holzfunde aus Samos', *A. M.* 95 (1980) 87–147, at 89–94.

4. See e.g. G. M. A. Richter, *Kouroi*, 3rd ed. (London, 1970), 6.

5. G. Lippold, *Die griechische Plastik*, Handbuch der Altertumswissenschaft. W. Otto, R. Herbig (ed.). Handbuch der Archäologie III (Munich, 1950), 92 n. 11.

6. Richter (n. 4) 154, no. 63a.

7. J. Ducat, *Les kouroi du Ptoion: le sanctuaire d'Apollon Ptoieus à l'époque archaïque* Bibliothèques des écoles françaises d'Athènes et de Rome, 219 (Paris, 1971).

8. Richter (n. 4) 51–3, no. 15; J. J. Coulton, 'Lifting in early Greek architecture', *J. H. S.* 94 (1974) 1–19, at 17.

9. Richter (n. 4) 51–3.

10. At least, this is how I understand the passage, with the relative clause *choris ho ti . . en* being dependent solely on *anathemata* and not on *agalmata* too; for if bronze and stone *statues* are excepted, then what sculpture worth mentioning is left? *graphe*, painting, points the same way: that is, to dedications in general, not to statues.

11. B. Isserlin *et al.*, 'Motya, a Phoenician-Punic site near Marsala', *Annual of the Leeds University Oriental Society* 4 (1965) 84–131, at 129.

12. N. Yalouris, 'Problems relating to the temple of Apollo Epikourios at Bassai', *Acta of the XIth International Congress of Classical Archaeology, London, 1978* (London, 1979), 89–104, at 91.

13. P. A. Ålin, Review of A. M. Snodgrass, *The Dark Age of Greece* (Edinburgh, 1971), *A. J. A.* 77 (1973) 238.

14. Whatever its remaining deficiencies, this paper has benefited from the criticisms of Dr P. A. Cartledge, Mr M. H. Crawford, Professor M. I. Finley and Dr R. G. Osborne.

CHAPTER 13

Interaction by Design: The Greek City State

This article, like Chs. 7 and 9 above, found a place in a collection otherwise dominated by prehistoric studies. It might not have survived the closer scrutiny of Classical colleagues, dealing as it did mainly in simple terminology, with a level of confidence that a later breakdown in the consensus could (and did) disrupt. In assuming, for example, that a discontinuity of political entities between the Mycenaean world and the system of the *polis* was something that could more or less be taken for granted (pp. 237–9), it failed to spot a 'cloud no bigger than a man's hand' in the shape of van Effenterre 1985, later to be reinforced by support from others (see Ch. 9 above, pp. 158–60).

On a more detailed point, the pair of temple buildings listed on p. 252 and assigned to the '8th century BC' in Table 13.1 have both been recently judged to belong to much earlier periods. The 'Temple of Hera' at Tiryns, though it may have ended its days in that guise, is now held, by an increasing number of scholars, encouraged by the view of the recent excavators of Tiryns (Kilian *et al.* 1981: 160), to have originated as a very late Bronze Age repair to the main unit of the Mycenaean palace. 'Megaron B' at Thermon (as again noted in Ch. 9 above, p. 166) has meanwhile been reassigned to the tenth century BC or earlier. Probably they would both be better eliminated from the comparison of dimensions in Table 13.1.

BIBLIOGRAPHY

Kilian, K., C. Podzuweit and H.-J. Weißhaar (1981), 'Ausgrabungen in Tiryns 1978. 1979: Bericht zu den Grabungen', *Archäologischer Anzeiger* 151–256.

van Effenterre, H. (1985), *La cité grecque: des origines à la défaite de Marathon*, Paris: Hachette.

Peer polity interaction, like many concepts recently under discussion in archaeological circles, is by no means the exclusive property of archaeology. On the contrary, one could argue that its best chances of validation will be found in cases like that dealt with in the present chapter, where it can be in part documented by historical evidence, which can show certain stages of the process in more or less unquestioned operation. Yet the presence of documentary evidence, in this case at least, no more brings about an immediate dissolution of the difficulties than does that of material evidence. An important stage in the history of any state is the stage of its formation; and one of the problems on which the model of peer polity interaction could be expected to throw light is that of the origins of the Greek (or any other) form of state. But for this epoch in Greek history an abiding difficulty – which is merely a facet of the general difficulty of applying modern concepts to past institutions – is that it is doubtful how far, if at all, contemporary consciousness of the emergence of a 'state' existed.

This may sound improbable. Could a people be unaware that, by setting up a central government to which it would owe certain obligations and from which it would expect certain benefits, it was taking an important new step? Furthermore, later citizens of these same Greek states were acutely aware of their distinctive characteristics, and some of their extensive writings on these matters survive. Yet these same writers, who offer us a range of confident statements about the foundation and early history of cults, about early warfare, oracles or legislation, are reduced to virtual silence on the question of the emergence of the entity of which they claimed citizenship. This would appear to suggest that that process had not made an indelible impact on their ancestors who had lived through it. Indeed, the very concept corresponding to our term 'statehood' is not one that is apparent in Greek political writings, even of the full Classical period.

How much does this matter? Very little, I would argue. The operations of peer polity interaction are by no means confined to fully-fledged states. For the sake of accuracy, it will be better to replace the familiar phrase 'city state', which I have used in my title, with the Greek term *polis*, denoting in its strict sense a polity consisting of a settlement and its territory, politically united with one another, and independent of other polities. But whether or not we choose to credit

'Interaction by design: the Greek city state'. From C. Renfrew and J. F. Cherry (ed.), *Peer Polity Interaction and Socio-political Change*, Cambridge: Cambridge University Press, 1986, pp. 47–58.

the polities of Classical Greece with 'statehood', with the specific attributes given to that term in the last few centuries of modern political thought, the fact remains that they represented a striking, innovatory and advanced system by the lights of their own age: if that had not been so, they would not have had such a profound impact on later Western thought. As such, they must have emerged at some time, and the earlier we date the beginning of that process, the more remarkable we are implying that the phenomenon was. We return, therefore, to our previous difficulty: the ancient Greek political analysts appear to throw little light on the origins of what they were analysing.

Such evidence as they do offer on the age and ancestry of the Greek *polis* has come to seem, in the light of modern research, extremely difficult to accept. Let us take one of the best-informed and most judicious of them, Thucydides of Athens. True to his aim of tracing events to their causes, he offers by implication (II. 15.2) an explanation of how the political organisation of fifth-century Attica came into being: it was Theseus, he says, who persuaded its people to give up their local political centres and adopt Athens as their centre of government. There is no suggestion that later generations had ever gone back on this act of 'synoecism', so that the origins of the Classical *polis* of the Athenians are thus firmly placed in the Heroic Age. This in turn implies that the decisive step had been taken some 800 years before Thucydides' days, and he shows by references elsewhere that he himself would have endorsed this modern calculation of the interval of time. Nor is this the only passage in Thucydides which carries the implication that the *polis* system was of such great antiquity. In the introduction to Book I he finds it necessary, in order to establish the unique historical importance of the contemporary war whose history he was writing, to give a searching critique of the accepted view of the greatest conflict of the Heroic Age, the Trojan War. He does this in quantitative and logistic terms; and since the commander of the Greek forces, Agamemnon, was king of Mycenae, this in turn involves him in a comparison between Agamemnon's capital and a contemporary *polis* like Athens (Fig. 13.1). The fifth-century *polis* of Mycenae had become a very small place; yet Thucydides assumes without question that he can use it as a measure of the size and power of Agamemnon's capital, and thus make a fair comparison with contemporary Athens. This suggests that he believed in the essential continuity of the *polis* of Mycenae over a period, once again, of about eight centuries (I. 10.1).

In these same chapters, he discusses the sea-power of Minos of Crete in language completely appropriate to the world of the *polis*,

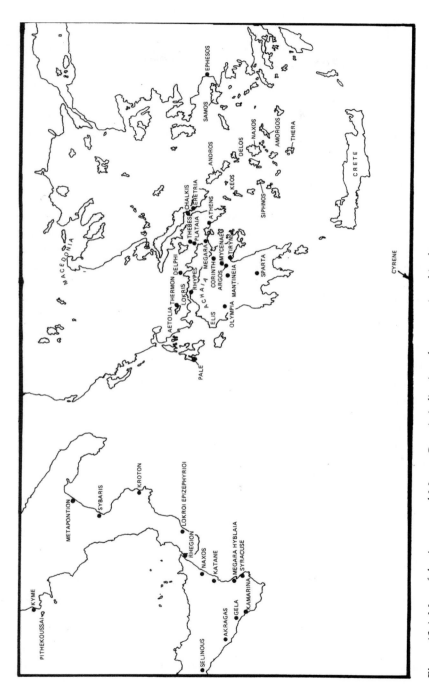

Figure 13.1 Map of the Aegean and Magna Graecia indicating places mentioned in the text.

which gives a further hint of the same attitude (I. 4; I. 8.2). Beside
Thucydides' account, we can set many more uncritical statements of
ancient authors, particularly those in which they retail the foundation
legends of Greek cities, usually giving them a setting in the Heroic
Age, and never betraying any recognition that important structural
changes might have occurred subsequently.

Why is it that modern scholarship has come to reject the implication that the political system of Classical Greece essentially goes back
to the Heroic Age? To begin with, the last hundred years have given
us some considerable independent knowledge of that 'Heroic Age'
by showing it to have its historical basis in what archaeologists call
the Late Bronze Age. This knowledge, although imperfect, is quite
enough to show that the political systems of the Aegean world at that
time were very different from those of the Classical age. The political
units conform to the model which is best described as 'redistributive':
relatively large, heavily centralised, minutely bureaucratic, they leave
little scope for an independent citizenry. Extravagant and laborious
steps are taken to secure the prestige and power of the rulers, to an
extent which is not matched even in the most deferential Archaic cities
of, say, the seventh century BC. Production and distribution were, it
seems, closely monitored (Renfrew 1972: 297–307, 462–5 etc.).

Next, there is the evidence of the Homeric poems. Here it is not
so much the few and faint memories which, even on the most positive view, Homer betrays of the political realities of the Late Bronze
Age Aegean; rather, it is the general (though not quite total) absence
from Homer's world of any awareness of the systems characteristic
of Greece in the Classical period. It is usual to conclude, on this and
on much other evidence, that a complete interruption had taken place
between the Late Bronze Age kingdoms and the rise of the *polis*; that
the Homeric poems, which portray a system that resembles neither
the one nor the other when examined in detail, are giving us a glimpse
of one or more stages within the period of the interruption; and that
the emergence of the *polis* is likely to have begun only at the time
when the poems were reaching their final form, that is, probably in
the eighth century BC (Snodgrass 1980: 27–31).

Such, at least, is the view taken here, and the main emphasis of
this chapter will be on developments which took place between approximately 750 and 650 BC. For the reasons given above, there will
be certain difficulties in extending these developments to include the
actual emergence of the Greek polities, though the attempt may still
be made. But whether or not it succeeds, there is a whole range of

further processes, only slightly later in date, which seems to me to illustrate the interaction of peer polities in an unusually clear way. Some of the evidence advanced will be archaeological, some historical; it will cover issues ranging from the fundamental question of the size and nature of the Greek *polis* itself, to such details as law-codes, warfare, burial practices, temple architecture and the production of painted pottery.

According to the model under consideration in this book, it will be maintained that an entity like the Greek *polis* is 'legitimised in the eyes of its citizens by the existence of other states which patently do function along comparable lines' (Renfrew 1982a: 289). Perhaps the first quality of the Greek *polis* which might stand in need of such legitimation is its small size. It has not been characteristic of the Greek-speaking world at other periods of its history that it should be composed of such a proliferation of small, mutually independent units. This is true not only (as would be expected) of the periods when Greece has been under the control of a major power, whether external (the Roman and Ottoman Empires) or in some sense internal (Macedon, Byzantium), but also of the other eras in which the Greek world has comprised a number of independent states. The Mycenaean kingdoms, for example, do not appear to embody the Classical principle that each major town and its territory should be autonomous (Gschnitzer 1971); nor, in the two-and-a-half centuries after the Fourth Crusade, when a series of independent baronies grew up in the Aegean lands, was any of these of such small compass (Miller 1964). To establish the political and – subject to a certain degree of inter-dependence – the economic viability of the numerous Greek *poleis* must have been an initial problem. But it is hard to believe in any general principle, applied at the time or even invoked later, such as would justify the more extreme cases of local fragmentation. Some representative figures for the territory sizes of Greek *poleis* are given by Ehrenberg (1969: 27–8). But it remains difficult to detect the rationale by which, for example, the small Cycladic islands of Keos (131 sq.km) and Amorgos (124 sq.km) each have their territory divided, at least in the earlier stages, between four and three separate *poleis* respectively, when larger neighbours such as Andros (380 sq.km) comprised a single *polis*, and when the *polis* of Naxos probably incorporated the archipelago of very small islands around it, in addition to its own 430 sq.km. Outside the Cyclades, these upper and lower limits of size were comfortably exceeded in either direction; but this very divergence in size of territory and in population is, in

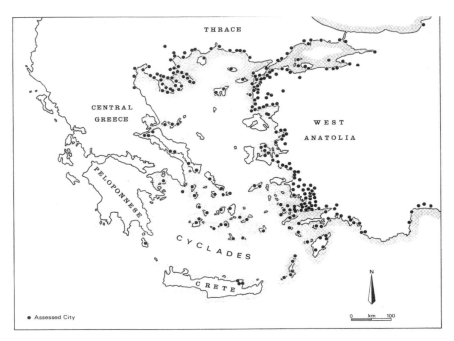

Figure 13.2 Map of the Aegean showing the distribution of polities assessed in the Athenian tribute lists during the later fifth century BC.

its way, a testimony to the strength of the '*polis* idea'. Later, towards the middle of the fifth century BC, more than two hundred of these once independent polities around the Aegean coasts became tributary allies of Athens (Fig. 13.2).

We may, in general, have little independent evidence as to how this and other formative steps in the emergence of the Greek *polis* were taken; but there is fortunately one large exception – that of the early Greek colonies. We know enough about several dozen of these in their early years – approximate or accurate date of foundation, identity of founding city, partial excavation of sites and cemeteries, occasionally more circumstantial accounts of the original settlement – to be able to make certain observations about them (see Hammond 1967: 657–60 for a table of dates and founding cities). One is that, if we set on one side a very few settlements which were emporia of a rather cosmopolitan kind, virtually every Greek colony was a *polis*. This at first sight predictable fact is made more interesting by two factors. First, the earliest of these colonies were sent out at a time when the *polis* system was, at most, a newly established feature of the Greek homeland;

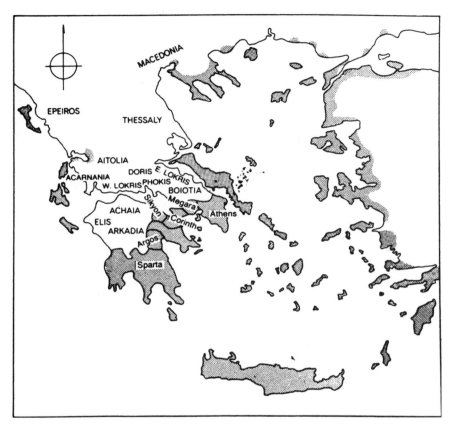

Figure 13.3 Mainland Greece and the Aegean: the extent of the *polis* system (shaded areas) in the Archaic period.

Sicilian Naxos, in 735 BC, may be the first colony for which we have a plausible and exact foundation date, but Pithekoussai (Ischia) and Kyme in the Bay of Naples were both appreciably older than that. Secondly, not every Greek in the homeland lived in a *polis*, either then or later; what is more, a number of important colonies in the west (Sybaris, Kroton, Metapontion, Lokroi Epizephyrioi) were actually settled from the regions of Achaia and Lokris, which were among those areas where the *polis* idea had not been adopted (Fig. 13.3). Instead, the inhabitants lived in scattered village settlements, linked by some more or less loose form of alliance which, in later centuries, became formalised into a confederation or league. The very fact that the founders of these colonies were recorded merely as 'Achaians' and 'Lokrians', rather than as coming from an individual town or district, must imply some capacity for concerted action, even in the early days, on the part of these regions of the homeland. Yet these 'ethnic' colonists seem to have adopted without hesitation the model of the *polis* when establishing their new settlements, complete with city, territory, individual land-plots constituting the title to citizenship, official cult of the patron deity, law-code and all the other appurtenances. There were of course incentives, at least initially, for doing so: only a concentrated settlement would stand a chance of surviving its early years on a fairly distant and potentially hostile continental shore. Nevertheless, this assimilation to the *polis* model does give an example of the kind of interaction that we are looking for. The very earliest colonists in the west had come from places – Chalkis and Eretria, Corinth and Megara – where the *polis* idea was accepted: their successors apparently followed the same practice because it had been seen to work in the colonial context, irrespective of whether or not they found it appropriate to their own circumstances at home.

Irrespective too, one might add, of a larger consideration: would not other and larger political units have proved even more effective in the colonial west? Whatever geographical determinants might be held to justify or explain the prevalence of small autonomous polities in the Greek homeland, such as the fragmentation of good farming land by the pervasive and barren limestone, they apply much less obviously to the landscape of southern Italy and Sicily. To take an immediate instance, why did not the three Achaean colonies of Sybaris, Kroton and Metapontion, strung out over more than a hundred miles of coastline along the 'instep' of Italy, come to form a single federal state, as their Achaean homeland was later to do? The answer must be in part that, at the early date when they were founded, the appeal of the *polis* to Greek minds was too strong to be resisted. Greek colonisation, in other words, exhibits in rapid succession two of the modes of interaction between peer polities that can occur in the context of emigration: first, the political systems of the earliest colonists are 'exported' and reproduced in a new geographical setting; second, the interaction between overseas polities of different stock becomes influential enough to override the native affiliations of later arrivals on the scene. In this case, only a single generation intervened between the two stages.

One part of this phenomenon, that is the weakening of native ties, seems to be a cultural equivalent of the 'founder principle' of genetics, recently discussed in the context of island colonisation by Cherry (1981: 61–2): an off-shoot of a larger parent population almost invariably becomes genetically distinct in its new habitat because it does not represent fully the gene pool of the parent population. But it is the other part, the assimilation to each other of groups of different origins coming together in the new environment, which, as Renfrew points out [Introduction, *Peer Polity Interaction and Socio-political Change*, ed. C. Renfrew and J. F. Cherry, Cambridge: Cambridge University Press, 1986, p. 5.], lacks obvious biological analogies and remains accordingly mysterious. One further illustration of this second process in the Greek colonial world may be given, from the field of burial practices. Within the general prevalence of the rite of inhumation among the early colonists (some of whose mother-cities favoured cremation), we may note a more particular phenomenon: the use of a form of crude sarcophagus, hollowed out from a single block of stone, into which the body was placed. This form of interment was popular in Corinth and, so far as we know, only in Corinth among the colonising cities. It is not unexpected, therefore, that it proves to have been equally popular in Syracuse, Corinth's colony. What is more interesting is that it is later found in the other Sicilian colonies of Megara Hyblaia, Gela, Selinous and Kamarina, of which only the last-named is linked with either Syracuse or Corinth; the others were founded from cities where the practice seems to have been unknown (Snodgrass 1971: 175–6, 199 n. 19).

The western colonies, like the pan-Hellenic sanctuaries (cf. Renfrew, p. 16), are a valuable testing-ground for the concept of peer polity interaction, in that they provided an area in which the members of different Greek polities came into contact. But it is time to leave them and return to the Greek homeland, where we may not be able to follow the process of the emergence of the *polis* to its very beginnings in the same way, but where episodes not very much later in date can be used to illustrate the same overall concept.

No clearer illustration could be given of the sheer power of *polis* rivalry and emulation than that of early Greek warfare. The emergence of the Archaic heavy infantryman (*hoplite*), with the attendant changes in equipment, tactics, social stratification and political obligation, stands close to the heart of the idea of the *polis* (Snodgrass 1980: 99–107). The notion that all citizens above a certain property qualification should be obliged to serve in the army of the *polis*, equipped at their own (considerable) expense, and that by so doing they secured certain minimal rights as citizens, arose sufficiently soon after the emergence of the *polis* itself to constitute, in many cases, our earliest and most positive proof of its reality. The hoplite phalanx was the

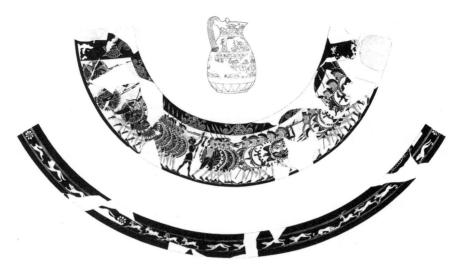

Figure 13.4 The close-order phalanx of Greek heavy infantry in action. Late Protocorinthian jug, Rome, Villa Giulia Museum, c. 640 BC.

embodiment of the *polis* idea translated into action (Fig. 13.4). At the same time, hoplite warfare, as has often been observed (e.g. Adcock 1957), had a strong element of the conventional, even of the ritualistic about it. In the Archaic period especially, armies were used in the main for a single tactical purpose (the pitched battle on level ground) and in a single formation (the close-order phalanx). Campaigns were decided by a single engagement, whose verdict was invariably accepted by both sides; there were no reserves worth mentioning since it was essential to field one's maximum strength for the first encounter, and the training of other arms, apart from the heavy infantry, was neglected. The use of long-range missiles was considered contemptible, winter campaigning unthinkable. The two-handled shield or *hoplon*, in which the hoplite engaged his left arm and from which he took his name, was a symbol of duty and at the same time a badge of privilege for the well-to-do citizen.

The rules of this game were apparently accepted without question by every Greek *polis*. The experience of foreign wars can only have served to reinforce this conviction, for hoplite armies fought with signal success against Etruscans, Persians and Carthaginians, and Greek hoplite mercenaries were in demand in many countries: a mere boat load or two of them, landing in the Nile Delta, were enough to tip the power struggle in Egypt in the 660s BC, according to Herodotus (II. 152). True, the economic basis for this system, a settled population of prosperous farmers, was not at the disposal of every Greek state; backward ethnic groups like the Aetolians might fight by different rules (Thucydides III. 94), and they could occasionally spring a surprise on the hoplite army of a *polis*. It was from a similar background that, centuries later, the Macedonian kings, with their strong cavalry, their lighter-armed troops using a pike held with both hands, and their winter campaigns, brought about the downfall of the hoplite system.

As long as success attended this form of warfare, however, the Greek polities conformed to it with what seems an excess of zeal. In many states the proportion of the free adult male population which qualified for hoplite service was of the order of one-third; this will have meant that, of the *total* population, something in the region of one-fifteenth would have been available for effective warfare. If a *polis* was small, therefore, it might produce an effective army of a really tiny size. We have a poignant illustration of this when the united army of the allied Greek *poleis*, representing something approaching their full muster of hoplites, took the field against the Persians at Plataia in 479 BC. The by now insignificant cities of Mycenae and Tiryns fielded a joint force of four hundred men; the *polis* of Pale in Kephallenia sent just two hundred. On this occasion, taking their place alongside the ten thousand Spartans and the eight thousand Athenians, their contribution was valued; but one is bound to wonder about their role in the much commoner circumstances of warfare against other Greek states. A city that could muster only two hundred men at arms would be utterly dependent on alliances with more powerful neighbours; logically, one would have thought, some other tactical system which could involve a wider section of the population would seem preferable. But a hoplite army had become a symbol of *polis* status, and that was enough. Here again, the neglect of wider considerations seems to underline the strength of the urge to conform to the practices of one's peers, even when it was only in order to fight them. War had indeed become 'a channel for communication' (Renfrew (see p. 243), p. 8).

A second essential principle of the *polis* system was the existence of codified law. By its mere existence and, even more important, by its exhibition in public, a law-code represented a major step in the advance of the *polis* idea, establishing that element independent of both ruler and ruled which is a necessary ingredient of statehood (Fig. 13.5). We do not know the sequence by which the Greek cities came to adopt this advance, but one thing is clear: interaction between cities played a large part. The commonest medium was that of a prominent individual who, having acquired a reputation as a lawgiver, was then called upon for his services by cities other than his own. There

Figure 13.5 Fragment of a law-code inscription from Dreros in Crete, late seventh century BC (photograph courtesy of Miss L. H. Jeffery).

are some surviving inscriptions with Archaic law-codes, but for the very earliest stages we have to rely on the statements of writers who, however authoritative (Aristotle's *Politics* is the most fruitful source), lived several centuries later. The first, rather isolated case is that of an exiled Corinthian nobleman, Philolaos, who was invited by Thebes to devise a law on a adoption. The motive for the invitation, 'to pre-serve the number of land-holdings', is one that lies at the very heart of the *polis* system, where 'citizenship' at first consisted of no more than the possession of a plot of land; if we can accept the dating of Philolaos' visit to the 720s BC, then it gives early confirmation of the adoption of the system at Thebes, and by implication at Corinth too. But this episode falls short of attesting a full codification of the law; and the tradition that Philolaos was an exile also detracts from his claims to represent an institutionalised structure. Our next body of evidence derives from the years towards the middle of the seventh century BC, and two areas figure prominently in it, the western colonies and Crete. Zaleukos of Lokroi Epizephyrioi (one of the colonies dis-cussed above), who became the most famous lawgiver of his day, is said to have been taught by a man who had learned his law in Crete, and the island is certainly the richest source of Archaic law-code in-scriptions. Later in the century, Epimenides the Cretan was called in by the Athenians to purify their city after an unsuccessful *coup d'état*; while, in the west, two pupils of Zaleukos established law-codes for their own cities, Rhegion and Katane. In the next century, Demonax, from Mantineia in Arkadia, was called in to reform the constitution of Cyrene; other examples can be found in, for instance, Jeffery 1976: 41–4, 145–6, 188–90. These activities once again suggest that the Greek *poleis* kept an alert eye on the constitutional progress of their peers, and were ready to learn from them.

In two of the fields which we have been considering, colonisation and codification of law, a prominent part was played by the pan-Hellenic sanctuary at Delphi and by its oracle of Apollo. Whatever rationalist interpretation we may care to put upon the oracular utterances of Apollo's priestess, their prestige, and the range of expertise with which they were credited, are undoubted facts. The function of the Delphic oracle is perhaps seen at its most remarkable in the context of colonisation (Forrest 1957). Most important Greek colonies boasted a foundation legend which began with a consultation of the oracle. Not only are many of the reported responses specific and well-informed about distant coastlines but, more striking still, the oracle frequently emerges not merely as an adviser but as an initiator. A typical story concerns, yet again, one of the Achaean colonies of southern Italy. Myskellos, an Achaean from the small town of Rhypes, went to consult the oracle about a private matter, his own childlessness; he was told that he would be granted children, but only when he had founded Kroton, an enterprise for which, not unnaturally since the place did not yet exist, he needed further directions. Following these, and finding the already established colony of Sybaris, he asked Delphi's permission to settle there; he was refused, and eventually Kroton was founded, traditionally in about 708 BC (Anderson 1954: 78). Even when due allowance is made for political manipulation, the role of the oracle remains an important one. Delphi was evidently acting as the main central clearing-house for information of a geographical and political kind which was of potential value to many different cities and their governments; it was also being used as an instrument of persuasion by pressure groups, and here too it could act across the lines of division between states. When, for example, the instruction to found a colony came as a surprise to a city's rulers and was unwelcome to many of its citizens, we may suspect that the pressure came ultimately from outside; such were the circumstances in our best-documented case of a colonial settlement, the foundation of Cyrene from Thera in the 630s BC (Herodotus IV. 150–8).

With legislation and codification, likewise, the Delphic oracle did not merely approve proposals – it initiated them. Sometimes, indeed, it is represented as taking a dangerously interventionist line, as when a Corinthian from outside the ruling circle of his city was encouraged to 'put Corinth straight'; he was Kypselos, who became the first Corinthian tyrant and the most powerful individual ruler in the Greek world of his day. The story of the oracle *might* indeed be dismissed as a propagandist invention, by Kypselos or his supporters, to justify his seizure of power. In the same way, the promoters of a lasting constitutional reform at Sparta, at about this time (perhaps the second quarter of the seventh century BC), presented their measures as having been initiated by Apollo, whereas it is much more likely that a pre-arranged 'package' was presented to the oracle for divine ratification. The fact remains, however, that in both these cases it was thought worth while to obtain the seal of Delphic approval; and in neither case did Delphi disown its attributed words. This must mean that, before 650 BC, Delphi had acquired great prestige as an arbiter who in some sense stood above the authority of any single *polis*; and this prestige in turn must have been at least partly based on the only earlier episode in which it had played a leading role, that of colonisation. One thing that all these activities had in common was success: the Greek colonisation of Sicily and southern Italy created polities which not only survived, but in several cases grew to overshadow their founding cities; Kypselos established a dynasty which ruled for 74 years and brought Corinth to the zenith of its power; the Spartan constitution became a by-word for political stability.

But, given that its initial successes were the foundation of its subsequent prestige, how was Delphi able to embark on this career in the first place? Like the Pope, it had no divisions, yet the most powerful cities felt the need of its sanction. If its role had been exclusively a religious one, and if the motive for soliciting its approval had been only piety, it seems unlikely that it could have played so complex a role. The explanation must surely be that a culture so politically fragmented as Archaic Greece was very much in need of a common arena, in which the innovations, advances and attainments of each individual *polis* could be rapidly communicated to others, when desired, or could, more simply, be displayed for admiration. The alternative of direct interaction, when there were more than two hundred separate polities, often many days' travel apart, would have required an extremely elaborate network of communications.

Delphi, although its possession of an oracle gave it an early primacy in certain spheres, was not the only inter-state sanctuary which could fulfil such a function. Its athletic festival, for example, was eclipsed by that of Olympia and was of much later foundation. But both sites show a parallel development. In the early days, there is evidence for geographical or political bias: the responses of the Delphic oracle may betray a partiality for Corinth and its allies (Forrest 1957), while the earliest Olympic victors were drawn from a restricted area of the Peloponnese. Already, however, the dedications show that *individuals*, some of them well-to-do, were being attracted from further afield (the Athenian tripods at Olympia, for instance, or the Cretan bronzes at Delphi). As the Archaic period advanced, the fact that both sanctuaries were relatively remote from the most powerful and innovatory centres of the Greek world came to matter less, and the advent of inscribed dedications proves that polities, as well as individuals, were cultivating Olympia and Delphi. The process reaches its peak with the construction of the treasury buildings in the later Archaic and Classical periods – a dozen at Olympia, at least 28 at Delphi. Whereas to muster a hoplite army was one way of staking a claim to be a fully fledged *polis*, to erect a treasury at a pan-Hellenic sanctuary was to put one's city forward as belonging to an élite among the *poleis*. Just as both activities were clearly inspired by the example of the peer polities, so both had the effect of impressing those peers: when little Siphnos, with its territory of 75 sq.km and its population of perhaps two to three thousand, built its splendid treasury at Delphi, it was directly challenging comparison with Corinth, which was more than ten times the size in both categories.

Some of the smaller dedications, and some surviving historical anecdotes, throw a little more light on the question of *how* these sanctuaries acted as media for interaction. The Olympic festival, in particular, was clearly the place at which to make any appeal, over the heads of the individual *polis* governments, for the adoption of a pan-Hellenic policy, or more simply for recognition outside one's own *polis*. Only after his overwhelming reception at the Olympic games of 476 BC, for example, did Themistokles feel that he had reaped his due harvest of honour for having played a leading role in delivering both Athens and Greece as a whole from Persian conquest, four years earlier. The policies of an individual city could be held up for condemnation, as when Lysias' speech at the festival of 388 BC provoked a riot against Dionysios, the tyrant of Syracuse, for his brutality and treachery towards fellow Greeks in the west. These examples from later history show that Greeks came to regard the great sanctuaries as offering a forum, superior to that offered by the channels of normal diplomacy, for communication with the citizens of other *poleis*. Can we detect any signs from the earlier, mainly archaeological evidence, for the exercise of a similar function?

The prominence of dedications of hoplite armour at Olympia (and to a much lesser extent at Delphi and other sites) suggests one answer (Snodgrass 1980: 105–7). The very fact that armour and weapons were dedicated at sanctuaries is important, for down to about 700 BC

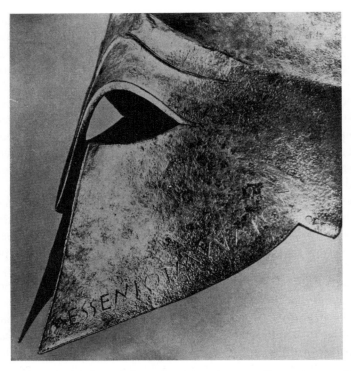

Figure 13.6 Inscribed helmet dedicated at Olympia, recording a victory of the *polis* of Messana over that of Mylai, both in northeastern Sicily, early fifth century BC (photograph courtesy of Deutsches Archäologisches Institut, Athens).

it had been a common practice to bury them with their owner in the grave, and this custom desists just as the dedications at Olympia begin. In a general way, this merely shows a switch of emphasis and loyalty from the individual and the family to the *polis*; but there was a second, concurrent change in that it now became the tendency to dedicate not one's own, but one's defeated enemy's arms. Such dedications were quite often inscribed, to rub home the message that they were intended to convey (Fig. 13.6). At a fundamental level, it is not unlikely that this contributed something to the spread of hoplite equipment and tactics across the Greek world; much more certainly, it will have impressed the citizens of other *poleis* with the prowess of one's own. The same message could be transmitted in a less obvious way through other types of dedication. Of the 24 statues of Zeus which the traveller Pausanias records his having seen at Olympia, for instance, one was (not unfittingly for a pan-hellenic sanctuary) a memorial to the

victory of the allied Greeks over the Persians at Plataia, another commemorated the Eleans' successful expulsion of the Arkadians from
Olympia itself, after the latter had temporarily seized control of the
festival, while yet another was a supplicatory offering for the intended
suppression by the Spartans of the serious internal revolt in 464–456
BC (Pausanias V. 23; V. 24.1; V. 24.3–4). In all these cases the choice
of an inter-state sanctuary is surely designed to communicate with
other polities and their individual members; one's own fellow citizens
or subjects could be more easily impressed by the commissioning of a
fine building, a statue or an armour dedication at home – as is shown
by the fact that all three (and other) forms of dedication are common
in the state, as well as the inter-state, sanctuaries.

In one respect at least, the pan-Hellenic sanctuaries can be said
to have developed more slowly than those of the individual cities:
this is in the acquisition of monumental temples. The earliest temples
at Delphi, Olympia or Delos are relatively small and unspectacular.
But at the same period, the most prosperous states were building
more pretentious temples at home, and one feature of these shows
how they, too, could act as a medium of rivalry between peer polities
(Table 13.1). Two of the very largest temples known from the eighth
century BC are the first temple of Hera on Samos and the long, apsidal temple of Apollo at Eretria. The Eretria temple is certainly the
later of the two, and its slightly larger dimensions could be seen as
dictated by a desire to outdo the Samians; there is other evidence
that the two cities were mutually unfriendly, and by the end of the
century they were almost certainly at war. A similar comparison may
be made between two smaller structures of approximately the same

Table 13.1 Comparative measurements of certain Greek temples

Temple	Length (m)	Width (m)	Area (sq. m)	Approximate date
Hera, Samos (first)	33.50	6.70	224	*c.* 800 BC (?)
Apollo, Eretria	35.00	7.00 (façade)	*c.* 240	*c.* 750 BC (?)
Hera, Tiryns (?)	20.90	6.90	144	8th century BC (?)
'Megaron B', Thermon	21.40	7.30 (at rear)	*c.* 150	8th century BC
Artemis, Ephesos (first)[1]	109.20	55.10	6,017	550 BC
Hera, Samos (fourth)[1]	111.00	54.40	6,038	530 BC
'GT', Selinous[1]	110.12	50.07	5,538	540 BC
Olympian Zeus, Akragas[1]	110.09	52.74	5,806	480 BC

[1] Measurements taken from Lawrence 1957: 331, 95, 325 and 326, respectively.

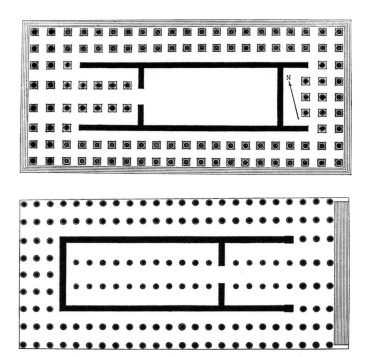

Figure 13.7 Competitive emulation in monumental temple-building: (top) the Archaic temple of Artemis at Ephesos, c. 550 BC; (bottom) the fourth temple of Hera on Samos, c. 530 BC.

date, the building which overlies the Mycenaean palace at Tiryns and is best interpreted as a temple of Hera, and the structure at Thermon in Aetolia, which almost certainly became a temple of Apollo, even if it was not originally built as such. The comparison of dimensions in these two cases may seem inconclusive, but as so often in Greek history one can strengthen the inference by appealing to later and clearer instances. The two largest Archaic temples in the Ionic order were the 'Old' temple of Artemis at Ephesos and the fourth temple of Hera at Samos (Fig. 13.7). Here again, we know that the larger temple – the ground area at Samos comes out at 6,038 sq. m as against 6,017 at Ephesos – was begun later, while mythology and geography alike suggest a tradition of political rivalry between the two cities. Among the western colonies, meanwhile, a similar competitiveness seems to have operated in the designing of giant temples in the Doric order. The temple known as 'GT', at Selinous in western Sicily, was begun in about 540 BC and held the field for about two

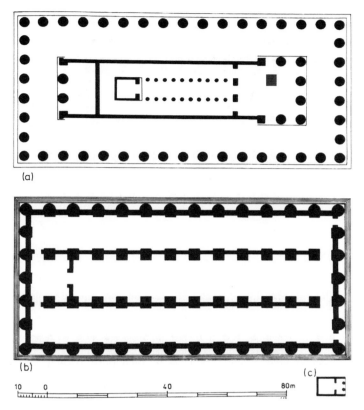

Figure 13.8 Plans of (a) the temple 'GT' at Selinous, c. 540 BC, (b) the temple of Olympian Zeus at Akragas, c. 480 BC and (c), for comparison of size, the treasury of the Athenians at Delphi, c. 500 BC.

generations until the neighbouring city of Akragas laid out a temple of Olympian Zeus with almost exactly the same length and a marginally greater width (Figs. 13.8 and 13.9). Yet again, there is a record of hostile political alignment for these two Sicilian cities. If the degree of geometrical nicety imputed by this view to the Archaic temple-builders seems improbable, it become less so in the light of the fact that Herodotus, in the following century, rightly describes the Samian temple as 'the largest of all those known to us' (III. 60.4) – a difficult point to establish had there not been a clear local tradition to this effect, and a deliberate intention behind it.

All the examples so far given are concerned with the activities of governments, rulers, rich patrons, or at least (in the case of hoplite warfare) the more prosperous land-owners – that is, in the main, of

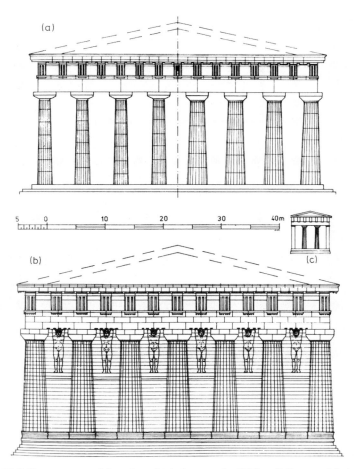

Figure 13.9 Reconstructed façades of (a) the temple 'GT' at Selinous, (b) the temple of Olympian Zeus at Akragas, and (c) the treasury of the Athenians at Delphi (cf. Fig. 13.8).

the policy-makers within the Greek states. But the material evidence indicates that comparable effects were taking place at the level of craftsmanship and art style; it can also show that these effects began to operate well before the emergence of the *polis*. Take, for example, the long series of changes in the method of decorating painted pottery, between the eleventh and the eighth century BC. We see in succession the adoption of the compass and the multiple brush, and of a range of motifs to which these aids lent themselves and which go to make up the style called Protogeometric; then more than a century

Figure 13.10 The appearance of figures in Greek Geometric art. Attic Late Geometric krater, National Museum, Athens, c. 740 BC (photograph courtesy of Deutsches Archäologisches Institut, Athens).

later a new style, the Geometric, emerged, distinguished by the use of new motifs like the meander and the swastika, and new devices like the cross-hatching of outline shapes; finally, the silhouette figure, human or animal, is adopted as the most important decorative element (Fig. 13.10). Each of these changes, as it happens, is believed to have originated in Athens; but each in turn is taken up by other local schools, one after another, the circle widening at each stage until the final change of fashion produces echoes from Sicily to Ionia (Snodgrass 1971: 45–94, 418–19). To attribute the changes to purely commercial competition, in these early centuries, would be quite inappropriate (Cartledge 1983); taste, if not deeper psychological needs (see e.g. Himmelmann-Wildschütz 1968), is likely to have counted for more than pursuit of profit. But the tastes were collective ones: groups of craftsmen, living in settlements whose political organisation was as yet primitive, were already emulating other groups in other such settlements. With sculpture, the case is changed somewhat by the fact that the client, rather than the artist, tended to be the greater arbiter of convention and change; but one can still point to the later spread of the *kouros* type of statue as evidence of the way in which the patron in one city was influenced by the taste of his counterpart in another.

The case of Classical Greece has thus, in my view, proved able to furnish a series of fairly concrete instances of the operation of peer polity interaction. It shows the process taking place before, during and after the emergence of a political unit, the *polis*, which at the least has some of the attributes of statehood. The Greeks' espousal of a small-scale polity in which the community of citizens could act in concert, later so resonant in the pages of Plato's *Republic* and *Laws* and Aristotle's *Politics*, appears to have been a strong factor from the very start; indeed, so widely unquestioned were the assumptions behind it that later Greeks appear to have forgotten how the idea first came into being. The Greek case has also served to show the interaction of peer polities at several different levels of activity: the formation of state policy, patronage of the arts and architecture, and the field of the individual craftsman himself.

But can the study of the Greek *polis* do more than that? Can it serve to enhance the model of peer polity interaction, rather than merely exemplifying it? Here I am more doubtful, save perhaps in one respect. The Greek example seems to me, in more than one instance, to indicate that peer polity interaction could be a *conscious* process. The people responsible for the foundation of the western colonies, for the formation of the early hoplite armies, for the marginal surpassing of the measurements of their rivals' temples, or for the equally direct provocation of setting up their city's treasury in a pan-Hellenic sanctuary, must have been aware not only of the structure within which they were operating, but of the scope which it gave for internal comparisons. In this case at least, therefore – and there are certainly other, if mostly much later, instances – the idea of peer polity interaction is seen to be not merely a modern intellectual concept imposed on its unsuspecting subjects, but something which those subjects were themselves practising, with some acumen and deliberation of purpose. There are not many models of which one can say as much.

BIBLIOGRAPHY

Adcock, F. E. (1957), *The Greek and Macedonian Art of War*, Berkeley and Los Angeles, University of California Press.
Anderson, J. K. (1954), 'A topographical and historical study of Achaea', *Annual of the British School at Athens* 49: 72–92.

Cartledge, P. (1983), ''Trade and politics' revisited: Archaic Greece', in P. D. A. Garnsey, K. Hopkins and C. R. Whittaker (eds), *Trade in the Ancient Economy*, 1–15, London, Chatto and Windus.

Cherry, J. F. (1981), 'Pattern and process in the earliest colonisation of the Mediterranean islands', *Proceedings of the Prehistoric Society* 47: 41–68.

Ehrenberg, V. (1969), *The Greek State* (2nd edn), London, Methuen.

Forrest, W. G. (1957), 'Colonisation and the rise of Delphi', *Historia* 6: 160–75.

Gschnitzer, F. (1971), 'Stadt and Stamm bei Homer', *Chiron* 1: 1–17.

Hammond, N. G. L. (1967), *A History of Greece to 322 BC* (2nd edn), Oxford, Clarendon Press.

Himmelmann-Wildschütz, N. (1968), 'Über einige gegenständliche Bedeutungsmöglichkeiten des frühgriechischen Ornaments', *Abhandlungen der Geistes- und Sozialwissenschaftlichen Klasse, Akademie der Wissenschaften und der Literatur, Mainz* 7: 261–346.

Jeffery, L. H. (1976), *Archaic Greece: the City-States, c. 700–500 BC*, London, Methuen.

Lawrence, A. W. (1957), *Greek Architecture*, Harmondsworth, Penguin.

Miller, W. (1964), *The Latins in the Levant: A History of Frankish Greece (1204–1566)* (Reprint of 1903 edn), Cambridge, Speculum Historiale.

Renfrew, C. (1972), *The Emergence of Civilisation: the Cyclades and the Aegean in the Third Millennium BC*, London, Methuen.

Renfrew, C. (1982), 'Polity and power: interaction, intensification and exploitation,' in C. Renfrew and J. M. Wagstaff (eds), *An Island Polity: The Archaeology of Exploitation in Melos*, 264–90, Cambridge, Cambridge University Press.

Snodgrass, A. M. (1971), *The dark age of Greece*, Edinburgh, Edinburgh University Press.

Snodgrass, A. M. (1980), *Archaic Greece: the Age of Experiment*, London, Dent.

CHAPTER 14

The Economics of Dedication at Greek Sanctuaries

This is a paper, like Chapters 18 and 25 later in this collection, originally published in a place where it could be easily missed. So it sometimes was, although it has been fully and supportively discussed by Whitley (2001: 311–13), who however suggests (with justification) that it underestimates the frequency of dedication of terracottas in Classical times.

BIBLIOGRAPHY

Whitley, J. (2001), *The Archaeology of Ancient Greece*, Cambridge: Cambridge University Press.

Many excavators, and even more readers of sanctuary excavation reports, must have observed the phenomenon which gives rise to this paper. Whether at Panhellenic sanctuaries – Olympia, Delphi, Delos – or at city and *ethnos* sanctuaries – Lindos, Perachora, Isthmia, the Argive and Samian Heraea, the Athenian Acropolis, Pherae – there is a very marked preponderance in the number of small dedications of Geometric and Archaic date, by comparison with those of later times. In some cases, 'decline' is too weak a word to describe the change in frequency: the lists of finds show a fall-off from hundreds or even thousands of specimens of a given artefact-type in the eighth, seventh and sixth centuries BC, to very few or none at all thereafter.

This profligacy of dedication was not a practice of time-honoured antiquity: in most cases, it had itself only come into being in the course of the eighth century BC.[1] We are thus dealing initially with an episode that is roughly co-terminous with the Archaic period. We shall have

'The economics of dedication at Greek sanctuaries', *Scienze dell'antichità* 3–4, 1989–90, 287–94.

occasion to compare it with the pattern of the ensuing centuries; and we may then try to explain the transition from the earlier pattern to the later. But it is important to realize at the outset that even the earlier pattern had enjoyed only a relatively short existence; and it may be worth considering, in due course, whether the explanations generally accepted for its *rise* have any bearing on the explanation for its later decline.

First, however, it is essential to understand the nature and scale of the phenomenon. We must immediately concede that it is a phenomenon which relates entirely to *preserved* dedications. It cannot take account of those which were intrinsically perishable, unless their existence is attested by other means. Nor can any accurate allowance be made for those other 'post-depositional' factors[2] which affect every kind of archaeology – in this case, the removal of dedications later in antiquity to locations where they are unlikely to be recovered, or the hidden biases in the manner of the (often nineteenth-century) excavation of sanctuary sites, which predisposed the excavators to find the materials of certain periods rather than others. What *can* be taken into account, however, is the wealth of other, non-archaeological evidence attesting to the existence of dedications which have disappeared or not been found: notably, temple inventories, dedicatory inscriptions, and the pages of Herodotus, Pausanias and certain other writers. For the Classical and Hellenistic periods, we lean heavily on such sources; but we must not forget that their inclusion can also result in a marked augmentation of the numbers of earlier dedications.[3] There can, however, be no real quantitative value in a comparison between two such different classes of evidence as archaeological finds and written lists of dedications. A more important lesson to be learned from comparing them is that a change in the *nature and value* of dedications took place in Greek sanctuaries, alongside and perhaps contemporaneously with the negative change in *frequency* with which we began; this is an important point to which we shall return.

To establish the scale of the change in frequency, we need quantification. As an exemplary instance, one may take a fairly recent publication: the study of the dedications of bronze jewelry at Olympia by Hanna Philipp.[4] This volume has the advantage of dealing not with one, but with six distinct types of artefact: pins, ear-rings, finger-rings, bracelets, fibulae and pendants. Thus any special factor affecting the currency of any one type of object may be balanced by those affecting others: a wide and representative range of human activity is covered. All the objects are items of jewelry, and primarily worn by females;

yet their popularity has fluctuated in independent ways throughout history, as we may reflect by noting that, in our own day, dress-pins and even hat-pins have almost completely disappeared; brooches certainly, and bracelets possibly, enjoy less currency than in the recent past; while finger-rings, pendants and ear-rings are probably as popular, or more so, than they have been for centuries past. To secure comparability of frequency, we may simply divide up the entire period covered by the finds into five sections of equal length (300 years each); 1351 finds are catalogued, but I omit from the calculations a few unusual pieces which are hard to date even loosely, and arrive at the following figures for the remainder:

c. 1050–750 BC:	49 finds
c. 750–450 BC:	948 finds
c. 450–150 BC:	77 finds
c. 150 BC–AD 150:	72 finds
c. AD 150–450:	184 finds

The figure for the second period stands out with startling clarity, set off both from what precedes and what follows it: the Archaic period accounts for something in the region of 70% of all the dedications of jewelry over a period of 1,500 years. Yet the other figures are enough to show that dedication of jewelry at Olympia was not abandoned altogether, as one might have expected if fashion in dress or religion had radically altered.

For another instance, we may turn to a set of figures already published sixty years ago.[5] They relate to a single class of find, the small lead figurines dedicated in vast quantities at the sanctuary of Artemis Orthia outside Sparta; yet, considering the wide range of subjects represented by the figurines, we may regard these too as a heterogeneous assemblage, reflecting different concerns on the part of different groups within the population. This time the periodisation is based on the excavators' pottery-classification in six stages, from 'Laconian I' to 'Laconian VI'; for the absolute dates of Laconian I and II, I give not the chronology of the excavators, but the revised one proposed by J. Boardman in 1963:[6]

pre-650 BC ('Lead 0'):	23 finds
c. 650–620 BC ('Lead I'):	5719 finds
c. 620–560 BC ('Lead II'):	9548 finds
c. 560–500 BC ('Lead III and IV'):	68822 finds
c. 500–425 BC ('Lead V'):	10617 finds
c. 425–250 BC ('Lead VI'):	4773 finds

This time, the size of the sample is vast, and the preponderance of the Archaic dedications even clearer at about 85% of the total, though the latter is admittedly spread over a much shorter period.

Parallel patterns of dedication, with a climax in the seventh and sixth centuries BC and a decline thereafter, can be observed in other categories of dedication, such as metal armour and weapons. At Olympia, for example, we have also a rich series of helmets which have been well studied: by the fifth century, the numbers are in decline and there are few examples of later date.[7] At Isthmia, the sequence of helmets begins rather later, with its main concentration in the sixth century, but terminates even more abruptly at about 470 BC with the destruction of the Archaic temple of Poseidon.[8] At virtually every sanctuary where arms were dedicated, the decline eventually comes; and in most cases it does so at a time when both the total population of the dedicant communities, and the external evidence for their prosperity, are still rising rather than falling.

How are we to account for this pattern? Let us start with the minimalist line of argument: that the whole phenomenon is the product of post-depositional factors. The most plausible line of explanation for a recurrent pattern like this would be in terms of a widespread change of practice by the ancient Greeks in the disposal of existing, unwanted dedications. This change would be assumed to have spread over the Greek world during the first half of the fifth century BC. We must agree that there was at least one post-depositional factor in operation, which may have tended to produce the result that we observe. This was the practice of clearing out the earlier dedications in bulk, by jettisoning them into pits (whose secondary nature is proved by the wide time-range covered by their contents) or, even more obviously, by throwing them into disused wells, or using them as ballast for earthen banks, as at Olympia. This practice is sometimes associated with major fifth-century building projects like the construction of a new Stadium at Olympia or the re-erection of the Temple of Poseidon at Isthmia; though the occasion is by no means always so obvious. Unquestionably, such activities increase the chances of the material in question surviving, to be recovered by excavation. But this explanation is no sooner advanced than it raises the further question: *why* were such practices so much commoner in, and shortly after, the Archaic period? Why did not the same problems of congestion continue to arise, and be solved in the same way, throughout later Classical, Hellenistic and Roman times? For the evidence, at least at the major Panhellenic and state sanctuaries with which we have been concerned, is that they did not. The answer to this question must be, at least in part, that the congestion was itself at its most severe in Archaic times. The written accounts of later centuries, especially those of Pausanias, make it clear that a major sanctuary remained a very crowded place, with dedications on every side. But in so doing, as already noted, they bring out the fact that the *nature* of these dedications had changed.

A second class of possible explanation is in depositional, rather than post-depositional terms. A whole series of such explanations has been offered in the past, for individual classes of dedication. Thus in the case of the lead figurines and other classes of dedication at Sparta, more than one contributor to the *Artemis Orthia* volume (n. 5) advanced the view that the progressive militarisation of Spartan society in the fifth century was responsible for the decline, both in quality and in quantity, of the dedications made. This explanation can, however, only be applied to the instance of Sparta, and may seem less than fully satisfying even for that case – for example, why should the numbers of warrior figurines fall off as an effect of militarisation? For armour-dedications, an attractive and widely-held view is that the growth of Panhellenic feeling, at the time of the Persian Wars, discouraged the continued dedication of spoils won by one Greek city from another. But again, this explanation applies only to one not outstandingly prolific class of dedication.

A third level of explanation would take the matter back to the pre-depositional stage: that is, in this case, to the pattern *of production* rather than merely that of dedication. Thus it has been contended, very persuasively, that the large bronze tripod-cauldrons, which had been among the most prominent dedications at important sanctuaries during the ninth and eighth centuries BC, simply went out of production early in the seventh, because the supplies of bronze were not adequate to meet both this need and the more pressing one of producing panoplies of bronze defensive armour for the infantry forces of the Greek cities.[9] It is certainly true that the tripod-cauldrons disappear from sites of all types, and that bronze panoplies for the first time become widespread at the same period. My only criticism of this theory arises from unease at the way in which it attributes to the Greeks the same scale of priorities as our own, with the production of functional objects having automatic precedence over that of largely non-functional votives. More important, however, is the fact that, even if such an explanation were invoked to cover the disappearance of other bronze votives, either individually substantial or smaller but more numerous, then it would still altogether fail to account for the parallel decline in the dedication of terracotta, ivory or faience objects – which is a fact. In a different way, the argument that the decline in certain kinds of dedication can be explained in terms of change in real-life fashion or habit – that people stopped wearing fibulae, for instance, or gave up using a certain type of helmet – can be easily countered by taking figures from publications that combine multiple types of artefact under a general heading, like *Olympische Forschungen* 13 (above, n. 4).

We must, I think, search for a level of explanation which extends more broadly, and runs more deeply, within human psychology. It must, at the very least, be deep and broad enough to apply to the whole variegated pattern of ancient Greek society and culture. One helpful observation of this kind might be that there was a certain diversion of cult, in the fifth and fourth centuries BC, away from the time-honoured sanctuaries of the Olympian deities, and towards those of what H.W. Pleket has called the 'assisting deities'.[10] Asklepios, Pan and the Nymphs in their cave-sanctuaries, the Kabeiroi and the Great Gods of Samothrace would all be examples of these latter. No doubt there is much force in this suggestion: in one way, the sanctuaries of such deities have proved as much, by yielding many later finds. Yet, once again, these finds also prove a greater truth: that, even in the cults of the 'assisting deities', there was a change in the nature of the dedications at the end of the Archaic period. This is well illustrated by an observation of B. Schmaltz in his publication of the metal figurines from the Sanctuary of the Kabeiroi in Boeotia. Here, as at Olympia and other sanctuaries of the major Olympian gods, bronze ox-figurines were a popular form of dedication but, as Schmaltz points out,[11] they disappear in the fifth century, their place being taken in this case by terracottas and vases. A change was passing over Greek religious practice, profound enough to affect the sanctuaries of very different kinds of deity.

It seems to me that this change, to which reference has now been repeatedly made, lies closer to the core of the matter than any of the other partial explanations that have been invoked. The best way to characterise the change, I think, is in terms of a dichotomy between 'raw' and 'converted' offerings. A 'raw' dedication is something like a weapon of war, a brooch, an ear-ring, a shield or a jumping-weight, which is an unmodified object of real, secular use. Its dedication involved no more than the simple act of surrender which Walter Burkert described in his contribution to the Uppsala Symposium.[12] Often the owner, or someone else, will have used it for a considerable time before its dedication. By contrast, a statue or statuette, though equally direct in expressing the piety of the dedicant, does so in a different way: it is a *conversion* of a part of his or her wealth, rather than a part of it in its own right; and in most cases it has been produced for the specific purpose of dedication. A *simulacrum* of a part of the human body, offered to a healing deity,[13] is a transformed or converted offering of a rather different kind. An inscribed plaque, representing in writing the piety (and sometimes the wealth) of the dedicant, would be a further example. All these 'converted' offerings are alike in that they have to be commissioned or bought (in the latter case, often on the spot) for the express purpose of dedication; they do not in themselves have a secular use, though they can in a variety of ways represent the activities of ordinary life.

Many of the phenomena that we have observed can be explained by reference to a change of preference, from 'raw' to 'converted' dedications, at a time close to the end of the Archaic period. With a state offering to commemorate a victory, for example, the 'raw' offering of captured arms has its 'converted' counterpart in the form of an inscribed statute or group. A woman who dedicates an ornate female statuette, where her grandmother would have offered her personal jewelry, exemplifies the same change.

It is not of course the case that all Archaic dedications were of the 'raw' type and all post-Archaic of the 'converted': the pattern is more complex. Some popular early dedications occupy a kind of intermediate status, such as the bronze tripod-cauldrons which were mentioned earlier: they simulate, in a grandiose way, a functional object of everyday life, yet we know them to have been in some cases produced on the actual sanctuary-site, for expressly religious purposes. Then there are those even commoner dedications of the Archaic and earlier periods, the animal-figurines. On the face of it, they are of the 'converted' class of dedication: yet many of them, at least when they represent cattle, sheep or pigs, must have been dedicated on the occasion of a sacrifice of an animal or animals of the species in question. Sacrifice is essentially an activity distinct from dedication, and for that reason has not been encompassed by this paper: yet in so far as it is comparable with dedication, it clearly falls into the 'raw' category. To this extent, also, the fact that sacrifices continued in post-Archaic times shows that 'raw' offerings were not abandoned. All the same, the overall balance between 'raw' and 'converted' appears to have undergone a reversal in the early fifth century.

This change, if its reality is accepted, invites two obvious observations. First, it represents a more sophisticated attitude to religion: to transform one's possessions before offering them to the god is to represent both the god and oneself in a less simple light. Secondly, 'converted' offerings must inevitably involve a greater economic outlay than 'raw' ones. The main reason for this is that the dedicant who commissions a specially-produced dedication, or even buys one ready-made at the sanctuary, must pay for the time and raw materials of the professional whose services are needed for its production. By contrast, the prudent dedicator of a 'raw' offering may well retain other examples of the same item for personal use, to the extent that the surrender of the dedication may scarcely be felt in economic terms.

Can this change in dedicatory practice then be dismissed as nothing more than the product of increased sophistication and/or prosperity? Such an answer would surely be oversimplified: one can hardly expect such processes to have other than a gradual effect, and the change in dedications is, especially in its negative aspect, relatively abrupt. Yet it may be that economic issues are involved. It is time to revert to a question raised at the beginning of this paper, as to the reasons for the *rise* in the mass-dedication of 'raw' offerings, at or shortly before the beginning of the Archaic period. That too had been a relatively abrupt change (see n. 1), and it is now a widely accepted view that, like the architectural development of the sanctuaries where the dedications were made, it is a phenomenon reflecting the growth of the communal idea of the *polis*. The roughly concurrent abandonment, over much of the Greek world, of the practice of putting very similar objects in graves would be the reverse side of the same coin: the subordination of private interest to public. But few would claim that the rise of the *polis* provides a complete explanation of the upward surge in dedication. In particular, it has been argued by Ian Morris[14] that the appetite for display and conspicuous consumption was merely given a new direction by the change-over from grave-goods to sanctuary-votives; that there was 'an unbroken continuation of competition through incremental gift-exchange', and that the use of the sanctuary for the disposal of wealth 'was linked to a need to represent aristocratic competition as having a wider communal value'. I would not wish to question the importance of competitive gift-exchange in early Greek society, but I doubt whether the mass of early, 'raw' dedications in the sanctuaries is the best exemplification of it. These dedications are too numerous and too cheap to be seen as motivated by competitive ostentation. To dedicate one's own bronze dress-pin can hardly be classed as conspicuous consumption, especially when one is adding it to a collection of which the archaeological residue, over two and a half millennia later, itself may run to thousands. Rather, I think that the sudden rise in the numbers of these standard offerings reflects a feature which Morris himself elsewhere identified: the egalitarian, communal spirit of the nascent *polis*, of which the new provision of formal burial for all citizens was a striking correlate.[15]

If the earlier pattern is viewed in this light, then how will this reflect on the change to the later one? As we have already seen, the 'converted' dedication is, in its nature, likely to be more costly than the 'raw'. A simultaneous decrease in the *frequency* of dedication, together with a general rise in the *value* of each separate dedication, invites a socio-economic explanation, even though other factors like the growth in religious sophistication were also operating. The fact that a much smaller proportion of the post-Archaic dedications actually survives, by comparison with what is described in the written sources, is a tiresome obstacle to quantitative comparison; but it does not undermine the kind of socio-economic explanation which is being suggested here. On the contrary, in so far as it implies the proneness of the post-Archaic offerings to later looting and expropriation, it reinforces the evidence for their greater value. By contrast, the humbler 'raw' dedications of earlier centuries were preserved for posterity mainly because they enjoyed less regard: even a prestigious dedication like the helmet captured by the Athenians from the Persians (probably at Marathon) was found to have been discarded after an 'exhibition life' of, at most, forty years.[16]

The substitution of 'converted' for 'raw' dedications reflects a fairly natural mental and social shift: it has indeed been noted without comment in much earlier publications.[17] My aim in this paper has been to draw attention to the thoroughness and relative abruptness with which the old preference for 'raw' offerings, of many well-attested types, was terminated at the close of the Archaic period. The logical conclusion of my last argument is that social and economic factors played a central role in that termination: that the egalitarian ethos of the early *polis*, which must have been at least partially responsible for the institution of the 'old order' of dedicatory practice, had been very much diluted by the fifth century. Social differentiation and even social polarisation are not unfamiliar features of the Classical Greek scene, even in a society with democratic political institutions like Athens.[18] Other processes, coinciding in time, served to accelerate the change and strengthen the impression of its abruptness. Rich state dedications were on the increase and, if only for reasons of space, they had a propensity for the 'converted' offering. The rise in popularity of the 'assisting deities' will have supported the trend, since some of their services (healing, protection of travellers) invited the 'converted' thank-offering more naturally than the 'raw'. It may be, too, that the increasing complexity of economic processes discouraged the continued disposal of portable wealth through dedication. Whatever the order of precedence that we give to these lines of explanation, the phenomenon that they seek to explain is a real one; and I think it will be agreed that its economic causes – and its economic effects, a whole separate question on which we have not even touched – are of central interest.

NOTES

1. See for example A. Snodgrass, *Archaic Greece*, London 1980, 52–63.
2. See D. L. Clarke, *Archaeology: the Loss of Innocence*, in *Antiquity* 47, 1973, 6–18 (16).
3. A good example is the statement (Herod., 8, 27, 4) that the Phokians on a single occasion in the sixth century BC dedicated 2000 Thessalian shields at Abae and 2000 others at Delphi. It is not known that a single one of the latter group is included among the shields excavated at Delphi.
4. H. Philipp, *Bronzeschmuck aus Olympia (Olympische Forschungen,* 13), Berlin 1981.
5. See A. J. B. Wace, *The lead figurines*, in R. M. Dawkins (ed.), *The Sanctuary of Artemis Orthia at Sparta*, London 1929, 249–284 (251–252).
6. J. Boardman, *Artemis Orthia and Chronology*, in *Ann. Brit. Sch. Athens* 58, 1963, 1–7.
7. See especially the studies by E. Kunze, in 6. *Bericht über die Ausgrabungen in Olympia*, Berlin 1958, 118–151; 7. *Bericht*, 1961, 56–137; 8. *Bericht*, 1967, 111–183.
8. Dr. A. H. Jackson, personal communication; but note the general conclusion of O. Broneer in *Hesperia* 28, 1959, 339, 'it cannot but impress the unprejudiced observer that so many of the valuable objects from our excavation are to be dated to the sixth century BC and so few to the fifth'.
9. S. Benton, *Further Excavations at Aetos*, in *Ann. Brit. Sch. Athens* 35, 1934–5, 255–361 (338–340).
10. H. W. Pleket, *Religious History as the History of Mentality*, in H. S. Versnel (ed.), *Faith, Hope and Worship*, Leiden 1981, 152–192 (155, 166, 176).
11. B. Schmaltz, *Metallfiguren aus dem Kabirenheiligtum bei Theben (Das Kabirenheiligtum bei Theben*, 6), Berlin 1980, 113, 164.

12. W. Burkert, *Offerings in Perspective: Surrender, Distribution, Exchange*, in T. Linders and G. Nordquist (edd.), *Gifts to the Gods. Proceedings of the Uppsala Symposium* 1985, Uppsala 1987, 43–50.

13. On these dedications, see especially F. T. van Straten, *Gifts for the Gods*, in H.S. Versnel (ed.), *op. cit.* (at n. 10), 65–151.

14. I. Morris, *Gift and Commodity in Archaic Greece*, in *Man* 21, 1986, 1–17 (12, 13).

15. I. Morris, *Burial and Ancient Society: the Rise of the Greek City-State*, Cambridge 1987, especially Chapters 10–11, 171–217.

16. See E. Kunze, *op. cit.*, 1961 (at n. 7), 136–137.

17. Compare the remarks of G. Dickins, *The Masks*, in R. M. Dawkins (ed.), *op. cit.* (at n. 5), 163–186, at 174–176.

18. See, for example, J. K. Davies, *Democracy and Classical Greece*, Glasgow 1978, 34–38.

CHAPTER 15

Archaeology and the Study of the Greek City

This is perhaps best treated as an updating of Ch. 11, published fourteen years earlier – but with a little more attention paid to the developed *polis*. It reports progress in some areas – the potential contribution of intensive survey is first recognised here (pp. 278–80) – and lack of progress in others; one or two over-emphatic claims have been toned down. There is a glimpse (p. 284) of the impending controversy which forms part of the discussion in Part IV below.

For well over a hundred years, people studied the Greek city as an entity without making more than negligible use of archaeological evidence. As late as 1969, in the translated second edition of Victor Ehrenberg's *Der griechische Staat*,[1] the reader has to search very hard indeed to find even a veiled recourse to archaeology. The historians of the polis saw themselves as dealing essentially with an abstraction; they avoided tawdry physical detail, much as they tended to eschew the whole diachronic approach; and both exclusions rendered archaeology superfluous. The archaeologists showed little sign of minding this: they carried on studying their temples, statues and pots, innocent not of *all* historical considerations – from the 1930s to the 1950s was, after all, the golden age of the 'political' interpretation of pottery-distributions – but certainly innocent of any concern with historical *entities* like the city-state.

Today, all that appears to have changed. Some books on aspects of the polis are being written by historians who make constant reference to archaeological findings; others are even written by archaeologists. What factors have brought about such a change? An important contributory factor has been the minor wave of new archaeological

'Archaeology and the study of the Greek city', from J. Rich and A. Wallace-Hadrill (ed.), *City and Country in the Ancient World*, London and New York: Routledge, 1991, pp. 1–23.

discoveries, relating especially to the era of the rise of the polis. But what generated this wave? The answer lies partially in an initiative on the part of historians: which brings us to a second and more fundamental factor. There has been a change of attitude, on the part of historians and archaeologists alike. The former are now no longer content to give, like Aristotle in the *Politics*, a more or less theoretical reconstruction of the advent of the polis, set in some indefinite early period: they feel an obligation to offer some kind of account of the date, causation and means whereby the entity that they are concerned with came into being. To do so, they must venture back into periods where the written sources on their own are manifestly inadequate. So they have called in the archaeologists, who in turn have been surprised to find that they are already sitting on a substantial body of existing evidence that is relevant to the problem, as well as responding to the call for new excavation to fill in the blank areas on the map of early Greece. The fact that so much of the evidence was long since available, however, must mean that it is this change of attitude that has been the decisive factor. In a nutshell, explanation has taken over from analysis and description as the prime aim, in both disciplines. I hope that, to most readers, these will be welcome developments.

These considerations all relate to one large area of the study of the polis, that of its origins and rise: this is indeed a topic where archaeology plays a major role, which is why it will feature prominently in this paper. But there is a second such topic in polis studies, which has likewise benefited from new archaeological work, and from a parallel change of attitude. It is the whole question of the physical basis on which the Greek city rested: the territorial sector and the rural economy. Here, the seeds of the change of attitude may be detected very much longer ago; but they were sown outside the boundaries of Classical scholarship (I have the name of Max Weber especially in mind) and, perhaps for that reason, they took an extraordinarily long time to germinate; indeed, but for the stubborn advocacy of Moses Finley, I rather doubt whether even now they would have burgeoned into the flourishing growth which they present today in ancient historical studies. In the archaeological field, they fell on even stonier ground, and I believe that the change of direction in archaeological studies has other causes. In passing, both sides alike should pay tribute to a third group, the epigraphists: with many of the relevant topics, from topography in general to the constitutional arrangements as they affected territories, to territorial boundaries, to agricultural slavery, it was they who were often first in the field.

The opening up of this second field of enquiry (or so I am suggesting) has come about through a fortunate coincidence of interests between recent historical and archaeological research. The historians, as soon as they became conscious of the need to examine the agricultural basis of the city, found that the evidence from the ancient written sources was seriously defective, and began to look round for alternative kinds of documentation. The archaeologists, having for so long followed the historians in their concentration on the urban sector of polis life, were in no position to assist. But help was at hand, and from an unexpected source. Archaeological colleagues in northern America were beginning to supplement, or even replace, excavation as the traditional medium of fieldwork with the new technique of area survey. Here was a technique which, unlike excavation, was designed to generate information on a regional scale, and with a rural bias. Methods which had been applied to the indigenous cultures of North America, by people who often had little interest in urbanised cultures and none at all in the Classical city, were found to be eminently applicable, first to pre-Roman or Etruscan Italy, then to the period of Roman rule in Italy and beyond, and finally to the world of the Greek city. A survey could provide a picture of the pattern of settlement over the whole territory of a medium-sized polis, or over parts of those of several poleis, and would also have an application in the more extended landscape of the average *ethnos* – exactly what the historians needed.

As a result of all these developments the study of the polis, at least when conducted at the generalised level, has become more and more deeply involved with the use of archaeological evidence. If we return to our first topic, that of the origins and growth of the city, we may begin our search for applications, actual or potential, of such evidence. In his opening chapter, Ehrenberg (1969) divided his treatment of this subject into five sub-headings: 'Land and Sea', 'Tribe and Town', 'The Gods', 'Nobles and non-nobles', and 'Forms of State'. Except for the last category, where the enquiry is essentially historical in nature and is conducted through backward projections from later documentation, I believe that archaeology can contribute in each of these spheres. It can offer not only the classes of evidence, referred to above, which are specific to the case of the Greek city, but also a body of recent work that is directed towards a general theory of state formation, based on anthropological research but later given an archaeological application.[2] Although such work has been mainly applied to non-historical cultures, some of its findings are relevant to the case of ancient Greece: notably, the idea of an 'Early State Module' that is essentially small in scale,[3] though hardly as small as the typical Greek polis. Indeed, a case could be made for treating even the polis, at its stage of formation, as a non-historical instance, since it is almost entirely lacking in contemporary documentation. This is generally true of early states: the discovery of writing seldom precedes state-formation by a long enough interval to generate coherent documents by the time of the political change.

A good starting-point for the discussion is the primary importance that Aristotle attached to 'community of place' – perhaps the earliest clear acknowledgment that the abstraction of the polis had an inseparable physical embodiment. Community of place incorporates both the *astu*, the central place, whose function was transformed when the state came into being, and the territory, which henceforth consisted of the sum of the landholdings of all members of the community. These are changes which can be expected to have manifestations in the archaeological record. What we must guard against is any expectation that these manifestations will be *uniform* in every case. The physical impact of polis-formation would vary according to the different prior conditions in the region where the particular polis arose. We know little enough about these prior conditions in any part of the Greek world, but what we do know can at least be expressed in archaeological terms. Thus there is the interesting fact, whose significance was spotted by Ehrenberg and has recently been enlarged upon by Nicolas Coldstream,[4] that the area of the Greek world where the Geometric style in pottery had reached its most advanced development (Fig. 15.1a), and the area where the polis was to prevail (Fig. 15.1b), roughly coincide. The priority of the archaeological phenomenon will stand unless we push back the rise of the polis to an improbably early date, nearer 900 than 800 BC. How much weight we attach to this coincidence will depend on our assessment of the importance of Geometric pottery: but we may at least recall the arguments advanced by Martin Robertson for thinking that, at this early period, painted pottery in general held a primacy among the visual arts which it never recovered later.[5] It may be that artistic sophistication was a foretaste of political progressiveness.

How then, precisely, might political transformation be reflected in the physical aspect of city or territory? We may begin with the *astu* itself, and assume that the circumstances were not those relatively simple ones where a physical *synoikismos* took place, with part of the population moving to a newly established urban nucleus, nor those even simpler ones of the colonisation of a new locality. In other

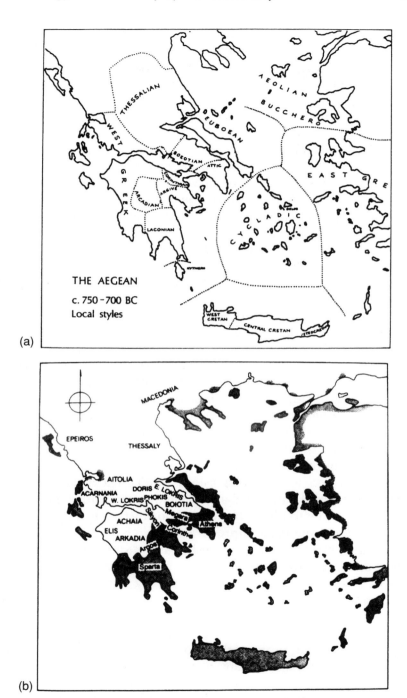

Figure 15.1 (a) Extent of the regional Late Geometric pottery styles (b) Extent of the polis system (shaded).

words, we assume that there *was* a pre-existing settlement, whose status was now transformed through its becoming the centre of a polis. How will this show? It is possible that some kind of concentration will have occurred at the site, with new functions and perhaps new inhabitants being transferred to it, and that this will show itself in a nucleation of buildings – possible, but by no means to be counted on. That a 'nucleus' could continue to take the form of a cluster of separate villages, long after the transition to polis status, is proved not only by Thucydides' well-known reference to fifth-century Sparta (1.10.1), but by the findings of survey archaeology elsewhere in the Greek homeland. That an *agora* would now be a necessary feature is no guarantee of its archaeological traceability. An acropolis would in many cases have been in existence long since, and archaeology has contributed here by showing how often it was the very same that had once served as a Mycenaean citadel. Administrative buildings, as is shown by the example of several cities, could at first be dispensed with. Sanctuaries are another matter, but they will be treated presently under the heading of religion. What we are looking for above all are the physical traces of *communal* activity, in the service of the polity as a whole.

Such traces have often been sought in the form of *fortification*. Here we must be more specific: the fortification must have clearly been designed to surround the whole inhabited nucleus, and not just a citadel; and that nucleus must be of an adequate size to represent a plausible *astu* for the territory and population in question, rather than being merely an isolated local stronghold. The second criterion is the one that invites most debate. We have, for example, a whole series of excavated sites in the Cyclades and other Aegean islands, where a fortification wall surrounds a nucleated settlement: the earliest of these begin in the ninth century BC, if not the tenth (Fig. 15.2) Perhaps the largest and most impressive or them is Zagora on Andros,[6] which may serve as an exemplar. It has a protecting wall (among the earliest dated structures on the site), areas of housing that show clear signs of planning, a probable contemporary temple, and plenty of open space for the siting of a hypothetical *agora*. Was Zagora then the centre of an early polis embracing the island of Andros? Given the low population figures estimated for Greece as a whole, and the islands in particular, in the earlier Iron Age, it is not impossible that the size of Zagora, at any rate, was commensurate with that function. But if this was an early experiment, it was a short-lived one for Zagora, like so many of this group of fortified island sites, was suddenly and permanently abandoned around 700 BC. Many of the other

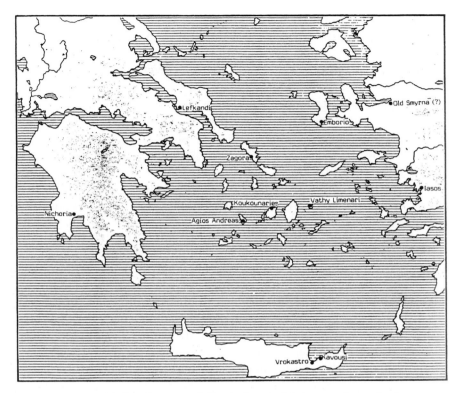

Figure 15.2 Fortified settlements of the ninth and eighth centuries BC in the Aegean.

sites in this group fail to match up to Zagora in one or more respects, principally those of size and of the location of the fortification. Thus, Emborio on Chios[7] was a sizeable village, but its fortified area was confined to a narrow hilltop with only one structure of recognisable domestic function within, plausibly identified as the chieftain's hall; much the same could be said of Koukounaries on Paros,[8] where the fortified area is also a small hilltop citadel, while other nucleated sites in its vicinity are relatively small; Agios Andreas on Siphnos,[9] and Kavousi[10] and Vrokastro[11] in eastern Crete, look more like tactically sited hilltop refuge sites than the centres of populated territories; Vathy Limenari is an almost inaccessible fortified headland on a small islet (Donoussa), and would be much more reasonably interpreted as a pirate stronghold than as an abortive polis-venture;[12] and so on. The mere fact that these fortifications are mainly confined to island sites, at a time when mainland and offshore-island settlements (even those concentrated in the same epoch, like Lefkandi in Euboea[13] and

Nichoria in Messenia[14]) were unfortified, suggests that some special geographical factor, rather than a ubiquitous political change, is responsible for the walls. The long delay in building city-walls round even the most famous mainland poleis, or even, as at Sparta, their permanent absence, is a matter of record.

Instead, I think that we should concentrate our gaze on the other almost invariable feature of these fortified island sites: their lasting abandonment, usually in the years around 700 BC. It is, I think, this negative feature which gives the strongest hint of political change. What concerted process, if not state-formation, would lead to the roughly simultaneous desertion of a range of sites which for the previous century or two had been not merely occupied, but in some instances places of real local prominence (Zagora, Emborio and on the off-shore island of Euboea, Lefkandi)? Was it not that their siting, and the original purposes that had prompted it, became suddenly obsolete with the advent of a new system? That their inward-looking, security-conscious orientation formed no part of a wider community which itself promised security through communal action? If such proves to be the case, then archaeology, virtually unaided, has provided the first secure indication of the date and nature of the earliest historical state-formation in the islands of the Aegean.

By that date, the colonising process had already begun to testify to the advent of the polis in rather different circumstances; and earlier still, there had been the 'pre-colonial' phenomenon of the Ionian Migration. It has been suggested that Zagora itself may represent a relatively late and half-hearted contribution to this latter process; while today we have, in the evidence of the large Protogeometric cemetery at Torone in the Chalkidike,[15] a considerably earlier and entirely unexpected manifestation of the same migratory spirit. Several of the sites, both of the Migration and of the later colonies, also show fortification as an early feature. I refrain from introducing yet again the site of Old Smyrna into this analysis, pending the radical reinvestigation by Turkish archaeologists of the dates of its first two fortification circuits; but there is another early wall reported at Iasos in Karia,[16] and in due course the early colonies often demanded walls. We have seen enough to appreciate, however, that local conditions often determined the construction of a fortification. City walls, as the mainland shows, were not at first a necessary condition of polis-formation; and our other instances are enough to cast grave doubt on any belief that they were a sufficient condition either.

Now that the colonial sites have been introduced to the discussion, we may note that they are the first to manifest another sign of that communal action that we have been looking for: the planned layout of an urban centre, with an *agora*, blocks of housing, and even individual plots provided for; Megara Hyblaia in eastern Sicily[17] has become a classic instance. From an historical point of view, however, such a discovery has limited significance, since it had never been doubted that the early colonies embodied the polis principle. Historically, much the most interesting question is whether this feature of the first colonies in itself presupposes the prevalence of the same principle in the homeland communities that sent the colonies out. I note in passing that the recent work of Irad Malkin[18] makes some use of archaeological evidence to answer this question firmly in the negative, and instead pursues the idea of the colonising experience as a 'trigger' for the relevant political developments at home.

Comparable physical evidence is, predictably, much harder to detect in the urban centres of Greece proper. Here the exercise of town planning was frustrated by the pre-existing structures, and the best that we can usually hope for is that the general layout of the settlement will bear some trace of reorganisation and re-location. The most fruitful investigation of this has been conducted in respect of the town of Argos,[19] but under severe handicaps of modern building and heavy dependence on burial evidence (Fig. 15.3). Otherwise, as with the abandonment of the fortified island sites, the clearest sign may be

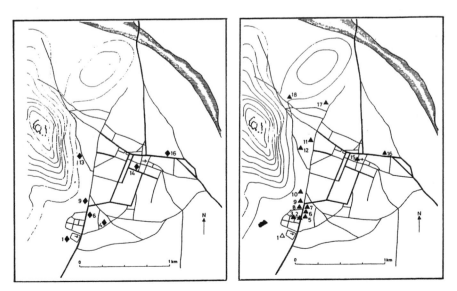

Figure 15.3 Early settlement traces from the city of Argos: Protogeometric Period (left) and Geometric Period (right).

a negative one. Where, as at Athens, the site of the subsequent *agora* had previously been given over to indiscriminate activities including burial, then the cessation of these activities may herald the new political order. In the case of Athens, this is detectable from shortly after 700 BC, when graves are progressively eliminated from an increasing area of the Agora site.[20]

But it is time to turn away from the urban centres, and look instead at territories. The territorial aspect is at once the most basic and the most neglected element of polis organisation. The frankest illustration of this neglect is to be found in the pages of almost any Classical atlas. Here you will look in vain for many features that one might expect to find in a map of a well-documented historical civilisation. The traditional atlas is constrained by its format to mark only the known and firmly located ancient toponyms, and such other data as the written sources convey. This excludes, most obviously, the unnamed sites excavated or otherwise investigated through archaeological means; but it excludes much else as well. There is unlikely to be a map showing the boundaries of the individual poleis of the Archaic and Classical periods. Then there are the second-order settlements, which must in reality have far outnumbered the *astea* themselves, but which in most atlases appear if anything less numerous; internal, district boundaries are correspondingly absent. Here the findings of epigraphy have proved invaluable, at least in the case of Attica,[21] but these too are generally not taken into account in an atlas. All of this explains why most Classical maps, unless they are drawn on a small scale, wear such a sparse look. You do not need a map of an abstraction and that, as we have seen, is exactly how the polis was seen by most of its earlier students.

It should be a primary aim of archaeology to fill in these blank spaces on the map and, as we have seen, the development of the technique of intensive area survey has given it the instrument that the task requires. The survey has to be intensive if it is to achieve two joint objectives: first, to discover the full range of settlement, in at least a sample area, from the *astu* itself down to the smallest isolated habitation; and secondly to estimate the frequency of settlements, of each level of importance, as it varies from period to period. A large-scale or 'extensive' survey will of course cover a much wider stretch of terrain, but at the cost of picking up only the most conspicuous – that is normally the larger – settlements, with the consequence that the settlement range is truncated, and the settlement distribution possibly also distorted, through neglect of unpromising (e.g. infertile or overgrown) terrain. By its total or near-total coverage of a given piece of territory, the intensive survey should be capturing a very large part of the history of occupation there; yet even the most intensive survey is not a precision instrument. For example, the level of chronological definition can never be sufficiently high to establish that a group of sites was in exactly simultaneous, rather than broadly contemporary, occupation; one needs further supporting indications, such as are provided in the case of the colonial land-allotments at Metapontum,[22] where the sites are not only contemporary but also very regularly spaced and located with respect to field-boundaries.

But at a less specific level, the broad trends of settlement between one period and the next can emerge very clearly from survey. Consider, for example, the maps and tables published by Dr John Bintliff and myself from the limited area covered by our first four seasons of survey in Boeotia (Fig. 15.4).[23] These show, in a space of 21 square kilometres, a maximum total of only 7 sites with occupation in the Geometric period, rising to a maximum of 23 in the Archaic, and a maximum of 76 in the Classical and earlier Hellenistic periods. Once one learns that the great majority of these are small, isolated rural sites, it becomes an inescapable conclusion that dispersed rural settlement took place over the first few centuries of the historical period and accelerated in the fifth and fourth centuries BC. Results like these

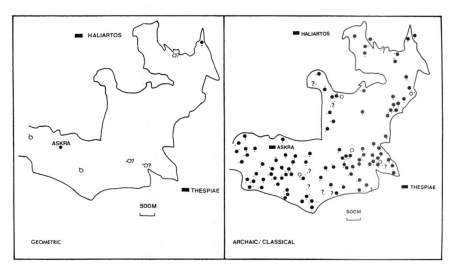

Figure 15.4 Boeotia survey: Distribution of Geometric sites (left) and Classical sites (right) (Slightly updated from Bintliff and Snodgrass, 1985).

can be first checked against those obtained by other surveys in Greece (which in several cases show similar patterns), and then monitored by the continuation of survey in the same area. In our case, three further field seasons (1984–86) have reinforced the overall proportions, but added more specific nuances. Thus, the seventy-odd additional sites investigated since the publication of the preliminary report include the two actual *astea* of Haliartos and Thespiai, in whose territory we have mainly been operating. These can now be added to the small group occupied from Geometric times onwards, showing that the population then existing was relatively nucleated. Thereafter, Thespiai provides the fuller sample, since at least two-thirds of our sites can be confidently allocated to its territory. This sample makes it virtually certain that there was no major dispersal of rural settlement from the city in the eighth, the seventh, or the greater part of the sixth centuries BC; nor was the *astu* of Thespiai itself a major nucleated settlement in these years, but rather a cluster of small village-sized settlements. It was only in the fifth and fourth centuries that Thespiai grew into a sizeable city, and (perhaps in concert with its second-order settlement of Askra) generated a dense scatter of rural settlement within its territorial boundaries.

This pattern is the more interesting because of the contrast that it presents with certain other cases, notably that of Athens. Whatever its precise explanation, an undoubted feature of the early growth of Athens is the proliferation of new sites in the Attic countryside during the eighth century BC, and an accompanying concentration of occupation in Athens itself.[24] Since we have already seen one reason for associating with this general period the rise of Athens to statehood, and shall shortly consider another, it does seem likely that this process in Athens was accompanied by a sharp increase in the size of the city, and the number of rural settlements. Where, though, does this leave Thespiai? Is it simply an illustration of the fact that the physical processes attendant on state-formation could be utterly different in different places? Are there grounds for the surmise that, in terms of power rather than of political form, Thespiai and perhaps other Boeotian cities developed late, and for that reason may have espoused the loose form of ethnic confederation that appears in later history as the Boeotian League? Politically, there can have been no significant time-lag, since we are fortunate enough to have the first-hand testimony of Hesiod as to the function of his own polis.

Our reconstruction will partly depend on the view taken of the dispersed rural sites. In eighth-century Attica, they look like a successful

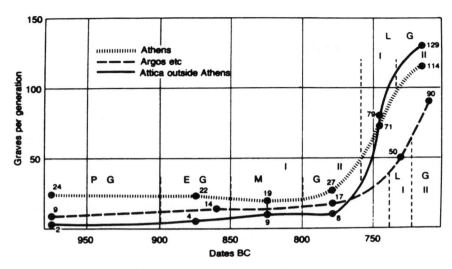

Figure 15.5 Unadjusted figures for the frequency of burials in (i) Athens, (ii) The Argolid and (iii) The Attic Countryside, c. 950–700 BC.

attempt to consolidate, by internal colonisation, an unusually large territory for which a single city now took responsibility. In Thespiai, with a territory of perhaps one-twentieth of the size, this move may have appeared neither necessary nor perhaps feasible with the available resources of population. This brings us directly to the obvious demographic question: had Athens experienced a dramatic rise in population, which aided and even partly caused the rise of the Athenian state? Ten years ago, I favoured a positive answer to these questions;[25] but there is little doubt that the interpretation then given was too simplistic. By calculating the numbers of extant burials, within and outside Athens, apportioned between successive generations (Fig. 15.5), I sought to show that the Attic population had risen exceptionally steeply, precipitating in at least this one case a political change. But one of the hypothetical or potential factors involved, which was explicitly left out of account, was an important one: the possibility of changing eligibility for formal burial. If the extant burials were not, at all periods, equally representative of both sexes, of all age-groups, and of all levels of society, then the count of graves is not a reliable indicator of the population of the settlement. In his new book *Burial and Ancient Society* (1987),[26] Ian Morris has argued convincingly that two at least of the above factors were indeed at work. From the mid-eleventh century BC to the mid-eighth, he believes, the extant

burials from Athens show a suspiciously low proportion of child-
burials, and an equally suspicious predominance of rich grave-goods.
The great upsurge in numbers at the middle of the eighth century
is partly, perhaps largely, accounted for by the suspension of these
two exclusions. This finding carries with it an extremely problematic
corollary: before about 750 BC, many poorer people and many children were being disposed of in some way that has not, so far at least,
proved archaeologically traceable. Despite this very unexpected implication, I think that Morris's detailed arguments will convince most
readers. He accepts that there was *some* increase in the Athenian population around the mid-eighth century; but this was on a much more
modest scale than I had believed, and historically it was less significant
than the abrupt change in the scope of the 'burying group'. Yet the
most striking thing is that Morris's explanation of this major social
change is in essence identical with the one that I had offered for the
supposed upsurge in population: that the advent of the Athenian polis
lies at the heart of it. What I had seen as a demographic explosion,
helping to precipitate the formation of the state, Morris interprets as
the newly-formed citizen body and their families, claiming their right
to a formal burial of a kind which had hitherto been a fairly select
privilege: a proximate cause has become an immediate result. Unless
we are both wrong, it seems increasingly likely that critical changes
began to take place in Athens in the eighth century.

In this survey of fortification, town planning, territorial settlement and demography, we have covered not only topics grouped
by Ehrenberg under 'Land and Sea', but also some of those of his
'Tribe and Town', or at least of its second element. But can archaeology contribute anything to the question of tribalism, and of the
pre-polis organisation of Greece? I think that today caution should
be the watchword: since the publication of Denis Roussel's *Tribu et
cité*,[27] it is difficult to sustain Ehrenberg's unquestioning faith in a
'tribal order' prevailing everywhere in the stage immediately before
state-formation. The archaeologist must content himself with repeating that, in eleventh-, tenth- and ninth-century Greece, pottery styles,
burial practices and some other criteria do project very clear regional
divisions in Greece, larger in scale than most later polis-territories.
Within each region, a degree of homogeneity prevails such that some
kind of communal feeling is suggested. Were these regions early political entities of a loose-knit kind? Caution is advisable not least
because the sequel does not mark a very clear break with this early
pattern, such as we would predict on a strictly political interpretation.

The partial fragmentation of these regional pottery styles in the eighth century, to which Coldstream (1983) has drawn attention, never even approximates to the point where each pottery-producing polis has its own individual style. To this one might reply that, even after the adoption of the polis system, the regional allegiances still count for much: there was an expectation that, other things being equal, the Ionian or the Argolic or the Boeotian cities would follow a similar policy. These regional divisions, which ultimately derive from the closing stages of the Bronze Age, must have influenced many aspects of early Greek life, whether or not these included the directly political ones; and archaeology can claim to have done most to draw attention to them, if not yet to have interpreted their meaning.

So we come at length to 'The Gods'. Here, the contribution of archaeology, in the context of state-formation, is a relatively clear one. The realisation that communal state cults stood at the very heart of the polis should have prompted the archaeologists to make this contribution much earlier. For over a century now, major state and inter-state sanctuaries have been under intermittent excavation, and a striking feature of many cases – Olympia, Delphi, Delos, and Ptoion, the Athenian Akropolis, the Temple Hill at Corinth, to name but a handful – has been the flood of light thrown on the early phases of the sanctuaries. What this has shown is that, apart from an unsettled debate on the degree of continuity from prehistoric times, by far the clearest phenomenon in this area of religious history is the sudden access of activity near the beginning of the historical period. I shall not rehearse again the different categories of evidence which reflect this feature;[28] it is enough to say that sanctuary after sanctuary displays the sequence of an abrupt increase in the frequency of small dedications, followed (sometimes quite quickly) by the building of a first monumental temple. Roughly contemporary with the first phase at the older sanctuaries, the picture is compounded by the institution of a wave of new cults: sometimes these lie at new sites in the territory of a given polis; sometimes they mark the first such foundation in what is to become a new polis. They include the cults of heroes, particularly those sited at prehistoric tombs, as well as deity-cults. When the sanctuary belongs to a polis, the building of a monumental temple seems a particularly significant step, especially when (as is usual) the earliest temple is that dedicated to the god who became the presiding or patron deity of that particular polis. If Apollo in his sanctuary on Temple Hill was the guiding deity of Corinth, then the institution of a temple for him was, in some sense, retrospective proof of the institution of the polis of Corinth. The building of such a temple was, in addition, a communal undertaking of a substantial physical kind.

But this whole argument has been given a new dimension by the publication of François de Polignac's book *La Naissance de la cité grecque.*[29] While reviewers have quarrelled with his conclusions in detail, nothing can detract from de Polignac's achievement of bringing the *territory*, as well as the *astu*, into the religious argument. He has shown that, for many cities, the establishment of greater and lesser sanctuaries in the territory, sometimes including a major one deliberately located near its boundary, was of comparable importance to the formalising of the central polis cult in the city itself. Among other things, these extra-mural cults served to bind the *astu* to the outlying territory, by means of an annual festive procession from the former to the latter; to warn neighbours of the extent of the territorial claims of the polis; and generally to proclaim to every citizen the implications of what had been undertaken. This argument touches the very heart of the polis idea.

It remains to say something about Ehrenberg's 'Nobles and non-nobles'. It is well-known that a social dichotomy of this general form persisted long after the rise of the polis, until tyranny or democracy sapped its strength. But there is one very important step along the road away from 'noble' rule whose reality has, until very recently, been uncontested; and it is a step which has been primarily established by archaeological evidence. I refer, of course, to the 'hoplite reform'. Whatever the nature of pre-hoplite warfare in Greece – a subject on which there is still room for the most radical disagreement – it must surely be agreed that the formation of a citizen-army and, even more clearly, the rapid rise of this army to dominance of Greek battlefields, was a decisive historical advance. Recent questioning of the reality of a 'hoplite reform'[30] cannot effectively detract from the historical consequences. Even if Homer's repeated use of the term *phalanges* implies the existence, in earlier times, of massed armies whose military effectiveness was greater than the Epic form allowed him to show, and even if these armies were well and uniformly equipped – a somewhat debatable inference from the text of the *Iliad* – the citizen hoplite embodied several major departures from such a system. The hoplite, in the first place, served primarily, and increasingly only, the state; secondly, he and his fellows comprised a substantial proportion (typically, about one-third) of the adult male population; thirdly he was, at his own expense, equipped and protected so well that for centuries he could only be resisted on the battlefield by other hoplites; fourthly, his pre-eminence sooner or later received the ultimate accolade, that nobles themselves came to fight as hoplites in the phalanx. Few if any of these attributes can have belonged to earlier mass armies. At whatever instigation they came into being, and at whatever point of time between the end of the eighth and the middle of the seventh century BC, hoplite armies shaped rather than merely echoed the history of the polis. The existence of hoplites is the clearest *a posteriori* proof of the existence of the polis, both in Greece generally and in each specific case; and the best evidence for hoplites remains the archaeological.

At a point rather earlier than the first clear evidence of the existence of hoplite armies, many communities in Greece had adopted another innovation that was closely linked with the hoplite phenomenon: the discontinuation of burial with arms (and of the corresponding provision of metal grave-goods for female burials). Everything about this change serves to underline its close connection with the rise of the polis: the fact that it primarily affected those of higher social status; the fact that it is not matched in other areas which rejected the polis idea (Lokris, Achaia and Thessaly continue to produce later warrior-burials); the fact that it finds a compensating feature in the sharp increase in dedications, of exactly the same classes of object, in the sanctuaries – the communal superseding the personal.[31] This change is most clearly dated at Athens and Argos, where it coincides fairly precisely with the end of the local Geometric style around 700 BC, and at Knossos in Crete, where it is later or more gradual, with a few isolated cases persisting into the first half of the seventh century. Like the mustering of the hoplite armies, it shows how rapidly the ethos of the polis came to override what might be seen as the private interests of its members. Once again, however, it is essentially an archaeological phenomenon: the ancient sources do not record it, and indeed one interpretation of the Thucydides passage on the 'Carian' graves at Delos (1.8.1) would imply that, by the fifth century, the old practice of burial with arms had been forgotten.[32]

Greek historians may have begun to wonder where this catalogue of archaeological pretensions will end. So let me cut it down to size myself by acknowledging, first that many, though by no means all, of the contributions claimed here for archaeology relate to the single epoch of the rise of the polis. All the evidence here considered has pointed to a date in the eighth century BC for that episode, or at least for its inception. But that, after all, was the date to which Victor Ehrenberg had assigned it, largely on quite other kinds of evidence, as long ago as 1937.[33] What archaeology has added is a huge body of circumstantial and confirmatory detail, of many different categories. Secondly, let me acknowledge that many of the archaeological arguments depend ultimately for their validity on *a posteriori* reasoning from the statements of ancient authorities, or from the inferences made by historians of later periods in the history of the Greek city. This paper is designed to help concert, not to usurp, the most interesting line of enquiry in the contemporary study of Greek history.

NOTES

1. Ehrenberg (1969).
2. See, e.g., Cohen and Service (eds.) (1978); Claessen and Skalnik (eds.) (1978); Cherry (1978 and 1984); Renfrew and Cherry (eds.) (1985).
3. See Renfrew (1975), who finds c. 1,500 sq.km to be a frequent modular size, and c. 40 km a mean distance between the central places of neighbouring modules. Both figures are far too high for the average Greek polis, notwithstanding the calculation of C.Doxiadis, cited by Renfrew at 14–16.
4. Ehrenberg (1969), 19; Coldstream (1983).
5. Robertson (1951), especially 152–4.
6. Cambitoglou *et al.* (1971); Cambitoglou (1981).
7. Boardman (1967).
8. See especially Schilardi (1983), with mention of other Parian sites at 180–82 and nn. 39–42.
9. Philippaki (1970).
10. See most recently Gesell *et al.* (1983) and (1985).
11. Hall (1914).
12. Zaphiropoulou (1967–71).
13. Popham *et al.* (1979–80).
14. McDonald *et al.* (1983).
15. For preliminary reports, see Catling (1983), 42–4 and (1986), 59–61.
16. Levi (1961–2).
17. Vallet *et al.* (1976).
18. Malkin (1971).
19. Hägg (1982).
20. Thompson and Wycherley (1972), 10, 12, 19; Camp (1985), 28, Fig. 11, and 34; neither account, however, brings out clearly the fact that from the end of the eighth century BC burials are excluded from the central area of the Agora and banished to locations on the periphery, where in turn they die out (apart from a couple of late burials in a family plot) at the end of the seventh.
21. See for example Eliot (1962) and Traill (1975), with their associated maps.

22. See especially Adamesteanu (1967).
23. For a preliminary report, see Bintliff and Snodgrass (1985).
24. Snodgrass (1977), 16–17, Fig. 3, and 29, Fig. 5.
25. Snodgrass (1977), 10–14 and, more fully, (1980), 21–5, Figs. 3–4.
26. Morris (1987).
27. Roussel (1976).
28. Snodgrass (1980), 33, 52–65.
29. de Polignac (1984).
30. E.g., by Pritchett (1985); Morris (1987), 196–201.
31. Snodgrass (1980), 52–4, 105–7.
32. So Cook (1955); for a somewhat different view, Snodgrass (1964).
33. Ehrenberg (1937).

BIBLIOGRAPHY

Adamesteanu, D. (1967), 'Problèmes de la zone archéologique de Métaponte', *Revue Archéologique* 1967, 3–38.
Bintliff, J. L. and Snodgrass, A. M. (1985), 'The Cambridge/Bradford Boeotian Expedition: the first four years', *Journal of Field Archaeology* 12, 123–61.
Boardman, J. (1967), *Excavations in Chios, 1952–55: Greek Emporio.* London.
Cambitoglou, A. (1981), *Archaeological Museum of Andros.* Athens.
Cambitoglou, A., Coulton, J. J., Birmingham, J. and Green, J. R. (1971), *Zagora* 1. Sydney.
Camp, J. M. (1985), *The Athenian Agora: Excavations in the Heart of Classical Athens.* London.
Catling, H. W. (1983) and (1986), 'Archaeology in Greece, 1982–83' and 'Archaeology in Greece, 1985–86', *Archaeological Reports* 29 (1982–3), and 32 (1985–6).
Cherry, J. F. (1978), 'Generalisation and the archaeology of the state', in D. R. Green, C. C. Haselgrove and M. J. T. Spriggs (eds.), *Social Organisation and Settlement. British Archaeological Reports* (S) 47. Oxford.
Cherry, J. F. (1984), 'The emergence of the state in the prehistoric Aegean', *Proceedings of the Cambridge Philological Society* 210, 18–48.
Claessen, H. J. M. and Skalnik, P. (eds.) (1978), *The Early State.* The Hague.
Cohen, R. and Service, E. R. (eds.) (1978), *Origins of the State: the Anthropology of Political Evolution.* Institute for the Study of Human Issues. Philadelphia.
Coldstream, J. N. (1983), 'The meaning of the regional styles in the eighth century BC', in R. Hägg (ed.), *The Greek Renaissance of the Eighth Century BC: Tradition and Innovation. Skrifter utgivna av Svenska Institutet i Athen* (Series 4°) 30. Stockholm.

Cook, R. M. (1955), 'Thucydides as archaeologist', *Annual of the British School at Athens* 50, 266–70.

Ehrenberg, V. (1937), 'When did the *polis* rise?', *Journal of Hellenic Studies* 57, 147–59.

Ehrenberg, V. (1969), *The Greek State*. London.

Eliot, C. W. J. (1962), *The Coastal Demes of Attica*. Toronto.

Gesell, G. C., Day, L. P., and Coulson, W. D. E. (1983), 'Excavations and survey at Kavousi, 1978–81', *Hesperia* 52, 389–420.

Gesell, G. C., Day, L. P., and Coulson, W. D. E. (1985), 'Kavousi, 1982–1983: the Kastro', *Hesperia* 54, 327–55.

Hägg, R. (1982), 'Zur Stadtwerdung des dorischen Argos', in D. Papenfuss and V. M. Strocka (eds.), *Palast und Hütte*, 297–307. Mainz.

Hall, E. H. (1914), *Excavations in Eastern Crete: Vrokastro*. Philadelphia.

Levi, D. (1961–2), 'Le due prime campagne di scavo a Iaso', *Annuario della Scuola archeologica di Atene* 39–40 (n.s. 23–4), 527–34.

McDonald, W. A., Coulson, W. D. E. and Rosser, J. (1983), *Excavations at Nichoria in Southwest Greece* 3: *Dark Age and Byzantine Occupation*. Minneapolis.

Malkin, I. S. (1987), *Religion and Colonization in Ancient Greece. Studies in Greek and Roman Religion*, 3. Leiden.

Morris, I. M. (1987), *Burial and Ancient Society*. Cambride.

Philippaki, B. (1970), 'Agios Andreas Siphnou', *Arkhaiologikon Deltion* 25, Chroniká, 431–4.

Polignac, F. de (1984), *La Naissance de la cité grecque*. Paris.

Popham, M. R., Sackett, L. H. and Themelis, P. G. (1979–80), *Lefkandi* 1: *The Iron Age*. London.

Pritchett, W. K. (1985), *The Greek State at War*, Part iv. Berkeley and Los Angeles.

Renfrew, A. C. (1975), 'Trade as action at a distance: questions of integration and communication', in J. A. Sabloff and C. C. Lamberg-Karlovsky (eds.), *Ancient Civilization and Trade*, 3–59. Albuquerque.

Renfrew, A. C. and Cherry, J. F. (eds.) (1985), *Peer Polity Interaction and the Development of Sociopolitical Complexity*. Cambridge.

Robertson, C. M. (1951), 'The place of vase-painting in Greek art', *Annual of the British School at Athens* 46, 151–9.

Roussel, D. (1976), *Tribu et cité*. Paris.

Schilardi, D. (1983), 'The decline of the Geometric settlement of Koukounaries at Paros', in R. Hägg (ed.), *The Greek Renaissance* [see above, under Coldstream 1983], 173–83.

Snodgrass, A. M. (1964), 'Carian armourers: the growth of a tradition', *Journal of Hellenic Studies* 84, 107–18.

Snodgrass, A. M. (1977), *Archaeology and the Rise of the Greek State*. Inaugural Lecture. Cambridge.

Snodgrass, A. M. (1980), *Archaic Greece: the Age of Experiment*. London.

Thompson, H. A. and Wycherley, R. E. (1972), *The Agora of Athens. The Athenian Agora*, 14. Princeton.

Traill, J. S. (1975), *The Political Organization of Attica. Hesperia Supplement* 14. Princeton.

Vallet, G., Villard, F. and Auberson, P. (1976), *Mégara Hyblaea* 1: *le quartier de l'agora archaïque*. Paris.

Zaphiropoulou, Ph. (1967–71), 'Donoussa', *Arkhaiologikon Deltion* 22, Chroniká, 467; 24, Chroniká, 390–3; 25, Chroniká, 426–28; 26, Chroniká, 465–7.

CHAPTER 16

The Nature and Standing of the Early Western Colonies

Here is a rather belated attempt to confront a topic which has long been prominent in scholarship, forming the primary focus of some historians' and archaeologists' work, briefly admitted to the mainstream of history for the period when it first arose but often excluded thereafter: the world of the Greek cities of the West. The paper was one of a 1994 seminar series, to be offered (unknown to him at the time) to my own former supervisor John Boardman. The term 'colonisation' with its cognates, still used here without compunction, was by then beginning to be found inappropriate and misleading when applied to the process which led to Greek (and other) overseas settlement in antiquity (compare the review of the resultant volume by Purcell 1997, and the comment at page 56 of his earlier (1990) paper, cited in the bibliography of the paper itself).

The topic of new settlement in the northern Aegean (pp. 298–300) is taken further in Ch. 8 above.

BIBLIOGRAPHY

Purcell, N. (1997), review of *The Archaeology of Greek Colonisation*, ed. G. Tsetskhladze and F. de Angelis, *Antiquity* 71: 500–2.

In an important paper of a decade ago, Jean-Paul Morel identified 'the motives for Greek colonisation' as one of a series of 'subjects of research that have become less important' (Morel 1984, 123–24).

'The nature and standing of the early Western colonies', from G. R. Tsetskhladze and F. De Angelis (ed.), *The Archaeology of Greek Colonisation: Essays Dedicated to Sir John Boardman*, Oxford: Oxford University School of Archaeology, Monograph 40, 1994, pp. 1–10.

This was one of the reasons why I declined the editors' request to take that as my subject. The rather awkward title that I have chosen reflects an intention to concentrate instead on the immediate *results* of the colonising movement, especially as they affected the colonists themselves. This will be a contribution too partisan to masquerade as a *bilan de recherches*: rather, it is stating a case, against the background of the past ten years of research in this field, in which some of the most important contributions have been made by non-archaeologists.

I begin by drawing particular attention to one of Morel's notable insights, the huge empty gaps in the map of the Greek colonies in the West, and the relatively wide spacing of the colonies that were established (1984, 127–29). We can see the force of this observation most clearly by comparing the western venture with another movement traditionally held to be roughly contemporary, and involving some of the same Greek cities, the settlement of the north coast of the Aegean. Here we have the feeling that every possible niche of settlement is being occupied: in the West, the picture is markedly and permanently different. We shall return to this contrast later. Meanwhile, let us note Morel's own interpretation of the pattern in the West: he concluded that the location of the colonies here was determined with a high degree of caution and hesitation on the part of the Greeks, as if they 'had drawn back .... wherever powerful and organised peoples were installed before them' (1984, 128). This may well have been true. I also take this pattern as testifying to what is the main theme of this paper, the unprecedentedly planned, deliberate and calculated nature of the movement to settle in the West. As subsequent history showed, it was, in a way that almost nothing done in Greece before the eighth century BC was, building to last and building for success.

One rather earlier insight into the pattern of Mediterranean colonisation generally is often overlooked today, perhaps because its implications are now uncontested. It appears in the preface to the *Penguin Atlas of Ancient History* (McEvedy 1967, 10–11 with Figs 4–5). Colin McEvedy used a kind of theoretical 'nearest neighbour analysis' to quantify the degree of *indentedness* of a coastline. He showed that one characteristic of indented coasts was that each coastal location was more likely to have, as its nearest neighbours, other coastal locations; and that even an inland settlement might have a majority of such neighbours, rather than other inland settlements. Finally, by superimposing a fine-grained grid of squares on the map of the Mediterranean, he was able to single out and shade in those stretches of coast where such conditions prevailed. The resultant map is, to all intents and purposes, a map of ancient (Greek and other) Mediterranean colonisation. Coupled with Morel's explanation of where and why the Greek expansion stopped short, it comes close to giving a predictive geographical model for the entire process of overseas settlement in the eighth, seventh and sixth centuries BC.

Another phrase from Morel's paper, his description of the Western Mediterranean as 'a fantastic cauldron of expanding cultures', has been quoted with strong approval by Nicholas Purcell (1990, 33). I would not dissent: indeed, I think that today we should be ready to add yet another ingredient to this mixture. We have long since accepted the idea that Greek and non-Greek elements lived side by side on many western sites. I think it is time to admit the likelihood that the Greek element was itself much more of a mixture – and not just in the joint ventures by more than one city – than the ancient historical accounts suggest; that the description of, say, Syracuse as 'a Corinthian colony' need mean little more than that the oikist and his immediate entourage came from Corinth. Does not Archilochos, with his cry that 'the ills of all Greece have come together in Thasos', imply just such a picture (fr. 102 West)? Only thus, I believe, can we account for the sudden bursts of colonisation, ostensibly by a single city in a short span of years, at a time when the population of Corinth, Chalkis or any other Greek city can hardly have sufficed to man a series of colonising expeditions, let alone be *compelled* by pressure of numbers into undertaking them.

Over-population and land-hunger, as motives for the colonising movement, have always had to confront the objection that, whatever the level of population in the Greek cities in the second half of the eighth century may have been, it was so much higher in the fifth, that supplementary factors must at least be called in to explain the early recourse to colonisation. The strongest of these factors, in my view, must have been the injustices, perceived or real, personal or collective, in the distribution of land and the access to power. Hunger, as we have learned in earnest in recent decades, can exist in a generally well-fed society; the same could easily have been true of the hunger for land in early Greece.

These are, however, not very controversial sentiments with which to overlay my general acceptance of one of the main tenets of recent scholarship on the settlement of the western Mediterranean, namely its cosmopolitanism. If belatedly, we have all come to recognise the degree of integration of indigenous and intrusive populations, and between intruders of different origins. The Phoenicians, in particular, have become as prominent in places – such as Sardinia and southern Spain – where we had not particularly expected to find them prominent, as they remain fugitive in places where Thucydides had expressly led us to look for them (vi. 2.6: 'all round Sicily'). But now it is time to take issue with another trend of recent scholarship that is on the way to general acceptance: I hope I shall be able to characterise fairly a view with which I am in radical disagreement.

During the 1980s, a new analysis has begun to find favour, which runs along something like the following lines: 'The isolation and backwardness of Greece during the Early Iron Age has been grossly exaggerated: so much so that it is unjustified to talk any longer of a 'dark age'. Greek venturers, with Euboeans to the fore, had been establishing overseas contacts since at least the tenth century' (the word 'commerce' may or may not be used here, but there is sure to be a reference to the finds at Lefkandi at this point). 'Presently permanent settlements began to be established, again with Euboeans to the fore, with Al Mina on the fringes of the eastern continental powers being succeeded by Pithekoussai on its western island site, the latter a forerunner of the new style of overseas expansion which we call colonisation (Euboeans yet again to the fore), but which is nothing more than a continuation of long-standing processes. Throughout this period, Phoenicians and Greeks are engaged in complementary activity, sometimes in rivalry, sometimes in collaboration, sometimes indistinguishable from each other. On the Greek side, these processes result in the linking of the Aegean world to a Mediterranean-wide network with itself at the centre, the colonies remaining firmly tied to the apron-strings of their mother cities'.

I do not wish to reject the entirety of this picture: in particular I accept, as already implied, the reality of early Phoenician activity in the West, though it is well to remember that, for them, the Aegean was itself part of 'the West'. What I wish to question is, first, the degree of Greek participation in all these earlier activities beyond Aegean waters. The evidence, however greatly we may differ in our assessments of its significance, will be agreed to be very much more impressive in respect of the inward movement of artefacts and practices to the Aegean, than of the corresponding outward transmission. On the one hand, we have not just portable objects – some of them of intrinsic value like the Lefkandi jewelry, others with a different significance like the inscribed bowl from Knossos – but also architectural evidence (the apparent Phoenician presence at Kommos), and evidence for the learning of techniques (the foundry deposit at the Lefkandi settlement). Presently there is the suggestion of resident Oriental goldsmiths (and later of bronze-workers) at Knossos and of a specialised unguent-bottling establishment in the Dodecanese. Behind all this, we have to envisage the likelihood of bulk importation of certain raw materials: most notably, copper and tin, from the time that bronze objects again begin to be plentiful in Greece. The striking features of this evidence are that it suggests a wide range of activities, certainly entailing the movement of people as well as goods; that it is geographically rather restricted – central Euboea, central Crete, Athens and the Dodecanese between them account for nearly all of it; and, no doubt partly as a consequence, that its visible impact on the material culture of Greece as a whole is not very great. Phoenician temple-plans are not generally imitated: Cypriot rod tripods are sparingly imported and, again, not widely imitated, at least in metal; gold jewelry and even cheap imports like faience beads are slow to spread beyond the original close circle of contact-points; resident craftsmen are hard to detect elsewhere; and so on.

Yet this evidence seems imposing indeed when we compare it with that of its counterpart, the outward-going movements from the Aegean. Cyprus may be regarded as a special case because of its already partially Greek-speaking population; but even if we include it, there is little more than a scatter of pottery, thinly if fairly widely spread, to cover the lapse of between two and three centuries, mostly from sites without the least hint of independent evidence for a Greek presence (for Al Mina see below). If it is a residual Hellenocentric prejudice which nevertheless urges us to interpret both sides of this picture as resulting primarily from Greek enterprise, then it has a very thin and unbalanced diet to feed on. A sceptical archaeologist with a different training, innocent of either the Classical or the Orientalist tradition, might even conclude that, between the time of the last major Aegean emigration to Cyprus, probably in the first half of the eleventh century BC, and the settlement of Pithekoussai in the first half of the eighth, there is no *proof* of any Greek having set foot beyond the Greek-speaking world of the Aegean, and perhaps its Cypriot extension.

Except of course at Al Mina, so often and so confidently described as a Greek *emporion* or even a Greek colony. But this foundation-stone in the edifice of early Greek overseas enterprise has been struck by two heavy blows in the past few years. The first was Rosalinde Kearsley's detailed study of the pendent-semicircle skyphos (Kearsley

1989). It was on the chronology of this type of drinking-cup that
the traditional date for the first Greek presence at Al Mina ('*c.* 825
BC') partly rested. Her study now proposes a partial revision of that
chronology, with 'Type 6' of the pendent-semicircle skyphos, including the great majority of the pieces from Al Mina as well as other
far-travelled examples, being assigned to the second half of the eighth
century (1989, 101–104, 142–45). The site was in existence earlier,
but she concludes that there is no proof of Greek presence or even
Greek participation at Al Mina before 750 BC.

I am well aware that her dating, and indeed her classification, have
been criticised, not least from the direction of Oxford (Popham and
Lemos 1992). But it seems to me that her evidence, particularly that
from Eretria and Paphos, strongly suggests that this type of skyphos
was still being produced in the later eighth century. Once we acknowledge this extension of the date-range, the Al Mina material begins
to wear a different look. It is common ground that the overwhelming preponderance of the early Greek pottery from the site dates to
c. 750 BC and later; if we can no longer insist on an earlier date for the
relatively few pendent-semicircle skyphoi, then they no longer have
to support, with the aid of only a handful of sherds of other types, the
heavy burden of proving a further 75 years of earlier Greek activity
at the site.

The second setback is more fundamental. The axiom of resident
Greeks at Al Mina, at any time before the sixth century, has itself
been increasingly questioned. That axiom was always based on the
pottery, like so much of the accepted picture of early Greek activity in the East: architecture, burial-practices and other aspects of the
material culture of Al Mina-gave little or no support for it. Even the
interpretation of the pottery has been beset by the doubts that arose
over the stratification of the early levels at the site. A laudable early
attempt to isolate one class of early Greek ware as having been actually made at the site (Boardman 1959) foundered on the rock of
scientific analysis, which pointed instead to Cyprus as the place of
manufacture (Jones 1986, 694–96). (In passing, the systematic tendency to underrate the role played by Cyprus has from the beginning
been a *Leitmotiv* of the study of early Greek expansion). Now, in a
new paper, J. Y. Perreault (1993) has concluded that Al Mina cannot
by any strict standard pass as a Greek *emporion*. He makes telling
use of the discovery of a sizeable collection of early Greek pottery at
Tyre, a site which other evidence forbids us to regard as in any sense
Greek. Al Mina must presumably carry with it Sukas and Bassit, two

nearby sites where the evidence for a Greek presence is either weaker or later. Perhaps I may also mention here the work of Joanna Luke in her Cambridge doctoral dissertation now approaching completion, which has led her to the same conclusion (Luke 1994). Al Mina does not meet certain clear criteria for the presence of a foreign community in a port of trade. Rather, the precise nature of the Greek pottery found – exclusively eating and drinking vessels – together with its inland distribution, points to the site's having functioned as a mere funnel for the transmission of table-ware to the élites of the more important administrative centres that lay inland.

The combined effect of these two lines of argument is to throw grave doubt on the evidence of Al Mina, in respect of both its significance and its claim to a precolonial date. But where does this leave the overall picture of overseas activity in the tenth, ninth and early eighth centuries BC? I am not going to emulate the imaginary archaeologist whom I conjured up just now, and argue that *none* of this activity need have been Greek; that all the goods transported in both directions could have been carried by others. An appropriate illustration may be found in the comparison of two contemporary distribution maps, and in the differing interpretations of them by two different scholars (Fig. 16.1). The glass bird beads shown in the first map have a distribution that by-passes the inner Aegean as it extends from the Levant to Italy; the 'Lyre Player seals' shown in the other map have a parallel distribution at both extremities, but this time cover the Aegean as well. For Hans-Georg Niemeyer who drew attention to the comparison (Niemeyer 1984, 29, Figs 20–21), it is the *difference* between the two that is significant, and it suggests to him that the former class of objects were carried by Phoenicians, the latter by Greeks. For John Boardman, there is a significant *resemblance* between them, in that both exclude the far western Mediterranean, a finding that seems difficult to reconcile with the view that the Phoenicians were the carriers in either case; in the absence of any evidence for sea-transport on the part of the Aramaeans who actually produced the Lyre Player seals, the implication is that Greeks are the likeliest carriers (Boardman 1990, 10–11, Fig. 20). For our purposes, the significant thing is that both interpretations agree in assigning some part of the eighth-century traffic to Greeks.

More generally, one cannot ignore the insistent appearance of the Euboeans, on both sides of the balance of imported and exported objects. This cannot be attributed either to coincidence, or to any superior quality in their pottery. It must mean that they in some way

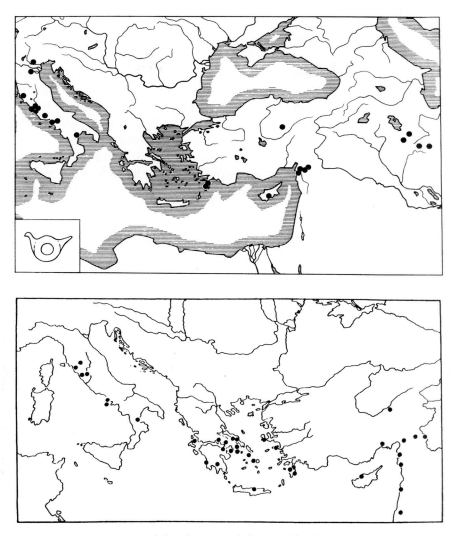

Figure 16.1 Comparison of distributions of glass bird beads (above, after Niemeyer 1984, 28, Fig. 20) and of Lyre-Player seals (below, after Boardman 1990, 10, Fig. 20).

controlled a privileged channel of communication into and out of the Aegean; while the sequel, their primacy in the movement to colonise, hints strongly that they were already well-travelled themselves. My overall response to this recent appraisal of precolonial Greek overseas activity is therefore that it is greatly exaggerated; that it shows a quite disproportionate preoccupation with painted pottery; that it is partly founded on dubious chronology; but that it is nevertheless not entirely imaginary.

We have been looking largely towards the East, because that is the direction in which nearly all the precolonial evidence points. But we should also acknowledge that a revision of the dating of pendent-semicircle skyphoi has repercussions in the West. Kearsley (1989, 101–4) assigned to her 'Type 6' the skyphoi from Veii and Villas-mundo, as well as most of those from Al Mina. What this implies is that some of the western 'pre-colonial' Greek trade need not be such; rather it is, to adopt a phrase which I first heard used by David Ridgway, 'para-colonial'. As such, it would cast a different light on our picture of the beginning of western colonisation; especially as, in the West as in the East, we have to accommodate the possibility of Phoenician or other non-Greek carriers taking Greek artefacts with them, a realisation which we owe primarily to the discoveries in the Phoenician sites of southern Spain.

Now I wish to direct attention briefly in another direction, nei-ther East nor West but North. I have already fleetingly referred to the Greek colonies on the northern coast of the Aegean. Here recent discoveries, which I hope to discuss more fully elsewhere (Snodgrass 1994), have so radically transformed our picture of the sequence of developments that I wish to suggest that it is here, and not in the shadowy appearances of Euboean pottery on western Asiatic sites, that we should be looking for understanding of the precedents for western colonisation. We have learned that settlement from central or southern Greece, of at least a durable and probably a permanent na-ture, may be found in sites of the Chalkidike peninsula from possibly the twelfth or eleventh, and at the very latest the mid-ninth, centuries BC. A most significant feature is the repeated appearance of pottery of Euboean type, together with local imitations. Partial comparison can be made with the ninth-century settlement, apparently also from Euboea, of certain of the Cycladic island-sites; chronologically, there must even be some overlap with the Ionian Migration. Here then is an episode which links – as indeed the ancient Greeks linked them – the earliest movements across the Aegean with the later *apoikiai* in the West.

The northward movement, unlike those to the Cyclades, involved a continental coast with a potentially or actually hostile indigenous pop-ulation in close proximity, a feature which links it to both the Ionian and the western settlements. But it differs from the Ionian Migration in bringing the Euboeans to the fore, in the context of durable colonial establishments, many years before the western ventures began. It also throws a discreditable light on the flimsy and mostly late historical evidence, on whose basis we used to assign the northern settlement to a date roughly contemporary with that of the western colonies – if anything (since Euboeans led the way in both and it is hard to imagine their undertaking them simultaneously) a shade later. Twenty-five years after he published *The Greeks Overseas*, John Boardman wrote that the book 'was criticised for taking too little notice of texts (it took too much)' (Boardman 1988, 796) – a judgment that some of us might echo about our own and others' writings in that period.

The great difference between northern and western Greek colonisation is of course that of distance. Whereas from the outer coast of Euboea to the tip of the Pallene promontory is a sail of only about a hundred miles, in which one can be in sight of land throughout, the journey to Pithekoussai is about eight times as long, including passages of much greater danger like the rounding of Cape Malea. When we couple this with the contrast, already noted, in the density of colonisation in the two areas, we may see a causal connection. The sites of the western colonies look as if they were chosen with a lot of circumspection, with regard not only (as Morel rightly said) to the 'powerful and organised peoples' who were there before them, but also to each other. Of course, the early settlers could not know that their new outposts would become prosperous and powerful; but one way to provide for that eventuality was to allow plenty of space for them to expand. There were exceptions – Megara Hyblaea was a little uncomfortably squeezed in between Syracuse and Leontinoi, and eventually its inhabitants were to pay the price for this – but they are few and far between. With the colonies in the Chalkidike, if overcrowding or any other cause made settlement no longer viable, an oared ship could return to the mother-city for consultation within two or three days and, in the direst emergency, the whole of a small community could be evacuated. In the West, the degree of commitment was so much greater that the founding of a new colony must have seemed more or less irrevocable to all concerned. We cannot know the strength of the ties which the early northern Aegean settlements maintained with their homeland; but with the western colonies we are in a stronger position ... and this brings me to my last argument, the degree of independence of the western colonial cities.

Here once more we broach Morel's list of 'subjects of research which have become less important', for 'the relations between mother cities and their colonies' were on that list. There has indeed been an apparently inconsequential sequence of swings in the pendulum of opinion on this subject, no doubt because a judicious selection of the evidence can be enlisted to support either side in the argument. Nevertheless I shall risk re-opening that argument, since independence is at the heart of my case, that western colonisation is to be set apart from anything that had preceded it.

One possible way to establish that case is to state, *a priori*, that we are now dealing, both in the Aegean and in the West, with the world of the *polis*, and that this therefore places western colonisation in a fresh category. But this is rather begging the question: one group of sceptics might ask how we can be so sure that institutions were not already in place at the time of the northern Aegean settlements, or even of the Ionian Migration; another (and I would number myself among them) might question whether the establishment of the colonies presupposes that the entire *polis* system was then already in place. There is no doubt that the western colonies rapidly came to exemplify that system in its most clear-cut form; but what of the argument that they may, in many ways, have been the *first* Greek settlements to do so?

Let us turn to rather more specific and empirical arguments. The last component in the 'straw man' case that I set up earlier on was the view that the whole process of early Greek expansion resulted in the creation of a sort of spider's web of contacts with the Aegean at its heart. Whatever the truth about the precolonial period, I maintain that the outcome of western colonisation was nothing of the kind; and I believe that the objectives, as well as the results, of colonisation reflect this fundamental difference. A reading of Irad Malkin's book (1987) provides us with a number of starting-points which are worth enumerating.

The religious and political measures taken when a colonising party set out for the West were far-reaching. Almost from the outset, the key role played by the Delphian Apollo can be documented, even if we choose to take a sceptical view of the very early oracular consultations (which I myself do not). The evidence from Delphi itself suggests that such a role would have been out of the question in periods before the eighth century (Morgan 1990, 106–147). The selection of the oikist was an even more important new feature: in political terms, because of the extraordinary powers with which he was endowed, and in religious terms because of his close linkage with Apollo himself, and also because of his subsequent destiny, to be commemorated with cult at the heart of the city that he had founded. A striking feature of Malkin's book is indeed his closing argument (1987, 261–66) that these cults may have been the very earliest instances of public, communal founder-worship in the Greek world.

The evidence now available for the early incidence of planned settlements in the western colonies also justifies a reappraisal of old assumptions. Politically, this planned element is one of the reflections of the power of the oikist; but culturally it is even more significant, in that it shows the Greek mind grappling with entirely fresh problems. Such at least is Malkin's view (1987, 135–186); and the clearest evidence for it is the demonstration that such planning often dictated religious decisions, by determining the location of the colonial cult-centres according to rational, secular principles. The sanctuaries were placed where they would fit best with the organisation of the settlement. I am not sure that this is necessarily the *first* time that such factors had operated: I think that something of the same kind may have happened with the location of the sanctuary at a site like Zagora on Andros, a century or so earlier. But it is certain that none of the established cities of the Greek homeland can have faced such decisions, or enjoyed such opportunities.

The apportionment of rural land is a topic briefly touched on in Morel's paper (1984, 140–141), but one that lies largely outside the scope of Malkin's book. Here it is difficult to trace any clear picture back to the initial years of western colonisation, though the attempt has been made. But here again we can declare in principle that the colonists were dealing with a fresh problem, for which life in Aegean Greece can have offered no full precedent. As with the lay-out of the main settlement, so in the allocation of rural land an entire community had to be provided for in 'a single rationally planned act' (Malkin 1987, 186).

One other area where we have a relatively full body of evidence is that relating, not to colonial life but to colonial death. Gillian Shepherd's study of burial practices in certain of the Sicilian colonies (Shepherd 1993 and forthcoming), in which she reveals a pattern of competition and emulation, not of the practices of the mother cities, but of those of other nearby colonies; some awareness of indigenous burial customs is also detectable. The overall picture is one of a robust independence, which forms early in the lives of the new settlements and increases steadily thereafter. Her thesis also re-interprets certain other features which had hitherto often been seen as indicative of a dependent or nostalgic hankering for the 'old country', such as the use made by colonial cities of the Panhellenic sanctuaries, above all

Olympia. It emerges that a better interpretation of the Western Greek policy of conspicuous dedication, and later of the erection of treasuries, is that these activities served less to satisfy provincial longing, than to assert colonial prowess and prosperity, in an arena chosen for its unavoidable impact on the consciousness of the cities of the homeland. It is after all a fact that, after not many generations had elapsed, the early colonies were already in a position to challenge the attainments of the Aegean cities, by a wide range of criteria – populousness, legislative innovation, temple-building, fortification, and almost any indicator of prosperity that one liked to choose. This result could not, as I have already admitted, have been predicted at the time of their foundation, but it was surely one of the long-term aims that dictated the choice of their locations.

This essential separateness of the colonial world is also a theme of Carol Dougherty's (1993) recent and pithily entitled paper, which focuses on the strange correlation between the office of oikist in a colony, and the status of social outcast in the homeland, often on grounds of criminal acts. The theme recurs often enough to reinforce the notion that to found one of the early colonies was to make an irrevocable, indeed an urgent break with the society of the homeland. It reminds me of a sentence, set in a rather different context, from Malkin's book: 'It is probable that in certain respects colonization resembled a crime because it took land from someone else; for this reason it was important that the act of colonisation receive moral sanction from Apollo' (Malkin 1987, 90). This time we are confronted with a kind of problem which would have been a commonplace within the world of the Aegean, in the Chalkidike, in Ionia and earlier still no doubt in Cyprus; but which was now for the first time arising in relation to peoples outside the confines of the known Greek world.

The outline of my case will by now be clear enough. The early western colonists may have persuaded themselves that they were following in the footsteps of predecessors in the Heroic Age, but they should not persuade us. They were attempting something without full precedent. By transposing practices rehearsed in the small world of the Aegean coasts and islands to a wider stage and to alien coasts, they were creating a whole new category. If their initial objectives included an element of extending the culture of the Greek world to new shores, this was very soon forgotten in the much greater challenge of founding a new world altogether. For that, in the end, is what they did.

BIBLIOGRAPHY

Boardman, J. 1959: Greek potters at Al Mina? *Anatolian Studies* 9, 163–69.

Boardman, J. 1988: Classical archaeology: whence and whither? *Antiquity* 62, 795–97.

Boardman, J. 1990: The Lyre-Player group of seals: an encore. *AA*, 1–17.

Dougherty, C. 1993: It's murder to found a colony. In Dougherty, C. and Kurke, L. (edd.), *Cultural Poetics in Archaic Greece* (Cambridge, Cambridge U.P.), 178–98.

Jones, R. E., 1986 *Greek and Cypriot Pottery* (Athens, British School at Athens).

Kearsley, R. 1989: *The pendent semicircle skyphos* (London, BICS, Supplement 44).

Luke, J. 1994: Since published as *Ports of Trade, Al Mina and Geometric Greek Pottery in the Lerant* (Oxford, British Archaeological Reports 5–1100, (2003). Unpublished Ph.D. dissertation, University of Cambridge.

Malkin I. 1987: *Religion and Greek colonisation* (Leiden, E. J. Brill).

McEvedy, C. 1967: *The Penguin Atlas of ancient history* (Harmondsworth, Penguin).

Morel, J. P. 1984: Greek colonization in Italy and the West. Problems of evidence and interpretation. In Hackens, T., Holloway, N. D. and R. R. (edd.), *Crossroads of the Mediterranean* (Louvain-la-Neuve, Université Catholique de Louvain / Providence, Brown University).

Morgan, C. A. 1990: *Athletes and Oracles* (Cambridge, Cambridge U.P.).

Niemeyer, H.-G. 1984: Die Phönizier und die Mittelmeerwelt im Zeitalter Homers, *JbRGZM* 31, 3–94.

Perreault, J. Y. 1993: Les *emporia* grecs du Levant: mythe ou réalité? In Bresson, A. and Rouillard, P. (edd.), *L'Emporion* (Paris, E. de Boccard, Publications du Centre Pierre Paris 26), 59–83.

Popham, M. R. and Lemos, I. 1992: review of Kearsley 1989, *Gnomon* 64, 152–55.

Purcell, N. 1990: Mobility and the *polis*. In Murray, O. and Price, S. (edd.), *The Greek city from Homer to Alexander* (Oxford, Oxford U.P.), 29–58.

Shepherd, G. 1993: *Death and religion in Archaic Greek Sicily: a study in colonial relationships*. Unpublished Ph.D. dissertation, University of Cambridge.

Shepherd, G. The Pride of Most Colonials: Burial and Religion in the Sicilian Greek Colonies, *Acta Hyperborea* 6. (Copenhagen).

Snodgrass, A. M. 1994: A new precedent for westward expansion: the Euboeans in Macedonia. *AION* 16 (volume *dedicato a Giorgio Buchner*).

The Early Polis *at War*

INTRODUCTION TO PART IV

We come first to the earliest paper in the book (Ch. 17), with its rather different sequel, Ch. 19. Because of the central part played by the heavy infantrymen or *hoplitai* in the Greek city, both on and off the battlefield, their study has always been a less specialised field than one might expect, attracting at least as much interest from literary scholars, anthropologists and sociologists (see recently Runciman 1998) as from historians or archaeologists.

Because of this interest, the questions dealt with in the 1965 paper were not new; and they have since been taken up by many others. From the 1970s to the 1990s, there was a whole series of treatments, mainly by Greek historians, of the issue of hoplite warfare, but this meant mainly the mature hoplite tactics of the full Classical period: for studies focused on the formative phase, see Greenhalgh 1973; Cartledge 1977; Salmon 1977; the two works by Hans van Wees listed later, under Ch. 19; and for close investigations of particular aspects, Pritchett 1971–85. A number of modifications of my conclusions, some of them mutually contradictory, were proposed; but the necessity for some kind of initial 'hoplite reform', whether gradual or abrupt, to bring the system into being, was not yet generally questioned. But, in an entirely unexpected quarter, the seeds were being sown for a much more radical reappraisal of this question: this will be discussed under Ch. 19 below.

I came to this subject only towards the latter end of my graduate study of early Greek arms. I have not preserved the lifelong attachment which many academics retain for the subject of their doctoral research – in the case of this particular topic, partly because I felt that it was another factor in the fencing off of the Classical from other branches of archaeology. But a few reversions to military themes have nevertheless taken place, among them Ch. 18 addressing a subject, fortification, which by contrast with hoplite warfare has remained rather forbiddingly specialised.

BIBLIOGRAPHY

Cartledge, P. A. (1977), 'Hoplites and Heroes: Sparta's contribution to the technique of ancient warfare', *Journal of Hellenic Studies* 97: 11–27.

Greenhalgh, P. A. L. (1973), *Early Greek Warfare: Horsemen and Chariots in the Homeric and Archaic Ages*, Cambridge: Cambridge University Press.

Pritchett, W. K. (1971–85), *The Greek State at War*, 4 vols, Berkeley: University of California Press.

Runciman, W. G. (1998), 'Greek hoplites, warrior culture, and indirect bias', *Journal of the Royal Anthropological Institute* n.s. 4, 4: 731–51.

Salmon, J. B. (1977), 'Political Hoplites?', *Journal of Hellenic Studies* 97: 84–101.

CHAPTER 17

The Hoplite Reform and History

The first paper can, after this preamble, be briefly introduced. There have been a number of subsequent archaeological discoveries which have filled out the picture available in 1965. Thus, 'the unparalleled nature of the find' of the Panoply Tomb at Argos (p. 314) has now been qualified by the excavation of two other contemporary burials at Argos, with helmets and other arms (Protonotariou-Deilaki 1971: 81–2, Fig. 13; 1973: 99, pl. 95). An important addition to the list of Attic Geometric vase pictures, one which has a direct bearing on the early use of such bronze cuirasses, has come with the publication of an amphora in Buffalo, NY, showing a horseman with what appears to be a cuirass over-painted on his torso (Alföldi 1967: 24, n. 94, pl. 7,1). Studies of specific items of early armour have multiplied (notably Jarva 1995 on body-armour), but the most important new addition to the actual finds has been the collection of pieces of seventh-century date from Cretan Arkades (Hoffmann 1972).

The more speculative excursion into the Etruscan, Roman and generally Italian use of hoplites (pp. 319–26) has not given rise to such intense discussion. But later syntheses of the evidence can be found in D'Agostino 1990 for Etruria; and in Cornell (1995) on the Etruscans (170–1), and early Rome (183–6). Both scholars fully accept the reality of the transmission of hoplite methods from the Greek world to Etruria and to Rome, though Cornell does not believe in any significant lapse of time between these two cases.

BIBLIOGRAPHY

Alföldi, A. (1967), 'Die Herrschaft der Reiterei in Griechenland und Rom nach dem Sturz der Könige', in *Gestalt und Geschichte: Festschrift für Karl Schefold* (*Antike Kunst*, Beiheft 4), ed. M. Rohle-Liegle, H. A. Cahn and H. C. Ackermann, Bern: Francke Verlag, pp. 13–47.

Cornell, T. J. (1995), *The Beginnings of Rome: Italy and Rome from the Bronze Age to the Punic Wars (c. 1000–264 BC)*, London: Routledge.

D'Agostino, B. (1990), 'Military organisation and social structure in Archaic Etruria', in *The Greek City from Homer to Alexander*, ed. O. Murray and S. Price, Oxford: Clarendon Press, pp. 59–82.

Hoffmann, H. (1972), *Early Cretan Armorers*, Mainz: von Zabern.

Jarva, E. (1995), *Archaiologica on Archaic Greek Body-Armor*, Rovaniemi: Pohjois-Suomen Historiallinen Yhdistys.

Protonotariou-Deilaki, E. (1971; 1973), 'Arkhaiotites kai mnimeia Argolido-Korinthias', *Arkhaiologikon Deltion* 25, B: 68–84 and 27, B: 80–122.

I have tried to analyse elsewhere[1] the archaeological evidence for Greek armour and weapons, and their possible effects on tactics, in the critical period of the eighth and seventh centuries BC. There, I was of necessity concerned with the monumental evidence, and did not look far beyond it. But there are historical implications which should be faced and also, I think, some further historical support for the conclusions there reached.

The conclusions were briefly these. The equipment of arms and armour, which modern writers tend to group together as the 'hoplite panoply', was originally a motley assemblage. Certain of its components – the long iron sword and spear – were part of the equipment of most warriors of the era, and of many periods before and since. Other items resemble those used by Mycenaean warriors some five centuries earlier: these include the bronze plate-corslet, the greave and (an optional accessory) the ankle-guard. I cannot believe, with some scholars, that such advanced and costly products of the bronze-smith had been produced continuously throughout the Dark Age that followed the fall of the Mycenaean civilisation; and indeed for at least 400 years there is no evidence of any kind that they were. Rather, they were revived or readopted: the corslet apparently under the influence of the metal-working cultures of Central Europe and Italy, the greave and ankle-guard spontaneously, although the Epic tradition had never forgotten their earlier use. Other items again, the closed helmet of the type that the Greeks called Corinthian, and the large round shield with arm-band and hand-grip, were Greek variants devised as an improvement on foreign models, principally the metal open-faced helmets and

'The hoplite reform and history', *Journal of Hellenic Studies* 85, 1965, 110–22.

round single-grip shields used by the Assyrians, Urartians and other Eastern peoples. The combination of all these elements together was an original Greek notion; as was their later association with a novel form of massed infantry tactics, the phalanx.

This brings us to the question of chronology. The adoption or read-option in Greece of each of these elements of the panoply, with the exception of the greave, can be shown to have taken place decid-edly earlier than 700 BC, though not probably earlier than *c.* 750. This conforms with the likeliest date at which the foreign models, whose influence we have posited, would become accessible. The Euro-pean metal-workers would be encountered at the beginning of Greek colonisation in Italy (*c.* 750), the Oriental perhaps with the new onset of the Assyrians on the Mediterranean seaboard under Tiglath-Pileser III (745–727). On the other hand, the full equipment is first definitely shown together, on one man, on Protocorinthian vases of *c.* 675 BC; and the massed tactics of the phalanx are first convincingly repre-sented, also on Protocorinthian, hardly before the middle of the 7th century. There may, of course, be other uncertain factors at work here: the tendency of the Greek artist to portray nudity where it would not occur in real life, and the great difficulty for the vase-painter of de-picting the phalanx at all. But the chance statements of contemporary poets, and the evidence of the only relevant grave-group, both sup-port the *prima facie* evidence of the artists: that the adoption of the 'hoplite panoply' was a long drawn out, piecemeal process, which did not at first entail any radical change in tactics.

This conclusion has, after all, a certain historical plausibility. Since there was no true precedent, but only partial parallels, for the new developments, it would have been extraordinary if the hoplite had sprung fully-armed from the head of some unknown genius, and at once taken up his position in the phalanx. Rather, we should expect that the different improvements in armour, coming as they did from a variety of sources and not all at the same moment, would be adopted, as occasion offered, by the warrior class of the period. This class was the aristocracy; and its methods of warfare are known to us, not only from Homer (whose evidence is usually ambiguous), but from the occasional remarks of poetic aristocrats like Archilochos, from the researches of Aristotle and other later writers,[2] and from the military scenes of the contemporary Geometric vase-painters, predominantly Attic and Argive. In such battles, the horse apparently played a con-siderable part, though its purpose may more often have been to serve as a transport animal, rather than as a charger in true cavalry warfare of the kind to which Aristotle refers. But to judge from the vase-paintings, infantry battles were commoner. In these the warriors on either side were armed with shield, sword and spears, but were for long without metallic protection for the head or body. The spears were predominantly used as javelins, and the engagements partly fought out at a distance, with archers, by the late eighth century at least, also taking a part.

Thus far, the picture of pre-hoplite warfare conforms to some extent with the Homeric descriptions. But one other feature appears often enough in the vase-paintings to be taken as characteristic: this is the beached warship, sometimes with an amphibious battle taking place at the point of landing. This cannot be entirely of heroic or mythological import, nor relevant only to Attica;[3] it therefore suggests a form of warfare in which raiding, by small parties of warriors, was a familiar tactic. Such raids will also have been possible on land for mounted men; and it may be that the Greek aristocrats of the late eighth century fought strategically, as they often did tactically, at long range, making armed forays of an offensive character against the territory of other cities. Whether they ever, in the battle itself, fought in a series of individual duels between rival champions, such as the Homeric poems portray, is far more questionable. The literary requirements, which may largely explain this picture, would not operate on the battlefield.

What would one expect to be the impact, on such a pattern of warfare, of the purely technological advances made in the later eighth century? Surely, that each improvement would be adopted by the aristocrats of the day, as far as possible within the existing mode of fighting. Thus there is the tradition that Timomachos the Aegeid, captor of Amyklai in the mid-eighth century, wore a metal corslet which was carried in processions in later days (see note 2). The horseman, infantryman and marine would benefit alike from having a metallic helmet, corslet and greaves. They would also theoretically benefit from having a larger and more protective shield, also faced with metal; but here arose the complications of weight and manoeuvrability. The Assyrian infantryman had gone into battle with a large, round, bronze-faced shield which he held in the time-honoured way, by a central handle, supported in some cases also by a strap passing round his neck. The Greeks, less robust or more ingenious, devised a new method of overcoming the weight of such a shield: the central arm-band, with the hand-grip shifted to the right-hand edge. It has been claimed that this simple improvement entailed a sweeping change in tactics, but this is an exaggeration. There are many later parallels in history for the use of such multiple-handled shields, without any such formation as the phalanx being entailed.[4] Certainly it would be hard to protect one's right-hand side with a shield so held; but so would it with any type of shield, save the long-extinct leather body-shields of the Bronze Age. One would expect the aristocrat, at least when fighting on foot, to make use of such a shield even in an era of missile-warfare. He could let go of the hand-grip to hold his spare javelins; and he would often have a horse (and no doubt a squire) at hand to relieve him of its weight before and after the fight.

Finally, emboldened by this protection, the warrior would tend to close the range at which he engaged. Having thrown his javelins, he would close with the sword; alternatively, he would exchange his two or three javelins for a single, heavy, thrusting-spear which would become his main weapon. All this could happen without any wider change in man-power, or in the general attitude to warfare.

Thus far, this has been a hypothetical argument: but it can be supported and illustrated, at almost every stage, by the evidence of archaeology or, more rarely, of contemporary literature. First one may make a general point: namely that, with the rather higher dating now provided for the introduction of many of the improvements, it follows that they were present in the Late Geometric era, the very period in which the painters are portraying the old, pre-hoplite style of warfare. Their presence is occasionally indicated by these artists; and the hoplite shield is unambiguously shown on two vases of the Late (but not the very latest) Geometric style.[5] In both cases it is carried by warriors who are following each other in a repetitive file round the vase; it is not yet shown being wielded in battle, and this may be significant. Possibly a distinction is to be drawn between such decorative subjects and the true battle-scenes; conceivably the latter are all intended to represent episodes from saga or mythology. It has been argued that both the chariot and the predominant type of shield (the 'Dipylon' form) in such scenes are merely heroic property, and do not correspond with contemporary usage.[6] But it would be unwarrantable to dispose of the whole body of contemporary pictorial evidence on such grounds. Even if the subject-matter of all these scenes were legendary, it would be extraordinary if the artist's depiction of them were not in some way coloured by his experience of contemporary warfare. We thus have evidence that the tactics of the Geometric battle-scenes could be, and were, combined with the use of the hoplite shield, and of the metallic helmet and corslet.

For the last two items, there is conclusive evidence from another source besides the paintings: the Late Geometric grave discovered at Argos in 1953.[7] The warrior buried here was a young man of substance; he may also, if the iron axes and huge fire-dogs in the shape of warships mean anything, have been a ship's captain or marine, as the excavator suggested. He wore a bronze helmet of early type, new to Greece but very soon to become obsolete with the development of the Corinthian helmet, and a superbly made bronze cuirass of the type which Greek hoplites wore for some two centuries afterwards. It might seem rash to conclude that he was an aristocrat; but the unparalleled nature of the find for its period, and the other indications of wealth, make this a natural inference. In addition, the connexion of the horse with a prominently drawn helmet, almost certainly metallic, is established by a small group of paintings, of Argive as well as Attic provenance.[8] In these, the helmeted warrior is shown either actually mounted, or holding the heads of one or two horses.

The next stage in the evidence is represented by the scenes on a number of vases, mainly Corinthian and Attic, of the first half of the seventh century. Here again there is ambiguity in the evidence. It has been claimed that certain features of these scenes are romantic survivals, while others are based on up-to-date observation; and that the scenes themselves, according to the presence or absence of these features, are sometimes legendary, sometimes contemporary in subject-matter, or else a mixture of the two.[9] I have no wish to ridicule such a theory, which in part at least is well-supported. But it seems better to make certain objective observations about these scenes:

(i) Only a very few of the latest scenes in the group (all Corinthian) unmistakably portray men operating in a close-packed formation that can be called a phalanx. In the main, the warriors are either alone, or engaging in a series of individual duels, or in a more or less loose formation, often with variegated equipment. It should be stressed that even uniform equipment and fairly close formation are not peculiar properties of the hoplite: New Kingdom Egypt, seventh-century Assyria and pre-hoplite Greece all show examples of these features.[10]

(ii) Of the scenes in which spears are carried, a majority give two spears to each warrior. This is most easily intelligible if one or both spears are to be thrown; and two even later Corinthian vases do clearly show twin spears with thongs attached for this very purpose.[11] The Classical hoplite, on the other hand, had only one spear, for thrusting.

(iii) A majority of the scenes show the warriors wearing something less than the full hoplite equipment: in particular, either the corslet or the hoplite shield is definitely absent in many cases.

(iv) The modes of fighting differ: in particular, one group of Attic vases shows warriors engaging in single combat with long swords.[12] This again is not hoplite practice, unless we are to imagine that these warriors have broken their spears.

I believe that these pictures are in fact the documentary evidence of a transitional stage in the development of Greek warfare. In this stage, there was as yet no crystallised formation or form of tactics; indeed, there was no standardised panoply, either of armour or of offensive weapons. Instead, the familiar tactics of the previous century were being gradually modified – for instance, there is now an overwhelming concentration on hand-to-hand fighting. But the equipment remains much the same as in the last generation, except that the helmet has been improved and the greave is now often present. It may also be possible to recognise glimpses of this kind of warfare in two contemporary poets. The use of the javelin, perhaps in conjunction with the hoplite shield, is twice indicated in the surviving poem of Kallinos of Ephesos; while the sword-duels (see (iv) above) may be recorded in Archilochos' prophecy that an imminent war in Euboea ‘$\xi\iota\phi\acute{\epsilon}\omega\nu \ldots \pi o\lambda\acute{\upsilon}\sigma\tau o\nu o\nu \ \acute{\epsilon}\sigma\sigma\epsilon\tau\alpha\iota \ \acute{\epsilon}\rho\gamma o\nu$', where the prospective participants are also referred to as ‘lords’.[13] Here there is no mention of the spear (except in the traditional epithet $\delta o\upsilon\rho\iota\kappa\lambda\upsilon\tau o\acute{\iota}$), although we know from other fragments that Archilochos fought with the hoplite shield and spear.[14] Furthermore the mounted warrior, though not yet a common figure in Greek art, is less rare in the early seventh century than in the late eighth.[15] He is seldom equipped as a true hoplite at this date, and may well represent a survival of the aristocratic ‘cavalryman’, who now probably used his horse mainly for transport.

It therefore seems unnecessary to believe that a radical change in the warrior class, with its social and political implications, had yet taken place. This would only occur after – if very soon after – the adoption of the phalanx. But it is an equally fundamental question, what the scope and effects of such a change would be when it did happen.

In seeking an answer to this question, we are fortunately not confined to the world of early Greece, with its extremely thin documentation. The superiority of hoplite equipment and tactics was such that they came to be adopted, in emulation of the Greeks, by several other peoples. Of these the Carians perhaps take first place chronologically, but their case is not an enlightening one.[16] The literary tradition, such as it is, is misleading; there is no evidence, nor is there ever likely to be, from artistic representation; while actual finds of armour have yet to materialise.

Far more rewarding is the study of the two stages whereby the new form of warfare first passed from Greece to Etruria, and then from Etruria to Rome. Part of its value lies in the fact that the nature of the evidence is so different from that in Greece. Admittedly there is much useful information here also to be gained from pictorial evidence, especially in Etruria. But in the case of Rome there is a literary account, diffuse if incoherent, and this account includes just enough about Etruria to confirm the natural inference from the archaeological material.

Before examining this, however, I think it is worth making a few observations on the whole subject of hoplite warfare. Sometimes the fundamentals stand in greatest danger of being overlooked.

First, the entire concept of a hoplite army must always be based on a qualification of wealth: the wealth necessary for the individual soldier to pay for his own panoply. This point has of course been made by many commentators, ancient and modern. In the state of society in which the system was invariably adopted, this qualification could be assessed primarily in one commodity only, landed property. The hoplite phalanx must, for a time at least, be recruited largely from the ranks of the farmers. These would hardly be mere smallholders; in a country as poor as Greece, one would judge that only a fairly substantial landed proprietor could afford a panoply which was not only intrinsically valuable, but which (particularly in the case of the Corinthian helmet) required exceptional skill in the bronze-smith and a considerable amount of his time.

There is also the question of an *upper* limit to the property qualification of the hoplite class. Can we believe that, from the first, the aristocrats and men of exceptional wealth took their place in the phalanx beside their supposed inferiors ? Any answer to this is largely dependent on the function that is allowed to the cavalry before and after the hoplite reform. The position, at least as far as Athens was concerned, was made clear by the researches of W. Helbig at the beginning of this century.[17] The Athenian $ἱππεῖς$, by a deft compromise, were able to keep their horses (and servants) and yet serve in the phalanx. The horse was used only for transport, and on the battlefield the aristocrat, already accoutred as a hoplite, dismounted and took his position in the line, leaving his horse to a squire.

Such an arrangement need not necessarily have gone back to the very beginnings of the phalanx, especially if there had been true cavalry warfare in the preceding period. Aristotle assures us that, in Euboea and Ionia at least, there was; and certainly, in some of the more backward areas of Greece, cavalry warfare was traditional and remained in use down into the Classical era. When Helbig applied his theory of mounted hoplites to early Rome and other more primitive communities, he was understandably challenged.[18] Nevertheless, it seems that Helbig was probably right in the main about seventh-century Greece. Neither in the monumental evidence, nor in contemporary literature, is there an instance of a Greek warrior going into action on horseback; while our one articulate aristocratic warrior of this period, Archilochos, certainly fought as an infantryman and almost certainly in hoplite equipment (see above).

If farmer and aristocrat stood side by side in the phalanx from early on, there would clearly be a degree of interdependence between the two classes. Of the farmers one can perhaps say more. For one thing, they would have no vested interest in war; on the contrary, it would be a double menace to their property, possibly leading to its devastation and certainly requiring their own absence from it. Nor had they, to judge from the evidence available, any tradition of service as a military unit. To say that they had a positive interest in maintaining the *status quo* would be an exaggeration; it is most unlikely, for instance, that the old system provided for any efficient protection of their property. But it remains difficult to see in the hoplite class a driving force for military or political innovation, let alone revolution.

The second general point is an even more obvious one: that fighting in a hoplite battle, if on occasion glorious, must almost always have been unpleasant. The soldier was well protected, it is true; but this made marching and fighting, under the Greek summer sun, a gruelling experience for him, and it also ensured that any wound he did receive was likely to be an agonising one, not necessarily bringing a quick death. We have it on the authority of many contemporary vase-paintings that the two thrusts habitually used with the hoplite spear were directed at the throat and at the groin. Tyrtaios gives a grim picture of the effects of the latter.[19] In steeling himself to this ordeal, the hoplite had to bear in mind that, accidents apart, the battle would continue relentlessly until a sufficient number of soldiers, on one side or the other, had been so disabled. The one attraction of this form of warfare to the ordinary hoplite will have been that a single engagement usually gave a clear-cut result and ended the campaign.[20]

These factors in combination will have produced an inevitable strategic effect: under the new system, offensive warfare became far less attractive. The hoplite who would willingly fight at his city's frontiers, or under her walls, might well baulk at a speculative foray into neighbouring territories. It will be observed that the seventh century is none the less a period of great expansion for many Greek states; but there were other military instruments besides the hoplite citizen militia for this purpose. In the first place, there were already mercenaries: such use of Carian hoplites and, less securely, of Thessalian cavalry and Cretan archers, is attested for this period.[21] Secondly, there were warships, a necessary accompaniment of colonising ventures overseas: Thucydides dates the first Greek naval battle to *c.* 664 BC.[22] Naval warfare at this time may still have been partly conducted on the old lines, with a fighting deck carrying marines armed as hoplites, and several contemporary pictures show ships of this type;[23] but the new tactics, in which fast, undecked longships were manoeuvred to ram, were already being introduced,[24] and these would make small demands, if any, on the hoplite class.

Lastly, there remained a traditional warrior class in the shape of the aristocracy. We have seen (pp. 314–15 above) that there is evidence for its continued activity in warfare after the introduction of hoplite *equipment*; only with the sharp increase in man-power, required by the adoption of hoplite *tactics*, would its supremacy in this field be affected.

The conclusion that I would draw from all these considerations is that there was not, and could not be expected to be, an enthusiastic rush to arms on the part of the more substantial property owners, the future 'hoplite class'. Even if the bait of political power had been held out from the first – which is perhaps improbable – this would hardly be enough to launch a voluntary movement which ran so entirely against historical precedent. Here again we may cite Tyrtaios: there are clear indications in his poems[25] that the Spartan army in the Second Messenian War needed constant, not to say desperate, exhortation to duty. This army, it is clear, fought in hoplite equipment; although its organisation can correspond only with a rudimentary version of the phalanx.[26] The case of Sparta is indeed the best-documented of all. The stage of confused tactics and reluctant hoplites, of which Tyrtaios is witness, is succeeded (it is now clear) by the stage of the lead hoplite-figurines found in such quantities at Sparta and the

Menelaïon.[27] These cheap, mass-produced dedications, a sign of a unified and self-conscious hoplite class, have at last been put in their correct place chronologically, and probably do not begin before *c.* 650 BC.[28]

Such a conclusion will almost certainly involve the question of the rise of tyranny. As Professor Andrewes' study has shown, the hoplite reform and the path to power of the early tyrants are subjects which impinge on one another in several cases.[29] But the relationship of the two events may have to be reconsidered. For instance, since it is particularly from Corinthian vases that we infer the appearance of the true hoplite phalanx at about the middle of the seventh century, can we believe that Kypselos in *c.* 655 gave political power to an established hoplite class ? And could Pheidon of Argos, whether his rise comes in the mid eighth century or (as most scholars believe), in the early seventh, have used the phalanx, drawn from a trained hoplite class, as an instrument for re-establishing the power of the monarchy against that of the aristocracy? And finally, to tread on still more dangerous ground, can the wording of the Spartan Rhetra be taken as a guarantee that a full hoplite assembly is envisaged ? If so, the date of that controversial document may have to be placed lower than the latest estimates would have it,[30] since political recognition of the hoplite class will hardly have preceded its vindication in war.

I will leave these questions to those better equipped to answer them, and pass instead to the rather less troubled waters of Italy, where the notion of the hoplite phalanx was among those ideas which migrated in the wake of the Greek colonists and traders.

The story of the adoption of hoplite equipment by the Etruscans is less complex. There is very little literary evidence: almost the only tradition worth noting is that the people of Falerii and Fescennium used Argive shields and other hoplite arms, a fact sometimes attributed to their being descended from Greek settlers.[31] But a large corpus of representations of warriors, covering much of the sixth and fifth centuries, seems to give an almost unanimous verdict, that the archaic Etruscan warrior had adopted part or all of the Greek hoplite panoply. These representations embrace a wide range of art, and to them we may add a number of actual specimens of hoplite armour found in Etruria; but many of these last lack secure dating contexts, as indeed they do in Greece itself. The process of borrowing did not apparently begin before 650; perhaps the best evidence of this is the fine series of Etruscan shields of single-grip, pre-hoplite type, ultimately derived

from the Near East, which begins in the eighth century and continues
only down to about the middle of the seventh.[32] It is regrettable that
the considerable numbers of hoplite shields[33] and greaves[34] found in
Etruria are not better documented, but at least their Greek inspiration
is evident. A recent find may help here: a shield-facing with bronze
blazons and other decoration, found at Fabriano in Picenum. In a very
full publication of this find,[35] Stucchi has argued that it is Attic work
of the mid seventh century. Almost certainly it is a hoplite shield, and
possibly of Greek workmanship; but I do not think that the animals
are as close to Attic models as Stucchi does, nor that a dating closer
than to the late Orientalising period is possible. Mr J. Boardman suggests that it could be from an Etruscan or West Greek workshop.[36]
Fabriano is not far outside Etruscan territory; but if this is a stepping-
stone on the way to Etruria, it is on a most unexpected route from
Greece.

By comparison with the actual examples, the representational evidence is profuse. I can only hope to give a selection of it here, and
it may be that I have omitted some important monument: but I do
not think that the conclusions will be affected. This evidence has one
great limitation, that one cannot always be sure that the appearance
in Etruscan art of figures in Greek armour is not simply due to the per-
vasion of Etruria by Greek artistic models and motifs. The example
of Greek hoplite-figures, executed in materials closely comparable to
their own, could have inspired artists who had never seen them in real
life. But the evidence allows a *prima facie* inference, that several of
the Etruscan city-states adopted hoplite *equipment* (as distinct from
tactics) during the late seventh or the early sixth century.

It is possible to make some differentiation in the quality of this
evidence. Of the early vase-paintings, for instance, two similar, late
seventh-century amphorae in the Villa Giulia and in London[37] show
warriors with pattern shield-devices clearly copied from Greek models, most of which represent hoplites.[38] They thus offer only the most
indirect evidence that the Etruscan artist had ever seen a hoplite. Of
similar date, but rather less ambiguous, is the oinochoë from Tragli-
atella with the scene of the Trojan Game,[39] in which the armed dancers
and the horsemen carry shields with bird- and animal-blazons, a sure
mark of the hoplite type. These are strange circumstances in which
to find the hoplite shield first represented; yet this, in a way, adds to
the strength of the evidence. Neither the style nor the subject-matter
of the scenes on this vase is likely to owe as much as usual to Greek
prototypes, and the blazoned shield may therefore quite possibly be
present in Etruria before 600 BC. Such a conclusion is also supported

by the less explicit scene of a hoplite duel on a bronze relief from the Tumulus of Castellina (Montecalvario).[40]

Greater certainty is possible with early sixth-century works: first, the find of bronze figurines made at Brolio in Northern Etruria in the last century, which includes three warriors which form a natural group.[41] These evidently served as supports to an object of furniture: they are distinctively Italian in style, and their pose, with the sharp turn of the head, is original. Yet they are wearing Greek helmets, of a form somewhat rarely seen in art: the so-called 'Illyrian' type, actually of Peloponnesian origin. The very slight development of the cheek-piece would date such helmets in Greece some way back in the seventh century.[42] but the Brolio figurines are normally placed just after 600. In addition, the figurines show, on their left arms, the unmistakable remnants of the arm-band and hand-grip of the hoplite shield. Now too representations in stone begin, with a fragmentary statue from Chiusi,[43] perhaps as early as the Brolio bronzes, of a warrior wearing a roughly carved Corinthian helmet and carrying a hoplite shield with a Gorgoneion device. This substantial piece of sculpture is perhaps even better evidence for Etruscan practices.

If we can identify Etruscan hoplites here, we may the more confidently detect them in many later representations which are more directly reminiscent of Greek models, though not always finer in execution. Outstanding among these is the fully-accoutred bronze warrior forming the handle of one of the cauldrons found with the Loeb tripods (apparently near Perugia).[44] Here we see not only the Corinthian helmet and hoplite shield, but also the corslet and greaves.[45] Also from the middle and later sixth century are examples of relief sculpture; in stone, such as the famous Avle Feluske stele which portrays a man partly equipped as a Greek hoplite although he also carries a double axe,[46] and a head and another stele from Orvieto which show Corinthian helmets;[47] in bronze, as one of the lateral reliefs of the Monteleone chariot,[48] and, most commonly, in terracotta.[49] Hoplite armour is also present in a wider range of art before the end of the sixth century – for example, on Etruscan black-figure[50] and incised bucchero vases,[51] and in aryballoi in the shape of a helmeted head.[52]

It is one of the stone funerary reliefs which provides perhaps the first instance of Etruscan hoplites ranged in a formation which could be an attempt to portray the phalanx.[53] This again is of the second half of the sixth century. But the most impressive evidence for the Etruscans having adopted the phalanx is literary: the repeated tradition of the Romans that they had learned from the Etruscans the technique of fighting χαλκάσπιδες καί φαλαγγηδόν.[54] This is a key passage for the whole question. No date is indicated for the event, which theoretically could have happened at any time from the sixth century to the fourth, when Rome went over to the manipular army on the Samnite model. Fortunately, however, there is supporting evidence on the Roman side which will enable us to determine closer limits.

For Etruria, the evidence summarised above shows that, beyond reasonable doubt, the Etruscans adopted the equipment of the Greek hoplite by the early sixth century. Indeed, from the presence of the Graecizing shield at Fabriano and the disappearance of the earlier Etruscan single-grip shield, I should be inclined to place the change rather earlier than 600 BC. It is conceivable that it could be connected with the migration of Demaratos of Corinth and his retinue.[55] The Etruscans also adopted the hoplite phalanx, probably during the sixth century.

This being so, it is worth noting two consequences. First, the change to the new equipment will have occurred during the period when the archaic monarchies were still in power in most or all of the Etruscan states. Secondly, it occurred in a society with a pronounced and lasting oligarchic trend, based on gentilicial lines, and there is no evidence that it was in any way compromised by the transfer of power to the aristocracies, which in most cases took place about the end of the sixth century. This is a very singular fact, as has been observed recently by Momigliano.[56] For if the hoplite system could be organised and maintained within an unregenerate oligarchic society in Etruria, by what right can it be assumed that its adoption in Greece had far-reaching and almost immediate social consequences?

We may also perhaps point to another analogy with Greece: the repeated evidence that the 'panoply' could be assumed piecemeal or only in part, and the pronounced time-lag between the first evidence for the equipment and the first evidence for hoplite tactics. Even against the misty landscape of Etruscan history, these facts seem to emerge unmistakably.

Roman hoplites are a different story again. It is true that there is some archaeological evidence of the same kind as in Etruria; and that, for the pre-hoplite period, there is abundant proof of Roman dependence on Etruria in things military.[57] For later times, there are again the architectural terracottas: we have noted that one of the Etruscan examples was found at Satricum in Latium (n. 49) and Rome itself has produced others.[58] But it is precisely because they are so Etruscan in style, and almost certainly from the hand of Etruscan visiting artists, that their value as evidence is limited. We cannot infer that the equipment and tactics of the hoplite had passed to Rome simultaneously with the artistic influence which led to their being portrayed. It is usual, therefore, to turn to the literary evidence for enlightenment of this question.[59]

It is equally usual to connect the adoption of hoplite tactics with the Centuriate reform attributed to Servius Tullius. Here one enters hazardous ground. In the first place, it is most unlikely that the details of the Centuriate reform, as recorded by Livy and others, all go back to the original Servian scheme; and secondly, even if Servius can be credited with introducing hoplites, the dating of this king is at the moment the very nucleus of a profound controversy.[60] But provided that Servius really did initiate a scheme, however rudimentary, of military classes based on property qualifications,[61] he can hardly be dissociated from the adoption of hoplites in Rome; and we may therefore pose the problem as a choice between two alternatives. Either Servius was king, in accordance with the traditional Roman chronology, some time in the sixth century, a period, on any account, of deep Etruscan influence on Rome, when it would have been natural for military advances to be taken over from Etruria in the way which Roman tradition remembered (pp. 321–2 above). Or, according to Gjerstad's view, based not only on archaeological evidence, he reigned in the first half of the fifth century, which is much nearer the time at which independent evidence suggested to Nilsson (n. 59) that the hoplite reform occurred. As a matter of fact, Nilsson's evidence is far from conclusive: he points to the creation of the *tribuni militum consulari potestate* and of the censorship in the mid fifth century. But the first of these reforms is now generally admitted to have been a political device to buy off Plebeian aspirations; while the second is hardly a sign of the original institution of a property census, which may have existed for some time within the sphere of other magistrates' duties.[62] Nilsson also cites the case of the Dictator, A. Postumius Tubertus, who in 432 or 431 BC put to death his own son for leaping forward from his place in the line to engage an enemy;[63] but this event, even if historical (which our ancient authorities doubted), would be only a *terminus ante quem* for the establishment of hoplite tactics.

Another piece of evidence much quoted in this context is the tradition that the Fabii went to war as a gens, with their clientes, against the Veientes and were annihilated at the Cremera in *c.* 477 BC.[64] For

Nilsson, who rejected any connexion of military reform with Servius Tullius, this was evidence that the hoplite system had not been adopted at that date. This seems at first sight a fair inference, even though the value of this story is to a slight degree offset by the fact that in the traditionally yet earlier battle of Lake Regillus, the Romans were said to have fought in the phalanx.[65] Momigliano however (n. 56) uses the Cremera incident to support a different view: that the Servian hoplite reform, enacted in the sixth century, had been allowed to lapse after the king's death, and was reinstated only when the Romans had learned, from such misfortunes as the Cremera, of the indispensability of hoplites.

This is a possible reconstruction, only if the lapse was a temporary, administrative failure, unconnected with equipment or tactics. The advantages conferred by the hoplite reform were too obvious for it to be annulled or abandoned by the state; and they would have been doubly so to the Romans who were continually confronted with Etruscan hoplites. Momigliano's own observation, that the Etruscans combined hoplite tactics with an aristocratic system of nobles and clientes, goes far to show how the Fabii could have used hoplites at the Cremera. Men *equipped* as hoplites could and did take part in the warfare of gentilicial factions: we have seen evidence for something much like this in Greece, and indeed Alkaios himself is a witness of it.[66] It may even have been possible to muster a phalanx from one's own entourage, and this, again, would be desirable when confronting hoplites as the Fabii were. Some social distinction might still be preserved by the nobility serving as mounted hoplites (see pp. 316–17 above).

I would accept the tradition that Servius was responsible for a military reform, and that this was designed to provide a citizen hoplite army. It also seems less difficult, on balance, to date him within the sixth century, though I cannot believe that his traditional dates (579–534) correspond in any way with the historical reality. From this it will follow that the introduction of hoplites in Rome was an extended process, allowing of such irregularities as the Cremera expedition in the early fifth century, and perhaps only systematised in the great period of constitutional reform that began with the Decemviral legislation.[67] What Servius' exact contribution was, one can hardly tell; but it was evidently an attempt to define the classes from which hoplites and other troops could be recruited, by some kind of property qualification. On this account, the hoplite system will first have been launched in the regal period, by a king in his capacity as head of state; and further, this will have happened before, or at the most during, a period of pronounced aristocratic ascendancy in Rome, in which a hoplite class as yet plays no recognisable part.

We may now return to the original starting-point, the hoplite reform in Greece. One cannot infer, from the cases of Etruria and Rome, that the sequence of events was necessarily the same in Greece; indeed it evidently was not. But one can make more general inferences.

First, the adoption of hoplite equipment, which after a time crystallised into a standard panoply, invariably took place in a period of aristocratic or regal domination, both military and political. There is also evidence, both from Greece and much more definitely from Italy, that the aristocratic ascendancy in warfare survived this event and continued for a considerable period after it. This phase could only be terminated by the growth of a substantial class of land-owners who had proved their worth by fighting in the phalanx. Yet the adoption of the phalanx did not inevitably have this sequel even then: we have no evidence in Etruria that the supposed social upheaval happened at all, and we have no grounds for thinking that it happened immediately in Rome. We cannot therefore assume that it followed at once on the adoption of the phalanx in Greece.

I do not think that this interpretation is contradicted by what Aristotle says in the *Politics* about the development of constitutions; indeed there are details in his account which hint at roughly the sequence of events that we have inferred. Aristotle says that the hoplite 'democracy' succeeded a phase of cavalry supremacy.[68] We can hardly identify or date this phase with precision, but I have suggested above (p. 315) that it continued for a time after 700 BC. In the previous sentence Aristotle makes a telling comment, that hoplite warfare is ineffective without organisation; and this is recalled at the end of the passage when he uses the same word ($\sigma \acute{v} \nu \tau \alpha \xi \iota s$) in a difficult phrase, best understood as meaning that the middle class were 'deficient in organisation' (including presumably military organisation). These remarks seem to presuppose a phase in which hoplites existed, but had not yet been organised, either tactically as a phalanx, or politically as a party.

The second conclusion is closely bound up with the first: that there would be no spontaneous movement on the part of the prospective 'hoplite class'. In Eturia we can infer, and in Rome we can be virtually certain, that the adoption of hoplite tactics took place, for purely military reasons, at the behest of the heads of state, who could apply compulsion to a possibly reluctant body of men. This is very much the pattern that we see in a remarkably late case of introduction of hoplites in Greece, the reorganisation of the Achaean army by Philopoemen in the third century BC;[69] and we see it again, many centuries later, in the Capitularies of Charlemagne.[70]

Charlemagne was expressly concerned, as the creators of the hoplite phalanx must have been, with the provision of metal body-armour and the infantry to wear it, and it may be worth looking more closely at his dispositions. First, in a series of ordinances (the earliest apparently in AD 779), he made it an offence to export mail-shirts from the realm. Later, in the *Capitulare de Exercitu promovendo* of 803, military service and provision of equipment is generally enforced for a wide range of land-owning Franks: all who possess one *mansus* of land or more.[71] The enforcement is much stricter for the nobility and richer land-owners; as one descends the scale of wealth, groups of two, and then of four, men are to combine to equip one of their number, the others being exempt from actually serving. The *Capitulare Aquisgranense* of 805 supplements this: each man who owns more than 12 *mansi* (about 95 acres) is to provide his own mail-shirt alone.

The Capitulary of 807 extends this arrangement. The lower limit for compulsory service is brought down to half a *mansus* or its equivalent in goods, and the obligations of the next higher class are slightly increased. The *Capitulare Bononiense* of 811 provides, among other things, for the requisitioning of spare mail-shirts by the king. Finally, the *Capitulare Aquisgranense* of 813 makes it compulsory for all the household men of counts, bishops and abbots to have their own metal helmet and mail-shirt.

The features that I should like to stress are these: the prevalence of land as a qualification, other property being introduced only for the additional lowest class of the Capitulary of 807: the comparatively high land-qualification (nearly 100 acres) for independent commoners providing their own equipment: the fact that it took a powerful and efficient king over thirty years to achieve a satisfactory proportion of heavy-armed infantry: and, in general, the atmosphere of compulsion and penalty which pervades these Capitularies and explains their existence.

It seems likely that the hoplite phalanx also owed its inception in the Greek cities to the action of the heads of state, whose foremost aim was the defence of the realm. Later on hoplites could and did partake in political struggles and win political rights, but it is in no case certain that they established their political or military leaders as tyrants.[72]

By the time of Solon, it is clear that the Zeugitai, to be identified with the Athenian hoplite class, formed a distinct group and had earned the political power that he gave them. It is also possible that they represent the disappointed δῆμος who had wanted a tyranny.[73] But Solon's poems are our earliest explicit evidence for this state of affairs, and his reforms suggest that in Athens it was a recent growth.

On this account, then, the Greek hoplite entered history as an individual warrior, probably in most cases an aristocrat. The adoption of the phalanx meant that he was joined by men, for the most part substantial land-owners, who had come not to seek a way to political power nor by any wish of their own, but because they were compelled to. These men, however stout-hearted as warriors, are not likely to have become, all at once, a revolutionary force in politics, even in Greece. The political rights which they came to possess could have been acquired gradually and peacefully τῶν ἐν τοῖς ὅπλοις ἰσχυσάντων μᾶλλον, as Aristotle says. They must have had political leaders, but I doubt whether we can number the early tyrants among them. Hoplites, in short, were an instrument before they became a force.[74]

NOTES

1. *Early Greek Armour and Weapons* (Edinburgh, 1964), esp. pp. 83–4, 89–90, 136–9, 193–204.
2. Aristotle, *Pol.* 1289b 36–40, 1297b 16–28: fr. 611, 51: cf. Strabo xiv 643: Plutarch, *Mor.* 760–1. Note also the metal corslet of Timomachos the Aegeid (Aristotle fr. 532 (Rose), in Schol. on Pindar, *Isthm.* 6 (7). 18; cf. on *Pyth.* 5. 101).
3. On this question see Kirk, *BSA* xliv (1949), 144–53.
4. E.g. the Romans and Dacians in Trajan's day: Cichorius, *Reliefs der Traianssaüle*, pls. 69 etc. The shield of the later Medieval knights: R. W. Oakeshott, *The Archaeology of Weapons*, figs. 132–3.
5. *BSA* xlii (1947), pl. 19A (Benaki Museum): lii (1957), pl. 3A (from Eretria, in Athens): *Early Greek Armour* 62. To these we may now add a sherd from the Kerameikos, *AA* 1963, 649, fig. 5.
6. Webster, *BSA* 1 (1955), 41–3 and *From Mycenae to Homer*, 169 f. on the shield: cf. *Early Greek Armour* 58–60, and 159–63 (chariot).
7. *BCH* lxxxi (1957), 322–86.
8. Attic: *AM* xvii (1892), pl. 10; Robinson, Harcum and Iliffe, *Greek Vases in Toronto* pl. 9. 120. Argive: *Tiryns* i, pl. 15. 5; *Argive Heraeum* ii, pl. 57. 4; *JHS* lxxiv (1954) pl. 8. 3; *BCH* lxxviii (1954), 413, Fig. 4; and another unpublished sherd from Argos, shown to me by Prof P. Courbin.

9. See especially Miss Lorimer, *BSA* xlii (1947), 80–108. This view was rightly criticised by Roland Hampe, *Ein frühattischer Grabfund*, 82–3.

10. Cf. Myres, *Homer and his Critics*, 183 and pl. 6.

11. Chigi Vase: *Antike Denkmäler* ii, pl. 44 (far left). Alabastron in Berlin: *AA* iv (1889), 93.

12. *CVA* Berlin i, pls. 28. I; 44. 2: *BSA* xxxv (1934–5), pl. 52 a: Hampe, *op. cit.* Fig. 37, upper right.

13. Kallinos i 5, 14; cf. 10. Archilochos fr. 3.

14. Frr. 2 and 6.

15. *CVA* Berlin i, pls. 42. 4; 44. 2; Welter, *Aus der Karlsruher Vasensammlung* (*Bausteine* i), pl. I. 2 (all Attic). *Artemis Orthia*, pls. 92. 3 and 104. I (Laconian). To these we may add many terracotta figurines of mounted warriors, such as *Tiryns* i 83 Fig. 20; *Perachora* i. pl. 100. 166; *Argive Heraeum* ii, pl. 48. 245.

16. See *JHS* lxxxiv (1964), 107–8.

17. *Mémoires de l'Académie des Inscriptions* xxxvii (1902), 157 f.: cf. *S. B. Bayr. Ak. Wiss.* 1911, 37 f.

18. Helbig, *Abh. Bayr. Ak. Wiss.* (*philos.-philol. Klasse*) xxiii. 2 (1905), 265–317: *Hermes* xl (1905), 101–115: cf. *CRAI* 1904, 190–201. Contrast Ed. Meyer, *Kleine Schriften* ii (1924), 274 f.

19. Fr. vi-vii, 21–5 (Diehl, ALG_3). See R. Nierhaus *JdI* liii (1938), 90–114 on this theme.

20. Cf. Adcock, *The Greek and Macedonian Art of War*, 7 f.

21. Carians: Archilochos fr. 24 Bergk (40 Diehl), Hdt. ii 152. Thessalians: Plutarch, *Mor.* 760–1. (These are perhaps semi-professional allies, rather than mercenaries.) Cretans: Pausanias iv 8. 3; 10. I (conquest of Messenia); iv 19. 4 (Second Messenian War).

22. i 13. 4.

23. Kirk, *BSA* xliv (1949), 119–23 with references.

24. Kirk, *op. cit.*, 137–9.

25. Fr. vi–vii and viii, *passim*.

26. See Eduard Meyer, *Kleine Schriften* ii, 271–2: M. P. Nilsson, *Klio* xxii (1929), 241–4: *Early Greek Armour* 181–2.

27. *Artemis Orthia* pls. 183, 191: *BSA* xv (1908–9), pl. 7, etc. An example was found at Tegea, *BCH* xlv (1921), 429, no. 377, Fig. 42.

28. Boardman, *BSA* lviii (1963), 1–7.

29. *The Greek Tyrants*, 41–2 (Pheidon as possible creator of the Argive hoplite army); 49 (Kypselos as champion of the Corinthian hoplite class); 72–3 (the Rhetra as the enfranchisement of Spartan hoplites). Cf. Huxley, *BCH* lxxxii (1958), 588–601 and *Early Sparta* 30 – a similar conclusion but a very different chronology for Pheidon; *ibid.* 49 (the Rhetra): Wade-Gery, *CAH* iii 551 on Kypselos.

30. See most recently W. G. Forrest, *Phoenix* xvii (1963), 157–79 and G. L. Huxley, *Early Sparta* 41–52, who both arrive at a date around 675 BC.

31. Dionys. i. 21: cf. Pliny, *Nat. Hist.* iii 51.

32. On these see A. Akerström, *Der geometrische Stil in Italien* 102 f., 113 f., 119 f.: E. Kunze, *Studies presented to D. M. Robinson* i 736 f.

33. E. g. Schumacher, *Antike Bronzen in Karlsruhe* 137, pl. 13. 13: Dennis, *Cities and Cemeteries of Etruria* i 171–2 (Bomarzo). *Stud. Etr.* vi (1932), pl. 25. I 3–4: *Olynthus* x 445, n. 221 (two unpublished examples in Florence and Palermo): Helbig, *Führer (Rom)* i 364, no. 613.

34. E. g. Hagemann, *Griechische Panzerung* 135–6, n. 3b, figs. 148, 150 (two pairs): Micali, *Monumenti Inediti* (1844), pl. 53. 4–5: Helbig, *Führer (Rom)* i 364, no. 612 (three pairs): Montelius, *Civilisation Primitive en Italie* ii pl. 178. 2: *Stud. Etr.* vi (1932), pls. 25. I 2a and 29. III 2. Greek helmets are rarer: cf. Babelon & Blanchet, *Catalogue des Bronzes, Bibliothèque Nationale* no. 2013 (Vulci).

35. *Rivista dell' Istituto nazionale di Archeologia e Storia dell' Arte* viii (1959) 1–58.

36. *Island Gems*, 64, n. 2.

37. *Stud. Etr.* xx (1948–9), 241–5, pl. 13: Walters, *Catalogue of the Greek and Etruscan vases in the British Museum* i. 2, pls. 23–4.

38. For similar 'Catherine wheel' patterns, compare *AM* xvii (1892), pl. 10: *BSA* xlii (1947), 76 ff., Figs. 6, 8b, 13: *Artemis Orthia* pls. 183. 13–15; 191. 13–15.

39. *Stud. Etr.* iii (1929), 111–159, pls. 23–6.

40. D. Randall MacIver, *Villanovans and Early Etruscans* 254, pl. 46.6.

41. Riis, *Tyrrhenika* 120 f.: cf. Lamb, *Greek and Roman Bronzes* 80, pl. 24a.

42. E. Kunze, *Olympiabericht* vi 125 f. ('Frühform').

43. *AM* xxi (1896), 1–10, pl. I: Riis, *Tyrrhenika* 114 A4.

44. *AJA* xii (1908), 297, Fig. 2, pl. 12: Riis, *Tyrrhenika* 127, 132.

45. The greave may have been a slightly late arrival, but not nearly so late as was thought by G. Karo (Daremberg-Saglio, s.v. 'ocrea', 147), and by E. S. McCartney, *MAAR* i (1917), 151–2, who misunderstood representations on terracottas.

46. M. Pallottino, *The Etruscans* 141, Fig. 4.

47. O. W. von Vacano, *Die Etrusker, Werden und geistige Welt*, 165, Fig. 69: Riis, *Tyrrhenika* 102, no. 3 and n. 3.

48. L. Goldscheider, *Etruscan Sculpture*, pl. 81.

49. E. g. Andrén, *Architectural Terracottas from Etrusco-Italic Temples*, pl. 24. 86, 88 (Tuscania); pl. 25. 91 (Poggio Buco); pl. 36. 124 (Civita Castellana); pl. 141. 492 (Satricum); pl. B. 2–3 (Caere). Commonest of all are the mounted hoplites (see above, p. 316, n. 17): *ibid.* pl. 5. 10–12, 8. 22 and 13. 45 (Caere); pl. 24. 87 (Tuscania); pl. 57. 188 (Vignanello).

50. E. g. Beazley, *Etruscan Vase-painting*, pl. 3. 3–4.

51. E. g. Martha, *L' Art Étrusque*, Figs. 316, 321.

52. E. g. von Vacano, *op. cit.* 61, Fig. 22 (Caere).

53. *Stud. Etr.* iv (1930), 101–2, pl. 10.

54. Diodor. 23. 2; Ined. Vat. iii (*Hermes* xvii (1892), 121): cf. Athenaeus vi 106.

55. See Blakeway, *JRS* xxv (1935), 129–49.

56. *JRS* liii (1963), 119–21.

57. See E. S. McCartney, *MAAR* i (1917), 121–67.

58. E. g. Andrén, *op. cit.* pl. 107. 382; pl. 105. 377, which is identical with examples from Velletri, *ibid.*, pl. 127. 445–6. Cf. also pl. 120. 424 from Segni.

59. As Nilsson, *JRS* xix (1929), 1–11.

60. See most recently Momigliano, *JRS* liii (1963), 95–121: Gjerstad, 'Legends and Facts', *Scripta Minora* (Lund), 1960–1, 2.

61. See Last, *JRS* xxxv (1945), 30 f., especially 34–5 and 42–4.

62. I am most grateful to colleagues in Edinburgh, particularly Drs T. J. Cadoux and P. G. Walsh, for discussion of these points.

63. Diodor. xii 64: cf. Livy iv 29.

64. Livy ii 48–50.

65. Dionys. vi 10. 2.

66. See especially fr. 15 Bergk (54 Diehl): *Early Greek Armour* 182–3.

67. Compare the conclusion of K. Hanell, *Das altrömische eponyme Amt* 197–8.

68. *Pol.* 1297 b 16–24: cf. 28.

69. Pausanias viii 50. I.

70. See Oman, *History of the Art of War in the Middle Ages* 77–82.

71. A *mansus* apparently equalled 12 *iugera*, or just under 8 acres.

72. Kylon of Athens was evidently not such a leader, since he required Megarian help to seize the Acropolis in *c.* 632 (Thuc. i 126). See also p. 319 above.

73. So Andrewes, *The Greek Tyrants* 35–6, 87–91. We may disbelieve, along with the rest of Chapter iv of the *Ath. Pol.*, the claim that Drakon extended rights ῾τοῖς ὅπλα παρεχομένοις᾽.

74. Prof. A. Andrewes and Mr John Boardman have given me much helpful advice on this subject, though they can in no way be held responsible for what I have written. The article is substantially in the form in which it was delivered to the Hellenic Society in November 1964.

CHAPTER 18

The Historical Significance of Fortification in Archaic Greece

This paper, first delivered at a conference in Valbonne in 1982, is an attempt to deconstruct the simple concept of 'fortification' by showing that, even within a single period, its nature could change radically, and that the building of defensive circuits could serve radically different ends. It concludes that the pre-Archaic and early Archaic fortifications of the Greek islands and Ionia differed from their successors in every way: their geographical distribution, their purpose, their durability and above all their independence of any influence from earlier Aegean, or contemporary Oriental, practices. It was only in the advanced Archaic period that the familiar fortified *enceintes* and towers of the Greek landscape first came into being.

Here is a subject which, as already indicated, has become the preserve of a dwindling handful of experts: the late A. W. Lawrence was, in this country, perhaps their last recognised representative. It was not therefore to be expected that the propositions advanced here would find a wide response; they are however in general accord with the brief statements to be found in later works on Greek warfare or the Greek city, such as Ducrey (1985: 148) and Owens (1991: 149–50).

BIBLIOGRAPHY

Ducrey, P. (1985), *Guerre et Guerriers dans la Grèce antique*, Fribourg (CH): Office du Livre S. A.
Owens, E. J. (1991), *The City in the Greek and Roman World*, London: Routledge.

If the study of Archaic Greek fortification is at present in an untidy state, this is at least in part because its first chapter has yet to be satisfactorily written. Indeed, only in the last decade or so has enough evidence been collected by recent excavation for us to begin writing that chapter. In addition, the writers of the text-books on Greek fortification have a natural bias away from the Archaic period and towards the latter end of their story: towards the epoch of the great siege-narratives, from Thucydides on Plataea to Polybius on Syracuse; to the epoch of the Hellenistic manuals; to the epoch, not least, of the most impressive surviving monuments – Aegosthena, Oeniadae, Messene, Heraklea-by-Latmos, Paestum and their like. Between the late fifth and the late third centuries BC, Greek fortification offers the Classical archaeologist something which his colleagues have to be content to dream about: a relative wealth of documentary evidence, bearing more or less directly on a large body of monumental evidence which also survives.

It is a waste of time to try to apply such standards to the early period; a fact which has perhaps disheartened the experts. To apply such texts as Thucydides i 7 to Archaic fortifications and expect to find the sort of correlation which might be achieved with, say, Vitruvius will only lead to bitter disappointment. Different approaches are needed if this branch of the subject is to be developed. Lacking the aid of coherent documentary accounts in Greek sources, lacking even the compensatory help of iconographic evidence which sometimes sustains him, the archaeologist must first look at the surviving monuments in their own right, before deciding whether they invite comparison with the much better-documented remains from the Levant and Asia Minor, to a point where they can be interpreted with the aid of these; whether the element of Bronze Age survival is strong enough to link them with that (also better-documented) epoch of fortification; whether they can better be explained a *posteriori*, as the first halting steps towards something which was only to be perfected only in the Classical Greek world; or whether, finally, they constitute an independent phenomenon, a response to circumstances some of which were temporary, which differed fundamentally from the responses of other contemporary people and of the Greeks themselves at other

'The historical significance of fortification in Archaic Greece', from P. Leriche and H. Tréziny (ed.), *La fortification dans l'histoire du monde grec*, Paris: Editions du CNRS, 1986, pp. 125–31.

periods. Let us examine each of these possibilities, in respect of the first phase of Archaic Greek fortification, but only (as I have already suggested) after looking at the principal surviving monuments: that is, the sites which have produced substantial walls of about 700 BC or earlier.

These early sites fall into two geographical groups, with half a dozen in each. From the western coast of Asia Minor and its large off-shore islands, we have Old Smyrna,[1] Kalabaktepe outside Miletos,[2] Emborio on Chios,[3] Melie[4] (Fig. 18.1), Iasos[5] and Vroulia on Rhodes.[6] From the Aegean islands, we have Zagora on Andros,[7] Vathy Limenari on Dhonoussa,[8] Koukounaries on Paros,[9] Kastro[10] and Agios Andreas[11] on Siphnos (fig. 18.2) and Phaistos in Crete.[12] In defining these groups, let us be clear about their negative counterpart: I mean, the major Geometric sites on the Greek mainland which did *not* have fortifications. The list is potentially long: we may begin by mentioning Eleusis, where the sanctuary was once reputed to have a Geometric fortification-wall: now both the Geometric date and the status as a fortification (rather than a revetment) have been called into question by Mylonas.[13] Next there is Lefkandi, whose excavators are silent about fortifications: Eretria, which lacks fortifications as early as this; Nichoria, where the only apparent 'fortification-wall' discovered turned out to be the packing-wall of a tholos tomb.[14] To these we may add the numerous sites where concentrations of Geometric burials prove the existence of large communities – Athens, Argos, Thorikos, Mycenae, Asine, Corinth, Thebes, Iolkos and others. In none of these was fresh Geometric defensive walling discovered, and at some of them it has been positively excluded. What probably happened instead – though this is difficult to prove – was that the walls of the local Bronze Age citadel were called back into use, perhaps after rehabilitation, whether the settlement now lay outside them (as at Athens and Argos) or partly inside (as Asine, Mycenae and probably Thebes). A mainland site where fortifications were actually *built*, at any time in the four centuries preceding 700 BC, is hard to find.

We are left, therefore, with the obvious fact that every one in my list of sites with Geometric fortifications is situated in the Cyclades, Crete or Ionia; and the further fact that every one of them is on, or within about 5 kms. of, the sea-coast. Before we try to assess the significance of these facts, however, we must look more closely at the individual examples while considering the overall hypotheses of interpretation mentioned above.

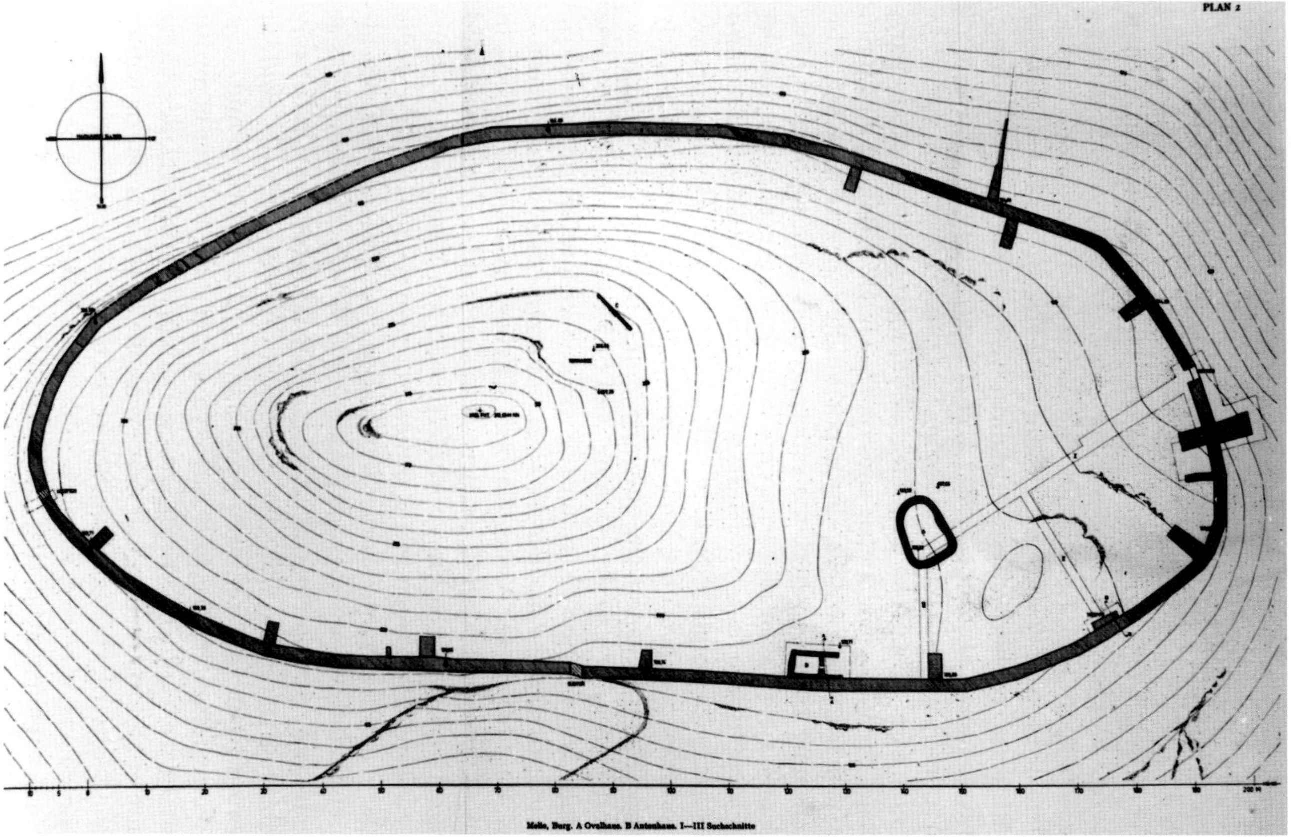

Figure 18.1 Mélië.

(i) *The theory of influence from the Levant and Asia Minor.* This view is detectable behind many writings on Greek fortification, and is most explicitly advanced in A.W. Lawrence's distinguished recent book *Greek aims in fortification*,[15] where however it is combined with theory (ii) below. Lawrence begins his book with the words 'Greek schemes of fortification were initially derivative', and devotes most of his first chapter to two sections entitled 'Fortification in Western Asia' and 'The formation of the Greek style'. On closer inspection, individual features of early Greek fortifications which betray Oriental influence are hard to find. Almost the only case that can be advanced is the solid rectangular salient beside the main gateway at Old Smyrna; but the excavators of the site saw no need for external influence here or elsewhere in the first, ninth-century circuit at Smyrna. The suggestion that the wall-builders of the ninth and eighth centuries had actually studied the great fortifications of Gordion, Bogazköy, Karatepe, Zincirli or Lachish (let alone Ashur or Nimrud) seems to me on reflection unlikely. These systems had been built, with colossal expenditure of man-power, to resist a type of military threat which did not come the way of the Greek world until at least a century after the building of the Greek walls that we are considering. I would suggest, not merely that an Assyrian siege-train would have seemed a remote threat to the builders of the first Ionian defences, but that they are unlikely even to have heard of it. Their bogey was not Shalmaneser III, but the nearest Carian war-band; while their numbers and resources could not match those available at the Oriental sites.

(ii) *The theory of continuity from the Prehellenic epoch.* This theory seems to find more immediate support from the evidence than (i) above. Lawrence is able to point to a number of general parallels in building practice: a preference for convex curvature in some Ionian wall-circuits (Old Smyrna, Melie, but hardly Iasos and definitely not Vroulia); a preference for a siting on a hill-slope which would reduce the amount of free-standing construction on the inner face; and more specifically the addition of a projecting spur near a gateway at Melie (Fig. 18.1). But it may be significant that one of his most convincing parallels, the design of a laterally-opening gateway at Melie, occurs not in the Geometric but in the early sixth-century circuit. And I confess myself baffled by the words with which Lawrence (p. 30) introduces this section of his book: 'So many Classical cities in Asia Minor occupied the sites of Mycenaean walled settlements that there must have been some continuity . . .'. *Bronze Age* walled settlements, perhaps; but true Mycenaean sites on this coast are, so far as present knowledge goes, few and far between, and the solitary instance that Lawrence (p. 424, n. 53) gives, 'Larisa'/Buruncuk, is emphatically not one of them.

If scepticism is aroused by this last point, then it can only be reinforced by closer inspection of the freshly fortified Geometric sites. The exceptional case of Agios Andreas on Siphnos, where for once we can trace the process whereby a partly-ruined Bronze Age wall was rehabilitated in Geometric times, will be dealt with in a moment. At Koukounaries, to judge from the preliminary reports available, the Mycenaean wall was either well-enough preserved to be serviceable as it stood, or was now dispensed with; at Old Smyrna the prehistoric walls were too ruinous either to act as a model or to provide practical protection. But at Agios Andreas (n. 11 above and Fig. 18.2 below) a new frontage, thinner than the faces of the Bronze Age wall, was erected a few metres in front of the latter, and the intervening gap filled with loose stones. Obviously the new fortification was in this sense dependent on its predecessor, but one of its most striking features, the series of straight stretches connected by 'jogs' between 15 and 40 cms. deep, is simply not present in the earlier wall; while conversely the bastions of the earlier fortification are not reproduced in the later one. From some points of view, therefore, it is the *lack* of continuity in design which is the more remarkable feature, considering that the two systems of fortification are immediately juxtaposed. Several other negative observations can be added to this argument. At Emborio, the prehistoric fortifications were in another locality altogether and were ignored. Vroulia, Zagora and Vathy Limenari are not only not on the sites of Bronze Age settlements, but embody a principle, the fortification of a promontory by means of a straight wall across the neck, from cliff to cliff, that was not a characteristic Mycenaean one. Miletos was, certainly, a major Mycenaean site, to whose significance we shall return in a moment; but the eighth-century walls here are sited on the Kalabaktepe hill where they can neither use nor even imitate the Mycenaean defences on the ground below (which indeed were being slighted at this very time by the building of Geometric constructions on top of their remains).[16] As for Phaistos, which on the scanty evidence so far published seems to be one of the more impressive known fortifications of early Iron Age Greece, the fact that its predecessor was not a Mycenaean citadel but a Minoan palace means that there was no local model for inspiration. Local forerunners are of course not a *sine qua non* for continuity of tradition, so

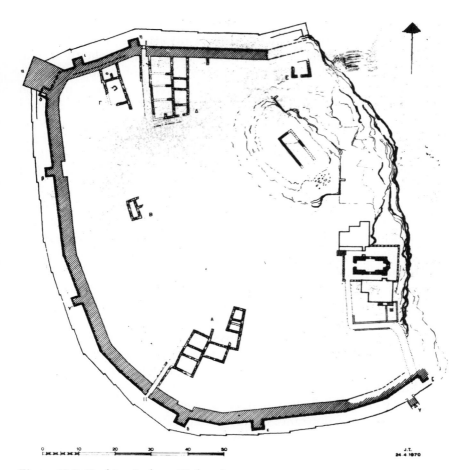

Figure 18.2 Haghios Andreas (Siphnos).

that the fact of Iasos and Melie having no Mycenaean predecessors is not the last word; but this leaves the onus on those who would argue from detailed similarities of practice.

In fact the overall picture, far from reinforcing belief in continuity, seems to me to be one of essential dichotomy. Many of the Geometric fortifications are built for different purposes, and on different kinds of site, from Mycenaean ones; the local shift of emphasis at Miletos and Emborio is telling evidence for this. Where the locations exactly coincide, the Bronze Age structures may be used, but are not copied. We are left with the few general similarities listed at the beginning of this section.

(iii) *The theory of continuity with later Greek fortification*. This view comes so naturally to any student of any aspect of Archaic Greek civilisation that it is implicitly assumed, rather than explicitly stated, in most accounts of fortification. Yet examination of some of the individual sites again provokes doubt as to the strength of the connection with later developments. At least three of our list of early fortified sites were abandoned after a not very long occupation; what is more, the date of their abandonment roughly coincides with the rise of the dominant political form of later Greek history, the *polis*. It is likely enough that the actual occasion for the desertion of Zagora and of Emborio was the formation of a central urban nucleus on their respective islands – that is, of the *poleis* of Andros and Chios. The desertion of Vathy Limenari on Dhonoussa, likewise, probably betokens the recognition that such a small island could not form a viable territory for an independent state. Then there are three further sites on the list, Kalabaktepe, Agios Andreas and Vroulia, which, though not immediately abandoned, were at this same period apparently displaced from their former function by the establishment of *polis* settlements elsewhere, under whose sway they now fell; and the same may prove true of Koukounaries on Paros. All of this suggests that, from the early seventh century BC, political requirements were changing so radically in the Greek world that it would be surprising if defensive requirements could develop by a simple linear progression.

There were exceptions, where early defensive provisions remained useful in later circumstances. Kalabaktepe, if not the true acropolis for Archaic Miletos, continued to be maintained for some purpose; so, more obviously, did the Kastro site as the acropolis for Siphnos, as demonstrated by its sixth-century rebuilding. Perhaps more significantly, an *enceinte* round a peninsular site such as Smyrna or Iasos could continue to serve the needs of a *polis*, provided that the latter remained small, or that security allowed of the extension of the city beyond the walls. We may therefore admit these few examples as true forerunners of the next generation of Greek fortifications, those of the age of the Archaic *polis*.

In so criticising the three theories that have been considered, I have by implication been advancing the claims of the fourth remaining view: that the earliest fortifications of Archaic Greece are to some extent an independent response to circumstances that were often temporary. In so far as there is a constant and positive factor behind their formation, I find it to be that of geographical location rather than any form of external inspiration or native inheritance. The first and most obvious sign of this is the fact that the earliest defended sites are all found in the Aegean islands and Ionia. It is surely a fact of great significance that the most important Bronze Age sites in these two respective areas, Phylakopi and Miletos, had also departed from the standard contemporary practices of mainland Greece, in that their walls were sited to enclose, not a royal citadel but a flattish area large enough to house a sizeable community. The geographical constraints, in other words, were strong enough to survive the gap in time between the Mycenaean and Archaic periods. What these geographical factors seem to boil down to is the fact that overseas expansion, of a colonial kind, was taking people into areas where they felt insecure; where there were threats different in kind from those which existed in the homeland. In the case of the islands, we can safely infer that in the early Iron Age the chief threat was from pirates, as Thucydides in a famous passage (i 5) asserts. The much earlier prehistoric fortifications of the Cyclades suggest that this was an old problem. That it waned in the historical period is shown, not so much by later developments in fortification as by the mere fact of the abandonment of such inhospitable sites as Zagora and Vathy Limenari. The case of Phaistos suggests that where in the Bronze Age Minoan dominance had made fortification unnecessary, the collapse of that dominance could bring the conditions of insular vulnerability even to a site that lay some kilometres from the sea on a coast that faced away from the Aegean. In the case of Ionia, the threat was from the indigenous non-Greek peoples, for the settlers of the Ionian Migration as for the founders of Mycenaean Miletos; in this case the threat, far from receding, was to intensify as the centuries went on.

If Ionia therefore emerges as being the more significant of the two areas in relation to long-term developments, this importance is enhanced by the fact that it also provided some kind of model for the next stage in Greek expansion and fortification, the foundation of the western colonies.[17] Here too the factor of indigenous and potentially hostile non-Greek inhabitants prevailed, and it is hardly surprising to find that the most durable fortification-type of Ionia, the peninsular *enceinte*, is also represented at sites like Taras and Sicilian Naxos. But some of the same historical constraints proved to apply: sites which prospered, like Leontinoi, soon outgrew their first fortifications; sites which remained within their original defensible area, like Naxos, were doomed to relative obscurity (recalling Iasos in Asia Minor).

If there is a general historical conclusion which emerges from the whole discussion so far, it is that early fortification, so far from

securing later success, rarely accompanies it. Apart from the fortified sites that were actually abandoned, or gradually supplanted, let
us recall that Smyrna was destroyed by the Lydians and Melie by the
other Ionians; and that Phaistos was for long overshadowed by her
neighbour Gortyn, before beig actually destroyed by her in Hellenistic
times.

The main phase of later Archaic fortification is, in my view, a different and in large part an independent story. Instead of representing
a series of tactical expedients governed by local considerations, Greek
fortification now becomes essentially a physical manifestation of the
workings of Archaic Greek politics. As such, not surprisingly, it shows
a degree of assimilation in each area where this political system prevailed, even though the starting-point for development was not the
same in the different areas.

On the *Greek mainland*, as we have seen, a start had virtually to be
made from scratch. Fortifications can have existed only in the form
of the walled acropolis, and even under this heading we have found
no instance where fresh building is attested earlier than 700 BC. It is
therefore universally assumed that protection was found in the surviving or rehabilitated Mycenaean citadel-walls and, although it is a little
disquieting to find no definite proof of the early practice of this expe-
dient, it was such an obvious and economical one that we need not
doubt its reality. The growth of the *polis*, meanwhile, meant that the
natural progression from this starting-point was to enlarge the fortified area outwards from the acropolis and sites like Eretria exemplify
this process very clearly. But the surprising feature of this process is
its slowness: there are many major cities, from Athens downwards,
where we are not even certain that there was a city *enceinte* by the end
of the Archaic period. This was perhaps because oligarchies continued to dominate many Archaic cities and because, as Aristotle says, 'a
citadel is suitable to oligarchies and monarchies'. Corinth even offers
an apparent example of separate fortified enclaves within an Archaic
city; as Winter observes,[18] this echoes Aristotle's further prescription
that, for an aristocracy, 'a number of strong places is preferable'. As a
final example of mainland Archaic fortification, let me draw attention
to the pattern in Boeotia (where, with the Cambridge/Bradford Boeotian Expedition, I have been conducting survey since 1978). There
extends across the whole country a thick scatter of at least 15 sites
with walling in the polygonal style; this does not of itself make them
of Archaic date, since the style is revived in Hellenistic times, but a
number of them are undoubtedly Archaic or early fifth century in

date. Some sites are merely the *acropoleis* of major cities but others, more interestingly, seem to be smaller walled towns. Here is a clear physical manifestation of the effect of the new political system on Greek practice.

In the *Aegean islands*, a fresh start was often equally necessary, but for the different reason that the site of an island's major settlement has been shifted. But here, too, a combination of written and archaeological evidence shows that some islands had acquired a wall-circuit surrounding a large part of the *polis* by the end of the Archaic period: Paros, Thasos and Naxos (Hdt. v 34) are examples. Of these, Thasos can provide as complex an example of the progressive expansion of Archaic fortifications as anywhere. The steps by which a small acropolis, lying a little inland, was extended until a circuit-wall enclosed much of the settlement on the coast below are not entirely clear: if, as Winter suggests,[19] there was at one stage a series of small citadels, then this evokes the parallel of Corinth (above) on the mainland and perhaps of Miletos (see below) in Ionia; if there was merely a repeated enlargement of the fortified area, then Leontinoi in the west and, probably, Eretria in Euboea are the Archaic analogues that come to mind.

In *Ionia*, the early precedents for a walled town at Smyrna and Iasos did not provide a very encouraging starting-point for later Archaic developments. That both these cities ran into difficulties because of the small compass of their walls is suggested, first by the substantial 'overspill' of extra-mural housing at Smyrna and then, much later, by the construction of the vast and unfinished circuit of the 'Mainland Wall' outside Iasos. In the event, Archaic fortification in Ionia echoes the pattern of the rest of the Greek world. Miletos, although its relationship to the nearby Kalabaktepe site remains obscure, had certainly acquired a fortified citadel or citadels on the peninsula below, and probably a complete circuit of walls, before the end of the Archaic period. But the classic example of Archaic defensive walling is that of 'Larisa'/Buruncuk where, before 500, a small part of the hill-top town was enclosed by a circuit with regularly-placed square or oblong towers. The occurrence of these towers, which find approximate counterparts at Archaic sites elsewhere[20] – Halieis and Eleusis on the Greek mainland, Megara Hyblaea in the West – brings us to the fact that it is really now, in the *second* phase of Archaic fortification, that we begin to find convincing examples of features recalling either Prehellenic Greek or contemporary Oriental practice: as witness the Mycenaean-type gateway in the later (and enlarged) circuit at Melie (above, p. 335), or in the perhaps slightly earlier Archaic circuit at Kalabaktepe; and the towers themselves, doubtless inspired as Lawrence and Winter suggest by non-Greek precedents in Asia, such as Gordion. We learn from Herodotus (i 26) that Ephesos was walled by the sixth century and (iii 54) that the circuit at Samos, by a somewhat later sixth-century date, incorporated towers. Extant remains add the towns of Mitylene and Eresos on Lesbos.

In the *Western colonies*, it is sufficient to note that the same steps in development occurred as in the Greek homelands:[21] extension of the fortified city area at Leontini and, probably, Taras; reliance on an original acropolis at Selinus and, more interestingly, apparent desertion of the original acropolis at Gela in favour of a more suitable location for the fortified *polis* (recalling perhaps Kalabaktepe and Miletos); complete walling of a city at Akragas. The case of Punic Motya, where the walls around the island's coast were not built until the sixth century, show a similar preoccupation to those of the Greek *poleis*; the area thus enclosed was, if anything, bigger than that required by any foreseeable expansion of the urban area, so that the earlier difficulties encountered by the fortifiers of Old Smyrna and Iasos (and, one might add, by the occupants of the early stronghold of Ortygia at Syracuse) did not arise.

All these defensive constructions of the second Archaic phase were built, unlike their Geometric predecessors, mainly to protect Greek cities against other Greek cities; that is, against enemies of a known capability, numerous and formidable though not skilled in the techniques of siege-craft. They were built to protect sizeable populations, either by directly shielding them or by providing them with a refuge; whereas their early forerunners were designed for small, in some cases tiny communities – let us recall Kinch's estimate (*Fouilles de Vroulia* p. 90) that the entire population of Vroulia, averaged over its life of somewhat more than a century, scarcely exceeded 40 people. The 'bridges' between these two phases of early Greek fortification are, in my view, few and far between; it is only the second which can be regarded as the true prelude to later Greek fortification; and it is the second, too, which offers the more convincing evidence for influences from earlier Aegean and contemporary Oriental practice.

NOTES

1. R. V. Nicholls. *Old Smyrna: the Iron Age fortifications and associated remains on the city perimeter*, in ABSA 53–54 (1958–9), 35–137.

2. A. von Gerkan, *Milet* i 8: *Kalabaktepe, Athenatempel und Umgebungen* (Berlin, 1925).

3. J. Boardman, *Chios: Greek Emporio* (London, 1967).

4. G. Kleiner *et al.*, *Panionion und Melie (Jdl Erganzungsheft* 23, 1967).

5. D. Levi. *Le due prime campagne di scavo a Iasos (1960–61)*, in *Annuario ASA* 39–40 (1961–2), 527–34.

6. K. F. Kinch, *Fouilles de Vroulia (Rhodes)* (Berlin, 1914).

7. A. Cambitoglou *et al.*, *Zagora* I (Sydney, 1971); *The Archaeological Museum of Andros* (Athens, 1981).

8. Ph. Zaphiropoulou, *ADelt.* 24 (1969), B2, 390–3; 25 (1970), B2, 426–8; 26 (1971), B2, 465–7.

9. Most fully, D. Schilardi, *The destruction of the LH III B citadel of Koukounaries on Paros*, in J. Davis and J.F. Cherry (edd.), *Papers in Cycladic prehistory* (Monograph xiv, Institute of Archaeology, University of California at Los Angeles, 1979), 158–179.

10. J. K. Brock and G. Mackworth Young, *Excavations in Siphnos, ABSA* 44 (1949), 1–92.

11. B. Philippaki, *ADelt.* 25 (1970), B2, 431–4.

12. D. Levi, *Gli scavi à Festos negli anni 1958–60*, in *Annuario ASA* 39–40 (1961–2), 397–418, with *Bollettino d'Arte* 41 (1956), 241.

13. G. E. Mylonas, *Eleusis and the Eleusinian Mysteries* (Princeton, 1961), 63–6.

14. G. Rapp. jr. and S. E. Aschenbrenner (edd.), *Excavations at Nichoria in Southwest Greece* i (1978), 116.

15. (Oxford, 1979).

16. C. Weickert *et al.*, *Die Ausgrabung beim Athena Tempel in Milet, 1957*, in *Istanbuler Mitteilungen* 9–10 (1959–60), 1–96.

17. See F. E. Winter, *Greek Fortifications* (London, 1971), 19–25.

18. Winter, *op. cit.* 64.

19. Winter, *op. cit.* 24.

20. Lawrence, *op. cit.* (above, n. 15), 34–6.

21. Winter, *op. cit.* (above, n. 17), 19–29.

CHAPTER 19

The 'Hoplite Reform' Revisited

Here is an example (see p. x above) of a re-entry into a controversy, defending an earlier thesis against radical later modification. The striking thing in this case was the wholly unexpected direction from which the rival interpretation came. The Homeric poems, almost unmentioned in my original paper (Ch. 17) because of the then near-consensus that they portrayed a system anterior to, and largely innocent of, hoplite armour and tactics, were suddenly reintroduced into the discussion by Joachim Latacz's new analysis of the Homeric battle scenes, cited at the start of the paper. His thesis presently won important support from historians and archaeologists: the implication was that any such episode as a 'hoplite reform', if indeed it had happened at all, did so at an earlier date than I had argued, in time for its effects to permeate the text of the *Iliad*.

My stand against this revised view rests on my conviction that certain of Latacz's claims for the Homeric battle-scenes are, on closer analysis, no longer tenable; and on certain propositions about hoplite arms and hoplite armies which seem to have been neglected by Latacz's supporters. Certain features in the narrative of the *Iliad* combine to present a picture that is still quite at variance with hoplite warfare: but this on its own is not enough to dismiss the possibility that such a method of fighting, even if inappropriately deployed by the poet, was nevertheless already a reality of contemporary warfare, and one that was known to him. We can note in passing that the subsequent movement to bring down the date of Homer and the final stage of the composition of the Homeric poems to the seventh century BC (above, p. 173) would, if widely adopted, have a dramatic effect on this and many other issues. Instead (p. 353) I turn to certain features which, for me, define hoplite warfare. The most important of these is that a hoplite force should be the prime, and often the only, determinant of the actions of its side in an engagement.

The elder Moltke, when asked for his views on the American Civil War, is said to have replied that he was not interested in a struggle between two armed mobs. It was no doubt arrogant of him to reject the many valuable lessons he could have learned from such a huge conflict. Yet it remains true that the operations, soon afterwards, of the regular German armies under his direction were to be very different in kind. The early hoplite commanders and their successors, by contrast, would have hastened to use the *Iliad* as an inspiration for their troops; but, here too, this implies nothing as to the similarity of their actual operations.

Since the publication of this paper, Hans van Wees has advanced a case for a quite different, at times conflicting, revision of the established view, making new use of the iconographic evidence (van Wees 2000; 2004: 47–52). His conclusion is that the process resulting in the full hoplite system, known to us from accounts of Classical battles, took far longer than even I had argued, and was not complete even by 600 BC. The combination of Latacz's and van Wees's propositions would result, on the orthodox chronology, in a process which lasted well over a century – too long, perhaps, for 'reform' to be the appropriate term for it.

My final answer to both these reinterpretations of the evidence is the same (cf. p. 356): that there is a substantial class of evidence, that of the actual surviving pieces of armour dedicated at Olympia and other sanctuaries, which is more robust than either new textual interpretations of Homer, or new readings of battle scenes in art. It tells a firmly consistent story, that the middle years of the seventh century saw a sharp rise in frequency of use of the 'classic' items of hoplite armour on Greek battlefields: something in Greek warfare changed significantly in these years. It also provides evidence, though in lesser quantity, for a process of transition over the previous two generations, in which Greek armourers worked their way, through experiment, towards these 'classic' forms of equipment. This body of data, which could have been more prominently emphasised in my original paper (Ch. 17: but see the later discussion and table in Snodgrass 1980: 105–7), should perhaps serve as the starting-point for any future discussion of this issue.

BIBLIOGRAPHY

Snodgrass, A. (1980), *Archaic Greece: The Age of Experiment*, London: J. M. Dent.

van Wees, H. (2000), 'The development of the hoplite phalanx: iconography and reality in the seventh century', in *War and Violence in Ancient Greece*, ed. H. van Wees, London: Duckworth, pp. 125–66.

van Wees, H. (2004), *Greek Warfare: Myths and Realities*, London: Duckworth.

It is a rare feat for an author, writing within one field of study, to bring about a complete revision of the accepted doctrine in a quite different field. Yet that is what Joachim Latacz achieved with the publication, in 1977, of his *Kampfparänese, Kampfdarstellung und Kampfwirklichkeit in der Ilias, bei Kallinos und Tyrtaios*.[1] Whatever its impact has been within Homeric philological scholarship, it can hardly match the transformation of thought which the book has brought about in early Greek military and social history. To some extent, that transformation only began to take effect from 1985, when W. K. Pritchett gave prominence to Latacz' conclusions, and upheld the most important of them, in volume iv of his *The Greek State at War*;[2] but the ground had been prepared by a series of favourable reviews of Latacz' work, with only one clearly dissenting voice[3] among the philological experts. Since 1985, the view has become widespread among historians that Latacz' findings require a complete reappraisal of a critical episode in early Greek history, the transition to hoplite warfare: I single out, as especially influential, the views of Ian Morris,[4] Victor Hanson[5] and Kurt Raaflaub.[6]

I will attempt to summarise, even if in too simplified a form, the main relevant conclusions that Latacz reached:

1) Mass armies, and not heroic champions, are the decisive element in Homeric battle, and the importance of their rôle is absolutely integral to the battle-descriptions;

2) These mass forces mainly play their part in two ways, and at two junctures: they partake in mass long-range exchange of missiles, before the *promachoi* engage in those exploits to which the narrative

'The "hoplite reform" revisited', *Dialogues d'Histoire ancienne* 19, 1993 (Hommage à Lucien Lerat), 47–61.

gives such prominence; and they join battle thereafter in mass hand-to-hand combat and close-order formation;

3) This latter phase, which decides the outcome of each major engagement, differs in no significant way from the warfare of the phalanx known from post-Homeric sources;

4) This Homeric phalanx-warfare is no mere literary conceit, but a consistent portrayal of what may well have been the contemporary historical reality;

5) As a consequence of 3) and 4) above, the whole conception of a dramatic change in Greek warfare in the period after Homer – the 'hoplite reform' or 'hoplite revolution' – must be abandoned.

In thus simplifying the arguments, I have omitted some important and interesting elements in Latacz' case, such as his closely-argued interpretations of the frequent Homeric terms *phalanges, stiches*, and *promachoi;*[7] but important as they are, I do not think that the main line of argument, as outlined above, actually *depends* on them for its validity. I therefore wish to set them aside here.

Let me begin my discussion, and indeed shorten it, by stating at once that I accept what I have called conclusion no. 1; indeed, like others, I see it as a striking new insight into the understanding of the battles in the *Iliad*. So much for those who thought in the 1960's, as I did, that future enlightenment on early Greek warfare must come from archaeology, since the parameters of the interpretation of the literary evidence were substantially fixed and immovable. We have learned that, however much the poet may choose to emphasise the prowess of his heroes, and even to present his theme as being the anger of just one of them, he has still accepted that the setting of his poem is a long war between two large armies, and acknowledges some of the implications of this in a realistic if intermittent way. Expressed in such words, this may not sound like a spectacular advance; yet the repercussions in historical scholarship suggest that such it is.

These repercussions, however, in large part result from the subsequent conclusions that I have numbered 2), 3), 4) and 5); and here, along with an apparently small number of other critics,[8] I begin to dissent. Let us concentrate our attention on no. 2, which relates to the phases of operation of the mass forces in the poetic narrative, since nos 3, 4 and 5 all to some degree presuppose its validity: only if there is consistent and regular depiction of phases of exclusive hand-to-hand combat in the *Iliad* can we use this literary depiction as a basis for historical conclusions.

Latacz holds that there is a common initial phase of *Massenwur-fkampf*, mass long-range exchange of missile-fire, which can on its own be decisive, but usually is not, and so makes way for the familiar interlude of exploits by the *promachoi*. These are then in turn brought to an end by a more decisive phase of *Massennahkampf*, mass hand-to-hand engagement.[9] Latacz freely acknowledges that the sequence is not invariable, but it is important to his argument that there should be this chronological separation of phases in the battle-narrative.

In truth, however, such a separation is highly debatable. It is prob-ably Hans van Wees (n. 8 above) who has looked most closely at Latacz' argument, and here I am borrowing and enlarging on some of his criticisms. To consider, first, the status of the phase of *Massen-wurfkampf*: there are four formulaic pasages which describe this in generalised, closely parallel terms: viii 66–7 and xi 84–5, which are identical, and xv 318–9 and xvi 777–8, which share the same second line. In each case, the poet tells us that 'As long as (so-and-so), so long were the missiles flying from both sides, and men kept falling'. The temporal expressions in the first line vary, but the picture is in each case one of a protracted period of missile-fire from both sides. The words hint at the inevitable sequel, that this picture will change and that one of the two sides will get the advantage. But at what stage in each engagement do these passages occur?

The answers are hardly what Latacz' analysis requires: the pas-sages are *not* always situated in a phase of unmixed missile-fire, nor are they located at the outset of the engagement. At viii 66, for exam-ple, we have heard only six lines previously that the two converging armies have clashed 'with an impact of shields ... their bossed shields collided together' (62–3). So it seems that the *Massennahkampf* has begun, just before the formulaic phrase encapsulating the *Massenwur-fkampf*. At xi 84, similarly, we have heard almost as shortly before that the Trojans and Achaeans 'fell upon each other ... it was level pegging ... they rushed in like wolves' (70–73) – not quite so explicit, but suggestive of much the same thing. If we move to xvi 777, the formulaic passage is set in the context of the struggle over the corpse of Kebriones: around him, the ground is 'bristling with javelins and arrows' (772–3). In this particular case, Latacz goes so far as to es-timate the distance between the two armies as 'some 40 metres'.[10] But there is something wrong here. Only a few lines before (762–3), we have learned that Hector has hold of Kebriones' head and Patro-clus of his feet. So these two enemies at least are at close quarters; and they are not alone. The other Trojans and Greeks have come together in a mighty clash (764), and rocks are crashing against the shields of 'those fighting over him' (sc. Kebriones) (775). Once again, a *Massennahkampf* or something like it is under way.

With the remaining passage, xv 318–9, there is a quite different problem, of a kind that will reappear later. This time, it does seem that the setting is one of pure missile-fighting: the difficulty is that one side in the exchange, the Achaean, consists of a small group of picked men who have been chosen for an explicit task, to cover the retreat of the main body of the army to the ships. Yet we hear in some detail of javelins finding their target, and the formulaic phrase 'and men kept falling' once again applies to both sides. To his credit, Latacz admits that here the repeated passage has been inappropriately inserted, as a set piece, through a failure of composition.[11] Just so: but this surely means that here, at any rate, the passage forms the weakest evidence for a regular literary, let alone a regular historical practice. These formulaic passages form the heart of the case for the integrity and the temporal priority of the *Massenwurfkampf*. Yet they show such a close juxtaposition of missile and hand-to-hand engagement that, *prima facie*, the most reasonable inference is that which Hans van Wees has drawn:[12] that the poet is saying that, *at one and the same time and place*, a large number of warriors were exchanging missiles while others were fighting it out hand to hand. But let us suspend final judgment until we have considered the *Massennahkampf* passages.

Latacz lists some 23 episodes of mass hand-to-hand engagement in the *Iliad*.[13] But once again, we find 'contamination' in their near vicinity. Take the very first general clash in the poem, which begins at iv 446: the two armies come to grips and 'shield clashed on shield', in exactly the formula that we encountered in viii 60–63 (p. 346 above). Yet almost at once, from line 457 on, we are in the throes of missile-fighting between individuals: twice in the later course of this engagement (iv 542 and v 167) the poet makes the general observation that there was 'a hail of missiles'. This turns out to be typical. In Book viii, as we have already seen, a classic *Massennahkampf* description at lines 60–63 turns into a *Massenwurfkampf* at lines 66–7. At xi 90, a diagnostic phrase of hand-to-hand battle, the 'breaking of the *phalanges*', is merely a brief glimpse between the missile-combat that comes before (xi 84–5, above, p. 346) and the mixed rout of infantry and chariots that follows when the Trojans give way; by line 163, it is from 'the flying missiles' that Zeus rescues Hector.

With Books xii to xvi, we enter the great battle around the beached Achaean ships; and here occurs a series of passages which constitute the most impressive evidence for the 'Homeric phalanx' of Latacz, since they combine a reference to mass in-fighting with a mention of a tightly-packed formation – a formation which Latacz compares, and indeed identifies, with the *synaspismos* of the Classical phalanx.[14] These two features, the *Massennahkampf* and the *synaspismos*, do not correlate very closely. Outside these Books, many of the mass engagements omit any mention of a tightly-packed formation; and conversely, many of the episodes of *synaspismos* take place in special, localised circumstances. Thus, at iv 532–3; it is only a small group of Thracians who form a close formation around their fallen leader Peiros; while at xi 592–4 the wounded Eurypylos is similarly protected by his companions, with their shields sloping back against their shoulders and their spears outstretched. When Patroclus is killed, the formation of his companions round his body is even more explicitly described, with a 'hedging' of shields (xvii 266–7; cf. 354–5). The size of force which can form around a single fallen man is not to be compared with a phalanx in the open field.

Much the same is true of the first occurrence within the battle at the ships (xiii 128–35): a group of the 'best' Achaeans, 'hand-picked', confront the Trojans with another 'hedge' of spears and shields. This is portrayed as a small task-force, specially mustered by Poseidon, not as a regular mass formation. Another passage which is given prominence in Latacz' account is the massing of the Myrmidons at xvi 211–17. When Achilles harangues them, they respond by bunching together as closely as stones in a wall. But these are men who are nowhere near action. Before they reach the enemy, they must cover a distance (line 258), and indeed emerge from among the beached ships (267). The famous simile of the swarm of wasps (259–65) is intended to describe an order of march, not an order of battle.

In the middle and later part of Book xiii, more convincing examples appear: massed forces are in action, they are continuously at close quarters, and the compactness of their formations is several times explicitly mentioned. At xiii 339–43 occurs a passage which, while making only scant reference to formations, clearly describes a mass engagement on both sides, and places unusual stress on the bronze armour: the cuirasses are, uniquely, 'newly-burnished', the shields 'gleaming', the spears 'grasped', not thrown. At 487–8, there is once again a grouping of 'companions' around Idomeneus, in response to his exhortation, with a repetition of the shield-drill found in xi 592–4 (see above). At 800–01, the Trojan forces advance *en masse*, rank upon rank and 'glittering with bronze'.

In these engagements, if anywhere in the *Iliad*, both the tactics and the equipment of hoplite warfare seem to invite recognition. But we have continually to remind ourselves where all this is taking place. At the end of Book xii, Hector had smashed down the gate in the Achaean rampart and the Trojans had swarmed inside. The fighting is now among the sterns of the beached ships, which some of the Achaeans will presently use as a fighting-platform. A certain confusion has sometimes been detected hereabouts: the reference to the *phalanges* of the Achaeans at xiii 806 seems inappropriate for the topographical situation. To state the position more broadly: no army which is hurled back on to the beaches in headlong retreat, as happens to the Achaeans at xii 470–1 (and again at xv 304–5), and is forced to make a stand with its back to the sea, has either the time or the freedom to adopt a formal battle-array like the phalanx. Its use of close-order formation is not a matter of choice, but of desperate necessity. As for the Trojans, it is equally impossible for them to attack their enemies in such circumstances without adopting a correspondingly dense formation.

Two provisional conclusions emerge from this discussion of what I have called 'conclusion no 2' in Latacz' argument. First, in the battles set in the open field, the narrative does not maintain a regular separation of phases of *Massenwurfkampf* and *Massennahkampf*. On the contrary, each is allowed to contaminate the other with, at times, as rapid an alternation between the two as is possible within the tempo of Homer's narrative. Secondly, when (as in Book xiii) there is a sustained account of a pure hand-to-hand engagement, it is in special circumstances which have nothing in common with a pitched battle in the open field, between two well-prepared adversaries. The significance of all this is that the integrity of a pure *Massennahkampf* in Homer, as a style of combat on a normal battlefield, seems unsustainable. Instead, we find the recurrent use of looser formations: formations in which there is room for individuals not only to hurl missiles, but to dodge them; which allow extreme freedom of movement to individuals across, the battlefield; and which – an important observation that I owe to Hans van Wees – allow repeated rally and re-formation after a phase of retreat or flight. This last feature makes possible the apparently endless ebb and flow of battle with which we are so familiar in the *Iliad*. It is also something of which the later hoplite phalanx was notoriously incapable.

We should not forget that chariots are also a regular element in Homeric battle. For Latacz' interpretation they pose a special problem, on top of the difficulties that they present to the rest of us. He postpones treatment of them until the second half of his penultimate chapter,[15] and his explanation of their use in the *Iliad* has attracted some criticism. For him, the chariot serves mainly as a transport vehicle, though it has also an important rôle in the context of pursuit and flight; during the main engagement, however, he believes that chariots are normally stationed behind the confronted armies. This case seems difficult to sustain. Quite apart from the promptitude with which chariots become available when their owners need them, there are a number of occasions where chariots are shown to be in the thick of the fighting, in the front line, at a time when the outcome of the battle is still in the balance. For an example, we need look no further than the opening engagement of the *Iliad* (iv 446 ff.). The Achaeans appear to be gaining the advantage, and at iv 507 Apollo rallies the Trojans. First to respond is Peiros with his Thracians, with a sequel that we have already noted (532–3, above, p. 350); but next, at the very beginning of the following book, the two sons of Dares charge at Diomedes in their chariot, though with equal lack of success (v 11–13). This is in the midst of a mass engagement, which only swings decisively in favour of the Achaeans at v 37.

The case for 'Homeric phalanx warfare' thus seems vulnerable from every side. If even its literary existence is highly debatable, then the grounds for believing in its resemblance to later tactics, in its probable historical origin and in the consequent rejection of any post-Homeric 'hoplite reform' – what I have termed conclusions 3), 4) and 5) in Latacz' argument – are, to say the least, very much weakened. Yet there is a further line of defence. I have based my own arguments throughout on a hypothesis which Latacz himself shares, along with perhaps a slight majority of other commentators. This is, that the battle-scenes of the *Iliad* are based on a coherent, if not always absolutely clear vision of a form of warfare; and that the poet is, apart from the occasional lapse, faithful to that vision. I have been arguing that, on this hypothesis, the systematic use of a pitched battle formation like the later phalanx, with tactics like those of the later *synaspismos*, has no part in this form of warfare.

But what if the hypothesis is itself unsound? Some commentators would argue that to reproduce faithfully such a vision would be at best irrelevant, at worst inimical to the poet's artistic purpose. Rather, the poet would draw on different and possibly incompatible modes of combat, known to him from whatever source, and weave them into a composite picture according to the dictates of a literary narrative.

On the point at issue here, the significant question might then be, not whether the poet uses the 'Homeric phalanx tactics' in a consistent and intelligible way, but whether he shows any awareness at all of their existence. It could be argued, on this view, that any reference at all to the use of massed troops in close-order formation for hand-to-hand fighting, especially with associated mention of bronze defensive armour, betrays a familiarity with the concept of the later hoplite phalanx. The 'threshhold of proof' will be very much lower than it has been in the argument as conducted up to this point.

This line of reasoning poses an obvious threat, not only to Latacz' case but to my counter-arguments as well. I have no devastating rejoinder to it, still less a way of proving it invalid. I merely argue that, even on this more sceptical (or perhaps more sensitive) reading of the *Iliad*, the case for a 'proto-phalanx' is still not made: much less does it follow that 'The general impression created by the poem is one of hoplites fighting in mass formation'.[16] Four essential elements of a hoplite phalanx were, first its use as a formation for pitched battle in an open field; secondly its density; thirdly its function as the main fighting force of an army; and finally its employment of (preferably uniform) bronze defensive armour. Never once, as far as I can discover, does the poet of the *Iliad* represent all four of these elements together. The most important missing element is usually the first, the use in pitched battle. The fact that one or two, and occasionally all three, of the other elements are found in some passages is an important discovery which we owe largely to Latacz' work. Yet it is certain that, for centuries and even millennia before Homer, armies in certain regions of the ancient world had had occasion to adopt the tactics of mass, close-order formation, and had at times also made use of bronze armour. Sometimes the circumstances of battle, the natural topography, or the technology of potential enemies invited or dictated such a response. At other times, these tactics were varied with looser formations, with more mobile operations, and with recourse to the help of specialised arms such as archers, cavalry or charioteers – just as happens in the battles of the *Iliad*.

But the measured clashes of hoplite phalanxes, which we know from the fifth century and which we believe we can detect in the seventh, imply something more. What were these further developments? What, in other words, remains of the case for a 'hoplite reform'? Pritchett sums up his own answer very succinctly, with the words 'a technical progress in arms'.[17] That is an element which is most certainly present and, in attempting to put forward a positive alternative

to the views of Latacz and Pritchett, I shall attend to it first. But I
hope also to make clear that it is not the whole story.

The battle-scenes on Attic Late Geometric pottery have a natural
place in this argument. They are used to good effect by Latacz in his
closing pages:[18] he finds valuable support for his conclusion about the
potential historicity of the Homeric mass-battles (no. 4 above, p. 347)
in the fact that Gudrun Ahlberg had independently reached parallel
conclusions about the Geometric paintings.[19] The apparently 'mixed'
tactics which they show, in her view, represent a natural sequence from
long-range to close-in fighting; the repeated scenes of single combat
are likewise seen as an 'abbreviation' for mass hand-to-hand engagements. The resemblances to Latacz' own interpretation of the battles
in the *Iliad* are indeed close, but the interpretation of these scenes is
so controversial, even among those who know them best, that it is
wisest not to press the arguments beyond general parallelisms.

It is on this level of general parallels, however, that I should like to
draw attention to a feature which can be observed without involving
much interpretation. This is, that Geometric depictions of warriors
regularly occur, often on the same vase, in two clearly separated contexts. There are action scenes, usually military or funerary, and there
are 'parade scenes', often below but sometimes above, in which files
of warriors follow each other uneventfully round the vase.[20] In the
early phases of the pictorial style, there is a compatibility between
the equipment and the style of drawing, as between the figures on
the two separate zones, which allows the viewer to assume that the
same kind of people are participating in both kinds of activity: in one
or two cases, the 'action' can even spill over into the 'parade'. But
in the latest scenes, those of 'Late Geometric IIB', this is no longer
so clearly the case. A group of late amphorae, from more than one
different workshop, show a funerary or chariot scene above, and a
file of warriors with twin spears, helmets and round shields below.[21]
Their equipment is uniform and modest. Both in general and in detail, this recalls the *Iliad's* distinction between the emphasized action
of individuals and the implicit recognition of the rôle of the mass of
the army. In both cases, the latter are foot-soldiers; the equipment of
spears, helmets and shields recalls the normally specified arms of the
laoi in the *Iliad*. Many of these are mentioned only at the moment
of their death, and they are not usually credited with, for example,
cuirasses or greaves.

Greater interest attaches to these group-portrayals on the vases
once the painters begin to show pictorial blazons on the shields, as

they occasionally do.[22] If we are right in seeing a close connection between the pictorial blazon on the outer surface of the shield (implying that it could only be held one way up) and the two-handled arrangement of the Archaic and Classical *hoplon* on its inner side, which likewise could not be inverted, then we have here a proof that the hoplite shield was already known to Athenian painters in the years around 700 BC. In the *Iliad*, by contrast, it is agreed that there is little if any sign of its presence; certainly its presence *as a norm* is entirely excluded by the recurrent shield-formulae. Hide appears as a standard material, for example, while wood is apparently unknown. With the hoplite shield, it was exactly the other way round.

If we accept the view that such a shield would *only* be used by warriors fighting in close formation, alongside others identically equipped, then we have here evidence of a dramatic change which, at least at Athens, had taken place by about 700 BC, but which appears entirely to post-date the composition of the *Iliad*. This view commands wide support, and has now been reinforced by strong new arguments, based on the weight and concavity of the hoplite shield, by Victor Hanson'.[23] Nor is there anything impossible about the swift sequence of change that it implies. Yet I am still inclined to doubt it, because of the clear iconographic evidence for the use of this shield in more varied types of fighting, and because of the still widely accepted interpretation[24] of the poetic evidence of Tyrtaeus, that the Spartan army in the mid-seventh century was still combining this equipment with a more open formation than the fully-developed phalanx. There is also the persistent portrayal, even later in this century, of formations of hoplites with twin spears, suggesting the survival of missile-combat as one of the functions of the early hoplite. This evidence led Latacz himself[25] to accept the reality of a long-drawn-out development, rather than a rapid introduction, of the phalanx of Classical type. On balance, I still find this broad, inductive evidence more persuasive than the strict deductive logic of the argument from the handle-arrangement, weight and shape of the hoplite shield. We cannot after all be certain, from the time of the very first depiction of a pictorial blazon, that the shield had all the attributes of weight and material that it presently came to possess.

With the metal helmet, cuirass and greaves, it is utterly different. No one can seriously dispute that warriors of various kinds might find it advantageous to adopt these. The fact is that all three are indisputably present in the battle-scenes of the *Iliad*; and that, concordantly, all three are attested by actual dated finds from a date earlier than even the indirect evidence for the hoplite shield. The greave occurs, both in a Cretan tomb and in an isolated dedication at Olympia, well before 700 BC and perhaps around 750.[26] The helmet and cuirass are most famously attested in the Panoply Tomb at Argos, of perhaps about 720,[27] and there is at least inferential evidence that each had passed through a phase of development before that. For the *use* of the cuirass, there is the corroborative evidence of the Attic Late Geometric amphora in Buffalo,[28] which shows one worn by an armed horseman. This evidence may be circumstantial, but is surely a more persuasive hint of the purpose of the Argive warrior's cuirass than the suggestion once mooted, that the dead man had been a sea-captain: not least, because it supplies a neat explanation of why the Argos tomb contained no shield, of hoplite or any other type.

On this account, we have the appearance, from well before the end of the eighth century, of a set of items of bronze defensive armour which are sporadically adopted by the exponents of the current forms of warfare. At the close of the century, there is added to these a form of shield designed for fighting on foot, in formations that gradually evolve into the true phalanx, in the form know from Classical times. But at the same period, the existing type of bronze helmet and greave are also modified, to a form that was equally suited to the tactics now evolving. The Corinthian helmet, heavy and vision-obscuring but immensely protective, was introduced and then, by the mid seventh century, modified so that it could be rested on the crown of the head and pulled down at the last moment before action. The greave acquired a new shape which enabled it simply to be slipped over the shin, again allowing for removal on the march and fitting just before action.

With these changes, the hoplite panoply was at last fully-formed. That hoplite tactics took a comparably long time to develop is *a priori* likely, since a substantial and by no means a natural or inevitable evolution lay between the adoption of heavy infantry in general, and the very specialised and somewhat artificial version of it that was the Greek hoplite phalanx.[29] At all events, the actual dedications from Olympia[30] confirm, in a quantitative way, that only from the middle of the seventh century did the panoply enjoy widespread popularity, just as the Corinthian vase-paintings more anecdotally suggest that only then did the tactics reach their finished form.

This then encompasses the 'technical progress in arms' of which Pritchett writes, though I give the phrase a wider application than he. But what else was entailed by acceptance of the developed hoplite phalanx? I should like to end by singling out one factor which seems to me of the highest importance, although it has no direct connection with the actual battlefield; and which at the same time underlines the essential differences from the picture given in the *Iliad*. This is the matter of the *enrolment* of a hoplite army. For Archaic and Classical Sparta, we know a considerable amount about the *agoge*, whereby a self-selected hoplite class was prepared for an adulthood in arms. For general purposes, however, our knowledge of the Athenian system is more likely to be helpful, since here as in most Greek *poleis* eligibility for service as a hoplite was not automatically self-defining. A certain minimum property standard had to be applied, above which service was normally compulsory, so that some mechanism to prevent 'draft-dodging' had to be available; and below which it might be equally unfortunate, militarily, to go, since it would lead to an unevenly equipped army – an army, I cannot forbear to add, such as we seem to be presented with in the strange and often condemned passage in *Iliad* xiv 370–382 where at Poseidon's behest three of the Achaean leaders set about re-distributing their troops' armour by compulsory exchanges.

In Classical Athens, this enrolment process was devolved to the level of the ten Cleisthenic tribes, though there is evidence of changes over time.[31] How is it likely to have been organised at the very earliest stage, in Athens and elsewhere? The natural answer would be on a local basis: someone in each community would be charged with the duty of mustering a given number of hoplites from their district. Ideally, this would require the existence both of a census and of a property register. Only thus could a count be made of those who were eligible and, equally important, a record kept *through time* to allow for new hoplites coming of age, and older ones dying, being killed in action, passing military age or falling on hard times economically. These mechanisms of later times sound improbably elaborate for the seventh century BC, and we may prefer to imagine a cruder system in operation, such as the calling of an assembly of the biggest land-owners, with each being sent away to recruit one or more men similarly equipped. Yet even this mechanism would be hard to operate without maintaining a nominal roll, or at least a tally, of the original group – that is, without some kind of durable written records, however simple. The question of training must also have arisen for some of the participants: it should not be strongly emphasised, any more than it was in antiquity, but there will always have been a minimum requirement.[32]

The whole issue of the organisation of hoplites takes us ever further away from the world of the *Iliad*. Even when the rôle of the mass armies in Homer has been given its due recognition, there was still a long stride, or rather a whole series of shorter strides, to be taken before the developed hoplite phalanx arrived. On the one hand, the mixed tactics, the free and volatile formations, the sharp contrast between a chariot-driving hero and a Thersites, 'counting for nothing in battle'; on the other, the streamlined uniformity of the hoplite phalanx, kept in step by the pipers so entirely absent from Homer, in which even the pretended descendants of that same hero would fight like anyone else, a uniformity dictated by peer-group pressure both within and between the separate *poleis*. I have always advocated the theory of a long and gradual evolution for the hoplite. I take the evidence of the *Iliad*, re-interpreted by Latacz' findings, as prolonging that evolution at its upper end, not as truncating it or eliminating it altogether.

NOTES

1. *Zetemata* vol. 66 (Munich, 1977).
2. (Berkeley and Los Angeles, 1985).
3. That of R. Leimbach, *Gnomon* 52 (1980), 418–425.
4. I. Morris, *Burial and ancient society* (Cambridge, 1987), especially 196–200.
5. V. D. Hanson, in V. D. Hanson (ed.), *Hoplites: The Classical Greek battle experience* (London, 1991), 66–67, n. 11–12.
6. K. Raaflaub, 'Homer und die Geschichte des 8. Jh. s v. Chr.', in J. Latacz (ed.), *Zweihundert Jahre Homer-Forschung (Colloquium Rauricum 2*, Stuttgart/Leipzig, 1991), especially 222–230.
7. Latacz, *op. cit.* (above, n. 1), 45–49, 141–171.
8. Notably H. van Wees, "Kings in combat: battles and heroes in the *Iliad'*, *CQ* 38 (1988), 1–24; *idem, Status Warriors / War, Violence and Society in Homer and History* (Amsterdam, 1992); and in a still unpublished paper that he was kind enough to show to me.
9. Latacz, *op. cit.* (above n. 1), 116–212, especially 117–8.
10. Latacz, *ibid.* 125 and n. 9.
11. Latacz, *ibid.* 124.
12. See the works cited above, n. 8, especially *CQ* 38 (1988), 2–12.
13. Latacz, *op. cit.* (above, n. 1), 178–212.
14. Latacz, *ibid.* 55–67.
15. Latacz, *ibid.* 215–223.
16. Pritchett, *op. cit.* (above, n. 2), 33.

17. Pritchett, *ibid.* 44.
18. Latacz, *op. cit.* (above, n. 1), 238–241 and 245.
19. G. Ahlberg, *Fighting on land and sea in Greek Geometric art (AIARS,* vol. 16), (Stockholm, 1971), 53–54.
20. On these see G. Ahlberg, *Prothesis and ekphora in Greek Geometric art (Studies in Mediterranean Archaeology,* vol. 32), (Göteborg, 1971) especially 306, 309 on the files of warriors.
21. Note especially the amphorae Athens, NM 894 (Ahlberg, *ibid.* (n. 20), 190, fig. 59); Berlin, 3203 (*ibid.* 183, fig. 58c); Hamburg, 1966–89 (*ibid.* no. 43, fig. 60c); Philadelphia, MS 5464 (*ibid.* 183, fig. 58d).
22. On the amphorae Athens, Benaki Mus., 7675 (Ahlberg, *ibid.* 28, no. 46, fig. 46a); Athens, NM 14763 and Copenhagen, Ny Carlsberg Glyptotek 3187 (J.N. Coldstream, *Greek Geometric Pottery* (London, 1968), 55, nos 8 and 12); and on a sherd from Athens, Kerameikos, *AA* 1963,649, fig. 5.
23. V.D. Hanson, *op. cit.* (above, n. 5), 67–71.
24. As for example by J. K. Anderson; in Hanson (ed.) (above, n. 5), 15–17.
25. Latacz; *op. cit.* (above, n. 1), 37–38.
26. See E. Kunze, *Beinschienen (Olympische Forschungen,* vol. 21) (Berlin and New York, 1991), 4–6 and n. 15.
27. But E. Kunze, VIII *Bericht über die Ausgrabungen in Olympia* (Berlin, 1967), 114, prefers a date no later than 740 BC.
28. Coldstream, *op. cit.* (above, n. 22), 59, no. 21a.
29. Compare the view of P. A. Cartledge, 'Hoplites and heroes', *JHS* 97 (1977), 11–27, especially 18–24.
30. See A. Snodgrass, *Archaic Greece* (London, 1980), 105–107.
31. See A. Andrewes, 'The hoplite *katalogos*', in *Classical Contributions: Studies in honor of M. F. McGregor* (Locust Valley, NY, 1981), 1–3.
32. Anderson, *op. cit.* (above, n. 24), 28–31.

Early Greek Art

INTRODUCTION TO PART V

Art history and archaeology are not the natural allies that they might appear. Even when they are dealing with identical subject matter, their objectives are often poles apart, while their interests – in both senses of the word – are always different and sometimes directly conflicting. Yet there are a few fields in the study of the past, among which Classical archaeology is prominent, where it has been traditional to merge the two disciplines together, and indeed to expect the same people to practise both at once. Critics of this tradition have argued that it produces a kind of hybrid sub-discipline, one which cannot be called 'art history' but which, at the same time, certainly does not satisfy any definition of 'archaeology' that would be accepted by the non-Classical branches of the other discipline. The charge was that the diligent pursuit of classification, of dating, of artistic parallels and, especially, of attributions had so preoccupied Classical art historians as to leave neither space nor inclination for the wider concerns of true art history – for which, elsewhere, these activities would have been seen merely as desirable preliminaries.

This criticism, though no doubt overstated, had a ring of truth for me – at least since the time when, over thirty years ago, I was invited to teach the second year of a degree course in History of Art, a year devoted exclusively to Classical art. The result – a course modelled on this same tradition of Classical art history – was less than satisfying to the teacher and to the students, who found little to connect it with their study of art in other periods and were baffled by some of the subject matter – especially vase-paintings – which they were expected to take seriously as art.

I pondered this experience for some years before venturing back into the field of Classical art, with two new convictions in mind. First, I sought to demonstrate the essential independence of the early Greek visual artist from literary influences – a kind of analogue of the independence of Classical archaeology itself from literary Classics (cf. above, p. viii). The first paper below (Ch. 20) was an early product of this conviction. Second, I reverted to the very early history of the discipline, to a time before the tradition just described had even reached a settled form, to revive a question which had then exercised some distinguished minds: by what technical means did Greek artists convey the passage of time, something essential to any narrative picture? Here, Ch. 21, a lecture delivered to an inter-disciplinary audience at New College, Oxford, is an early specimen.

These concerns led in turn to others, some of them embodied in works not here included, but two of them represented by Chs. 22 and 23 below.

CHAPTER 20

Poet and Painter in Eighth-century Greece

An attempt to separate comprehensively these two areas of creativity from each other, this paper was addressed to fellow Classicists who did not, as I had half expected, take offence but showed their usual broad-mindedness in the ensuing discussion. But in the years since 1979, the whole study of Classical art has blossomed in such a variety of ways, most of which owe nothing to my own contributions, that it is no longer recognisable in the terms of the tradition criticised above. I single out just a few very recent works which have in part followed roughly parallel lines of argument to those used here, though not always to the same ends, and often over a much wider time-span: Stansbury-O'Donnell 1999; Hedreen 2001; Burgess 2001 (Part Two); Small 2003. In a separate category belongs Luca Giuliani's book (2003), a profound and subtle treatment of mythological scenes over the whole range of Greek art, informed by a fundamental distinction between 'descriptive' and 'narrative' pictures. His denial of true narrative status to the Geometric scenes and consequent relegation of the scenes discussed here to the descriptive category, is not necessarily a fatal blow to the claims made in the paper for a 'generalised heroic' interpretation of Geometric scenes; but a certain tension can already be detected between our views (compare p. 381 below, on the paper which follows).

Since this paper was unillustrated, it may be helpful to point out that, a year later, I again discussed some of the same monuments, and illustrated a few of them, in the paper referred to at n. 30 below (Snodgrass 1980), not included here.

On tomb-cults and hero-cults (pp. 373–4), the definitive work has since appeared in Antonaccio 1995. The specific problems posed by the 'Dipylon Shield' (pp. 377–8) have since been confronted, to very disparate effect, by Boardman 1983 and Hurwit 1985. I should confess, finally, that the 'Hesiodic' fragment referred to on pp. 375–6 is not recognised by modern expert opinion, as it was in antiquity, as the authentic work of that poet:

rather, it belongs a century or more later, and the argument at that point is accordingly weakened.

BIBLIOGRAPHY

Antonaccio, C. (1995), *An Archaeology of Ancestors: Tomb Cult and Hero Cult in Early Greece*, Lanham, MD: Rowman and Littlefield.

Boardman, J. (1983), 'Symbol and story in Geometric art', in *Ancient Greek Art and Iconography*, ed. W. G. Moon, Madison: University of Wisconsin Press, pp. 15–36.

Burgess, Jonathan S. (2001), *The Tradition of the Trojan War in Homer and the Epic Cycle*, Baltimore and London: Johns Hopkins University Press.

Giuliani, L. (2003), *Bild und Mythos*, Munich: C. H. Beck.

Hedreen, G. (2001), *Capturing Troy: the Narrative Functions of Landscape*, Ann Arbor: University of Michigan Press.

Hurwit, J. (1985), 'The Dipylon shield once more', *Classical Antiquity* 4: 121–6.

Small, Jocelyn P. (2003), *The Parallel Worlds of Classical Art and Text*, Cambridge: Cambridge University Press.

Snodgrass, A. (1980), 'Towards the interpretation of the Geometric figure-scenes', *Athenische Mitteilungen* 95: 51–8.

Stansbury-O'Donnell, M. D. (1999), *Pictorial Narrative in Ancient Greek Art*, Cambridge: Cambridge University Press.

The relationship between poetry and the visual arts is seldom close and never simple. But special difficulties attend the study of it in the eighth century before Christ in Greece, when evidence is not only in excessively short supply but, when it does come, is almost by definition ambiguous. On the whole question of the interpretation of Late Geometric vase-painting and other eighth-century art, there are well-established opposing positions: each new discovery finds a different interpretation on the part of what may be called the optimists – those who seek for correspondences between the Homeric epics and the visual arts – and of the sceptics, who habitually argue that there is no evidence for anything of the kind. Each party appears to have found an outlet for the promulgation of its view, inasmuch as many

'Poet and painter in eighth-century Greece', *Proceedings of the Cambridge Philological Society* 205, 1979, 118–30.

general or semi-popular accounts of Geometric and other early Greek art present it as having a major mythological content derived from epic poetry,[1] while many closer scholarly studies, deploying an array of iconographical learning and strict logic, nowadays reach the opposite conclusion, that there is little or no narrative content of any kind, mythological or otherwise, and no significant contact with epic, until the end of the Geometric period.[2]

I wish to begin, however, with an attack on the one important common assumption shared by both sides in this dispute. Those who believe in the mythological content of Geometric art have tended, at least since the time of T. B. L. Webster's article of 1955,[3] to link this expressly with the diffusion of the Homeric epic; Webster's paper was significantly entitled 'Homer and Attic Geometric vases'. By pointing out correspondences between specific Homeric passages and specific figure-scenes, the 'optimists' have either sought to establish the artists' general familiarity with the Homeric way of life (especially warfare), or gone further and identified narrative representations of particular episodes. Their theory assumes that the spread of the Homeric epic across the Aegean to Attica, in something like its final form, had happened early enough for the Athenian Geometric vase-painter to desire, and his customer to recognise, illustrations of Homeric scenes; and that means no later than 750 BC. They also, even more obviously, assume that these artists had the technical means for expressing narrative, that is for presenting a scene in a form, preferably unique but in any event sufficiently distinctive for it to be recognised for what it was, and not mistaken for a scene of everyday eighth-century life. But the central article of their faith is the literary one: that the prestige of the epic drew the painters, like a magnet, into attempting some kind of graphic depiction of subjects that their public already knew and loved.

Their opponents seek to refute these arguments at every stage – except one. At the fundamental level, they question whether a contemporary could ever have recognised mythological content in such scenes as the great battle-fragment Paris A 519, and whether the potential for narrative content existed anywhere in the Geometric figure-style.[4] In this last point, I think they go too far: the painter of a teeming, dramatic battle-scene such as this, with perhaps fifty participants when the picture was complete, can hardly have failed to convey *some* kind of story, even if only a generalised one. When Professor Coldstream dubbed this particular composition 'the death of a hero', he was being rightly cautious; anything far short of this would be unreasonable.

For this is hardly some ordinary event on a eighth-century battlefield, as is shown – quite apart from the controversial accoutrements of chariot and shield – by the discrepancy of scale in the figures, both upright and fallen. However, I am anticipating too much; it remains true that this is not a recognisable picture of any mythical episode known to us.

Next, the 'sceptics' have little difficulty in showing that most of the proposed identifications with events from epic involve episodes which, in Homeric terms at any rate, are of great obscurity and would therefore make curious choices; and conversely that the great Homeric set-pieces are curiously absent. Here I agree with them, and there is more evidence to come as we shall see. But now we encounter a difficulty for the sceptics' case. It is a fact that the next stage of Greek art, from about 700 BC on, shows recognisable mythological scenes becoming so common in vase-painting that they probably predominate among scenes of human action. Why this change? The sceptics have their answer ready: it is that it was only now that the diffusion of the epic really took place, producing almost immediately a rich crop of mythological illustrations. By this argument, they make common cause with their opponents in the matter of the influence of epic poetry. According to both sides, it is only the prestige of Homer and his followers which is sufficient to explain the phenomenon of the upsurge of legendary subjects in vase-painting. If we could only date the spread of the Homeric epic more readily, both sides suggest, then we should have a *terminus post quem* for heroic scenes in art. We cannot do that, but the sceptics still adduce arguments for placing this process around 700 BC, their opponents for putting it fifty years earlier.

It seems natural to ask the question: what if both sides are mistaken in this assumption of dependence on Homeric epic, perhaps even on epic of any kind? Is there not another equally likely and much simpler explanation of the popularity of legendary scenes in early Greek art, from whatever date it begins – namely, that there was a great web of vernacular, orally-transmitted mythology which penetrated every part of the Greek world, which was known to everyone of whatever level of education, and which did not need to depend at all on epic poetry? The range of Greek mythological stories is so vast that at no time, not even by the very end of antiquity, was it all able to find its way into surviving written literature, let alone the narrower scope of epic. We can support this statement by pointing to a series of much later vase-paintings which portray unquestionable episodes from legend – but episodes nowhere recorded in surviving literary in sources. Some are unique even in art, some are repeated many times.[5] But common sense alone would tell us that mothers will have told stories to their children without reciting them in hexameters and, what is more important, without having to wait for the recitation of the latest epic (to which, after all, not everyone would be admitted) to acquaint them with heroic stories. If this was still possible in the Athens of the sixth centuries BC, when Homer's prestige stood high and the *Iliad* had been familiar for generations, then is it not much more likely to have been so two centuries earlier, in an age of general illiteracy and relative backwardness? That the stories had in many cases been known much earlier even than this is virtually certain; a few years ago Professor Kirk rightly reminded us that Homer and Hesiod represent quite an advanced stage in the organisation of the body of legend with which they deal.[6] The question is, how far this process had been the exclusive preserve of the poets during the long period between the fall of Mycenae and the final appearance of the *Iliad*.

Rather than try to answer this question directly, I should like to lead some evidence from, once again, the ensuing period between about 700 and 650 BC, simply because this is the first phase of Greek art in which we really know what we are talking about in terms of subject-matter. I shall use as my text the very thorough and devastatingly sceptical treatment of early Greek mythological iconography in Klaus Fittschen's Tübingen dissertation of 1969 (n. 2 above); a mythological interpretation which is accepted by Fittschen can be taken as established indeed. I have extracted from his catalogue those representations of the period down to 650 BC which he recognises as definite, or at least reasonably likely, portrayals of specific legends. They number some 68.[7] Which legends are included among them, and does Homer have a great predominance? The answer is uncompromisingly blunt. Homer, that is the entire sequence of events narrated in the *Iliad* and *Odyssey*, accounts for something between 7 and 9 out of the 68. But perhaps this is being too strict and narrow; what about the events of the rest of the Trojan cycle, to the earlier and occasionally the later episodes of which Homer often refers? It is true that there are about 17 other pictures in Fittschen's catalogue which show episodes from the *Kypria, Aithiopis, Little Iliad, Ilioupersis* and *Oresteia*;[8] but even if we could accept that all the subjects chosen could have been inspired by knowledge of the two Homeric epics (which we hardly can; see below p. 371), then that would still account for well under half the total. There is a further question: in what form, if any, did the poems known collectively as the Epic Cycle exist between 700 and 650 BC? I note from Jasper Griffin's recent and persuasive article[9] that he accepts the arguments of Wilamowitz and Wackernagel for a relatively late date of composition; and follows Lesky in inclining towards the late seventh century as the absolute date for the version of the poems which later antiquity knew.

Again there is an obvious counter: that there were earlier poems on the same episodes. Is it not well-known that *Odyssey* 12.70 implies the existence of a pre-Homeric epic on the Argonauts? In this case, yes, although one would hesitate to say how early it needs to have been composed. But if the epics were already so extensive as to cover the same range as the early representations in art, then the early poets had been busy indeed. What we have, among the pictures of the period before 650 BC, is by Fittschen's strict reckoning as follows: about 26 representations of five or six separate exploits of Herakles, more than half of which show one or other of his encounters with Centaurs (Pholos or Nessos); six scenes of Perseus and the Gorgons; three each of Bellerophon and the Chimaera and Theseus and the Minotaur; two of the Lapith/Centaur story; one each of the Rape of Europa and the Birth of Athena. These, with the scenes from the Homeric epics and the rest of the Trojan cycle mentioned above, make up the total of 68. Herakles is, in this as in other periods of Greek art, the most favoured subject; and it is relevant that the celebration of Herakles in epic is, for us at least, an obscure topic, with the *Oikhalias Halosis*, the *Shield* and other seemingly late and mediocre efforts in the epic manner constituting some of our earliest evidence.[10] But it now seems that we are to posit, by 700 BC, a Herakles epic or epics sufficiently diffuse to cover his confrontations with Nessos, Pholos, Geryones, the Hydra and the sons of Aktor, not to mention the more doubtful case of the Nemean lion: an extraordinarily motley collection of exploits which it would be difficult to accommodate within one poem. By the same period, too, we should have to assume a sort of proto-*Aithiopis*, a proto-*Ilioupersis* and a proto-*Oresteia*, together with a proto-*Theogony* to narrate the Birth of Athena. All of this by 700; within the next few years at the latest, we should have to add early epics on Perseus, Bellerophon and Theseus, as well as a proto-*Kypria* and *Little Iliad*. I find this quite a lot to swallow, but I concede that it is quite possible.

With the Homeric poems, however, there is also the factor that the whole bias of the artistic evidence runs counter to that of the direct or indirect literary evidence. If we read the *Iliad* with an open yet retentive mind, we shall of course end up with the events actually narrated in the poem most clearly imprinted on our memories. These apart, the main focus of our interest will probably lie in a few episodes from other sagas whose dramatic date was earlier than that of the *Iliad*,[11] notably, the Theban saga (one thinks of the repeated comparisons of Diomedes with his father Tydeus), the Bellerophon story (*Iliad* 6), the Meleager story (*Iliad* 9), a Pylian saga commemorating the earlier deeds of Nestor, and of course the antecedent stages of the Trojan saga itself, as later enshrined in the *Kypria*. But what do we find in Fittschen's catalogue of the artistic evidence? The first, shaky, appearance of the *Kypria* is not until about 675, the *Iliad* itself comes in later still, the Bellerophon story, in its full form, later again; the Theban saga and the Meleager story make no definite appearance at all until after 600. The Pylian saga does have two doubtful early occurrences, which will be mentioned again (pp. 375–6); but they are as likely to represent one of the exploits of Herakles.[12]

Conversely, we may look at the episodes which *do* appear earliest in the artistic evidence. Certain deeds of Herakles are recognisable by about 700, but they are not the ones which Homer emphasises; and as for the other subjects which make an early appeal to the artists, they might have been hand-picked for the obscurity, cursoriness or total omission which they receive at Homer's hands. The Amazon-battle of the *Aithiopis*, for example, or the recovery of Achilles' body by Ajax in the same poem – what artist could be put in mind of these by familiarity with the *Iliad* and *Odyssey*? The choice faces us in the same form as before: either to posit the existence, on the Greek mainland presumably, of a large body of pre-Homeric (or at any rate non-Homeric) epic; or to deny any connection with poetry at all. I do not think that it is necessary for us to settle exclusively for either of these alternatives. But as for the *Iliad* and *Odyssey*, I find it hard to see how they can have contributed significantly at any time.

I should like to turn to a quite different argument. In the past few years, a series of remarkable, probably royal, burials have been excavated at Salamis in Cyprus. Their excavators, Vassos Karageorghis and the late Porphyrios Dikaios, have reasonably claimed that they show striking correspondence with Homer. They mark, in any case, an abrupt departure from previous Cypriot practice: all contain cremations, whereas the rite for the previous six thousand years in Cyprus had been an almost invariable one of inhumation. More important, there are other practices which are equally unprecedented in Cyprus and have direct and resonant Homeric echoes. Tomb 1 at Salamis shows the ashes of the dead wrapped in a cloth and deposited in a metal vessel (as in *Iliad* 23.243 and 24.795); it also contained jars of oil, placed by the tomb, while horses had been sacrificed outside the chamber (23.170–2, again from Patroklos' funeral). Tombs 3 and 79 repeated, respectively, the wrapping of the ashes and the deposition of oil jars, but a little later. Tomb 2, also a little later, actually involved two or more human sacrifices (compare 23.175), as well as the sacrifice of cattle (23.166). Finally, tomb 79 also contained three wooden thrones, one of which was completely clad in ivory plaques, while a second was decorated in both silver and ivory, like Penelope's chair in *Odyssey* 19.55f.[13]

The last item in this list should be set on one side, since there is an obvious common external explanation for ivory thrones, whether in Homer or in Cypriot graves, namely Assyrian court furniture and other luxury Oriental work. But that type of explanation cannot be applied to the funerary practices, where there must be something approaching a direct connection. This makes the initial date of the Cypriot burials an interesting question. The earlier burial in tomb 1, which had the features just listed, dates from about 750 BC. This poses serious problems. It is perhaps just worth pausing a moment to entertain the notion that Homer might have modelled the passages in Patroklos' and Hektor's funerals on a newly-adopted practice in Cyprus; but only just. When we consider the circumstantial evidence for the interest in the whole heroic idea in the eighth century, not least in Cypriot Salamis, traditionally founded by Teukros after the Trojan War, it seems overwhelmingly more likely that the influence would be in the reverse direction. But can we believe that a climactic episode of our *Iliad* like the funeral of Patroklos was not only composed in its present form, but also transmitted to Cyprus and emulated there, all as early as 750 BC? Perhaps; but there is a way out of this difficulty:[14] a school of thought in Homeric scholarship holds that behind the episode of Patroklos' burial and funeral games there lies an earlier version in which the deceased hero was none other than Achilles himself; hence, most obviously, the otherwise surprising abstention of Achilles from competing in the games. It seems to me that the Cypriot evidence fits best with this notion of a pre-Homeric funerary description, already incorporating some of the features of *Iliad* 23. Stasinos of Cyprus is at least a later witness for the acceptance and familiarity of Ionian epic in the island. Here again, as with the iconographic evidence, the difficulties are eased as soon as we no longer insist on a specifically *Homeric* inspiration for the phenomena.

I am not sure that there are necessarily any very significant implications for Homer in all this, and even if there were I should hardly be
competent to explore them. But the implications for life and the arts
in eighth-century Greece are substantial. We can now, in approaching
the Geometric figure-scenes, open our minds to a far wider range of
possibilities than those offered by Homeric epic. We can also look
at the evidence for 'heroic' practices in contemporary life, without
having to seek a direct justification in the *Iliad* and *Odyssey* for the
ideas which seem to lie behind them. Since this latter field lies outside
the scope of my title, I shall be brief. There is first the phenomenon of
the eighth-century hero-cults at Mycenaean graves.[15] These cults take
place, without exception, at built or rock-cut tombs of the Bronze Age,
all of which are predictably inhumations. Now one of the most obvious features of this practice is its utter irreconcilability with Homeric
descriptions: the Homeric dead are cremated and placed under tumuli, whereas the recipients of the eighth-century cults are inhumed
in tholoi and chamber-tombs on sloping ground. Would a generation
that was inspired by the type of funeral in *Iliad* 23 and 24 to look
for physical traces of the heroic dead have turned its back so completely on the literary guidance? There is a further difference in the
kind of hero selected for worship: in most cases, they seem to have
been local figures of great obscurity, sometimes perhaps eponyms of
the district, sometimes anonymous even to their worshippers, as we
know from a dedication inscribed simply 'I am the Hero's'. Finally,
there is the question of the initial date: as with the different practice
of actual 'heroic' burial in Cyprus, the main onset of dedications can
be traced to the years around and after 750 BC, but there are one or
two awkward cases where cult seems to begin as early as 900.

At the very end of the eighth century, there appears a further, and
in my view quite different, phenomenon. This is the establishment
of sanctuaries to major heroes, not usually at tombs – the Agamemnoneion below Mycenae, the Menelaion above Sparta – and perhaps
also to minor but still epic figures such as Iphigeneia at Brauron or
Phrontis, the steersman of Menelaos in *Odyssey* 3.282, at Sunion.[16]
Much has been made of this by the adherents of the 'sceptical' view
mentioned earlier, who use it to argue that it was only around 700 BC
that the Homeric epics began to spread to the mainland. They may
well be right thus far, although I have questioned their wider inferences from this. In particular, I have doubted the connection between
this and the earlier practice of grave-cult. There may be a parallel here
in Martin West's recent comments on the distinction between the two

separate meanings and contexts of the word ἥρως, as used in epic and as associated with hero-worship: he concludes, 'Each represents, I suggest, a particular facet of a system, separately developed in the Dark Ages.'[17]

There is a third practice of this period which may, like the grave-cults, be susceptible of an explanation independent of Homer, although it has invariably been linked with Homer by the commentators, myself included. This is the writing of hexameter inscriptions on vases, which begins with the Dipylon jug in Athens, probably of the 740's, and continues with the Nestor inscription from Ischia (about 720) and another series of verses, painted this time, on a vase from Ithaka (c. 700).[18] Striking as it is to find hexameter verse so prominent among early Greek alphabetic inscriptions, the hard fact is that none of them is actually a quotation from the *Iliad* or *Odyssey*. The reference to Nestor's cup in the Ischian inscription, incised probably by a Euboean on a Rhodian cup, may but need not imply familiarity with *Iliad* 11.632f. These inscriptions at least do not discourage the belief that non-Homeric epic could have been in the process of composition in Attica, Ithaka and the Western colonies during the second half of the eighth century.

But it is to the painted scenes on vases that I wish finally to return, encouraged by the external evidence which we have reviewed so far. We have found that interest in the heroic age in eighth-century Greece was sufficiently widespread to lead to the strange, pseudo-archaeological practice of unearthing purported heroic graves and honouring them with sacrifice, together with rarer manifestations such as inscribing verses with the names of heroic figures or even (in Ionia at least) calling royal children by such names as Hektor and Agamemnon.[19] Secondly, since vase-painters show a similar interest in heroic subjects from about 700 BC onwards, we may expect them to show it before 700 as well unless there are express grounds for thinking otherwise. Thirdly, since even in the seventh century, when the *Iliad* at least must be known, Greek artists show a curious disinclination to take their subjects directly from the two Homeric poems, there is no reason whatever to expect them to depend on Homer in the eighth century. Instead, there is reason to look for non-Homeric epic as a focus of public interest at this time, and to suggest that influences could also have existed outside the sphere of poetry altogether. These are all inferences from the external evidence: can we add anything from the internal evidence of the vases themselves?

I am not going to embark on a laborious series of analyses of single pictures; it is more profitable to select the widespread, or at least repeated, subjects in Geometric vase-painting. The obvious theme to begin with is the apparent 'Siamese twin' picture, which occurs no less than ten times on seven separate works of Geometric art, as well as on one slightly later one. Fittschen in his treatment is inclined to accept only three or five of the latest examples as genuine portrayals of Siamese twins;[20] and there is an intimidating range of arguments, brought forward by him and the other sceptics, against accepting the earlier pictures as representing the mythological pair of Siamese twins, the sons of Aktor. It is argued that these pictures merely embody a device for representing two warriors standing close together, on the analogy of the portrayals of horses in which, when short of space, the Geometric painters drew a single body with eight legs and two heads; that, since the double figures occur more than once in the same scene, they cannot be individualised; that no surviving work of art from later times can be shown to represent the sons of Aktor; that the two Homeric episodes involving Nestor and the twins are brief and obscure, and make no very explicit reference to the twins' deformity anyway, so that they would make an unlikely inspiration for the artist; and finally that old favourite, awkwardly combined with the preceding argument, that the hypothetical diffusion of the Homeric epic around 700 BC would explain neatly why a piece of Geometric iconographical shorthand, with two figures shown overlapping, should have been transformed into a handy means of portraying a case of legendary deformity.

I hope I have said enough to show that I consider the last two arguments almost entirely worthless. Nearly twenty years ago, my predecessor Robert Cook wrote of those who looked for connections between Homer and Geometric vase-scenes: 'Curiously, they rarely or never test their assumptions on Hesiod'.[21] This is an entirely fair criticism, and I should like to make an overdue attempt to meet it, though hardly in the way in which it was intended. It had long been known from later references that Hesiod had somewhere made mention of the twin sons of Aktor, and in terms which somehow implied the nature of their deformity. But recently Merkelbach and West published for the first time a fragment of a papyrus preserving part of the passage in question;[22] fragmentary as the text is, it is clearly describing the twins as having two heads, four legs and four arms, springing from a joined body. I am rather impressed by this evidence. If a Boeotian poet exhibits such detailed anatomical interest in a legendary being, then this surely constitutes evidence for the intentions of the artists, mostly Attic and Boeotian, who at the same period represents what looks like a similar being? Am I therefore simply substituting Hesiod

for Homer as the literary inspiration for contemporary artists? By no
means; it is much more likely that a common earlier source, perhaps
in vernacular mythology, lies behind the two different manifestations.
The sons of Aktor, we may note, were finally confronted and killed by
Herakles; Fittschen points out that, in one of the three latest pictures
where the intention to portray Siamese twins is unquestioned, their
opponent carries a quiver, which would be appropriate for Herakles
but not for Nestor.[23] Maybe all three of these pictures show Herakles,
thus again detaching them from Homeric influence. As for the earlier
pictures, one of them, an Attic jug of around 730 BC, already shows
a tell-tale detail: the helmet-crests are joined together at the back, an
ingenious way of indicating Siamese twins when the more obvious
signs of deformity were covered by a shield.[24] The only obstacle to
accepting this explanation of all the early representations is that of
logical consistency, namely that the double figure is portrayed more
than once in the same scene; but this is an argument of limited validity for Geometric art (see below, p. 377). Since the earliest picture
of a double figure belongs at the very beginning of Geometric figure-
painting, probably before 750 BC, the implications are important; it
looks as if this is a mythological subject present in the artists' minds
from the start.

It is nevertheless true that many specialists reject, root and branch,
the notion of eighth-century mythological representations. They
maintain that these scenes are generic in kind and derived from contemporary life: the funerals are eighth-century funerals, the battles
eighth-century battles, the narrative content (such as it is) of eighth-
century biographical intention. It is this last issue which is really fundamental: if the narrative content is severely limited or non-existent,
does this exclude the possibility of mythological subject-matter? I
would argue that, once we forget about Homer and do not even insist on any necessarily poetic inspiration, we are no longer bound to
expect the portrayal of unique events or the narration of immediately
recognisable stories; we can look rather for a generally heroic *am-
biance*. Once again, in seventh- and sixth-century art there are numerous examples of scenes which have no specific narrative content, but
are nevertheless unmistakably heroic in setting.[25] If the analogy holds
here, then it can be extended so as to allow us to expect the occasional
case of a portrayal of a myth unknown to us from literary sources.

With this much wider brief, we can look at Geometric vase-
paintings with a view, not so much to identification as to classification; we can search them, not for unique elements but for generic

signals which might have conveyed their heroic import, at least to contemporaries. This would be an easier task if only we knew more of what life and death in the eighth century were like. We have, for example, several hundred Athenian graves of this period, almost all of them very modest in their construction and other appointments; we have also about fifty Athenian Geometric funerary vases of the same date, showing an elaborate ritual with mourners and warriors massed round the corpse as it lies in state, often associated with a procession of chariots, and sometimes with funerary games as well.[26] In the literary sources, such accompaniments appear only in heroic or in aristocratic funerals; yet the vases appear in about 10 per cent of all Attic burials of the period. Is it possible that, in eighth-century Athens, such majestic overtures regularly led to such modest conclusions? It seems more likely that, to say the least, a degree of glorification, of 'projection', is taking place. If the chariots are shown in battle (as they rarely are) then we can speak a shade more strongly, and say that this feature was more probably strange to, rather than a mere glorification of, eighth-century military reality.

When the scenes include the exotic 'Dipylon' type of shield, then we come to grips with an argument which has been sustained for the past twenty-five years, since Webster first argued that this shape of shield was itself used by the Geometric artists (as is was, in a slightly different form, by their successors) as a sort of 'heroic prop'. In terms of numbers, at any rate, the sceptics have had much the better of the debate,[27] realising as they do that this shield-form is so frequent in the pictures that to concede its heroic status would be to yield virtually the whole battlefield to their opponents.[28] They argue, rightly, that the shield is not consistently used by the artists, who show it in the same scene with perfectly acceptable eighth-century shapes such as the circular. But it would be easy to show that such internal consistency is not really a quality of the Geometric vase-painters, who are happy to show a profile view of a four-legged bier (that is, with only two legs showing), alongside a horse portrayed with all four legs, or both wheels of what is usually taken to be a two-wheeled chariot.[29] Decorative variety was, for them, at least as constant an ideal; which is incidentally why I think they felt free to include more than one Siamese-twin figure in the same scene (above, p. 376), another instance where the argument from consistency has been used to refute a heroic interpretation.

I have tried elsewhere to give a more detailed answer to this and others of the sceptics' arguments on the 'Dipylon' shield,[30] and do not wish to dwell on the question here. There are, however, two relatively fresh arguments with which the sceptics will have to reckon, and perhaps I may summarily refer to them. First, we know that a shape of shield almost identical to that of the 'Dipylon' type was shown in Mycenaean art of the fourteenth and thirteenth centuries BC so that, if this form really did exist in the eighth century, it was at least 500 years old.[31] Which is more likely, unchanged survival (with no supporting evidence from the intervening centuries), or a purely artistic revival in the eighth century? Secondly, there is a strange contemporary work from Cyprus, by an artist of the day who so far misunderstood the 'Dipylon' shield as not to realise that it was a shield at all. Cyprus had some direct contact with Attica at this time, and a shared concern with the heroic past; this artist clearly did not understand Geometric art, but could he really have been so ignorant of Geometric life? Even on the mainland of Greece, there are representations from this period which betray a suspiciously defective understanding of this shield.[32]

I am sure that sufficient ingenuity exists to counter these new arguments, as happened with those originally advanced by Webster. But I would argue that it is simpler and more sensible to admit that these figure-scenes are somewhat hard to reconcile with what we know of the realities of eighth-century life; and that they may therefore represent something else. Part of the reluctance to accept this is, I think, an unwillingness to give up so much precious contemporary evidence for the life and thought of the period. But we would not really be giving it up at all: on the contrary, it would be telling us that eighth-century Athenians were like most other people, in being much preoccupied with what social scientists call projective systems. Professor Colin Renfrew once aptly quoted Eliot's

> human kind
> Cannot bear very much reality.[33]

I suggest that Geometric vase-painting, re-interpreted in this way, could prove a surprisingly rich source of understanding.

In particular, I have submitted some evidence that the painter and the poet were and are independent types of creative artists, with different sources, different interests, different techniques. Practitioners of the visual arts, throughout history, have looked at literature less often than they have drawn on their own perceptions and experience, or studied the work of earlier artists in their own field. When King George I, in his only well-known utterance, said 'I hate all Boets and Bainters', his implication that they were two indistinguishable categories was nearly as objectionable as his tastes. The status of the vase-painter may not have been high in antiquity, but this need not have made him dependent on the poets; it is more likely to have distanced him from them. Among Classicists, with their inborn reverence for ancient literature, such a conclusion may rank as unorthodox; but in many disciplines I think it would be regarded as almost self-evident.

NOTES

1. For example, K. Schefold, *Myth and legend in early Greek art* (1966) (original German edition 1964) 21–8; B. Schweitzer, *Greek Geometric art* (1971) (original German edition 1969) 56–7.
2. For example, N. Himmelmann-Wildschütz, 'Erzählung und Figur in der archäischen Kunst', *AAWM* 1967, 2, 73–101, esp. 83, 87; K. Fittschen, *Untersuchungen zum Beginn der Sagendarstellungen bei den Griechen* (1969); J. M. Carter, 'The beginnings of narrative art in the Greek Geometric period', *ABSA* 67 (1972) 25–58, esp. 38–9.
3. *ABSA* 50 (1955) 38–50.
4. J. N. Coldstream, *Geometric Greece* (1977) 113, fig. 33b; quotation, *Gnomon* 46 (1974) 395.
5. Two famous vases in the Vatican will serve as examples of each: respectively, the red-figure cup showing Jason disgorged by the dragon, J. D. Beazley, *ARV* ed. 2 (1963) 437. 116; and the black-figure amphora with Achilles and Ajax playing dice, Beazley, *ABV* (1956) 145–13.
6. G. S. Kirk, *Myth, its meaning and functions in ancient and other cultures* (1970) 238–41; cf. id. *The nature of Greek myths* (1974) 97–8.
7. The count is rendered approximate by the need to estimate the degree of conviction on the author's part. But rightly or wrongly I have included Fittschen's M 4, 7–8 (pp. 68–75); L 32–3, 42 (76–88); SB 1–18 (111–28, esp. 126); GS 1 (129–31); SB 27–31, 35 (147–50); SB 39–44 (152–7); SB 55–7 (157–61); SB 63–5 (166–8); SB 72, 74, 80, 82–3, 88–90, 93–4, 98–107, 111–13, 115 (169–94); SB 118 (197–8). One might add that, even if one extended the period down to as late as 600, Fittschen's lists make clear that the strictly 'Homeric' scenes would still account for no more than 10% of the total.
8. These are SB 72, 83, 88–90, 93–4, 98–107.
9. 'The Epic Cycle and the uniqueness of Homer', *JHS* 98 (1978) 38–53, esp. n. 9
10. Cf. Kirk, *The nature of Greek myth* 180, 182.
11. Discussed by Kirk, *The songs of Homer* (1962) 326–8, 348.
12. I am referring to Fittschen's (n. 2) M 4 and M 8 (pp. 72, 75).
13. The evidence is assembled most accessibly in V. Karageorghis, *Salamis in Cyprus, Homeric, Hellenistic and Roman* (1969) 26–8, 31–2, 70–2, 92, 94.

14. I am most grateful to Mr. A. F. Garvie of the University of Glasgow for first pointing this out to me; discussions can be found in K. Reinhardt, *Die Ilias und ihr Dichter* (1961) 349–77; and more briefly M. M. Willcock, 'The funeral games of Patroclus', *BICS* 20 (1973) 1–11, esp. 5.

15. See J. N. Coldstream, 'Hero-cults in the age of Homer', *JHS* 96 (1976) 8–17; 10 for the anonymous inscription.

16. See respectively J. M. Cook, 'Mycenae 1939–52: Part III. The Agamemnoneion', *ABSA* 48 (1953) 30–68; H. W. Catling in *AR* 22 (1975–6) 14; 23 (1976–7) 35–42; J. Papadimitriou, 'Anaskaphai en Braurôni', *PAAH* 1955, 119; 1956, 76–7; 1957, 44–5; Ch. Picard, 'L'hérôon de Phrontis au Sunion', *RA* (6ᵉ série) 16 (juillet–septembre 1940) 5–28.

17. Hesiod, *The Works and Days*, ed. M. L. West (1977), Excursus I, 370–3; cf. 186 *ad* 1. 141.

18. See L. H. Jeffery, *The local scripts of Archaic Greece* (1961) 68, 76 no. 1; 235–6, 239, no.1; and 230, 233, no.1, respectively.

19. Cf. T. B. L. Webster, *From Mycenae to Homer* (1958) 145, 152.

20. Fittschen (n.2) 75, M 4, 7–8 and more vaguely M 5–6. His 71, n.375 gives useful references to earlier sceptical views.

21. R.M. Cook, *The Greeks till Alexander* (1961) 48.

22. *Fragmenta Hesiodea*, edd. R. Merkelbach and M.L. West (1967), fr. 17(a).

23. Fittschen (n. 2) 72 on M 7.

24. Uncharacteristically, Fittschen (n.2) 68, 70 on M 2 misses this vital detail.

25. A classic example would be the dinos Acropolis 606 (Beazley *ABV* 81.1 and *The development of Attic black-figure* (1951) pl. 13, 1–2).

26. See G. Ahlberg, *Prothesis and ekphora in Greek Geometric art* (1971).

27. Fittschen (n. 2) 36–9 marshals their arguments with typical clarity.

28. Compare Ahlberg's candid remark in her *Fighting on land and sea in Greek Geometric art* (1971) 65.

29. See, for example, the krater fragment Paris A 517: Coldstream (n. 4) 110, fig. 33a; Schweitzer (n. 1) pl. 36.

30. To appear in *MDAI(A)* 95 (1980).

31. See P. Cassola Guida, *Le arme difensive dei Micenei nelle figurazioni* (*Incunabula Graeca* 56, 1974) 38–44.

32. Cypriot bowl, Otterlo inv. 50V: see most recently M. van Vloten and A. N. Zadoks-Josephus-Jitta in *BABesch* 48 (1973) 101, where possible but less obvious analogies in mainland Greek Geometric vase-painting are mentioned; V. Karageorghis and J. des Gagniers, *La céramique chypriote de style figuré: Âge du Fer* (1974) Texte, 27.

33. *Four quartets: Burnt Norton* 44–5.

CHAPTER 21

Narration and Allusion in Archaic Greek Art

This, the Eleventh J. L. Myres Memorial Lecture, intermittently makes contact with the work of that scholar, who had shown some interest in the narrative techniques of artists from the Aegean Bronze Age onwards.

Here again, this is an early encounter with problems to which I have returned later and in greater detail (e.g. in Snodgrass 1998: 57–66). But here too potential tension arises with Giuliani's views (Giuliani 2003, above, p. 365), when towards the end of the paper I develop the insights of Nikolaus Himmelmann and others into the depiction of the passage of time in Geometric vase-scenes (pp. 395–403 below). This is still compatible with the undoubtedly valid conclusion (Giuliani: 77) that 'Geometric vase-paintings reflect the cognitive common ground. They show the world as it is, or better, as we want to see it and believe that we know it to be'; but it can hardly be reconciled with the view (Giuliani: 160) that the stereotypical form of the Geometric figures precludes their involvement in temporal sequences. This last became a problem that attracted the concern of later Greek artists for generations on end: that the Geometric painters should have been the first to grapple with it is, to me, not only credible, but something readily paralleled in many another feature of early Greek culture. This, however, is far from being a conclusive argument.

BIBLIOGRAPHY

Giuliani, L. (2003), *Bild und Mythos*, Munich: C. H. Beck.
Snodgrass, A. (1998), *Homer and the Artists*, Cambridge: Cambridge University Press.

A recurrent theme of Sir John Myres' writings was the extended analogy between poetry and the visual arts. In describing painting and other visual media, we all tend to use words which in their strict and original sense are applied to the spoken or written word: terms like the 'narration' and 'allusion' in my title, 'reading', 'episode' or even 'syntax'. Myres was not afraid to reverse the process too, and to write of 'frieze-composition' in Homer, and of 'economy of essential figures' in Homeric similes. He was in fact one of the few writers in English who have ventured into the narrative methods of ancient artists, a province which has generally been the preserve of German scholars. This year indeed marks the exact centenary of the publication of Carl Robert's *Bild und Lied*, on which all subsequent studies have built, from those of Robert's younger Viennese contemporary Franz Wickhoff down to our own times, when the subject has been taken up in a series of penetrating studies by Professor Nikolaus Himmelmann-Wildschütz, and in the writings of other scholars like Hans von Steuben, Frank Brommer and Irmgard Raab.[1]

The story can however be traced back much more than a hundred years, and to no less a figure than Goethe. In a letter of 27th February 1789 to his friend Heinrich Meyer, Goethe wrote words of such truth and relevance that they can serve as an ideal text for what I have to say today:

> 'Die Alten sahen das Bild als ein ab- und eingeschloss'nes Ganze an, sie wollten in dem Raume alles zeigen, man sollte sich nicht etwa bey dem Bild denken, sondern man sollte das Bild denken und in demselben alles sehen. Sie rückten die verschiedenen Epochen des Gedichtes, der Tradition zusammen und stellten uns auf diese Weise die Succession vor Augen, denn unsere leiblichen Augen sollen das Bild sehen und geniessen.'[2]

> 'The ancients saw a picture as an enclosed and separate whole; they wanted to show everything within the given space; one was not to think something about the picture, one was to *think the picture* and see everything in it. By putting together the various stages of the poem and of the tradition, they set the sequence before our eyes; for our bodily eyes are to see the picture and enjoy it.'

In writing thus about 'the ancients', Goethe of course had access to only a small fraction of the evidence which exists today; yet it proves the essential rightness of his claim. What he and Meyer were

Narration and Allusion in Archaic Greek Art. Eleventh J. L. Myres Memorial Lecture, New College Oxford, 29 May 1981, London: Leopard's Head Press [21 pp.].

directly concerned with was a work of Annibale Carracci: the *Ulysses and Circe*, one of the series of mythological frescoes painted between 1595 and 1597 in the lunette fields of the ceiling of the Camerino of the Farnese Palace.[3] It shows Circe handing the magic potion to Ulysses, intercepted by Mercury who reaches up in the nick of time to put the equally magic antidote, the *moly*, in the cup. Goethe knew, and credited Carracci with knowing, that in Homer the god had given the *moly* to Odysseus much earlier. He therefore understood the painter to be including this episode as a kind of explanatory feature, in defiance of time. Whether Goethe was right or not in his assumptions, it is surely true that a less learned spectator could read Carracci's picture in a more literal sense: Mercury has only a moment in which to act, and presumably is using his supernatural faculty of invisibility (and perhaps of flight as well), to do so *now*. This kind of ambivalence, between knowledgeable allusion on the one hand and literal simultaneity on the other, will often occur in the works of Archaic Greek art to which I now turn. But in many cases it becomes clear that early Greek artists included in their pictures allusions to events which, in any version of a story, must take place at different points in the narrative, whether earlier or later. Goethe's generalisation was right. Carracci's picture presents a further feature which we shall see again before long: the form of metamorphosis which the bewitched sailor of Ulysses, shown reclining in the lower right-hand corner, has undergone. His head has become that of a wild boar, but his body remains human. There is no authority in Homer for this variant, and its appearance here raises those intriguing problems of the antique sources on which Renaissance and Baroque artists drew, for which I believe that Carracci provides a rich field.

Modern authorities, in describing the various methods which Archaic Greek artists used for representing narrative, differ sharply from each other not only in their terminology but also, more important, in their assessments of the relative significance and temporal sequence of development of the different methods. I will not burden you with an attempt to form a concordance of their terms; suffice to say that there appear to be four main methods by which an Archaic artist conveys a story. First, there is the 'monoscenic' method in which one essential and dramatic moment is portrayed. Secondly, there is what I prefer to call the 'synoptic' method, the one to which Goethe referred and on which I shall be concentrating today: in this, the artist includes within a single picture two or more successive episodes in a story, but without repeating any individual figure. Thirdly, there is the 'cyclic'

Figure 21.1

method, in which the story is broken up into a number of separate scenes with the figure of the protagonist, and sometimes other figures too, appearing in each. This method seems to appear later than the first two, and is particularly appropriate to a series of separate panels like the sculptured metopes of the Doric frieze. Fourthly, there is the closely-related and even later 'continuous' method, in which a series of scenes with a repeated figure or figures is again used, but this time without any explicit division of the picture into separate panels or units. Since Wickhoff, we have associated this last method inseparably with Roman art; but the third, 'cyclic' method, or something almost indistinguishable from it, is found on a few late Archaic and Classical vase-paintings of the deeds of Theseus (Figure 21.1 shows an example).'[4]

But the most complex, the most interesting and I think the most important of methods listed above is the second, the 'synoptic'. As it happens, the picture always chosen to express its very quintessence is an Attic black-figured cup (Figure 21.2) of about 550 BC whose subject is the very same that we found handled by Annibale Carracci: Circe

Figure 21.2 Photograph © 1981 Museum of Fine Arts, Boston

and Odysseus.[5] In the centre, Circe hands the magic potion in a cup to one of the sailors, stirring it with her other hand as she does so. Yet he, together with three of his companions, has already been transformed into an animal as far as his head is concerned (and the others in respect of their arms too). So far, then, we have two manifestly successive episodes represented in a way which we today would understand as meaning that they were simultaneous. But then when we look at the right-hand end of the picture, a third phase is shown: Eurylochos, the sailor who in the *Odyssey* lurks suspiciously outside Circe's house and runs away to give the alarm to Odysseus, is shown doing just that. And finally, towards the left-hand side Odysseus himself is shown, in an episode which must of course follow later still, advancing with a drawn sword with which he will threaten Circe into reversing the transformation of his men. Thus the picture embraces four episodes, of which (2) must be later in time than (1), and (4) than (3), while (3) is also best understood as following (2). Before we leave this vase, I hope that I may be forgiven for suggesting, in the most tentative way, that there may possibly be an allusion to yet another episode in the story, as told by Homer. Circe is altogether exceptional for a woman in an Archaic mythical picture in being shown nude, and in the striding posture of a male *kouros*. The experts explain this as a reference to her supernatural powers, a 'hieroglyphic' or 'hieratic' expression of the sorceress' attributes. But could it not rather refer to the very next episode in the *Odyssey* version, the erotic interlude which follows Odysseus' arrival on the scene? If so, I admit that it would conflict with certain other features of this and other vase-paintings: features which underline the *independence* of the painting from Homeric, or other literary, versions of the story.

The first warning sign of a departure from the *Odyssey* version of this story is the nature of the transformation of the sailors: in Homer they simply become pigs (though the 'crowd of lions and wolves' around Circe's house represent earlier victims of her spells). For this artist, they remain at least three-quarters human in form, and three of them have acquired the heads, not of pigs but of a lion, a horse and a ram respectively. The reason is surely iconographic: either the artist (like most of his successors who showed this subject) wanted a composition of upright figures, not grovelling animals, and also welcomed the variety which the different animal types offered; or, more sophisticatedly, he wished to express the passage of time by indicating a half-way stage in the transformation. This last explanation is not fully compatible with the 'synoptic' method as outlined above, since it would involve representing different individuals at the *same* moment of time; yet the fact that the other sailors have animals' forelegs, while the latest victim still has human arms, tells in favour of it. For one further insight into this remarkable picture, I am indebted to a singularly appropriate source: it was Sir Michael Weir, our Ambassador in Cairo, who suggested to me at a lecture in Nicosia in March 1980 that the painter's vision of the metamorphosis might owe something to the figures of Anubis, Horus and other animal-headed deities in Egyptian art. The date is highly plausible for Egyptian influence on Greek vase-painters, as has been shown in a number of parallel cases by Professor John Boardman.[6]

The Boston Circe cup, in short, is an outstanding example of the synoptic method, representing it in an elaborate form, with the main outlines quite unambiguous, but with other, subtler nuances that we cannot be sure of taking correctly. It shows familiarity with the *Odyssey*, yet paradoxically at the same time declares its independence of literary influence; this independence is shown, not merely by the artistic considerations mentioned in the last paragraph, but more fundamentally as well. No poet or writer could really use the synoptic method as practised here; the words must follow each other, on the page or on the lips of the rhapsode; and when a writer adopts (as Homer does) the technique of the 'flashback', or the portentous allusion to a character's future fate, he does so explicitly, at least in ancient literature. It is surely clear that the synoptic technique was evolved by the practitioners of the visual arts, for a public who could either be educated to understand it, or else do so instinctively.

I should now like to consider a series of questions about this method of narration, which arise from the acceptance of its independent quality. First, how prevalent in early Greek art was this synoptic technique? Next, how far is it to be regarded as a sophisticated, or alternatively as a naive, method intellectually? How far back in time, from the date of the Circe cup, can its pedigree be followed? And finally, in what circumstances is the method likely to have first evolved?

The first question about the relative frequency of this method of narration might seem to involve a simple matter of fact; yet recent authorities, partly because they turn out to be using different terminologies, have given startlingly different answers to it. My own finding is that, given certain clear external limitations on its use, the synoptic method is employed very frequently indeed: almost as frequently as the subject-matter allows, at least until the middle and later Archaic period. To put it negatively, when the synoptic method is *not* used, this is almost always because the story chosen simply does not offer scope for the portrayal of successive episodes within one picture. Some of the Greek myths most favoured by the artists are ones in which there really *is* only one episode worth showing. To take their favourite single character, Herakles: several of his deeds involve merely the killing or capture of a supernatural or animal adversary: he killed or captured them and that is all there is to be said. The artist will show him doing so in a single scene, not because he has suddenly grasped the principle of the 'monoscenic' picture with its single moment of time, but because that is the most obvious way of doing it.

Where the artist wished to show his hero involved in a more complex sequence of expedients, the rules of the synoptic method imposed a constraint of their own; for they prescribe that he can only show the protagonist (or anyone else) *once* in the picture. He could show four episodes in the Circe picture simply because each of them involved a different agent or subject: it was *Circe* who mixed the drink, *the sailors* who were transformed, *Eurylochos* who gave the alarm and *Odysseus* who came to the rescue. Even if I am right to see an allusion to a fifth episode, in which Circe seduces Odysseus, this episode is not 'narrated' but simply alluded to by Circe's nudity. Allusion of this kind can be seen, if one looks for it, in many other pictures. What can the artist do if his subject is, say, Herakles and the Nemean Lion, and he wants to convey the tradition that Herakles tried in vain to pierce the lion's invulnerable hide with one weapon or another, before resorting to throttling it? The answer is that he often does quite a lot: he frequently shows Herakles' quiver hanging on a tree in the background, Herakles' club being held by Iolaos, and once even Herakles' bent

Figure 21.3

sword lying below the struggling group of hero and animal (Figure 21.3):[7] all of these are surely meant as allusions to the earlier stages of the fight. Once we are prepared to accept this kind of allusion as a substitute for the actual depiction of earlier or later episodes, then we can recognise numerous other pictures as being 'synoptic' by extension. The story of the Birth of Athena, for example, contains at most two central episodes: Hephaistos cleft Zeus' skull with his axe, and the fully-armed Athena emerged from her father's head. To show both events actually happening at once would hardly have made an intelligible picture, so the artists do the next best thing (Figure 21.4): they show Hephaistos standing by, or walking away, with his axe, and Athena emerging.[8]

If we grant that these pictures give at least a hint of the 'synoptic mentality', then we may detect it, as Himmelmann notably has, in a whole series of scenes which could be, and have been, quite differently interpreted as aberrations, curious or macabre, on the part of artists who deviated from the literary version of their story. Several vase-paintings of the sack of Troy, for example, show Neoptolemos combining the two deeds of brutality which he performed on that occasion: he uses the body of Astyanax as a weapon with which to strike down the aged Priam or, in an even more grisly way, employs

Figure 21.4

Astyanax's head as a missile.[9] It is most unlikely that the artists knew
of some lost literary version in which this gratuitous and barbaric
gloss was put on to the traditional account, or that they consciously
devised such an alternative for themselves. If we accept that their
innate desire was, as Goethe said, to compress as much as possible
into the one space, then this on its own will suffice as an explanation. Likewise, the equally numerous pictures of Priam's earlier visit
to Achilles' tent, which show Achilles dining with his enemy's corpse
lying under the couch, are making reference – allusive rather than

narrative this time – to the purpose of Priam's visit and the status of Achilles as Hektor's conqueror. There is still, perhaps, an element of doubt about interpretations like this: the pictures *are* ambiguous and, as with a problematic text, one searches for the interpretation that will yield the best sense. Fortunately, however, one can also point to a number of scenes which are synoptic in a quite unproblematic way.

They are found not only in Athenian art, but in that of Corinth, Lakonia, the Cyclades and the western colonies; they occur not only in vase-painting, but earliest and most frequently in that medium, a point to whose significance we shall return at the end. Between the beginning of the seventh century BC and the later part of the sixth, the synoptic method is used (or so I would argue) whenever the story chosen is sufficiently episodic, or involves a sufficient number of participants, to allow of it. One story which gave an early opportunity was the blinding of Polyphemos: our earliest picture, on the famous Eleusis emphora, already shows Polyphemos holding the cup which will lead to the drunkenness which will bring on the sleep which will give Odysseus the chance to blind him – as he is simultaneously shown doing. A Laconian cup-painter, over a century later, goes a step further and introduces the stage before the drinking of the cup – the horrific devouring of the sailors whose dismembered limbs Polyphemos clutches – as well as the cup itself and the blinding (Figure 21.5).[10] If we return to the early Archaic period and move to the Cyclades, we find the amusing scene on the relief-pithos from Mykonos, where the Greek heroes debouch from a Trojan Horse which is helpfully (if improbably) equipped with windows, through which arms are being passed out; yet one of them has taken up a posture of combat and some have seen, in the figures coming up from the sides, their Trojan opponents.[11] Even a single figure can be synoptically shown, as we see from the numerous pictures of the Medusa which show her with her head firmly on her shoulders, yet already clutching Pegasos or Chrysaor (or both), the offspring who in the legend emerged from her decapitated trunk when Perseus killed her.[12] Another story which later became popular was the episode of Achilles and Troilos at Troy: on the François Vase of about 570 BC we see not only Polyxena and Troilos pursued by Achilles, but Antenor reporting the disaster to Priam and Hektor and Polites sallying forth from the gate of Troy in response: not to mention allusions to past and future implications, represented by the watching deities and the fountain-house where the ambush is laid.[13] Another well-known example is the slightly later

Figure 21.5

Corinthian vase with the departure of Amphiaraos, in which allusions to past and future episodes (the necklace of Eriphyle, the hero's drawn sword, the seer's despair) are piled on to a central episode which itself turns out to be split into temporally incompatible phases (the charioteer's drink and the horses already at the trot).[14] A contemporary Lakonian dinos carries a remarkable scene of Herakles, Pholos and the other Centaurs on Mt. Pholoë, where we are at a loss to say where the artist (as I think likely) is making an unusually bold use of the synoptic method, or whether once again he has in mind some unknown and illogical aberration from the accepted version of the story. In the latter, Herakles meet Pholos and is hospitably received by him, only for the smell of the wine to stampede the other, less civilised Centaurs with whom Herakles then fights. Yet here (Figure 21.6) the Centaurs are shown in disarray, wounded or in flight, while Herakles is only just greeting Pholos in the centre of the composition.[15] As on the Circe cup, so here it seems simplest to read the events on either side as set in the future, relative to the central group. Finally, to show that even

Figure 21.6

an uneventful scene can generate the use of the synoptic method, we may turn to an Attic plate by Lydos where Achilles is shown arming, in the presence of his parents and apparently on his departure for the Trojan War; yet beside the fourth figure, a grown man on the right-hand side, there is inscribed the name of Neoptolemos, who at this point should be no more than a child.[16] The painter, once again, has defied time, perhaps because he wanted to show three generations of heroes in their prime.

I hope that I have now given enough examples to show that the method called 'synoptic' is widespread and deeply-rooted in the mentality of the early Greek artist. If I have laboured the point, it is because this feature is so very easy to miss in a casual glance: I suspect that today most of us, most of the time, look at these works without realising that they conflict with our own notions of pictorial time. Partly, no doubt, this is because we are less than closely familiar with the stories that form their subjects; partly, too, because our own preconceptions, nourished by two and a half millennia of later art and then strongly reinforced by the invention of photography, have disposed

Figure 21.7

us automatically to reinterpret the scenes as showing momentary and simultaneous actions; for often, as we have seen, there is no very obvious difficulty in doing so. I must also concede that there are some early works of Greek art which do demand this interpretation, and which thereby embody the very different and more modern-seeming notion of 'photographic' representation. We shall come to the very earliest instances in a moment; but even as late as the first half of the fifth century, contemporary Greeks may have found it a striking *tour de force* when the sculptors of the East Pediment of the Temple of Aphaia at Aigina portrayed figures in the act of falling over backwards (Figure 21.7), or when the Niobid Painter introduced into an Amazonomachy picture the motif of a sword in mid-air, falling from the hand of a wounded Amazon.[17] These are perhaps experiments in a direction that was about to be more thoroughly explored by others: it is with the Eleatic school of philosophy of the mid-fifth century, and above all with Zeno, that we associate the systematic attention to problems of space and time.

The majority of the 'monoscenic' pictures, in my view, are not to be judged in the same way. They are monoscenic not from the deliberate intention to confine the representation to a single moment in the chosen story, but from the fortuitous choice of a subject whose narrative did not involve any substantial lapse of time, or which contained only one episode of interest to the artist. How then are we to judge the intellectual quality of the 'synoptic' method as against the equally common 'monoscenic' one? We must at all costs avoid anachronistic modern conceptions. Franz Wickhoff had a different name for the method that I have been calling 'synoptic', and this betokened his very different understanding of it. He used the term 'komplettierend', and persuaded even Carl Robert to follow him in this usage in his later writing on the subject. This term implies that such scenes are built round a central moment or episode, to which the subsidiary actions are then added to 'complete' the presentation of the story. It was Himmelmann who eventually pointed out the serious objections to this view.[18] There are, as he showed, a number of scenes like that on the Circe cup where we should be hard put to it to say which is the original, central moment and which are the subsidiary, 'komplettierende' elements. In others, like the Lakonian dinos mentioned just now (Figure 21.6), there is no doubt which is compositionally the central episode, but it is highly questionable whether the more exciting scenes on either side are added merely to fill out the story. Himmelmann's point becomes critically important once we consider the psychological background of the artists' choice of methods. Wickhoff's theory of the 'komplettierend' composition presupposes an evolution from a 'natural' notion of a single, momentary action to the 'completion' of it by the addition of other episodes. It thus imposes on the Archaic artist what may be an anachronistic idea of what is 'natural'; and it begs the whole question of how the second, more 'developed' notion evolved. Once we abandon the preconception that temporal simultaneity within the spatial frame of a single picture is the 'natural' thing, I think we shall find that a very different sequence of development will emerge from the evidence. So far from being a sophisticated elaboration of an original, naive conception, the synoptic method in my view grew up independently and more or less contemporaneously alongside the monoscenic one, as a result not of increasing sophistication, but of the demands of a different kind of subject-matter.

This brings us to our next question: the date at which the synoptic concept arose. I shall be using, in what follows, a wider definition of the term 'narrative' than would be accepted by some authorities (such as, most recently, Meyboom).[19] There is a sense of the word 'narrative' which covers every scene in which even one distinctive action is shown, whether that action is taken from a recognised legend or from the ordinary experience of contemporary life; so that an instance of the synoptic method can in principle occur whenever two or more distinctive actions of *any* kind are represented in a single picture. This is the sense in which I shall be using the term 'narrative' and, in approaching the field of Greek Geometric art as I now do, it enables me to avoid the vexed question of whether or not mythological scenes are present in Geometric art and indeed whether, on some stricter definition of the term, their content could be called 'narrative' at all.

Himmelmann concludes that the method which I am calling 'synoptic' was an original discovery of the early Greeks; my own, doubtless much more cursory examination of the evidence has given no ground for disagreeing with him. Oriental art seems to offer no true forerunners;[20] nor does the art of the Aegean Bronze Age, though Myres himself argued persuasively for the use here of a very different concept, one more akin to the 'continuous' method mentioned at the beginning.[21] In the famous Toreador Fresco from Knossos, he claimed, the positions of the performing acrobats can be 'read' as indicating the successive positions of a single figure; while the Lion Hunt dagger-blade from Mycenae can equally be understood as showing successive phases in one action. If we find no true precedent here for the synoptic method, we must revert to later Greek art; and it is reasonable to begin our search in the figure-scenes on Late Geometric vases, which offered the first real artistic opportunity after the Mycenaean period.

On the liberal interpretation of the term 'narrative' given above, we have simply to look for narrative depictions of action complex enough to involve a temporal succession of two or more episodes. The figures on Geometric vases exhibit some features which equip them very well for inclusion in a 'synoptic' picture. Himmelmann has shown the way here by observing[22] that they already have the quality that he calls 'hieroglyphic' – that is, they retain certain permanent attributes by which their status can be recognised (as a hieroglyph can), whether or not these attributes are relevant or suitable for the action that the figures are currently performing. In later art, this is exemplified by those depictions of the Judgment of Paris in which the hero, who according to the story is living incognito as a shepherd on Mount Ida, is nevertheless shown (Figure 21.8) regally accoutred and sceptred, because this is an essential and permanent attribute of a king's son;[23] a similar explanation was, as we saw, given by Himmelmann for the nudity of Circe on the Boston cup, though I have tentatively suggested an alternative one. But this 'hieroglyphic' quality is also entirely characteristic of the figures, human and even animal,

Figure 21.8

on Geometric vases: stationary male figures have lightly-bent knees
and striding legs to indicate their potential mobility; horses stand with
their rear hooves on tiptoe for the same reason; hunters and Centaurs
wear helmets to indicate their prowess as fighters. Another feature
of the Geometric scenes which is germane to the idea of synoptic
narrative is their awareness of pictorial space: as Irmgard Raab has
argued, it was in the Geometric period that the Greeks re-discovered
the idea of a clearly demarcated panel within which the artist suggests
the presence of a space which is not literally 'there'.[24] This device is a
necessary precondition for the use of the synoptic technique, and for
the spectator to be able to distinguish it from, say, the 'continuous'
method (at least with a style as austere and sparing of distinctive detail
as the Geometric). But does Geometric art show evidence of anything
beyond a general compatibility with the synoptic method?

The commonest theme in all Geometric figure-painting is the *prothesis*, the lying in state of the deceased with attendant mourners; often
this is combined with the depiction of a chariot-procession, whether
in the same frieze or panel, or in a separate one lower down the
vase. When, as in Figure 21.9, the two are combined in one zone, it
can be argued that a simple form of synoptic narrative is being attempted. For our knowledge of Greek funerary ritual, combined with
sheer common sense, tells us that the lying in state will have taken

Figure 21.9

place in the house of the deceased, or at least its courtyard, while
the chariot procession must be out of doors. Furthermore, the two
events are likely to have happened in succession rather than simultaneously, since otherwise the participants could not witness both. In
this observation I am again following Himmelmann, though he has
doubts, which I do not share, arising from the fact that the chariots
face the same way;[25] he sees this as a hint of the common and largely
decorative motif of a chariot-frieze running right round the vase. But
this painter has explicitly demarcated his picture, enclosing two of the
chariots, as well as the *prothesis*, with multiple vertical lines at the
sides; beyond these, the subject changes abruptly to one of naval warfare (though the chariot-procession is resumed in the frieze below).
I think that he meant us to see the central panel as a single, closed
composition.

But there are other pictures which give less grounds for doubt. One
may take, for instance, an oenochoë in the Louvre which has attracted
much interest since 1961, when K. Friis Johansen suggested that it was
a portrayal of the duel in book vii of the *Iliad*. It was Himmelmann,
yet again, who convinced learned opinion that this must be wrong,[26]
supplanting it with a more convincing if less exciting interpretation
of his own: that the scene represents the capture and disarming of
prisoners of war (Figure 21.10). Close examination shows that the
figures numbered 2, 4, 5, 8, 10 and 12 must be on one side, the

Figure 21.10

losing side. Yet 2, 5, 10 and 12 retain their shields, while 8 has lost his and is about to have his remaining weapons removed; 4 sinks to the ground in an apparently dying condition, which suggests that 7 and 14, who are already dead, may have been murdered after being disarmed, rather than killed in the preceding fight. Whether this last inference is justified or not, the whole picture is most easily understood as showing several successive stages in the operation, which is the essence of the synoptic method.

This vase, whose date is not much after 750 BC, is the earliest on which I have been able to find a likely instance of the application of the synoptic technique: it stands significantly close to the beginning of multiple-figure painting on Geometric vases. In the ensuing generation, the idea seems to become more widespread. On an oenochoë in Tübingen (Figure 21.11), some of the dancers are shown with their linked hands raised above their heads, some with their hands down; Renate Tölle has observed that it is far more likely that the form of dance required *everyone* to raise their hands and lower them alternately, than that some would have their hands up while others had theirs down.[27] In a small-scale way, then, this picture too would seem to incorporate a temporal succession within itself. Again, I choose one of the many Geometric war-scenes, on an oenochoë in Copenhagen (Figure 21.12):[28] a warrior falls, pierced by arrows, while an enemy archer stands by him, holding his bow and arrow ready-drawn, at

Figure 21.11 Raab (above, n.1), 99.

point-blank range. The painter is surely saying that this is the archer who fired the fatal arrows, not that he is in the act of firing another into the doomed man's head. Then there are two vases which have often been advanced as examples of scenes recognisable from Epic; whatever the truth of that question, I think that both can be argued to contain the seeds of synoptic narration. The bowl in the British Museum with the departing warship (Figure 21.13)[29] shows the rowers in mid-stroke, as if already at sea, yet the position of the two large figures at the left-hand side reveals that they are at an earlier stage in the action, when the ship is still beached. Even more clearly, a well-known oenochoë from the Athenian Agora (Figure 21.14)[30] shows

Figure 21.12

Figure 21.13

Figure 21.14

Figure 21.15

two attacking warriors, in the presence of their enemy, who appear to be thrusting with their swords and hurling their javelins simultaneously: the true sense is surely that they first use the long-range weapon and then close with the sword. Finally, let me show a chariot-scene on a very late Geometric amphora in Hamburg (Figure 21.15): at first sight a standard example of the genre, it contains (as was pointed out this time by Gudrun Ahlberg)[31] the odd feature that the armed men accompanying the charioteers are facing alternately backwards and forwards on each successive chariot. Her explanation, which I find attractive, is that this records a kind of martial feat in which the warrior had to turn round as the chariot raced along; so that the artist seems once again to be showing his different figures at different points of time.

In all but one of the Geometric scenes that we have looked at, there is an absence of any single, central episode to act as a prime focus of attention, with the other episodes subordinated to it: the 'komplettierend' model fails here as well. In several cases we have seen, on the contrary, a binary division of the figures or of the actions into two groups of approximately equal weight: this was true of the Tübingen dancers and the Hamburg charioteers and, in a different way, it is true of the balancing figure of archer and victim on the Copenhagen jug, and of the balancing actions of the warriors from the Agora. Only on the London bowl do I feel that the artist, by his use of a gigantic scale for the two figures on the left, has indicated that the moment of embarkation is the focus of interest, and that the oarsmen

are there to show us what will happen shortly. As for the scene of the
prisoners of war on the Louvre jug, it seems almost to rival the Circe
cup of two centuries later in its temporal complexity. Here then is
a confirmation of one of Himmelmann's main arguments: the origin
of this method of visual narration does not lie in the extension of a
central, dominant moment by the addition of earlier and later episodes
in the story; it springs from the conception of a picture incorporating
the passage of time, from the very start.

I am not claiming that this was the sole and exclusive conception
of narrative art that Greek artists had, in the Geometric period any
more than later. There is, for example, a remarkable series of pictures,
spanning two centuries and more, in which an identical subject is
treated in a very similar way, one that is almost the antithesis of the
synoptic method. The subject is that of dancers leaping to the music
of a piper or lyre-player, with one or more dancers shown in mid-
air. It is striking to find that there are already instances of this in the
Geometric period; a kantharos in Athens (Figure 21.16) will serve as
an example.[32] A century and a half later, an aryballos from Corinth
(Figure 21.17) elaborates on this theme of instantaneous action by
showing the leading dancer in mid-leap while his companions stand
in a taut, attentive pose which strongly suggests that they are waiting
for their turn to come.[33]

Figure 21.16

Figure 21.17

We come to our last question: in what circumstances did this original, persistent and deep-seated concept of the early Greek artist first
emerge? One part of the answer, the most obvious and perhaps the
most important, is simply that the notion must first have arisen among
vase-painters. There is no other medium in which, at the middle of
the eighth century BC, Greek artists had the opportunity to apply the
idea. Only several generations later did a sculptural medium arise, in
the form of the long compositions in relief on a temple pediment or in
the Ionic frieze, where the concept could be applied on a monumental
scale. As for wall-paintings, we do indeed know that they ultimately
provided a field for the use of the synoptic method, but our evidence
is much later and involves works which survive, not in the flesh, but
in the pages of Pausanias. He describes, for example, the mural of
the battle of Marathon painted between 480 and 460 BC on the walls
of the Stoa Poikile at Athens, by Panainos or Mikon: here, in one
large composition, were shown the first joining of battle; then, in the
centre, the Persians fleeing in disarray; finally, the fight at the ships.

The leading Athenians – Miltiades, Kallimachos, with sundry heroes and deities – appeared at different points in the narrative; and they appeared only once each.[34] This famous and large-scale deployment of the synoptic method, after the end of the Archaic period, is one of the highest tributes to the strength and adaptability of the original conception. The whole sequence of development from the eighth century to the fifth seems to me to provide confirmation of the view propounded in a paper some thirty years ago by Professor Martin Robertson: the 'inescapable conclusion' which he then reached was 'that vase-painting was the dominant art of its time' – that is, the Late Geometric period.[35] The evidence that he used was quite different from what I have been talking about, so that this is independent confirmation. If a notion first employed by vase-painters in eighth-century Greece, and then developed for several generations by their successors in the same medium, could later find acceptance with artists in the more monumental art-forms of relief sculpture and mural painting, then this is indeed evidence for the prestige of early vase-painters and their works; and not only in artistic circles, one might add, since the success of the method depended on its ready comprehension by the general public.

The burden of my argument has been that the synoptic method was not a 'sophisticated modification of a more "natural" concept of narrative' in which the portrayal of a single episode or moment had been the aim. On the contrary, the synoptic method was one of the oldest, and presently became the most prevalent, means by which the early Greek artist conveyed a narrative. There were alternatives, such as that exemplified by the motif of the leaping dancers; but the commonest of these alternatives, the 'monoscenic' method in its broader form, had come into existence at the dictates of the subject-matter, not because of its inherent 'natural' quality. 'Sophistication' came when allusion took the place of straight narration within the synoptic technique. It may have been this last route which in the end led the artists of the Late Archaic and Classical periods to an alternative which was more satisfying to their intellect and tastes.

If I have pressed my case rather hard at times then I feel that the fault is one that Sir John Myres might have condoned. I began with a quotation from one German genius, so let me end with one from another, the man who perhaps achieved more than any in combining the visual arts with the different media of drama and music. 'I scarcely move' says Richard Wagner's Parsifal in the Transformation Scene of

Act I, 'yet I feel myself already far away'. As the back-drop of the forest rolls past them, Gurnemanz replies:

'Du siehst, mein Sohn,
zum Raum wird hier die Zeit'.

'My son, as you see, here space and time are one'.

NOTES

1. See especially N. Himmelmann-Wildschütz, 'Erzählung und Figur in der archaischen Kunst' (*Abhandlungen, Akademie der Wissenschaften und der Literatur, Mainz: Geistes- und Sozial-wissenschaftliche Klasse* 1967, 2, 73–101), with a very constructive review by J. M. Hemelrijk, *Gnomon* 42 (1970), 166–71; H. von Steuben, *Frühe Sagendarstellungen in Korinth und Athen* (Berlin, 1968); F. Brommer, *Die Wahl des Augenblicks in der griechischen Kunst* (München, 1969); I. Raab, *Zu den Darstellungen des Parisurteils in der griechischen Kunst* (*Archäologische Studien* 1, Frankfurt, 1972), especially 92–102.
2. Cited by C. Robert in *Archäologische Hermeneutik* (Berlin, 1919), 423.
3. See D. Posner, *Annibale Carracci* (London and New York, 1971) I 79, 82, 166; II 39, no. 92, pl. 92f.
4. Cup by the Kodros Painter, London BM E 84; J. D. Beazley, *Attic Red-figure Vase Painters*, 2nd ed. (Oxford, 1960) (hereafter *ARV*²), 1269. 4.
5. Cup by the Painter of the Boston Polyphemos, Boston 99.518; J. D. Beazley, *Attic Black-figure Vase Painters* (Oxford, 1956) (hereafter ABV) 198.
6. See J. Boardman, *The Greeks Overseas*, new ed. (London, 1980), 148–51.
7. Amphora in Rome, Villa Giulia M 472 (*ABV* 291, with references).
8. Amphora by the Painter of the Birth of Athena, London BM E 410 (*ARV*² 494. 1).
9. See Himmelmann (above, n. 1) 76–7 with fig. 1 and pl. 8 a–b.
10. Cup by the Rider Painter, Paris, Cabinet des Medailles 190: C. M. Stibbe, *Lakonische Vasenmaler des sechsten Jahrhunderts v. Chr.* (Amsterdam and London, 1972), 285, no. 289, pl. 94; for the Eleusis amphora, see e.g. P. Arias, M. Hirmer and B. B. Shefton, *A History of Greek Vase-painting* (London, 1962), 274, pls. 12–13.
11. See e.g. J. Boardman, J. Dörig, W. Fuchs and M. Hirmer, *The Art and Architecture of Ancient Greece* (London, 1967), pl. 83; discussed by K. Fittschen, *Untersuchungen zum Beginn der Sagendarstellungen bei den Griechen* (Berlin, 1969), 182–3, no. SB 99.
12. See for example the Medusa on the Corfu pediment, Boardman *et al.* (above, n. 11), pl. 101.

13. See Arias *et al.* (above, n. 10), 290–1, pl. 44.
14. Himmelmann (above, n. 1), 90, 98–100, fig. 8.
15. Dinos by the Rider Painter, Paris, Louvre E 662: Stibbe (above, n. 10), 286–7, no. 313, pls. 110–1.
16. Plate by Lydos, Athens NM 507 (*ABV* 112. 56).
17. Aegina, East Pediment figures O III and O VIII: D. Ohly, *Die Aigineten, I: die Ostgiebelgruppe* (München, 1976), pls. 73–4, 45–6. Volute-krater by the Niobid Painter, Palermo G 1283: see Arias *et al.* (above, n. 10), 356–7, pl. 179.
18. Himmelmann (above, n. 1).
19. P. G. P. Meyboom, 'Some observations on narration in Greek art', *Mededelingen van het Nederlandsch Historisch Instituut te Rom* 40 (1978), 55–82.
20. See J. M. Carter's valuable article, 'The beginnings of narrative art in the Greek Geometric period', *Annual of the British School at Athens* 67 (1972), 25–58, especially 26–7.
21. 'Homeric art', *Annual of the British School at Athens* 45 (1950), 229–60, especially 233, 245.
22. Himmelmann (above, n. 1), 87–92.
23. Hydria in Bristol, H. 801: this is no. A IV a. 1 in I. Raab's catalogue (above, n. 1), discussed along with other examples by her, 62, 174.
24. Raab (above, n. 1), 99.
25. Krater fragment, Paris, Louvre A 517: Himmelmann (above, n. 1), 83, pl. 1.
26. Oenochoë, Paris, Louvre CA 2509: K. Friis Johansen, 'Ajax und Hektor: ein vorhomerisches Heldenlied?', *Historisk-filosofiske Meddelelser det Kongelige Danske Videnskabernes Selskab* 39, no. 4 (1961); N. Himmelmann-Wildschütz, 'Nach der Schlacht', *Marburger Winckelmannsprogramm* 1961, 1–5.
27. Oenochoë, Tübingen 2657: R. Tölle, *Frühgriechische Reigentänze* (Waldsassen, 1964), 11–12, 56–7, pls. 1–2.
28. Oenochoë, Copenhagen 1628: see G. Ahlberg, *Fighting on Land and Sea in Greek Geometric Art* (Stockholm, 1971), 29–30, no. B.4, figs. 31–3.
29. Bowl, London BM 99.2 – 19.1: discussed by Fittschen (above, n. 11), 51–9, no. AA 1.
30. Oenochoë, Agora P 4885: see Fittschen (above, n. 11), 68–75, no. M 2.
31. Amphora, Hamburg 1966.89: see G. Ahlberg, *Prothesis and Ekphora in Greek Geometric Art* (Göteborg, 1971), 28, 189–90, no. 43, pl. 60a.
32. Kantharos, Athens NM 14447: Tölle (above, n. 27), 12–13, 61, pl. 3.
33. Aryballos in Corinth Museum: see M. C. and C. A. Roebuck, 'A prize aryballos', *Hesperia* 24 (1955), 158–63, pls. 63–4.
34. Pausanias i 15, 4.
35. 'The place of vase painting in Greek art', *Annual of the British School at Athens* 46 (1951), 151–9, especially 153.

CHAPTER 22

The Uses of Writing on Early Greek Painted Pottery

This paper was first delivered at a conference in my old University, Edinburgh, in March 1999. In the same year a paper was published (Slater 1999: see especially pp. 154–8) which, as its main title suggests, quite independently reached a similar view of the prevalence of reading written texts out loud, at least in the earlier periods of Greek history. Later, there appeared a point-by-point rejoinder (Boardman 2003), challenging each of my contentions both primary and incidental, including the fundamental case for the practice of reading out loud. Boardman rests his own case on a series of propositions whose validity readers must judge for themselves.

BIBLIOGRAPHY

Boardman, J. (2003), ' "Reading" Greek vases?', *Oxford Journal of Archaeology* 22: 1, 109–14.
Slater, Niall W. (1999), 'The vase as ventriloquist? *kalos* inscriptions and the culture of fame', in *Signs of Orality*, ed. E. Anne Mackay, Leiden: E. J. Brill, pp. 143–61.

καθάπερ τὰ τῶν ἀρχαίων γραφέων, εἰ μή τις ἐπέγραψεν, οὐκ ἐγνωρίζετο τί ἐστιν ἕκαστον.
Aristotle, *Topica* 140a21–2

'Just as in the case of the paintings of olden days, unless they were inscribed, one did not know what each thing was.' Whatever the 'old

'The uses of writing on early Greek painted pottery', from N. K. Rutter and B. A. Sparkes (ed.), *Word and Image in Ancient Greece*, Edinburgh: Edinburgh University Press, 2000, pp. 22–34.

paintings' that Aristotle had in mind, the reference is certainly to large-scale work; and we know from Pausanias' detailed descriptions that the practice of inscribing still prevailed when Polygnotos and Mikon were executing their famous murals, something over a hundred years before Aristotle's time of writing. In fourth-century parlance, their work could perhaps already be counted as 'ancient'. The analogy that Aristotle is making is with definitions which are insufficiently precise and exclusive to do their job effectively. We note that this purports to be a statement of fact rather than an inference: literally, 'it used not to become known' what the paintings showed. Whether or not we believe that Aristotle was right about this, it is at least clear that he regarded the practice as obsolete and no longer necessary in his own times. What is more, when we turn our attention to vase-painting, we shall find evidence to support this temporal distinction in general terms.

The interplay of image and word had long been ubiquitous in the culture of ancient Greece. But there are very few places where the two come so close together as in the painted inscriptions on Greek vases: indeed, inasmuch as the inscriptions at times seem to be located with a view of filling gaps in the figure-scenes, the word can actually become a *part* of the image. This was a phenomenon that had a fairly rapid growth, then a pronounced peak, then a steady decline. Even at its peak, in the high archaic period, it was a minority practice among vase-painters; yet it was widespread enough, within and beyond Athens, to pass with little extended comment from scholars nowadays. By the full Classical period, it had become rather rare and by the fourth century, as Aristotle's parallel suggests, even more so.

In 1990 appeared Henry Immerwahr's long-awaited[1] *Attic Script: A Survey*. The title of the book hardly conveys the fact that vase-inscriptions heavily preponderate in its content, though it fairly represents the treatment that follows, which is epigraphical first and last. There is, for example, little or no discussion (nor an index) of the range of types of pot chosen for inscription, the main aspect with which I shall be dealing here. Nor can ceramic considerations have been uppermost in the author's mind when he gave 'the backwardness of Attica' as the explanation for the relative dearth of early inscriptions there (Immerwahr 1990: 8): 'backwardness' is hardly the first word that springs to the mind of anyone contemplating the unquestioned leadership of the Attic ceramic industry in the eighth century BC. When pottery provides the writing-surface for more than three-quarters of a body of extant inscriptions, as it does in this case, then to neglect the generations of painstaking study which that material has received in its own right is to set aside all potential investigation of the *context* of the writing.

The François Vase[2] stands just at the point when the flood-gates were about to open on the inscribing of vase-scenes at Athens; but they opened rather earlier elsewhere. Probably our first painted inscription, a maker's one from the rim of a krater, belongs more than four generations earlier than this, around 700 BC, and comes from one of the furthest outposts of Greek culture, the island of Ischia.[3] Such 'signature' inscriptions form what is not only the earliest, but to later ages the most readily intelligible, category of painted inscription. Presently, in the middle years of the seventh century BC, it is joined by a second category which will provide the greater part of the material for this paper, the 'tag'– or 'caption'– inscription. Here (as on the François Vase) a name is painted beside a human or divine participant in a figure-scene or, much less frequently, beside an object. There is thus a difference of context, as well as of purpose, from the first category, in that only a representational scene will provide an opportunity for its use.

Thirdly, and *not* reserved exclusively for figural scenes, there is perhaps the best-known of all categories of painted inscription on vases: the ΚΑΛΟΣ names, praising the beauty of an individual, which can also occur as incised *graffiti*, unconnected with the production of the vase and scratched at some later time. The ΚΑΛΟΣ names begin much later and are clearly in a separate class: direct communications to the user which may or may not relate to a primary visual communication. Most intelligibly, it is the *anonymous* ΚΑΛΟΣ inscriptions which point the viewer directly to the picture: there is not much point in writing, for example, hO ΠΑΙΣ ΚΑΛΟΣ ('the boy is beautiful') unless there is a picture of a boy to go with the message. Conversely, when a name *is* given, ΛΕΑΓΡΟΣ ΚΑΛΟΣ, alongside a picture which may or may not actually represent Leagros, there is the possibility of confusion: this very confusion has posed problems for modern scholarship. Nevertheless, there are cases of what Beazley called the 'tag-ΚΑΛΟΣ' and Immerwahr the 'caption-ΚΑΛΟΣ', where a name, real or invented, is written beside, and is clearly meant to be taken with, an image.

Fourthly, and this time once more confined to figural scenes, there is the much rarer category of what we may call 'bubble'-inscriptions. The orthodox view of their first appearance is that it belongs latest of the four, in the latter part of the sixth century BC. But in 1987 Gloria

Ferrari proposed recognising an instance of this type in what had been taken as one of the very earliest specimens of the caption-inscription, the Menelas stand from Aigina, which probably dates from before 650 BC and which had for nearly a hundred years presented a serious puzzle to art-historians and others (Ferrari 1987). A line of identically dressed men processes round this conical stand, each holding a spear. In front of one, otherwise indistinguishable from his companions, is painted the word, ΜΕΝΕΛΑΣ, which gives the piece its name. If the artist were really identifying this figure as Menelaos, as had been universally assumed, then there is a first difficulty in locating the context of this not very warlike procession. Even if that problem were solved – by identifying the scene as an assembly of the suitors of Helen, or less plausibly as the later gathering of the Achaean leaders for the Trojan War – there would remain a broader problem of iconography. Why should the artist name only Menelaos, among companions who would be certain to include some major heroic figures? Why should he show them in uniform and unheroic guise? The dress was indeed the clue which led Ferrari to her conclusion: these are dancers or singers, a lyric chorus in fact. 'Menelas' is not the name of one of them, but the title (and perhaps the first word) of the song that they are all singing: hence the fact that the name is written in Doric, the dialect of lyric. 'Not convincing' was the brief and rather icy comment which Immerwahr devoted to this suggestion in a late footnote to his book (Immerwahr 1990: 10, n. 7).

By contrast, I find this to be one of those insights which, because they unravel a whole skein of difficulties at a stroke, must be right. 'Bubble'-inscriptions are at all periods rare enough — occurring perhaps on less than one figured scene in a thousand — for it to be unremarkable that we have to wait more than a century for the next parallel. Imagine what later ages might make of a nineteenth-century picture showing a concert-group in military dress uniform, inscribed with the words 'Some talk of Alexander'. Might they falter in learned perplexity, knowing that there was a famous British commander in World War II who was also called Alexander, yet recognising that this picture was of a much earlier date? Would not they too jump at the explanation that it was the first line of a song? Be that as it may, there eventually comes a time when undoubted 'bubble'-inscriptions provide a fourth category, as in one of the several scenes of Odysseus and the Sirens, on a jug of about 500 BC,[4] where a constrained and only partially literate hero (ΟΛΥΤΕΥΣ) cries out ΛΥΣΝ (ΛΥΣΟΝ without the O) – 'untie me!', 'set me free!'.

Such written utterances lead directly on to one of the neglected insights about all these *dipinti* inscriptions on vases, whether they are signatures expressing the pride of the artist, captions to aid the understanding of his pictures, direct communications to the user like the ΚΑΛΟΣ inscriptions, actual 'bubbles' or of any other category. This is that, as far as our current understanding goes, they must very often have been designed for oral utterance – in that silent reading was probably not yet practised in the earliest stages of antiquity and, when it began to prevail, did so primarily as a time-saving device in the reading of long texts. This seems to me to have wide implications, especially but not exclusively for inscriptions on pottery. It is Jesper Svenbro, in his *Phrasikleia*, who has most fully and recently treated the general scope of these implications (Svenbro 1988), though I appreciate that his is not the last word on the subject. In particular, one must acknowledge the important contribution made in a recent paper by A. K. Gavrilov, with its equally valuable postscript by Myles Burnyeat (Gavrilov and Burnyeat 1997). But Svenbro's exploration of the cultural consequences of reliance on reading aloud remains valuable, even if it was not universally prevalent as he assumed. His own interests may lie chiefly with literary writing, and with inscriptions that aspire to a literary quality. But his arguments apply *a fortiori* to the decidedly non-literary specimens of writing that most often confront us on painted pottery, and to their destined readership, which is likely to have been, at least, around the average level of literacy for archaic and classical Greece.

Svenbro stresses the rôle of the reader as 'deliverer' of the writer's message, in a culture which practises reading out loud. In the case of our inscriptions, it will clearly be the owners and users of these vessels who take on that rôle. Its importance will have increased when the use normally took place in the presence of more than one person: there will then have been an oral communication from the current holder of the vessel to one or more other people. So what do we know of the context of use of these inscribed vases? In some cases, fortunately, quite a lot; and especially for the case of Athens, which provides the material for Immerwahr's corpus.

I shall therefore use Immerwahr's catalogues, not as an exhaustive list of Athenian painted inscriptions (which he never claims them to be), but as a large and unquestionably valid sample of Athenian practice over the period, from *c.*660 to *c.*350 BC, to which they belong; and, almost as confidently, for the period (rather longer at both ends) in which such inscriptions occur in the Greek world as a whole.

There are altogether some 877 inscriptions catalogued in his book, but these include substantial numbers of incised *graffiti* on pottery, which are most often secondary to the actual production of the pots and which in some cases, like the numerous *ostraka*, are by definition entirely independent of the purpose for which the pots were made. The catalogues also include a selection of extant Attic inscriptions on stone and on lead from this longish period. There remain some 544 painted inscriptions on vessels which are themselves sufficiently well preserved for us to identify their shape and function. On the latter aspect, one can usefully turn to Max Kanowski's invaluable compilation (Kanowski 1983).

Of these 544, just under two-thirds turn out to belong to categories which we can definitely associate with perhaps the best-documented of all ancient social contexts, the *symposion* (Table 22.1). Cups and other drinking-vessels form much the largest category; then come kraters and other wine-mixing bowls; then vessels more or less closely linked with the dispensing and cooling of wine (stamnoi and psykters); then wine-jugs of various kinds; painted bowl-stands; and finally ladles. One can also most easily place here the few cases of plates and dishes which, even if they did not feature at the *symposion* proper, would at least have featured at social occasions involving the serving of food. That makes a sub-total of 358, all in the broader class of table-ware and the vast majority specifically tied to the *symposion* itself.

To reconstruct the rôle of these inscribed vases at the *symposion* is not difficult, given the wealth of literary and iconographic evidence that we have for that institution. Just as the numerous visual portrayals of symposiasts on these vessels would fit in smoothly with the real-life enactment of very similar scenes, so the presence of writing would have its place in the atmosphere of convivial challenges, competitive recitation and singing, amorous discourse and table-games which we know prevailed. A drinker would read out the inscriptions to his neighbours and thereby, especially in the case of caption- or portrait-ΚΑΛΟΣ inscriptions, find himself involved in a sort of impromptu and involuntary exposition of the scenes to which they belonged. He would be identifying for the company the heroes portrayed in a legendary scene; or the boys or *hetairai* in a genre picture – with the faint possibility that the latter, at least, were physically present to hear the performance. He would likewise have to divulge the subjects of the detached ΚΑΛΟΣ inscriptions without a picture, and perhaps to describe or more fully identify their subjects for the benefit of the

Table 22.1 Functions of inscribed vase-shapes (Attic)

Sympotic	
cups, skyphoi etc.	239 wine-drinking
kraters, dinoi, lebetes	63 wine-mixing
stamnoi	10 wine-dispensing
psykters	15 wine-cooling
oinochoai, choes	21 wine-pouring
stands	2
kyathoi	2 ladles
plates and dishes	6
	Sub-total 358

'Generally banausic'	
amphorae, pelikai	74 storage; but including wine
hydriai	41 water-transport and storage
louteria	3 washing-basin
aryballoi	2 male bath-accoutrement
	Sub-total 120

Female use	
pyxides, lekanides	12 boxes for jewellery etc.
alabastra	4 female bath-accoutrement
epinetron	1 guard for wool-carding
bobbin	1 for thread
	Sub-total, without the hydriai above 18; with, 59

Funerary	
lekythoi	36 for grave unguent
pinakes	8 funerary plaques
loutrophoroi	3 for purification of the corpse
phormiskos	1 suspended at grave-side
	Sub-total 48

Note: Immerwahr's (1990) sample: total of ascertainable shapes, 544.

uninitiated. He might even – though this is harder to imagine – read out the painters' and makers' signatures: a suggestion that becomes slightly less far-fetched in the case of the drinking cups, where the physical attributes of the vessel will have played some rôle in its user's performance at the game of *kottabos*. The likelihood that a participant at a *symposion* could bring his own cup with him, as was certainly sometimes the case, gives an added edge to this imaginary picture. The cup would then serve not only as a talking-point at the party (with the added, near-literal sense that an inscribed cup would be 'talking' itself), but as a source of pride to its owner, who could repeatedly present its iconography and inscriptions to new audiences.

None of this is problematic. In fact, it is so readily reconstructed that the impact of the proportion of sympotic shapes begins to reverse itself: if the application of painted inscriptions to the *symposion* is so self-evident, then the remarkable fact is not that so many, but that *only* some two-thirds of the inscriptions are on vessels which lend themselves to this context. We may now return to the remainder of the sample offered by Immerwahr's catalogues.

They include some 120 vessels which I have loosely grouped together as 'generally banausic' in purpose (Table 22.1). There are fairly frequent occurrences of inscriptions on amphorae, pelikai and hydriai of varying forms; and rarer incidences on two other shapes, the louterion or washing-bowl and the aryballos which served for male ablutions. Several of these 'banausic' shapes are in fact rather equivocal in their status. The amphorae could well have been included with the sympotic vessels, thus swelling that category further. As storage-vessels, they might be thought to have spent the greater part of their lives out of the sight of anyone but the owner and his family. Yet one of their functions was indeed to store wine and, especially in the case of the finer specimens with inscribed figure-scenes, it is hard to believe that they would not be shown off to the drinkers of the wine. Bulkier than our own wine-bottles, they were also relegated by the peculiarities of Greek drinking-practice to that stage in the preparations when the pure wine was being initially mixed with water, most often in a krater. Yet there is no reason to exclude the possibility that this operation was carried out in front of the eyes of the guests.

The hydriai are equivocal in a different way. As water-jars, they fall within a sphere of activity which, in Greek society, seems to have been largely the preserve of women. As such, they could well be brought into association with a smaller group of inscribed vessels (Table 22.1) which are more expressly destined for use by the female gender: the pyxis and lekanis, whose prime rôle seems to have been as boxes for prized female possessions, the epinetron, which was used as a knee-guard in wool-carding; the bobbin for spinning; and the alabastron, which may have been the female counterpart of the aryballos for ablutions. If taken together with the hydriai, these make up the quite impressive total of 59 painted inscriptions whose primary readers (and therefore speakers) would be expected to be women.

It has been assumed throughout this discussion that the users of these vessels had the capacity, indispensable for any use of inscriptions whatever, of being literate. Put thus simply, this is too sweeping. It would suffice for the company, at the *symposion*, in the household or at the fountain, to include at least one person who could read out the messages. But in respect of the inscriptions directed at women, there is an important point to be made. It is a fact well known to the small group of scholars who have worked on this subject that, among the scenes in vase-painting which show a mortal person (as distinct from, say, a Muse) holding up or reading from a book-roll, a remarkably high proportion – about half – show women doing so.[5] From this, it is a reasonable inference that the wives and daughters of educated Athenians could often read and write. I infer therefore that Athenian women quite often read aloud to their children, servants or men-folk; and this makes it less surprising that the short messages painted on hydriai or pyxides should have been normally designed for female customers.

There remains one final category of painted inscriptions on ceramic objects on Table 22.1: those that are presumptively or exclusively associated with funerary practice. The biggest element here is formed by the lekythoi, which can have other uses, but which in this case include a number of specimens of the white-ground lekythos, exclusively funerary in purpose. To them we can add the cases of painted funerary plaques, of loutrophoroi, and of the phormiskos which was designed for suspension at funerals, giving a total of 48 in all. Here we are presumably to imagine the inscriptions being read out as contributions to the formal burial utterances; and it is comforting that, in at least one case of a 'bubble'-inscription, the words are clearly designed for just this purpose (Immerwahr 1990: 74, no. 436, figs 98, 99a–b).

But there is one rather awkward element which has not yet been worked into the argument, and which should be: the 'nonsense' inscriptions. These are, first, fairly numerous and, secondly, particularly prevalent in Athens. Immerwahr, who had earlier drawn up a skeleton typology for the 'nonsense' inscriptions according to the degree of relation to sense that they bear (Immerwahr 1971: 54, 59–60, n. 8), is particularly helpful here. In his 1990 book he draws attention to the important fact that the same painter can write both orthographically and in nonsensical letters, even on the same vase, sometimes in regular, firm characters for both (Immerwahr 1990: 44–5). But because the largest single group of vessels inscribed with nonsensical letters is the 'Tyrrhenian amphorae', expressly designed in Athens for export to Etruria, theories had earlier been advanced to the effect that the letters were designed to tease the Etruscans; or alternatively, that it was not worth the trouble of writing Greek correctly for Etruscan customers; or again that the 'nonsense' letters would make sense in some language other than Greek (though unfortunately it has not proved possible to make sense of them in Etruscan). Immerwahr is content to say that 'they give the illusion that the story is also told in words and show that the painter can write, even where he lacks the precise words or the time to put them on'; and that painters like those of the 'Tyrrhenian amphorae' 'use a certain type of nonsense as a kind of "trade-mark"'. This account is perhaps not fully satisfactory, resting as it does on the questionable assumption that it is easier and quicker to write just any letters rather than letters which make sense. But it is at least compatible with all the evidence on this puzzling phenomenon – a phenomenon which, I admit, may require a slight further dilution of the assumption that I have just been making, about basic literacy, or access to literacy, on the part of producers and customers alike.

I should round off the whole issue of the internal classification of the shapes of inscribed vessels by saying that, despite the positive and definite counter-examples which have been adduced, it is the *symposion* which remains the prime field for the deployment of these inscriptions. Only here do we have the full, complex interplay of different levels of reality, with depictions of sympotic activity being used in the activity itself; with actual sympotic vessels carrying depictions of other sympotic vessels; with inscriptions often relating to the *symposion* inviting utterance by the participants in it; and occasionally (since it is on sympotic vessels that 'bubble'-inscriptions are least rare) with three levels of reality, with painted figures uttering painted words which the real user must then himself utter.

I turn finally to a quite different aspect of the *dipinti* on pottery, namely the dating and the possible causes of their use and subsequent fall in popularity as a cultural phenomenon. I have already given the outer time-limits within which they prevail in Athens and Attica: between 660 and 350 BC. For Greece as a whole, the time-span is a little longer, from roughly 700 to 300 BC. But within this bracket there are very marked gradations of popularity. This is most clearly shown by a couple of simple statistics: a mere ninety-odd years, from the time of the François Vase in about 570 to the end of the archaic

Table 22.2 Chronology of inscribed Attic vases (Immerwahr's periods)

Period	No. per generation
Pre-François Vase (*c*.660–570 BC)	8
François Vase generation (*c*.570–550 BC)	25
Developed black-figure (*c*.550–530 BC)	255
Red- and black-figure (*c*.530–500 BC)	154
Late Archaic (*c*.500–480 BC)	129
Early Classical (*c*.480–450 BC)	83
Classical (*c*.450–420 BC)	55
Late Classical (*c*.420–350 BC)	17

period in 480 BC, accounts for nearly five-sixths (81 per cent) of all the surviving Athenian painted inscriptions; even the half-century between *c*.550 and 500 BC provides over half of them. For those who prefer a more nuanced picture, Immerwahr divides his material into shorter periods of varying lengths. It is possible to adjust his figures to the common standard of a number *per generation of thirty years*. The total sample, some 635 inscribed pots and fragments, would if spread evenly give about 61 per generation. The actual distribution gives the very different results seen in Table 22.2.

So there is a huge and abrupt surge in popularity at the mid-sixth century BC, then a fairly steep but even decline over the next century and three-quarters. It seems that we are dealing with a sudden craze in Athens, which later lost its attraction and gave ground steadily for six generations or so, before virtually disappearing (in Athens, that is: in one distant part of the Greek world, the colonial West, it was to linger almost as long as figural scenes on pottery did). How are we to explain such a pattern and profile?

No one, I trust, will suggest that it simply reflects changes in the prevalence of literacy. Although its rise may be explained in terms at least loosely connected with this, its decline cannot have a corresponding significance. In an equally relevant, but more specialised, comparison, we note that its sudden rise and akme are linked to the equally swift rise and akme of the Athenian black-figure style; and that the *beginning* of the decline of the one occurs at much the same date as the much more complete decline of the other, the black-figure technique. This rough correlation could be significant. There *is* a technical reason why the addition of inscriptions to a picture would have been easier in black-figure: it is that writing could simply be added in the

course of the first stage of figure-decoration, when the black silhouette was being laid out with a fine brush on the clay background. In
the red-figure technique, by contrast, the painter had to change implements and paints, picking up a finer brush than the one he had been
using to black in the background, and writing in added red paint on
top of this black background – which in turn meant waiting until it
had dried. Yet the fact remains that, when the red-figure technique
was adopted, not only was a method found, and frequently employed,
to persevere with inscriptions, but this method was to live on in use
for nearly two centuries. Once again, then, we have found that it is
easier to explain the timing of the rise of Attic painted inscriptions
than to account for their long, slow decline.

It seems to me that we should be looking for something more in
the nature of a cultural than of a technical explanation. This would fit
more easily with the pattern of sudden popularity followed by a gradual falling out of fashion. There is a feature of Athenian (and Greek)
art which, without conforming at all closely to the same timetable,
does follow a broadly parallel trajectory through time – it is the use
of what has been called the 'complementary' or 'synoptic' method of
visual narrative; and it relates to exactly the same medium as the great
majority of the painted inscriptions – that is, to the representational
figure-scenes on vases. In this narrative technique, a scene (often but
not invariably legendary in subject) is shown as a succession of more
than one episode of the same story within the same frame; but without
any single figure being allowed to appear more than once.

I have toyed with the notion that the use of 'caption'-inscriptions,
easily our most prolific category of *dipinti* on vases, was first conceived
as a viewer's aid for the comprehension of these 'synoptic' pictures.
For, without needing to enter here into the thorny issues which have
arisen over the intellectual presuppositions which lay behind the use of
the 'synoptic' technique (for a recent survey, see Stansbury-O'Donnell
1999: 1–17), we can probably agree that scenes of this kind are more
difficult to 'read', simply because they lack the element of unity of
time.

The prime difficulty is that such pictures were first introduced
into Greek vase-painting very much earlier than the first 'caption'-
inscriptions. The technique is unquestionably present in some of the
mythological scenes of the first half of the seventh century BC, notably
in Corinth and Athens; and I myself have argued that it is already a
feature of certain Attic Geometric paintings of the late eighth (most
recently, Snodgrass 1987: 153–7). The conclusion would therefore

have to be that it took time for this to be perceived as an obstacle to interpretation, or for the solution of inscribed names to be found, by vase-painters. At the other end of the process, however, it can at least be argued that the decline in favour of the 'synoptic' treatment, like that of the painted inscriptions, was a gradual one, surviving well after the introduction of red-figure. In the medium of large-scale painting with which we began, we may note that one and the same era exemplified a relatively late survival of both practices. It is as clear that the great early classical murals of Athens and Delphi were inscribed with names (some of them obscure enough to be taken as the painter's inventions – see, for instance, Pausanias x.25.3) as it is that, in the mural of the Battle of Marathon in the Stoa Poikile at Athens, for example, the painting took the form of a diachronic narrative of the battle, unfolding from one side to the other, with each leading figure appearing once only (Pausanias i.15.4). Later on in the classical period, we do find that narrative scenes tend to become simpler in construction, with fewer figures and a concentration on a single moment taken from a story – just as the painted inscriptions begin to drop away (Table 22.2). Thus far, there is a very loose fit between the two phenomena: both are (in a broad sense) archaic devices, with which the classical age increasingly dispensed.

The argument cannot, however, be pressed home. An attempt to correlate the incidence of especially complex 'synoptic' pictures with that of painted inscriptions might find a few good individual correspondences,[6] but would soon run into counter-examples. All that we have uncovered are two roughly parallel cultural developments, each of them closely related to the problems of framing narrative scenes in art. I would claim no more than that this general line of explanation is likelier to be on the right track than, on the one hand, those which are more narrowly technical and, on the other, those which appeal to historical frameworks on the grand scale, such as the rise of Athenian prosperity in the sixth century BC under the rule of the tyranny.

Whatever our view on this issue, it is surely clear that the *dipinti* on Attic pottery are a unique source of evidence on 'everyman's' use of writing. Produced for users who might or might not belong to the élite, by artisans who definitely did not, they throw a flood of light on several quite different aspects of ancient cultural life, ranging from male entertainment to the status of women, and from artists' conventions to the attitudes of their public. For all of these, we badly need the evidence of their alternative voice.

NOTES

I am most indebted to Professor Stephen Halliwell for knowledge of the apposite quotation that heads this chapter; and to members of the Edinburgh audience – especially Professor Robin Osborne – for some enlightening comments on other parts of the chapter.

1. Its forthcoming appearance had been announced as much as forty-four years previously, by Richter 1946: 167, n. 21 *ad fin.*
2. For the most perceptive discussion, see Beazley 1951/1986: 26–37/24–34. Immerwahr (1990: 24) characteristically described the vase, with its 270 figures, as 'a major monument of Attic epigraphy'.
3. See Buchner 1970–1: 67, fig. 8; Ridgway 1992: 96, fig. 26.
4. For an illustration, see Boardman 1974: 150, 201, fig. 286.
5. See most recently Cole 1981: 223, nn. 21–3, citing especially the earlier lists of such scenes drawn up by Immerwahr in 1964 and 1973.
6. As, for example, with the striking scene of Neoptolemos at Troy (Snodgrass 1987: 142–6, figs 37–8), where the viewer badly needs the help of the inscriptions to identify an unfamiliar episode, and would lose much by failure to do so.

REFERENCES

Buchner, G. (1970-1), 'Recent work at Pithekoussai (Ischia), 1965–71', *AR*, 17, pp. 63–7.

Cole, S. G. (1981), 'Could Greek women read and write?', in Foley 1981: pp. 219–45.

Ferrari, G. (1987), 'Menelas', *JHS*, 107, pp. 180–2.

Foley, H. P. (ed.) (1981), *Reflections of Women in Antiquity*, New York, London and Rome: Gordon and Breach.

Gavrilov, A. K. and Burnyeat, M. F. (1997), 'Techniques of reading in classical antiquity' and 'Postscript on silent reading', *CQ*, 47, pp. 56–73 and 74–6.

Henderson, Jr, C. (ed.) (1964), *Classical, Mediaeval and Renaissance Studies in Honor of Berthold Louis Ullman*, I, Rome: Edizioni di Storia e Letteratura.

Immerwahr, H. R. (1964), 'Book rolls on Attic vases', in Henderson 1964:17–48.

Immerwahr, H. R. (1971), 'A projected corpus of Attic vase inscriptions', in *Acta of the Fifth International Congress of Greek and Latin Epigraphy, Cambridge 1967*, Oxford: Blackwell, pp. 53–60.

Immerwahr, H. R. (1973), 'More book rolls on Attic vases', *AK*, 16, pp. 143–7.

Immerwahr, H. R. (1990), *Attic Script: A Survey*, Oxford: Clarendon Press.

Kanowski, M. G. (1983), *Containers of Classical Greece: A Handbook of Shapes*, St Lucia, London and New York: University of Queensland Press.

Richter, G. M. A. (1946), *Attic Red-figure Vases: A Survey*, New Haven CT: Yale University Press.

Ridgway, D. (1992), *The First Western Greeks* Cambridge: Cambridge University Press.

Snodgrass, A. M. (1987), *An Archaeology of Greece: The Present State and Future Scope of a Discipline*, Berkeley CA and Los Angeles: University of California Press.

Stansbury-O'Donnell, M. D. (1999), *Pictorial Narrative in Ancient Greek Art*, Cambridge: Cambridge University Press.

Svenbro, J. (1988), *Phrasikleia: anthropologie de la lecture en Grèce ancienne*, Paris: La Découverte; English translation, *Phrasikleia: An Anthropology of Reading in Ancient Greece*. Ithaca NY and London: Cornell University Press, 1993.

CHAPTER 23

Pausanias and the Chest of Kypselos

This paper is just one example of the remarkable recent access of interest in this once-despised writer – not only nor even mainly on the part of the archaeologists, by whom he has always been seen as a prolific source of information. Other aspects of his work and its reception have been handled in papers not here included (Snodgrass 1977: 2003). Even those who cannot fully share in Paul Veyne's enthusiastic verdict on our author (p. 426 below) have begun to realise that his is an interesting mind, from which there is much to be learned whenever we grapple, eighteen centuries after him, with the same problems as he. He has to some extent benefited from the parallel but broader resurgence of literary interest in the movement of the 'Second Sophistic', of which he may perhaps be called an honorary member.

BIBLIOGRAPHY

Snodgrass, A. M. (1977), 'Cretans in Arcadia', in *Antichità Cretesi: Studi in onore di Doro Levi*, ed. G. P. Carratelli and G. Rizza, vol. II, pp. 196–201, Catania: Università di Catania.
Snodgrass (2003), 'Another early reader of Pausanias?', *Journal of Hellenic Studies* 123: 187–9.

Plodding the galleries, we ask how can
    That century of the Uncommon Man
Sovereign here in paint, bronze, marble, suit
    The new narcissism of the Also-Ran.

C. Day Lewis, *An Italian Visit*, Part 5,
'Florence: Works of Art' (1953)

'Pausanias and the Chest of Kypselos', from S. E. Alcock, J. F. Cherry and J. R. Elsner (ed.), *Pausanias: Travel and Memory in Roman Greece*, Oxford: Oxford University Press, 2001, pp. 127–41.

Sightseeing is a notoriously tiring activity. Every user of a guidebook will hope and expect that, from time to time, there will be occasions when the author will call a halt and describe what can be seen from a more or less stationary position. The user of Pausanias's guide will know that he provided a few such occasions for his ancient readers, by offering long and detailed descriptions of objects or groups of objects. This, I suggest, is his counterpart for the *ekphrasis*, in which his more demanding literary forerunners and successors so revelled.[1] Pausanias's passages have not hitherto been taken in this way, because of the extreme restraint and self-effacement with which he presents his material, here and elsewhere; certainly his descriptions, by comparison with the gushing set pieces of some writers of the Second Sophistic, are dry indeed. They are entirely without that overt empathy with the work of art which we encounter in, say, Philostratus or Lucian; and I would not exclude the possibility that this represents an early and deliberate move in the long-running debate between 'empathy' and 'objectivity' in art criticism, an open espousal of a contrasting approach. Yet their purpose, if I am right, is rather similar: to vary the pace of the itinerary, just as Philostratus varies the pace of his narrative, by calling up a heightened pause and holding the reader's gaze in a single direction.

This considerate provision on Pausanias's part has earned him scant gratitude from the modern commentators, who for the most part are using his work from the already stationary position of their armchairs and grow impatient at the prolixity of his accounts of long-lost objects. I doubt that W. Gurlitt was the first to call him 'dry, sober and pedantic' on the evidence of such detailed excursuses.[2] Even Pausanias's stalwart recent champion, Christian Habicht, has concurred, citing as examples of the author's pedantry the unnecessary enumeration of the sixty-nine altars at Olympia (5.13.4–15.12), the long description of Phidias's statue of Zeus (5.11.1–11), the list of the forty founder-cities of Megalopolis (8.27.3–4), and the accounts of the Chest of Kypselos (5.17.5–19.10) and, longest of all, of the two big murals of Polygnotos in the Lesche of the Knidians at Delphi (10.25.1–31.12).[3]

The simple practical motive that I have ascribed to Pausanias does not apply to all these cases: the founder-cities of Megalopolis are not works of art, and no immediate visual impetus provokes their listing. The artistic set pieces, even if a somewhat deeper programmatic aim lurks behind them as I have tentatively suggested, are perhaps not fully accounted for either. The question, seldom asked, why Pausanias devotes *quite* so much space to these objects may have different answers in different instances. The first, general aim of this chapter is to explore his motivation in the specific case of the Chest of Kypselos; but there are others, which relate to his broader role in the interpretation of early Greek art.

Pausanias's account of the Chest of Kypselos is his second-longest descriptive excursus: even though truncated at its beginning, it takes up some 170 lines in the best-known text,[4] as against 255 for Polygnotos's painting of the Underworld, 164 for his companion piece of 'Troy taken,' a mere 80 for the statue of Zeus – all of them much better-known works of the fifth century BC – and 70 for the Archaic throne of Apollo at Amyklai (3.18.9–19.2). The account of the chest stands out from his work as a whole, even from the last-named monument, because of the very early date of its subject. For the last hundred years, the learned consensus has been that Pausanias had been misled by his guides when he relayed the story that the chest was the actual one in which the infant Kypselos, later tyrant of Corinth, had been concealed; this would have happened at some date in the early seventh century BC by our reckoning. Yet the remarkable correspondences between Pausanias's account of the iconography and epigraphy of the chest and the iconography and inscriptions on surviving Corinthian vase scenes are enough to prove beyond reasonable question that he was describing a genuine product of Archaic Corinth, dating perhaps from somewhat after 600 BC. In principle, I see no reason why the plain cedarwood chest itself cannot have been much older, and the ornate decoration applied to it later in the lifetime of the dynasty that Kypselos founded, precisely because of the dramatic role that it was believed to have once played in the family's fortunes. But that is an unimportant speculation. The interesting issue is Pausanias's choice of a real antique, already some seven and a half centuries old in his time and now long since disappeared, for such full treatment. Apart from the basic circumstance that presumably, because of its location in what was probably then the joint temple of Hera and Zeus, it had once been dedicated to one or both deities, it made an unlikely focus for those religious convictions that Pausanias's subject aroused in him. It was decorated and inscribed in a style that even a Greek-speaker must by then have found obscure, hard to interpret, and aesthetically relatively unrewarding.

The 'century of the Uncommon Man,' which dominated the impressions of Cecil Day Lewis throughout the long poem which provides my epigraph, was the Renaissance; for Pausanias, the period from the Persian Wars to the time of Epaminondas filled a parallel role, but not to so exclusive an extent. He does show intermittent appreciation of older, Archaic works of art,[5] and doubtless mere age on its own would be the source of a certain interest for the users of his *Guide*. But his whole approach to the chest suggests something far beyond that. In the first place, his own personal interest is clearly aroused: he feels that the chest represents a challenge to his interpretive skills. Thus, after a few perfunctory words on the manner of execution of the decoration and a further few lines on the history of the chest (all in 5.17.5), he proceeds first to the inscriptions, then to his much fuller account of the iconography of the scenes.

The latter has attracted by far the greater attention from modern scholars; yet it is the inscriptions that Pausanias puts first, stressing their unfamiliarity and difficulty of reading, and to which he repeatedly returns later in his text. He reads off the caption inscriptions to identify some of the figures, cites many of the poetic epigraphs in their entirety, gives the exact location of the writing (5.18.2, 5.19.4), comments on the nomenclature used (5.18.5), and, in the case of the metrical inscriptions, specifies the scansion (5.18.2 again, 5.19.3). But for his ability to read the Archaic Corinthian script, he would clearly have been unable to offer a convincing interpretation for many of the scenes, as is shown by his palpably less successful efforts in the case of the third zone from the bottom (5.18.6–8), which evidently lacked inscriptions, and of the fifth and last zone (5.19.7–9), which he specifically states was uninscribed.

Once again, what might have been thought a creditable achievement by a writer of the late second century AD has for the most part brought him scorn. Pausanias is the only source for the poetic fragments inscribed on the chest, and it is surely to his credit that he saved them for posterity. But this section of his work, understandably in view of its literary interest, has been claimed by the classical philologists as their property. The tone was set early on by Wilamowitz, whose contempt for Pausanias was based at least partly on the discreditable personal grounds that Habicht has now brought to light.[6] The scribal errors that Pausanias inevitably made in reading and scanning the lines were seized on, at times with something approaching glee, at times with greater patience. Emendations were proposed on the assumption that Pausanias got the meter right but the readings wrong;[7] alternatively, results have been achieved by assuming the opposite, that the readings are more or less correct but the meter not always correctly identified.[8] Some of the lines carry conviction in the form in which Pausanias gives them, while it has proved possible to emend and restore others in a convincing way.

But there was a second line of attack on Pausanias's account of the inscriptions: to deny him the credit for the readings. For a time, the prevailing theory was that the entire description of the chest, along with other extended passages in Pausanias, had been taken over from an earlier writer (Polemo of Ilion being the favorite choice). This view implied an outright rejection of a number of explicit claims to autopsy on Pausanias's part and, in the case of the chest, of his implicit but clear suggestion that he had looked at the object in the same sequence which he prescribes for his readers, since he twice (5.18.7–8, 5.19.7) offers his own interpretation of a scene. I trust that Christian Habicht's reassessment of the work as a whole, in which comparative evidence from every part of it is brought into play, will have done enough to discredit this line of argument permanently.[9] But the persistent skepticism about Pausanias's ability to read Archaic Corinthian script has also taken a more specific form: it is suggested that, for the *inscriptions* (on the chest and elsewhere at Olympia) but not for the rest of his account, he made use of a local repertory of inscriptions and copied its readings.[10] Such an argument overlooks the fact that this is not the only place where Pausanias apparently achieved a reading of a fairly early Corinthian script: he seems to have deciphered, at least in part, the inscriptions on the Corcyrean bull, which was dedicated at Delphi around 480 BC and cannot have appeared in any putative handlist of inscriptions at Olympia.[11]

It is surely the most economical hypothesis that he himself managed, no doubt with difficulty and with some help from his guides, to master the letter-forms used in Archaic Corinth and the principle of *boustrophedon* writing, which he evidently (5.17.6) found an interesting curiosity. For the average modern classicist, familiar with the language but epigraphically challenged, Pausanias's efforts with an epichoric Archaic script will excite fellow-feeling and mild admiration rather than contempt. Paul Veyne's assessment of our author–'not a mind to be underestimated ... the equal of any of the great nineteenth-century German philologists or philosophers ... The precision of his descriptions and the breadth of his knowledge are astounding'[12]– may have struck some readers as over-enthusiastic, even after the partial rehabilitation of Pausanias that has now taken place; it would certainly have given Wilamowitz apoplexy. But his engagement with the Corinthian script typifies that serious scholarly motivation which Veyne detected in Pausanias.

From the inscriptions, Pausanias moves abruptly to the main subject matter, both of his account and of this chapter: the decorative scenes and their iconography. There were at least thirty separate subjects, almost all of them legendary in nature, treated in different parts of the chest. As with the inscriptions, so here the faithful recording of what Pausanias observed has enabled modern scholars to treat the chest almost as if it still survived. Its decoration has been completely reconstructed on paper more than once[13] (see Fig. 23.1), and the iconographers, like the epigraphists, have been able to offer their own emendations of Pausanias – in this case, of his identifications of certain scenes. In his statistical study of the incidence of legendary subjects in earlier Archaic art, Robert Cook lists the chest in exactly the same way as the surviving vases and sculptures.[14]

It is in fact an observation of Cook's that provides the starting point for this section of my argument. He points out that only a minority of the subjects on the chest (perhaps eight in all) are taken from either the Trojan or the Theban cycle of legends; and that, of these, precisely two figure in the Homeric poems: the duel between Ajax and Hektor that is portrayed in *Iliad* 7.225–312 and the much more obscure fight between Agamemnon and Koön over the body of Iphidamas, Koön's younger brother, from *Iliad* 11.218–63.[15] Now Cook's calculations reflect the results of modern scholarship, rather than Pausanias's own reckoning, which would have added at least one and probably two scenes from the *Odyssey* and one from the *Iliad*, all in the fifth and uppermost zone of the chest. At 5.19.7, he offers his own identification of a scene showing a man and a woman reclining on a bed in a cave: 'I thought [or possibly, since he uses the first-person plural, 'The guides and I thought'] that they were Odysseus and Kirke,' an interpretation which he backs by a learned comparison of the number and actions of the serving women described in *Odyssey* 10.348–74 with those here shown next to the couple. At 5.19.9, he reports, 'As for the two young women riding in a cart drawn by mules . . . they [i.e., his local informants] consider that one is Nausikäa and the other her servant'–thus relating the picture to the episode in *Odyssey* 6.71–84. He does not this time endorse the identification himself, but he offers no alternative view. Both suggestions, however, are weakened by Georg Loeschcke's clever alternative interpretation of well over a century ago that what was really portrayed, in an extensive scene of

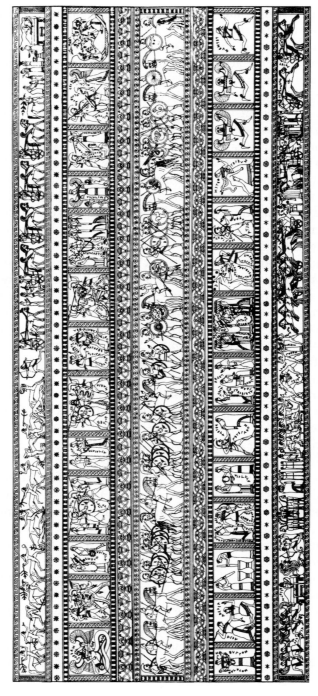

Figure 23.1 Reconstruction of the Chest of Kypselos. (After W. von Massow, 'Die Kypseloslade,' *Mitteilungen des Deutschen Archäologischen Instituts, Athenische Abteilung*, 41 (1916): 1–117.

which the first of the 'Odyssean' groups formed the climax, was the wedding of Peleus and Thetis, set in a cave on Mount Pelion according to one tradition at least as old as Euripides (*Iphigeneia at Aulis* 704–707), with the bridal pair reclining and the guests arriving in couples in a row of chariots.[16]

Loeschcke's theory has won almost unanimous support ever since. Much later, K. Friis Johansen added an important gloss to it: that the setting and personae were as Loeschcke had proposed, but that the moment represented was a later one, when Achilles had reached manhood and was about to leave for Troy.[17] Thus the reclining couple would be long since safely married, and decency would be preserved. The only other serious criticism of Loeschcke had come almost immediately, when W. Klein objected that he had not gone far enough: why not also include 'Nausikää and her servant' in the interpretation and make them one of the pairs of divine guests arriving in their chariot?[18] Loeschcke himself refused to go along with this extension of his explanation,[19] and indeed it is not free of difficulty, since it posits a failure on the part of Pausanias's informants (and, by implication, of Pausanias himself) to detect the difference between a cart and a chariot, and perhaps also between mules and winged thoroughbreds; but these would be venial errors. On the whole, it seems easier to reject an incongruous and isolated portrayal of 'Nausikää' amid the two extensive scenes which otherwise take up the whole of the fifth zone–the reception at Peleus and Thetis's cave, and Herakles fighting the Centaurs–and thus to eliminate the second 'Odyssean' subject along with the first. If this is right, then there is a nice modern parallel for the same misrecognition of Nausikää in a scene actually involving Peleus and Thetis.[20]

Assuming that Loeschcke's main interpretation of the setting is sound, there is a third case in this passage where Pausanias entertains the idea of a strictly Homeric setting for a scene that does not truly belong to either Homeric poem. This is where he discusses the arms that Hephaistos was shown bringing to Thetis. On Loeschcke's account, these must of course be the arms to be presented to Peleus, passed on to his son Achilles as his *first* set of armor, and then in turn loaned, with fatal consequences, to Patroklos.[21] As such, they play a minor part in the narrative of the *Iliad* at several points: they are described in some detail at 16.130–44 and their history is related by Achilles at 18.82–87. But their original *presentation* is not an Iliadic episode. What Pausanias says, once again deferring to his guides, is: 'They maintain that this relates to Patroklos's death, with the Nereids in chariots, and Thetis taking the arms from Hephaistos.' By these words, he clearly implies that the arms were taken to be the *second* set acquired by Achilles, which were indeed occasioned by Patroklos's death, whose making forms the subject of the famous set piece dominating Book 18 of the *Iliad*, and which are handed over by Thetis (though without the assistance of the Nereids) at the beginning of Book 19.

What is fascinating about the iconographic confusion here (if such it is) is that, once again, precisely the same difficulty has arisen for twentieth-century art historians in establishing the iconographic distinction between the two occasions on which Thetis received armor from Hephaistos and subsequently passed it on to Achilles. The recent consensus has been, following the arguments first propounded by K. Friis Johansen,[22] that the majority of the earlier representations on vases show the *first* presentation, set in Phthia before Achilles's departure for Troy, and with the Nereids often shown in attendance – just as in the scene on the chest, if Loeschcke's view is accepted, the first stage in the history of this armor was portrayed. So, on this view, most of the 'Arms for Achilles' scenes cannot after all be taken to illustrate one of the climactic episodes of the *Iliad*; though I must add that, in a recent paper, Steven Lowenstam has dissented.[23] Whatever the true solution to our own problems of interpretation, the strong probability remains that Pausanias's informants were mistaken in *their* identifications, both here and immediately before. Hephaistos, Thetis, and the Nereids from *Iliad* 18–19, cheek by jowl with Odysseus and Kirke from *Odyssey* 10, make an infinitely less convincing reading of an extended scene than one that, like Loeschcke's, binds the figures together. These mistakes are not without bearing on our own deliberations over surviving works.

There is, first, an important general lesson for the art historian, to be learned both from the paucity of truly Homeric scenes on the chest and from Pausanias's palpable errors in trying to add to their number. From the former, the implication is most clearly drawn by Cook when he concludes, from his study of legendary scenes in Archaic art down to about 530 BC: 'So it seems that there is little or no evidence that artists in this period knew the *Iliad* or the *Odyssey* themselves or, if one or two knew them, that all the others did.'[24] This is a theme upon which I have enlarged at much greater length elsewhere.[25] In brief, Cook's view is the one to which any cool and unprejudiced survey of the evidence must point; yet it is difficult to reconcile with the

approach of some standard and quite recent works in the field of
Homer and early Greek art.[26] There seems to be a predisposition to
find a Homeric inspiration for any scene where any case for it at all
can be made. Literary scholars too have shown a natural tendency
to accept the gift that this approach offers them, of a series of 'illustrations' of scenes from the Homeric epic. As Cook points out, this
tendency has not gone unchallenged in recent years;[27] but, at least
outside the narrower confines of Classical art history, it seems still to
hold the field.

The Chest of Kypselos, as we have seen, offers cold comfort for the
upholders of this view. Its makers were familiar with their *Iliad*, as is
shown not so much by the often-illustrated duel of Ajax and Hektor,
which is prominent in the poem but may well have enjoyed some
currency outside it, as by the relatively obscure choice of the fight
between Agamemnon and Koön, which passes almost unnoticed in
the *Iliad* and is totally unknown from any other source. Yet despite
this, neither the Corinthian craftsmen nor the tyrants who employed
them show any sign of a wish to privilege Homeric subjects. Long
ago, Sir James Frazer, with his eye on the choice of the Muses and the
personifications of abstract and natural forces shown on the chest,
offered the more perceptive comment that the scenes appear to owe
more to Hesiod than to Homer.[28]

The inscribed verses, which were evidently composed for the occasion and to which we briefly return, also do little to direct our attention back to Homer. On the contrary, when presented with a rare
opportunity, in the scene of Agamemnon, Koön, and Iphidamas, to
cite the Homeric source for a rather obscure episode, the Corinthian
poet preferred to improvise two somewhat banal hexameters of his
own, one describing the whole scene, the other inscribed on the shield
of Agamemnon and making perhaps a veiled and incomplete allusion
to the description of its device at *Iliad* 12.37–38. Pausanias (5.19.10)
offers the conjecture that this poet was Eumelos, author of a processional hymn to Delian Apollo which he elsewhere attributes (4.4.1)
and quotes from (4.33.2). Once again, the proposal has met with rejection, mainly on the chronological ground that Eumelos would be
far too early for the apparent iconographical dating of the chest. Yet
it has the merit of being roughly compatible with *Pausanias's* date
for the chest, which could have fallen within the lifetime of Eumelos.
Pausanias may well have made his conjecture in awareness of this: if
so, it would suggest yet another way in which he has been underrated.

A more specific lesson has emerged from this reexamination of the iconography of the chest: namely, that the 'Homerist hypothesis' in the interpretation of early Greek art, which was alluded to just now and whose impact can be seen in the nineteenth and even more strongly in the twentieth century of our era, may itself go back to Pausanias's time. It is clear that the guides at Olympia, when they fashioned their interpretations of the uninscribed scenes on the chest, were positively looking out for scenes of Homeric inspiration and so settled happily on 'Nausikäa and her servant' and 'after the death of Patroklos.' Pausanias himself, who had a special interest in things Homeric, followed them with his 'Odysseus and Kirke,' which is at least as likely to be mistaken. In this predisposition, they may well reflect the prevailing artistic climate of Roman Imperial times, when the long-standing prestige of Homer in literary, political, and philosophical circles had been largely appropriated into the artistic community as well: a series of major and minor works, extending from Sperlonga to the Vatican *Odyssey* landscapes, suggest that this was so. But looking beyond the visual arts, one can see that they also reflect an attitude that finds fuller expression in the movement of the Second Sophistic. Elsner has drawn attention to some passages where the 'Homerizing' of Pausanias goes even further than that of other writers.[29] When Homer is treated as the ultimate authority on every subject, it becomes axiomatic that artists too should draw their inspiration from him.

By their readings of the scenes on the chest, Pausanias and his contemporaries betray the assumption that this had *always* been the situation, since the first diffusion of the Homeric epics. Here, as I have said, they pointed a way that modern art historians have eagerly followed. This has not come about by chance: the still largely unacknowledged influence of Pausanias on J. J. Winckelmann, the founding father of Classical art history, is at the very root of the process. There is neither the space nor the appropriate occasion to deploy here the counter-arguments to show how improbable a view of Greek art this assumption embodies; but there is some satisfaction in detecting how long it has been around.

This criticism, however, must not be permitted to cloud the broader appreciation of Pausanias as a fellow toiler in the effort to comprehend Greek art. Again and again in his description of the chest, he makes comments that can be heard, in much the same words, in any classroom of the 1990s where Archaic Greek art is being studied for the first time: 'The inscriptions are written in twisting lines which are difficult to make out' (5.17.6). 'It is perfectly obvious that this is Herakles' (5.18.4). 'Artemis (I have no idea why) has wings on her shoulders' (5.19.5). 'The Centaur does not have all four horse's hooves, but his front feet are human' (5.19.7). Here is an observant and intelligent mind, confronted with an early or mid-Archaic work for perhaps the first time, and struggling with its many unfamiliarities. Pausanias and his Olympia guides had many advantages over us: the better preservation of what they saw, the sharing of a language with the producers of the art, the possession of a much fuller literary record to help understand it, and, above all, the survival of a rich oral tradition which is almost completely lost to us. True, they lacked the wealth of archaeological comparanda that we have in the shape of excavated vases and bronzes. But there is some comfort in the fact that they still went wrong, and that eighteen centuries later we can still show that they did so.

There remains the question posed at the outset: why did Pausanias devote so much space and trouble to an antique curiosity like the Chest of Kypselos? The same explanation can hardly apply as in the case of his other long excursuses: certainly not that of the throne of Apollo at Amyklai, the nearest parallel in terms of date, where he significantly curtails his account with the words 'anyway, most of its workmanship is already familiar' (3.18.10). This judgment stands in stark contrast to that implied by his account of the chest. In a different way, the statue of Zeus was a wonder of the ancient world, the murals of Polygnotos had a literary interest in addition to being masterpieces from the great age of Greek painting, while the foundation of Megalopolis marked perhaps the greatest *bouleversement* in all Greek history: by comparison with these, the chest calls for a special motivation. The decision to include it at all may have been influenced by the fact that, just a century before, Dio Chrysostom (*Orations* 11.45 – an early speech, probably of the '70s AD), alone of other ancient writers, had made brief mention of the chest; but not the decision to treat it at such length.

Dio remarks that the chest was to be found in the *opisthodomos* of the temple of Hera, an out-of-the-way location which could only be reached after walking all round the temple to its back (western) end. Pausanias may have said the same in the missing opening lines of his account. But Arafat has now drawn a different inference: that the chest had been moved, since Dio's time, into the main *cella* of the temple, where it would have been much more conspicuous.[30] His grounds for this view are that Pausanias has already 'visited' the *opisthodomos* (5.16.1) and has now moved on into the *cella*. But the mention in

5.16.1 is part of Pausanias's brief summary of the *architecture* of the temple, where he remarks in passing that one of the columns in the *opisthodomos* was of timber. He next retails a few Olympic legends and then, from 5.17.1 to 5.20.5, he enumerates the *works of art* within the temple. The long description of the chest comes in the middle of this account, it is true; but no seasoned reader of Pausanias can exclude the possibility that he would move from one part of the temple to another (and, for that matter, back again) without explicitly telling us so. It is surely most economical to assume that the chest was still standing where it had been a century earlier, in a spot where it could not impose itself on the casual visitor. Its historical associations with the Corinthian tyranny, though not negligible, represented an episode with which few later Greeks could whole-heartedly empathize. Its materials, which included gold and ivory, were fairly costly, but by no means uniquely so. Most of the scenes carved on it were very small: even if the chest were 2.5 m long, which seems very unlikely, the size of the mostly two- and three-figure compositions in the second and fourth zones would work out at less than 15 cm square – a scale which, like their style, would not have differed markedly from that of a large Corinthian vase. The hexameter inscriptions within these scenes must have been written in tiny letters. The iconography was severely Archaic and, as the description testifies, full of unexpected obscurities. Yet Pausanias persevered until he had given some account of every figure, apart from the groups described collectively in the third and fifth zones, and until he had deciphered every inscription (unlike Dio, who, for the only scene on the chest that he described, was content to report that there was 'an inscription in ancient letters' attached to it).

It is possible that the chest had, by Pausanias's time, acquired a certain religious aura as a goal for pilgrimage: if so, this would certainly have been enough to commend it to Pausanias. But two arguments incline me to doubt the force of this explanation. First, many a Greek sanctuary housed relics that purported, however fraudulently, to be of far greater antiquity than the age of tyranny: Pausanias himself saw and described a number of these, but never at anything approaching this length. Second, there is the contrast already noted with his comment on the throne at Amyklai: for me, this carries a strong hint that the chest, far from being spotlighted because of its renown and prestige as a religious attraction, was in fact being picked out for special treatment on roughly the opposite grounds, that its workmanship was *not* 'already familiar.' I think that we shall move closer to the truth by appealing to the unusual elaboration of the chest's iconographic program: for this is a feature shared by the statue (and especially the throne) of Zeus, the large-scale murals at Delphi, and the throne at Amyklai, on all of which Pausanias also dilates at length.

Besides serving the practical purpose suggested at the very beginning of this chapter, the exposition of this, or any other, lengthy iconographic programme provided an ideal opportunity to inculcate certain academic and pedagogic principles for the description of works of art (as I have also, more tentatively, suggested). But what made the chest stand apart was the *difficulty* of its exposition, seven and one-half centuries after it was designed. This, I believe, Pausanias found to be its most attractive aspect. The challenge of its difficult subject matter aroused in him an enthusiasm that he wanted to communicate to his readers. Proud of his newfound expertise as an expositor of very early Greek figural scenes, he felt able to venture on to original interpretations of his own, just as he had done with the less forbidding works of later centuries. Few writers are entirely averse to occasional showing off, and here was an opportunity that not even the modest Pausanias could resist.

In his espousal of exact, dry, and objective description of works of art, as in his bent for the *interpretatio Homerica* as a clue to its understanding, Pausanias emerges as the true father of Classical art history. But in his bafflement at the Corinthian letter forms, in his fascination at the surprises of Archaic iconography, and, not least, in his satisfaction at his own success in unraveling it, he is something much closer: he is one of us.

Appendix: J. G. Frazer's (1898) Translation of Pausanias 5.17.5– 5.19.10

(5.17.5)...There is a chest made of cedar-wood, and on it are wrought figures, some of ivory, some of gold, and some of the cedar-wood itself. In this chest Cypselus, who became tyrant of Corinth, was hidden by his mother when at his birth the Bacchids made diligent search for him. As a thank offering for his escape his descendants, the Cypselids, dedicated the chest in Olympia. Chests were called *kupselai* by the Corinthians of that time, and it was from this circumstance, they say, that the child got the name of Cypselus. (6) Most of the figures on the chest have inscriptions attached to them in the ancient letters: some of the inscriptions run straight on, but others are in the form which the Greeks call *boustrophedon*. It is this: the second line turns round from the end of the first as in the double race-course. Moreover, the inscriptions on the chest are written in winding lines which it is hard to make out.

If we begin our survey from below, the first field on the chest exhibits the following scenes. (7) Oenomaus is pursuing Pelops, who has Hippodamia: each of them has two horses, but the horses of Pelops are winged. Next is represented the house of Amphiaraus, and some old woman or other carrying the babe Amphilochus: before the house stands Eriphyle with the necklace; and beside her are her daughters Eurydice and Demonassa, and a naked boy, Alcmaeon. (8) But Asius in his epic represents Alcmena also as a daughter of Amphiaraus and Eriphyle. Baton, who is driving the chariot of Amphiaraus, holds the reins in one hand and a spear in the other. Amphiaraus has one foot already on the chariot and his sword drawn, and is turning round to Eriphyle in a transport of rage ⟨as if he could hardly⟩ keep his hands off her. (9) After the house of Amphiaraus there are the funeral games of Pelias, and the spectators watching the competitors. Hercules is represented seated on a chair, and behind him is a woman: an inscription is wanting to tell who this woman is, but she is playing on a Phrygian, not a Greek flute. Chariots drawn by pairs of horses are being driven by Pisus, son of Perieres, by Asterion, son of Cometes (Asterion is said to have been one of those who sailed in the *Argo*), by Pollux, by Admetus, and also by Euphemus. Euphemus is said by the poets to have been a son of Poseidon, and he sailed with Jason to Colchis. He it is who is winning in the two-horse chariot-race. (10) The bold boxers are Admetus and Mopsus, son of Ampyx: between them a man stands fluting, just as it is now the custom to play the flute when the competitors in the pentathlum are leaping. Jason and Peleus are wrestling on even terms. Eurybotas, too, is represented throwing the quoit: no doubt he was some famous quoit-thrower. A foot-race is being run between Melanion, Neotheus, Phalareus, Argeus, and Iphiclus. The last is victorious, and Acastus is handing him the crown. He may be the father of the Protesilaus who went with the army to Ilium. (11) There are also tripods, no doubt prizes for the victors; and there are the daughters of Pelias, though Alcestis alone has her name written beside her. Iolaus, who voluntarily shared in the labours of Hercules, is represented victorious in the four-horse chariot-race. Here the funeral games of Pelias stop. Next we see Hercules shooting the hydra (the beast in the river Amymone), and Athena is standing beside him as he shoots. As Hercules is easily recognised both by the subject and his figure, his name is not written beside him. Phineus, the Thracian, is represented, and the sons of Boreas are chasing the harpies from him.

(5.18.1) In the second field on the chest we will begin to go round from the left. A woman is represented carrying a white boy asleep on her right arm: on her other arm she has a black boy who is like one that sleeps: the feet of both boys are turned different ways. The inscriptions show, what is easy to see without them, that the boys are Death and Sleep, and that Night is nurse to both. (2) A comely woman is punishing an ill-favoured one, throttling her with one hand and with the other smiting her with a rod. It is Justice who thus treats Injustice. Two other women are pounding with pestles in mortars: they are thought to be skilled in drugs, but there is no inscription at them. The man followed by the woman is explained by the hexameters, which run thus:—

> Idas is leading back the daughter of Evenus, fair-ankled Marpessa,
> Whom Apollo snatched from him, and she follows nothing loath.

(3) There is a man clad in a tunic: in his right hand he holds a cup, and in the left a necklace, and Alcmena is taking hold of them. This is to illustrate the Greek tale that Zeus in the likeness of Amphitryo lay with Alcmena. Menelaus, clad in a breastplate, and with a sword in his hand, is advancing to slay Helen: the scene is clearly laid at the taking of Ilium. Medea is seated on a chair: Jason stands on her right and Aphrodite on her left; and beside them is an inscription:—

> Jason weds Medea, for Aphrodite bids him do so.

(4) The Muses, too, are represented singing, and Apollo is leading the song; and there is an inscription at them:—

> This is the son of Latona, the prince, far-shooting Apollo;
> And round him the Muses, a lovely choir, and them he is leading.

Atlas is upholding on his shoulders, as the story has it, heaven and earth; and he bears also the apples of the Hesperides. Who the man with the sword is that is coming towards Atlas there is no writing beside him to show, but everyone will recognise Hercules. There is an inscription at this group also:—

> This is Atlas bearing the heaven, but the apples he will let go.

(5) There is also Ares clad in armour, leading Aphrodite: the inscription at him is Enyalius. Thetis, too, is represented as a maid: Peleus is taking hold of her, and from the hand of Thetis a snake is darting at him. The sisters of Medusa are represented with wings pursuing Perseus, who is flying through the air. The name of Perseus alone is inscribed.

(6) Armies fill the third field of the chest: most of the men are on foot, but some are riding in two-horse chariots. By the attitudes of

the soldiers you can guess that though they are advancing to battle,
they will recognise and greet each other as friends. Two explanations
are given by the guides. Some of them say that they are the Aetolians
under Oxylus, and the ancient Eleans, and that they are meeting in
recollection of their old kinship, and with mutual signs of good-will.
Others say the armies are advancing to the encounter, and that they
are the Pylians and Arcadians about to fight beside the city of Phea
and river Jardanus. (7) But it is incredible that Cypselus' ancestor,
who was a Corinthian, and had the chest made for himself, should
have voluntarily passed over all Corinthian history, and should have
caused to be wrought on the chest only foreign scenes, and scenes, too,
which were not famous. The following conjecture suggested itself to
me. Cypselus and his forefathers came originally from Gonussa, the
town above Sicyon, and Melas, son of Antasus, was an ancestor of
theirs. (8) But, as I have said in my account of Corinth, Aletes refused
to allow Melas and his host to enter and dwell in the land, for he was
alarmed by an oracle which he had received from Delphi, till at last
by coaxing and wheedling, and returning with prayers and entreaties
as often as he was driven away, Melas extracted a permission from
the reluctant Aletes. We may surmise that it is this army which is
represented by the figures wrought on the chest.

(5.19.1) On the fourth field of the chest as you go round from
the left there is Boreas with Orithyia, whom he has snatched away:
instead of feet he has the tails of snakes. There is also the combat
of Hercules with Geryon: Geryon is three men joined together. There
is Theseus with a lyre, and beside him Ariadne grasping a crown.
Achilles and Memnon are fighting, and their mothers are standing
beside them. There is Melanion, too, and beside him Atalanta with
a fawn. Hector is fighting Ajax according to challenge, and between
them stands Strife, a most hideous hag. In his picture of the battle
at the Greek ships, which may be seen in the sanctuary of Ephesian
Artemis, Calliphon of Samos represented Strife in a similar way. On
the chest are the Dioscuri, one of them beardless still, and between
them is Helen. (3) Aethra, the daughter of Pittheus, clad in black
raiment, is cast on the ground under the feet of Helen. Attached to
the group is an inscription consisting of a single hexameter verse with
the addition of one word:—

> The two sons of Tyndareus are carrying Helen away, and are drag-
> ging Aethra / From Athens.

(4) Iphidamas, son of Antenor, is lying on the ground, and Coon
is defending him against Agamemnon. Terror, a male figure with a

lion's head, is depicted on Agamemnon's shield. Above the corpse of Iphidamas is an inscription:–

> This is Iphidamas, Coon is fighting for him;

and on the shield of Agamemnon:–

> (5) This is the Terror of mortals: he who holds him is Agamemnon.

Hermes is leading to Alexander, son of Priam, the goddesses to be judged by him touching their beauty. This group also has an inscription:–

> This is Hermes: he is showing Hera, Athena, and Aphrodite
> To Alexander, to judge of their beauty.

I do not know for what reason Artemis is represented with wings on her shoulders: in her right hand she grasps a leopard, and in the other hand a lion. Ajax is represented dragging Cassandra from the image of Athena; and there is an inscription at him:–

> Ajax the Locrian is dragging Cassandra from Athena.

(6) There are also the sons of Oedipus: Polynices has fallen on his knee, and Eteocles is rushing at him. Behind Polynices stands a female figure with teeth as cruel as a wild beast's, and the nails of her fingers are hooked: an inscription beside her declares that she is Doom, implying that Polynices is carried off by fate, and that Eteocles has justly met his end. Dionysus is reclining in a cave: he has a beard and a golden cup, and is clad in a tunic that reaches to his feet: round about him are vines and apple-trees and pomegranate-trees.

(7) The uppermost field, for the fields are five in number, presents no inscription, and we are left to conjecture the meaning of the reliefs. There is a woman in a grotto sleeping with a man upon a bed: we supposed them to be Ulysses and Circe, judging both from the number of the handmaids in front of the grotto, and from the work they were doing; for the women are four in number, and are doing the works which Homer has described. There is a Centaur not with all his legs those of a horse, but with his forelegs those of a man. (8) Next are the chariots drawn by pairs of horses, with women standing in them: the horses have golden wings, and a man is giving arms to one of the woman. This scene is conjecturally referred to the death of Patroclus, it being supposed that the women in the chariots are Nereids, and that Thetis is receiving the arm from Hephaestus. Besides, the man who is giving the arms is not strong on his feet, and behind follows a servant with a pair of fire-tongs. (9) As to the Centaur, it is said that he is Chiron who, having quitted this mortal world, and having been found worthy to dwell with gods, has yet to come to soothe the grief of Achilles.

As to the maidens in the mule-car, one holding the reins, the other with a veil on her head, they believe them to be Nausicaa, daughter of Alcinous, and the handmaid driving to the washing-troughs. The man shooting at Centaurs, some of whom he has already slain, is clearly Hercules, and the scene is one of his exploits.

(10) Who the craftsman was that made the chest we were quite unable to conjecture. As to the inscriptions on it, though they may perhaps be by a different poet, yet on the whole I am inclined to guess that they are by Eumelus, the Corinthian, chiefly on the ground of the processional hymn which he composed for Delos.

NOTES

1. See esp. Elsner 1992.
2. Gurlitt 1890: 126.
3. Habicht 1985: 161 and n.82.
4. Hitzig and Blümner 1896–1910.
5. See Habicht 1985: 131–33; and now Arafat 1996: 43–79.
6. Habicht 1985: 165–75 (Appendix I: "Pausanias and His Critics").
7. As by Robert 1888: 436–44.
8. As by Gallavotti 1978: 12–14.
9. Habicht 1985.
10. Gallavotti 1978: 3.
11. See Vatin 1981: 440–49, on the now rediscovered inscriptions; Habicht 1985: 75–77.
12. Veyne 1988b: 3.
13. E. g., Stuart Jones 1894; von Massow 1916 (from whom Fig. 23.1 is taken).
14. Cook 1983.
15. Cook 1983: 3–4.
16. Loeschcke 1880: 5ff. [*non vidi*].
17. Johansen 1967: 247–49.
18. Klein 1885: 16.
19. Loeschcke 1894: 512–13, n. 2.
20. See the exchange between Brommer 1980 and Boardman 1981.
21. So von Massow 1916: 96.
22. Johansen 1934: 52–72, 1967, 92–127.
23. Lowenstam 1993.
24. Cook 1983: 5.
25. Snodgrass 1998.
26. Most notably, Johansen 1967; Schefold 1964, 1978, 1981, 1989, 1993; Schefold and Jung 1988.
27. Cook 1983: I, n. I.

28. Frazer 1898, vol. 3: 606.
29. Elsner 1995: 316–17, n. 30.
30. Arafat 1995: 465.

BIBLIOGRAPHY

AM Mitteilungen des Deutschen Archäologischen Instituts, Athenische Abteilung

BABesch Bulletin antieke beschaving. Annual Papers on Classical Archaeology

BCH Bulletin de Correspondance Héllénique

BSA Annual of the British School at Athens

JHS Journal of Hellenic Studies

JWalt Journal of the Walters Art Gallery

Arafat, K. W. (1995), 'Pausanias and the Temple of Hera at Olympia', *BSA* 90: 461–73.

Boardman, J. (1981), 'No, no Nausicäa.' *JWalt* 39: 38.

Brommer, F. (1980), 'Theseus and Nausicäa.' *JWalt* 38: 119–20.

Cook, R. M. (1983), 'Art and epic in Archaic Greece', *BABesch* 58: 1–10.

Elsner, J. R. (1992), 'Pausanias: a Greek pilgrim in the Roman world', *Past and Present*, 135: 3–29.

—— (1995), *Art and the Roman Viewer: The Transformation of Art from the Pagan World to Christianity*, Cambridge and New York: Cambridge University Press.

Frazer, J. G. (1898), *Pausanias's 'Description of Greece'*, 6 vols, London: Macmillan.

Gallavotti, C. (1978), 'Le copie di Pausania e gli originali di alcune iscrizioni di Olimpia', *Bollettino del Comitato per la Preparazione dell'Edizione Nazionale dei Classici Greci e Latini (Accademia dei Lincei)*, n. s. 26: 3–27.

Gurlitt, W. (1890), *Über Pausanias Untersuchungen*, Graz: Leuschner & Lubensky.

Habicht, C. (1985), *Pausanias' Guide to Ancient Greece* (Sather Classical Lectures 50), Berkeley: University of California Press.

Hitzig, H. and H. Blümner (1896–1910), *Pausaniae Graeciae Descriptio*, 3 vols, Leipzig: Reisland.

Johansen, K. F. (1967), *The Iliad in Early Greek Art*, Copenhagen: Munksgaard.

Klein, W. (1885), *Zur Kypsele der Kyspeliden*, Vienna: Carl Gerold's Sohn. Originally published in *Sitzungsberichte der phil.-hist. Classe der Kaiserlichen Akademie der Wissenschaften* 108 (1884): 51–83.

Loeschke, G. (1880), *Observationes Archaeologicae (Archäologische Miszellen)*, Dorpat: Schnakenburg.

Lowenstam, S. (1993), 'The arming of Achilles on early Greek vases', *Classical Antiquity* 12: 199–223.

Robert, C. (1888), 'Olympische Glossen', *Hermes* 23: 424–53.

Schefold, K. (1964), *Frühgriechische Sagenbilder*, Munich: Hirmer Verlag. English translation: *Myth and Legend in Early Greek Art*, London: Thames and Hudson, 1966.

—— (1978), *Götter- und Heldensagen der Griechen in der spätarchaischen Kunst*, Munich: Hirmer Verlag. English translation: *Gods and Heroes in Late Archaic Greek Art*, Cambridge: Cambridge University Press, 1992.

—— (1981), *Die Göttersage in der klassischen und hellenistischen Kunst*, Munich: Hirmer Verlag.

—— (1989), *Die Sagen von den Argonauten, von Theben und Troia in der klassischen und hellenistischen Kunst*, Munich: Hirmer Verlag.

—— (1993), *Götter- und Heldensagen der Griechen in der früh- und hoch-Archaischen Kunst* (new edn. of Schefold 1964), Munich: Hirmer Verlag.

—— and F. Jung (1988), *Die Urkönige: Perseus, Bellerophon, Herakles und Theseus in der klassischen und hellenistischen Kunst*, Munich: Hirmer Verlag.

Stuart Jones, H. (1894), 'The Chest of Kypselos', *JHS* 14: 30–80.

Vatin, C. (1981), 'Monuments votifs de Delphes', *BCH* 105: 429–59.

Veyne, P. (1988), *Did the Greeks Believe in Their Myths? An Essay on the Constitutive Imagination*, trans. P. Wissing, Chicago and London: University of Chicago Press.

von Massow, W. (1916), 'Die Kypseloslade', *AM* 41: 1–117.

PART VI

Archaeological Survey

A setback for the major intellectual movements of the last forty years in archaeology has been their failure to capture the public imagination, in the same way that their unreconstructed predecessors did. Much the same could be said, respectively, of intensive archaeological survey and excavation. I suspect that many general readers have been mystified by the hold that field survey has taken on archaeologists in the Mediterranean lands. It can further be argued that some of the initial ambitions nursed by its early pioneers have, in the generation that has since elapsed, fallen seriously short of fulfilment: compare p. 5 above.

These are reasonable attitudes. The best counter to them is perhaps to present a selective but considered case, based not on expectation but on several years of experience, for what rural survey can contribute. This is what Ch. 24 aims to do, picking out one main finding that should be of central concern to Classicists and of some interest to archaeologists of all kinds.

CHAPTER 24

Survey Archaeology and the Rural Landscape of the Greek City

The revelation that, in Boeotia and certain other areas of Aegean Greece, the Classical countryside was covered by a network of small but closely-spaced activity areas (to use a neutral term) was clearly apparent by 1990 when this paper was published. A degree of support for this basic finding is claimed (pp. 456–7 below) from many other survey projects in Greece; but for the *interpretation* of the finding, that the 'activity areas' are in fact the remnants of isolated farmsteads, occupied at least seasonally by agriculturalists, a much more dramatic confirmation came a few years later, with the publication of Hans Lohmann's work (Lohmann 1993) in a different part of Greece, south-eastern Attica. Here (as further discussed in Ch. 25) there were visible architectural remains, often of some pretension, at rural sites of exactly the same period, primarily the fifth and fourth centuries BC. Even this is not in itself proof that a similar pattern of dispersed Classical settlement prevailed in Greece as a whole; but it surely lays, on those who maintain other explanations of the same widespread phenomenon, the immediate burden of disproof. The whole issue is thoroughly discussed in Whitley 2001: 377–91.

BIBLIOGRAPHY

Lohmann, H. (1993), *Atene: Forschungen zu Siedlungs- und Wirtschaftsstruktur des klassischen Attika*, 2 vols, Cologne and Weimar: Böhlar Verlag.
Whitley, J. (2001), *The Archaeology of Ancient Greece*, Cambridge: Cambridge University Press.

'For all scholars' good intentions the study of the ancient city has remained the study of the town.'[1] This chapter is addressed to those (surely the great majority) who think that this statement is true, and especially to those – still I think a majority – who think that it ought not to be true. Most studies of the *polis* at least pay lip service to the axiom that it formed an indissoluble union between town and countryside but, when and if they move from the abstract level to the physical, they find that they have embarrassingly little to say about the second element in this partnership. I shall not linger here on the reasons for this state of affairs: we can, if we wish, comfort ourselves by laying a good part of the responsibility on the ancient Greeks, first for using such an infuriatingly ambivalent term as *polis*, and secondly because their surviving authors do in fact show an almost exclusive preoccupation with the urban component of the physical make-up of the *polis*, at the expense of the rural.

What can we do, at this late stage, to counteract a bias which can be traced all the way back to antiquity, and which nearly two centuries of organized archaeological work in Greece have only served to reinforce? In a general way, we can take a leaf from the book of other schools of modern classical studies, and adopt approaches from other disciplines. Thus in the present case, it was at first left to non-Classical scholars – most notably, the sociologist Max Weber – to draw attention to the degree of dependence of the ancient city on agriculture. Weber's insight met with prolonged resistance from within the guild of classicists; but when it eventually won the very widespread acceptance among ancient historians which it now commands, the effect on their work was profound: much valuable work on the agricultural economy and especially its demographic implications has already resulted. On literary classicists, constrained as they are to share the predilections of their chosen ancient authors, the effect has been much less conspicuous. Even if the great majority of these authors themselves owned and worked pieces of farming-land, one would hardly guess as much (at least for the Greeks among them) from their surviving writings.

Equally muted has been the effect on classical archaeologists, until the last few years; and for this there is, I think, a special explanation. It

'Survey archaeology and the rural landscape of the Greek city', from O. Murray and S. Price (ed.), *The Greek City from Homer to Alexander*, Oxford: Clarendon Press, 1990, pp. 113–36.

is that the traditional medium of archaeological research, excavation, is in its nature ill-suited to illuminating the rural sector of the ancient world. All the greatest achievements of excavation in the historical periods of ancient Greece and Italy have been associated with urban sites, with the cemeteries that these towns produced, and with the major sanctuaries that either arose within the towns, or themselves grew to the scale of conurbations. The excavator who works in an urban site can be certain of results, even if they do not match in quality, or correspond in period, with what he anticipated. By contrast the ultimate nightmare of the excavator, that of finding quite literally nothing, is a real possibility in a rural context; actual instances, though of course the annals are silent about them, survive in the memory of oral folk-lore among the archaeological fraternity.

In defence of excavation as a source of knowledge of the rural sector, it should be acknowledged that there have been a few outstanding investigations of isolated rural sites. Many archaeologists would also make the further claim that the excavation of a regional centre contributes information on that region as a whole.[2] This argument has a certain instinctive appeal: a capital is after all held to be 'representative' of the country that it controls, in one sense of that word. The trouble is that it is the wrong sense for the purpose under consideration. With the Greek city-state, with its regular verbal identity between the main conurbation and the *polis* as a whole, the temptation to make this semantic slip is all the greater. In ideal conditions, if first the entirety of a city-site were to be excavated, and secondly the entire range of finds were to be recorded, including not only manufactured durables but also more perishable natural commodities, then the claim would have greater substance. As things are, however, the only approximations to the fulfilment of the first condition took place at a time when the second requirement was not yet envisaged; and today financial and political conditions combine to make the first aim an increasingly unrealistic one. Instead, excavators must content themselves with a small sample of the chosen urban site; in terms of representativeness, the best that they can hope for is that the choice of their sample will be determined by scientific criteria rather than (as is more usual) by irrelevant constraints such as the existence of later standing structures or the selective availability of land for purchase.

One natural reaction to this quandary is to abandon the rural sector of urbanized societies, as being archaeologically unapproachable; another, less defensible, is to dismiss it as uninteresting. But a moment's thought will reveal the annihilating effect that either attitude would have on archaeological work in cultures that are not only pre-urban, but sometimes pre-agricultural and even non-sedentary. In all these areas, non-classical archaeology has some impressive past achievements to its credit; but most exciting of all are the very recent results, and the prospects for future ones.[3] Here is a case in point of the desirability of learning from other disciplines, or from other branches of the same discipline. The key to the most successful attainments in these fields has been, above all, a technique of site-location of a kind that has hardly been called on in traditional classical archaeology, together with the scarcely less important dogma that the business of archaeology is the entire material culture of past societies, which itself has a major bearing on what constitutes a 'site'.

Thus we come at last to the topic of archaeological survey. Even when prefixed by 'archaeological', the word 'survey' remains distressingly ambiguous and is uniquely generative of misunderstandings even among professional archaeologists. In the sense in which it was used in the previous paragraph, it need mean no more than a desirable preliminary to later excavation – which is exactly the sense to which many would confine it, descriptively and often prescriptively as well. The idea that a survey, alone and in its own right, can generate worthwhile archaeological results still has to be tirelessly promoted and defended today. In part, this is because some notable surveys have been carried out by those who reject any such idea. In part, too, it arises from the arguable claim that survey is parasitic upon excavation in a different way: namely, that survey archaeologists have constant recourse to knowledge acquired through previous excavations. How else could they date their pottery, recognize a piece of an olive-press, or interpret a fragmentary Doric cornice? As a matter of fact, there is more than one answer to these rhetorical questions – stylistic studies, textual descriptions, and standing monuments have played a part comparable with that of excavation in the understanding of such finds – but let that pass. Supposing that the claim were wholly justified, would it have any bearing on the utility of survey? Would any doctor dismiss diagnosis for being 'parasitic' on anatomy or surgery? In the advance of a discipline, any technique that is developed later is likely to draw on those already established.

But even in those archaeological circles where survey is fully accepted, there is still room for radical disagreement on a further issue: the exact nature of survey to be undertaken. Should a survey cover a smaller but contiguous block of land, or should it proceed by carefully sampling a larger block? If the latter, on what principles should the sample be chosen? Should the survey be concentrated on the period or periods in which its directors have an established interest and competence, or should it deal with all periods? Finally, should it be intensive, to the point of aiming at total coverage of the chosen territory?

The last question is the most important one, and an answer to it determines one's answers to the other questions. When the intensive technique was first tried out in the 1970s, there was room for honest doubt about its value. But enough has resulted from the subsequent decade's work to make only one view tenable today. For one thing, it has been demonstrated[4] that intensive surveys (predictably) find many more sites than 'extensive' ones, which proceed by investigating only the likely site-locations: in some cases, the intensive method yields more than 100 times as many sites per unit of territory. Whatever riposte is offered to this observation, it will have to be a good one to justify a method that can be predicted to miss up to 99 out of any 100 knowable archaeological sites (to say nothing of the others that even the intensive method may miss). In the particular case of the ancient Greek landscape, which has now been shown to have been a populous one (at least at certain periods), and which produces surface material in quantities undreamed of in the areas where the intensive survey technique was pioneered like North America and northern Europe, I think that the need to explore every kind of terrain is absolute.

This finding, if accepted, does not preclude the use of a well-planned sampling technique, though I think it does tip the scales in favour of using what is called a 'stratified' sample: that is, one in which scope is given to pre-existing knowledge about boundaries, preferences of soil-type, and historical evidence generally, rather than allowing purely mathematical factors to determine the locations of the sampled tracts. The finding does also point to an answer to our remaining question, whether to have a selective concentration of period. For intensive survey is a slow, laborious, and taxing technique for everyone involved in it. To invest so much time and labour in a territory, only to dismiss the finds of many of its periods of settlement as being of no direct concern to the project, is an enormous waste of energy. In the same way, the exponents of the older ethic of excavation, who hacked their way impatiently through the post-classical levels of a site in order to get at their chosen period, were sentencing themselves to much unproductive labour.

They were also, of course, guilty of permanent destruction of the evidence in question. This brings us to the final justification of survey – what might be loosely called the environmental one. Survey is unlike excavation in that it does not directly involve the destruction of the evidence with which it works. A given stretch of terrain may be re-surveyed, if not indefinitely, then at least several times over, and adequate material can be taken from the surface each time under most conditions. For it is the repetition of the cultivation process, year after year, which provides surface survey with its diagnostic evidence; wherever this continues, and in some cases even where it does not, and natural erosion performs the work instead, this material will continue to appear. Intrinsically, this material is almost always unspectacular: once recorded and analysed, it can be packed away economically, making slight demands on museum storage, and virtually none on exhihition space. This explains its lack of attraction to one kind of archaeological mentality, but in these days of excessive pressure on museum space in Greece, it can be reckoned as a further advantage.

To sum up the generalizations in the first part of this paper: archaeological survey, pioneered in very different conditions and for very different purposes elsewhere, has come to fill a specific need in Mediterranean archaeology. It is uniquely adapted to cope with the long-standing void of relative ignorance in our understanding of the rural territory of the ancient city. In the process of transplantation from the plains of North America and the sparser archaeological landscapes of temperate Europe to the dense palimpsest of Mediterranean settlement, it has inevitably undergone changes: in particular, as it spread first to Italy and then to Greece. After some epoch-making pioneer work at a less intensive level, it was the 1970s which saw the first attempts to apply the total-coverage survey in Greece proper. Pride of place may be given to the Argolid Exploration Project, inaugurated by an American team in 1972 and resumed in 1979–83.[5] The outstanding project of the mid 70s was the Melos survey, which like the Argolid project grew up in association with the excavation of a major site or sites within the territory surveyed.[6] In 1979 came the inauguration of the Cambridge/Bradford Boeotian Expedition, whose work will form the subject of the rest of this paper.[7] The early 1980s saw a proliferation of similar projects, mostly again of Anglo-Saxon initiative, which are not yet fully published: the Megalopolis survey of the University of Sheffield, the Greco-Anglo-American survey in northern Keos and the Nemea Valley Archaeological Project which involved some of the same team, the Methana survey and the Laconia survey of the British School at Athens, and the Strymon Valley project. (This list is a selective one, omitting several undertakings which are either directed at specific periods or less intensive in their coverage.)[8]

Between them these projects have involved dozens of researchers, in a number of disciplines besides archaeology, and their existence and concentration of date show that a wave of activity in intensive survey has swept across the scene of Greek archaeology. That such activity is misdirected or unproductive is coming to seem increasingly unlikely.

It is time to turn to specifics, and record some of the experiences of the Boeotian project which I direct jointly with Dr John Bintliff of the University of Bradford. By the time that we took the field in 1979 we had become convinced advocates of an intensive, all-period approach aiming at total coverage. In choosing Boeotia, we are not committing ourselves to the territory of a single *polis*, but rather to that of a loose federation of cities with a slightly qualified degree of independence. In the event, our area of operation within Boeotia was one that quite definitely included parts of the territories of at least two of these cities, since it embraced the urban centres of Thespiai at one extremity and Haliartos at the other (Fig. 24.1). By ranging from the centres of cities to the borders of their territories we placed ourselves to assemble comparable data for every facet of the classical *polis*, in addition to our findings for other periods to which such divisions are inapplicable. The account that follows will be highly selective, omitting whole millennia that range from the sparse finds of the Upper Palaeolithic to the surprisingly positive picture of the Turkish period; selective, too, in making little reference to the very detailed patterns of growth and decline, shift and abandonment that emerged from our study of the city-sites themselves, since the main purpose of this chapter is to cast some light on the rural landscape.

First, some overall figures. To date, seven seasons of field-walking and two study sessions have been carried out. In that time, we have covered some forty square kilometres, and it is chastening to reflect that this represents little over 1.5 per cent of the land surface of ancient Boeotia. The area covered forms a single block, if of rather straggling shape, and this means that on strict statistical criteria it has no validity as a sample of Boeotia as a whole. However, we see our findings as complementary to those of the other expeditions working elsewhere on the Greek mainland and islands: it is ancient Greece in its totality that we are combining to sample, and we draw much encouragement from the fact that many of our most important findings for the classical period are being replicated in the results of these other expeditions. Indeed, it will be a matter for specific mention when a finding is *not* so replicated, but seems rather to be peculiar to Boeotia.

Figure 24.1 Map of part of western Boeotia. Stipple shows the area covered by survey in 1979–1986.

In these forty square kilometres we have found about 150 sites, maintaining steadily from season to season a frequency of just under four sites per square kilometre. The density is rather high, and already hints at the fact that the great majority of these sites are very small. The figure of 150 of course covers all periods; but the fact is that a large majority of the sites (well over three-quarters) show occupation in the age of the *polis* (more precise specifications will be given presently). Here it is important to mention a subsidiary part of the surveying process which has a bearing on the definition and interpretation of these small sites. From 1980 onwards – that is, in all seasons but the first – we have been systematically recording the density of artefacts over the whole landscape, between, around, and within the sites. This practice has brought into sharp focus two features of the archaeological landscape which would otherwise have remained vague impressions. First, there are whole areas of generally very high and generally very low density of finds in the 'off-site' sector, such that, at times, what would qualify as a 'site' in a 'low' area passes unnoticed, as a stretch of standard 'off-site' density in a 'high' area. In other words, the criterion for defining a 'site' has to be relative to its surrounding level of find-density, and not an absolute one, if absurd results are to be avoided. In case this sounds like a mere piece of sophistry, let me say that, once we tackle the problem of explaining how this scatter of 'off-site' artefacts came to be generated, and why it should vary so greatly in density, we shall thereby also be offering an explanation of the variations in prominence of the actual sites.

The second observation arising from the overall recording of finds will set us on the path towards tackling that problem. It is that, around almost every site, there is a clear 'halo' of finds, whose level of density is decidedly lower than that of the site itself, but equally higher than the standard 'off-site' level of the surrounding area. Typically, it is of a moderately high density in a generally 'low' area, and very high in a generally 'high' area. It usually extends over an area several times larger than the site itself, often on all sides, and regularly extends up-slope as well as down-slope from the site. Figure 24.2, which shows a detail from one of our overall density plots, is taken from an area of generally extremely high density, in the western approaches to the city site of Thespiai itself; it shows a scatter of small rural sites, each with its 'halo', standing out from the unusually high background density. What is the genesis of these haloes? Are they the product of natural processes, geomorphological or climatic, which have eroded or washed the material out from the nucleus of the site? Or are they rather generated by the endlessly repeated human activities of cultivation, with the plough carrying artefacts every year a little more or a little further, down to and beyond the present day? Any of these answers would reduce the archaeological significance of the haloes almost to vanishing point. But fortunately (as we see it) there are some clinching arguments that deny anything more than a minor contributory role to these incidental processes.

First, the observation already made: that the haloes run uphill as well as downhill from their sites, sometimes for fifty or a hundred metres. There is no mechanism whereby weathering could bring about this result, nor can the plough drag small sherds over such distances.

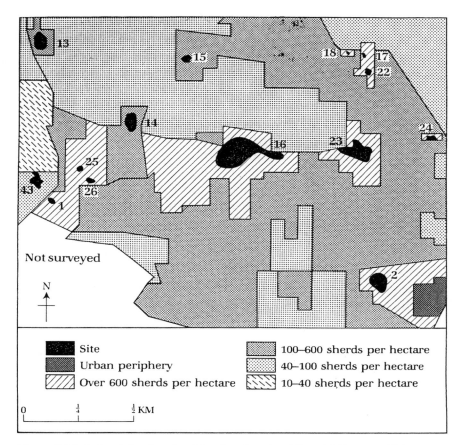

Figure 24.2 A sherd density plot. The site of ancient Thespiai lies just off the bottom right-hand corner. In the northern sector, the ground slopes steadily from north to south; in the sourthern it is virtually level.

Secondly, there is the fact that the background scatter of finds continues where the haloes leave off, often at a far from negligible level of density, and seldom dropping to the zero level. It is too much to believe that every one of these scattered artefacts has got there by means of random subsequent dispersal from the nearest site. Finally, the density of the off-site scatters, the strength of the haloes, and the frequency of the sites themselves are all features that are clearly correlated with each other. Where sites are thin on the ground, individual artefacts in general become correspondingly fewer.

There is one explanation which will answer the facts better than any of those so far considered, and we are inclined to accept it as having played the greatest single part.[9] It is that the activities of cultivation are indeed responsible for the spreading effect: but that these were activities contemporary with the occupation of the sites, and involved fertilizing rather than ploughing operations. The prime fertilizing agent in antiquity was animal manure, collected up from the locations where livestock was stalled or tethered, and then carried out to the fields by cart or on donkey- or mule-back. Since the livestock would normally be kept in or near structures where other activities took place, and since in antiquity many of these other activities involved the use (and therefore the breakage) of pottery, it would be a commonplace thing for rubbish including broken tile and potsherd to be mingled with the manure. When the manure came to be spread on the land, a certain proportion of sherds would go with it: even a single piece in every load of dung, repeated on each journey and augmented by occasional mishaps and deliberate disposals, would be enough to produce the pattern that we see. The relatively high density of the halo around the site itself would have several plausible explanations. Most importantly, there was a common practice of locating very intensive in-field cultivation, of the nature of gardening more often than agriculture, in the immediate vicinity of a town or farm. As far as accidental deposition goes, it is also true that every radial journey must pass through the immediate environs of the centre-point, and that the density of the radii is at its highest there.

If this explanation is adopted, it has some important implications. First, it means that the level of off-site density is an index of agricultural activity, and specifically of contemporary (that is, in this case, ancient) agricultural activity. The general areas of high density are areas of intensive ancient cultivation. Since in many cases these will coincide with areas of similar but later activity, we can see why it is that sites in the low-density area are not only few, but also 'weak', in the sense that their interior density of finds is low: there has not been the same frequency of farming operations over the subsequent centuries to bring their material to the surface. Next, and even more important from the viewpoint of the survey archaeologist's self-confidence, the presence of the haloes serves to confirm the reality of the sites, and indeed to show that they were foci of ancient agricultural operations. We shall see the significance of this last point in a moment.

We had been surveying in Boeotia for some seasons before all these points became clear to us. But meanwhile, virtually every intensive survey in Greece was replicating our main observation about site-distribution: that the scatter of rural sites reached, in the Classical period, its highest peak of density at any point in the past, and that the great majority of these Classical sites were very small. Not every survey, however, was reporting the same subsidiary features in the pattern: thus, the Nemea Valley Project finds that the haloes are much less distinct, while from the southern Argolid it is even stated that '... artifacts occurred for the most part in discrete clusters.... Few were found in between; there was little background scatter.'[10] These differences may perhaps in some way relate to the distinctive feature for which, above all, Boeotia was notorious in antiquity, the rustic preoccupations of its inhabitants.

It is time now to face the central question arising from this pattern of classical settlement: the interpretation of the sites and the explanation of their distribution. Let us first tabulate their salient features:

(i) *Small size.* In Boeotia, the typical classical rural site occupied less than one half of a hectare – that is, it measured 70 metres or less across – even after the effects of local dispersal had operated.

(ii) *Frequency.* With an overall density of above three per square kilometre, and an average size as described, it follows that the distance between any two classical sites was frequently of the order of 500 metres, and sometimes much less. They also occurred within this relatively short distance of the major city-sites.

(iii) *Foci of activity.* Almost every site was seen to have formed the centre of a sequence of agricultural operations, which we have identified as being primarily directed at fertilization.

(iv) *Characteristic finds.* These form the most fundamental feature of all, since it is by them that the site is recognized and defined as such. On Classical sites, they normally consist of numerous roof-tiles; appreciable quantities of coarse or semi-coarse household pottery; lesser amounts of fine glazed pottery; occasional pieces of cooking ware, burned with use; and occasional pieces of building material.

It is worth mentioning here the interesting cases of a correlation in the *absence*, rather than the presence, of features (iii) and (iv) above. With a very few sites, there was neither the halo that we associate with cultivation, nor any sign of roof-tiles, while the pottery showed an unusual preponderance of fine painted ware. These sites we interpret as rural grave- or cemetery-sites; and their presence in the landscape is not without significance for the interpretation of the very much larger group of 'standard' classical sites.

We are now face to face with the question: what form of rural activity is most consonant with the small size, dense distribution-pattern, and indications of use that these sites present? Our hypothesis about the haloes implies the presence of farm animals, but are the other attributes compatible with structures that were *only* used as animal-shelters? Surely not. These attributes imply at least the intermittent use of the sites for human occupancy. The haloes suggest that they were used as bases from which cultivation was carried out, while the household pottery suggests that they were more than mere barns or implement-sheds. Further, the occasional interleaving of burial locations among these occupation-sites at a distinctly close human attachment to the land, and therefore presumably also to the structures on it.

So far, everything appears to point to one conclusion: our Classical rural sites are isolated farmsteads. But no sooner is this hypothesis advanced than it is seen to bristle with difficulties. If these sites represent rural dwellings which were the only residence of the landowner in question, then why did such landowners choose to build them within very close distances of the city (particularly in the case of Thespiai, Fig. 24.2)? Everything that we know about Greek society, ancient and modern, suggests that the amenities of living in a town or village would be rated far too highly to be sacrificed merely in order to save oneself a ten- or fifteen-minute walk to one's land. Next there is the difficulty about Greek inheritance law – again, both ancient and modern. Since the practices of partible inheritance and dowry tend inexorably to result in the fragmentation of a given family's land-holdings, the construction of a farmstead on any one plot would be a questionable step in the first place, and a diminishing asset with the passage of every generation thereafter. The presumptive preference for living in the town would become a choice with no reasonable alternative.

Somehow, these a priori arguments have to be reconciled with the empirical findings from the evidence. There are at least possible ways out of the impasse. Thus the objection based on partible inheritance is at its weakest in the circumstances of a fresh apportionment of land – an event most familiar from the colonial context (as has been most strikingly confirmed by the survey evidence from Metaponto where, sure enough, rural farmsteads were regularly built[11]), but not an unknown phenomenon in the history of the cities of the Greek homeland. Is it possible that some such step was taken in classical Thespiai, and the other regions of Greece where a similar pattern of settlement is emerging? Again, human occupancy is not synonymous with owner-occupancy: many of these putative farmsteads could have been occupied by the eldest son, bailiff, or slaves of the landowner, without any visible difference in the material evidence. Nor should we exclude the possibility of second homes, expressly recommended by Plato in the *Laws* (745E 4–5) and later disparaged by Aristotle in the *Politics* (1265[b] 25–6) on the grounds that they made life awkward. Both passages date from the general period under discussion, and each in a different way implies that its author was not unfamiliar with the idea of double residence.

The final alternative is to brazen the matter out, and state flatly that at certain periods Boeotians and other Greeks, in contrast to their modern descendants and in default of much other positive evidence to this effect, actually did prefer to reside permanently in farmsteads built on their lands, even when these lay quite close to their city. After all, Brasidas' acceptance into Amphipolis was preceded by his capture of 'the property of those Amphipolitans who were living all over the district' (sc. between the bridge over the River Strymon and the city; Thucydides 4. 103. 5); it is, I think, implied by the phrase 'all over' that they lived in homesteads rather than hamlets or villages. There are also Hellenistic inscriptions from Boeotia, and even from Thespiai itself, which testify to the existence of permanent buildings, of unspecified use but appreciable monetary value, associated with land-holdings in the open country.[12] The history of the study of the ancient Greeks is littered with instances of the overturning of long-established dogmas, and it may be that this is another case in point.

It is at this stage in the argument that critics, and even uncommitted bystanders, invariably ask: 'Surely you must excavate one or more of your rural sites to get the answers?' To us, the belief that excavation would necessarily, or even probably, provide these answers appears ingenuous. We may note that even the admirably-conducted excavation of one such isolated house, above Vari in Attica,[13] did not reveal such farm equipment as would have proved its agricultural use, nor other evidence to determine what was the status of its occupants, nor whether it was their only home. Certain other questions, for example those relating to the size and plan of a small rural structure, would undoubtedly be answered by excavation; but here we can point to the practice of geophysical survey with the electric resistivity meter, which in favourable circumstances can provide an outline plan of buried buildings without disturbing the surface.

I turn now to the question of the distribution of these small sites, tentatively identified as farmsteads, in the Classical period.

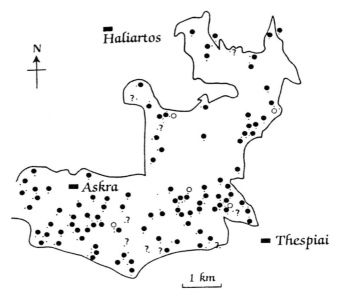

Figure 24.3 Distribution of sites found in 1979–1984. The survey was later
extended to include the sites of Haliartos and Thespiai.

Figure 24.3 covers the area walked to the end of our 1984 season
only, which explains why it contains only just over 100 definite or
possible sites of the period, plus nine others designated as 'uncertain'
because the relevent evidence is imprecisely dated. The sites shown
fall within a fairly long period, from the later Archaic to the early Hellenistic periods, roughly between the limits of 600 and 200 BC. Within
this bracket, greater precision is possible in a large number of cases:[14]
thus, for example, only a very few of the sites marked can be proved
to have been in occupation before the fifth century, while the vast majority show clear proof of habitation in the fourth, which appears to
mark the all-time peak of dispersed settlement in this part of Boeotia.
This finding, naturally, still falls well short of proving that this large
group of sites was actually in *simultaneous* occupation: the difficulty
is the acute shortage of imported or otherwise closely dateable pottery: so that, here again, excavation would not necessarily settle the
matter.

The distribution shown in Figure 24.3 is dense, but it is not evenly
so. There is a band of almost empty territory running across the middle
of the map, roughly in the latitude of Askra. We tentatively identify
this as the border-zone between the *chora* of Thespiai and that of

Haliartos, two cities that at times pursued sharply contrasting policies. The line roughly coincides with the border as shown in Figure 24.1, which is based on the placing of this feature by Paul Roesch in his book on Thespiai,[15] even though Roesch himself notes the discovery of Thespian inscriptions (perhaps moved in more recent times) to the north of this line. The line runs closer to Thespiai than to Haliartos, reflecting the fact that the former city had ample territory to the south, whereas that of Haliartos was circumscribed on the north by the shore-line of Lake Copais (now drained). Here, however, our survey has shown that the size of the lake in antiquity was appreciably smaller than in the nineteenth century, prior to the modern drainage. We have surveyed well within the nineteenth-century shore-line, and found that the background scatter disappears only at a line some way north of the shore as it appears in all classical atlases.

Only at one other period does the density of sites even approach that of the classical period, and this is in the 'Late Roman' epoch, a period whose limits are determined by certain classes of plain pottery, whose life is known to have extended from about AD 300 to 600. At that time, many of the actual sites of the classical period were reoccupied, suggesting that the ruined structures could still be rehabilitated, while a few new sites were added. This resettlement, however, is heavily concentrated in the putative Thespian territory; on the land of Haliartos, well under half the number of the classical sites was reoccupied, reflecting the fact that, since its destruction by the Romans long before in 171 BC, Haliartos had effectively ceased to exist as a city. More relevant to our purpose here, however, is the very much lower density of sites at other periods within the lifetime of the *polis*, whether in its independent heyday or in its survival as an administrative unit under the rule of the Hellenistic kingdoms and the earlier Roman empire.

Here I return to chronological sequence, and consider first the interesting pattern of settlement in the formative age of the later Geometric and earlier archaic periods (*c.* 800–600 BC). Today these centuries are widely recognized as having witnessed the rise of the *polis* system. Yet the distribution of sites does little to foreshadow the rural dispersal of the classical period. On Thespian territory, we have only the larger sites of Thespiai and Askra in occupation at this time, plus a very small number (three at the most) of the small outlying sites. But within the area of the actual city of Thespiai, the pattern is interesting: Geometric and earlier archaic sherds are concentrated not in one location, but in three or four, suggesting a cluster of villages rather than an urban nucleus, in a manner recalling Thucydides' description of Sparta (1. 10. 1). Haliartos, however, presents a different picture. In the city itself, Geometric settlement is apparently confined to the area of the later acropolis; but outside, there is a string of small sites, stretching from 500 to 2500 metres away to the east, whose occupation in each case begins not far from 700 BC. Clearly, contrasting patterns of *polis* growth could coexist, even in directly adjacent cities.

This general sparseness of early settlement, with the main centres as yet being few and of modest size, and very limited rural dispersal, suggests a further conclusion about at any rate some parts of Boeotia. The 'take-off' of population-growth, which in many parts of Greece leads to a sudden access of new rural sites, and signs of rapid growth at the major centres, within the eighth century BC, simply did not happen here. No such phenomenon is detectable until some two centuries later, with the evidence already considered for the later Archaic and Classical periods. Boeotia, on this evidence, developed late; and this may explain why it is not until the fourth century that we hear of its reputation for populousness, and see its fruits in the short-lived Theban hegemony in Greece.

The picture of a relatively late and steep growth to the Classical peak is roughly mirrored by the decline that follows. In the later part of the Hellenistic period, the whole process goes into reverse. Of the large sites, Thespiai and Askra both shrink perceptibly in size, while Haliartos (for the historical reason that we have just seen, p. 461) is utterly deserted. Of the small rural sites, something over half are also abandoned at this time, in a few cases for ever, more often for a period several centuries long. The survivors among these rural sites tend to be larger ones. The opening centuries of Roman imperial rule bring no more than the slightest reversal of this decline, and it is not until the remarkable 'Late Roman' revival of the fourth and later centuries that rural settlement recovers; even then this is not fully matched in the main centres, and not at all in Haliartos. There is some literary and epigraphic evidence to substantiate this picture of agricultural depression (and even to suggest some of the reasons for it), which has been rehearsed elsewhere.[16] Our inclusion of the main city-sites within the area of the survey has borne fruit here by showing that the sequence of growth and decline in rural settlement, far from being compensated for it by the cities, is echoed by them: the picture is a total and consistent one.

I turn finally to another conspicuously neglected feature of the Greek rural scene, the *komai* or second-order settlements, which held a dependent status within the territory of a *polis*. They must have been many times more numerous than the actual *poleis*; yet immeasurably fewer of them have been excavated or investigated in detail. Thespiai is altogether exceptional among Greek cities in having three *komai* firmly located with its territory – Askra, Eutresis, and Kreusis – not to mention the extremely controversial case of Leuktra, which may not have been the name of an actual settlement at all. In our survey area, there are a dozen rural sites which comfortably exceed the norm of size, and a range from one to five hectares in extent; in the Classical period, at any rate, one would incline to interpret these as hamlets, villages, or in one case a probable sanctuary, rather than as very large farms. But at the end of our 1981 season, we located a site that was larger by a further order of magnitude: originally we reckoned its maximum size at 25 hectares, but intensive coverage of the site has reduced this figure to between 10 and 15 hectares, this peak falling as usual in the later classical period. It lay at an altitude of over 1,500 feet, midway up the Valley of the Muses, and we soon became convinced that it was none other than Askra, the home village of Hesiod (though even he does not unequivocally state that he lived *in* Askra, rather than in a nearby farm).

Once again, the arguments for the identification of the site have been set out by me elsewhere;[17] it should suffice to say here that the literary and epigraphical testimonia, coupled with the absence of any other plausible candidate within the area surveyed, make it difficult to avoid the conclusion that our site is indeed Askra. Hesiod's name was sufficiently closely associated with the place for his bones to be repatriated there, at some time after his death, only for them to be carried off to Orchomenos when (also at an uncertain date) Askra suffered the unreasonably cruel fate of being destroyed by its own *polis*, Thespiai.[18] Whatever the circumstances of this strange episode, it is enough to suggest that Askra was quite a substantial place at the time in question.

The reconstruction of Askra's history by means of surface survey presents an obvious contrast, both in method and in the details of the results, with that of another Thespian *kome*, Eutresis, which was the scene of an excavation two generations ago;[19] but the two are alike in having had very interrupted histories. The Early Helladic period sees both sites quite densely settled, but thereafter the parallel breaks down, for Askra shows no sign of occupation for almost a thousand years after the very beginning of the Middle Bronze Age, while Eutresis continued to flourish. After the end of the Bronze Age, however, it is Askra which appears to have recovered first. Pottery of the later Protogeometric period, and of several phases of the ensuing Geometric, is found at Askra, but only in the same limited sector, towards the north-western extremity of the later classical site, as the Early Helladic settlement had occupied. This belated return to the very same location recalls the correspondence that we have observed between the classical Greek and Late Roman settlements (p. 461); this time, the interval of apparent desertion is even longer, but the likelihood of visible ruins surviving is still considerable.

The small village of Hesiod's lifetime was to prosper for many centuries: the Archaic and Classical periods see a steady expansion southwards and eastwards, till the settlement bordered on the permanent watercourse that runs southwards to join the main river of the Valley of the Muses. It is possible that Askra, lacking the Mycenaean heritage of Eutresis, felt the need to protect itself with a fortification at some point in this period: round the southern perimeter of the site at its greatest extent, there runs a rather abrupt break of slope, with large blocks visible, embedded in the ground where it temporarily steepens; while within the area of the site itself, we found several worked 'polygonal' blocks, with curving joints between the corners, of a kind known from Archaic to fifth-century walls in Boeotia. They seemed too massive to have belonged to house-walls. Outside the settlement to the west another feature was visible: a small enclosure or *temenos*, whose southern and eastern walls, with their junction, partially survive. Inside this the foundations of a rectangular structure can be made out, with four large oblong blocks set on end: these show exactly the same measurement in their long axis, and are clearly re-used. Presumably they were originally orthostats for the walls of a public building, up-ended at some later time to form a crude barricade. We interpret the whole as an extra-mural sanctuary.

In the Hellenistic period Askra begins to show signs of shrinkage, and a falling density of artefacts; but the site is still on too large a scale to be interpreted as another Hellenistic country house, of the kind found by the excavators of Eutresis outside their site. In earlier Roman imperial times, evidence of occupation appears to die away altogether, an observation that is important for the identification of the site, since Pausanias (9. 29. 1) reports that at Askra in his day there was 'a tower and nothing else to remember it by'. The 'Late Roman' era, however, sees a revival at Askra that is as impressive as at any of our sites: the settlement regains most of its former size, and densities are once again very high. Askra survived even the Early Byzantine period (the only epoch, after the opening centuries of the

Iron Age, which finds our whole territory almost completely barren of settlements, whether large or small); and it lived on, by now much reduced in scale, through the later Byzantine centuries and the opening years of Turkish rule, before quietly reverting to the vineyard and arable cultivation which cover the site today. All this time, however, the nucleus of the settlement was gradually shifting south-eastwards, to the point where the original Early Helladic settlement and the final Byzantine-Turkish one have no overlap at all. The occasion for the final desertion of the site may be sought in the reoccupation of another site a short way to the east ('Valley of the Muses 4') which, long deserted, resumes strongly in the seventeenth century of our era and was actually seen in occupation by at least one of the early travellers to Greece.

One other loose end remained to be tied up by the survey: the 'tower' mentioned in the Pausanias passage. There can be little doubt that this is the watch-tower of the fourth century BC which still crowns the hill immediately to the west of Askra, and gives it the name of 'Pyrgaki' today. Indeed, a too literal reading of Pausanias' text had led many earlier authorities to place the site of Askra on the barren, stony summit of this hill, 2,150 feet above sea-level. It now emerges that Pausanias used this tower merely as a loose landmark for the location of Askra. Nevertheless, the hill-top itself did present some interesting features: in the first place, it produced a little Mycenaean pottery, absent from the site below, which hinted that, once before, Askra had suffered desertion by reason of a move elsewhere. In later times, however, from the Archaic to the Hellenistic periods, the hill probably served as an acropolis for Askra. There was some pottery from these centuries and, more substantial, the evidence of a wall-circuit enclosing an area of about one-third of a hectare around the fourth century watchtower. Inasmuch as this fortification had at one point had to be re-aligned to make room for the tower, it could be shown to have been an earlier feature of the site, and its style of masonry is perfectly compatible with an earlier Classical date. The size of the fortified enclosure would be appropriate to house the population of a *kome* in an emergency.

Our examination of Askra has, I think, revealed the strengths and weaknesses of survey in approaching a larger settlement; they differ from those which apply in the uncovering of the rural settlement pattern *in extenso*, and the limitations may be rather more apparent here. We have been able to place the site in its local context, that of the settlement and exploitation of the fertile valley in which it lies, at various periods of human history. We have charted the episodes of growth, decline, and shift in the history of the site, in general terms. We can explain its location in terms of water-supply, and general economic base (the finds include wine-jars and bee-hives), and we can detect one industrial activity in the making of pottery: 'kiln-wasters' (mis-fired vessels which would be discarded in the vicinity of the kiln) were found from both Hellenistic and, especially, the Late Roman periods. But we are unable to match the potential of excavation in answering more specific questions: was the settlement walled, and if so when? When did the historically-attested destruction of Askra take place? What exactly was the state of the site in Hesiod's lifetime, or at the moment of Pausanias' visit?

These conflicting thoughts may serve to epitomize the contribution of surface survey to the understanding of the Greek *polis* and its rural territory. Its strength lies in the diffuse nature of its results. As applied to the rural landscape *in extenso*, it is not merely the best, but at present virtually the only systematic source of fresh knowledge. Only the investigation of a sizeable stretch of territory can produce results that are truly representative. Next there is the indispensable function of site-location; and for this, too, a survey of some kind is necessary. Only in the final stage, when the focus narrows to single locations, and the interior of an individual site, does the picture presented by survey become blurred and relatively imprecise. But, for the present, it is the territorial aspect of the Greek city for which we stand in the greatest need of enlightenment; and for the immediate future, it is survey alone that can supply that need.

NOTES

1. R. G. Osborne, *Classical Landscape with Figures: The Ancient Greek City and its Countryside* (London, 1987), p. 9.
2. See 'The Analysis of Data from Surface Surveys', an exchange of views between R. Hope-Simpson and J. F. Cherry, *J. Field Archaeol.* 11 (1984), 115–20, especially Cherry on p. 119.
3. For some outstanding examples, see L. R. Binford, *In Pursuit of the Past: Decoding the Archaeological Record* (London, 1983).
4. See J. F. Cherry, 'Frogs Round the Pond: Perspectives on Current Archaeological Survey Projects in the Mediterranean Region', in D. R. Keller and D. W. Rupp (eds.), *Archaeological Survey in the Mediterranean Area* (Oxford, 1983), pp. 375–416, especially p. 391 and fig. 1.
5. See most recently T. H. van Andel and C. Runnels. *Beyond the Acropolis: A Rural Greek Past* (Stanford, 1987).

6. C. Renfrew and M. Wagstaff (eds.), *An Island Polity: The Archaeology of Exploitation in Melos* (Cambridge, 1982).

7. For an interim report, see J. L. Bintliff and A. M. Snodgrass, 'The Cambridge/Bradford Boeotian Expedition: The First Four Years', *J. Field Archaeol.* 12 (1985), 123–61.

8. For an instance of the latter, S. Bommeljé and P. K. Doorn, *Aetolia and the Aetolians: Towards the Interdisciplinary Study of a Greek Region* (Utrecht, 1987).

9. See J. L. Bintliff and A. M. Snodgrass, 'Off-Site Pottery Distributions: A Regional and Inter-Regional Perspective', *Current Anthropology*, 29 (1988), 506–13.

10. van Andel and Runnels (n. 5), p. 33.

11. See e.g. D. Adamesteanu, 'Problèmes de la zone archéologique de Métaponte', *Rev. Arch.* 1967, 3–38, especially p. 26 and fig. 32.

12. The references are collected in my *An Archaeology of Greece: The Present State and Future Scope of a Discipline* (Berkeley, 1987), p. 118 n. 4.

13. J. E. Jones, A. J. Graham, and L. H. Sackett, 'An Attic Country House below the Cave of Pan at Vari', *BSA* 68 (1973), 355–452, esp. pp. 418–19.

14. See the period tables in Bintliff and Snodgrass (n. 7), pp. 158–60.

15. P. Roesch, *Thespies et la Confédération béotenne* (Paris, 1965), p. 39, map 2, and p. 52 n. 5.

16. See Bintliff and Snodgrass (n. 7), pp. 145–7.

17. 'The Site of Askra', in G. Argoud and P. Roesch (eds.), *La Béotie antique* (Colloques internationaux du CNRS, Paris, 1985), pp. 88–95.

18. See Snodgrass (n. 17), p. 94 for the evidence for this episode.

19. H. Goldman, *Excavations at Eutresis in Boeotia* (Princeton, 1931).

CHAPTER 25

Rural Burial in the World of Cities

The final paper addresses a narrower, but rather more secure finding that arose from our intensive survey in western Boeotia: that there were small isolated burial sites, sporadically interspersed with the 'activity areas' of the same rural landscape, and presumably accommodating members of families of landowners. This time, the finding could not be reinforced by many such survey discoveries elsewhere in the Greek world. But meanwhile, an irrefutable parallel had again emerged from Lohmann's discoveries in Attica (see above, under Ch. 24), where family burial plots with the remains of built funerary monuments were found in the vicinity of several farm sites.

My paper is short and exploratory: it can be criticised for not paying sufficient attention to literary and epigraphic evidence of similar date. I would single out three especially interesting pieces of testimony which could have been cited.

First, there is an early fifth-century inscription from Gortyn in Crete (Guarducci 1935–50, iv: 45–6, no. 46B) which seems to legislate for precisely the circumstance of isolated burial in a rural location, by prescribing when a funerary procession might or might not cross someone else's property on the way to that of the family of the deceased, where the burial is to take place. (The decisive factor, the presence or absence of a public road, was one briefly touched on at p. 476 below). Second, in a private speech usually attributed to Demosthenes (Demosthenes 55, *Against Callicles*: 11–14), there is a rather detailed description of the rural properties of the two litigants, in which Demosthenes' client bases part of his argument on the presence of ancestral burials on his own plot. Finally, though rather later in date, there is an inscription of the third century BC from Gonnoi in Thessaly, where the issue at stake is the larger one of a dispute between two cities as to the rightful possession of some marginal land close to their joint border (Helly 1973, ii: 100–7, no. 93), where again the presence of the burials of former citizens of Gonnoi is cited as vital evidence of their city's ownership of the land in question.

In this last case, there is the added bonus (relevant to the argument in Ch. 24 above) that in more than one case these men are explicitly stated to have *lived* on their remote land-holdings. By contrast, the situation described in the Demosthenes speech is argued by Osborne (1985: 17–18) to imply that the owners were not resident on their lands. Thus burial on a rural plot of land, on its own and in default of supporting evidence, would fall short of demonstrating residence on that land – a question raised towards the end of the paper, pp. 476–7.

BIBLIOGRAPHY

Guarducci, M. (1935–50), *Inscriptiones Creticae*, 4 vols, Rome: Libreria dello Stato.

Helly, B. (1973), *Gonnoi*, Amsterdam: A. M. Hakkert.

Osborne, R. (1985), *Demos: The Discovery of Classical Attica*, Cambridge: Cambridge University Press.

Without careful definition, a concept such as 'rural burial' is nothing. The first and most obvious point is that it has no meaning except in eras where there is an opposition between an urban and a rural sector. In a society without sizable nucleated settlements, there can be no 'rural sector' and the urban/rural contrast in burial location, as in much else, gives way to other polarities with a different significance, such as intramural and extramural, or single and grouped. This is the significance of the second half of my title: it is only in a 'world of cities' that burial-location could in principle become capable of conveying any message of the kind that I hope to discern here. Thus the archaeology of the most prehistoric societies is not relevant to this topic. One cannot exclude the possibility of the same processes operating in the case of a society with well-developed nuclear settlements such as Mycenaean Greece; but in this particular case, as it happens, the phenomenon is hard to identify, partly perhaps because so many Mycenaean settlements have had their very existence

'Rural burial in the world of cities', from S. Marchegay, M.-T. Le Dinahet and J.-F. Salles (ed.), *Nécropoles et Pouvoir: idéologies, pratiques et interprétations*, Paris: de Boccard, 1998, pp. 37–42.

inferred from the presence of a cemetery, partly perhaps because of the specific natural setting – a hill-slope – required for the most popular Mycenaean grave-types, which encourages burial in sizable group-ings. Single, isolated Mycenaean graves have at times been reported (usually tholos tombs in Messenia, and chamber tombs elsewhere in the Aegean area), but it has often been suspected that these are merely the visible portion of a larger cemetery.

'Rural burial' must be defined even more strictly for the purposes of this paper. One important element will prove to be the notion of property; another is that of distance from nucleated settlements, large and small. I therefore define rural burial as 'burial on a site sufficiently distant from any nucleated settlement to be inexplicable in terms of the location of such settlements, in a location chosen on grounds of the ownership of rural land'. Thus a grave or cemetery which has merely been pushed to the edges of a built-up zone (or even beyond), through the desire to exclude the dead from the cur-rent (or projected) habitation area, will *not* qualify as a case of rural burial. Nor will a grave or cemetery associated with a small hamlet or village, even though we would often describe that settlement itself as 'rural'. Instead, I wish to direct attention towards instances where the choice of a burial-site appears to have been influenced by other factors, primarily the ownership of land. This is something difficult to demonstrate by archaeological means. We do however have doc-umentary evidence, at least by the Roman Imperial period, that this was an important, indeed an indispensable factor. In the *Digest*, there are several passages which derive from the Roman legal tenet that burial of a corpse conferred the status of a *locus religiosus* on the location chosen: that is, that it thereby became consecrated ground – but only on certain conditions. The most important of these was that those responsible for the burial (not necessarily the person actually buried) must have a legal title to the ownership of the land in ques-tion. Thus *Digest* i 6, 4 cites the view of Marcian that '*Religiosum autem locum unusquisque sua voluntate facit, dum mortuum infert in locum suum*': see Mommsen, Krueger and Watson (edd.), 1985, i 25–26, with the translation 'Being religious is, however, a quality which every single person can impose on a site of his own free will by burying a corpse in a place *which one owns*'; while no one can be barred from burying in a place *to which they have a right* (xi 8, 1, 7; Mommsen *et al.* i 356 – my emphasis in both cases). Elsewhere in the *Digest*, the importance of this last condition is elaborated in a number of passages, which deal with such issues as whether one is entitled to dig up a corpse which someone else has buried on one's property (xi, 7, 8: Mommsen *et al.* i 350); whether on selling a property one could retain a right to bury on it (xi 7, 10, *ibid.*); and even whether an heir burying on ground inherited by a conditional legacy, while the condition is pending, can thereby consecrate the ground (xi 7, 34: Mommsen *et al.* i 354). I do not know whether there is any evidence for parallel provisions in Greek law but, if and when burial outside regular cemeteries was countenanced, the principle involved was an obvious one. An important distinction which we must bear in mind, however, is that between *ownership* and actual *residence* on the land: to this we shall return at the end.

In the nature of things, it is rural survey rather than excavation that is likely to find archaeological exemplification of such practices; but at the same time, by comparison with excavation, it is obviously much harder for survey methods conclusively to demonstrate the funerary nature of the locations found. Typically, burial-sites of this kind are presented in one of two forms: either exposed graves, uncovered through past agricultural activity and thereafter an obvious target for spoliation, so that their contents have usually disappeared; or surface scatters, where the small extent of the scatter and the unusual quality of its contents suggest an origin in a burial or burials, rather than in settlement or sanctuary debris. The second category, being almost by nature susceptible of dating, is the more useful, provided that the case for a funerary origin can be supported by convincing arguments. The elements of such a case are usually that the pottery is significantly less abraded than settlement material, often showing recent breaks, with the possibility of finding joins and occasionally of restoring complete shapes; that these shapes conform to the funerary usage of the region and epoch; and that the surface scatter is exceptionally small and concentrated. But the first category, where a funerary nature is usually self-evident, need not necessarily be devoid of dating evidence, even in the total absence of surviving grave-goods.

It was in fact the field experience of the Boeotia Survey, directed since 1979 by Dr. John Bintliff and myself, which first alerted me to the possibility of the practice of rural burial in antiquity (see Bintliff and Snodgrass 1985, p. 140). It was a phenomenon inherently unlikely to feature in the documentary sources, combining as it does two elements (rural life and burial custom) each of which is notoriously neglected by the ancient writers. But from 1981 until our last full field season in 1991, we encountered a minority of sites which did not conform to the common pattern of our rural concentrations of surface material. They were decidedly small in size (seldom more than 10 m in diameter), and they displayed in their make-up the other qualities listed above. The distinctively Boeotian feature was the predominance of black-glazed *kantharoi* in a suspiciously good state of preservation, suggesting that the adoption of a deeper plough had led to a recent disturbance of their contents, without uncovering the actual structure of the grave or graves.

There was another factor which strongly influenced our interpretation of these sites, although it is one which has proved not to be universally applicable in the survey archaeology of Classical Greece. This was that, unlike the great majority of our rural sites whose presence was suspected well before it could be confirmed, thanks to the existence of a more extensive 'halo' of scattered material around the nuclueus of the site, these sites presented themselves as a sudden and unexpected occurrence in the landscape: the survey team had not been forewarned of their likely presence by such a halo. Inasmuch as the most widely accepted explanation of such haloes is in terms of ancient agricultural practices deriving from the sites at their centres – specifically, from the spreading of manure fertiliser in which potsherds had previously become embedded – it is a reasonable inference that sites which lack them also lacked an agricultural purpose. It is true that a small rural sanctuary would also conform to such a description; but the likely or possible cases of such sanctuaries that we encountered (with, for example, inscribed dedications) were very much more extensive in area: the difficulty was to distinguish them from settlement localities of a comparable size, rather than from these small concentrations of relatively choice pottery.

Once the hypothesis of burial-sites had been adopted, the interesting question became that of their location in relation to the identified *loci* of settlement. A reasonably clear pattern emerged: these burials were situated at some way from the nearest nucleated settlement, and at a shorter but nevertheless distinct distance from the nearest small rural site; yet they were by no means removed from the area of past agricultural activity in general. On the contrary, they occurred only where there was independent evidence, from the nature of the soil and from the unbroken scatter of ceramic material of their period, for intensive cultivation at the time of their deposition. This makes plausible a further inference, even in the absence of any direct evidence for the location of field-boundaries: that the burials were located on cultivated landholdings. A detailed map of part of the survey area (Fig. 25.1) shows that they lie in the interstices between the

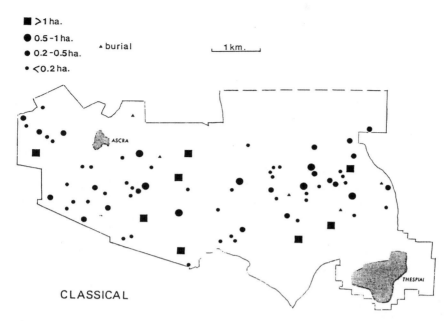

■ >1 ha.
● 0.5 - 1 ha.
● 0.2 - 0.5 ha.
• <0.2 ha.

▲ burial

⌐ 1 km. ⌐

ASCRA

THESPIAI

CLASSICAL

Figure 25.1 Part of the territory of the Boeotia survey, showing urban, rural and burial sites in the Valley of the Muses (left) and the approaches to Thespiai (right). After OPUS 6–7 (1987–89), p. 69, fig. 4.

canonical small rural sites of the same general period, the fifth to third centuries BC.

These canonical sites we, along with virtually every other director of an intensive survey in the Aegean area, interpret as Classical farmsteads. There is an impressive concurrence between these two phenomena, the uniquely dense phase of rural settlement during the Classical period and the incidence of isolated rural burials in the same epoch: neither is easy to match at any other period.

In the published accounts of most of these other surveys, burials – at least of the kind under discussion here – do not feature very prominently. Two fully-published Greek projects, the Northern Kea and the Southern Argolid surveys (see respectively Cherry, Davis and Mantsourani 1991; Jameson, Runnels and van Andel 1994), exemplify much the same picture. Apart from finding groups of graves of prehistoric date, the Kea survey reports a substantial cemetery of the historical period (Cherry *et al.*, p. 85, site 17) and two larger settlements that were fairly closely associated with, respectively, four rock-cut graves and a probable cist-grave (*ibid.* p. 90, 121, sites 24 and 62). In the terrain of the Southern Argolid, there were again some relatively isolated prehistoric burials, but for the lifetime of the Classical civilisations, the pattern encountered seems to have been one of organised cemeteries, and most of these were in the close vicinity of the well-documented city-sites of Halieis (Jameson *et al.*, p. 425–426, site A21; 427, site A25) and Hermion (p. 488–489, site E19), or of the second-order settlement of Mases (p. 466–467, 474–475, sites C11 and C41). With preliminary publications, one cannot expect the level of detail that would draw attention to single isolated burials, but nevertheless a similar picture of organised cemeteries in the vicinity of nucleated settlements is presented by, for example, the Lakonia Survey (Cavanagh 1991, p. 112, at Palaiogoulas, probably the ancient Sellasia) and the Nemea Valley Archaeological Project (Wright *et al.* 1990, p. 615–616, at ancient Phlious); while the Megalopolis Survey in 1981 reported the discovery of a Classical burial site, with much human bone and a funerary inscription (J. A. Lloyd and J. Roy, personal communication), but this was in the general vicinity of one of two sites that were 'by far the largest' in the survey area, and it too is perhaps best interpreted as a village cemetery.

The greatest advance in the understanding of the phenomenon first encountered in Boeotia came with the publication of Dr. Hans Lohmann's work in southern Attica in his full and impressive two-volume study *Atene* (Lohmann 1993). The study area is unusual – indeed, so far unique – in the survival and preservation of the actual architectural evidence of rural settlement: farmstead walls, terraces, agricultural installations, inscriptions and even boundary-walls between properties. What elsewhere were merely reasonable inferences in the interpretation of such sites become, in this case, almost certain deductions. It is thus of the greatest interest that a feature of a number of these rural sites was a *Grabterrasse*, a family burial-plot in fairly close proximity to the actual farmstead – in most cases, at a distance ranging between 40 and 200 metres. These rural burial-plots generally belong to the first of the two categories distinguished above (p. 471): they are visible structures, whose ceramic evidence has in some cases entirely disappeared. It was thus often not possible to *prove* the contemporaneity of the *Grabterrassen* and the associated farmsteads, which again are heavily concentrated in the fifth and fourth centuries BC, although the typology of the monuments goes some way towards doing this, and common sense suggests a close link between two phenomena that are so unusual a feature in the history of this landscape.

A fairly typical instance was that of site LE 16 (Lohmann 1993, i, p. 165–166 with Fig. 34; ii, p. 513–515), where a farmhouse of the fifth to fourth centuries has a small grave-plot located some 40 metres to the north of it, at the top of a slope with agricultural terrace-walls presumably belonging to the lifetime of the farm, but without any direct dating evidence for the *Grabterrasse*. Here and in other cases like that of site CH 8 (i, p. 176 with Fig. 46; ii, p. 359–360) the very close proximity of farmstead and *Grabterrasse* is the strongest argument for their association together. As far as the identification and interpretation of the *Grabterrassen* is concerned, clear evidence comes from site PH 3 (i, p. 188–193 with Fig. 53–55; ii, p. 414–415), where a decidedly monumental group of burial-monuments could be partially reconstructed, and the pottery gave a clear dating to the end of the fourth century BC and the beginning of the third; but in this case the association with a farmstead was not so self-evident, the best candidate being the comparably large and pretentious farm PH 2 some hundreds of metres to the north, said to be the largest known from Attica (i, p. 161–164 with Fig. 33, *cf.* 136, n. 1056; ii, p. 409–414), and certainly in use at the same period. Another imposing funerary monument was found at site CH 14 (i, p. 126–129 with Figs. 14–15; p. 253; ii, p. 362–363), but this was on the edge of a settlement which, at more than 2,5 hectares, was exceptionally large for a farmstead (CH 15, ii, p. 363–367; but see also i, p. 126–129).

The other cases described by Lohmann are similar and numerous enough to make his general interpretation unassailable, even where either the date or the identity of the burial-site is open to argument. Thus at site CH 3 we have a probable *Grabterrasse* (3C) a short distance away from a pair of 'tower' farmhouses (i, p. 139–141 with Figs 19–20; ii, p. 352–356); at TH 36, there is a definite (and datable) *Grabterrasse* near the contemporary farmstead TH 35 (i, 177 with Fig. 47; p. 221 with Fig. 65; ii, p. 478–480), and at TH 29/TH 30 a more problematic case, because of the unusual architecture of the former (i, 186 with Fig. 52; ii, p. 474–476). Other less than certain instances occur with the pair of sites TH 58/TH 57 (ii, p. 489), and in the inferred presence of graves at site TH 37 (ii, 480). Further north, the pair of sites AN 15/AN 14 provide a final probable example (i, 69; ii, p. 500–501). In addition to all these cases, Lohmann interprets two circular features as the perimeters of isolated tumulus graves (CH 38 and GA 7, i, p. 193–194 and ii, p. 379, 405), a class of monument well-known elsewhere in Attica.

The evidence is thus very strong from Attica, and relatively unambiguous from Boeotia, that isolated single burials or groups of burials were often associated with small rural sites. At present, it is difficult to extend the picture beyond these two regions. But an interesting parallel has arisen in the rather different circumstances of the Balboura Survey in Lycia, where instead of the relatively inconspicuous burials of the Classical Greek homeland, there was a tradition of prominent monumental tombs, at least for one stratum of society. Here the preliminary reports (Coulton 1992, 1993, 1994) refer to a number of cases of façade tombs, rock-cut sarcophagi and stone tumuli in apparently isolated locations, sometimes close to ancient roads, and of Hellenistic or Roman date. This may be a regional manifestation of the same phenomenon that we have discerned in Greece proper.

We have, I think, proved the existence of a practice, heavily concentrated in the Classical period of Greek history, of the burial of individuals or families in rather isolated rural locations, often associated with probable or definite farmsteads, in at least some regions of the Aegean world. Lycia may be a different matter, but in Attica and Boeotia at least we can say with certainty that this practice went on in a society where regular collective cemetery plots, on the edge of towns or villages, were the norm, and where strict constraints were put on their location and use. To this extent, the rural burials come as a surprise. But what exactly do they tell us?

Lohmann's discoveries have been the most important in this field, and he himself offers a confident interpretation of them: they prove that their associated rural sites were indeed inhabited farmsteads (an argument that he uses for instances where that might be otherwise debatable, e.g. Lohmann 1993, i, p. 69). But it could be argued that this slightly overstates the case in one respect. Rural burial on an agricultural holding does indeed suggest a close attachment to that piece of land, but perhaps does not necessarily prove actual residence at that location. It might reflect only a kind of aspiration, on the part of the individual or family, to have their name linked in perpetuity to an agricultural property, without their having actually resided on it. Just as today (at any rate in Protestant or entirely secular societies) people sometimes request in their wills that their ashes be scattered in their favourite beauty-spot, so it might be argued that, in the case of Lycia for example, the Balbourans had their tombs set up in a spot chosen for its conspicuousness or territorial significance, rather than as a token of ownership. If there is still a burden of proof on those survey archaeologists who (like myself) have argued that the majority of their isolated rural sites are indeed owner-occupied farmsteads, then even the discovery of these burials may not quite discharge that burden. They certainly demonstrate the importance that small farmers attached to their holdings: the tomb architecture (in Attica) and the grave-goods (in Boeotia) are powerful arguments that the persons buried belonged to a free, land-owning class rather than being slaves or tenants. Yet this might still allow of the view that the actual structures built on these holdings were for occupation by the tenants, agents, slaves or even animals of the absentee owner, who remained resident in the city or village in his lifetime, and repossessed his property only in death.

I put this alternative, perhaps 'post-modern' interpretation mainly out of deference to the sceptical view, which holds that the phenomenon of widespread rural residence on the part of Classical Greek farmers is so unexpected a finding that it still needs to be conclusively demonstrated. I do not myself believe in this interpretation. I think it much more likely that so close an association in death implies the closest possible association in life, that of permanent residence on the land. To return for a moment to the later Roman period with which we began: even in the very different circumstances and period of the 'serf' burials at the Late Roman *villa rustica* at Halieis (Rudolph 1979, p. 297–305), support can be found for this view: the owner buried them there because, as the *Digest* confirms, he had the right to do so, but the deceased were presumably buried on the estate because their whole life had revolved round it.

Rural burial is thus, at the least, another of the surprises that the systematic examination of the rural landscape has brought to the understanding of Greek history.

BIBLIOGRAPHY

Bintliff (J. L.), Snodgrass (A. M.), 1985, 'The Cambridge–Bradford Beotian Expedition: the first four years', *Journal of Field Archaeology* 12, p. 123–61.

Cavanagh (W. G.), 1991, 'Surveys, cities and synoecism', Rich (J.), Wallace-Hadrill (A.) edd, *City and Country in the ancient world*, London, p. 97–118.

Cherry (J. F.), Davis (J. L.), Mantsourani (E.), 1991, *Landscape Archaeology as Long-term History: Northern Keos in the Cycladic Islands*, Los Angeles.

Coulton (J. J.), 1992, 'The Balboura Survey', *Anatolian Studies* 42, p. 6–8.

Coulton (J. J.), 1993, 'The Balboura and district research project', *Anatolian Studies* 43, p. 4–6.

Coulton (J. J.), 1994, 'The Balboura and district research project', *Anatolian Studies* 44, p. 8–10.

Jameson (M. H.), Runnels (C. N.), van Andel (T.), 1994, *A Greek countryside: the Southern Argolid from Prehistory to the present day, Stanford.*

Lohmann (H.), 1993, *Atene: Forschungen zu Siedlungs- und Wirtschaftsstruktur des klassischen Attika*, vols. i and ii, Köln/Weimar/Wien.

Mommsen (Th.), Krueger (P.), Watson (A.) edd, 1985, *The Digest of Justinian*, vols. i-iv, Philadelphia.

Rudolph (W. W.), 1979, 'Excavations at Porto Cheli and vicinity', *Hesperia* 48, p. 294–324.

Wright (J. C.) and others, 1990, 'The Nemea Valley Archaeological Project: a preliminary report', *Hesperia* 59, p. 579–659.

Index

Note: As far as seems reasonable ('Aitolia' but not 'Akhilleus'), a consistently 'Greek' spelling is used in this index, regardless of the variant spellings used in different Chapters.